10/10

D0923166

Broadway

Broadway

An Encyclopedia of Theater and American Culture

VOLUME 2: M–Z

Thomas A. Greenfield, Editor

GREENWOOD
An Imprint of ABC-CLIO, LLC

A B C ⬤ C L I O

Santa Barbara, California • Denver, Colorado • Oxford, England

Copyright 2010 by Thomas A. Greenfield

All rights reserved. No part of this publication may be reproduced, stored in a
retrieval system, or transmitted, in any form or by any means, electronic, mechanical,
photocopying, recording, or otherwise, except for the inclusion of brief quotations in a
review, without prior permission in writing from the publisher.

Library of Congress Cataloging-in-Publication Data

Broadway : an encyclopedia of theater and American culture / Thomas A. Greenfield, editor.
    p. cm.
  Includes bibliographical references and index.
  ISBN 978–0–313–34264–6 (set: hardcover : alk. paper) — ISBN 978–0–313–34265–3
  (set: ebook) — ISBN 978–0–313–34266–0 (vol. 1: hardcover : alk. paper) —
  ISBN 978–0–313–34267–7 (vol. 1: ebook) — ISBN 978–0–313–34268–4 (vol. 2: hardcover :
  alk. paper) — ISBN 978–0–313–34269–1 (vol. 2: ebook)
1. Theater—New York (State)—New York—Encyclopedias. 2. Broadway (New York, N.Y.)—
History—Encyclopedias. 3. Broadway (New York, N.Y.)—Biography—Encyclopedias. I.
Greenfield, Thomas Allen, 1948–
PN2277.N5B62   2010
792.09747′103—dc22   2009045720

14 13 12 11 10   1 2 3 4 5

Greenwood Press
An Imprint of ABC-CLIO, LLC

This book is also available on the World Wide Web as an eBook.
Visit www.abc-clio.com for details.

ABC-CLIO, LLC
130 Cremona Drive, P.O. Box 1911
Santa Barbara, California 93116-1911

This book is printed on acid-free paper ∞

Manufactured in the United States of America

REF
792
.09747
BRO
2010
v. 2

For Alice Hermoine Rogstad
Suzanne Margaret Rogstad Greenfield
and
Alex Jee Rogstad Greenfield

*Home with my own
when company's expected . . .
. . . well protected.*

Contents

❦

Alphabetical List
of Entries

Volume 1

Volume 2

Guide to Related Topics

This list divides entry names (headwords) by broad topic. Note that some entries are listed under more than one topic.

Actors and Actresses

Andrews, Julie

Barrymore Ethel

Barrymore, John

Booth, Edwin

Brando, Marlon

Brice, Fanny

Cantor, Eddie

Channing, Carol

Cobb, Lee J.

Cohan, George M.

Cronyn, Hume

Davis, Ossie

Drake, Alfred

Ferrer, Jose

Fiske, Mrs. (Minnie Maddern)

Fontanne, Lynn. *See* Lunt, Alfred, and Fontanne, Lynn

Forrest, Edwin

Gilpin, Charles S.

Grey, Joel

Hagen, Uta

Harris, Julie

Harrison, Rex

Hayes, Helen

Jones, James Earl

Keene, Laura

Lane, Nathan

Lansbury, Angela

Le Gallienne, Eva

Lunt, Alfred, and Fontanne, Lynn

LuPone, Patti

Martin, Mary

McClendon, Rose

McDonald, Audra

Merman, Ethel

Raitt, John

Robards, Jason, Jr.

Robeson, Paul

Tandy, Jessica

Taylor, Laurette

Verdon, Gwen

Williams, Bert

Broadway and Main Street

High Schools, Theater Education in
High Schools, Theater Performances in
Regional Theaters

Touring Productions
Tourism

Broadway Entertainment Components

Broadway (Location)
Broadway's Theaters and Theater
   District
Critics

Off-Broadway
Playwrights
Producers

Choreographers and Dancers

Balanchine, George
Bennett, Michael
Champion, Gower
de Mille, Agnes
Fosse, Bob

Robbins, Jerome
Stroman, Susan
Tune, Tommy
Verdon, Gwen

Composers and Lyricists

Berlin, Irving
Bernstein, Leonard
Brown, Jason Robert
Comden, Betty, and Green, Adolph
Gershwin, George, and Gershwin, Ira
Gilbert and Sullivan
Hart, Lorenz
Herbert, Victor
Herman, Jerry
Kander, John, and Ebb, Fred

Kern, Jerome
Lerner, Alan Jay, and Loewe, Frederick
Lloyd Webber, Andrew
Loesser, Frank
Porter, Cole
Robbins, Jerome
Rodgers, Richard, and Hammerstein,
   Oscar, II
Sondheim, Stephen
Styne, Jule

Ethnicity, Gender, and Identity

African American Dramatic Theater
African American Musical Theater
Asians and Asian Americans
Gay Culture
Jewish American Musicals
Jewish American Playwrights

Latino Americans
Religion
Women and Broadway: The Early
   Years, 1845–1939
Women and Broadway: The Later
   Years, 1940–Present

Media and Journalists

Atkinson, Brooks
Critics

Nathan, George Jean. *See* Critics
Sullivan, Ed

Organizations

The Actors Studio
American Theatre Wing—Tony
   Awards
Disney Theatrical Productions
Federal Theatre Project
Group Theatre
Nederlander Organization

Neighborhood Playhouse
Provincetown Players
Shubert Organization. *See* Shubert
   Brothers
Theatre Guild
Theatrical Syndicate

Performing Arts, Entertainment, and Literature

Comic Strips
Dance and Choreography
European "Megamusicals"
Film
Musicals
New Media and Technology
Novels (American)
Operetta
Puppetry
Radio

Regional Theaters
Show Tunes: From Tin Pan Alley to
   Pop Radio
Show Tunes: The Rock Era, Disney,
   and Downloads
Solo Performance
Sports
Television
Vaudeville

Plays

Angels in America
Barefoot in the Park
The Black Crook
Cats
A Chorus Line
Company
The Cradle Will Rock
The Crucible
Death of a Salesman
*for colored girls who have considered
   suicide/when the rainbow is enuf*
Gypsy

Hair
In the Heights
Long Day's Journey into Night
My Fair Lady
Oh! Calcutta!
Oklahoma!
Othello
Our American Cousin
Our Town
Pal Joey
The Phantom of the Opera
Porgy and Bess

The Producers (The Musical)
A Raisin in the Sun
Rent
Show Boat

Shuffle Along
A Streetcar Named Desire
West Side Story
Who's Afraid of Virginia Woolf?

Playwrights and Authors

Albee, Edward
Anderson, Maxwell
Belasco, David
Booth, Edwin
Burrows, Abe
Champion, Gower
Clurman, Harold
Crothers, Rachel
Fierstein, Harvey
Fitch, Clyde
Glaspell, Susan
Hansberry, Lorraine. See *A Raisin in the Sun*
Hellman, Lillian
Hwang, David Henry
Inge, William
Kaufman, George S.
Kushner, Tony

Larson, Jonathan. See *Rent*
Laurents, Arthur
McNally, Terrence
Miller, Arthur
Norman, Marsha
Odets, Clifford
O'Neill, Eugene
Shakespeare
Shange, Ntozake. See *for colored girls who have considered suicide/when the rainbow is enuf*
Shaw, George Bernard
Simon, Neil
Wasserstein, Wendy
Wilder, Thornton
Williams, Tennessee
Wilson, August

Producers, Directors, Theater Owners, and Managers

Abbott, George
Disney Theatrical Productions
Fields, Lew
Fosse, Bob
Group Theatre
Kazan, Elia
Keene, Laura
Logan, Joshua
Mackintosh, Cameron
Merrick, David
Nederlander Organization
Neighborhood Playhouse
Nichols, Mike
Papp, Joseph

Pastor, Tony. *See* Vaudeville
Prince, Harold
Provincetown Players
Quintero, Jose
Richards, Lloyd
Shubert Brothers
Strasberg, Lee
Stroman, Susan
Taymor, Julie
Theatre Guild
Theatrical Syndicate
Wolfe, George C.
Ziegfeld, Florenz

MACKINTOSH, CAMERON (1946–)
PRODUCER

Best known as the groundbreaking producer of visually spectacular **European megamusicals**, Cameron Mackintosh is the single most important and influential Broadway producer of the past 30 years. He masterminded production of the three longest-running Broadway hits in history, respectively, ***The Phantom of the Opera*** (1988), ***Cats*** (1982), and *Les Misérables* (1987) as well as several other Broadway successes. Apart from the massive revenues and attendance numbers he generates with his hit shows, Mackintosh has revolutionized the way Broadway musicals are staged, marketed, and presented for touring. Before reaching the age of 50, he had earned a reputation as one of Broadway's legendary producers, comparable with such historic figures as **David Belasco**, **Joseph Papp**, and **David Merrick**.

Mackintosh began his theatrical career in his home country of England. He claims that he knew he wanted to produce musicals at the age of eight when he saw *Salad Days*, a London hit of the 1950s. As a teenager, he worked on and off as a stagehand both in London's West End theater district and in **touring productions** of **musicals**. In 1969, he scraped together enough money to produce his first West End musical, a revival of **Cole Porter**'s *Anything Goes*. Despite Porter's historic popularity with London theatergoers, Mackintosh's production flopped and closed after two weeks.

Mackintosh produced a number of small shows in and out of London over the next several years, finally achieving a modest degree of success with *Side by Side by Sondheim* in 1976, a tribute revue of songs by Broadway's preeminent composer at the time. (The show would open on Broadway the following year, produced by **Hal Prince** not Mackintosh.) More success followed in the late 1970s with well-received London revivals of *My Fair Lady* and *Oklahoma!*, but it was not until Mackintosh collaborated with **Andrew Lloyd Webber** that he began his unparalleled rise in London and Broadway theater production.

The first true blockbuster Mackintosh produced was Lloyd Webber's *Cats*, which opened in the West End in 1981 and transferred to Broadway the following year. With no name stars and an obscure source (a book of verse about cats by the modernist poet T. S. Eliot), *Cats* unexpectedly became a monumental success with both critics and audiences. It ran on Broadway for 18 years. His next endeavor was producing *Les Misérables* (1987) by the French composer and lyricist team of Claude-Michel Schönberg and Alain Boublil. *"Les Miz"* became another box-office smash as, this time, wildly enthusiastic word of mouth response trumped tepid reviews. (This phenomenon would repeat itself throughout Mackinosh's career, causing many people to describe his work—not always kindly—as "critic-proof.")

In 1988, already Broadway and London's hottest new producer, Mackintosh's second collaboration with Andrew Lloyd Webber, *The Phantom of the Opera*, would surpass in commercial terms anything ever accomplished or even seriously dreamed of for a Broadway show. In its 20-plus-year Broadway run (with numerous worldwide tours, resident sitting companies, and an epic cross-marketing and merchandising campaign) *Phantom* is now the most lucrative single production of any kind in all of entertainment history. The show's gross box-office receipts from all authorized productions is now estimated at US $5 billion, nearly tripling the international gross of the all-time highest grossing film, *Titanic*.

Within a span of six years, Mackintosh had altered the landscape of both London and Broadway musical theater. A new term—"megamusical" (or European megamusical)—emerged to describe Mackintosh's productions, a circumstance necessitated by the fact that there was neither a phrase nor a precedent to account for what he had accomplished. The term also refers to his penchant for jaw-dropping technological feats on stage ("gimmicks" to detractors), which have included the flotation and ceiling-high drop of a one-ton chandelier (*Phantom*), the hydraulic launch skyward of a gigantic automobile tire (*Cats*), and the stupefying onstage landing of a military helicopter in Schönberg and Boublil's Vietnam-era love story *Miss Saigon* (1991), which prior to its Broadway premiere broke the record for largest box-office advance ticket sales of any show in history. Such visual pyrotechnics were altogether new to modern Broadway, representing a stark contrast to the scaled-down sets of popular "concept musicals" such as Stephen Sondheim's *Company* (1970) or **Michael Bennett**'s *A Chorus Line* (1975) and dwarfing even the most elaborate productions of traditional book musicals and **operetta** revivals.

Through innovative advertising and marketing techniques, Mackintosh universalized his biggest hits, shrewdly expanding markets for his shows all over the world. For example, before bringing West End musicals to the United States, he would first circulate the London recordings to American test audiences, building interest and creating excited speculation about the next arrival. He also created logos for his shows that were simple and eye-catching, using a main symbol from each show while minimizing the show's title or not even including it at all. The textbook example of this marketing technique is the logo for *The Phantom of the Opera*, a plain white theatrical mask on an unadorned black background. It is now one of the most recognizable "corporate logos" in the world. By placing simple but powerful symbols at the forefront of the marketing campaign, Mackintosh built interest among a much wider audience than commercial theater producers traditionally pursue or attract.

His first U.S. national tours of *Cats* and *The Phantom of the Opera* in the 1980s were so successful that they revolutionized the Broadway touring industry. Mackintosh became the first producer in history to insist that tours of his premiere licensed shows (*Phantom* and *Cats* in particular) replicate in every detail his Broadway and London productions with virtually no compromises to accommodate smaller venues. This move generated theater renovation and construction throughout America toward the end of the twentieth century and was a significant impetus for the development of multipurpose performing arts centers in several American cities. Road demand for his top shows is so strong that he has often negotiated local stays or "sit down" residencies for weeks or months instead of the typical one or two week runs of shows in a local "Broadway season" subscription series.

Still actively producing, since the year 2000 Mackintosh has yet to produce a hit of the magnitude of his earlier epic works. Revivals of *Oklahoma!* (2002), *Little Shop of Horrors* (2003), and a limited run of his own *Les Misérables* (2006) each ran less than two years. His most recent Broadway success has been the staging of Disney film favorite *Mary Poppins* (2006), a transfer of the West End production he coproduced with **Disney Theatrical Productions**. Although the show is running successfully after three years, many observers doubt that it will have the kind of staying power of his greatest successes.

Cameron Mackintosh has expanded the role of the modern Broadway producer in production and marketing, although not all current producers can afford or desire to follow his model. Like great producers before him, such as Belasco and Papp, Mackintosh has insisted on being expressly involved in the creative process and not just the "production end" of his shows. But unlike even the most successful of his peers, he has created branding and marketing strategies that have brought heretofore unknown fame, riches, and influence to live musical theater—especially the considerable portion of it that he created and owns.

Thomas A. Greenfield and Mary Hanrahan

Further Reading

Dorbian, Iris. *Great Producers: Visionaries of the American Theater.* New York: Allworth Press, 2008.

SIMMS LIBRARY
ALBUQUERQUE ACADEMY

Morley, Sheridan, and Ruth Leon. *Hey, Mr. Producer!: The Musical World of Cameron Mackintosh.* New York: Back Stage Books, 1998.

MARTIN, MARY (1913–1990)
ACTRESS

Dubbed by press and theatergoers as "The First Lady of **Musicals**" during the 1950s, Mary Virginia Martin originated some of post–World War II Broadway's most important roles. A three-time Tony winner for Best Actress in a Musical, Martin is best remembered for her ebullient performances as Nellie Forbush in *South Pacific* (1949), the title role in *Peter Pan* (1954), and Maria von Trapp in *The Sound of Music* (1959). Her remarkable ability to perform a number in a perfect "pop song" singing style while dancing and staying in character had audiences singing her solos as they left the theater and buying up sheet music and hit recordings of songs she introduced onstage.

Martin was born in Weatherford, Texas, to Preston and Juanita Presley Martin, a lawyer and a violin teacher, respectively. A self-admitted tomboyish farm girl, Martin's childhood in many ways foreshadowed her future career in theater. Her enthusiasm for physical activity, as it would later in her professional life, could subsume her concern for her own safety. (A youthful attempt to "fly" off of the roof of her garage landed her with a broken collarbone. She would eventually fare better flying, singing, acting, and dancing in midair above Broadway audiences in *Peter Pan*, one of the most visually enduring performances in musical theater history.)

Martin married Benjamin Hagman when she was 16 and became a mother at 17. At the same time she opened a dance school in Weatherford and tried to balance the multiple roles of marriage, motherhood, and dance. Finding marriage and motherhood increasingly tedious and dance and performance increasingly enticing, she left her husband and young son (the future television star Larry Hagman) to pursue a show business career in California.

While performing at a nightclub in Los Angeles she caught the attention of veteran Broadway producer Laurence Schwab, who was captivated by Martin and became her principal manager and career guide thereafter. With Schwab's help, Martin landed an audition in New York for **Cole Porter**'s *Leave It to Me* (1938). Martin so impressed Porter with her tenacity and talent that he had her cast immediately in a featured role. The show was very successful, running for almost 300 performances, and Martin triumphed in her solo number "My Heart Belongs to Daddy," the most famous hit song from the show.

Leave It to Me led to a **film** contract with Paramount Pictures in 1938. However, Martin was neither happy nor successful working at Paramount. Martin met her second husband at Paramount, movie story editor Richard Halliday, but returned

Choreographer and director Jerome Robbins, left, and Mary Martin, dressed in her Peter Pan outfit, fly through the air during a rehearsal for the television production of Peter Pan *in 1955. (AP Photo)*

to New York in 1943 and refrained from doing film work for most of the rest of her life.

Despite the lapse of five years since her first and only Broadway appearance, Martin found success immediately upon her return to the Broadway stage. She starred in Kurt Weill's *One Touch of Venus* (1943), which ran for 18 months and over 500 performances. The Asian-themed *Lute Song* (1946), a "play with music" rather than a full musical, ran for only a few months, but Martin impressed critics and audiences as soloist on five of the production's eight songs. After the *Lute Song* she starred in a very well-received national tour of *Annie Get Your Gun* (1946), while **Ethel Merman** was still starring in the original Broadway production.

In 1949 Martin, already a highly respected and popular musical theater performer, began her ascent to stardom by agreeing to play Ensign Nellie Forbush in **Rodgers and Hammerstein**'s *South Pacific* (1949). Rodgers and Hammerstein tailored the role and the songs to Martin's voice and talents, a decision that paid off handsomely for all concerned. Martin commanded the show with her boundless youthful energy and natural charm, even as she played off skillfully against the mature continental sophistication of co-star Ezio Pinza. She stopped the show with songs as varied as "Cockeyed Optimist," "I'm Gonna Wash That Man Right Out of My Hair," and "Some Enchanted Evening." She won the Tony Award for Best Actress in a Musical and "captained" the production to a 1,925 performance, five-year run—the longest of any Rodgers and Hammerstein musical with the exception of *Oklahoma!* (1943).

Martin's next major role was as the title character of *Peter Pan* (1954), in which she memorably flew over the audience in an aerial ballet choreographed by director **Jerome Robbins**. Her dazzling high-flying performance garnered Martin her second Best Actress Tony Award. Although the original Broadway show ran for a modest 152 performances, NBC television broadcast two live, nationwide original-cast productions of the show (1955 and 1956) and aired a videotaped version of the production twice during the 1960s. No less a telegenic performer than a stage star, Martin's television appearances as Peter cemented her in the minds of a generation as the mythical boy who never grew up.

Martin's third Best Actress Tony came with her next musical: as Maria von Trapp in Rodgers and Hammerstein's *The Sound of Music*, the final collaboration of the legendary composer/lyricist team. (Hammerstein died a few months after *The Sound of Music*'s opening night.) Martin gave a stunning performance, turning the songs "The Sound of Music" and "My Favorite Things" into popular song standards and "Do Re Mi" into a rare Broadway children's song classic. As successful as she was onstage as Maria and Nellie Forbush, Martin turned down the starring film roles in *The Sound of Music* and *South Pacific* owing to her earlier disappointing Hollywood experiences.

After the run of *The Sound of Music* Martin appeared in an ill-conceived star vehicle, *Jenny* (1963), which closed in two months. Three years later she had her final Broadway success starring opposite Robert Preston in *I Do! I Do!* (1966), a shrewd musical adaptation of the **Hume Cronyn/Jessica Tandy** 1955 comedy *The Four Poster*.

After the run of *I Do! I Do!* in 1968 Martin at 52 retired as a career Broadway theater performer. Over the next several years she appeared in some special, one-night events in theater and television as well as an unsuccessful Broadway romantic comedy, *Do You Turn Somersaults?* (1973). In 1986 she toured the country with **Carol Channing** in *Legends*, a play that has never made it to Broadway despite high expectations and vigorous promotion as a **touring production**.

During the 1940s and 1950s Golden Age of musicals, no actress's career was more gilded than Mary Martin's (although she famously turned down the role of Eliza Doolittle in *My Fair Lady* [1956]). As Broadway historians and audiences have continued to honor the charm, wit, and cockeyed optimism of the Rodgers and Hammerstein era, Martin's Broadway performances have emerged as a definitive body of work from that period and a landmark theatrical legacy.

Mary Martin died of cancer in 1990 in Rancho Mirage, California.

Thomas A. Greenfield and Mary Hanrahan

Further Reading

Kirkwood, James. *Diary of a Mad Playwright: Perilous Adventures on the Road with Mary Martin and Carol Channing.* New York: Applause, 2002.
Martin, Mary. *My Heart Belongs.* New York: Morrow, 1976.

McClendon, Rose (1884c.–1936)
Actress, Director, Producer

Rose McClendon was the premiere African American stage actress during the 1920s and 1930s. With 12 different productions, she had more lead or featured acting roles on Broadway than any other African American actress of the twentieth century. Capable of enormous emotional range and possessed of a powerful stage presence, McClendon won the admiration of many Broadway luminaries of her day including *New York Times* theater critic **Brooks Atkinson**, who openly lamented that the relative paucity of her Broadway appearances was not commensurate with the enormity of her talent. She was also a noteworthy theater company manager, having founded the Negro People's Theater in 1935 and served briefly thereafter as co-director of the influential New York Negro Unit of the **Federal Theatre Project**.

McClendon was born in Greenville, South Carolina, but was raised in New York City. She was educated in New York's public schools and performed and directed in amateur community and church theater in New York through the 1910s. In the hopes of improving her craft and landing roles in commercial theater, McClendon enrolled in New York's American Academy of Dramatic Art. As an African American woman in her thirties, she was at that time a rare presence in the prestigious Academy.

Well-known within New York theater circles, if not yet famous, McClendon began taking roles in major commercial productions in the 1920s. Her first mainstream professional break came on a national tour in 1924 as a member of an all-black cast production of Nan Bagby Stephens's *Roseanne*, "a tale of Negro life in the South" by a white writer. The play had run in New York the year before—improbably with an all-white cast—but closed quickly. In 1926 McClendon made an auspicious Broadway debut in the Laurence Stallings's musical *Deep River,* for which she received rave notices. Her other prominent roles on Broadway included that of Serena in the original production of Dorothy and DuBose Heyward's *Porgy* (1927), with which she also toured throughout the United States and in Europe,

Rose McClendon, as Medea, in a 1935 photo by Carl Van Vechten. (Library of Congress, Prints & Photographs Division, Carl Van Vechten Collection, LOT 12735, no. 788 P&P)

and the **Theatre Guild**'s first Broadway production, Paul Green's *The House of Connelly* (1931). Her starring role in *Never No More* (1932) was hailed by Atkinson as presenting the most effective and "harrowing" scene of cruelty and inhumanity he had ever witnessed on stage.

By the early 1930s, McClendon had become an heroic figure among African Americans in New York, especially to those involved in the arts. In 1935 she helped establish the Negro People's Theatre in Harlem, one of several prominent African American theater groups that emerged during the Harlem Renaissance. (After her death, the group was renamed the Rose McClendon Players in her honor.) By virtue of her work with the Negro People's Theatre and the high regard in which she was held among New York's African American community, she was appointed, along with John Houseman, to head the New York Negro Unit of the Federal Theatre Project—the unit that produced Orson Welles's groundbreaking 1936 black-cast *Macbeth* (sometimes called the "Voodoo Macbeth" because of its nineteenth-century Haitian setting). However, at the time McClendon was beginning her run on Broadway in Langston Hughes's *Mulatto* (1935) during which she would become fatally ill. The bulk of the administrative work for the Negro Unit soon fell to Houseman.

McClendon's final Broadway appearance was as Cora, *Mulatto*'s long-suffering black mistress to a patriarchal southern white plantation owner—a part written by Hughes expressly for her. Although Hughes was furious that a gratuitous rape scene had been added to the Broadway production by the show's producer, McClendon's performance, which featured several showstopping monologues, was an unequivocal triumph for both playwright and star. *Mulatto* ran for an astonishing 373 performances and, until Lorraine Hansberry's **A Raisin in the Sun** opened in 1959, was the longest-running drama written by an African American author in Broadway history.

McClendon contracted pleurisy and then pneumonia during the run of *Mulatto* and had to leave the show. She died in her home in Harlem on July 13, 1936, from complications related to her illnesses. Although hardly known today even among many knowledgeable theater people, McClendon was one of the most prolific and highly regarded African American Broadway actors or actresses of the twentieth century.

Thomas A. Greenfield

Further Reading

Robert, Lewis. "Rose McClendon." *Negro: An Anthology*, ed. Nancy Cunard and Hugh D. Ford. New York: Continuum International Publishing Group, 1996.

Wintz, Cary D., and Paul Finkelman, eds. *Encyclopedia of the Harlem Renaissance*. New York: Routledge, 2004.

McDonald, Audra (1970–)
Actress

Audra McDonald has had the fastest rise on Broadway of practically any contemporary actress and the most prodigious Broadway career of any African American performer of her generation. Although not yet 40 she has earned four Tony Awards and two more Tony nominations. An accomplished recording artist, she has also won two Grammy Awards and numerous other honors. Successful in both **musicals** and dramas, McDonald also appears in operas, on the classical concert stage, and in popular cabaret concerts. She has worked in film and TV movies, and recently ventured into serial television in the *Grey's Anatomy* spinoff, *Private Practice*. But she considers Broadway her home.

McDonald was born in 1970 in Germany and raised in Fresno, California, in a musical family. Her mother played piano and sang, and a quintet of aunts toured as a gospel group, the McDonald Sisters. She went to a performing arts school, performed regularly with a local dinner theater company in Fresno, and then went to New York to study classical voice at Juilliard. Barely a year after her graduation, she won her first Tony Award for her featured role as Carrie Pipperidge in director Nicholas Hytner's 1994 revival of **Rodgers and Hammerstein**'s *Carousel*. This would not be the first time that McDonald would be cast in a role historically performed by a white actress. In Hytner's incarnation of the musical, the grit of the original production is heightened and the cast is multiracial.

Immediately following *Carousel*, she was cast with Zoe Caldwell in **Terrence McNally**'s *Master Class* (1995) for which she won a second Tony Award for Best Featured Actress. Caldwell, who won the Tony for Best Actress, portrayed opera diva Maria Callas in her later years, teaching aspiring opera singers. McDonald portrayed Sharon, one of Callas's students. The musical *Ragtime*, based on the E. L. Doctorow novel of the same name, followed with McDonald playing Sarah, a young woman who has a child by an itinerant ragtime piano player. In this show, the social restrictions on Sarah as an African American woman, the departure of the baby's father, and her own inability to cope with life cause her to try to kill her own child. The portrayal earned MacDonald her third Tony Award. She was 28.

McDonald's extraordinary versatility as an actress and singer make her an ideal interpreter for some of the new and diverse trends emerging from today's younger musical theater composers. Her debut solo album, *Way Back to Paradise* (Nonesuch Records 1998), featured young Broadway composers **Jason Robert Brown**, Jenny Giering, Adam Guettel, and Michael John LaChiusa. This young generation of composers is known for combining popular and classical traditions, and for complex drama captured in music—a perfect match for McDonald's own eclectic tastes and wide-ranging abilities. LaChiusa wrote McDonald's next Broadway project, *Marie Christine* (1999), specifically for her skills as a singer and an actress. Based loosely on the Medea myth reset in nineteenth century New Orleans, the show's book and lyrics drew unfavorable reviews but McDonald earned strong praise for her first leading Broadway role. (She was nominated for a Best Actress Tony but did not win.)

For much of the early twenty-first century, McDonald has been branching out into opera, concert appearances, film, and television, but has still taken on several notable Broadway roles. She played Ruth opposite Phylicia Rashad in Broadway's 2004 revival of *A Raisin in the Sun* and repeated the role in the made-for-TV movie for ABC. McDonald won her fourth Tony and earned an Emmy nomination for her portrayal of Ruth.

In 2007 McDonald starred as Lizzie Curry in a revival of *110 in the Shade*, which had been a minor hit in the mid-1960s. As had been the case in *Marie Christine*, McDonald drew critical praise as a standout in a show that generally did not impress critics.

McDonald has been so successful in so many ways that, while still early in her career, she can "call her own shots" and take her considerable talents in virtually any direction she chooses. This is an extraordinary position for a young African American performer. She has already helped weaken commercial theater casting color barriers that have historically limited minority performers' opportunities to play "traditional" white roles. In so doing, she has fashioned an extraordinary career while reminding critics and audiences alike that talent and excellence know no barriers beyond themselves.

Melanie N. Blood

Further Reading

Pendergast, Sara, et al. *Contemporary Black Biography.* Detroit: Gale, Cengage Learning, 2008.

Singer, Barry. *Ever After: The Last Years of Musical Theater and Beyond.* New York: Applause Theatre & Cinema Books, 2004.

McNally, Terrence (1939–)
Playwright, Writer

Widely recognized as one of the America's most versatile dramatists, Terrence McNally is best known for uncompromising explorations of gay and lesbian issues in his works. Skilled in writing farce, serous drama, and books for musicals, McNally won four Tony Awards in the 1990s, two each for Best Book of a Musical (*Kiss of the Spider Woman*, 1993, and *Ragtime*, 1998) and Best Play (*Love! Valour! Compassion!*, 1995, and *Master Class*, 1996). With the arguable exception of **Neil Simon**, McNally was the most successful American Broadway dramatist of the decade. Now in his seventies, he remains active writing for **Broadway**, **Off-Broadway**, and **film**.

McNally was born in St. Petersburg, Florida, in 1939 and grew up in Corpus Christi, Texas. In 1956, he moved to New York City to study at Columbia University. After college, he worked as stage manager for New York's **Actors Studio** and came in contact with many of the major dramatic and literary artists of the day. He befriended, among others, **Elia Kazan**, **Lee Strasberg**, and John Steinbeck. (The latter engaged McNally as a tutor for his children.) He became a friend and protégé of noted playwright **Edward Albee**, with whom he had a personal relationship for many years.

After writing a few uncelebrated pieces for Broadway, McNally gained his first commercial and critical success for his farce *The Ritz* (1975). Set in a gay bathhouse, the play was groundbreaking for its time. Running a full year on Broadway, *The Ritz* benefited from even as it helped expand mainstream interest in gay culture, especially in the wake of the famous Stonewall Riots and the subsequent emergence of a highly visible national gay rights movement.

In 1984 McNally wrote his first Broadway musical. Entitled *The Rink* (1984), the production starred famed musical actresses Liza Minnelli and Chita Rivera but was ultimately a critical failure. McNally would not write again for Broadway for nearly a decade but returned with the longest-running Broadway show of his career, *The Kiss of the Spider Woman* (1992). Set in a South American prison, *Spider Woman* explores the intricate relationship between two imprisoned men. Although hardly typical musical fare even for audiences familiar with the dark themes of *Cabaret* (1966) or *Sweeney Todd* (1979), the show was a hit with critics and audiences. The production also represented a triumphant return to Broadway (after an eight-year absence) of veteran Chita Rivera, who won the Tony for Best Actress in a Musical in the title role.

McNally followed *Spider Woman* with *Love! Valour! Compassion!* (1995), a drama that examines the relationships of eight gay men who spend summer holidays together. **Nathan Lane** starred on Broadway but did not participate in McNally's 1997 movie adaptation that featured the rest of the original Broadway cast. Jason Alexander, then at the height of his fame from the television show *Seinfeld*, took Lane's role for the movie, which did not receive widespread distribution or commercial promotion. For the remainder of the 1990s until 2002 McNally enjoyed a string of critical and commercial successes, including *Master Class* (1995), a character study of legendary opera singer Maria Callas that ran for almost two years, *Ragtime*, *The Full Monty* (2002), and a Broadway production of McNally's earlier Off-Broadway success, *Frankie and Johnny in the Clair de Lune* (2002). He also wrote the book for Chita Rivera's autobiographical revue, *Chita Rivera: The Dancer's Life* (2005).

In 2007 a revival of *The Ritz* starring rising Broadway and film actress Rosie Perez failed to meet expectations. In the same year, however, a moderately successful new play, *Deuce*, starred **Angela Lansbury** and Maria Seldes. *Deuce* was a wistfully humorous portrait of two retired women tennis champions-partners-rivals reuniting for a public appearance. The limited engagement run, powered by publicity over Lansbury's first Broadway appearance in 14 years, received mixed reviews from critics but was embraced enthusiastically by fans of the actresses and the author. A new play, *Unusual Acts of Devotion*, which explores the lives and loves of several Greenwich Village apartment dwellers, opened at the Philadelphia Theatre Company in 2008 to outstanding reviews but has not as yet been professionally produced in New York.

Thomas A. Greenfield and Sean Roche

Further Reading

Tipton, Nathan G. "Terrence McNally." *Contemporary Gay American Poets and Playwrights*, ed. Emmanuel S. Nelson. Westport, CT: Greenwood Press, 2003.

Zinman, Toby Silverman. *Terrence McNally: A Casebook*. New York: Garland, 1997.

MEISNER, SANFORD (1905–1997)
ACTOR, DIRECTOR, ACTING TEACHER

Sanford Meisner is best known as one of a handful of New York–based acting teachers to adapt Konstantin Stanislavsky's method to an American theater and film milieu. Teaching at the **Neighborhood Playhouse** from 1935 until 1990, he influenced generations of well-known actors and developed a unique approach to acting that is best summarized by his own slogan that "acting is living truthfully under imaginary circumstances." Meisner himself acted frequently into the 1960s, performing in over 35 Broadway productions as well as a handful of television and film roles (including his final professional acting performance, a 1995 episode of *ER*).

Meisner was born to Hungarian Jewish immigrant parents in 1905 in New York City. As a teenager he acted at the Chrystie Street Settlement on the Lower East Side. In 1924 he made his Broadway debut in *They Knew What They Wanted* by Sidney Howard for the **Theatre Guild**. For seven years he honed his skills acting in plays for the Theatre Guild, such as **George Bernard Shaw**'s *The Doctor's Dilemma* (1927) and **Eugene O'Neill**'s *Marco Millions* (1928), as well as studying at the Theatre Guild's acting school.

Meisner was an original member of the **Group Theatre**, formed in 1931 by **Harold Clurman**, Cheryl Crawford, and **Lee Strasberg**. He acted in many key Group Theatre productions, including Sidney S. Kingsley's *Men in White* (1933) and **Clifford Odets**'s *Awake and Sing!* (1935) and *The Golden Boy* (1937). The Group used Stanislavsky's acting techniques to achieve extraordinary degrees of naturalism in performance and to develop a tight ensemble that sustained itself, with difficulty at times, across a span of ten years. That feat has not been duplicated in Broadway history. Rarely playing starring roles, Meisner learned from the Group the importance of ensemble acting and the need for actors and directors to develop supporting roles—principles that would shape his teaching philosophy for the rest of his career.

The Group Theatre splintered in 1940, largely over artistic differences. Like Stella Adler, another Group Theatre actor who was to become an important acting teacher, Meisner disapproved of the heavy influence on emotional memory emphasized by Strasberg, the Group's principal acting instructor. Adler and Meisner would develop their own techniques in a different direction from that of Strasberg and his followers.

Meisner began teaching acting at the Neighborhood Playhouse in 1935 becoming head of its acting program in 1936. Although he would take on other projects in California and elsewhere throughout this career, his legacy rests on his 50-plus-year association with the Neighborhood Playhouse.

Meisner's most famous teaching innovations came in the form of acting exercises that required actors to repeat words with a partner. His goal was to train the actor to focus on what is really present in the room, in one's partner and in one's self. Other hallmarks of Meisner training included the privileging of instinct over intellect in character development. All of his acting principles were taught with a heavy emphasis on improvisation.

Meisner was mostly beloved by his students, but he was also known for unusual, sometimes controversial methods. He saw each actor as unique and sought to train each one individually. A list of his most successful students reads like a who's who of show business in the mid and late twentieth century, including actors Gregory Peck, Joanne Woodward, Diane Keaton, Jon Voight, Robert Duvall, Grace Kelly, Mary Steenbergen, Peter Falk, Lee Grant, Tony Randall, Jeff Goldblum, as well as director Sydney Pollack and playwright David Mamet. Richard Pinter and a group of acting teachers, all of whom trained with Meisner, carry on his technique at the Neighborhood Playhouse to this day.

After his retirement from the Neighborhood Playhouse in 1990, Meisner moved to North Hollywood and founded another acting school, the Sanford Meisner Center. Martin Barter, who worked with Meisner for years in New York, is the master teacher.

Meisner died on February 2, 1997, in his home in Sherman Oakes, California. His philosophy and teaching techniques still exert a significant influence upon actor training on both coasts.

Melanie N. Blood

Further Reading

Bartow, Arthur. *Training of the American Actor.* New York: Theatre Communications Group, 2006.

Meisner, Sanford, and Dennis Longwell. *Sanford Meisner on Acting.* New York: Vintage Books, 1987.

MERMAN, ETHEL (1908–1984)
SINGER, ACTRESS

"The First Lady of Musical Comedy," Ethel Merman's Broadway career spanned 35 years, from her first role in *Girl Crazy* (1930) to her nostalgic farewell return as Annie Oakley in *Annie Get Your Gun* (original, 1946; Merman revival, 1966), and over a dozen **musicals** in between. Although she never had professional voice training, Merman possessed extraordinary vocal range and volume control—natural qualities that allowed composers and orchestrators enormous freedom in creating musical numbers for her. Her powerful, brassy singing voice and her infectious song delivery style became closely associated with some of the biggest musical hit songs in Broadway history, including "I've Got Rhythm" and "Anything Goes" from **Cole Porter**'s *Anything Goes* (1934), "There's No Business Like Show Business" from **Irving Berlin**'s *Annie Get Your Gun*, and "Everything's Coming Up Roses" from **Jule Styne** and **Stephen Sondheim**'s *Gypsy* (1959). Merman remains an iconic figure in Broadway history—very much a female counterpart to **George M. Cohan**: a diva who embodies the Broadway musical's hyperenergetic, joyously in-your-face demand for attention.

Merman was born as Ethel Agnes Zimmerman in Astoria, New York, on January 16, 1908. As a teenager she sang at local shows and area army bases. After graduating high school, she took secretarial day jobs while landing occasional engagements as a nightclub singer. She quickly impressed both audiences and local show business professionals with her club performances. At age 22 Merman debuted on Broadway in a featured role in **George and Ira Gershwin**'s new musical *Girl Crazy* (1930). The show was very successful, and Merman earned rave reviews for her three songs, including "I've Got Rhythm," the first of Merman's string of showstopping numbers that were to become identified with her fill-the-house voice and personality. She appeared next in a revue, *George White's Scandals* (1931), and a musical comedy, *Take a Chance* (1932).

In 1934, Merman began a fruitful series of collaborations with composer Cole Porter in the musical *Anything Goes*. The show ran for an impressive 420 performances led by Merman's stand-out comic acting and knockout delivery of such songs as "Anything Goes," "I Get a Kick Out of You," and "You're the Top," all songbook standards to this day. *Anything Goes* made Merman a Broadway star. She appeared next in Porter's moderately successful *Red, Hot, and Blue* (1936), in

Ethel Merman, in the role of lady sharpshooter Annie Oakley, and Ray Middleton, in the role of Frank Butler, are seen in the original production of the Broadway musical comedy Annie Get Your Gun, *at the Imperial Theater in New York City, in 1946. (AP Photo)*

which she and co-star Bob Hope immortalized the song "It's De-Lovely." The sardonic song, "Down in the Depths (on the 90th Floor)," which Merman performed solo in *Red, Hot, and Blue*, eventually became an underground anthem in gay/lesbian culture. In 1939 she graduated to her first starring role in Porter's *Du Barry Was a Lady*, which also ran for over 400 performances. This time Merman and co-star Bert Lahr introduced the Porter novelty hit, "Friendship." The Porter/Merman 1940 collaboration *Panama Hattie* was even more successful than *Du Barry*, running 501 performances. Their wartime spirit lifter *Something for the Boys* (1943) ran for a solid year.

Although she had established herself as a major Broadway performer by the time she was 25, Merman also aspired to be a film star. She landed some film work in the 1930s, including an appearance with Bing Crosby in the 1933 musical film

We're Not Dressing and 1938's *Alexander's Ragtime Band*. She also appeared in two film adaptations of her own Broadway musicals, *Anything Goes* (1936) and later *Call Me Madam* (1953). But as quickly and easily as success had come on Broadway, Merman struggled in Hollywood. Her brash, full-out stage persona did not translate effectively to film, and she was later passed over for the screen adaptations of two of her biggest Broadway roles: Annie Oakley in the film version of *Annie Get Your Gun* and Mama Rose in the film of *Gypsy*.

Notwithstanding her Broadway successes as a young songstress prior to and during World War II, Merman achieved even greater stage success and fame as she approached middle age—to this day a career rarity for musical actresses and virtually unheard of at the time. In *Annie Get Your Gun*, Merman wowed audiences as the feisty Annie Oakley, who as a small-town teenager conquered sharpshooter Frank Butler in marksmanship and romance. Merman was 38. Produced by **Richard Rodgers and Oscar Hammerstein** with music composed by Irving Berlin, the show remained on Broadway for almost three years. In Berlin's *Call Me Madam*, Merman played the "age-appropriate" central character based on famed socialite, activist, and diplomat Perle Mesta. Merman earned outstanding reviews for her measured performance as well as her only Tony Award for Best Actress. (In 1972 she received a Special Tony Award recognizing her lifetime of accomplishments in American theater.)

In 1954 Merman announced she was retiring from Broadway to devote time to domestic life and family matters, but she returned two years later to star in *Happy Hunting* by the team of Harold Karr and Matt Dubey. A surprise hit, *Happy Hunting* ran for a full year and produced the very popular "Mutual Admiration Society," sung at the finale by Merman and co-star Fernando Lamas. Then, with her brilliant career seemingly coming gracefully to a close, at age 51 Merman delivered the defining role of her life: Mama Rose in *Gypsy*. Arguably the best female role ever written in the history of the Broadway musical, Merman's Mama Rose displayed amazing vocal and emotional ranges throughout the performance. Rose's closing song, "Rose's Turn," is one of the most dramatically moving "self-declaration" songs in the annals of American musical theater.

The show ran on Broadway for two years and has only grown in popularity through national tours, four Broadway revivals, and countless amateur and professional stagings across North America and Europe. Merman's final Broadway show was as the title character in *Hello, Dolly!* (1964), which she joined in 1970. The show and its main character, Dolly Levy, had originally been written for Merman by young composer and lifetime Merman fan, **Jerry Herman**. But she originally declined the part. Forty-year-old **Carol Channing** originated the role on Broadway instead and launched the next four decades of her career on that character. However, Merman came in as a replacement to finish the last season of the show's six-year Broadway run. Now over 60 years old, Merman delivered the show's big numbers to great effect, including Dolly's famous regal descent down a stage-smothering staircase as the entire chorus—if not the entire universe—sings the title song.

The uniqueness of Merman's talent is the stuff of Broadway legend. Increasingly, since the 1970s decades, Broadway musical performers have been using microphones and voice amplification to deliver a big musical sound—something that for Merman, at least, would have been as unthinkable as it was unnecessary. Her astounding voice, having no Passagio (i.e., no break between her "head voice" and "chest voice," essentially making of her voice a perfectly seamless instrument), gave her an ease of delivery even across huge note ranges that was unique among Broadway performers of her day. The power of her breathing, which came completely naturally to her, outstripped that of most professionally trained and practiced singers, and gave her a command of the musical stage that by all accounts was matchless for its stamina, energy, and impact.

Merman died in New York City on February 15, 1984, of complications relating to a brain tumor.

Shannon Kealey

Further Reading

Flinn, Caryl. *Brass Diva: The Life and Legends of Ethel Merman*. Berkeley, CA: University of California Press, 2007.

Kellow, Brian. *Ethel Merman: A Life*. New York: Viking, 2007.

MERRICK, DAVID (1911–2000)
PRODUCER

The most prolific Broadway producer from 1950 to 1980 and one of the most successful in Broadway history, David Lee Merrick produced more than 80 shows in a career spanning five decades. Known as "the abominable showman," Merrick became a legend for staging outrageous stunts to promote his shows and engaging in highly publicized feuds—which he himself often helped publicize. For years Merrick defied prevailing economic trends of post–World War II Broadway and, in the manner of the early **Shubert Brothers**, **Theatrical Syndicate**, or **David Belasco**, he would mount several productions simultaneously, counting on the hits to compensate for the inevitable commercial losers. His production history includes some of the biggest hit musicals and most significant prestige dramas of his era, including *The Matchmaker* (1955), *Gypsy* (1959), *Hello, Dolly!* (1964), *The Persecution and Assassination of Marat as Performed by the Inmates of the Asylum of Charenton Under the Direction of the Marquis de Sade* (1965), *Travesties* (1975), and *42nd Street* (1980). He is credited with having launched or significantly enhanced the careers of Barbra Streisand, Jerry Orbach, **Ethel Merman**, Robert Morse, and **Carol Channing** among others. Despite Merrick's legendary personal and professional conflicts within the industry, he is among the most honored and decorated figures in the history of American theater.

Producer David Merrick, second from right, listens to composer Burt Bacharach at the piano for the first rehearsal of the Broadway musical Promises, Promises, *1968, New York. Also contributing to the original play were, from left to right, actor Jerry Orbach, actress Jill O'Hara, director Robert Moore, author Neil Simon, Merrick, and actor Edward Winter. (AP Photo/Bob Wands)*

Born David Lee Margulois on November 27, 1911, Merrick was the youngest (by nearly ten years) of five children. Stagestruck since boyhood, Merrick attempted to see every live play, musical, or concert that came to his native town of St. Louis. After graduating from high school Merrick entered nearby Washington University. While at Washington he won second place in a playwriting contest defeating, among other fellow students, a young **Tennessee Williams**. He later transferred to St. Louis University, where he earned a law degree in 1937. At both universities, Merrick tried directing as well as playwriting before deciding that production was the aspect of theater that most appealed to him. Merrick practiced law for seven years in New York while he saved up money to attempt to break into the production business.

Merrick launched his career as a Broadway producer and his reputation for outlandish publicity stunts at about the same time. In 1949, he made his first venture into Broadway theater when he coproduced *Clutterbuck*. The play earned only mediocre reviews but enjoyed a good run largely due to Merrick's novel promotional efforts, including having "Mr. Clutterbuck" paged by bellboys in the lobbies of Manhattan's busiest hotels. As a publicity gimmick for *The Matchmaker* (1955), Merrick arranged for a horse-drawn "cab" to drive up and down Broadway; the cab appeared to be driven by a monkey (the actual driver was concealed behind curtains in the back) with a sign reading, "I am driving my master to see *The Matchmaker*." Retaliating against theater critics for panning his musical *Subways Are For Sleeping* (1961), Merrick found people in the New York phone book with the same names as the city's leading theater critics and secured their permission to advertise the show by attributing favorable quotes to them by name. Merrick produced over 20 shows between 1954 and 1961; almost all of them were successful. In addition to the aforementioned *The Matchmaker* and *Gypsy*, he also mounted *Jamaica* (1957), *Irma La Douce* (1960), and *Carnival* (1961) during this remarkably productive period. In 1960, he set a record as producer or co-producer for 11 shows running simultaneously on Broadway.

In 1964 Merrick produced *Hello, Dolly!*, which became the second longest-running Broadway show to open in the 1960s—behind only *Fiddler on the Roof* (also 1964). *Hello, Dolly!* ran for 2,844 performances and replaced **My Fair Lady** (1956) as the longest-running Broadway musical at the time. The show elevated composer/lyricist **Jerry Herman** to the ranks of Broadway's premiere musical creators, defined lead actress Carol Channing's public persona for the next 30 years, and revived the dormant career of jazz great Louis Armstrong who, at age 63, had an improbable Number 1 pop hit with the show's title song. *Hello, Dolly!* swept the Tony Awards for the season, winning in ten categories, including Best Musical, Best Director of a Musical, and Best Actress in a Musical (won by Channing). A powerful moneymaker, *Hello, Dolly!* was revived three times on Broadway, including an all-black production in 1975. The show was also adapted into a popular film starring Barbra Streisand, and, owing to Channing's performances and durability on the road, became one of the most successful national touring shows of the 1970s and 1980s.

The late 1960s and 1970s saw a period of decline for Merrick. A number of his productions closed after only a handful of performances or even in tryouts or previews. Merrick took an unprecedented (for him) five-year hiatus from Broadway and turned his attention to commercial film. He produced a handful of respectable films, including *The Great Gatsby* (1974), *Semi-Tough* (1977), and *Rough Cut* (1980) but never achieved in Hollywood anything approaching his Broadway success.

In 1980, Merrick made a comeback on Broadway producing what would become the longest-running show of his career, *42nd Street*. The show ran for 3,486 performances over eight and a half years. Opening night became the subject of some extra unexpected media publicity when Merrick announced, following 11 curtain calls and in front of an army of journalists, that the show's director and choreographer, **Gower Champion**, had died just hours before the performance. Some observers would later accuse Merrick of using Champion's death as a promotional ploy. *42nd Street* would be Merrick's last successful production.

In 1983 Merrick suffered a debilitating stroke. The resulting impairment to his health and some legal battles over his business affairs crippled his career. In the next 13 years he would produce his last three shows, none of which was successful: a revival of Joe Orton's crime farce *Loot* (1986), an all-black cast revival of a 1926

Gershwin musical, *Oh, Kay!* (1990), and a stage adaptation of **Rodgers and Hammerstein**'s film musical *State Fair* (1996).

Merrick died of natural causes in London at the age of 88 on April 25, 2000.

Kathy Dreifuss

Further Reading

Dorbian, Iris. *Great Producers: Visionaries of the American Theater.* New York: Allworth Communications, Inc., 2008.

Horn, Barbara Lee. *David Merrick: A Bio-bibliography.* Westport, CT: Greenwood Press, 1992.

MILLER, ARTHUR (1915–2005)
PLAYWRIGHT

For at least two decades prior to his death, Arthur Miller was generally regarded as America's greatest living American **playwright**. He earned this reputation during a 60-year career in which he achieved critical success on Broadway in the 1940s with the dramas *All My Sons* (1947) and ***Death of a Salesman*** (1949). In the 1950s he premiered ***The Crucible*** (1953) and famously refused to "name names" before the House Un-American Activities Committee (HUAC), a decision that enhanced his stature in theatrical and literary circles for the rest of his life. His high-profile marriage in 1956 to film star Marilyn Monroe accorded him media celebrity status serious writers rarely acquire. Although best known as a literary and public figure of the 1940s and 1950s, Miller wrote plays throughout his life as well as numerous essays and a critically acclaimed autobiography, *Timebends* (1987). For half a century following World War II, his writings served as the moral voice for American theater.

Arthur Miller was a born in Manhattan. The family owned a successful coat and suit factory and lived in a large apartment overlooking Central Park. However, the business collapsed just before the Stock Market Crash of 1929, and in 1928 the Millers relocated to a small six-room house in Brooklyn. The move to Brooklyn and the onset of the Depression were the defining events of Miller's youth. Miller graduated high school in Brooklyn but poor grades and family finances initially kept him out of college. In 1934, he entered the University of Michigan where he began his writing career, twice winning the college's major writing award. After graduation, Miller moved back to New York. He joined the **Federal Theatre Project**, writing half-hour radio plays while also working in the Brooklyn Navy Yard. In 1940 he married Mary Slattery, a fellow student.

Miller's first Broadway play, *The Man Who Had All the Luck* (1944), opened to almost universally negative reviews and closed after four performances. However, his next Broadway play, *All My Sons* (1947), was a hit, winning the Tony Award for Best Play and earning Miller widespread audience acclaim. With *All My Sons*, Miller began his professional and personal association with the play's **Elia Kazan**, one of the most prominent directors of the day.

In late 1948, Miller wrote what many consider to be his masterpiece, *Death of a Salesman*. When the play, directed by Kazan, opened in 1949, critical reaction was overwhelming. It ran for 742 performances, winning the Tony Award and the Pulitzer Prize. Within a year of its premiere, *Salesman* was playing in every major city in the United States and had begun its astonishing record of international productions that continues to this day. Miller then wrote an adaptation of Henrik Ibsen's

Arthur Miller poses at his typewriter in New York City, 1949. Miller won the Pulitzer Prize in 1949 for drama for Death of a Salesman. *(AP Photo)*

nineteenth-century classic *An Enemy of the People* (1950), subtly updating it to reflect his outrage at the Army/McCarthy and HUAC investigations. High-profile celebrities were called before these committees and pressed to confess to alleged radical pasts. Elia Kazan was subpoenaed by HUAC and "named names" of celebrities he had encountered at Communist Party meetings during the 1930s. Kazan's testimony caused a breach in his relationship with Miller that would last until the next decade, when Kazan would direct *After the Fall* (1964).

Deeply troubled by the larger social and moral issues raised by the HUAC hearings, Miller saw a connection between the congressional investigations and the seventeenth-century witch trials in Salem, Massachusetts. After traveling to Salem to research the trials, he wrote *The Crucible* (1953). The play opened to mixed reviews, but won the Tony Award for Best Play. A searing indictment of government and society's susceptibility to mob hysteria and self-righteous power mongering, *The Crucible* has since joined *Death of a Salesman* as the most frequently performed American dramas ever written.

Miller's next play, *A View from the Bridge* (1955), explored the Sicilian immigrant society of the Brooklyn docks; it was well received by audiences and critics. Miller then entered a period of personal and political turmoil that kept him from the Broadway stage for nine years. He embarked on an affair with film star Marilyn Monroe and divorced his wife. He suspected that the publicity over his marriage to Monroe would draw the attention of HUAC to his alleged leftist activities, which, indeed, it did. During his testimony, he admitted his attendance at a meeting of Communist writers a decade earlier, but refused to give the names of others. He was tried for contempt of Congress and found guilty. His sentencing was deferred for appeal; in 1958 a federal appeals court overturned his conviction.

In 1960 he revised a short story, "The Misfits," into a screenplay for Monroe, but Monroe and Miller's marriage was already faltering during the filming. Her emotional insecurity and inconsistent work habits among other problems caused an irreparable rift between them and the two divorced. *The Misfits* (1961) would be Monroe's final film. She died in 1962 at age 36, presumably a victim of suicide although speculation and gossip to the contrary persist to this day.

In 1962, Miller married Ingeborg Morath, a renowned photographer, whom he had met on the set of *The Misfits*. In 1964, Miller's first Broadway play in nine years, *After the Fall*, premiered for the new Lincoln Center Repertory Theatre. Critical reaction was negative, especially to the decidedly unsympathetic portrayal of the character Maggie—widely assumed, then as now, to represent the deceased Monroe, who was still an iconic figure in American culture. Notwithstanding its controversial reception, as Miller's first play dealing with the Holocaust *After the Fall* holds a significant place in his canon. He eventually wrote three more plays dealing with the topic: *Incident at Vichy* (1964), *Playing for Time* (teleplay 1980, stage script 1985), and *Broken Glass* (1994).

In the late 1960s, 1970s, and 1980s, Miller continued expressing his political opinions in a variety of writings and activities. He publicly protested the Vietnam War. As President of International P.E.N. (Poets, Essayists, and Novelists), he was an internationally respected critic of intellectual repression and literary censorship. His 1977 play *The Archbishop's Ceiling*, which opened in Washington, D.C., condemned repression of writers in Soviet-controlled Eastern Europe. The play reflected his recent experiences visiting Eastern Europe where he discovered that some of his own conversations were "bugged."

Returning to Broadway with *The American Clock* (1980) Miller chronicled his family's fall into poverty during the 1920s and 1930s, combining their traumatic stories with those of other Americans. In the original production Miller's sister, Joan Copeland, played Rose Baum, a character based upon their mother. Although a favorite of Miller enthusiasts, the Broadway production was unsuccessful.

In the 1980s Miller wrote four one act plays: *Elegy for a Lady* (1982), *Some Kind of Love Story* (1982), *I Can't Remember Anything* (1987), and *Clara* (1987), all of which premiered at the Long Wharf Theater in New Haven, Connecticut. Miller was also engaged, as ever, in politics: supporting the Polish Solidarity movement, protesting Israel's West Bank settlements, and defending the rights of artists and writers in repressive governments such as Turkey and the Soviet Union. Miller's railing against the 1989 Tiananmen Square massacres in China was particularly relevant because he had directed an acclaimed version of *Death of a Salesman* in Beijing in 1984. Miller also began to increasingly criticize the state of the American theater in essays and interviews.

The last 15 years of his life represented a period of remarkable creativity for Miller. *The Ride Down Mount Morgan* premiered in London in 1991 but did not have its Broadway debut until the 2000 season. *The Last Yankee* (1993) opened at the Manhattan Theatre Club on Broadway. *Broken Glass* (1994) received a Tony Award nomination for Best Play, although it ran for only 73 performances. Miller also wrote the screenplay for *The Crucible* (1996) for which he received an Academy Award nomination. In 1999, a fiftieth anniversary Broadway revival of *Death of a Salesman* was a critical and commercial sensation. Miller received a Tony for Lifetime Achievement that year.

Although his early Broadway successes established him as a major playwright, Miller found it difficult to find success on Broadway during the middle and end of his career. His three Tony Award–winning plays, *All My Sons*, *Salesman*, and *Crucible* all premiered between 1947 and 1953. He wrote new plays throughout his life, but after 1970 he never had another major original Broadway hit. After 1970 many of his works premiered in **regional theaters** and, often by Miller's choice, some never had a Broadway opening. While Broadway revivals of his earlier works were plentiful and often well received during this period, Miller frequently expressed dismay at Broadway's commercialization and its attendant toll on production of serious drama.

Miller's final play, *Finishing the Picture* (2004), opened at Chicago's Goodman Theatre, a few months before his death of heart failure. Miller died on February 10, 2005, at his home in Roxbury, Connecticut.

Stephen Marino

Further Reading

Brater, Enoch. *Arthur Miller's America: Theater and Culture in a Time of Change*. Ann Arbor: University of Michigan Press, 2005.
Miller, Arthur. *Timebends: A Life*. New York: Grove Press, 1987.

MUSICALS

The Broadway musical is a distinctively American theatrical tradition that developed principally in New York City in the **Broadway theater district**. The repertoire comprises thousands of works dating from the 1910s to the present, with a particularly rich flourishing in the so-called "Golden Age" of Broadway musicals in the 1940s, 1950s, and mid-1960s. While the Broadway musical owes its origins to many sources, the most important is European classical opera. In fact, the Broadway musical may be viewed as an American national tradition of light opera analogous to the English operetta of **W. S. Gilbert and Arthur Sullivan** and its French and Spanish equivalents, *opéra comique* and *zarzuela*, respectively. The principal ingredients of a Broadway musical—songs, often with amorphous introductory verses followed by strictly constructed refrains, dances, and grandiose choruses—all derive from the operatic tradition. Indeed, the very idea of a theater in which music is an essential dramatic element, the *dramma per musica* or "music drama," is the foundational idea of all European operatic traditions and Broadway as well.

Like those European traditions, the Broadway musical is a popular tradition, surviving without court or government patronage and responsible always to the tastes of its audience. Until relatively recently that audience was composed primarily of middle-class people in metropolitan New York. Production of musical plays is a business, and commercial priorities influence the creation of nearly every work. A successful musical in these terms is simply one that earns more than the sum of its investment and continuing production costs; a failure is one that does not.

Opinion is divided about whether fiscal constraints on the artists have helped or hampered the development of the musical as an art form, but in any case, the genre has certainly taken its place as one of the world's significant theatrical traditions. International recognition came as early as 1950 when **George Gershwin**'s *Porgy and Bess* toured Europe, and in 1959 when productions of Richard Rodgers's *Carousel* and **Leonard Bernstein**'s *Wonderful Town* were mounted at the Brussels World's Fair. Since then American musicals have entered the repertoires of major opera houses such as Vienna's Theatre an der Wien, and revivals of classic musicals have been recorded by the some of the best-known opera stars.

Historical Outline

At the turn of the twentieth century Broadway had been home to a number of musical traditions antecedent to the mature musical: American burlesques of literary classics such as Longfellow's *Evangeline* (1873); **vaudeville** (theatrical variety shows combining skits, songs, dances, tricks, stunts, and other wholesome entertainments for middle-class audiences); and **operettas** of Gilbert and Sullivan, imported since 1879. Operettas were shows with more serious, exotic, and romantic plots with music to suit. **Victor Herbert**'s *Babes in Toyland* (1903), *The Merry Widow* (1907, an English adaptation of Austrian Franz Lehar's *Die Lustige Witwe*), and Sigmund Romberg's *The Desert Song* (1926) are famous examples that found popular success with American audiences in the early twentieth century. Shows with humorous plots and light musical numbers were "musical comedies." Elements from all these traditions coalesced into a complex hybrid of narrative plot, song, and dance that was variously known as "musical play," "book musical," or simply "musical." An important engine for the growing Broadway musical theater was the burgeoning American sheet music industry known as Tin Pan Alley, which offered a ready commercial outlet for the most popular songs from these various kinds of shows and at the same time provided an entrée for composers aspiring to break into the business of musical theater.

The evolution of these various traditions into the mature musical was not at all smooth and linear. Theatrical producers of the 1920s and 1930s trusted known success formulas to make profits and were instinctively suspicious of innovations. The formulas could be quite rigid: a show must begin with a chorus number; everything must orbit the star actor; reprises of the hit tunes must occur late in the second act; no character may die; and there has to be a happy ending. Nevertheless, certain artists who had secured their reputations with strings of such traditional successes could experiment from time to time and did so. From 1915 to 1918 **Jerome Kern** composed a series of intimate shows for the small Princess Theatre in midtown Manhattan that aspired to an unconventional continuity between song and story. He later brought this experience to fruition in the landmark musical *Show Boat* of 1927. George Gershwin broke off his string of musical comedy successes beginning with *Oh, Kay* (1926) to begin a series of political satires starting with *Strike Up the Band* (1930). He then composed on his own initiative his great folk opera *Porgy and Bess* (1935).

Such experiments in the 1930s of combining music and drama underlay what is often called the "Golden Age" of the American musical, a prolific two decades bounded by **Richard Rodgers and Oscar Hammerstein II**'s *Oklahoma!* (1943) and Jerry Bock and Sheldon Harnick's *Fiddler on the Roof* (1964). The Golden Age brought forth an extraordinary pool of talent in musical composition, lyric writing, dance and theatrical direction, set design, and visionary production combined with a heightened consciousness of the aesthetics of music drama and, above all, a rich and popular musical language suited perfectly to such aims. Most of the famous "classic American musicals"—the musicals that are widely regarded as having established the genre as both a legitimate art form and a major American contribution to international popular culture—date from this period.

A falloff in the production of musicals in the mid-1960s and 1970s had many causes. After decades of love story plots, there was perhaps an inevitable move to different dramatic themes such as ethnic identity in *Fiddler on the Roof*, the validity of marriage in **Company** (1970), the forces of history in *Jesus Christ Superstar* (1971) and *Evita* (1979), and personal success in **A Chorus Line** (1975), but new themes have not had the consistent success of the earlier classical formulas. A second change affected the musical theater even more. The advent of rock music ushered out the supple rhythms and modulations of the Romantic style of Tin Pan Alley that had served the musical theater well for six decades. *Hair* (1968) by Gerome Ragni, James Rado, and Galt MacDermot, is generally considered to be the first Broadway "Rock Musical," having paved the way for rock-influenced shows such as *Grease* (1972) and *The Who's Tommy* (1993) as well as the now popular "jukebox musicals" like *Mamma Mia!* (2001) and *Jersey Boys* (2005)—full Broadway shows based on the familiar tunes of pop and rock stars.

As experience has shown, unadulterated rock music is not well suited for traditional music drama. Its driving beat, static harmonies, and unchanging key expresses political protest and overt sexuality very well, but cannot accommodate a character's changing point of view. Consequently, since the 1960s there has been a cultural rift between the music of the theater and the music of the popular culture

Table 2
The Golden Age of Musicals

Title	Date	Composer	Lyricist
Oklahoma!	1943	Richard Rodgers	Oscar Hammerstein II
One Touch of Venus	1943	Kurt Weill	Ogden Nash
Carousel	1945	Richard Rodgers	Oscar Hammerstein II
Annie Get Your Gun	1946	Irving Berlin	Irving Berlin
Street Scene	1947	Kurt Weill	Langston Hughes
Finian's Rainbow	1947	Burton Lane	E. Y. Harburg
Brigadoon	1947	Frederick Loewe	Alan Jay Lerner
Kiss Me, Kate	1948	Cole Porter	Cole Porter
Where's Charley?	1948	Frank Loesser	Frank Loesser
South Pacific	1949	Richard Rodgers	Oscar Hammerstein II
Guys and Dolls	1950	Frank Loesser	Frank Loesser
The King and I	1951	Richard Rodgers	Oscar Hammerstein II
Paint Your Wagon	1951	Frederick Loewe	Alan Jay Lerner
Wonderful Town	1953	Leonard Bernstein	Betty Comden, Adolph Green
Kismet	1953	Alexander Borodin	George Forrest, Robert Wright
The Pajama Game	1954	Richard Adler	Jerry Ross
Peter Pan	1954	Mark Charlap, Jule Styne	Carolyn Leigh, Betty Comden, Adolph Green
Damn Yankees	1955	Richard Adler	Jerry Ross
Fanny	1954	Harold Rome	Harold Rome
The Most Happy Fella	1956	Frank Loesser	Frank Loesser
My Fair Lady	1956	Frederick Loewe	Alan Jay Lerner
Candide	1956	Leonard Bernstein	various
West Side Story	1957	Leonard Bernstein	Stephen Sondheim
The Music Man	1957	Meredith Willson	Meredith Willson
The Flower Drum Song	1958	Richard Rodgers	Oscar Hammerstein II
The Sound of Music	1959	Richard Rodgers	Oscar Hammerstein II
Fiorello!	1959	Jerry Bock	Sheldon Harnick
Gypsy	1959	Jule Styne	Stephen Sondheim
Camelot	1960	Frederick Loewe	Alan Jay Lerner
How to Succeed in Business Without Really Trying	1961	Frank Loesser	Frank Loesser
A Funny Thing Happened on the Way to the Forum	1962	Stephen Sondheim	Stephen Sondheim
Hello, Dolly!	1963	Jerry Herman	Jerry Herman
Fiddler on the Roof	1964	Jerry Bock	Sheldon Harnick

at large that had never existed before—even as the music of popular culture has made advances into Broadway musical production, to the dismay of traditionalists. In addition, a shift away from music drama as the chief dramatic value of a Broadway musical to other elements, such as dance, spectacle, or social criticism, represented a third significant change in musicals since the Golden Age of the 1940s and 1950s. Partisans of the classical concept "music drama" see this later period as the beginning of a decline in the musical's integrity that persists to this day. They point out that in recent years the most exciting new musicals on Broadway have not been original creations but revivals of classic shows; others simply see the movement away from classical musicals to newer forms and production values as a natural transformation of the genre into a different kind of theater.

The past three decades have seen further transformation. The cost of producing new shows has severely limited their numbers, and to be a hit one must aim at a national or even worldwide audience in contrast to the local audiences of the early and mid-twentieth century. Hit musicals have become tourist sites of New York City, things to be visited as the Statue of Liberty and the Empire State Building are visited. Popular musical plays have spawned musical films since the 1930s. But now new musicals, such as **Disney Theatrical Productions'** *Beauty and the Beast* (1994) and *The Lion King* (1997), are created after the release and distribution of blockbuster movies whose popularity ensures a name recognition for tourists. Such interests have created the "megamusical," a theater piece not only gigantic in all its production aspects—music, dance, sound, light, and, above all, special effects—but also in its marketing. These musicals are produced simultaneously in many cities of the world, each production exactly like another down to the look of the actors and the precise blocking of their movements, so that the musical theater has now approximated the unchanging nature of the cinema. The world market has inspired international sources of material and perhaps affected the internationalization of the genre. The French composer Claude-Michel Schönberg's *Les Misérables* played on Broadway from 1987 until 2003. Originally conceived, composed, and produced in France, if it is now to be viewed as a "Broadway" musical—as it is widely considered to be—then the genre is no longer American in the strictest sense.

Landmark Works

From time to time the Broadway musical tradition, like any other living tradition of art, produced particularly influential works that articulate its history. *Show Boat* (1927), with music by Jerome Kern and both lyrics and book (libretto, spoken script) by Oscar Hammerstein II, is generally regarded as the first mature musical play. At a time when the American musical theater connoted diversion and frivolity more than anything else, *Show Boat* told a rambling tale of love and desertion, addiction, and racism. But the mature themes would not ensure the work's survival were they not bound up in a network of musical characterizations and thematic references that make the opening scene one of the most substantial in Broadway's history. *Show Boat* gave the first evidence of the drama of which the Tin Pan Alley style was capable.

Hammerstein also wrote the lyrics and book for *Oklahoma!* (1943), with music by Richard Rodgers, thus initiating the most successful composer/lyricist collaboration in the history of the musical. The show is known as the first major exponent of the "integration" principle, which means not that the distinction between spoken dialogue and sung lyric is effaced or even blurred, but that all the theatrical elements are justified by the dramatic action underlying the play. In most earlier musicals, reprises of the best songs occurred in the second act in order to reignite the audience's flagging interest. In *Oklahoma!*, reprises may occur within a few minutes of the original, when the ever-changing situation can reveal a new meaning by providing a new context. In Rodgers and Hammerstein's work, the singing of a single isolated couplet can have devastating effect.

In **West Side Story** (1957), techniques of integration expanded significantly in two ways. Director and choreographer **Jerome Robbins**, whose conception of adapting **Shakespeare**'s *Romeo and Juliet* to a street gang setting was the musical's origin, made dance move the drama at every turn. Leonard Bernstein's music, with lyrics by **Stephen Sondheim**, has an unprecedented tightness of musical structure on every level from the smallest *motif* (a distinct musical phrase or passage) to the large sets of songs that would follow in rapid succession at key points in the story. These large structures made the slow pacing of tragedy possible. The death of the lead character at the play's end is shrouded in singing and underscoring that capture its moral significance. Broadway's music drama at this point had encompassed tragedy.

Although composer Stephen Sondheim dislikes the term, the "concept musical" first finds wide application to his musical *Company*. The show has no linear plot, but rather presents a series of musical vignettes depicting the friends of Bobby, the one principal character, in various states of matrimony. By avoiding the conventional boy meets girl, boy loses girl, boy gets girl formula, and instead offering a critique of its logical conclusion, *Company* created new possibilities and standards for musical theater, ushering in an era of enormous variety and little consensus about what a proper musical play should be.

One of these possibilities was realized five years later in *A Chorus Line*. Created by director **Michael Bennett** from conversations recorded from dancers, the show is a series of intertwined dancers' biographies. Musical integration is of little concern; in fact, the composer Marvin Hamlisch and lyricist Ed Kleban were brought in to collaborate only after the show was fully formed. *A Chorus Line* blasted all previous records for an opening run, playing for 6,137 performances before it closed on April 28, 1990, one of the first shows to be sustained by a national audience. It redefined what it meant to be a Broadway musical "hit."

The classic nineteenth-century French novel *Les Misérables* of Victor Hugo was set to music and lyrics by French composer Claude-Michel Schönberg and French lyricist Alain Boublil in the manner of a modern Broadway show, with discrete songs, reprises, chorus numbers, and dramatic choreography. It enjoyed a rousing success in limited engagement in France in 1980 before being adapted and translated for an even greater success in London (1985). Its transfer to Broadway in 1987 and blockbuster success closes the circle. The American musical tradition, exported abroad and imitated by French creators, creates a hit that returns to triumph in the home of its ancestors.

Traditions of Composition

The composer of a Broadway musical must be familiar with certain traditions of composition. Except for the work of Bernstein, Sondheim, and a few others, these forms are small-scale compared to their European forbears. This is because the Broadway musical genre derived from popular sources and traditions, and most Broadway composers, until quite recently, were not professionally trained musicians in the European manner, but rather self-taught. **Irving Berlin** required a musical secretary to write down what he composed at the piano by ear. Naturally they learned their art from listening to others' works, which accounts for the consistency of the tradition from 1920 to 1970. During this period, no composer could hope to succeed without the ability to write a good Tin Pan Alley song. Such a song began with the "verse" usually one or two quatrains set to a melody that adhered closely to the rhythm of the words, wandered through various keys, and had little sense of musical meter or of musical organization in general. These technical aspects combined to produce a rather vague and formless music, not usually memorable, that served as a bridge from the spoken dialogue to the "real" tune, just as *recitative* (monologues or dialogues sung to music) may do in some forms of classical opera. The real tune was known as the "refrain."

Compared to the verse, the refrain is a very well-articulated tight structure, with a strong sense of meter and tonal center, all of which makes the tune much more memorable. The refrain is almost always based on a model of 32 measures (bars), composed in four 8-measure phrases. The first two phrases have nearly identical music; the third phrase, the "bridge" or "release," is different, often in a new key; and the fourth sounds close to the first two and makes a strong cadence (ending) in the original key. Thus the typical Tin Pan Alley form: A A B A. Examples of the A A B A show tune are legion and include some of Broadway's best-known songs: "Ol' Man River" from *Show Boat*, "I Could Have Danced All Night" from *My Fair Lady*, and "Matchmaker" from *Fiddler on the Roof* among them. Not all refrains have exactly 32 measures—Richard Rodgers's songs, for example, often attach an extension to the last phrase that prolongs the tension just before the end. But virtually all classic Broadway songs ground themselves in the perceptual symmetry of the 32-bar model even when they depart from it.

Except for Irving Berlin, **Cole Porter**, **Frank Loesser**, Stephen Sondheim, and a few others, composers do not write the lyrics for their songs, but collaborate with specialists, lyricists who are essential contributors to the art of the musical. Which comes first, music or lyrics? Richard Rodgers first worked with the master comic lyricist **Lorenz Hart**, who never wrote a lyric without first hearing Rodgers's tune, fitting the words to the music's rhythm and melodic contour. Then Rodgers collaborated with Oscar Hammerstein II, who sent him entirely finished lyrics in the mail, to which Rodgers composed his songs. Obviously both practices can work, but it is more common for a composer to have the lyrics, at least in draft, before he begins writing a song.

A composer and lyricist might compose as many as 20 or 25 songs for a show, of which 10 to 20 might be retained after tryouts and cuts. These tunes would also provide the material for the overture and dances in the show. Most Broadway shows begin with an instrumental overture of some kind. Most common is the "medley" overture, a very loose organization that plays four or five of what the producers believe to be the most attractive tunes, separated by brief modulating transitions, leading to a rousing finish that brings up the curtain (e.g., *Oklahoma!*, *My Fair Lady*). There is no relation among the tunes in the overture except that they come from the same show. Subtler openings, often called "preludes," try to establish deeper musical relations, usually character motives, with the play that is to follow. The original opening to *Show Boat* and the dance prelude to *West Side Story* are fine examples.

Refrain tunes sometimes provide the basis for another, more ambitious form of vocal composition called the "ensemble," which has a long tradition in European opera. An ensemble is composed for more than one singing character, each of whom maintains his or her specific perspective on the dramatic situation. It is therefore distinct from the duet where two characters share the same lyrics, tune, and emotional expression such as "People Will Say We're in Love" from *Oklahoma!* and from the chorus number, where all the singers represent one point of view, such as "One" from *A Chorus Line.* But when, in the great quintet "Tonight" from *West Side Story*, Riff and the Jets sing in fierce anticipation of their oncoming street brawl, as do Bernardo and the Sharks from their side, while Anita looks forward to a romantic night and the doomed lovers Tony and Maria plan their escape from a violent world, each with distinct lyrics and contrasting music, all wrapped up in a single continuous composition, we have an ensemble. The ensemble does what spoken dialogue cannot: summarizes a dramatic situation, often conflicting, in a simultaneous expression by various characters. The construction demands considerable ingenuity on the composer's part. The ensemble "One Day More" that ends the first act of *Les Misérables* manages to combine in musical counterpoint three tunes already heard over a repeating bass melody.

The dances of a show often appear as extensions to a song. There is no rigid dance form comparable to the verse-refrain song form, but the symmetrical phrasing of the refrain supplies an organization that dancers can follow. Often, the form of the dances is not finalized for a Broadway opening until the show has had tryout performances or a preliminary run in other locations.

Although the composer is credited with the songs, much of the musical work is usually accomplished by another musician, the orchestrator. After the composer writes the songs at the piano, the orchestrator takes the manuscripts and decides how the orchestra is to play them. Often the orchestrator uses the refrain tunes to create the overture and, in collaboration with the choreographer, the dance numbers as well.

Since the 1960s composers and lyricists have experimented with other musical forms. New compositional strategies include the "parody" or "contrafactum," whereby the tune of one set of lyrics is applied to another, often quite different set of lyrics. Important examples occur in **Andrew Lloyd Webber**'s *Evita* and Schönberg and Boublil's *Les Misérables*. Stephen Sondheim often purposefully composes stylistic anachronisms—idioms of music from the past that can recall a certain atmosphere, time, or place.

Ingredients of a "Classic Musical"

Musical introduction—Opening scene. The standard formula for musicals of the early decades of the twentieth century, adapted directly from European opera, was the medley overture with the curtain coming up on a stage full of characters in striking costumes: the arrival of the show boat at the wharf (*Show Boat*); the tenants of Catfish Row gathered outside on a hot summer's evening (*Porgy and Bess*); the gangs of New York in choreographic confrontation (*West Side Story*); the people of the village Anatevka celebrating their Jewish traditions (*Fiddler on the Roof*). But there were many variations on this conventional opening. In *Fiddler*, the musical introduction is a single 8-bar violin tune. In *Oklahoma!* and *Mame* (1966) the crowd arrives only after the opening song.

Rodgers and Hammerstein's *Carousel*, a show especially rich in the conventions of the classical musical, combines the functions of musical introduction and spectacular vision in a single composition and, thus, serves as a particularly instructive model of the form. *Carousel* begins with quiet, mysteriously chromatic strains in the orchestra. It quickly builds to a grand waltz and the curtain rises to reveal a turning carousel surrounded by a happy crowd at a seaside town in Maine. The action is entirely mimed, no words are spoken, and yet the action conveys the immediate attraction of the rough-edged carousel barker, Billy Bigelow, and a shy young woman, Julie Jordan. When the waltz reaches its brilliant conclusion, the play's action is well underway.

Double romance. Billy is a deeply conflicted man who, in his struggles to express himself, does allow an obscure inner goodness to shine out. Julie is equally introverted, yet becomes his redeeming woman. Playing against this romance of utmost seriousness is a comic one between Julie's friend Carrie and the pompous self-made man Mr. Snow. In *Carousel* Carrie and Mr. Snow's conventional yet musically deep engagement makes a value of social convention against which Billy rebels, and so is essential to the play's action. But the comic romance also provides the narrative with relief of its serious moral tone, and because of this secondary love interest the plot can afford to slow the progress of the principal romance and thus fill out the action of the play. This is why so many successful musical plays make the double romance, one serious and one comic, the backbone of their narrative form.

Scene integration. The essential problem for the creators of a classic musical—composer, lyricist, librettist—is how to unite the music with the action in a way that allows all the elements of music, lyrics, spoken dialogue, set, character development, dance, and action to cohere. The ways to accomplish this are myriad but fragile. In *Carousel*, to have either Julie or Billy say "I love you" to the other would be a contradiction of character and would undermine the play's central dramatic interest. Thus the composer and lyricist had to confront the difficulty of portraying the progress of the romance implicitly. Julie and Billy sit together on a beach park bench and muse what it would be like "If I Loved You." The confession of love never passes their lips, but it arises from the music, especially through the harmonic references to the opening carousel scene, and at the end when he kisses her with the song's most climactic melodic phrase played by the orchestra. Music connects the scene with everything that preceded it in numerous ways. The scene makes no sense, and is dramatically void, without its music.

Musical character. Most musicals have "character" songs that do little more than establish the principal stock types in the narrative, usually near the beginning of the play. "I Can't Say No" of the lovelorn comic heroine Ado Annie in *Oklahoma!* is an excellent example, as is "If I Were a Rich Man" from *Fiddler on the Roof.* Sometimes these songs do more. When the male lead character Porgy sings "When Gawd Make Cripple" in the opening scene of *Porgy and Bess*, his first lyric melody, it presents his deep loneliness as his defining characteristic that will drive the entire drama. When Tony, the male lead character in *West Side Story*, sings of his inchoate expectation in "Something's Coming," the main musical motive ties his feelings to his future lover Maria. *Carousel*'s Billy Bigelow's moment of self-revelation comes late in the first act. "Soliloquy (My Boy Bill)" paints a superficial self-portrait as he imagines the future of his newly announced child, a boy of course. The music sounds like little else in the play, because the picture we are given is not real. When the thought strikes him that the child might be a little girl, the music recovers the introspective idiom of the carousel scene and the bench scene. We hear Billy begin to come to terms with himself. In this case, the song is much more than one of character definition; it is also a medium of dramatic action, since the action of Billy connecting and not repressing his own inner goodness is at the center of the drama.

Reprise. The idea of using music as a symbol to represent some element of the drama is as old as opera itself. Its most famous application is the leitmotif operas of Richard Wagner, in which a readily identifiable musical phrase or passage is associated specifically with a certain character or other discrete aspect of the story. George Gershwin follows this practice in *Porgy and Bess*. In Broadway musicals, the musical symbol is carried out as a reprise of a song heard earlier in the show.

There are many forms and uses of the reprise. In the musical comedies of the 1920s and 1930s, it was principally a device to maintain audience engagement. The best song of the first act would be reprised in the second, whether the situation demanded it or not. We hear this as late as 1950, when the finale of *Guys and Dolls* brings back the title song simply to make a loud, happy, choral ending and for no other reason. Even the reprise of "Do You Hear the People Sing" at the very end of *Les Misérables* recalls this practice.

In more sophisticated uses the reprise makes a dramatic point. It can do this, without changing any words or notes, because as a musical symbol it is interpreted not only by itself but also within its dramatic context, ever changing in the course of the play. When Magnolia sings "Why Do I Love You?" to her daughter Kim in Act II of *Show Boat*, the audience can instantly sense the transfer of her love from her runaway husband to her daughter, because everyone recalls how she sang it to him in Act I. The reference need not be lengthy; in the great tragic reprise of "There's a Place for Us," sung by Maria to her dying Tony in *West Side Story*, the pair cannot even complete three phrases.

Another masterly reprise occurs near the end of *Carousel* when Billy's spirit, dispatched after his suicide, is allowed to return to earth for a time to make amends with Julie, to whom he has never confessed his true feelings. Here there is a slight, but all-important change of lyric: "If I Loved You" becomes "How I Loved You," and so recalls Billy's struggle to express his own love, consummated with the music that should have done so in the first act.

Finale. Each of the two acts almost always concludes with an extended musical finale, a practice in common with European classical opera. Typically, the stage is full of people, symmetrical with the opening scene. The first act finale emphasizes the main conflict of the drama and leaves the audience wanting to see its resolution. Thus the first act of *Carousel* ends shortly after "Soliloquy," when Billy decides on a desperate course of action to provide for his future child. The second act finale contains the musical resolution of the dramatic action; Billy and Julie reconcile, his spirit touching her from beyond the grave.

Types of Dramatic Action

Despite the consensus about the necessary elements of a good musical, a consensus that began to fray in the 1960s, the musical has proved itself adaptable to many kinds of dramatic action told through music. This range of dramatic structures can be accounted for in part by the variety of sources that composers, writers, and lyricists have used for creating Broadway musicals. Legitimate plays and novels are the principal sources, but musicals have sprung from epics both classical and modern (*The Golden Apple* from Homer; *Les Misérables*), religious texts (*Godspell*), biographies (*Fiorello!*; *Evita*), historical episodes (*1776*), collections of poetry (**Cats**), short story collections (*Guys and Dolls*; *Fiddler on the Roof*), fable (*Brigadoon*), a set of interviews (*A Chorus Line*), and even from an impressionist painting (*Sunday in the Park with George*). The creators of successful shows saw in these varied sources a dramatic action that could be realized, and a means to accomplish the artistic goal of musical theater: to use music, songs especially, as a dramatic agent.

In doing so, the musical seems to have followed the life cycle typical of a vital artistic genre. It grew from a local business to first a national and then an international phenomenon. It developed and then lost a symbiotic relationship with the popular culture. It coordinated disparate elements of varied theatrical traditions

Table 3
Tony Awards for Best Musicals, 1949–2009

Year	Musical	Composers and Lyricists
1949	*Kiss Me Kate*	Music and lyrics by Cole Porter
1950	*South Pacific*	Music by Richard Rodgers; Lyrics by Oscar Hammerstein II
1951	*Guys and Dolls*	Music and lyrics by Frank Loesser
1952	*The King and I*	Lyrics by Oscar Hammerstein II; Music by Richard Rodgers
1953	*Wonderful Town*	Music by Leonard Bernstein; Lyrics by Betty Comden and Adolph Green
1954	*Kismet*	Music by Alexander Borodin; Adapted and with lyrics by Robert Wright and George Forrest
1955	*The Pajama Game*	Music and lyrics by Richard Adler and Jerry Ross
1956	*Damn Yankees*	Music by Richard Adler and Jerry Ross
1957	*My Fair Lady*	Lyrics by Alan Jay Lerner; Music by Frederick Loewe
1958	*The Music Man*	Music and lyrics by Meredith Willson
1959	*Redhead*	Music by Albert Hague, lyrics by Dorothy Fields
1960	*The Sound of Music* (tie)	Lyrics by Oscar Hammerstein II; Music by Richard Rodgers
1960	*Fiorello!* (tie)	Lyrics by Sheldon Harnick; Music by Jerry Bock.
1961	*Bye Bye Birdie*	Music by Charles Strouse; Lyrics by Lee Adams
1962	*How to Succeed in Business Without Really Trying*	Music and lyrics by Frank Loesser
1963	*A Funny Thing Happened on the Way to the Forum*	Music and lyrics by Stephen Sondheim
1964	*Hello, Dolly!*	Music and lyrics by Jerry Herman
1965	*Fiddler on the Roof*	Music by Jerry Bock; Lyrics by Sheldon Harnick
1966	*Man of La Mancha*	Music by Mitch Leigh; Lyrics by Joe Darion
1967	*Cabaret*	Music by John Kander; Lyrics by Fred Ebb
1968	*Hallelujah, Baby!*	Music by Jule Styne; Lyrics by Betty Comden and Adolph Green
1969	*1776*	Music and lyrics by Sherman Edwards
1970	*Applause*	Music by Charles Strouse; Lyrics by Lee Adams (Book by Betty Comden and Adolph Greene)
1971	*Company*	Music and lyrics by Stephen Sondheim
1972		Music by Galt MacDermot; Lyrics by John Guare

Year	Musical	Composers and Lyricists
	Two Gentlemen of Verona	
1973	*A Little Night Music*	Music and lyrics by Stephen Sondheim
1974	*Raisin*	Music by Judd Woldin; Lyrics by Robert Brittan
1975	*The Wiz*	Music by Charlie Smalls; Lyrics by Charlie Smalls
1976	*A Chorus Line*	Music by Marvin Hamlisch; Lyrics by Edward Kleban
1977	*Annie*	Music by Charles Strouse; Lyrics by Martin Charnin
1978	*Ain't Misbehavin'*	Music by Thomas "Fats" Waller, in addition to songs by various artists
1979	*Sweeney Todd*	Music by Stephen Sondheim; Lyrics by Stephen Sondheim
1980	*Evita*	Music by Andrew Lloyd Webber; Lyrics by Tim Rice
1981	*42nd Street*	Music by Harry Warren; Lyrics by Al Dubin
1982	*Nine*	Music and lyrics by Maury Yeston
1983	*Cats*	Music by Andrew Lloyd Webber; Lyrics based on *Old Possum's Book of Practical Cats* by T. S. Eliot
1984	*La Cage aux Folles*	Music and lyrics by Jerry Herman
1985	*Big River*	Music and lyrics by Roger Miller
1986	*The Mystery of Edwin Drood*	Music and lyrics by Rupert Holmes
1987	*Les Misérables*	Music by Claude-Michel Schönberg; Lyrics by Herbert Kretzmer
1988	*The Phantom of the Opera*	Music by Andrew Lloyd Webber; Lyrics by Charles Hart
1989	*Jerome Robbins' Broadway*	Songs by various artists, including Leonard Bernstein, Irving Berlin, Richard Rodgers, and others
1990	*City of Angels*	Music by Cy Coleman; Lyrics by David Zippel
1991	*The Will Rogers Follies*	Music by Cy Coleman; Lyrics by Betty Comden and Adolph Green
1992	*Crazy for You*	Music by George Gershwin; Lyrics by Ira Gershwin
1993	*Kiss of the Spider Woman—The Musical*	Music by John Kander; Lyrics by Fred Ebb
1994	*Passion*	Music and lyrics by Stephen Sondheim
1995	*Sunset Boulevard*	Music by Andrew Lloyd Webber; Lyrics by Don Black and Christopher Hampton

Table 3 (continued)

Year	Musical	Composers and Lyricists
1996	*Rent*	Music and lyrics by Jonathan Larson
1997	*Titantic*	Music by Maury Yeston; Lyrics by Maury Yeston
1998	*The Lion King*	Music by Elton John; Lyrics by Tim Rice
1999	*Fosse*	Songs by various artists, including Cole Porter, Cy Coleman, Dorothy Fields, John Kander, and others
2000	*Contact*	Music and lyrics by various artists
2001	*The Producers*	Music and lyrics by Mel Brooks
2002	*Thoroughly Modern Millie*	New music by Jeanine Tesori; New lyrics by Dick Scanlan
2003	*Hairspray*	Music by Marc Shaiman; Lyrics by Scott Wittman and Marc Shaiman
2004	*Avenue Q*	Music and lyrics by Robert Lopez and Jeff Marx
2005	*Monty Python's Spamalot*	Music by John Du Prez and Eric Idle; Lyrics by Eric Idle
2006	*Jersey Boys*	Music by Bob Gaudio; Lyrics by Bob Crewe
2007	*Spring Awakening*	Music by Duncan Sheik; Lyrics by Steven Sater
2008	*In The Heights*	Music and lyrics by Lin-Manuel Miranda
2009	*Billy Elliot, The Musical*	Lyrics by Lee Hall; Music by Elton John

Sources: Internet Broadway Database. http://www.ibdb.com/advancesearchaward.asp; American Theatre Wing. "Tony Awards" [Search Past Winners]. http://www.tonyawards.com.

into a mature tradition, and then, after a period of success and ever more conscious awareness, fragmented the tradition into a wild diversity of self-conscious styles.

Joseph P. Swain

Further Reading

Banfield, Stephen. *Jerome Kern. Yale Broadway Masters*, gen. ed. Geoffrey Block. New Haven, CT: Yale University Press: 2006.

———. *Sondheim's Broadway Musicals*. Ann Arbor: University of Michigan Press, 1993.

Block, Geoffrey. *Enchanted Evenings: The Broadway Musical from* Show Boat *to Sondheim*. New York: Oxford University Press, 1997.

———. *Richard Rodgers. Yale Broadway Masters*, gen. ed. Geoffrey Block. New Haven, CT: Yale University Press: 2003.

Bordman, Gerald. *American Musical Theatre: A Chronicle*. New York: Oxford University Press, 2001.

———. *American Operetta: From H.M.S. Pinafore to Sweeney Todd*. New York: Oxford University Press, 1981.

The Cambridge Companion to the Musical, ed. William A. Everett and Paul R. Laird. New York: Cambridge University Press, 2002.

Carter, Tim. *Oklahoma! The Making of an American Musical*. New Haven, CT: Yale University Press, 2007.

Engel, Lehman. *The Making of a Musical*. New York: Macmillan, 1977.

McClung, Bruce D. *Lady in the Dark: Biography of a Musical*. New York: Oxford University Press, 2006.

McMillin, Scott. *The Musical as Drama: A Study of the Principles and Conventions Behind Musical Shows from Kern to Sondheim*. Princeton, NJ: Princeton University Press, 2006.

Mordden, Ethan. *Beautiful Mornin': The Broadway Musical in the 1940s*. New York: Oxford University Press, 1999.

———. *Coming Up Roses: The Broadway Musical in the 1950s*. New York: Oxford University Press, 1998.

Most, Andrea. *Making Americans: Jews and the Broadway Musical*. Cambridge, MA: Harvard University Press, 2004.

Snelson, John. *Andrew Lloyd Webber*. Yale Broadway Masters, gen. ed. Geoffrey Block. New Haven, CT: Yale University Press, 2004.

Sternfeld, Jessica. *The Megamusical*. Bloomington: Indiana University Press, 2006.

Swain, Joseph P. *The Broadway Musical: A Critical and Musical Survey*. Rev. and expanded ed. Lanham, MD: Scarecrow Press, 2002.

Walsh, David F. *Musical Theater and American Culture*. Westport, CT: Praeger, 2003.

MY FAIR LADY

Broadway Run: Mark Hellinger Theatre (March 15, 1956 to February 24, 1962); Broadhurst Theatre (February 28, 1962 to April 14, 1962); Broadway Theatre (April 18, 1962 to September 29, 1962)
Opening: March 15, 1956
Closing: September 29, 1962
Total Performances: 2,717
Book: Alan Jay Lerner, adapted from *Pygmalion* by George Bernard Shaw
Lyricist: Alan Jay Lerner
Composer: Frederick Loewe
Choreographer: Hanya Holm
Director: Moss Hart
Producer: Herman Levin
Lead Performers: Rex Harrison (Henry Higgins), Julie Andrews (Eliza Doolittle), and Stanley Holloway (Alfred P. Doolittle)

From the unlikeliest of source material came *My Fair Lady*, which the *New York Times* called a "perfect" **musical**. That *My Fair Lady* became the most celebrated and commercially successful musical of the 1950s, surpassing the record set by ***Oklahoma!*** for the longest-running musical, could hardly have been expected from the play on which it was based, **George Bernard Shaw**'s *Pygmalion*. The

1916 Shaw play had frustrated a number of celebrated composers and lyricists who had attempted to adapt it as a musical until it fell to the team of **Alan Jay Lerner** and **Frederick Loewe**. The plot revolves around the attempt on the part of Henry Higgins, a British speech professor, to pass off a Cockney flowergirl, Eliza Doolittle, as a duchess at an embassy ball. Higgins trains her in proper speech to test his notion that only English properly spoken separated British social classes. What usually worked on Broadway at the time were musicals with romance at their center, but *My Fair Lady* had no romance to speak of, not even a kiss. In this musical, the major romance is with language, "the greatest possession we have," declares Higgins. Even Shaw felt the need to write an epilogue to the original play stating in no uncertain terms how wrong it would be for Higgins to wed the flowergirl Eliza. Lerner and Loewe would tackle this Shavian dilemma with imagination and inspiration, creating one of the most literary and intelligent musicals Broadway would ever see. The cultural dynamics among English social classes during the 1910s would hardly seem the stuff of which popular American musicals were made in the 1950s, yet this most un-American theme was made irresistible to Broadway audiences owing to a witty and sophisticated script and score. The seamless transition from "spoken Shaw" to "sung Lerner" left audiences wondering where one author left off and the other began.

Alan Jay Lerner (Juilliard and Harvard trained) and Frederick Loewe (whose checkered career saw stints as a Prohibition pianist, busboy, and boxer) began work as a team in 1942 for a rewrite of a show titled *Life of the Party*, which closed in Detroit. They followed it with *What's Up?* (1943) and *The Day Before Spring* (1945), each gaining modest critical support. Finally, they got their first hit in the fantasy *Brigadoon* (1947) and followed it with the California Gold Rush musical *Paint Your Wagon* (1951). Lerner and Loewe were initially approached about turning *Pygmalion* into a musical in 1952 by film producer Gabriel Pascal who owned the film rights to all of Shaw's work. Their early attempt proved fruitless and the project was set aside. Lerner was then engaged by producer Herman Levin to write a musical version of Al Capp's comic strip *L'il Abner* (with composer Arthur Schwartz), but he struggled with it. When Pascal died in 1954, Lerner decided to take another look at *Pygmalion*.

This time Lerner saw a way to make it work musically and convinced Levin that this was the project that he should be producing. Since the play was essentially composed of a series of drawing room scenes, it would need to be opened up so that a chorus could be introduced into the musical. Lerner and Loewe turned to Shaw's own screenplay for the 1938 film for inspiration. Shaw's play ends with Eliza leaving, but in his screenplay's final scene, Eliza returns to Higgins's study and Higgins asks her for his slippers. Lerner lifted the film's scene practically intact providing an ambiguous ending that pleased both Shaw purists and hopeful romantics. Lerner took advantage of the new scene locations in the screenplay and added the Ascot racetrack and the embassy ball, places a chorus could be comfortably inserted. Eliza's dustman father, Alfred Doolittle, had two musical numbers that echoed the style of the English Music Hall and provided an opportunity

Rex Harrison as Henry Higgins and Julie Andrews as Eliza Doolittle in a scene from My Fair Lady *at the Mark Hellinger Theater in New York City, March 1956. (AP Photo)*

for the chorus to break into a traditional Broadway production number ("Get Me to the Church on Time").

Musical comedy up to this point demanded a good singing voice over acting skills. *My Fair Lady* reversed that notion to spectacular effect. Creating a leading role for the accomplished stage and film actor **Rex Harrison**, composer Loewe famously said of Harrison that he had a singing range of one and a half notes. (By contrast, twenty-one-year-old **Julie Andrews**, playing Eliza, had a beautiful four-octave soprano voice.) But Harrison did possess an excellent sense of rhythmic speech. The songs for the musical's Henry Higgins became a combination of rhythmic speaking and an occasional sung note, creating a musical comedy model that would be copied by other composers and lyricists for years to come.

The production began rehearsals on January 3, 1956, and played out-of-town tryouts in New Haven (where two songs were cut) and Philadelphia. It opened on March 15, 1956, on Broadway to unanimous rave reviews. When *My Fair Lady* ended its Broadway run, it had been seen by over 3 million people and had earned nearly $40 million. Warner Brothers purchased the **film** rights for over $5 million, and their film version, which premiered in 1964, would go on to win eight Oscars, including Best Picture and Best Actor.

Adding to the impact of the show was the extraordinary success of the original cast album. Columbia Records, prodded by record producer Goddard Lieberson, had bankrolled the entire stage production ($400,000) and secured the rights to produce the cast album. This turned out to be an extraordinarily smart business decision. The album spent 15 weeks at No. 1 in the charts and became the top-selling album of both 1957 and 1958. With the advent of new recording technology came another first, as the stars of the original cast recorded a second cast album during the London run, this time in stereo.

Lerner and Loewe would never achieve the unparalleled success of *My Fair Lady* in subsequent collaborations, although the 1958 film score for their Oscar-winning *Gigi* was widely admired. *Camelot* (1960) became their final Broadway offering, with Loewe retiring and Lerner continuing to work with a number of different composers (including Burton Lane, Charles Strouse, **Leonard Bernstein**, and John Barry). Of all his later musicals, only *On a Clear Day You Can See Forever* (1965) would enjoy modest success.

My Fair Lady became a musical that bravely broke rules and in the process established a new standard of creativity in American musical theater. The elegant and stylish lyrics of Lerner wedded with the romantically tinged music of Loewe were the perfect match to the wit and cynicism of Shaw. Together, they created one of the most durable, beloved, and revived shows in musical theater history.

Daniel Yurgaitis

Further Reading

Lees, Gene. *The Musical Worlds of Lerner and Loewe*. Lincoln, NE: Bison Books, 2005.
Walker, Alexander. *Fatal Charm: The Life of Rex Harrison*. London: Orion Books, 2002.

N

NATHAN, GEORGE JEAN

See **Critics**.

THE NEDERLANDER ORGANIZATION
THEATRE OWNERS, PRODUCERS

The Nederlander Organization, named for the family that founded the organization and runs it to this day, has been a major force in Broadway theater ownership and theater production since the late 1960s. The Nederlander Organization (alternately, "The Nederlanders") stands today along with its older rival and occasional partner, the **Shubert Organization**, as the premier family-originated Broadway production company and Broadway's second largest theater owner. Unlike other major theatrical companies, including the present-day Schubert Organization, the Nederlander Organization is still managed by family members, as it has been since its founding. (The Shuberts' theatrical affairs have been managed by nonfamily members since the 1970s.) Family management makes the Nederlanders not only a unique entity among producers but also an historical "throwback" to pre–World War II Broadway production, when famous individuals or families, rather than corporations and large investment groups, were often personally identified with the shows they produced and the theaters they owned.

The Nederlander Organization was formed in 1912 in Detroit to support family ownership of a single theater there. David T. Nederlander was originally a Detroit jewelry store owner, who credited **Shubert Brothers** J. J. and Lee for his education in the theater business. In 1912, Nederlander entered into a shared ownership with the Shuberts of Detroit's Shubert-Lafayette Theatre and shared management with them of the Detroit Opera House. The partnership lasted over 40 years until the federal government filed an antitrust suit against the Shuberts, forcing them to sell off some of their theater interests. Nederlander ultimately became sole owner of the Shubert-Layfette in 1957. His son, James M. Nederlander, expanded the family business to New York City in the 1960s, purchasing the famous Palace Theatre in the heart of Broadway.

Originally built as a **vaudeville** showcase, the Palace had been a "dark" stage for years, showing only movies and hosting an occasional concert by the likes of Harry Belafonte or Judy Garland. The newly arrived Nederlanders won great praise from the Broadway community by bringing legitimate theater back to the Palace, starting auspiciously with the 1966 hit *Sweet Charity*. The Palace is still a Nederlander-owned mainstay of Broadway, housing such modern day hit musicals as *Legally Blonde* (2007) and the five-year run of **Disney**'s *Beauty and the Beast* (1994). Over the next 20 years, the Nederlander Organization acquired eight additional theaters in the city, tailoring most of their purchases toward larger venues that could house "big stage" mainstream musicals, including the Lunt-Fontanne (*The Little Mermaid*, 2008), the Minksoff Theatre (*The Lion King*, 2006), and the Marquis (2004 revival of *La Cage aux Folles*).

The Nederlanders' strategy of buying and adapting their theaters for big musicals proved to be both a cause and an effect of the rise of spectacle and effects-driven musical productions (sometimes called megamusicals) on Broadway at the close of the twentieth century. In 1980 the Nederlander family renamed their Trafalgar Theatre after their patriarch, David, who had died in 1967. The Nederlander Theatre tends to house straight plays and small-scale musicals rather than the family's trademark big hit musical spectaculars.

The family-oriented Nederlander Organization now relies heavily on its third generation of family management. David Nederlander's five sons—James M., Joseph, Harry, Fred, and Robert—have all been involved in the business at some point. Joseph Nederlander managed the Detroit Office, and James M. Nederlander, the current chairman, and his son James L. Nederlander, the current president, are based in New York.

The Nederlander Organization currently owns the largest number of Broadway theaters of any single entity other than the Shubert Organization, with whom the Nederlanders have a turbulent past. The Nederlanders and Shuberts have engaged in bidding wars and sometimes compete fiercely over production rights to shows and theater purchases. (At one point, the Shubert Organization canceled seats reserved for the Nederlanders in their theater.) Over the years, the rivalry has occasionally carried over into headline-making quarrels. Yet, despite competitive disagreements, the two organizations have engaged in some fruitful collaborations over the years, including a revival of *Fiddler on the Roof* (1976) and the heralded epic production of *Nicholas Nickleby* (1980).

As with the Shuberts, the Nederlanders' investment in theater throughout the country has led them directly into production of national tours of Broadway shows, which play in their own out-of-town theaters as well as others. The Nederlanders have produced and backed some of the most successful touring productions of Broadway shows in the past several years, including national tours of *Cats*, *Rent*, *The Producers*, and *Wicked*.

Thomas A. Greenfield and Christy E. Allen

Further Reading

Berkowitz, Gerald M. *New Broadways: Theatre Across America, 1950–1980.* New York: Rowan & Littlefield, 1982.

Rose, Philip. *You Can't Do That on Broadway!: A Raisin in the Sun and Other Theatrical Improbabilities: A Memoir.* New York: Limelight Editions, 2001.

NEIGHBORHOOD PLAYHOUSE
THEATER COMPANY, PRODUCERS

The Neighborhood Playhouse in lower Manhattan has had two distinct incarnations, each significant to the history of Broadway but for decidedly different reasons: first was the experimental semiprofessional theater company and then came the influential school for actors.

In the 1910s and 1920s, the Neighborhood Playhouse was one of a triumvirate of New York City "little theatres" that were to revitalize Broadway repertoire, design, and acting styles. When the Neighborhood Playhouse closed its theater company down in 1927 and abandoned their downtown theater building, a few of the artists affiliated with the company founded the Neighborhood Playhouse School of the Theatre further uptown on East 54th Street. Still operating 80-plus years later, the Neighborhood Playhouse School has produced countless well-known actors and served as the resident teaching home of two great American performing arts masters: Martha Graham taught modern dance in the 1920s and 1930s and, in the 1930s, **Sanford Meisner** developed his acting technique with generations of Neighborhood Playhouse students (he retired from teaching in 1990).

The young artists of the Neighborhood Playhouse—along with the Washington Square Players/**Theatre Guild**, and the **Provincetown Players** (all founded in 1915)—deliberately stepped outside of the restrictions of commercial theater, as their colleagues in Europe had done roughly 20 years before. They hoped to develop an American version of the European little theater movement that introduced what came to be known as New Stagecraft.

In the 1910s, commercial theater was completely controlled by the monopolistic practices of the **Shuberts**, which had recently wrested control from the equally monopolistic **Theatrical Syndicate**. Broadway was no home to innovation; the profit motive prevailed and popular melodramas and musical reviews were the typical fare. America had yet to find a national playwright, as European nations had found Henrik Ibsen, **George Bernard Shaw**, and John Millington Synge. Moreover, America and had yet to adopt the new visual and performance styles associated with modern art across the Atlantic.

Agnes Morgan, a Radcliffe student in George Pierce Baker's first 47 Workshop, was encouraged by her professor to go to Europe and study these new styles. Sisters Alice and Irene Lewisohn, New York City heiresses who loved both travel and performing arts, also were inspired by what they saw in European and Asian performance. Morgan, the Lewisohns, and Helen Arthur, a lawyer who had worked for the Shuberts, founded the Neighborhood Playhouse on the Lower East Side and built the theater on Grand Street. These four women became the producing staff of an experimental theater dedicated to training young, primarily immigrant, artists and to exploring new visual, dance, and performance styles.

Neighborhood Playhouse artists were probably the first Americans trained in Konstantin Stanislavsky's system. In the summer of 1923 Richard Boleslavsky of the Moscow Art Theatre and the Neighborhood actors lived and worked at the Lewisohns' Pleasantville house and developed a production of *The Bacchae*. More than the other little theaters, the Neighborhood Playhouse artists explored the nonverbal elements of drama. They were inspired by theatrical elements of ritual and regularly used music, dance, expressive gesture, symbolic scenery, and experimental lighting techniques to explore their topics. The works they developed themselves in this style they termed "lyric dramas," but the lyric style was also used as an approach to the eclectic mix of American and international works produced on the Playhouse stage.

Several of Neighborhood Playhouse's successful productions were revived for future seasons (*The Little Clay Cart*, *Salut au Monde*, *The Dybbuk*), and a few were so successful downtown that they were moved to Broadway, like Granville-Barker's *The Madras House* (1921) and the annual sketch revue *The Grand Street Follies* (1922 and subsequently 1924–1929). However, for the most part, the little theaters, including the Neighborhood Playhouse, attracted an audience of artists and intellectuals to see their theatrical experiments.

The designers, directors, actors, and finally playwrights nurtured by the Neighborhood and the other little theaters slowly made headway on Broadway through the 1920s. The most important contributions of the Neighborhood Playhouse were in developing designers who used the New Stagecraft, like Aline Bernstein, Esther Peck, and Donald Oenslager. The Neighborhood also became a center for development of the new field of modern dance: Anna Sokolow, who would later choreograph **Leonard Bernstein**'s *Candide* (1956) among other Broadway shows, began at the Neighborhood Playhouse, while Martha Graham taught there for many years. Many actors from the Playhouse company made careers on Broadway or in Hollywood, but none is a household name: Aline MacMahon, Paula Trueman, Dorothy Sands. In addition, the company had provided a venue for young composers like Lily May Hyland and directors such as Augustin Duncan, who would act in and/or direct some 20 different Broadway productions in the 1920s alone.

When Alice Lewisohn married and moved abroad, the glue that had held the dance and drama components of the Neighborhood Playhouse together dissolved. After 1927, Agnes Morgan went on to direct on Broadway and off before settling into a long career as Artistic Director at the Paper Mill Playhouse in New Jersey. Arthur lived and worked with Morgan before her death in 1939. Irene Lewisohn and Rita Wallach Morgenthau, who served as the school's director, continued and expanded the training program. She remained director until 1963.

The most famous acting teacher at the Neighborhood Playhouse has been **Sanford Meisner**, whose approach to actor training is still the basis of the Neighborhood's conservatory program. His parents were Jewish immigrants in the fur trade. In his youth he did some acting in lower Manhattan where he met and befriended **Lee Strasberg**. He began to study as a pianist but found work with the Theatre Guild as an actor. From his connections with Strasberg, he became a founding actor with the **Group Theatre**. In his later career, he enjoyed teaching more than performing and developed a unique technique described in his book *Sanford Meisner on Acting*. Meisner actors are taught not to say anything until impelled, so they do not attempt to act without genuine motivation.

Although Meisner passed away in 1997, acting teachers at the Neighborhood Playhouse still carry on his approach. Additionally, the Neighborhood Playhouse actor training program pays homage to its little theater roots by emphasizing the fusion of the many arts that go into theatrical practice.

Today the Neighborhood Playhouse offers a variety of educational programs for both adult and youth actors. Alumni of the Neighborhood Playhouse include many mainstays of Hollywood and Broadway, including **Bob Fosse**, Jeff Goldblum, Tony Randall, Lee Grant, as well as playwrights **Arthur Miller** and David Mamet.

Melanie N. Blood

Further Reading

Crowley, Alice Lewisohn. *The Neighborhood Playhouse: Leaves from a Theatre Scrapbook*. New York: Theatre Arts, 1959.

Hart, Victoria. "Sanford Meisner Technique." *Training of the American Actor*, ed. Arthur Bartow. New York: Theatre Communications Group, 2006.

http://www.neighborhoodplayhouse.org/history.html.

Longwell, Dennis, and Sanford Meisner. *Sanford Meisner on Acting*. New York: Random House, 1987.

NEW MEDIA AND TECHNOLOGY

New media and technology—including the Internet, cell phones, computerized lighting and image projection, interactive marketing, and even reality television —began exerting their considerable influence on American culture toward the end of the twentieth century and continue to do so to this day. As new mass media technologies gained in popularity, they made a significant impact on both American theater space and theater marketing and, thus, Broadway production as a whole. The example of one Broadway musical, originally produced in the 1960s but revived on Broadway in the era of new media, pointedly illustrates the significant role that new technology plays on the American stage.

The musical *How to Succeed in Business Without Really Trying* has been produced twice on Broadway. Both the 1961 original, which ran for 1,415 performances, and the 1995 revival, which was nominated for a Tony Award, were financially and critically successful. Both were housed in the same New York theater space on Forty-sixth Street; the script, score, props, and costumes were nearly the same. However, the producers of the 1995 revival introduced a significant change in their restaging of the show—media technology. The 1960s art deco set design, which provided a cartoonish atmosphere in the original production, was reenvisioned in the 1995 production as technological space. The most prominent feature of the revival production's set was an enormous video backdrop consisting of 32 video cubes. These projections were specifically designed to help the viewer understand the staged space and the characters that interact within that space.

Set in a business complex (the World Wide Wicket corporation), the 1995 play's projections helped the audience make visual transitions through various parts of the building. Video projections served as windows, elevators, the company logo, as well as a number of other shapes that helped the audience understand the structure and design of the workspace the characters inhabit. Projections also altered the space to underscore important, often subtle differences in each unique space of the World Wide Wicket building. They presented the viewer with visual knowledge of the characters. (At one point flames consume the corporate insignia when a female character with the power to dismantle the company arrives on the scene. The projected flames provided the audience with insight into the character's agenda.) Characters' thoughts and feelings were also revealed through the technology-enhanced space. At one point, J. Pierpont Finch's (Matthew Broderick) love interest Rosemary Wells (Sarah Jessica Parker) sings "Happy to Keep His Dinner Warm." Projected animated images propelled the audience from the city scene to a lovely house with a white picket fence, allowing the audience to see the details of her fantasy home.

The technology used in the 1995 production illustrates just some of the ways that theater messages can be delivered to audiences who themselves live in a media-saturated culture. While the expectation of mediatized Broadway productions is a given for contemporary theater audiences, the history of Broadway theater's interaction with new media technologies actually begins with the advent of **television** in the 1940s. From that point forward the intersection between theater and media has been an important and dynamic facet of Broadway theater production.

Broadway and Television in the New Media Age

Television became a fixture in American homes in the years following World War II. While early television was publicly popular, it lacked substantive content. To remedy this lack of content, television producers hired Broadway writers, directors, and actors to create quality programming content for television programs. Throughout the mid-part of the twentieth century anthology programs like the *United States Steel Hour* (1953–1963), *Ford Television Theater* (1948–1957), and *The Producers Showcase* (1954–1957) provided small, home-based audiences all over the country with access to successfully mounted Broadway productions on the live television in their living room. Weekly programs, particularly *The Ed Sullivan Show* (1948–1971), exposed audiences to Broadway stars and proven Broadway productions.

By the time *The Ed Sullivan Show* went off the air, interest in promoting Broadway theater to the television audience was waning. From the 1960s to the 1990s television audiences began showing preferences for television dramas and situation comedies crafted specifically for the small screen. During this period televised versions of live Broadway theater took on event status and were not presented weekly as they had been in past decades. The Public Broadcasting System (PBS) and other networks like the National Broadcasting Network and the American Broadcast Company (ABC) intermittently aired full-length Broadway shows that had been recorded during their Broadway run. Some of these include *She Loves Me* (1979), Frank Loesser's *The Most Happy Fella* (1980), which was taped live in performance, and *Sunday in the Park with George* (1986), which was aired for television after the play was featured on the Tony Awards telecast of that same year.

Commercial networks also produced variety shows, Broadway musical concert events, or documentary events that promoted Broadway to television audiences. *On the Road to Broadway* (1982, CBS) featured actors Debby Boone, Dionne Warwick, and other members of the cast of the musical *Seven Brides for Seven Brothers* (1982) as they prepared for their Broadway opening. Another notable production included *Les Misérables in Concert* (1995), which was taped in London's Royal Albert Hall. The cast for the concert, billed as a "dream cast," featured stars from the original Broadway production, subsequent Broadway tours, and other worldwide productions of the show. The concert version was steeped in celebrity and spectacle featuring 17 Jean Valjeans in its final scene.

In addition to promoting itself through event programming like those described above, the Broadway theater also promoted itself through public advertisement of its product. A noticeable threshold for Broadway marketing occurred in 1972 when it aired the first television commercial for a Broadway Production. The commercial, for the musical *Pippin*, featured stars Ben Vereen and Ann Reinking performing a key dance sequence from the production. The ad ran for 120 seconds and included the tag phrase, "If you liked this minute, just wait until you see the other 199 of them!" Long-form television promotions that introduced general television audiences to Broadway's most notable work also began to air during this period, including the American Theatre Wing's Tony Award Show. First televised in 1967 as a part of the National Broadcasting Network's special programs division, the Tony Awards are still presented live to television audiences across America.

Reality Television, Cellular Technology, and the Broadway Stage

Since the year 2000 Broadway has benefited from a new kind of connection to television and related new technologies: Reality television or "Reality TV." Reality TV programs present ostensibly unscripted events featuring ordinary people. The genre gained popularity through its ability to document the lives and actions of real people in heightened realities. One particularly popular format in this genre is the elimination game, in which contestants compete and are often propelled into stardom through popular votes cast by the television audience.

The most successful of these reality competitions is the Fox network's *American Idol* (*AI*), which has had a significant impact on the music industry in general and Broadway musical theater in particular. Beginning in 2002, the program has sought out through nationwide auditions the best unknown young singers it can find. A small group of audition survivors then compete in a weekly sing-off, with winners determined by public voting over cellular phones. Broadway producers soon began to use the program, which included a public audition format as a screening, as a source for replacement casting in running Broadway shows. *American Idol* finalists who have landed replacement roles on Broadway include the *AI* season-three winner Fantasia Barrino, who starred as Celie in *The Color Purple* (2005), season-three runner-up Diana DeGarmo who played Penny Pingleton in *Hairspray* (2002), and season-two runner-up Clay Aiken, who did a well-publicized turn as Sir Robin in *Spamalot* (2005). In 2009 Constantine Maroulis, a finalist in season four, landed a starring role in the original Broadway cast of *Rock of Ages*, earning a Best Actor in a Musical Tony nomination and glowing reviews. It appears that ticket sales and press interest invariably increase when a popular *American Idol* singer joins a Broadway cast.

Cross promotions between *American Idol* and Broadway led to an airing of a "Broadway Week" as part of the season-long singing competition. During Broadway Week contestants perform classical and contemporary selections from the Broadway musical theater catalogue (despite the fact that the judges on the program have occasionally used the phrase "too Broadway" as a derisive critique of performances during non-Broadway weeks). *American Idol* airs in over 100 nations, exposing millions of viewers to the contestant's musical theater selections. During the 2008 season, **Andrew Lloyd Webber** appeared on Broadway Week, coaching the young singers and promoting his upcoming sequel to ***The Phantom of the Opera*** (1988) titled *Love Never Dies*.

American Idol exposes viewers to the contestants' **show tune** performances, allowing Broadway producers and songwriters to benefit from the regular promotion and sale of *American Idol* music downloads. In 2008 the co-creators and producers of *AI* entered into a partnership with Apple Computers to sell 99-cent downloads of all of the contestants' live performances. Music and video downloads were also available for purchase during the run of the show and are promoted into the next year, providing additional ways for viewers to enjoy their favorite contestants' performances—including performances of show tunes—and for producers to reach customers who might not regularly attend Broadway musicals or otherwise spend money on Broadway songs or recordings.

This ability to advertise to a new audience through televised programming led Broadway producers to seek out other relationships with reality television production companies. In 2007 co-creators Andrew Lloyd Webber and David Ian developed a reality television series that followed unknown singer/dancers as they auditioned for the male and female leads in a Broadway revival of *Grease*. The program, titled *Grease—You're the One That I Want*, averaged 8 million viewers per night and led to several million dollars in advanced ticket sales for the Broadway production. The *Grease* revival opened to considerable audience enthusiasm in August 2007, starring the Reality TV show winners as Danny and Sandy. (In a notable case of Reality TV/Broadway inbreeding, *American Idol* season-five winner Taylor Hicks joined the cast of the Reality TV–generated *Grease* production in June 2008 as singing spirit Teen Angel.)

This ability to advertise to millions of viewers and introduce newcomers to Broadway led to additional partnerships with television, including two successful promotional deals with Music Television Network (MTV). In fall 2007 MTV produced a live-televised version of the Broadway show *Legally Blonde the Musical* (2007). The following spring MTV launched a reality program that allowed fans to select the replacement star for Elle Woods, the leading character in *Legally Blonde the Musical*. The voting was conducted entirely by cellular phone texting. The use of viral marketing that includes audience interface with the production through television, cell phones, and Web sites provides access to a new and largely untapped youthful Broadway audience. While reality programming to date has focused on the casting of Broadway plays, there is certainly potential to explore other variations of interactive television programming to bring new fans to Broadway in the future.

New Technologies, Scenic Design, and Theatrical Space

While television has had a great influence on the distribution and marketing of Broadway to mass audiences, media technologies such as video and projection images have also influenced scenic design and theatrical space. Artists in the 1950s avant-garde theater began to experiment with media technology as a means of theatrical meaning making. The work of Czech stage designer Josef Svoboda was particularly influential with other artists who used technology as a means of creating powerful images on stage. Unlike other Eastern European director/designers, like Irwin Piscator and Bertold Brecht, who used media technology as a means of educating audience members about their ideological perspectives, Svoboda saw the complex and integrated use of film and other moving images as a means to project emotive and lyrical atmospheres to audiences.

Influenced by Svoboda, who himself did relatively little work on Broadway, producers of multi-image lighting and sets began to create projected effects for Broadway stages in 1964. The first show to introduce projection design as a part of the scenic and lighting concept was the 1964 musical revival of **Clifford Odets**'s *Golden Boy*. The projection designer, Richard Pilbrow, subsequently infused projections into many lighting plots prepared for the Broadway stage. Pilbrow's combination of projection design and lighting design initiated other attempts to infuse projections into set and lighting designs. In this vein Boris Aronson's work in the original production of **Stephen Sondheim**'s *Company* (1970) is also noteworthy. Aronson's successful use of projections in the design of *Company* were lauded by the Broadway theater community when he won the Tony Award for Best Scenic Design (1971) and other awards.

In the early days of its inception, the role of the projection designer was considered that of an assistant to the lighting designer. However, the frequent use of projection technology has propelled multi-image producers and projection designers into a more central role in the creative, collaboration process in contemporary productions. Evidence of this new centrality is abundant. In 2007, for example, the United Scenic Artists, the union that represents scenic, lighting, and sound designers, created a new category of representation specifically for projection designers. The Drama Desk committee (who give the drama critics' annual awards for achievement in theater) established a new award for "Outstanding Projection and Video Design" in the same year.

The work of projection designer Wendall K. Harrington has been influential in establishing video and projection displays as a necessary component of theatrical settings. Harrington began her work as a multi-image producer in the original Broadway production of *They're Playing Out Song* (1979) and has continuously worked on Broadway in such shows as *My One and Only* (1983), *Beauty and the Beast* (1994), and *Ragtime* (1998). While there is no formal training for projection designers, Harrington has developed a cadre of designers through mentored apprenticeships on a variety of Broadway productions.

Today the use of projection designs in contemporary plays can take the form of integrated effects that augment or enhance set pieces, contributing to the atmosphere of the play, such as those created by Elaine McCarthy for *Wicked* (2003) and *Spamalot* (2005). Designs can also act as entire scenic backdrops. For example, *The Woman in White* (2005) relied solely on projection design to create the play's entire environment. All of the physical settings in the play were three-dimensional, computer-generated images projected onto a white wall. Similarly the 2007 revival of *Sunday in the Park with George* made visual the interior thoughts of two artists in its innovative and technologically updated animations projected onto white space. Both of these examples signal how the work of the projection designer has altered the way directors, designers, and audiences think about theatrical space.

Projection-based sets allow for a new multidimension space that can be cinematic or photographic in nature. Some projected images remain stationary like a photograph or a painting, while others can indicate vast changers in space or indicate rapid movement through time and space. Most importantly, the use of projection design offers audiences a new means of visually navigating the world of a play.

Web 2.0 and the Broadway Stage

While projection designs allow for changes in the spatial environment of the theater, new capacities of the Internet allow for more interactivity between audiences and the Broadway stage. In the early part of the twenty-first century the Internet provided a new means of disseminating knowledge about Broadway. Social networking sites, wikis, and affinity-based communication tools became venues of expression and connection for a new Broadway fan culture. In the early part of the twenty-first century information about Broadway began to be disseminated through databases like the Internet Broadway Database (IBDB.com). Created by the research department of the Broadway League, the IBDB provides a basic history of shows produced on Broadway as well as historical information about theater venues and statistics about individual theater seasons and critically acclaimed or popular productions. Since the 1990s Broadway affiliates have also offered *Playbill Online*, a free news-gathering Web site that provides readers information about operating Broadway theaters, national tours, and international productions as well as current cast biographies, cast photos, links to articles written about plays, and tickets. The Internet also provides opportunities for new interconnectivity between global audiences and popular Broadway musicals. For example, video captured portions of popular musicals, including **Disney**'s *The Lion King* (1997), *Wicked*, and *Legally Blonde* appear on the video-sharing Web site YouTube. Vignettes showcased on YouTube are often professional footage of musicals that have been prepared for awards shows or promotional advertisements. However, YouTube also presents illegally filmed footage of live shows created and posted on the interactive Web site by fans of a given musical for other fans who may not be able to see the live show. YouTube is also a virtual space where fans pay homage to the musicals by posting Webcasts and video footage of their own performance versions or school productions that mimic or replicate characters, music, and dialogue from segments of popular musicals.

Broadway fan culture is further advanced through promotional Web pages on social networking Web sites in which user-submitted networks of friends share personal blogs, video logs, music, and photos all related to their Broadway interests, aspirations, and experiences. Social networking Web sites like MySpace have entire sites dedicated to fan participation in the popular culture network of a given musical or play. Commercial entities can also use networking and affinity-based Web pages to promote musicals and plays. Emphasizing online activity, these sites allow fans to purchase tickets, create fan profiles, get information about the Broadway and touring versions of the musical, contribute to virtual discussion boards about the characters, setting, and themes in the musical, and participate in virtual contests related to the musical of their choice.

Amy Petersen Jensen

Further Reading

Burian, J. M., ed. *The Secret of Theatrical Space*. New York: Applause Theater Books, 1993.

Burian, Jarka. *The Scenography of Joser Svoboda*. Middletown, CT: Wesleyan University Press, 1971.

Chapple, Freda, and Chiel Kattenbelt. *Intermediality in Theater and Performance*. Amsterdam and New York: Editions Rodopi B.V., 2006.

Dixon, Steve. *Digital Performance: A History of New Media in Theater, Dance, Performance Art, and Installation*. Boston: MIT Press, 2007.

Giannachi, Gabriella. *The Politics of New Media Theater.* New York: Routledge, 2007.

Giesekam, Greg. *Staging the Screen: The Use of Film and Video in Theater*. New York: Palgrave Macmillan, 2007.

Jensen, Amy Petersen. *Theater in a Media Culture: Production, Performance, and Perception Since 1970*. Jefferson, NC: McFarland & Company, 2007.

Playbill Online. http://www.playbill.com/index.php.

Thompson, John B. *The Media and Modernity: A Social Theory of the Media*. Cambridge, U.K.: Polity; Stanford, CA: Stanford University Press, 1995.

Wickstrom, Mauyra. *Performing Consumers: Global Capital and Its Theatrical Seductions*. New York: Routledge, 2006.

NICHOLS, MIKE (1931–)
DIRECTOR, PRODUCER

As a contributing artist to the American musical theater, director-producer Mike Nichols has existed prominently on its periphery. His keen perceptions of human nature and relationships plus his uncanny knack for developing a theatrically satisfying event that appeals to a broad audience is as much in evidence in his work on **musicals** and plays as it is in his work for **film**, **television**, and even spoken word recordings. Winner of six Tony Awards for directing productions as varied as **Neil Simon**'s early comedies, Tom Stoppard's *avant-garde* puzzler *The Real Thing* (1984), and the farcical musical sensation *Monty Python's Spamalot* (2005), Nichols is the best-known and most successful director currently working in all three media of stage, television, and film.

Mike Nichols was born Michael Igor Peschkowsky in Berlin, Germany, to Jewish parents of Russian and German extraction. Although his father, Paul, was well established in the medical profession, his mother's side of the family was peopled with intellectuals, one of whom, Hedwig Lachmann, had translated Oscar Wilde's *Salome* into German. This translation would become the basis of Richard Strauss's libretto for his opera of the same name.

As the backlash against German-Jewish citizens began to reach its strongest point in 1938, the Peschkowskys immigrated to the United States. His father adopted the surname Nichols, earned his license to practice medicine in New York state, and set up practice in New York City. Nichols's mother joined the family three years later. The family functioned as a unit until Paul Nichols died of leukemia in 1944. His mother, Brigitte, would struggle through a series of low-paying jobs to keep her family together during the rest of the 1940s.

Though Nichols suffered a great deal of privation, he received an excellent education. He enrolled at the University of Chicago with the intent of becoming a psychologist, but while at college he flirted with theater and the entertainment industry, acting in campus productions and doing a short stint as a radio announcer for Chicago's first classical music station. His involvement in theater became life altering when he met fellow University of Chicago student Elaine May; they performed with an improvisational troupe in Chicago called the Compass Theater. Then, as a comic duo in the late 1950s, they would achieve fame on television, through recordings of their material, and, finally, on Broadway, with their innovative, improvisational two-person show *An Evening with Mike Nichols and Elaine May* (1960). The show received rave reviews and ran for almost a year.

The year performing on Broadway brought Nichols into the center of New York's theater community, which was about to experience a Renaissance in comedy thanks to the emerging talents of young **playwrights** Neil Simon, Herb Gardner, and Murray Schisgal, among others. Nichols made an auspicious debut as a director for Neil Simon's early Broadway hit *Barefoot in the Park* (1963). The comedy was a sensation, earning Nichols his first Tony Award and launching Simon and the 32-year-old director into the elite levels of Broadway stardom. Nichols followed *Barefoot* by directing Schisgal's *Luv* (1964), the biggest hit of Schisgal's career, and Simon's *The Odd Couple* (1965), winning another Tony for Best Director of the 1964–1965 season for both plays. He directed other Simon plays, including the hits *Plaza Suite* (1968) and *The Prisoner of Second Avenue* (1971), and the rare failure *Fools* (1981), while expanding his repertoire and seemingly inexhaustible energies into directing and even producing other writers' comedies, serious dramas, and musicals as well as directing films.

The themes that served as the frame of Nichols's work with Elaine May and the early Neil Simon plays, especially those of complex male-female and parent-child relationships, would come to bear on the three musicals that Nichols has contributed to as a director, producer, or both. For the first, Sheldon Harnick and Jerry Bock's *The Apple Tree* (1966), Nichols was hired to replace **Jerome Robbins** as director after having successfully guided Richard Burton and Elizabeth Taylor to well-reviewed performances in his screen coadaptation of **Edward Albee**'s *Who's Afraid of Virginia Woolf* (1965). *The Apple Tree*'s original concept, which was explorations of man, woman, and the devil, would be reworked by Nichols. The resulting show became both an award-winning success and a cult classic. Nichols himself received a Tony nomination as best director of a musical for the piece but lost to **Harold Prince** for *Cabaret* (1967).

Nichols's second and third encounters with the American musical would be even more successful. In 1977, Nichols was invited to produce the then-struggling *Annie*, based on the well-known comic strip by Harold Gray. Nichols preserved the intent of the show, which was to serve as an antidote to the more adult-themed cynical shows of the 1970s such as *Chicago* and *A Chorus Line* (both 1975). Nichols won the Tony Award for the now widely beloved and oft-revived 1977 show. Eighteen years later, Nichols returned to the musical as director of the hit *Spamalot* (2005), based on the cult film success *Monty Python and the Holy Grail* (1975). Audiences loved this latest in a series of wildly successful film-to-stage transfers; Nichols won a Tony as Best Director of a Musical to accompany the many he had won as a director of plays.

If Nichols's career were composed only of his Broadway work, his would be a distinguished career as an innovative artist and visionary producer. Yet he is also a four-time Oscar nominated film director, having won for the 1968 classic *The Graduate*. He has also won four Emmy Awards as both co-producer and director for television film adaptations of **Tony Kushner**'s *Angels in America* (play 1993, teleplay 2003) and Margaret Edson's Pulitzer Prize–winning *Wit* (teleplay 2001; no Broadway production to date). Now in his late seventies and working in his fifth decade of creating Broadway and Hollywood successes, Nichols recently completed directing the popular Tom Hanks film *Charlie Wilson's War* (2007) and a limited engagement Broadway revival of **Clifford Odets**'s *The Country Girl* (2008).

Darryl Kent Clark

Further Reading

Ephron, Nora. "Interview with Mike Nichols." *Wallflower at the Orgy*. New York: Bantam Books, 2007.
Schuth, H. Wayne. *Mike Nichols*. Boston: Twayne Publishers, 1978.

NORMAN, MARSHA (1947–)
PLAYWRIGHT, SCREENWRITER, NOVELIST, LIBRETTIST

Marsha Norman is one of the most important contemporary dramatists whose work first came to Broadway by way of American **regional theater**. She is best known for her riveting, Pulitzer Prize–winning play *'night, Mother* (1983), which accounts a daughter's final interaction with her overly dependent mother before killing herself. Norman has also written the book for Broadway musicals, including the highly successful *The Secret Garden* (1991), for which she won a Tony Award. She received a Tony nomination for the book of the long-running musical *The Color Purple* (2005), which she adapted from Alice Walker's novel of the same name. Norman is often associated with two important cultural trends of the

1980s and 1990s: the emergence of feminist authors born after World War II and a shift in the mission of major regional theaters toward self-consciously cultivating future national (including Broadway) theater artists and, in particular, discovering new plays and playwrights.

Norman's parents were fundamentalist Methodists, and her childhood in Louisville, Kentucky, was relatively isolated. Because of her mother's religious views, she was not able to play with some neighborhood children, go to the movies, or watch television. The one creative outlet allowed her was an occasional visit to see plays for children at the Actors Theatre of Louisville, one of the most highly regarded regional theater companies in America. Norman maintained her interest in theater throughout her childhood. After graduating from Agnes Scott College in Georgia, she returned to Louisville and began to work as a journalist, writing reviews of books, plays, and films. In so doing, she stayed in contact with Actors Theatre of Louisville (ATL), which would become instrumental in launching her professional playwriting career.

Norman's first professional play, *Getting Out*, was written specifically for ATL and was produced there in 1977. At the time, ATL's Jon Jory was one of a handful of regional theater artistic directors seeking to expand the role of "regionals" in nurturing new theatrical talent. Jory was particularly interested in cultivating new **playwrights**, and he urged Norman to write a play for ATL. Norman turned for inspiration to her personal experience working with troubled adolescents at a Kentucky hospital. *Getting Out*, an intense account of a woman paroled after serving a prison sentence for murder and other crimes, was cited by the American Theatre Critics Association as the best new play produced in regional theater that year.

After the success of *Getting Out*, Norman moved to New York City, where she wrote *'night, Mother* (1983). This play, too, opened in regional theater at the American Repertory Theater in Cambridge, Massachusetts, before coming to Broadway. Once on Broadway *'night, Mother* was a critical sensation and enjoyed a healthy one-year run. The show earned Norman the Pulitzer Prize, a Tony Award nomination, and widespread critical acclaim. She also adapted the play for a 1986 film version starring Sissy Spacek and Anne Bancroft. Norman went on to write many more plays over the next several years although none was produced on Broadway.

She returned to writing for Broadway with *The Secret Garden* (1991). Revisiting a familiar subject, troubled children, Norman adapted Frances Hodgson Burnett's Edwardian-era novel of a despondent young girl's spiritual revival in the magic of an English garden. She also wrote the lyrics. In addition to earning Norman a Tony nomination, the production had the distinction of seeing Daisy Eagan, as the girl, become at age 11 the youngest actor ever to win a Tony Award (Best Featured Actress in a Musical). Norman followed *The Secret Garden* with the book and lyrics for a musical *The Red Shoes* (1993). Despite music by the venerable **Jule Styne**, whose 45-year musical theater career ended anticlimactically with this show, *The Red Shoes* had a disastrous preproduction history and a no-less ignominious demise on Broadway. It closed in three days. Norman did not write again for Broadway for 12 years but returned in grand style as author of the book for *The Color Purple*, thus far the longest-running Broadway show of her career.

Although she remains active in New York theater in a number of capacities—including educational and philanthropic as well as artistic—Norman writes in a variety of genres. Most notably she wrote for several seasons on the hit television show *Law & Order: Criminal Intent.* A product herself of initiatives intended to develop young playwrights, she cochairs the playwriting department at Juilliard School in New York and teaches Graduate Playwriting at the Tisch School of the Arts at New York University. *'night, Mother* still enjoys frequent revivals in regional and university theaters, and her plays are taught regularly in college courses in American drama and women's literature.

Molly Smith Metzler

Further Reading

Brown, Linda Ginter. *Marsha Norman: A Casebook.* New York: Garland, 1996.
Gussow, Mel. "Entering the Mainstream: The Plays of Beth Henley, Marsha Norman and Wendy Wasserstein." *Women Writing Plays: Three Decades of the Susan Smith Blackburn Prize*, ed. Alexis Greene, Emilie S. Kilgore, and Marsha Norman. Austin: University of Texas Press, 2006.

NOVELS (AMERICAN)

Broadway is omnivorous in its appetite for new material, and thus the canon of American writers has been extensively plundered as inspiration for both plays and **musicals**. Notwithstanding the wealth of available information, a linear chronology of adaptations of American novels is difficult to construct because of the heterogeneous nature of the history of bringing fiction to the stage. Some writers participated in the adaptation of their own work; some did not. Some authors' works were adapted during their lifetimes while some were seized on decades after a novel was first published. Some novels were turned into plays, some musicals—a few were transformed into both. Perhaps most significantly, some adapted novels fared well on the stage but many more did not. The best generalization that can be offered on the subject of bringing American fiction to Broadway is that staging a successful show is a difficult, risk-laden enterprise and starting with a critically acclaimed or best-selling novel (or even one that is both) is no guarantee of success.

There are, of course, crucial formal differences between a novel and a play, making any potential adaptation extremely tricky. The novel as a form imposes no restrictions on time or space and can cover hundreds of years and thousands of miles in the service of plot and characterization. In addition, anything that can be described in words is representable—a sperm whale or the Mississippi River, for example. By contrast, notwithstanding the considerable ingenuity of Broadway theater artists, works on stage are constrained by a number of practical considerations: in general one has three hours or less to tell a story and must represent all settings on the finite space of the stage with sets, lighting, and technological effects. Novels often feature complex figurative language, provide copious exposition, and, through the use of perspective, can literally read the minds of its characters. On the stage this material must be expressed as dialogue and action. The transition to stage is even more difficult when a novel is made into a musical. Story is required to become song and dance. The best novels are so complexly rendered as to offer multiple levels of interpretation and often defy closure of plotline or characterization. These kinds of tensions are virtually unrepresentable onstage, especially for traditional musicals that employ the popular convention of staging a final song-and-dance number that involves the entire cast and wraps up all loose ends.

Early History

The first American novel successfully adapted for the American stage was Harriet Beecher Stowe's radical antislavery work, *Uncle Tom's Cabin*, published in 1851. The best-selling novel of the nineteenth century, it was first published serially, and unauthorized dramatic adaptations (as yet no laws existed for copyrighting fictional material for stage use) began appearing even before the serialization was complete. Ultimately, there were countless versions and parodies of the novel on stage, but most gutted Stowe's political content and instead combined her work's most melodramatic incidents with the already-popular American stage tradition of blackface minstrelsy. Scholars estimate that at least 3 million people saw these plays, ten times the book's first-year sales. One of the best-known versions was George Aiken's production at the National Theatre in Lower Manhattan (1852). This production set a number of important precedents for theater in New York. This dramatization was the first work to fill an entire evening's bill (until this point theater productions were basically variety shows), it featured the first matinee performances, it was a pioneer of long runs, and it brought new audiences to the theater when the Puritan tradition still considered theatergoing immoral.

In the 1890s, the novelist Henry James (Jr.) was a notorious failure as a **playwright** (albeit in London rather than New York). He attempted both adapting his own work and writing original plays, none of which was received well. Commercial theater must appeal to a mass audience and James's work has never appealed to a mass audience. After his death, however, his oeuvre has proven to be very attractive to Broadway producers, with most of his major novels and short stories having been adapted for the stage at some point. The most successful is probably *The Heiress* (1947, revived 1976) based on his 1880 novel *Washington Square*.

Modern Broadway and the Modern Novel

The rise of modern Broadway in the early part of the twentieth century coincided not only with the Jazz Age but literary modernism. In general, the years between

World Wars I and II were the period during which contemporary fiction was most likely to be adapted to the stage and also when the original writer was most likely to participate in the adaptation process. With the development of new artist-friendly copyright laws during this period, the movement from page to stage began to seem more attractive to successful fiction writers, especially if the writer and his material had some connection to New York. For example, F. Scott Fitzgerald sold the rights to his 1925 novel *The Great Gatsby* to Broadway **producers**; the resulting 1926 show was so successful it earned him more than sales of the book had and led to the sale of **film** rights. Edith Wharton helped to adapt her own 1905 novel *House of Mirth* for a theatrical version that was a dismal failure in the following year. But years later she had much greater success when she turned over the adaptation duties to others. *The Age of Innocence* (novel 1920, play 1928), *The Old Maid* (novella 1924, play 1935), and *Ethan Frome* (novel 1912, play 1936) were all successful on New York stages both critically and commercially.

By the late 1930s novelist John Steinbeck's writings were so popular and so sought-after by Hollywood and Broadway producers that he retained an agent specifically to negotiate film and theatrical rights to his work. Steinbeck is an especially interesting case in that several of his most famous works, including *Of Mice and Men*, *The Moon Is Down*, and *Burning Bright,* were written in a unique form he called "play-novelette." Conceived as plays but then written as fiction, these works were relatively easy to adapt, and Steinbeck generally wrote the adaptations himself. Yet another of his novels, *Sweet Thursday*, was adapted into the musical *Pipe Dream* (1955) by **Richard Rodgers and Oscar Hammerstein II**. The production was tepidly reviewed and was considered a failure. This brought an end to Steinbeck's fascination with theater, and he turned permanently back to fiction.

As in other arenas of American life, African American writers have faced repeated discrimination and unequal access to Broadway. The Harlem Renaissance coincided with the rise of Broadway as a force in New York culture, but this did not mean blacks were accurately represented on stage nor warmly welcomed into the new burgeoning community of commercial theater artists. Not only did black writers have to deal with the racist theatrical legacy of blackface minstrelsy, of the dozen or so plays with African American themes that appeared on Broadway during the Harlem Renaissance, only three were written by black authors. The first notable adaptation of an important novel by a black writer does not come until decades later. The Broadway adaptation of Richard Wright's 1940 novel *Native Son* (1941) was highly anticipated. The show was produced by a group that included Orson Welles (who also directed the production) and well-known actor/producer John Houseman. But Paul Green, the white writer who wrote the adaptation, changed Bigger Thomas from a black revolutionary into a Christ figure and Wright felt he was in no position to argue; the show was a failure. More recently, it took the power and pocketbook of talk-show host and impresario Oprah Winfrey to bring Alice Walker's 1981 novel *The Color Purple* (2005) to the stage in what proved to be a very successful, long-running production. But the body of work of perhaps the most important African American novelist, Toni Morrison, remains virtually untouched: there is only a single **Off-Broadway** adaptation of her 1970 novel *Bluest Eye* (2006).

Key Fiction-to-Stage Adaptations

For what are arguably the two most successful and influential musicals based on novels, ***Show Boat*** (1927) and *The Pajama Game* (1954), somewhat ironically, the source material is mostly forgotten. The latter is based on a 1953 novel by Richard Bissell, *7-1/2 Cents*. The show won the 1955 Tony Award for Best Musical. While Bissell, then and now, is considered a minor humorist and regionalist, *The Pajama Game* continues to be popular, having inspired a 1958 film adaptation starring Doris Day, a 2006 Broadway revival starring popular jazz singer Harry Connick Jr., and countless high school and community theater productions throughout the United States. Edna Ferber, the author of the 1926 novel *Show Boat*, was very well-known in her own time but is now little read and studied. Perhaps best characterized as a writer of popular middlebrow fiction, Ferber did win a Pulitzer Prize for her 1924 novel *So Big*, but her longevity comes from her 25-year partnership with **George S. Kaufman** and their ability to repeatedly bring successful comedies to the stage from the late 1920s to the early 1940s.

Somewhat like Ferber, a few decades later another popular middlebrow writer, James A. Michener, made an important contribution to Broadway. Michener enlisted in the U.S. Navy in World War II and turned his experiences into the short story collection *Tales of the South Pacific*, published immediately after the war. *Tales* won a Pulitzer Prize for fiction in 1948 and a year later became Rodgers and Hammerstein's groundbreaking musical *South Pacific* (1949), which dealt seriously with themes of American imperialism and racism. The show swept the 1950 Tonys, winning nine awards. *Tales* was Michener's first published book, and although he would go on to be one of the most prolific and popular writers of the twentieth century, publishing more than 40 titles, none of his other works was adapted to the Broadway stage.

The Pajama Game and *South Pacific* were two of several "classical" or "Golden Age" musicals of the 1940s, 1950s, and mid-1960s that were inspired by American fiction writers. Others included the highly successful *Guys and Dolls* (1950) based on Damon Runyan's trademark low-level urban gamblers and small-time crooks. Ruth McKenney's popular 1930s novel *My Sister Eileen* was the inspiration for **Leonard Bernstein**, **Betty Comden**, and **Adolph Green**'s highly successful *Wonderful Town* (1953). C. Y. Lee, who immigrated to the United States from China as a teenager and earned a Master's degree in writing from Yale University, saw his 1957 novel *Flower Drum Song* about life in San Francisco's Asian American community adapted in 1958 to a hit musical of the same name. *Flower Drum Song* was the first major Broadway musical to feature **Asian or Asian American** performers, setting, and themes. The all-but-forgotten writer Douglass Wallop and his all-but-forgotten 1954 novel *The Year the Yankees Lost the Pennant* provided the source for one of Broadway's best-known and most beloved musicals of all time, *Damn Yankees* (1955).

Children's Literature on Broadway and Other Considerations

Writers of what we might broadly refer to as literature for children have been popular sources for updating. Louisa May Alcott's 1868 novel *Little Women* falls into this category (adapted multiple times, most recently as a musical in 2005) as does the work of Frances Hodgson Burnett. *Little Lord Fauntleroy* published in 1886 and *The Secret Garden* in 1909 are probably her best known. Mark Twain, while certainly not exclusively a children's writer, has had most of his most popular and beloved stories serve as source material, most recently with *The Adventures of Huckleberry Finn* as the inspiration for the musical *Big River* (1985). And then there is the book that keeps on giving, Frank Baum's 1900 novel *The Wizard of Oz*. This work generated not only the 1939 family film classic with Judy Garland, but also inspired the musical *The Wiz* (1975), an adaptation featuring exclusively African American actors. Finally, Gregory Maguire's 1995 novel *Wicked*, a revisionist retelling of the Oz story clearly intended for adults, was refashioned as a family entertainment long-running musical under the same name in 2003. The success of that show generated what Broadway producers came to refer to as the "*Wicked* market"—pre- and early teenage girls, a heretofore relatively weak demographic for Broadway theater, who dragged their parents in droves to see the musical.

American novels have also inspired some of the Broadway musical's most notorious flops. The musical based on Truman Capote's 1958 best-selling novella *Breakfast at Tiffany's* (1966) never made it out of previews. Stephen King's 1976 horror-thriller novel *Carrie* (1988)—despite being first produced by the Royal Shakespeare Company in London before coming to New York—holds the honor of being one of the most expensive failures in Broadway history, closing after only five performances. More recently *Lestat* (2006), based on Anne Rice's series of top-selling vampire novels, could not be saved from commercial and critical oblivion even with music and lyrics from pop/rock music icons Elton John and Bernie Taupin. What these three shows have in common, however, is that each production *followed* a successful film adaptation, so perhaps the lesson is the material should have been left well enough alone. But sometimes the choice to stage or not to stage a musical is a "no-brainer." E. L. Doctorow's 1975 novel *Ragtime*, which takes its title from the popular musical style that predates jazz, is even set in the 1920s. The 1981 film version, directed by Miloš Forman, was nominated for eight Oscars and featured Hollywood icon James Cagney in his final role. The 1997 musical that followed enjoyed a healthy run on Broadway for two years.

Ambitious artists have sometimes turned to great American novels for a challenge. The Steppenwolf Theatre Company received rapturous reviews for its 1988 stage adaptation, by Steppenwolf member Frank Galati, of Steinbeck's Depression-era classic *The Grapes of Wrath*. The production moved to Broadway, where it won a Tony Award for Best Play in 1990. Orson Welles, an important innovator in both American theater and film, took on Herman Melville's nineteenth-century classic *Moby-Dick*. Welles labored on the script for eight years and created *Moby-Dick—Rehearsed* (London production 1955). His version was a play within a play and concerned a traveling theater company who themselves staged the novel. This approach allowed the production to be staged without scenery and, thus, Welles avoided having to represent some of the more imposing visual aspects of the novel on stage, including the ship, the ocean, and the whale. The play opened first in London to much praise from critics. However, seven years later when it finally opened on Broadway the New York critics were less generous, and the show lasted only ten performances.

One final way that American writers can appear on Broadway is as themselves. These productions are typically one-character shows that take their material from a whole life's work, a kind of subgenre of celebrity impersonation that extends far beyond just writers. This category includes personalities such as **Lillian Hellman**, Truman Capote, and Diana Vreeland. The most famous one-character show involving an American novelist is Hal Holbrook's *Mark Twain Tonight!*, which premiered in 1966 and has been updated and performed multiple times on Broadway and in national tours ever since. Robert Morse won a Tony for Best Actor in a Play as novelist Truman Capote in *Tru* (1989), a solo show written and directed by Jay Presson Allen based on Capote's writings." In 2007 novelist, scriptwriter, and journalist Joan Didion adapted for Broadway her 2005 book *The Year of Magical Thinking*, a personal account of depression and madness she endured when her husband and daughter died a few months apart. The great British actress Vanessa Redgrave gave a standout performance portraying what she and author Didion referred to as "a character named Joan Didion." Critics hailed the work as a career milestone for both author and actress as well as a public relations boost for the often marginalized one-character Broadway show.

Alice Rutkowski

Further Reading

Benstock, Shari. *No Gifts from Chance: A Biography of Edith Wharton*. New York: Charles Scribner's Sons, 1994.

Berg, Chuck. "Moby-Dick—Rehearsed." In *Encyclopedia of Orson Welles*, ed. Chuck Berg and Tom Erskine. New York: Checkmark Books, 2003, pp. 268–69.

Birdoff, Harry. *The World's Greatest Hit: Uncle Tom's Cabin*. New York: S. F. Vanni, 1947.

Brady, Frank. *Citizen Welles: A Biography of Orson Welles*. New York: Charles Scribner's Sons, 1989.

Brantley, Ben. "Risks of Making Literary Voices Sing Onstage." *New York Times*, December 9, 1996.

———. "Storyteller at Work: 'Mark Twain Tonight!' and as Ever." *New York Times*, June 10, 2005.

Courtney, Angela. "Edna Ferber." In *Dictionary of Literary Biography*, ed. Christopher J. Wheatley. Detroit: Thomson Gale, 2003, pp. 79–87.

Gilbert, Julie Goldsmith. *Ferber: A Biography*. Garden City: Doubleday & Company, Inc., 1978.

Lott, Eric. *Love and Theft: Blackface Minstrelsy and the American Working Class*. New York: Oxford University Press, 1995.

May, Stephen J. *Michener: A Writer's Journey.* Norman: University of Oklahoma Press, 2005.

Meyers, Jeffrey. *Scott Fitzgerald: A Biography.* New York: Harper Collins, 1994.

Novick, Sheldon M. "Henry James on Stage: 'That Sole Intensity Which the Theatre Can Produce.' " In *Henry James on Stage and Screen*, ed. John R. Bradley. New York: Palgrave, 2000, p. 1–22.

Parini, Jay. *John Steinbeck: A Biography.* New York: Henry Holt and Company, 1995.

Rich, Frank. "A New Era for 'Grapes of Wrath.' " *New York Times*, March 23, 1990.

Swaab, Peter. "The End of Embroidery: From *Washington Square* to *the Heiress*." In *Henry James on Stage and Screen*, ed. John R. Bradley. New York: Palgrave, 2000, pp. 56–71.

ODETS, CLIFFORD (1906–)
PLAYWRIGHT

Clifford Odets was the only **playwright** to emerge from the highly influential Depression-era radical theater company, the **Group Theatre**. Between 1935 and 1940, the Group Theatre produced 11 productions of seven different Odets plays, by which Odets became the premiere American social dramatist of the decade. Although his creative output and influence waned in the years following World War II, Odets remains an icon of the powerful social and political reformist sensibilities that still resonate within New York's theater community and among its playwrights in particular. His major plays, especially the naturalistic *Awake and Sing* (1935) and the political agitprop *Waiting for Lefty* (1935), brought a high level of craftsmanship and human emotion to American political drama.

Clifford Odets was born in Philadelphia in 1906 but moved with his family to New York City when he was six. A high school dropout, he took a number of odd jobs in the 1920s, including working as a radio announcer and acting in various theater groups. Among those early acting jobs were minor acting roles for the **Theatre Guild**. In 1930, he was invited to join the newly formed Group Theatre, an offshoot of the Guild dedicated to exploring new and radical approaches to acting, directing, and theater production. Odets originally joined the Group as an apprentice actor. However, his acting was viewed by his colleagues (and especially Group lead director and acting teacher **Lee Strasberg**) as adequate at best. To his frustration he was cast only in minor roles in early Group productions. Nevertheless, Odets stayed with the company and slowly began experimenting with playwriting. By the end of 1934, the combination of the Group's declining fortunes with their current season of plays and the support of Group co-founder **Harold**

Clurman for Odets's writing efforts (Strasberg was still not a fan) led the Group to produce in succession Odets's newly written one-act *Waiting for Lefty* and a full drama *Awake and Sing*. New York theater mythology surrounds the opening night of *Waiting for Lefty* (January 5, 1935) in an **Off-Broadway** theater in lower Manhattan. The play centers on a taxi driver's union dispute with its corrupt, antistrike union officials. A series of short scenes, demonstrating how the company and the pro-company union leaders are destroying families and society at large, culminate with a final confrontation: striking cabbies join with audience members to shout down the betrayers in the union and declare, famously, STRIKE! STRIKE! STRIKE!

With no press in attendance, director Harold Clurman's account of the opening night audience's response, has passed with little challenge into theatrical folklore ("an event . . . to be noted in the annals of American theatre"). He recounts a spontaneous surge of audience connection with the revolutionary fervor of the production, climaxing in a joint audience/cast quasi-labor demonstration subsuming the curtain call (1983, 147–48). However, even if unaided by Clurman's generous self-assessment, the play would have found the enthusiastic critical audience response it did. It played later that year on Broadway and then on tour. Opening a month after *Waiting for Lefty*, Odets's *Awake and Sing*, a deceptively subtle and moving drama about the withering effect of poverty on a family's love and loyalties, showed a remarkable level of artistry for a new playwright. Critics and audiences responded enthusiastically. The sudden parallel success of *Awake and Sing* and *Waiting for Lefty* brought immediate fame to Odets and new energy to the Group Theatre. Later in 1935 Odets and the Group would mount his anti-Nazi protest drama *Till the Day I Die* and *Paradise Lost*, a Depression-era family drama that critics tended to compare unfavorably to *Awake and Sing*. In the next three years, Odets added to the Group's repertoire with the remarkably successful *Golden Boy* (1937), a young boxer's rags to riches story, and *Rocket to the Moon* (1938), an unsuccessful family drama. (In 1964, *Golden Boy* was revived and adapted successfully as an all-black cast musical that ran for 17 months.)

When the Group Theatre ceased operations in 1941, Odets continued to write plays, enjoying some sporadic successes. He reconciled with Lee Strasberg who directed Odets's *The Big Knife* (1949) and co-produced with Odets his most successful post–Group Theatre play, *The Country Girl* (1950). Odets also directed his own new play *The Flowering Peach* in 1954. It would be his last new play produced on Broadway. Odets also attempted to parlay his theatrical successes into a career as a Hollywood scriptwriter, even as he continued writing plays for Broadway. His best-known screenplays are *The General Died at Dawn* (1939) starring Gary Cooper and *Humoresque* (1946) starring Joan Crawford. By the mid-1950s, however, Odets was no longer actively writing for either theater or film. Odets died of stomach cancer in 1963 in Los Angeles.

In some respects, Odets's theatrical legacy is tied to the Depression era—and arguably only the period between 1935 and 1937 when his most enduring works were first produced. But historians persuasively credit him more than any other playwright of the time with endowing Broadway with an indelible, if not always predominating, social consciousness. Although his most politically oriented plays are rarely revived in anything other than school settings, *Waiting for Lefty* and *Awake and Sing* are canonical works of Depression-era social literature.

Thomas A. Greenfield

Further Reading

Clurman, Harold. *The Fervent Years: The Group Theatre and the 30's.* New York: DaCapo, 1983.

Herr, Christopher J. *Clifford Odets and American Political Theatre.* Westport, CT: Praeger, 2003.

OFF-BROADWAY

Off-Broadway theater has existed as a supplement to the offerings of mainstream New York commercial theater since the early part of the twentieth century. Although the meaning of the word, introduced by theater critic Burns Mantle in the 1930s, has evolved over the years, "Off-Broadway" as a term and a concept have consistently retained their usefulness in the ever-changing New York theater scene.

In today's commercial theater industry the terms "Broadway" and "Off-Broadway" actually serve a relatively narrow function: to classify specific Manhattan theater venues by a criteria-based designation as one or the other (see sidebar "Broadway, Off-Broadway, and Off-Off Broadway Today—By Definition"). With rare exceptions, the plays and **musicals** produced in these venues will share the Broadway or Off-Broadway designation of the theater that houses them. However, in New York theater history, "Off-Broadway" has more broadly referred to the collective efforts of artists creating professional theater in New York away from midtown's most famous commercial theaters. At any given time Off-Broadway has represented a haven for theater artists disillusioned with, ignored by, competing against, or aspiring to reach Broadway. Throughout the twentieth and into the twenty-first century, Off-Broadway's greater predisposition for experimentation and lower potential for financial return have been its defining characteristics.

The Early Twentieth Century: Toward a Meaningful Theater

In the early decades of the twentieth century theatergoers were offered a selection of popular entertainments in Broadway theaters that varied from musical revues to melodramas to frivolous musical comedies. What was largely missing from the commercial theaters was serious social and political drama that would appeal to New York City intellectuals, of which there were many. In response to this need, throughout the 1920s, 1930s, and 1940s numerous literary theater groups and drama clubs (collectively known as the Little Theater Movement) sprouted up as theater artists and patrons of literary theater struggled to supply what they strongly felt was missing on Broadway. Many groups, such as the leftist Progressive Stage Society, disappeared quickly, although a few survived longer. One of these successful groups, the Washington Square Players, eventually became the **Theatre Guild**, which gained fame in the 1920s and 1930s for producing high-quality, commercially appealing work. The Theatre Guild's more important shows included original productions by **Eugene O'Neill**, Broadway premieres of plays by **George Bernard Shaw**, and *Green Grow the Lilacs* (1937)—the play that inspired the landmark musical *Oklahoma!* (1943).

Most of the earliest little theater groups had no permanent theater buildings in which to house their operations and, in fact, often gave little more than casual readings wherever they could muster up a space and an audience. Frequently this meant staging plays in coffeehouses, recital halls, nightclubs, and churches in New York's Greenwich Village and other downtown neighborhoods that became the center for Off-Broadway production in the 1910s. In time some groups, including the Washington Square Players, grew increasingly professional and established permanent home stages, although often in spaces not originally intended as a theater. The **Neighborhood Playhouse** was originally housed in the Henry Street Settlement House on Manhattan's Lower East Side. The **Provincetown Players** built a stage in what had been at one point a bottling plant on MacDougal Street in Greenwich Village. The building came to be known as the Provincetown Playhouse and, as an active theater venue, outlasted the group itself. It is currently owned by New York University, which uses it primarily as a performing arts teaching and performance facility.

Some of the little theater groups produced radical avant-garde plays that pushed artistic and political boundaries. However, some offered classic works or contemporary plays with literary merit by lesser-known or unknown **playwrights**. Most notably, for example, the Provincetown Players in the 1910s formed a partnership with neophyte Eugene O'Neill, performing his earliest plays and launching both his career and theirs. The 1920 production of O'Neill's *The Emperor Jones*, directed by Provincetown Players co-founder George Cram Cook, marked the first time an Off-Broadway play made an almost immediate jump to a successful run on Broadway—a phenomenon that would happen again in the following decades and, eventually, become almost commonplace in the closing decades of the twentieth century. But at the time, many theater groups shunned Broadway, preferring the hardships of creating artistically meaningful theater over the demands of pleasing large uptown audiences and mainstream critics. These groups often made a conscious decision to select plays that they knew would never succeed on Broadway, freeing directors and actors to experiment with interpretations, techniques, and stagecraft.

Social reform became the hallmark of Off-Broadway in the late 1920s and 1930s. During this period the attention of many New York artists, politicians, journalists, and, for that matter, citizens in general was focused upon the plights of factory workers, African American migrants, and immigrants struggling to survive in the Depression-torn city. New theater groups sprang up in response to the Depression, including the Jewish Workers' Theatre and the Workers' Dramatic League. They tended to produce straightforward, *agitprop* (agitation-propaganda) labor dramas in the hopes of enlightening and inspiring the political sensibilities of audiences that now included, along with intellectuals, citizens from various walks of life working for social justice. Such productions increased public interest in New York theater in general, inasmuch as this new audience was composed of many people who did not regularly patronize the revues, light musicals, or even the occasional serious literary plays that represented Broadway fare of the day. The **Group Theatre**, founded by former members of the Theatre Guild—**Harold Clurman**, **Lee Strasberg**, and Cheryl Crawford—became the most famous and prestigious of the social reformist little theater groups, launching to eventual theatrical stardom playwright **Clifford Odets** and director **Elia Kazan** as well as the three founders. Nevertheless, up through the 1930s, Broadway producers, directors, and actors largely viewed Off-Broadway productions with suspicion, as did many theater **critics**. Still, stalwart theater practitioners continued to mount noncommercial productions that slowly raised the public's awareness of theater's potential as an important and meaningful art form.

The financial difficulties that plagued the Little Theater Movement from its beginnings through the 1930s were a predictable outcome of its philosophy and practices, which included charging low ticket prices in order to make theater accessible to everyone. Some groups successfully cultivated patrons. The wealthy Lewisohn sisters (Alice and Irene, an actress and producer, respectively, as well as theatrical "angels") helped support the Neighborhood Playhouse. Actress **Eva Le Gallienne**, although not wealthy herself, skillfully marshaled support of a few wealthy backers for her Civic Repertory Theatre, which she founded in 1926. Other groups sold season subscriptions, enabling them to produce risky, experimental plays without having to sell tickets show by show. Several of the early Off-Broadway theater groups also encountered legal troubles. Owing to the fact that many of the groups mounted plays in spaces that were not real theaters, some had trouble with city licensing authorities. In some instances, by licensing and advertising a theatrical venue as a restaurant, a theater company could skirt certain licensing restrictions and, at the same time, sell food and beverages to generate additional revenue. Others ran into trouble in their effort to assess "fees" (i.e., admission ticket charges) from audience members and had to pass the hat after performances to see any revenue return at all.

The financial exigencies of Off-Broadway were so persistent in the first half of the twentieth century that something akin to a deprivation ethos evolved around Off-Broadway productions and the internal culture of Off-Broadway itself. Early Off-Broadway productions generally had little or no scenery, few props, or costumes. Wages for "professional" actors were often legendary in their miniscule size if they were available at all. (Fifteen dollars a week for a professional "full time" actor was not unusual during the Depression era.) Some dedicated actors lived communally in the performance space while rehearsing and performing their plays, often resulting in very intense performances and personal relationships. Rather than invest in a fine lobby, elaborate scenery, and costumes, Off-Broadway focused its attention on a play's text, the playwrights' meaning, and the acting. Those working in this milieu were quick to say that they performed for themselves to give life to a play, to explore human relationships through the text for their own benefit, rather than to entertain or even enlighten an audience.

By the 1940s, little theater movements and some of the serious American playwrights they had nurtured began to gain a wider reputation as serious artists. In the 1920s and 1930s several little theaters had produced Pulitzer Prize–winning plays, including O'Neill's *Strange Interlude* (1928, produced by the Theatre Guild) and **Susan Glaspell**'s *Alison's House* (1930, produced by the Civic Repertory Theatre). In the early 1940s Random House and other major publishers began releasing popular anthologies of "favorite" or "best plays" for general sales, sometimes including works that were first produced Off-Broadway.

Post–World War II: Impoverished Respectability

Off-Broadway offerings increased noticeably after World War II as many theater groups began to attain respectability, at least among the literary theatergoers. The *New York Times* principal theater critic of the 1930s and 1940s, **Brooks Atkinson**, began writing about and regularly championing Off-Broadway productions, often extolling their virtues over mainstream commercial theatrical productions. The Cherry Lane Theatre and the Provincetown Playhouse, both located in Greenwich Village, flourished in the postwar years, offering plays by such playwrights as Odets, O'Neill, **Tennessee Williams**, and Sean O'Casey. In 1950 producer Theodore Mann and director **José Quintero** opened the Circle in the Square—so named because their original stage was a semicircular dance floor in the former Sheridan Square nightclub—and quickly found a champion in Atkinson. Williams's play *Summer and Smoke* had been unsuccessful on Broadway in 1948, but the play blossomed under the direction of Quintero in his 1952 Circle in the Square production. Drawing rave reviews from audiences and critics alike, the production was a watershed event that signaled changing attitudes about the quality and viability of Off-Broadway. With *Summer and Smoke* and other critical successes, including 1954's *The Girl on the Via Flaminia* by Alfred Hayes, the Circle in the Square proved that there was a growing audience in New York for serious drama in Off-Broadway venues and that there were talented directors and actors capable of delivering it. Circle in the Square felt that its production of *The Girl on the Via Flaminia* was so strong that when New York City officials closed the theater down for fire code violations that year, *Flaminia* transferred to Broadway. However, the show flopped on Broadway as did other strong, well-reviewed or well-received Off-Broadway shows that transferred uptown in the 1950s. The Circle in the Square had several failed productions in the mid-1950s but followed those up with a glorious success in 1956. Just as Eugene O'Neill's plays had found a home with the Provincetown Players in the 1920s, the Circle in the Square's production of his

The Iceman Cometh reintroduced the theatergoing public to his intense explorations of American dreams. Director Quintero, long known for giving new acting talent a chance, chose a young **Jason Robards** to play the main character, Hickey. Extravagant praise followed for Robards's performance as well as Quintero's direction, and Circle in the Square made money on the play for two years.

Also in 1954, *The Three Penny Opera* at the Theater de Lys signaled to the world that Off-Broadway was truly a force to be reckoned with. Situated near the Hudson River at the far west end of Lower Manhattan's Christopher Street, the Theater de Lys's isolated location complemented the sinister tone of the dark musical by Kurt Weill and Bertolt Brecht. Featuring Lotte Lenya (Weill's widow), *The Three Penny Opera* was a commercial and critical success. Although the producers had to close the play temporarily because of another commitment in the theater, they brought the play back later and, with a rotation of cast replacements, enjoyed a run of six years.

Off-Broadway saw numerous successes in the decades that followed. In many cases, rather than move to Broadway, producers decided to keep their hit show Off-Broadway. In 1960, despite wild commercial success, *The Fantastics*, a lighthearted, sentimental musical featuring Jerry Orbach, stayed at the Sullivan Street Playhouse for a phenomenal 42 years, by far the longest run of any Off-Broadway show. *Little Shop of Horrors*, a rock musical takeoff of a black comedy B-movie, opened in 1982 at the Orpheum. Despite critical and commercial success, the producers decided it belonged Off-Broadway, where it stayed for five years. The show eventually came to Broadway with moderate success in 2003 with a different set of producers.

Even in the 1950s, with quality Off-Broadway shows enjoying increasing recognition and patronage from the theatergoing public, transitions from Off-Broadway to Broadway often proved to be highly problematic. In some cases, the original production lost its intimacy in the larger Broadway venues; in other cases it appeared that the Broadway audiences had different expectations than did their Off-Broadway counterparts. It would still be a number of years before Off-Broadway to Broadway transfers would become a major trend in Broadway production, but the growing success and prestige of Off-Broadway in the 1950s laid the foundation for that to happen.

At about the same time that Circle in the Square was gaining critical attention, other Off-Broadway companies with very dissimilar outlooks opened, signaling a new era of complexity in Off-Broadway theater that continued throughout the twentieth century. The Phoenix Theater sought to emulate the theaters of Europe's great cities while Julian Beck and Judith Malina's Living Theatre brought the influences of European postmodernism, absurdist, and avant-garde theater to New York. Unlike many other Off-Broadway theaters that evolved organically, the Phoenix started in 1953 with many financial backers and a renovated theater on the corner of 12th Street and Second Avenue. The first production, *Madam, Will You Walk?* with **Hume Cronyn** and **Jessica Tandy**, was a critical and financial success. A few months later, a musical called *The Golden Apple* also succeeded but failed when it transferred to Broadway. After a few years of struggle, the

Phoenix reorganized as a nonprofit theater to take advantage of foundation support and grants from corporations, a move that allowed them to continue for many years to come. They introduced new acting talent in plays by classic writers such as Anton Chekhov, **Shakespeare**, and Shaw, but also nurtured new writers such as Arthur L. Kopit (*Oh, Dad, Poor Dad, Mama's Hung You in the Closet and I'm Feeling So Sad*, Off-Broadway 1960; Broadway 1963). The Phoenix even enjoyed a major commercial transfer to Broadway during this period with *Once Upon a Mattress*, which opened at the Phoenix in 1959 and transferred later that year.

Another Off-Broadway theater company with a new outlook, the Living Theatre, was led by director Julian Beck and actor-director Judith Molina, a husband-and-wife team that saw theater as art and process—never as commercial product. Their unconventional productions of poetic plays were reminiscent of the early twentieth-century theater groups as well as the radical experimentation that would later become the distinguishing characteristic of Off-Off Broadway (see sidebar "Broadway, Off-Broadway, and Off-Off Broadway Today—By Definition"). The Living Theatre garnered significant critical attention with productions such as Jack Gelber's shocking play presaging the coming nationwide drug problem, *The Connection* (1959), Kenneth H. Brown's intense military prison drama *The Brig* (1964), and the bizarre audience-participation piece *Paradise Now* (1968). The group was plagued by building and fire code violations and tax problems among other legal difficulties and was forced to close down several times. Touring frequently as an ensemble theater for many years—in part to keep working when performing in New York proved unfeasible—the Living Theatre returned proudly to the city for a number of well-received productions in the late twentieth and early twenty-first century.

Joseph Papp and the New Off-Broadway

Before **Joseph Papp**, founder of the New York Shakespeare Festival and the Public Theater, began producing plays in New York during the late 1950s, Off-Broadway was a distinctly separate entity from Broadway. If an Off-Broadway production moved to Broadway, it did so in spite of, not because of, its production values. However, largely because of Papp's influence, since the 1970s Off-Broadway has been frequently used to "workshop" certain productions, especially productions chosen for, among other considerations, their potential appeal to a large general audience. As a result, today many Off-Broadway shows are produced with a "transfer-to-Broadway" mind-set and are often indistinguishable from Broadway fare in terms of themes, creative talent, and even some aspects of design and staging. This relatively recent role of Off-Broadway as Broadway incubator would have likely forced virtually all truly experimental theater out of the professional New York theater scene had it not been for another of Joe Papp's innovations: taking money earned by transferring large productions to Broadway and, in keeping with Off-Broadway's earliest traditions, mounting small, experimental productions highlighting the work of new writers and actors.

In 1956, Papp started producing free Shakespeare plays in city parks, cultivating a new level of interest in the theater throughout New York's diverse population. Hailed for these efforts by theater critics, the press, the public, donors, and theater professionals around the country, Papp soon moved the New York Shakespeare Festival (as it had been renamed) into a permanent theater, the Delacorte in Central Park. He later purchased a performance space, the historic Astor Library in Lower Manhattan, and in 1967 founded the Public Theater. His goal for the Public Theater was to offer modern plays in between his Shakespeare productions, and to that end he built five theaters of different sizes in the Astor. (Papp's development of multiple theaters of various sizes in the same building has influenced theater construction and refurbishment both in New York and across the country ever since.)

The Public Theater's inaugural production, a new musical *Hair*, garnered mixed response from critics, but theatergoers made it a success. The controversial antiwar "rock musical" (the first of that now familiar subgenre of musicals) shocked some with its nudity, but nevertheless enjoyed a four-year run on Broadway and became one of the best-loved musicals of the past 40 years. Papp used the profits from the transfer to Broadway to fund further productions, a formula that he and subsequent directors at the Public Theater have maintained for years (including well after Papp's death in 1991). After *Hair*, successful Public Theater transfers to Broadway became almost commonplace and included *That Championship Season* (1972), *A Chorus Line* (1975), *for colored girls who have considered suicide/when the rainbow is enuf* (1976), *Twilight: Los Angeles, 1992* (1994), *Bring in 'Da Noise, Bring in 'Da Funk* (1995), and *Caroline, or Change* (2003). By funding new productions and fostering new talent with profits derived from Off-Broadway to Broadway transfers, Papp created the blueprint for one of the most important ways that contemporary commercial theater fosters artistic experimentation.

The Turn of the New Century

Papp's innovations allowed Off-Broadway to thrive at the end of the twentieth and into the twenty-first century. The list of productions that started Off-Broadway (whether in Papp's Public Theater or elsewhere) and ended up on Broadway includes some of Broadway's most notable recent hits, such as *Urinetown* (2001), *Avenue Q* (2003), *I Am My Own Wife* (2003), *Doubt* (2004), *Spring Awakening* (2006), and *Grey Gardens* (2006). Indeed, 23 out of 25 Tony Awards handed out for the 2006–2007 season went to productions with ties to nonprofit theaters.

Some people within the theater industry are unhappy, however, with what they see as the new commercially driven purpose of Off-Broadway in its attempt to serve as a feeder for Broadway. Detractors of the current situation, observing the decrease in the number of successful shows that remain Off-Broadway for a sustained run, complain that almost any production that finds even mild success Off-Broadway is immediately groomed for transfer. However, proponents of the Off-Broadway to Broadway transfer phenomenon are quick to point out that, under current contractual arrangements, Off-Broadway theaters now share in the many

BROADWAY, OFF-BROADWAY, AND OFF-OFF BROADWAY TODAY—BY DEFINITION

Broadway. The Broadway League (the leading organization of professional theater producers), the American Theatre Wing (overseers of the Tony Awards), and the major theater publications currently recognize 40 venues as official Broadway theaters. In all cases these theaters have seating for at least 500. With the exception of the Vivian Beaumont Theater, located on West 65th street in Lincoln Center, all of them are located in the midtown Manhattan theater district, between 41st and 54th Street, within two blocks east or west of Broadway. They are primarily used for theatrical productions (plays and musicals) rather than music or dance concerts or other performances. Thirty-five of them operate as for-profit theaters under Actors' Equity Broadway production agreements, which include higher minimum salaries for virtually all unionized creative personnel than are required for Off-Broadway productions. Four are controlled by nonprofit companies that have separate contract agreements but also offer higher minimum salaries for unionized cast and crew. These official Broadway theaters are the only theaters whose shows are eligible for Tony Award consideration. (See list in **Broadway** entry.)

    Off-Broadway theaters have 100 to 499 seats and are located in Manhattan. By contract Off-Broadway plays are scheduled to run more than one week and, unlike "workshop" productions or semiprofessional shows and readings, must be offered to critics as well as general audiences. While the term "Off-Broadway" still retains some of the imprecision and fluidity it possessed when first introduced in the 1930s, the League of Off-Broadway Theatres and Producers, founded in 1959, oversees the professional interests of Off-Broadway theater, negotiating Off-Broadway contracts with Actors' Equity and other unions and presenting its own awards for eligible Off-Broadway shows. However, the term "Off-Broadway" can also apply more broadly to any number of New York professional theater productions that may abide by Actors' Equity and other Off-Broadway union contracts but may not be affiliated with the League of Off-Broadway Theatres and Producers per se. In general, Off-Broadway production and running costs still amount to a small fraction of those of Broadway productions.

    Off-Off Broadway technically refers to any professional or semiprofessional New York production staged in a venue with fewer than 100 seats. From this single criterion it is possible to stage an Off-Off Broadway play in the geographical area covered by the midtown Manhattan theater district. However, as a colloquial term, it generally implies a location away from the theater district.

benefits to be derived from launching a "Broadway show," including increased post-transfer recognition and revenue for the original producing company. Further criticism has been aimed at Off-Broadway producers who hire well-known actors from **film** and **television** to take starring roles in their productions—a practice pointedly at odds with Off-Broadway's original intention to develop new talent. Yet defenders of the practice argue that the presence of well-known actors in Off-Broadway shows creates networking and mentoring opportunities for the less experienced theater artists working in these productions as well as obvious promotional benefits for the Off-Broadway theater and its show.

Despite Broadway's unwavering appeal to theater professionals, there are still numerous productions that open, succeed, and remain Off-Broadway for a long time. Many of them tour successfully in the United States and throughout the world before opening on Broadway—if, indeed, they ever do. *Blue Man Group* (1991), *Oleanna* (1992; Broadway 2009), *Stomp* (1994), and *Alter Boyz* (2005) are among the best known of Off-Broadway's relatively recent successes. David Mamet's *Oleanna* represents one of numerous recent examples of a play that was originally produced in a **regional (resident) theater** outside of New York before it moved to Off-Broadway and then Broadway. ***In the Heights***, which debuted in Waterford, Connecticut, and then opened Off-Broadway in 2007, is one of the more noteworthy recent productions to find success as a regional-theater-to-Off-Broadway-to-Broadway transfer. It opened on Broadway in 2008, where it became the surprise hit of the 2007–2008 season. *Passing Strange* (2008) opened in Los Angeles before transferring to the Public Theater and then to Broadway for a critically heralded run.

Despite the contrast between Off-Broadway and Broadway's current close relationship and their "world's apart" philosophies that emerged in the early years of the twentieth century, the benefits of the current relationship accrue to so many segments of both nonprofit and commercial theater that the future is likely to yield more cooperation between the two rather than less. Purists' objections to the contrary, most observers agree that the relationship shores up weaknesses in both sectors. Commercial theater provides Off-Broadway with greater access to revenues and publicity than it could attract on its own. Off-Broadway and other nonprofits generate a far larger pool of plays and musicals than the handful of active Broadway producers could cultivate on their own. And Broadway audiences seem quite happy to see good theater come into midtown no matter where it originated.

Thomas A. Greenfield and Sue Ann Brainard

Further Reading

Auerbach, Doris. *Shepard, Kopit, and the Off Broadway Theater*. Boston: Twayne, 1982.

The Broadway League, http://www.livebroadway.com.

Little, Stuart W. *Off Broadway: The Prophetic Theater*. New York: Coward, McCann, and Geohegan, 1972.

Stone, Wendell C. *Caffe Cino: The Birthplace of Off-Off Broadway*. Carbondale: Southern Illinois University, 2005.

Wetzsteon, Ross. "I Lost It at the Obies: A Chronicle of Forty Years of Off Broadway." *The Village Voice*. May 30, 1995, p. 87.

OH! CALCUTTA!

Broadway Run: Eden Theater (June 17, 1969–closing date unverified) and Belasco Theatre (February 25, 1971 to August 12, 72)
Opening: June 17, 1969
Closing: August 12, 1972
Total Performances: 1,314
Music and Lyrics: Members of the Open Window (Robert Dennis, Peter Schickele, and Stanley Walden) and Jacques Levy
Book: Kenneth Tynan, Samuel Beckett, Robert Benton, Jules Feiffer, Dan Greenburg, John Lennon, Jacques Levy, Leonard Melfi, David Newman, Sam Shepard, and Sherman Yellen.
Choreographer: Margo Sappington
Director: Jacques Levy
Producers: Hillard Elkins, in association with Michael White, Gordon Crowe, and George Platt
Leading Performers: Robert Dennis (Open Window Performer), Bill Macy (Performer), Alan Rachins (Performer), Margo Sappington (Performer), Peter Schickele (Open Window Performer), Stanley Walden (Open Window Performer).

Oh! Calcutta!, British theater critic and writer Kenneth Tynan's full-frontal nude revue, was nothing short of a cultural phenomenon on Broadway and in Europe. Although reviewers dismissed this collection of sketches and musical acts as banal, juvenile, and patently unerotic, audiences flocked to this self-described "most controversial show in Broadway history" that aimed to arouse and to entertain. With a 1969 original run lasting for three years and a 1976 revival lasting nearly 13, *Oh! Calcutta!* was a mainstay of the New York theater scene in the 1970s and 1980s, briefly becoming the longest-running show in Broadway history. *Oh! Calcutta!* drew crowds when it played across the Atlantic as well, running for 12 years in London and 9 years in Paris. Its longevity defied all expectations. Despite mediocre material, an assessment with which even some of the show's creators agreed, the revue clearly struck a chord with diverse audiences in the two decades that it ran. *Oh! Calcutta!*'s greatest impact on the theater world and on American culture writ large was its demonstration that nudity and performances explicitly and exclusively about sex and sexuality could be viable, mainstream commercial fare. And Broadway has shown that influence periodically ever since.

Certainly, Tynan's show was not the first to feature or attract an audience with promises of bawdiness, licentiousness, and eroticism. Nor was it the first theater event to combine music and the removal of one's clothes. In addition to revues, *Oh! Calcutta!* contains vestiges of early twentieth-century burlesque, a form that in its day periodically ran afoul of censors and faced public outcries over "indecency" and "vulgarity." More recent predecessors like *Marat/Sade* (1965) and **Hair** (1968) had certainly contained more frank expressions of eroticism than post–World War II Broadway was used to. Moreover, **Off-Broadway** performances by The Living Theatre group (among many others) had contained controversial moments or scenes involving nudity since the 1950s. Yet with *Oh! Calcutta!*, nudity and simulated sex acts were prominent throughout the entirety of the show and constituted its very reason for being (and for attending). Building on sentiments of freedom and liberation from the 1960s, *Oh! Calcutta!* became a household name and, ultimately, Broadway's reigning symbol for the sexual revolution of the 1960s and 1970s.

Tynan, a highly influential **critic** for *The London Observer, The New Yorker*, and *Playboy* from the 1950s through the 1970s, had been a tireless advocate for free expression in theater throughout his career. He was a major force in the passage of England's Theatres Act of 1968, which ended the Monarchy's centuries-old authority for regulating moral content of London playhouses. *Oh! Calcutta!* was yet another calculated effort in Tynan's ongoing campaign to break down social taboos, and to that end, he asked writer friends and colleagues for contributions about eroticism, sexual fantasies, and fetishes. He solicited sketches that would titillate, but that had no pretense toward artistic or literary merit. Tynan invited Off-Broadway director (and professional psychologist) Jacques Levy to stage the project. The show's iconic onstage nudity was Levy's, and not Tynan's, lasting stamp on *Oh! Calcutta!* Levy recognized that conditions were right in New York City at the end of the 1960s to open a piece that used nudity not merely as a symbol or metaphor, but as the subject itself—the unabashed celebration of the human body and sexuality.

The name of the revue was taken from twentieth-century French painter Clovis Trouille's *Oh! Calcutta! Calcutta!*, which depicts the bare backside of a reclining nude. (The painting's title itself is a French pun; "O quel cul t'as" roughly translates to "What an ass you have!") Similarly naughty lyrics, skits, and scenes by the likes of Samuel Beckett, Jules Feiffer, John Lennon, and Sam Shepard appeared in the show. Offerings from contemporary playwrights Joe Orton and Eugene Ionesco were included in the London and Paris productions, respectively. Virtually all of the scenes and songs more or less dealt with the pursuit of happiness through sex. Between *Oh! Calcutta!*'s opening striptease number and its finale (a choreographed all-cast "grope and hump") were scenes and songs about group masturbation, sexually oriented personal ads, novice swingers, and sexual experimentation.

Midway through *Oh! Calcutta!*'s 1969 run, the production transferred from Off-Broadway to the Broadway Belasco Theatre. A Broadway revival later opened in 1976 at the Edison Theater and, astonishingly, ran for nearly 6,000 performances, making it, along with the 1996 revival of *Chicago*, one of the two longest-running revival productions in the history of Broadway. *Oh! Calcutta!* remained fluid throughout its runs. For example, some of the sketches encouraged actors to improvise, and some pieces that were printed in the published script were cut during the previews, only to be added back for different iterations of the show. A film of a performance was screened in cinemas across the United States (though many cities banned its presentation), and it has since been released on video and DVD. *Oh! Calcutta!* played for over 20 years in New York City and around the world, employed thousands of actors, and reached millions of audience members in its many incarnations (live performance, script, film). Considering its anomalous history, it is difficult, and maybe unnecessary, to articulate which one of its numerous versions might be considered *the* landmark production, but it is unquestionably a landmark show in the history of Broadway.

Beyond its legacy of prompting public discussions about censorship, morality, obscenity, and sexuality, *Oh! Calcutta!* also suggested that there was a profitable niche in the **musical** theater world for nude revues. It laid the groundwork for long-running Off-Broadway shows such as *The Dirtiest Show in Town* (1970), *Let My People Come* (1974), and *Naked Boys Singing* (1998). Tynan's entertainment is now so dated as to make a major twenty-first-century revival unlikely. In a sense, though, it may have helped achieve Tynan's lifelong goal of loosening society's inhibitions. In 1969, *Oh! Calcutta!* was breaking sexual barriers, or at least, exposing them as ridiculous; by 1989, when the Broadway revival production closed, social mores had both relaxed and transformed to such a degree that the politics and spectacle of *Oh! Calcutta!* had lost much of its novelty and its vaunted ability to shock.

Zachary A. Dorsey

Further Reading

Allyn, David. *Make Love, Not War: The Sexual Revolution, An Unfettered History.* New York: Little, Brown & Co., 2000.

Houghton, Norris. *The Exploding Stage: An Introduction to Twentieth Century Drama.* New York: Weybright and Talley, 1971.

OKLAHOMA!

Broadway Run: St. James Theatre
Opening: March 31, 1943
Closing: May 29, 1948
Total Performances: 2,212
Composer: Richard Rodgers
Lyricist: Oscar Hammerstein II
Book: Oscar Hammerstein II

Choreographer: Agnes de Mille
Director: Rouben Mamoulian
Producer: The Theatre Guild
Lead Performers: Alfred Drake (Curly), Joan Roberts (Laurey), Howard
DaSilva (Jud Fry), and Celeste Holm (Ado Annie)

Oklahoma!, **Richard Rodgers** and **Oscar Hammerstein**'s first collaborative effort, changed almost everything a single production could possibly change about Broadway and American musical theater: how **musicals** are written, written about, choreographed, staged, marketed, and perceived by audiences and American culture at large. The first Broadway show ever to run for over 2,000 performances or more than five years, it redefined what a hit show could be. The first of the modern "literary" or "book" musicals, *Oklahoma!* launched what many view as Broadway's Golden Age of musical theater—a 20-year period in which thoughtful integration of story line, dialog, song lyrics, melody, character differentiation, and choreography became the standard for excellence and the formula for success. A melodramatic love triangle set against turn-of-the-century frontier conflicts over land rights, *Oklahoma!* almost single-handedly rendered *passé* the musical's long-standing reliance on joke-infested dialog and stand-alone hit songs.

Curly, played by Alfred Drake, and Laurey, played by Joan Roberts, ride in "The Surrey with the Fringe on Top" in this scene from the original production of Oklahoma!, *which opened on Broadway March 31, 1943. Other principals (left to right directly in front of the surrey are Lee Dixon, Celeste Holm, and Joseph Buloff, who portrayed Will Parker, Ado Annie, and Ali Hakim, respectively. (AP Photo)*

The original cast album of *Oklahoma!* was so popular that it launched the modern practice of generating an original cast record album as a *pro forma* aspect of producing and marketing a Broadway musical. Original cast albums became a staple of Broadway's economy, and for the remainder of the twentieth century the genre occupied a healthy niche in the recording and broadcast music industries. The successful 1955 movie adaptation helped reinvigorate public interest in the Broadway musical movie. The newly formed partnership of Rodgers and Hammerstein became the most successful and revered creative team in American musical theater history, to the point that the phrase "a Rodgers and Hammerstein–type musical" has become a common descriptor of any and all musicals, regardless of authorship, that craft music, lyrics, choreography, and staging around the literary qualities of plot and character.

In 1942 Richard Rodgers had just completed an astonishingly successful run of nearly 20 years as the composing half of the team Rodgers and Hart. Rodgers and **Lorenz Hart** had written over 20 Broadway musicals, including *On Your Toes* (1936) and *Pal Joey* (1940), and had numerous hit songs to their credit, including the now American classics "The Lady Is a Tramp" and "Blue Moon." However, by the early 1940s, Hart's health problems and professional unreliability were undermining the partnership. Rodgers, just turning 40, was not interested in resting on his laurels or his wealth, although he clearly could have. Seeking other projects and other collaborators, his interest was whetted at the possibility of doing a musical adaptation of Lynn Riggs's 1931 play *Green Grow the Lilacs. Lilacs* was one of the **Theatre Guild**'s short-run literary dramas that often drew admiration from New York's intelligentsia if moderate interest from Broadway's broader audiences.

At the same time lyricist Oscar Hammerstein II had also been a long-standing presence on Broadway. However, unlike Rodgers, Hammerstein had collaborated with many partners and had been decidedly less successful than Rodgers over the previous 15 years. Although Hammerstein made history and money with composer **Jerome Kern** on the groundbreaking *Show Boat* (1927), he had since written a string of marginal productions and outright flops. An **operetta**-influenced lyricist with a greater gift for emotion and sensibility than urbane wit and ironic observation, Hammerstein's work had been bested throughout the 1930s by the cleverer, snappier tunes of the likes of **Cole Porter**, **Irving Berlin** and, indeed, Hart. Both Hammerstein and Rodgers became intrigued with the idea of adapting the Riggs play, in part because they sensed they could experiment with it in ways that defied current practice.

As is often the case at the outset of groundbreaking projects, *Oklahoma!*'s potential for failure seemed to overwhelm its probability for success. Hammerstein, then in his late forties, was widely seen as past his prime. (Before World War II the careers of Broadway's wordsmiths tended to crest in their late twenties and thirties.) The reputation of the Theatre Guild, producers of both the musical and the original Riggs play, was faring little better than Hammerstein's. Noted more for short-run, prestige dramas than musicals (or commercial successes of any kind), the Guild had produced only one original musical in the previous seven years and that one had closed in a week. The Guild, too, was widely seen as having made its theatrical mark in decades past with **Porgy and Bess** (1935) and **Eugene O'Neill** premieres, and was now occupying a small niche in New York theater while living off a venerated if somewhat stodgy legacy of former glory. The subject matter itself seemed problematic. Frontier romance and conflict, big winners in movies, had little precedence for the Broadway audience, which, in the World War II era, was far more local and northeast-based than it is today. The audience for the show would have as little firsthand identification with Oklahoma cowboys and farmers as did the musical's New York City born and bred composer and lyricist.

Nevertheless, from the outset *Oklahoma!* was a colossal success. Rather than opening with a clichéd big production number, the action starts with male lead **Alfred Drake** as Curley strolling up to his love interest Laurie's house while singing a solo, "Oh! What a Beautiful Morning." With Drake's stunning delivery, this deceptively forceful paean to rural landscape transformed Oklahoma's golden-hazed meadows with its winking maverick calves into an all-American paradise. New York **critics** and audiences approved from day one. Rodgers and Hammerstein followed *Oklahoma!* on Broadway with *Carousel* (1945), *South Pacific* (1949), and *The King and I* (1951), each a masterwork of the new literary musical form. The Rodgers and Hammerstein era was launched in earnest. The partnership would last until Hammerstein's death in 1960 but would exert its influence on virtually every major Broadway composer and lyricist to come in the twentieth century.

In the intervening six decades since *Oklahoma!*'s Broadway opening, scholars, dramaturges, directors, and audiences have continuously revisited its wonders and mystique, making of it a major artifact of twentieth-century American culture. *Oklahoma!* has been variously credited with quelling American anxieties during World War II, enhancing America's postwar self-confidence, validating the modern musical as a worthy indigenous American art form, bringing mature sexuality to the Broadway musical without being salacious or prurient, and enlisting sophisticated choreography to advance dramatic characterization. Perhaps most importantly, *Oklahoma!* seems to have convinced America once and for all that Broadway musicals can connect meaningfully to the lives of Americans beyond the reaches of New York's East Side, West Side, and Times Square.

Thomas A. Greenfield

Further Reading

Jones, John Bush. *Our Musicals, Ourselves: A Social History of the American Musical Theater.* Lebanon, NH: Brandeis University Press/University Press of New England, 2004.

Hischack, Thomas, ed. *The Rodgers and Hammerstein Encyclopedia.* Westport, CT: Greenwood Press, 2007.

ONE-CHARACTER SHOW

See **Solo Performance**.

O'NEILL, EUGENE (1888–1953)
PLAYWRIGHT

Eugene O'Neill defines American drama. Almost all studies, even those that begrudge O'Neill his towering status, trace the history of the American theater and the development of American drama using O'Neill's emergence and lasting impact as context. Despite some peripheral academic debate, ***Long Day's Journey into Night*** (1956) is generally admitted to be the greatest American play. Among his other masterpieces are *The Iceman Cometh* (1946), *A Moon for the Misbegotten* (posthumous Broadway premiere, 1957), and *A Touch of the Poet* (posthumous Broadway premiere, 1958). These plays were written at the conclusion of O'Neill's writing career, and this is one of the most extraordinary things about him: he wrote his best plays at the end of his career. Turning away from experimentation and innovation, O'Neill's final plays draw inspiration from the playwright's own tortured soul and bleak vision of existence. Almost all of his previous plays used sources or devices that somehow separated them from the playwright's direct experience. Late in life, debilitated by a degenerative Parkinson's-like neurological disorder and knowing his time was short, O'Neill tore away all dramaturgical masks and wrote the plays he had been preparing for his entire life.

O'Neill's life is compelling in itself. He was the son of one of America's most popular actors, James O'Neill, who had made a career playing in and producing *The Count of Monte Cristo*. O'Neill grew up in the theater, touring with his father and even performing with him, but he came to despise his father's world as the "show shop." He also rejected the genteel security his father's profits from *Monte Cristo* provided and took off to roam the world as a sailor. (O'Neill's proudest achievement was his certification as an "Able Bodied Seaman.") Between voyages he "bummed around" and wrecked his health; he survived a suicide attempt in 1912 but found that he had contracted tuberculosis. Sent to a sanatorium, the confinement caused him to focus his furious creativity. He began writing plays. He knew though that his efforts were lacking.

Determined "to be an artist or nothing," as he wrote to George Pierce Baker in his application letter to join the 47 Workshop at Harvard, O'Neill honed his craft and submitted to the discipline, if not the aesthetic, of Baker's methods. O'Neill's first plays offer clues to his genius. His first short play was a vaudeville sketch entitled "A Wife for a Life," copyrighted in 1913. A more important early play by O'Neill is "The Web," a one-act melodrama about a tuberculosis-stricken prostitute and her baby. Though its copyright is 1914, O'Neill considered it his first play.

Two other early works include "Before Breakfast" and "Ile." "The Web" contains two motifs that would concern O'Neill throughout his early career: tuberculosis and criminals. "Before Breakfast" is significant both in its obvious debt to Swedish playwright August Strindberg's "The Stronger" and that it is a monologue. O'Neill would always pay homage to Strindberg as the modern playwright to whom he was most indebted; throughout O'Neill's career he would rely on long speeches to present characterization. His experimental drama *Strange Interlude* would particularly depend on long asides that were the spoken thoughts of the characters.

The most significant one-act plays that he wrote are the "Glencairn cycle" of sea plays that involve the sailors of the tramp steamer of the same name. Here O'Neill draws on his own experiences. The plays include "Bound East for Cardiff" (1916), "The Long Voyage Home" (1917), "The Moon of the Caribbees (1918), and "In the Zone" (1919). Rejecting almost all contemporary conventional plot or characterization devices, these are evocative mood pieces completely different from other America plays of this time. The first production of a play by O'Neill was "Bound East for Cardiff" in July 1916 at the Provincetown Playhouse on Cape Cod in Massachusetts. This date is usually identified as the beginning of the modern American theater, and thus O'Neill began his fitful partnership with the **Provincetown Players** on Cape Cod and later in Greenwich Village.

By 1920 O'Neill had had enough avant-garde theater experience. Henceforth, O'Neill's life was consumed by his art. He would give up drinking and everything else that interfered with his work. His plays become the index of his life. Through the efforts of drama critic **George Jean Nathan** and others he was able to have his first Broadway production. *Beyond the Horizon* (1920) was a triumph and won the Pulitzer Prize. (He would win four more.) Virtually overnight O'Neill was recognized as the leading American dramatist. *Beyond the Horizon* is about the struggle of two brothers, one an artistic dreamer who longs to go to sea, the other a practical farmer. Both love the same woman. This causes the dreamer to stay on the farm and marry the woman and the other brother to leave and go to sea. The result is disaster for all. Here appear typical O'Neillian themes about the longing for freedom that only the sea can provide, the entrapment of marriage, and the sustaining "pipe dreams" that keep human beings functioning during our dreary existence.

Another important play of the 1920s is *The Emperor Jones* (1920), the first American drama to have the leading role of a black man played by a black actor. This expressionistic drama details the downfall of the self-proclaimed emperor of a Caribbean island. *Anna Christie* (1921) draws on the sea's psychological power. The title character is a reformed prostitute who finds love with a rough, but tender sailor and understanding from her frustrated barge captain father. *The Hairy Ape* (1922), O'Neill's finest expressionistic play, is a drama of "Yank," the brutal stoker who desperately attempts to find out where he "belongs"—a recurring theme in O'Neill's work. *Desire Under the Elms* (1924) is O'Neill's successful adaptation of the Hippolytus and Medea myths to a New England farm setting. *The Great God Brown* (1926) is an experimental play using masks to depict split personality. O'Neill was frequently critical of the adulation of commercialism, and *Marco Millions* (1928) is a satire of American businessmen using the legendary figure of Marco Polo to show how material success comes at the expense of one's true self. The culminating play of this decade in O'Neill's career is *Strange Interlude* (1928)—his self-described "woman play." It is the mammoth saga of Nina Leeds and "her three men," and was notorious in its time for its frank depiction of female sexuality. Even though the play is seven hours long (with a break for dinner) it was a great success. The parody of the play's aside-type monologues featured in the Marx Brothers' 1928 musical and subsequent film *Animal Crackers* (Groucho's "strange interludes") reveals O'Neill's celebrity. By now he was a fixture in the media—even though he shunned it—his grim visage was featured on *Time*'s cover three times.

In 1932 O'Neill again presented Greek tragedy adapted to a New England setting with *Mourning Becomes Electra*, a trilogy based on Æschylus's *Oresteia*. It takes place in the aftermath of the Civil War and concerns two generations of the Mannon family. A group of townspeople serves as a chorus. Adultery, murder, and matricide take us through the first play as in the Greek original. In the final two plays the tragic curse is played out via O'Neill's modern day applications of psychology as the guilty children accept their fate. This play was largely responsible for the Nobel Prize for literature that he won in 1936.

O'Neill's only comedy *Ah, Wilderness!* (1933) is a bittersweet recollection of the sort of family life and boyish romance that O'Neill wished he could have had. The play is not quite the sunny valentine to days gone by that it appears to be though. It was a hit, but O'Neill was upset that it was seen as a vehicle for the legendary **George M. Cohan**, who starred in the production. This fed his growing professional exasperation with Broadway, and after the 1934 failure of *Days Without End* O'Neill abandoned Broadway and immured himself to complete his final masterpieces.

O'Neill believed his last project would be a great cycle of 11 plays about the development of the United States, entitled: "A tale of possessors self-dispossessed." He declared, "We are the greatest failure in history—no other country was given so much—and look at what we have done with ourselves. I can't help but think of the words what profit it a man if he gain the whole world, but loses his own soul? We've lost our soul" (Agee 1946, 71). O'Neill labored for years, but failed to satisfy his own vision. In the midst of this titanic artistic struggle, illness intervened, and O'Neill was forced to curtail his historical project and complete a far more personal one. Confronted by the immediacy of his physical decay, O'Neill wrote the plays about his family and friends that would overwhelm the world.

In 1939 he wrote *The Iceman Cometh* inspired by the low-life comrades of his youth. The denizens of Harry Hope's saloon are a collective hero who await the annual return of Hickey, the traveling salesman who gives them free booze and good times. This visit is different; Hickey has foresworn liquor and is determined to force them all to face reality and free themselves from their "pipe dreams." Through choral and antiphonal dialogues O'Neill creates a brilliant "illusion" of his own, that the play is a realistic depiction of a backroom dive.

Long Day's Journey into Night (1941) and *A Moon for the Misbegotten* (1941–1943) are the most frankly autobiographical of his plays. The latter is a sequel of sorts to *Long Day's Journey*, showing us the fate of James Tyrone Jr. It is more than a valedictory for Tyrone, though. Its New England farm setting places it within themes developed by O'Neill since *Beyond the Horizon*.

Three years after O'Neill's death, the 1956 revival of *Iceman* directed by **José Quintero** at the Circle-in-the Square revived O'Neill's moribund reputation with critics and the theatergoing public, confirmed "**Off-Broadway**" as the creative locus of American theater, launched the career of actor **Jason Robards**, and led to the epochal Broadway production of *Long Day's Journey into Night* later that season. As he had in life, the late Eugene O'Neill led the way for American drama.

Thomas F. Connolly

Citation

Agee, James. "The Ordeal of Eugene O'Neill." *Time*, October 21, 1946, pp. 71–78.

Further Reading

Gelb, Arthur, and Barbara Gelb. *O'Neill: Life with Monte Cristo*. New York: Applause Theatre & Cinema Books, 2000.

Sheaffer, Louis. *O'Neill: Son and Playwright*. Little, Brown & Co., 1968.

———. *O'Neill: Son and Artist*. Little, Brown & Co., 1973.

OPERETTA

Operetta is a form of musical theater rooted in nineteenth-century European light opera traditions and is probably the single greatest influence on the evolution of the American Broadway musical. In the United States it was adapted to the styles of Broadway and Hollywood throughout the first half of the twentieth century. Historically, some see the development on Broadway of the integrated musical play, of which **Rodgers and Hammerstein** were the most prominent exponents, as an extension of operetta into post–World War II American musical theater. Through revivals of early operettas and operetta-influenced **musicals**, operetta's occasional influence upon contemporary musicals, and a lasting repertoire of songs, parodies, and movie adaptations, endures as an important musical influence on Broadway.

Shows characterized as operettas frequently include a distinctive spectrum of traits. Musically, they emphasize nineteenth-century European meters and rhythms, such as the march, polka, can-can, and, above all, the waltz. "Big" love songs, another common feature of operetta, tend to have a wide melodic range, demanding the vocal techniques of opera. Ensembles and choral numbers are often complex and multilayered. The settings that typify operetta are found either in

Continental Europe—particularly Paris, Vienna, and imaginary picturesque European kingdoms—or in other locales ripe for exoticizing, such as the Middle East or Asia.

The shows now commonly grouped together as operettas originally went under numerous labels: opéra-comique, opéra-bouffe, musical play, comedy opera, romantic opera, and, most often in the United States, comic opera. Following the opera tradition, early European and American operettas were usually orchestrated by the composer (not, as with most musical comedy, by separate arrangers). "Operetta" literally means "little opera," and, culturally and aesthetically, the genre is viewed as occupying a middle ground between opera and musical comedy.

European Background

Starting in the 1850s, there consolidated a new wave of musical theater in European music capitals. The new forms were lighter than opera in music and/or plot and often included spoken dialogue in alternation with the sung material. A trio of composers represented this tradition at its major urban centers: Jacques Offenbach in Paris, Johann Strauss II in Vienna, and Arthur Sullivan in London. Offenbach's 1858 *Orphée aux Enfers* was a bawdy, irreverent satire of Greek mythology —an international hit that is still regarded as a landmark of the genre. His *La Grande Duchesse de Gérolstein* took New York by storm in 1867 and played the city repeatedly through the late nineteenth century. Johann Strauss's famed operetta *Die Fledermaus*, which premiered in Vienna in 1874, became another American favorite. This prototypical Viennese operetta tells of a conflicted married couple reuniting when the wife, in disguise at a masquerade ball, flirts with her own errant husband. *Die Fledermaus* has been produced on Broadway three times (1885, 1900, and 1954) by light opera companies. It has also enjoyed two successful "modern" Broadway adaptations. *Champagne Sec* (1933) with lyrics by American Robert A. Simon ran for over 100 performances. *Rosalinda* (1942) was a major hit, running for over 600 performances primarily on the strength of choreography by American ballet master **George Balanchine**.

The international triumphs of Offenbach and Strauss served as a spur for British composer Arthur Sullivan, who eventually found a similar level of success teaming with poet W. S. Gilbert, a phenomenally clever lyricist and **playwright**. The two created a canon of comic operas that dominated London musical theater from the 1870s to the 1890s. American theater, and New York theater in particular, had been relying heavily on "imported" European hits and performers since the eighteenth century and, accordingly, **Gilbert and Sullivan** operettas caught on in America right away. They were represented in successful Broadway productions almost every season during the late nineteenth and early twentieth centuries, and revivals of their works are still common. Particular favorites with American audiences include their first Broadway hit, *H.M.S. Pinafore* (1879), *The Pirates of Penzance* (1879), and *The Mikado* (1885). Each has been revived on Broadway at least 24 times, not counting various adaptations for stage and other media.

Victor Herbert and Early American Operetta: 1890 to 1910

Three American composers of operetta rose to prominence in the 1890s. The American-born, European-educated Reginald De Koven matured through various local Chicago productions to achieve national success, especially with a series of comic operas set in England. His breakthrough score was *Robin Hood* (1891), which also proved to be the first nationwide success for librettist Harry B. Smith, the most prolific wordsmith for American operetta. The show featured the popular male drinking song "Brown October Ale," a De Koven/Brown example of that well-established operetta convention. The best-remembered song from the show, "Oh Promise Me," was written by De Koven and lyricist Clement Scott. It was introduced into the play during its touring schedule and for decades thereafter was a wedding ceremony standard. "Oh Promise Me" can also be heard in the 1980 film *S.O.B.*, sung by **Julie Andrews**.

John Philip Sousa, American-born of Portuguese-Spanish-German descent, is renowned for his marches, including the patriotic "Stars and Stripes Forever." But he was also a composer of comic operas. The two most successful were vehicles for the famous comic Broadway actor, DeWolf Hopper: *El Capitan* (1896) and *The Charlatan* (1898). A refrain from the former is the foundation for the famous "El Capitan March," which, as with most of Sousa's marches, is still a favorite of amateur and professional brass bands.

The most important of the early American operetta composers was **Victor Herbert**, who is generally viewed as America's chief exemplar of the form. Born in Dublin, half-Irish, half-German, Herbert was trained in Germany. He was a prominent cellist, married to an even more famous opera singer, soprano Therese Förster. The two emigrated to the United States in 1886, when she was engaged at New York's Metropolitan Opera House. Later, Herbert led the Pittsburgh Symphony, giving it up in 1903 to compose for the popular stage. He had already had success with comic operas, starting with *Prince Ananias* (1894). His operas were performed by prominent touring repertory companies, such as the Boston Ideal Opera Company, or that of renowned soprano Alice Nielsen. (Herbert's *The Fortune Teller* [1898], featuring the famous "Gypsy Love Song," was composed specifically for Nielsen.) Herbert quickly found success in numerous genres, from fairy-tale extravaganzas (*The Lady and the Slipper* [1912]) to revues (*The Century Girl* [1916]). Nevertheless, viewed from the perspective of the styles of later decades, all of his works are apt to seem like operettas.

Herbert's *Babes in Toyland* (1903), which included the song "Toyland," is the best-known American operetta from the pre–World War I era. He also had success with *Babette* (1903), *Mlle. Modiste* (1905), and *Naughty Marietta* (1910) among others. When he died in 1924, Herbert was among the most beloved figures in American music. Recordings of his songs and filmed versions of three Broadway operettas sustained his fame and influence throughout the twentieth century. *Babes in Toyland* saw several film adaptations between 1934 and 1997. *Naughty Marietta* (1910) was filmed in 1935 and featured the Nelson Eddy/Jeanette MacDonald classic duet "Ah! Sweet Mystery of Life." The 1938 film version of *Sweethearts*

(1913) featured an extraordinary ballad, "For Every Lover Must Meet His Fate," and "Sweethearts," a two-octave waltz.

While De Koven, Sousa, and Herbert were still producing Broadway works, Viennese operetta was entering a second peak of prominence, exemplified by Franz Lehár's *The Merry Widow* (1907). This international success debuted in Austria in 1905, in English translation and adaptation in London in 1907 and, later that year, on Broadway in much the same adaptation as the London production. The cultural effect of this hit show was colossal. It produced several hit songs: the story song "Vilia," the galloping "Women," the jaunty "Maxim's," and the most famous Viennese waltz after those by Strauss, "I Love You So (The Merry Widow Waltz)." These songs highlighted a sparkling score united with an urbane script about the reconciliation of overly proud lovers who cannot confess their love but allow the waltz to do it for them. Fads inspired by the show swept the nation. There were Merry Widow hats, corsets, cigars, shoes, *objects d'art*, dolls, sheet music, records, and piano rolls of the top songs. Numerous songs and burlesques parodying the show only fueled the vogue.

A 1925 silent movie version of *The Merry Widow* was followed by a 1934 sound film adaptation starring French star Maurice Chevalier and Jeanette MacDonald (just prior to her teaming with Nelson Eddy). By 1934 Chevalier and MacDonald, together and separately, had already starred in a series of movie operettas inspired by *The Merry Widow*, such as *The Love Parade* (1929), *Monte Carlo* (1930), *One Hour with You* (1931), and *Love Me Tonight* (1932). These films brought the élan of Viennese operetta to American cinema and are still acclaimed for their sophistication, wit, style, and charm.

In 1943, a major stage revival of *The Merry Widow*, produced in full Viennese style by émigrés who had fled war-torn Europe (stars Jan Kiepura and Marta Eggerth; conductor Robert Stolz; choreographer George Balanchine), enjoyed success both on Broadway and on tour. In 1952, Hollywood again retranslated and revised the property for movie audiences, this time to a mixed reception. The operetta continues to be among the most popular in opera houses throughout the world.

The Next Generation: Friml and Romberg, 1910s to 1940

Following in the wake of *The Merry Widow* were other successful Viennese imports to the U.S. stage, many composed by Oscar Straus (*The Waltz Dream* [1908] and *The Chocolate Soldier* [1909]) and Emmerich Kálmán (*Countess Maritza* [1926] and *The Circus Princess* [1927]). During the same period as the final successes of the De Koven and Herbert generation, and the mid-career successes of Lehár, Straus, and Kálmán, two émigrés from Eastern Europe were creating a fresh cycle of American operetta: Rudolf Friml and Sigmund Romberg.

Rudolf Friml was from Prague. His career jump-started with the 1912 hit *The Firefly* and peaked with three plays starring dashing baritone Dennis King: *Rose Marie* (1925), *The Vagabond King* (1925), and *The Three Musketeers* (1928). These latter followed up on the heroic-historic-romantic style of Herbert's

Naughty Marietta. The rendition of Friml's "Indian Love Call" by Macdonald and Eddy in the much-altered 1936 movie version of *Rose Marie* is widely viewed as the quintessence of operetta's romanticism and full-bodied melodic writing as well as its theatrical excesses.

Sigmund Romberg was born in Hungary in 1887 and by 1914 was contributing to Broadway musical comedies and revues as well as operettas (the genre for which he felt the strongest affinity). He found early success in operetta by adapting a German work for America as *Maytime* (1917), which ran for nearly 500 performances. His career peaked with the bittersweet *The Student Prince* (1924), the heroic *The Desert Song* (1926), and *The New Moon* (1929). All three were made into films, spreading their influence beyond Broadway and urban opera houses.

Both Friml and Romberg also composed in a lighter, even jazzy vein. But it was their operetta-influenced works that left the strongest impression, happily coexisting on Broadway in the years between the world wars with the breezy musical comedies and revues that produced the great song standards of jazz and pop music. Of their many famous songs suited for trained voice, Romberg's "Lover, Come Back to Me" (from *The New Moon*) has been the most often adapted to jazz renditions and was among the most-recorded songs of the era. Crucial to the pair's biggest successes were their lyricist-librettists, such as Rida Johnson Young, Dorothy Donnelly, Otto Harbach, Oscar Hammerstein II, and others.

Hammerstein and . . .

From the 1920s onward Oscar Hammerstein II proved to be a critical link between various operetta-influenced composers and shows. Early in his career, he worked with Friml (most notably on *Rose Marie* [1924]), Romberg (for most of his best work, including *The Desert Song* [1926]), **George Gershwin** (*Song of the Flame* [1925]), Herbert Stothart (co-composer of *Rose Marie* and *Song of the Flame*), and most crucially with **Jerome Kern**. Hammerstein and Kern wrote two operetta-influenced shows that explore both the idyllic and troubled aspects of the American past: the landmark ***Show Boat*** (1927) and *Sweet Adeline* (1929). They then reunited for *Music in the Air* (1931), another of the musicals Kern composed in this period that traversed the boundaries between operetta and other genres, featuring European settings, waltzes, big-voiced ballads, and dramatically complex musical scenes.

Meanwhile, George Gershwin, with his lyricist-brother Ira, was creating his own style of works that crossed over into the terrain of either opera or Gilbert-and-Sullivan-inspired comic opera. The most notable of these were their political satire *Of Thee I Sing* (a tremendous success in 1931) and the "folk opera" ***Porgy and Bess*** (1935), depicting a poor African American fishing community. These works of Kern and Gershwin among others helped put a fresh American emphasis on such operetta conventions as lengthy musical scenes, extensive underscoring, and complicated ensemble effects, including the complex first act finales that had previously been more typical of European-influenced operettas.

In the 1930s Hollywood stole from Broadway much of the audience for extravagantly romantic, European-tinged operetta. However, the **Shubert Brothers**, the giant theatrical agency that retained a nationwide chain of theaters, in addition to Broadway venues, found that operettas could draw audiences on national tours even as Broadway was becoming less accommodating to the form. As they often did with shows they staged, the Shuberts obtained all or partial performance rights to a number of operettas they toured, including Romberg's *Blossom Time*. The Shuberts determinedly never sold the movie rights to this and other valuable operetta properties. The effect of their decision is that shows and composers that were once household American names are now completely unfamiliar to all but aficionados and scholars.

Alongside Hollywood's operetta successes, a few interesting new stage works spun off of the operetta tradition. A fictionalized biography of Johann Strauss, setting his melodies with new words, appeared around Europe under various names and on Broadway as *The Great Waltz* (1934). The show was radically revised, with new lyrics by Hammerstein, as a 1938 Hollywood film of the same title. *The White Horse Inn* (Berlin [1930], on Broadway [1936]) was a loosely constructed, scenically spectacular farce-operetta with a patchwork score composed by Ralph Benatsky and several others. The New York production, with Irving Caesar's lyrics, proved that Americans were quite susceptible to the romantic appeal of this cookie-cutter picture of the Austrian Tyrol.

May Wine (1935) saw Romberg, Hammerstein, and librettist Frank Mandel experimenting with operetta form (no opening chorus, no concerted finales) and with juxtaposing a typical nineteenth-century Viennese operetta setting with the distinctly twentieth-century theme of psychoanalysis. It was their most successful Broadway production of the mid-to-late 1930s. *Lady in the Dark* (1941), composed by German-immigrant Kurt Weill in partnership with **Ira Gershwin**, also explored psychoanalytic themes using extended operetta-like musical scenes.

In the early 1940s, operetta still found a Broadway audience. *Die Fledermaus* played its successful run as *Rosalinda*, the Balanchine-choreographed 1943 revival of *The Merry Widow*, ran for over a year, and *Porgy and Bess* was successfully edited down to a speech-and-song version that made the opera more like an American musical.

Hammerstein, Rodgers, and the "Golden Age"

This was the theatrical milieu from which Richard Rodgers and Hammerstein's *Oklahoma!* emerged in 1943. The first American musical to fully adopt the principle of "integration" of plot, character, song, and choreography toward an artistically unified production, *Oklahoma!* became the biggest hit in Broadway history and set a lasting standard for excellence in American musical theater. Hammerstein's operetta-influenced lyrics, and Rodger's ability to compose melodies to accommodate Hammerstein's style, were essential to establishing this breakthrough achievement. Soon **Frederick Loewe**, German-born son of an Austrian operetta star, was successfully streamlining his Lehár-like melodies for American integrated musicals, creating with librettist-lyricist **Alan Jay Lerner** *Brigadoon* (1947), *My Fair Lady* (1956), and the movie *Gigi* (1958). Other operetta-influenced hit shows included 1943's *Carmen Jones* (in which Hammerstein adapted Georges Bizet's 1875 opera *Carmen* to a contemporary, African American setting), *Carousel* (1945), *Kiss Me, Kate* (1948), *The King and I* (1951), and *Fanny* (1954), all of which drew freely from operetta elements: lengthy musical scenes, romantic locales, high passions, and a relative seriousness. Among these, Rodgers and Hammerstein's *The Sound of Music* (1959) holds a special place due to its phenomenally successful movie version. The movie has familiarized audiences with such operetta elements as a nostalgically viewed Austrian backdrop for a Cinderella-like story, yodels, ländlers, and waltz songs. The period between *Oklahoma!* and the mid-1960s is widely viewed as the apex or Golden Age of musicals, with Rodgers and Hammerstein leading the way by adapting operetta conventions and sensibilities to the modern American musical.

Another significant thread of operetta influence during this period lay in the works of George Wright and Robert Forrest. They had learned their craft in Hollywood, rearranging stage scores for movies starring Jeanette MacDonald and others. In the mid-1940s, they began to adapt preexisting classical music into the form of Broadway songs. They clung closely to the operetta style of Romberg's *Blossom Time* for a fictionalized biography of composer Edvard Grieg, *The Song of Norway* (1944; filmed in 1970). They achieved something like an "integrated" musical comedy with the exotic, sexy *Kismet* (1953), using melodies of Alexander Borodin to create the hits "Stranger in Paradise" and "Baubles, Bangles, and Beads."

Decline and Legacy

During each season of the 1950s, the New York City Center hosted numerous limited-run stagings of operettas and operetta-influenced works. Opera-trained singers kept alive the traditions of premicrophone vocal production and its associated compositional styles, including tenor Mario Lanza in Hollywood movies (from which came his 1950 operetta-styled hit single "Be My Love"). On Broadway, bass Ezio Pinza introduced "Some Enchanted Evening" in *South Pacific* (1949) and baritone Robert Weede starred in *The Most Happy Fella* (1956). Long-playing original-cast recordings of operetta scores abounded. These were usually reorchestrated to match 1950s expectations, as with Lanza's 1954 million-selling album of songs from *The Student Prince* and other shows. These activities, however, spelled the last gasp for large-scale acceptance of the traditional operetta aesthetic. By the late-1960s, operetta was marginalized in a popular music scene increasingly dominated by youth culture, and even operetta-influenced integrated musicals were giving way to other forms and styles.

One prominent legacy of operetta lies in popular culture parodies of is excesses. Ironically, prior to becoming known for his operetta-like compositions, Richard

Rodgers, with 1920s–1930s partner **Lorenz Hart**, mocked the conventions of operettas in the one-act "Rose of Arizona" from their revue, *The Garrick Gaieties* (1926). Starting its long run in late 1959, the **Off-Broadway** *Little Mary Sunshine* managed to convey both the charm and the inanity of 1920s American operettas. Critics, too, made fun of the style as did television comics like Carol Burnett, Sid Caesar, and Bob Hope, who found easy laughs in lampooning pretentious, gaudily dressed operetta characters and actors.

More recent Broadway composers occasionally allude to the operetta tradition, as **Stephen Sondheim** does in "One Kiss" from *Follies* (1970) and in his entire score for *A Little Night Music* (1973). Cy Coleman recalls the operetta in *On the Twentieth Century* (1977) and the song "Love Makes Such Fools of Us All" from *Barnum* (1980). Other creators, however, feel less connected to the operetta tradition. In the final decades of the twentieth century, sung-through, tear-jerking historical epics and romances, such as *Les Misérables* (1987) and *The Scarlet Pimpernel* (1997), were sometimes nicknamed "poperettas," owing to their resemblance to operetta. **Andrew Lloyd Webber**, the composer of the longest running of these, *The Phantom of the Opera* (1988), feels indebted to the Rodgers and Hammerstein–era tradition, but admits little connection with the old-time operetta style that preceded it. Nevertheless, as with other still-popular shows, *Phantom* revels in a "little opera" aesthetic and a luxuriant romanticism that resembles operetta at its most extravagant. Through such works and the continued availability of older shows, movies, recordings, and repertoire, operetta's legacy remains embedded in American culture.

Michael G. Garber

Further Reading

Bordman, Gerald. *American Operetta: From H.M.S. Pinafore to Sweeney Todd.* New York: Oxford University Press, 1981.

Everett, William A. "Romance, Nostalgia and Nevermore: American and British Operetta in the 1920s." In *The Cambridge Companion to the Musical*, ed. William A. Everett and Paul R. Laird. Cambridge, U.K.: Cambridge University Press, 2002, pp. 47–62.

———. *Sigmund Romberg.* New Haven, CT: Yale University Press, 2007.

Franceschina, John. *Harry B. Smith: Dean of American Librettists.* New York: Routledge, 2003.

Ganzl, Victor. *The Musical: A Concise History.* Boston: Northeastern University Press, 1997.

http://musicaltheatreguide.com/.

http://www.johann-strauss.org.uk/

http://www.musicals101.com/

Knapp, Raymond. *The American Musical and the Performance of Personal Identity.* Princeton: Princeton University Press, 2006.

Lamb, Andrew. *150 Years of Popular Musical Theater.* New Haven, CT: Yale University Press, 2000.

Mordden, Ethan. *Broadway Babies: The People Who Made the American Musical.* New York: Oxford University Press, 1983.

Traubner, Richard. *Operetta: A Theatrical History.* New York: Oxford University Press, 1983.

OTHELLO

Broadway Run: Shubert Theatre
Opening: October 19, 1943
Closing: July 1, 1944
Total Performances: 296
Playwright: William Shakespeare
Production Designer: Robert Edmond Jones
Director: Margaret Webster
Producer: The Theatre Guild
Lead Performers: Paul Robeson (Othello), Uta Hagen (Desdemona), José Ferrer (Iago), Margaret Webster (Emilia)

When **Paul Robeson**, notable actor and concert singer, walked onto the stage of the Shubert Theatre in 1943 and spoke Othello's first line (" 'Tis better as it is."), the 45-year-old actor made social, political, and stage history as the first African American to play **Shakespeare**'s Moor on Broadway. For the first time in a Broadway theater, a black actor played one of the greatest parts ever written and with an interracial cast in a play that made a social statement about ideals and hopes for racial tolerance and equality. Those who wrote about the production confirmed that Robeson's commanding presence, powerful baritone voice, and imposing ethnicity brought an incalculable sense of reality to the importance of the play's racial divisions and tragic outcome.

Robeson had recruited the noted Anglo-American director Margaret Webster to join him in staging and financing a tryout production of Shakespeare's play. He had seen her staging of *Hamlet* with Maurice Evans as the Dane on Broadway, and she had seen his performance as Othello opposite Peggy Ashcroft as Desdemona in London in 1930. At the time, she thought Robeson was ill-equipped in training and vocal technique to master Shakespeare's verse. However, the actor convinced her that he was ready to undertake Shakespeare's troubled hero again and that Broadway audiences were ready in 1942 to see a black actor in the title role.

Unable to persuade mainstream producers and backers to underwrite the production, they set out, themselves, to produce tryout productions with campus audiences in Cambridge and Princeton where artistic and financial risks were minimal. Earlier, Webster, who had staged four of Shakespeare's plays on Broadway, said

Singer Paul Robeson is shown as Othello and Uta Hagen as Desdemona in Othello *at the Shubert Theatre in 1943. (AP Photo)*

that producers did not trust the American public to tolerate the issues raised by the 400-year-old play that required a black man to love, marry, and murder a white woman. Once the show was an unqualified success with the Boston **critics**, New York producers asked for "a piece of the show." Because of Webster's previous work with the venerable **Theatre Guild**, known for its prestige dramas and mannered comedies, they chose the Guild as lead producer for the New York production. Nevertheless, the production was delayed for over a year due to Robeson's concert commitments.

At the outset the production was controversial. For the first time on Broadway, a black actor was playing one of the greatest parts ever written with an integrated cast, and in a play whose social content reverberated with ideals and hopes for racial tolerance and equality. Both Robeson and Webster were in agreement over the unambiguous racial identity of Othello and approached the play's social and political issues with resolve. They were convinced that audiences, in the presence of a black Othello, could believe in the central reality that Othello could command Venice's armies while remaining a stranger to its society. Nonetheless, established actors declined the roles of Desdemona and Iago, including Maurice Evans who refused to play Iago. Webster turned to the youthful married couple **Uta Hagen** and **José Ferrer**, who had appeared separately in Broadway productions of *The Sea Gull* and *Charley's Aunt*. To simplify a short rehearsal period, Webster, herself an established actress, took the role of Iago's wife.

When the final curtain came down on opening night in mid-October 1943, the response was electric. The audience erupted into cries of bravo and applauded for over 20 minutes. Critical praise for the production and performances was unqualified. Reviewers for New York's major newspapers agreed that Robeson's performance was memorable, towering, and unbelievably magnificent. Hagen's Desdemona was described as simple, unaffected, and beautifully spoken; and Ferrer's Iago was called the epitome of egomania, cynicism, and passionless evil. Webster was hailed for satisfying the needs of the modern stage with a production of seriousness coupled with blazing theatricality.

Known for its subscription audiences in cities and towns across America, the Theatre Guild planned a 36-week tour from coast to coast. It had to be carefully arranged to avoid discrimination against the cast or reprisals against audiences. Moreover, the company refused to perform in theaters whose managements discriminated against the seating of African Americans as members of the general audience. As a consequence, the Robeson *Othello* was not seen in the nation's capital where theater audiences were not integrated at the time. Nevertheless, *Othello* set an all-time Broadway record for consecutive performances of a Shakespeare play and the national tour proved to be a professional and political milestone. Generating exceptional box-office grosses across the country, the tour also overcame racial barriers in many theaters, restaurants, and hotels in towns and cities.

Featured in a stellar Broadway season with *One Touch of Venus*, *I Remember Mama*, and *On the Town*, the Robeson *Othello*, as it was soon called, had an enormous impact on the careers of African American performers in the commercial theater by expanding options beyond musical revues and common stereotypical roles. The production also set a precedent for multiracial casting in touring and resident companies, and enhanced the reputation of William Shakespeare as a "box office" **playwright** in America.

Not only did the Robeson *Othello* break attendance records for a Shakespeare play, but, with a black actor in the title role, it proved a landmark in the American theater by transcending racial boundaries and abrading the raw edges of social prejudice. Almost all blacks and many whites regarded Robeson's *Othello* as a racial event of a magnitude that transcended its artistic significance. This response confirmed Paul Robeson's belief in art as a powerful weapon for social change.

Before the momentum of the Civil Rights Movement in the late 1950s, the country's progress toward mutual understanding and racial equality was felt more keenly on Broadway's stages in the 1943–1944 season (and in the next decade) than in the country at large. Shakespeare's remonstrations in *Othello* against racial division and social injustice, along with Paul Robeson's groundbreaking performance, have remained a permanent part of theatrical and social history in the United States since the middle of the last century.

Milly S. Barranger

Further Reading

Barranger, Milly S. *Margaret Webster: A Life in the Theatre*. Ann Arbor, MI: University of Michigan Press, 2004.

Duberman, Martin B. *Paul Robeson: A Biography*. New York: Knopf, 1989.

OUR AMERICAN COUSIN

Broadway Run: Laura Keene's Theatre (October 18, 1858–Closing date unknown)
Opening: October 18, 1858
Closing: Closing date unknown
Total Performances: Approx. 140
Playwright: Tom Taylor
Producer: Laura Keene
Staged by: Laura Keene
Lead Players: Joseph Jefferson III, E. A. Sothern, Laura Keene

For most Americans the story behind English playwright Tom Taylor's comedy about an inheritance dispute between a gentrified snooty English family, the Trenchards, and their country bumpkin American cousin Asa lies buried in the events surrounding the assassination of Abraham Lincoln. Having been brought to Washington, D.C., Ford's Theatre in April 1865 by **Laura Keene**, the producer of the play's Broadway premiere, *Our American Cousin* was a well-established hit comedy on the fateful night that President and Mrs. Lincoln came to see it. Seven years earlier in New York, the play had become one of Broadway's first long-running contemporary plays and an unqualified triumph for Broadway's first truly successful woman producer.

Laura Keene had been a popular actress in her home country of England and in New York when, in 1855, she leased a Broadway theater and became the first woman manager of a major commercial New York theatrical venue. She hit her stride as a producer between 1857 and 1863 when, as manager, producer, director, and frequent performer in Laura Keene's Theatre, she became a competitor and clear threat to her male peers. No production did more to establish Keene as a force among Broadway producers than did Tom Taylor's *Our American Cousin*, a play, by all accounts, she did not particularly like on first reading and ended up producing as an afterthought.

Tom Taylor was an English lawyer and government bureaucrat as well as a prodigious writer of humorous essays and comedic plays. Many of his comedies had played successfully on London stages in the 1840s and 1850s. Generally considered something of a commercial hack by English critics, some of Taylor's plays had been nonetheless popular with English audiences. Around 1857 or early 1858 Taylor sent a copy of his new American-themed comedy, *Our American Cousin*, to New York theater producers in the hopes of breaking it into the Broadway market. (The play had not yet been performed in London.) It was first rejected by John Wallack, an English-born producer who had been producing plays in the United States for years. (In 1852, Wallack had brought Keene to the United States from England to star in his American productions.)

In preparation for opening her fall 1858–1859 season, Keene, who had become successful producing both popular shows and prestige legitimate theater, was hoping to mount a large production of *A Midsummer Night's Dream*. Production delays caused her to scramble for a filler play to put on for a couple of weeks—just long enough to sort out matters with the troubled **Shakespeare** project. Accounts vary as to whether Keene had already secured performance rights to the less-than-promising Taylor script or had it brought to her attention by others who knew she needed a limited-run show to open in place of the Shakespeare play. Some of her associates, most notably her star comic actor Joseph Jefferson, saw some potential in the play. Between her colleagues and employees' enthusiasm for the play and her own shortage of options, Keene approved the play for production.

The play was a dazzling success. Jefferson (by his own account in his autobiography as well as that of others) was triumphant as the fish-out-of-water American Asa blustering his way through the rebuke of his English cousins. Audiences loved the hilarious stuffy British versus down-home American cultural conflict and supported the show for an estimated 140 performance run—a then virtually unheard of stretch for a nonmusical production. (The run ceased only because Keene, who also performed in the show, wanted to move on to other projects.) The play was the hit of the Broadway season. While thwarting Keene's own plans to mount the Shakespeare play, *Our American Cousin* decimated any hopes harbored by rival male producers of knocking the upstart, barely 30-year-old woman out of the theater producing business any time soon. Jefferson, already famous, became almost legendary in the role of Asa. Another comic actor, E. A. Sothern, a heretofore somewhat frustrated second banana in Keene's company, played boldly against Jefferson as the snooty nobleman Lord Dundreary. Although Dundreary had only a few lines in the original script, Sothern and Jefferson kept ad-libbing and enlarging Sothern's scenes throughout the run. The two expanded Dundreary's part from a cameo to a show-stealing featured role, which launched Sothern to new fame and riches.

As a manager and a performer, Keene eventually grew quite fond of the play. Under her guidance it had become an audience favorite both in and beyond New York, significantly enlarging her reputation and her coffers. She toured with the play frequently, especially after 1863 when she gave up her management duties at her Broadway theater.

Other than Keene herself, none of the original cast performed in Washington, D.C., on the night Lincoln was assassinated. The printed program for the April 14, 1865, performance, which openly touted the anticipated attendance of the president, hailed the play as the "eccentric comedy" that had played under Laura Keene's management for "one thousand nights." After the assassination, virtually everyone associated with the evening suffered personal and/or professional setbacks—most notably famed actor **Edwin Booth**, brother of the assassin, who had no connection with the production whatsoever. The play itself became stigmatized for some time. Even a 1908 Broadway revival, celebrating the fiftieth anniversary of its premiere (and starring E. A. Sothern's son, E. H. Sothern, reprising his father's role as Dundreary) met with controversy. The final Broadway revival of *Our American Cousin* was staged in 1915, eerily enough in the Booth Theatre, which had been posthumously named in honor of Edwin Booth two years earlier. The play fell entirely out of fashion shortly thereafter.

Our American Cousin remains first and foremost part of the historical iconography of Lincoln's assassination. It is a disturbing legacy tempered by the highly important, if decidedly less well-known, role it played in establishing a nonmusical play as a long-running Broadway hit and bringing a woman to the forefront of big-time commercial theater production.

Thomas A. Greenfield

Further Reading

"History of 'Our American Cousin.' " *New York Times*, January 26, 1908. Retrieved June 19, 2009, from http://query.nytimes.com/gst/abstract.html?res=940DE1DB1F3EE233A25755C2A9679C946997D6CF.

McCarther, Benjamin. *The Man Who Was Rip Van Winkle: Joseph Jefferson and Nineteenth-Century American Theatre.* New Haven, CT: Yale University Press, 2007.

Sothern, Edmund H. *The Melancholy Tale of "Me": My Remembrances.* New York: C. Scribner's Sons, 1916. Digitized June 4, 2008. Retrieved June 19, 2009, from http://books.google.com/books?id=hU6wAAAAIAAJ&pg=PR16&dq=melancholy+tale+of+me.

Our Town

Broadway Run: Henry Miller's Theatre (February 4, 1938 to February 12, 1938); Morosco Theatre (February 14, 1938 to November 19, 1938)
Opening: February 4, 1938
Closing: November 19, 1938

Total Performances: 336
Author: Thornton Wilder
Technical Director: Raymond Sovey
Producer and Director: Jed Harris
Lead Performers: Frank Craven (Stage Manager), John Craven (George Gibbs), Martha Scott (Emily Webb), Helen Carew (Mrs. Webb), Marilyn Erskine (Rebecca Gibbs), Phillip Coolidge (Simon Stimson), Arthur Allen (Professor Willard), Tom Fadden (Howie Newsome), Jay Fassett (Dr. Gibbs), and Thomas W. Ross (Mr. Webb)

Some 70-plus years after it first enchanted Broadway audiences and won the Pulitzer Prize for Drama, **Thornton Wilder**'s *Our Town* is still one of the most frequently produced American plays ever written. With the passage of time, professional theater has generally ceded ownership of the poignant, mythic tale about Grover's Corners, New Hampshire, to school drama programs, community theater, and regional and summer stock. Nonetheless, so many theater professionals hold such strong feelings of reverence, nostalgia, and respect for the play that it still inspires professional production (including a highly regarded **Off-Broadway** revival in 2009). With its fully exposed half-bare stage, minimalist sets, and improbable centrality of a stage manager/narrator/philosopher, the original 1938 Broadway production was, at the time, radically innovative for a mainstream theater piece. Yet Wilder and director Jed Harris, despite a rocky collaboration, managed to fix the audience's attention upon the beautifully drawn characters and masterfully understated themes to the point that the far-reaching, almost gimmicky staging ultimately proved to be the only way this story could be told.

The play begins as the Stage Manager wanders almost haphazardly across a nearly bare stage to tell the story of Grover's Corners between the years 1901 and 1913. The story soon focuses on the relationship between George Gibbs and Emily Webb. Act One, titled "Daily Life," covers the seemingly innocuous comings and goings of the people of Grover's Corners, including the first hints of an innocent youthful romance between teenage neighbors George and Emily. Act Two ("Love and Marriage") favors all with George and Emily's wedding. The Stage Manager also takes the audience back in time to a scene depicting George and Emily first falling in love. In the final act ("Death") the audience learns that Emily has died in childbirth.

In one of the most emotionally evocative scenes in all of American drama the Stage Manager, as a prelude to Emily's funeral, gives the audience a tour of the Grover's Corners cemetery. The town's dead are seated on stage dressed for a funeral as living embodiments of their gravesites. They are waiting, as the Stage Manager informs us, "for that eternal part of them to come out." They proceed to comment philosophically, insightfully, even comically on the lives lived in their town and all our towns: the familial, the familiar, the romantic, the spiritual, and the meanings of life and death.

The literary richness of *Our Town* clearly reflects the background and disposition of its author. In 1938 Wilder, an Ivy League–educated humanities scholar, was already a successful literature professor and author with a Pulitzer Prize–winning novel to his credit: *The Bridge of San Luis Rey* (1927). *Our Town* was his first fully formed play. He wrote the play over the course of several years, developing its experimental framework while familiarizing himself with some of the new literary *avant-garde* movements emerging in America and Europe. He befriended some of the movements' leading intellectual figures, including Gertrude Stein, who became a close friend and literary advisor during this period. In the course of writing the play he made several visits to the MacDowell artists' colony, a famous retreat for writers and artists in the small town of Peterborough, New Hampshire. His walks throughout Peterborough and nearby towns and his countless conversations with town residents gave the play its setting and much of its endearing texture. (Not surprisingly, an amateur theater company performs *Our Town* in Peterborough every summer.)

Once the script for *Our Town* was complete, Wilder persuaded Jed Harris, a personal friend and one of Broadway's most successful **producers** and directors, to mount a production of it. The knowing serenity that informs so much of the play belies the heated conflicts that ensued between **playwright** and director. Once rehearsals began, Wilder wanted to exert more influence over the production than Harris would allow. For his part Harris's direction struck Wilder as intruding upon the writing and storytelling, which Wilder viewed as his exclusive domain. Wilder was eventually banned from rehearsals because he made the actors nervous, shaking his head at Harris's stage directions and making additions to the script. Even with the astonishing success of their joint venture, Wilder's and Harris's friendship never recovered. Even when Wilder had to fill in briefly as the Stage Manager (played by Frank Craven) during the run, he did so only on the condition that Harris not be allowed in the theater during his performances. However, the cast as a whole felt the experience of performing the play to be a remarkable, even "transcendent" experience. The players realized they were contributing to the development of a newly maturing American theater and that *Our Town* might eventually be viewed as one of America's defining literary achievements. They were right.

Our Town premiered to a standing-room-only audience with a single performance at the McCarter Theatre in Princeton, New Jersey, on January 22, 1938. The Princeton performance was to be followed by a two-week run in Boston before heading to Broadway. Despite a negative local review in Princeton, Wilder was pleased with the audience response. In Boston critics were confused by the *avant-garde* practices and reviews were mixed. Harris decided to end the Boston run after only one week, gambling on an early Broadway opening. Wilder was by all accounts a wreck over Harris's decision, but Harris's gamble paid off—in part because he shrewdly covered his bet once he got to New York.

Harris was sufficiently well connected in New York theater circles that he could prevail upon *New York Times* critic **Brooks Atkinson** to attend a working rehearsal of *Our Town* a few days before the show opened. Harris hoped that Atkinson's preview would allow the highly influential critic to acclimate himself to the lack of scenery and other theatrical oddities that had so alienated out-of-town **critics**.

Harris got what he wanted. Once the show opened, New York reviews were mixed, but owing in large measure to an effusive write-up by Atkinson in the *Times*, people came to see the production. Four months into the run *Our Town* won the Pulitzer Prize and secured its place of honor in American theater and literary history.

Wilder went on to write several more plays, most notably the Pulitzer Prize–winning *The Skin of Our Teeth* (1942) and *The Matchmaker* (1955), which was later adapted into the musical hit *Hello, Dolly!* (1964). However, *Our Town* is by far the best known of all his literary works, fiction or drama.

It seems fitting that a play so concerned with the infinite value of human life should age as well as *Our Town* has. At century's end, *Our Town* was advanced by many cultural critics as *the* great American play of the twentieth century (rivaled by the likes of **Eugene O'Neill**'s ***Long Day's Journey into Night*** and **Arthur Miller**'s ***Death of a Salesman***). After World War II, as Broadway audiences and critics became acclimated—or at least less reflexively hostile—to the *avant-garde* theatrical innovations of such playwrights as Bertolt Brecht, Samuel Beckett, and **Edward Albee**, Wilder's dramatic achievement only grew in stature. No longer an idiosyncratic theatrical curiosity, *Our Town* now stands among the first important contributions of the United States to modernist theater as well as a canonical work in American literature.

Carissa Cordes

Further Reading

Goldstone, Richard. *Thornton Wilder: An Intimate Portrait*. New York: E. P. Dutton & Co., 1975.

Konkle, Lincoln. *Thornton Wilder and the Puritan Narrative Tradition*. Columbia, MO: University of Missouri Press, 2006.

Shuman, R. Baird. *Great American Writers: Twentieth Century*. Tarrytown, NY: Marshall Cavendish, 2002.

P

PAL JOEY

Broadway Run: Ethel Barrymore Theatre (December 25, 1940 to August 16, 1941); Shubert Theatre (September 1, 1941 to October 21, 1941); and St. James Theatre (October 21, 1941 to November 29, 1941)
Opening: December 25, 1940
Closing: November 29, 1941
Total Performances: 374
Composer: Richard Rodgers
Lyricist: Lorenz Hart
Book: John O'Hara
Choreographer: Robert Alton
Director: George Abbott
Producer: George Abbott
Lead Performers: Gene Kelly (Joey Evans), Vivienne Segal (Vera Simson), and Leila Ernst (Linda English)

By the time they collaborated on *Pal Joey*, **Richard Rodgers** and **Lorenz Hart** had been partners for over 20 years and had created many of the most popular **musicals** of the 1920s and 1930s. Their earlier shows—most notably *A Connecticut Yankee in King Arthur's Court* (1927), *On Your Toes* (1936), *Babes in Arms* (1937), and *The Boys from Syracuse* (1938)—were created with an eye toward a tighter integration between music and story than was typical for musical comedies of the period. Incorporating ballet within *On Your Toes* and adapting **Shakespeare**'s *The Comedy of Errors* into *The Boys from Syracuse*, the team was well-known for taking risks that stretched musical comedy as a genre.

They pushed artistic boundaries once again with *Pal Joey*, in which the decidedly unsympathetic title character commands the stage, and were reprimanded by *New York Times* theater critic **Brooks Atkinson** for their trouble. (Atkinson famously questioned whether one could "draw sweet water from a foul well.") *Pal Joey* was not a typical musical comedy in 1940. The fact that it has been revived and revised three times since then—1952, 1995, and 2009—and adapted into a **film** in 1957 suggests that later audiences and critics have become more comfortable than Atkinson with the show's amoral center.

John O'Hara, well known for his short stories and novels that focused on issues of class and social ambition, adapted his *New Yorker* short stories about a womanizing con man, Joey Evans, for the Broadway stage. In doing so, he maintained the cynical edge of this deceptive charmer who lacked the expected heart of gold, and he kept much of the slangy, rhythmic language he was known for in his fiction. In Chicago, Joey (Gene Kelly)—a second-rate dancer who thinks he is first-rate—is dating the apparently sweet Linda English (Leila Ernst), a secretary. He soon dumps her for the wealthier, older, and married Vera Simpson (Vivienne Segal) in the hopes that she will help him finance his own nightclub. Vera easily sees through Joey's charms, but is initially happy enough to enjoy them and pay his way through life, eventually funding Joey's dream with "Club Joey." But Joey's happiness and success are short-lived. Linda vindictively warns Vera that Joey plans to blackmail her, so the ever-pragmatic Vera dumps Joey in his turn and leaves him destitute before the blackmail can materialize. The musical ends with Joey, having lost everything but the shirt on his back, back on the hunt for a new girlfriend/meal ticket.

Pal Joey's setting within the nightclubs of Chicago gave Rodgers and Hart many opportunities to satirize the popular entertainment of the day. For example, "The Flower Garden of My Heart" turns **Florenz Ziegfeld**'s glorification of chorus girls on its head when the women who parade on the stage in various flower costumes turn out to be anything but lovely roses. Although numbers such as this can be viewed as purely comedic, the numerous parodies also highlight a central theme of *Pal Joey*: people are very good at deluding themselves. Joey assumes he is a good dancer, Linda believes Joey loves her, Vera pretends she is not getting old, and chorus girls think they will get the lead in the next production.

The show's explicitly cynical take on love, relationships, and sex, paired with its beautiful score, well-crafted songs, and excellent acting, put its first critics and audiences in an awkward position. How could one root for such despicable characters who seem destined to keep repeating their sins? In part, the question was answered by the original performers, especially Kelly and Segal. At bottom, Joey was an unredeemable cad who by the musical's end had learned nothing, but Kelly's performance was able to blunt some of Joey's sharper angles while maintaining his sex appeal. The fact that Kelly was an accomplished dancer, in contrast to the character he played, only added to his charm. Segal, a popular actress with a beautiful soprano voice who in her early career was famous for her roles in **operettas** like *The Desert Song* (1926), turned what was on paper a coldly calculating woman into someone who could be viewed as potentially sympathetic. Certainly her performance of "Bewitched, Bothered, and Bewildered," in which Vera reveals her complex relationship with Joey, cast its own spell over audiences. In this regard, the musical laid the groundwork for similar casting choices in *Carousel* (1945) and *Sweeney Todd* (1979) when the morally questionable characters of Billy Bigelow and Mrs. Lovett were, respectively, cast against type with likeable stars **John Raitt** and **Angela Lansbury**.

Groundbreaking in 1940 for its adult content, *Pal Joey* also anticipates by decades the dark tones and moral ambiguities of many of **Stephen Sondheim**'s plays. However, in terms of its internal structure as an integrated musical comedy, *Pal Joey* could be viewed as another variation on the backstage musical. Rodgers and Hart were certainly more thoughtful than many of their contemporaries when considering how to tie together music, dance, and story, but many of the song and dance numbers are presentational in nature. That is, the production numbers do not advance the story nor do they provide any insights into the characters; the songs exist simply to entertain and rely on the nightclub setting to justify why a character suddenly breaks out into song. In this regard, *Pal Joey* has much in common with musical comedies from the 1920s and 1930s. That said, what sets even the more presentational production numbers apart from regular musical comedy fare of the same timeframe is Rodgers and Hart's ability to execute transitions between dialogue and song in a naturalistic manner that predates the **Rodgers and Hammerstein** collaboration with *Oklahoma!* (1947) by three years.

When *Pal Joey* was revived in 1952, the show's musical comedy roots, rather than its aspirations for integration, were highlighted. This change in emphasis required the reassignment and rearrangement of some of the show's songs, such as "Plant You Now, Dig You Later," which was transformed from a song that related to the plot into a straightforward nightclub number. Ultimately the changes, which did not significantly alter the sardonic spirit of the show, helped the revival to succeed; it ran longer than the 1940 original. The 1957 film adaptation starring Frank Sinatra, Rita Hayworth (as Vera), and Kim Novak (as Linda) achieved critical success when initially released, but is now generally thought to suffer from 1950s' concerns about how to represent sex and therefore to lack the Broadway production's original bite. In addition, the film adaptation removed *Pal Joey* still further from the integration that had made it stand out in 1940 by interpolating four Rodgers and Hart songs—most famously "My Funny Valentine"—from three of their earlier musicals into the movie's score.

Pal Joey, while not as well known as *Oklahoma!*, also opened up new possibilities for musical theater. It not only dared to integrate song and story, it imagined a musical comedy world populated by relatively unpleasant characters who are not guaranteed a happy ending, pointedly rejecting the idea of a stable community so often celebrated by American musicals.

Kathryn Edney

Further Reading

Furia, Phillip, and Michael Lasser. *The Stories Behind the Songs of Broadway, Hollywood, and Tin Pan Alley*. New York: Routledge, 2006.
Jones, John Bush. *Our Musicals, Ourselves: A Social History of the American Musical Theater*: Lebanon, NH: University Press of New England, 2004.

PAPP, JOSEPH (1921–1991)
PRODUCER, DIRECTOR

Joseph Papp (Papirofsky) combined an extraordinary ability to merge the idiosyncrasies of cutting-edge innovative theater with mainstream commercial taste and marketing. From the 1960s through the 1980s, he nurtured produced, promoted, and brought to fruition all manner of not-for-profit theater to large audiences both on and off Broadway. His Broadway triumphs comprised a vast range of atypical Broadway fare—from innovative **Shakespeare** revivals, to expressionistic storyless dance-centered productions, to artistically and socially controversial dramas and **musicals**. For an entire generation of theater artists and audiences, Papp fostered the hope and brought to reality the idea that Broadway can embrace radical artistic innovation along with safe, derivative mainstream fare. Nearly 20 years after his death, **Off-Broadway** and not-for-profit resident theater remain major sources for new Broadway shows—a testimony to Papp's vision of an American theater that both thrives on and profits from bold, artistic creativity and innovation.

Papp was born and raised in Brooklyn, New York, and took an interest in drama while still in school. As a teenager, he saw several Shakespearean performances on Broadway, forming a precociously early taste for unmannered, naturalistic Shakespearean acting over the British "schooled" Old Vic formal style of presentation. Serving in the navy from 1942 to 1946, Papp supervised an entertainment unit that produced touring shows for American military bases and ships.

That Papp became a central figure in Broadway production was a seemingly unlikely result of his major forays into theater promotion, which were decidedly noncommercial in their focus. After leaving the navy, he joined the Actors Lab in Los Angeles, a not-for-profit, left-wing theater group composed largely of former members of the defunct radical New York–based **Group Theatre**. Papp remained with the Lab until its breakup in 1950, due in combination to fallout from HUAC investigations of high-profile members and the ambitions of many Lab members to abandon theater for lucrative film careers.

Moving back to New York in 1951, Papp took a low-level job with CBS television, eventually working his way up to the position of stage manager. At CBS Papp used his proximity to actors and directors to form a small theater group that put on productions of prestige dramas in the summer in the Catskill Mountains—the famed summer resort area outside New York City. By 1954, the combination of his experiences with the navy entertainments, the Actors Lab, CBS, and his Catskills shows gave Papp enough experience and ambition to launch a full time theatrical producing career. In 1954 he cajoled the City of New York and the State Education department officials to support his effort to create a public theater that would offer quality drama, particularly Shakespeare plays, as both free entertainment and educational experiences for New Yorkers. On November 4, Papp launched an evening of Shakespeare scenes in a Greenwich Village church, and the New York Shakespeare Festival was born.

Although well received from the outset, the Festival struggled for several years with a peripatetic schedule of productions in a variety of New York locations. But in 1962, Papp secured the outdoor Delacorte Theater in Central Park as a perma-

Theatrical producer Joe Papp is shown in his office at the Public Theater in New York City in 1974. (AP Photo)

nent home for the Festival (alternatively known as Shakespeare in the Park). The New York Shakespeare Festival soon grew into a national phenomenon, garnering fame for imaginative stagings that attracted big name stars (such as **James Earl Jones**, Kevin Kline, and Colleen Dewhurst), providing training grounds for young performers, and creating a national model for public presentation of Shakespeare that was eventually emulated by many cities around the country.

In 1966 Papp secured partial control of the historic Astor Library in Greenwich Village, a Civil War–era library built by the financier John Jacob Astor. Papp converted part of it to an Off-Broadway theater, which he called the Public Theater. Papp's new project quickly became a major force in commercial as well as noncommercial theater, showcasing innovative productions by new artists and often generating enough attention to warrant transfer of their productions to Broadway. The Public Theater launched its first production in 1967 with a decidedly noncommercial musical, *Hair*. Written by two unknown actors and an unknown composer, the musical combined rock music with a plot, of sorts, based on the quasi-tribal 1960s youth sex-and-drug counterculture—heretofore inconceivable material for Broadway. Nevertheless, *Hair* transferred to Broadway the following year, playing for 1,750 performances, bringing a whole new generation of young people to Broadway theaters, placing several hit songs on the rock and pop charts, and ushering in the now common Broadway rock musical.

The Public Theater would continue this line of daring "noncommercial" experimental productions, transferring important productions to Broadway on a regular basis. A champion of minority playwrights, Papp transferred his production of Charles Gordone's Pulitzer Prize–winning play, *No Place to be Somebody* (1969), the year following *Hair.* Papp's groundbreaking production of Ntozake Shange's choreopoem ***for colored girls who have considered suicide/when the rainbow is enuf*** (1976) remains the longest-running Broadway play ever written by an African American. Jason Miller's *That Championship Season* (1972) won both the Tony Award for Best Play and the Pulitzer Prize for Drama. Most improbably of all, ***A Chorus Line*** (1975), which began in Papp's Public Theater as a workshop project, eventually became the longest-running American-produced show in Broadway history, running for nearly 15 years. More recently Suzan-Lori Parks *Topdog/Underdog* (2001), the first Pulitzer Prize–winning play by an African American woman, transferred from the Public Theater to Broadway. Richard Greenberg's *Take Me Out* (2003), one of the most important gay-themed plays of the decade, originated in the Public Theater and eventually won the Tony Award for Best Play.

Beyond the sum total of his Off-Broadway and Broadway successes and the legacy of the New York Shakespeare Festival, Papp was a vital force for quality, self-assertive American theater throughout his career. An irrepressible, headline-grabbing opponent of censorship, devotee of left-wing causes, and philanthropist for theater in his own right, Papp became a national symbol for unyielding innovation, integrity, quality, and public involvement in theater—both commercial and noncommercial.

Papp died in New York City of prostate cancer on October 31, 1991. The Public Theater (now named the Joseph Papp Public Theater) and the New York Shakespeare Festival have been producing plays continuously ever since. Since the 1980s, not-for-profit resident or **regional theaters** around the country have become major sources for showcasing new Broadway productions, a direct result of Papp's success and vision.

Thomas A. Greenfield

Further Reading

Horn, Barbara Lee. *Joseph Papp: A Bio-bibliography.* Westport, CT: Greenwood Press, 1992.

Turan, Kenneth, and Joseph Papp. *Free for All: Tales from the New York Shakespeare Festival.* New York: Broadway Books, 2009.

PASTOR, TONY

See **Vaudeville**.

THE PHANTOM OF THE OPERA

Broadway Run: Majestic Theatre
Opening: January 26, 1988
Closing: Still Running
Composer: Andrew Lloyd Webber
Lyricist: Charles Hart, Richard Stilgoe
Book: Richard Stilgoe and Andrew Lloyd Webber
Choreographer: Gillian Lynne
Set and Costume Design: Maria Bjornson
Director: Harold Prince
Producer: Cameron Mackintosh and The Really Useful Theatre Company Ltd.
Lead Performers: Michael Crawford (Phantom of the Opera), Sarah Brightman (Christine Daaé), Steve Barton (Raoul), and Judy Kaye (Carlotta Guidicelli)

When **Andrew Lloyd Webber**'s *The Phantom of the Opera* opened in New York in January 1988, it helped usher in a new era in the history of the Broadway **musical**. The quintessential megamusical, complete with a large cast, cutting-edge pyrotechnics, elaborate opulent sets, and crashing chandeliers, *Phantom* offers its audiences pure theatrical spectacle combined with a classic melodramatic story. While some critics disparaged its slight lyrics and simplistic plot, audiences embraced the show's romantic tale and ambitious staging. Not only was the show a smash hit in London and New York, but subsequent national tours continued to take advantage of its popularity. These tours continue to this day and still fill houses for two- to three-week runs 20 years later. Moreover, *Phantom* joined earlier **European megamuscials** *Cats* (1982) and *Les Misérables* (1987) in benefiting from a sophisticated worldwide marketing campaign built around the proliferation of a single, iconic image. The Phantom's mask graced all manner of licensed merchandise—from posters, to T-shirts, to buttons, to refrigerator magnets—creating an international marketing phenomenon on a scale heretofore unknown in commercial theater promotion.

The Phantom of the Opera recounts the tale of the lonely, masked Phantom who lives in the elaborate catacombs beneath the Paris Opera House. With the Opera House coming under new management, the Phantom sees an opportunity to place his pupil and love, chorine Christine Daaé, in the role of lead soprano and, in so doing, assert control over the theater. When the new owners refuse his requests and when the Phantom realizes his love for Christine is not returned and that she has pledged it to another, various tragedies ensue: the death of a stagehand, the sudden illness of Carlotta (the previous lead soprano), and the dramatic fall of the famed chandelier. As a result, an angry mob descends upon the Phantom's lair beneath the theater seeking revenge, only to find his discarded mask.

The musical is based on French novelist Gaston Leroux's early twentieth-century novel *Le Fantome de l'Opera*. While the initial printing of the **novel** was hardly a success, the subsequent serialization of the story in English, French, and

American newspapers found an enthusiastic audience. In 1925, a film version staring Lon Chaney premiered and eventually became a horror classic that led to various other attempts to put the story on the big screen. In addition to the screen, others sought to bring the story to the stage and other venues.

A 1984 stage adaptation of Leroux's story using excerpts from the public domain operas of Verdi, Gounod, and Offenbach was performed at an East London fringe theater. The production caught the attention of composer **Andrew Lloyd Webber**. Lloyd Webber had already made a name for himself with shows like *Jesus Christ Superstar* (1971) and *Joseph and the Amazing Technicolor Dreamcoat* (1982) and was looking for material for his next show. He initially believed that the source material might best be developed into a campy musical along the lines of *The Rocky Horror Show* (1975). He even went as far as to contact producer **Cameron Mackintosh** about mounting such a project for a London West End theater. However, after reading Leroux's original novel, Lloyd Webber decided that the work was actually more of a genuinely romantic and heartfelt tale and that a musical adaptation should highlight those characteristics rather than exploit them for humor.

Lloyd Webber elected to write the score himself and tapped Richard Stilgoe to serve as his co-adapter and lyricist. He also convinced **Harold Prince**, one of Broadway's most successful producer/directors, to direct the show. (Prince had directed Lloyd Webber's 1979 hit *Evita*.) A summer festival tryout of the first act left Lloyd Webber wanting a more romantic approach to the songs, so he sought out an additional lyricist. Charles Hart was approached and accepted after **Alan Jay Lerner** (*My Fair Lady*) and Tim Rice (*Jesus Christ Superstar*, with Lloyd Webber) both turned Lloyd Webber down.

The Phantom of the Opera initially opened in London in 1986 with Michael Crawford as the Phantom and Sarah Brightman as Christine. Both Crawford and Brightman transferred with the show to New York two years later. Both performers left indelible marks on the production for two rather different reasons. Michael Crawford met with almost universal acclaim for his portrayal of the Phantom both in London and New York. Crawford had previously only really appeared in film versions of *Hello, Dolly!* and *A Funny Thing Happened on the Way to the Forum* and a variety of British films and television shows. Sarah Brightman was also a relative newcomer when she won the role of Christine. Unlike Crawford, however, her performance did not receive the same glowing notices in part due to charges of nepotism leveled at her since she was married to Lloyd Webber at the time. While many people who came to the show went to see Crawford's revelatory performance, others were enticed by the publicity surrounding the real-life romance between the show's creator and its female star.

Ultimately the show's initial success owed less to either Crawford or Brightman than to *Phantom*'s over-the-top theatrical moments—including the crashing of the chandelier at the end of the first act. The replica of the Paris Opera House chandelier is still in use at New York's Majestic Theatre, which has housed the Broadway production for its 20-plus year run. The dazzling beaded replica is nearly three feet wide and weighs approximately one ton. The centrality of this technical marvel clearly marked *Phantom* as part of the new megamusical trend wherein the theatrical machinery and spectacle played as much a central character as any actor. The chandelier actually opens the show, providing the transition from the auction house (where the opera house is being sold) back in time to the incidents at the opera house itself. As the overture soars, the chandelier springs to life, lighting up and slowly rising to the ceiling as large swaths of fabrics appear to magically fly away to reveal the opulence of the historic opera house. Throughout the first act, the chandelier actually hangs out over the audience only to come crashing down to the stage at the hands of the Phantom to end the first act. Audiences marveled at the chandelier as they did the floating tire in *Cats* (1982), the barricade in *Les Misérables* (1987), and yet again at the helicopter in *Miss Saigon* (1991).

The popularity of the show on Broadway and its clever, successful marketing strategies led to countless national tours and international staging that aimed to re-create the Broadway production as closely as possible. With such an emphasis on spectacle and a reproducible product in the show's advertising, **touring productions** had to figure out ways to make the show portable and feasible for constant travel. Audiences in Atlanta or Seattle wanted to see the same show in their city's theaters that they could see in New York. As a result, the touring productions employ as many as 27 large trucks to transfer the massive set from city to city.

Phantom's continued popularity has also resulted in another film version and a second permanent production in Las Vegas. A film version of the musical directed by Joel Schumacher and starring Gerald Butler as the Phantom and Emmy Rossum as Christine took advantage of cinema's visual possibilities and re-created the musical's environment in ever-greater opulence than on stage. The Las Vegas production reunited most of the original creative team including director Hal Prince who all came together to convert the over two and a half hour musical into a roughly 90-minute version more suitable to the city's casino audiences. The production, which now plays daily in a custom-designed theater at the Venetian Hotel and Casino, took the opportunity to enlarge the spectacle and employs a number of stuntmen and stuntwomen. For example, at one point, the Phantom, or his stunt double, uses the chandelier to swing across the ceiling of the theater. While other Broadway transfers have come and gone in Vegas, *Phantom* has remained enormously popular since it opened in 2006.

On January 6, 2006, Andrew Lloyd Webber's *The Phantom of the Opera* surpassed *Cats*, another Lloyd Webber musical, to become the longest-running show ever on Broadway. No one disputes the *Phantom*'s official Web site's claim that it is the most financially successful musical in history, and theater reporters and researchers generally accept the staggering statistics put forth by the show's producers: the show has been seen by over 80 million people in 124 cities throughout 25 countries, generating a worldwide box-office gross estimated to be in excess of $5 billion ("Facts and Figures").

Chase Bringardner

Citation

"Facts and Figures." *The Phantom of the Opera* (official Web site). Retrieved October 20, 2009, from www.thephantomoftheopera.com/the_show/facts_and_figures.php.

Further Reading

Citron, Stephen. *Sondheim and Lloyd-Webber: The New Musical.* New York: Oxford University Press, 2001.

Snelson, John. *Andrew Lloyd Webber.* New Haven, CT: Yale University Press, 2004.

PLAYWRIGHTS

Early Broadway to World War II

By 1820 New York City was the center of American theater, but "Broadway," as the theater district of the borough of Manhattan has come to be known, is the product of a flurry of theater construction that began 75 years later. By 1920 there were over 80 theaters in the district, but the evolution of the serious American playwright was delayed by the lack of an identity and the lack of intellectual property rights. Evert A. Duyckinck's 1855 *Cyclopedia of American Literature* declared American plays "thoroughly and essentially English." As late as 1909, English critic William Archer said he could not name a single American dramatist who had made any impact on European theater. Not until **Eugene O'Neill** won the first of his four Pulitzer Prizes with *Beyond the Horizon* in 1920 did a truly American drama of international quality exist.

The slow development of American playwriting is attributable to many factors, including aesthetics, economics, lack of copyright protection, residual Puritan antipathies to theater, and a pervasive Eurocentrist attitude toward the arts, culture, and the conduct of civilization in general. Prior to the establishment of meaningful copyright law, American playwrights had little control over their own work. For most of the nineteenth century the production rights to a play were lost to the author the moment the play was published. If the rights were sold to a producer, that producer would frequently refuse to let the play be published in order to maintain his production monopoly. The few nineteenth- and early twentieth-century playwrights who made money—Dion Boucicault, Steele MacKaye, Augustin Daly, **David Belasco**, and so on—were usually producers themselves. The prolific Elmer Rice, although not a producer during this period, enjoyed some success and fame with such plays as *On Trial* (1914) and *The Adding Machine* (1923), but his legacy has been largely overshadowed by O'Neill's.

Another obstacle to the independence of the Broadway playwright was the forming of the **Theatrical Syndicate** in 1896. Because the Syndicate controlled 95 percent of U.S. and Canadian theatrical bookings in the early 1900s, producers were forced to rent Syndicate road theaters to get a profitable tour route, and to only produce plays in New York that the Syndicate managers thought would be potentially successful on the road—thus moving artistic decisions from the hands of artists to those of marketers (businessmen).

Playwrights received some protection toward the end of the nineteenth century as copyright law and enforcement gradually improved. After 1870 registration of plays at the Library of Congress gave playwrights some national recognition as genuine writers, and Congress's 1891 acceptance of the International Copyright Agreement prevented managers from using "free imports" from foreign writers. The U.S. Copyright Act was revised in 1909, and the Minimum Basic Agreement, negotiated by the Dramatists Guild in 1926, prohibited producers from changing scripts, selling motion picture rights, or selecting directors and casts without playwright approval.

With the emergence of a community of serious playwrights in control of their intellectual property came waves of theater construction and production. Between 1924 and 1929, 26 new playhouses were either built or converted from other buildings in the Manhattan theater district. The 1926–1927 season saw an all-time high of 188 new plays on Broadway, followed by 53 new **musicals** in 1927–1928.

These numbers were never to be exceeded as Depression-era economics and Manhattan real estate prices deflated the 1920s boom. In the twenty-first century, despite a seasonal box office of nearly a billion dollars, only one Broadway offering in five makes money. Modern Broadway wields a three-pronged staff over the sea of red ink that forever threatens to engulf commercial theatrical production: (1) lowering production costs; (2) raising ticket prices; and (3) offering patrons what they have liked before. The higher ticket prices and familiar titles are synonymous with musicals and revivals. Nearly three out of every four Broadway productions are musicals, and only one in ten is a new American play. The latter traditionally is where the lower production costs can be seen. Nevertheless, in the eight decades since the halcyon days of the late 1920s, the occasional combination of an insightful text, experimental design, inspired acting, and innovative direction have given the world a drama that compares favorably with that of any other period in history: The American Broadway Play. "The American theater," **Arthur Miller** once said, "is five blocks long, by about one and a half blocks wide." The following playwrights strode it like colossuses.

Eugene O'Neill, the Provincetown Players, and the Coming of Age of American Drama

Notwithstanding admirable works by such nineteenth-century American playwrights as Bronson Howard and James Herne, the introduction of noteworthy modern American playwriting on Broadway is generally credited to Eugene O'Neill (1888–1953). The son of a famous stage actor (later notoriously immortalized as the alcoholic, self-absorbed James Tyrone in O'Neill's *Long Day's Journey into Night*, 1956), O'Neill owed his first Broadway opportunity to Richard Bennett, a matinee idol and friend of his father. Bennett, performing on Broadway in a faltering production of Elmer Rice's *For the Defense* (1919), convinced his producer to stage O'Neill's *Beyond the Horizon* in the afternoons at the same theater. The Rice play eventually folded but *Beyond the Horizon* continued for a run of 111 performances.

A college dropout who worked as a sailor and at a series of odd jobs in his early twenties, O'Neill was introduced in 1916 to the **Provincetown Players**, an experimental group formed a year earlier by playwright **Susan Glaspell**, George "Jig" Cook (Glaspell's husband), and other young artists summering on the Massachusetts coast, to provide American playwrights an opportunity to write and experiment, free from commercial pressures. After O'Neill read them some of his plays, the group began to focus its energies on getting them produced.

That fall the Provincetown Players moved to Greenwich Village in lower Manhattan, where by 1925 they had presented 93 plays by 47 authors, including 14 by O'Neill and 11 by Glaspell. But in O'Neill's great success lay the seeds of Provincetown's destruction. The Playhouse practice of having amateurs produce programs of one-act plays for limited runs soon dissatisfied O'Neill and the growing audience for his work. The groundbreaking *Emperor Jones* (produced at a cost of $502 in 1920) transferred uptown to Broadway for a substantial run and then went on the road for two years. However, similar transfers of plays by Glaspell and Cook failed. Another avant-garde pioneer, Arthur Hopkins, took over the production of O'Neill's *Anna Christie*, which won the 1922 Pulitzer Prize, and handled the uptown transfer of O'Neill's expressionistic *The Hairy Ape* from Provincetown that same year.

The original Provincetown Players suspended production in 1922 and closed down permanently in 1929. However, the Players left a crucial legacy of innovative, literate dramatists producing in the shadows of Broadway and sporadically but persistently infusing commercial theater with thoughtful, ambitious, serious plays. In addition to O'Neill, the Players launched the career of the first major American woman playwright, Susan Glaspell. In recent years Glaspell's one-act *Trifles* (1916) has become very well-known for its prescient feminist insights, and her last play, *Alison's House*, won the 1931 Pulitzer Prize.

The Theatre Guild, the Group Theatre, and Clifford Odets

The Washington Square Players, a highly respected experimental amateur theater group whose history paralleled the Provincetown Players, gave rise in 1919 to the fully professional **Theatre Guild**. Dedicated to the production of plays of "artistic merit not ordinarily seen on the commercial stage," the Guild survived early setbacks through strong patronage and a fortunate 1919 actors strike, which closed every Broadway house except the co-operatively run Garrick Theater where a Guild production was playing. From its inception into the 1970s, the Guild produced 228 plays on Broadway. Seven were by O'Neill, but an American play was a rarity in the Guild's early seasons. The Guild, with its imports from the modern European repertoire (including 18 productions of **George Bernard**

Shaw's plays), so successfully educated its audience that it found itself competing for them with the commercial managers it sought to supplant. By 1928 the Guild had a subscription season in six cities outside New York, and, observers noted, had become very much a part of the establishment against which it had rebelled.

In 1931 three younger employees of the Guild—**Harold Clurman**, Cheryl Crawford, and **Lee Strasberg**—formed the **Group Theatre**, introducing America to the Moscow Art Theatre's heralded Stanislavsky method of acting. As parting gifts to Clurman, Strasberg, and Crawford, the Theatre Guild yielded rights to plays that were to be the first two Group Theatre productions: Paul Green's *The House of Connelly* and Claire and Paul Sifton's *1931*. *Connelly* established the Group's production reputation. Another ex-Guild playwright, John Howard Lawson, opened the Group's 1932 season with his attack on advertising, *Success Story*, but the Group's first financial success was Sidney Kingsley's *Men in White*, the 1934 Pulitzer Prize winner about a young doctor's maturation under fire.

When later projects faltered **Clifford Odets**, a heretofore undistinguished Group actor, offered his own works. Odets's plays became synonymous with the Group's style and mission, marking him as the most important American social dramatist of the Depression Era. The performance of *Waiting for Lefty*, Odets's episodic, pro-labor, left-wing agitprop masterpiece (which he co-directed and acted in) as a fund-raiser for the Marxist New Theater League on January 5, 1935, is a defining moment in American theater history. Clurman was already rehearsing a second Odets play, called *Lefty*, a depiction of the 1934 New York taxi drivers' strike, "the birth cry of the thirties." *Awake and Sing!*, the contemporary saga of the agony, exultation, and disintegration of the Berger family, opened six weeks later at the Belasco Theatre to 15 curtain calls and ecstatic reviews. By the end of 1936 it had played in Philadelphia, Baltimore, Chicago, Cleveland, and Newark, and was to return to New York in Hungarian and Yiddish productions.

Waiting for Lefty soon became the mantra and economic angel of left-wing and labor groups throughout America, playing in 104 cities by the end of August 1935. To accompany *Lefty*'s Broadway premiere, Odets hastily composed an antifascist underground one-act, *Till the Day I Die*, and the double bill opened for a solid run on Broadway in March 1935. *Paradise Lost*, which followed a well-educated, middle-class Jewish business family into a Depression-imposed decline, succeeded the *Lefty* double bill in December. Initially unsuccessful, *Lost* is now lauded for its poeticizing of common city life, and is arguably Odets's most significant and most frequently revived work. Other non-Odets failures followed, and by 1936 the Group was broke again.

Odets came to the rescue again with *Golden Boy* (1937), the Group's biggest hit. *Rocket to the Moon* (1938), about a dentist whose sense of life's possibilities is slowly atrophying, was Odets's last successful collaboration with the Group. The Group itself had ceased to exist by the time Odets's *Clash by Night* failed at the end of 1941. Odets did mostly **film** writing in the 1940s and had only one other major theatrical success after the Group folded. *The Country Girl* (1950), Odets's best play since *Golden Boy*, depicts an actor unable to deal with responsibility, the wife who is both his support and the mirror of his failure, and the director who tries to understand both. The show ran for a healthy 236 performances, earning **Uta Hagen** the first of her two Best Actress Tony Awards. A 1954 film adaptation won an Academy Award for Grace Kelly. The play saw Broadway revivals in 1972 and 2008 as star vehicles for **Jason Robards** and Morgan Freeman, respectively. Odets was still working as a screenwriter when he died in 1963, but with the rising of the twin suns of Arthur Miller and **Tennessee Williams**, his dramatic star faded after World War II. Yet, Odets, like O'Neill, brought a poetic sensibility to social realism, and the legacy of his plays and his acknowledged influence on Miller and countless other playwrights has surpassed that of the Group Theatre with which he was first identified.

The successes of theater collectives like the Provincetown Players, the Theatre Guild, and the Group Theatre in nurturing and launching quality drama inspired many American playwrights from the 1930s to 1950s to develop both short-term and long-term associations with like-minded artists. In 1938 playwrights Elmer Rice, **Maxwell Anderson**, Robert Sherwood, Sidney Howard, and S. N. Behrman formed the Playwrights Producing Company. These playwrights, assuming the role of producers, guaranteed each author final say in all production matters within the confines of a preestablished budget. As an organization the Playwrights Company lasted until 1960, mounting over 60 Broadway productions by its members and other writers, including the postwar classics *Tea and Sympathy* (1953) by Robert Anderson and *Cat on a Hot Tin Roof* (1955) by Tennessee Williams.

Comedy: George S. Kaufman and Company

Notwithstanding the central role of stage comedy in the success of **vaudeville** and burlesque through the 1930s, the American popularity of G. B. Shaw's comedies of ideas, and J. M. Barrie's more subtle social commentary, the comedy of the early American commercial theater has not aged well. Unlike the novels from which he adapted them, the sentimental comedies of American Booth Tarkington, including *The Man from Home* (1908) and *Seventeen* (1918), died with the era that produced them. Playwrights Company co-founder S. N. Behrman created an American comedy of manners with *The Second Man* (1927) and *Biography* (1932), and Philip Barry wrote prolifically about the same social class in such classics as *Holiday* (1928) and *Philadelphia Story* (1939). However, no one dominated pre–World War II American comedy like **George S. Kaufman**.

Counting plays, musicals, adaptations, and revue contributions, his authorial presence can be documented in at least 45 Broadway productions from 1918 to 1955. Kaufman's record of having something he had written or directed on Broadway every season for 37 years (1921–1958) will never conceivably be challenged. He cowrote two Pulitzer Prize winners including *Of Thee I Sing* (1931), the first musical so honored, and the ever popular *You Can't Take It with You* (1936). He was constantly in demand as a director for projects that ranged from his own plays, to Hecht and MacArthur's *Front Page* (1928), to the Marx Brothers stage comedies, to the musical *Guys and Dolls* (1950), for which he won a Tony Award for directing. Kaufman achieved much of his theatrical success while working as the Drama Editor of the *New York Times* from 1917 to 1930, doctoring other people's plays, writing many screenplays, building a reputation as a radio personality, and sharing the notorious Algonquin (Hotel) Round Table with fellow New York intellectuals and wits Dorothy Parker, Robert Benchley, and Harpo Marx, among others.

Known as "The Great Collaborator" because of his ability to work with other writers, Kaufman's Broadway successes included shared credits with Marc Connelly (*Beggar on Horseback*, 1925), Edna Ferber (*The Royal Family*, 1927), Morrie Ryskind (*Animal Crackers*, 1928, and *Of Thee I Sing*), and most notably Moss Hart. Kaufman and Hart wrote eight Broadway comedies, the best known of which are *You Can't Take It with You* (1936) and *The Man Who Came to Dinner* (1939). The unique Kaufman and Hart method of collaboration—*You Can't Take It with You* was cast and the theater rented before Kaufman and Hart wrote a line—is now the stuff of American playwriting legend. His characters were genuinely likable people who triumphed over self-serving cynicism, unthinking conventionality, or bureaucratic oppression. Kaufman's plays offered trenchant social commentary dispensed in wisecracks—a legacy that has dominated Broadway, television, and modern film comedy ever since. A despiser of sentimentality himself, he consistently chose collaborators whose human warmth he could focus with his impeccable stagecraft. After his partnership with Moss Hart ended with *George Washington Slept Here* (1940) and World War II approached, Kaufman seemed less in touch with theater audiences. The 1942–1943 season was the first since 1921 that did not feature a new Kaufman play. His later works seemed at odds with the times and his acerbic, irreverent wit—eminently quotable on radio and in gossip columns before the war—was less acceptable on television in the McCarthy era. Although he died in 1961, his mastery of technique shaped American comedy writing for the remainder of the century.

The Educator: Thornton Wilder

During his lifetime only six of **Thornton Wilder**'s plays were produced on Broadway (seven, counting *Hello, Dolly!*, the musical adaptation of his *The Matchmaker*, 1955). He thought so little of his first, *The Trumpet Shall Sound* (1926), that he never bothered to publish it. The most famous member of a brilliant family of diplomats, biologists, and authors, Wilder was educated in China and Rome, taught French in New Jersey, comparative literature at the University of Chicago, and poetry at Harvard. His best-known Broadway plays reflected his scholarly command of the humanities. The Pulitzer Prize–winning **Our Town** (1938) was inspired by his friend Gertrude Stein's 1925 novel *The Making of Americans*. *The Skin of Our Teeth* (1942), which also won the Pulitzer Prize, was heavily influenced by novelist James Joyce's 1939 masterpiece *Finnegan's Wake*. Wilder's most successful play, *The Matchmaker*, had an even longer lineage traceable through two nineteenth-century European works—the Viennese Johann Nestroy's

Einen Jux will er sich machen ("He Will Have a Wild Time") and John Oxenford's one-act farce *A Day Well Spent*—as well as his own unsuccessful *The Merchant of Yonkers* (1938). Wilder's one-act, *The Happy Journey to Trenton and Camden* (1944), presented as a curtain raiser to a Broadway production of French writer Jean-Paul Sartre's *The Respectful Prostitute*, readily complemented Sartre's iconoclastic existentialist drama.

Wilder had a greater impact on American culture than on Broadway itself. He inspired few imitators—a testimony to the singularity of his talent more so than any lack of admiration from others. But the cultural legacy of *Our Town* cannot be overestimated. In the 1930s O'Neill and Odets loomed larger in professional theatrical circles. But American schools and community theaters have embraced Wilder's probing universal themes and true, if not strictly realistic, depiction of young people's lives. Inasmuch as Wilder always thought of himself as a teacher rather than a writer, *Our Town* appropriately still stands with Miller's **Death of a Salesman** and **The Crucible** as well as Williams's *The Glass Menagerie* as the starting point for countless American students' education in American drama.

Beyond Glaspell: Rachel Crothers, Lillian Hellman

Women playwrights scored some notable Broadway successes during and after the era of Susan Glaspell. Zona Gale's 1921 Pulitzer Prize for *Miss Lulu Bett* is nestled between two Pulitzer wins for Eugene O'Neill, and Zoe Atkins was similarly honored for *The Old Maid* in 1935. Sophie Treadwell's *Machinal* (1928) holds a historic place in the small but highly admired canon of American Expressionistic dramas, while Mary Chase's *Harvey* not only defeated Tennessee Williams's *The Glass Menagerie* for the 1945 Pulitzer Prize, it ran three times as long on Broadway. Anne Nichols's *Abie's Irish Rose* (1922) remains the second longest-running nonmusical in Broadway history with an astonishing 2,327 performances. Anita Loos penned the historic *Gentleman Prefer Blondes* (1926) as well as the comedy *Happy Birthday* (1946), one of the most successful plays of **Helen Hayes**'s storied career. Clare Boothe's *The Women* (1936), a comedy of betrayal and divorce with speaking parts for 33 women and no men, ran an impressive 657 performances. However, in the first half of the twentieth century, only two women playwrights developed Broadway careers the equal of any of their male counterparts: **Rachel Crothers** and **Lillian Hellman**.

Crothers was a true theater professional. Between 1906 and 1937, 24 of her plays were produced on Broadway—half of them substantial hits, which she mostly produced and directed, and occasionally acted in. Her last and most popular work, *Susan and God* (1937) was the first Broadway play to be televised with its original cast. Following her rediscovery by feminists in the 1970s, ironically Crothers is best known today for two initially less successful plays about the double standard for men and women: *A Man's World* (1910) and *He and She* (1920). The protagonist of *A Man's World*, a successful novelist who takes a male *nom de plume* to avoid biased criticism of her work, rejects a lover who refuses to take responsibility for a child he fathered out of wedlock. In *He and She* Crothers played the role of a sculptress who wins a commission of career-making importance in competition with her husband. Discovering that her neglected teenaged daughter is about to elope with a chauffeur, the sculptress must choose between artistic fulfillment and the needs of her family, and yields the commission to her husband.

Possessed of a notoriously contentious personality, Lillian Hellman was herself a subject for drama as intriguing as that in her plays, famously refusing to "cut my conscience to fit this year's fashions" during her 1952 testimony before the House Un-American Activities Committee (HUAC). Between 1934 and 1963 Hellman wrote eight original dramas for the Broadway stage and adapted two novels as well as two French plays. Her dominant themes, which she frequently mixed to the discomfort of audiences and critics, were politics and sexuality. Her first play and biggest box-office success, *The Children's Hour* (1934), showed the lives and careers of two young teachers destroyed by a malicious child's charge of lesbianism. The child's ruse is ultimately discovered, but in the aftermath one of the teachers realizes the underlying truth of the accusation and commits suicide. Hellman always claimed that the point of the play was not homosexuality but the destructive power of the unfounded accusation—an assertion made clearer when its 1952 Broadway revival (directed by Hellman) followed her defiant HUAC appearance. In 1935, however, the Pulitzer committee refused to consider *The Children's Hour* because of its unsavory subject matter.

Hellman spent much of her childhood in the South, the setting of four of her plays. Among these *The Little Foxes* (1939) is generally considered to be her best work. In a turn-of-the-century Alabama town on the brink of switching from an agrarian to an industrial economy, the avaricious Hubbards willingly destroy anything in their path, even their own family members, to finance the cotton mill that will make their monetary and social fortunes. Marc Blitzstein, who composed and wrote the protest musical **The Cradle Will Rock** (1937), adapted *The Little Foxes* into the 1949 opera *Regina*. Hellman shows the Hubbard family at an earlier stage in their development in *Another Part of the Forest* (1946), her first directing effort. *The Autumn Garden* (1951) is indebted to *The Seagull* and *Uncle Vanya* by Anton Chekhov, whose collected letters Hellman edited in the 1950s. More overtly political are the wartime dramas *Watch on the Rhine* (1941), which powerfully advocated for direct opposition to rising fascism in Europe, and *The Searching Wind* (1944), which singled out those whose appeasement made that fascism possible. However, her refusal to denounce Stalinism in the face of the Russian leader's brutal treatment of his own people drew harsh public criticism even from generally like-minded liberal thinkers. Hellman, who died in 1984, remains one of the most enigmatic figures in twentieth-century American letters.

Tennessee Williams and Arthur Miller

The names of Tennessee Williams and Arthur Miller are forever linked as the giants of the post–World War II American theater. Their successes in the late

1940s through the 1950s heralded a new acceptance of serious, literate, and even courageous drama on Broadway. As independent artists they flourished on Broadway without affiliation with "little theaters" or the activist playwright groups that had forged a short-lived but durable link between mainstream commercial theater and serious American playwriting prior to World War II.

Even though Williams and Miller continued to write until their deaths in 1983 and 2005, respectively, the works that established their reputations were produced on Broadway between 1945 and 1961. Williams, the Southern Gothic homosexual, closeted onstage by Cold War conformity, and Miller, the socially conscious assimilated Jew, had more in common than parallel chronologies. Both came from middle-class families devastated by the Depression, which forced them into menial labor—Williams in a St. Louis shoe factory (recalled in *The Glass Menagerie*, 1945) and Miller in a Brooklyn auto parts warehouse (recalled in *A Memory of Two Mondays*, 1976). Both began their writing careers with the Works Projects Administration's Federal Arts Project—Williams at the Writers Project and Miller as a scriptwriter for Federal Theatre Radio. Their first Broadway efforts failed: Williams's *Battle of Angels* closed in Boston tryouts in 1940 and Miller's *The Man Who Had All the Luck* (1944) closed after six performances. Both playwrights were realists who experimented with expressionism, as evidenced by the stage directions for Williams's *The Glass Menagerie* and the dream sequences in Miller's *Death of a Salesman* (1949). Both had productive relationships with director **Elia Kazan**—Miller with *All My Sons* (1947) and *Death of a Salesman* (1949), and Williams with *A Streetcar Named Desire* (1947), *Cat on a Hot Tin Roof* (1955), and *Sweet Bird of Youth* (1959). They both eventually feuded with Kazan. Miller did not speak to Kazan for ten years after the latter "named names" before the House Un-American Activities Committee. Williams felt that Kazan compromised *Cat on a Hot Tin Roof* by forcing him to write a commercially acceptable ending.

Williams wrote at least 30 full-length plays, numerous short plays, five volumes of essays and short stories, two volumes of poetry, and a novella. An obsessive craftsman he constantly reworked material until he found its proper shape. His compulsion to revise had a profound effect on what theater audiences saw of his work. *The Glass Menagerie* began as a short story and evolved through a screenplay to its present form. Traces of four earlier Williams one-acts are evident in *Streetcar*, of which 12 manuscript versions exist.

Williams called *The Glass Menagerie*, his first Broadway success, "a memory play": a three-part structure in which a profound experience causes an "arrest of time" for the protagonist, during which the experience must be relived until the protagonist can make sense of it. Audiences and critics were enraptured by the lyrical quality of the play and the masterful performance of **Laurette Taylor** as Amanda Wingfield. By the 1950s *The Glass Menagerie* had become a staple of **regional theater** and **high school drama programs** and reading lists. In 1947 *Streetcar* brought to commercial theater a new depth of emotional intimacy and volatility in adult relationships. Moreover, **Marlon Brando**'s performance as Stanley Kowalski, which he later re-created in the 1951 film adaptation, single-handedly immortalized the play, the character, and the actor in the annals of popular culture. Williams also enjoyed commercial success with *Sweet Bird of Youth* (1959) and *Night of the Iguana* (1961).

Although he continued to write prolifically in the years between *The Night of the Iguana* and his death in 1983, Williams never had another Broadway success. His earlier successful hits, however, have seen numerous revivals on Broadway as well as in London and other international theater centers. *The Glass Menagerie* has been revived on Broadway in each decade since the 1960s. *A Streetcar Named Desire*, the imposing legacy of the original notwithstanding, has been revived six times. *Cat on a Hot in Roof* has had four Broadway revivals, including an all-black cast production in 2008. Williams's last two Broadway efforts, *Kingdom of Earth/The Seven Descents of Myrtle* (1968) and *Vieux Carre* (1977) closed quickly.

If a Tennessee Williams play is about the individual crushed by society, an Arthur Miller play is about the mutual responsibility (fulfilled or unfulfilled) of the individual and society. The Great Depression was the shaping event of his life, but, as he often asserted, an event with surprisingly positive lessons about interdependency and personal vulnerability forgotten in the self-serving, hedonistic final decades of the twentieth century. Miller's theatrical ideal was the Group Theatre, which was in the process of breaking up in the late 1930s as Miller began writing for the Federal Theatre. His biggest influence as a playwright was Clifford Odets, and he viewed Group Theatre founder **Harold Clurman**—who later coproduced *All My Sons* (1947) and directed *Incident at Vichy* (1964)—as a high priest of social drama. When former Group Theatre member Elia Kazan—the director of *All My Sons* (1947) and *Death of a Salesman*—named former friends and colleagues before the HUAC hearings, Miller broke with him. Miller's next play was *The Crucible* (1953), an undisguised linking of HUAC, McCarthyism, and the seventeenth century witch trials in Salem. *The Crucible* was to become the one of the most frequently produced plays ever written by an American.

Typically the plot of an Arthur Miller play owes much to nineteenth-century Norwegian playwright Henrik Ibsen's use of the "Hidden Secret," an action by the protagonist, unknown to the public, often occurring before the action of the play itself and, thus, undermining the moral stature of the protagonist's subsequent actions. Wartime munitions manufacturer Joe Keller in *All My Sons* allowed cracked cylinder heads to be shipped to the Air Force (leading to the crash of 21 planes) in order to save his business for his sons. Eventually Keller admits, prior to killing himself, that the pilots who crashed were in a moral sense "all my sons." Willy Loman in *Salesman* climactically dredges up the 17-year-old memory of his son, Biff, discovering him in a hotel room with "the Woman in Boston." *The Crucible*'s John Proctor, who had a past secret sexual relationship with young Abigail Williams, hesitates to challenge accusations of witchcraft by the girls of Salem until it is too late to stop his own wife from being arrested. In *The Price* (1968), Miller's only successful play of the 1960s, the chair belonging to a long-dead father sits in the center of an abandoned apartment where he lived out his life after losing his fortune in the 1929 Stock Market Crash. Victor, the younger of two grown sons, bitterly recounts having abandoned his education to support his father, only to discover years later that his father had hidden money. Dismayed at this revelation, Victor struggles to understand the life-altering sacrifices he made decades ago.

Shortly after the 1960s, Miller and Williams plays as well as those of other serious playwrights of the 1950s began to fail more frequently on Broadway—victims of soaring production costs and shifting audience tastes. About the same time, however, producers were developing the concept of the limited run, which, with cooperation from the unions and negotiations with stars who were available for only fixed periods of time, could showcase quality dramas. Williams did not ultimately benefit from this new approach, but Miller and other playwrights did. It was under such circumstances that two new Miller plays came to Broadway in the last decade of his life. In *Broken Glass* (1994), the wife of a well-to-do Jewish American banking executive experiences paralysis when the news of *Kristallnacht*, the November 1938 destruction of Jewish businesses, homes, and synagogues in Germany, reaches America. Miller's last original Broadway production, *The Ride Down Mt. Morgan* (2000), had premiered in London in 1991. The play is a wry comment on 1980s America's self-centeredness that Miller associated with the presidency of Ronald Reagan. A revised comic version reached Broadway featuring a President Bill Clinton–like protagonist endlessly able to justify his appetites. Here Miller returned to the story of an adulterous salesman— symbolically named "Lyman" instead of "Loman"—who cannot separate his ability to manipulate a client from the bigamous need to fulfill himself by marrying two different women. When he crashes his Porsche on an icy road, both wives are summoned to the hospital and eventually come to terms with a man who feels no guilt about having met both their needs by meeting his own. The play closed after 121 performances, the longest run of an original Miller play since *The Price* 32 years earlier. Yet, as with Williams, periodic Broadway revivals of the earlier hits, especially *Salesman* and *The Crucible*, sustain Miller's theatrical legacy as an essential if rarified part of postwar Broadway.

Although Williams and Miller dominated Broadway drama, others labored in their shadow with varying degrees of success. In the 1950s **William Inge** (1913– 1973) gained a reputation as a Midwestern Tennessee Williams. Although his first play *Come Back, Little Sheba* was revived on Broadway in 2008, Inge seems distinctly a 1950s phenomenon. Horton Foote (1916–) debuted on Broadway as early as 1944 (*Only the Heart*), won a Pulitzer Prize for *The Young Man from Atlanta* (1995), and saw his *Dividing the Estate* open in 2008. However, Foote has never had a Broadway play run longer than seven weeks. Like most playwrights who began careers in the 1940s and 1950s, Foote, William Gibson (*The Miracle Worker*, 1959), and Paddy Chayefsky (*The Tenth Man*, 1960) had to find other ways to earn a living—usually writing for Hollywood dramatic television shows. *The Miracle Worker* (1959), Gibson's best and most successful play, premiered on CBS's *Playhouse 90* in 1957. Gibson did not have another solid success until 2003, when *Golda's Balcony*, a one-woman show starring Tovah Feldshuh as Israeli Prime Minister Golda Meir, set the all-time record for Broadway **solo performances** with 493.

African American Playwrights and Broadway

Although **African American musicals** had made an impact on Broadway since the 1920s (and arguably earlier from black minstrelsy), with few exceptions black Broadway playwriting is a post–World War II phenomenon. The first African American writer to have a drama produced on Broadway was Willis Richardson, whose melodrama *The Chip Woman's Fortune* ran briefly in 1923. The most celebrated African American writer of the 1930s, Langston Hughes, also wrote the only African American Broadway hit drama before World War II, *Mulatto* (1935). **Rose McClendon**, the premiere African American actress of her day, starred as the mistress of an aristocratic Southerner with whom she had three children. *Mulatto* ran for a year after its premiere and toured another eight months. Nevertheless, it had taken Hughes five years to find a Broadway producer, who added an unauthorized rape scene to the play while Hughes was out of the country. In the 1940s and 1950s the Great White Way was mostly true to its name. Richard Wright's *Native Son* (1941) ran 114 performances, but much of the adaptation was executed by its white co-author Paul Green and staged by white producers Orson Welles and John Houseman. In 1947 *Our Lan'*, Theodore Ward's tragedy of the U.S. government's betrayal of black colonizers of a post–Civil War Georgia island, transferred briefly from **Off-Broadway** to Broadway. Louis Peterson, who had acted in *Our Lan'*, wrote *Take A Giant Step* (1953), the story of a middle-class black boy separated from his roots by his family's upward mobility. The play enjoyed a successful Off-Broadway revival in 1956 and was filmed in 1958. In 1957 Hughes, who had previously adapted his newspaper column character Simple into a novel and a series of short stories, adapted Simple to a musical, *Simply Heavenly*, which transferred briefly from Off-Broadway to Broadway. However, Hughes's Broadway legacy arguably owes more to a line of his poetry than any of his plays. His poem "A Dream Deferred" speaks of dreams that dry up like "a raisin in the sun."

The premiere of Lorraine Hansberry's ***A Raisin in the Sun*** in 1959 marked a turning point in African American history. The most celebrated African American play ever written, it was to affect the future of black theater in ways no one could have predicted. The play won for Hansberry, who died of cancer at 34 in 1965, the Drama Critics Circle Award for best play—the first African American and to date the youngest playwright (then 29) ever so honored. Mainstream Broadway audiences and critics embraced the young playwright at a level heretofore unimaginable for an African American dramatist; she was a star, invoking hopeful comparisons with Miller, O'Neill, and other leading playwrights of the time. Director **Lloyd Richards** became the first African American to direct a Broadway show and went on to head the Yale School of Drama. Original cast members Sidney Poitier, Ruby Dee, and Louis Gossett went on to long successful careers as actors, with Poitier eventually attaining "Superstar" celebrity status in Hollywood. Cast member Lonne Elder III earned a Pulitzer Prize nomination for writing *Ceremonies and Dark Old Men* (1969) and became the first African American nominated for a Best Screenplay Oscar (*Sounder*, 1973). *A Raisin in the Sun* gave actor/playwright

Ossie Davis (Poitier's Broadway replacement) leverage to secure backing for Broadway production of his play *Purlie Victorious* (1961), which established his reputation and career. Robert Nemiroff, Hansberry's former husband and literary executor, later adapted *A Raisin in the Sun* as the musical *Raisin* (1973), which ran for 847 performances and won the Tony for Best Musical.

Black theatrical representation in the turbulent 1960s and 1970s was easy to find in New York, but not necessarily on Broadway. James Baldwin's *The Amen Corner* (1965), which explores the religious and social tumult of the author's Harlem youth, had to wait 11 years for its Broadway premiere. It might have waited longer without the sensation raised in 1964 by Baldwin's *Blues for Mister Charlie*, the **Actors Studio** production of Baldwin's depiction of interracial tension in a small southern town. *Mister Charlie* helped white audiences understand the most influential black writer of the period, LeRoi Jones (later to call himself Amiri Baraka), but while Baldwin shows some sympathy for his bigoted white characters, Jones/Baraka does not. In his four Off-Broadway productions of 1964—including *Dutchman*, which won an Obie Award and a place in the world repertoire—Jones's protagonists see no permanent relationship between the races other than murderer and victim. Jones/Baraka is, proudly, not a Broadway playwright, but his work exerted a profound influence on future African American dramatists, including some who wrote for Broadway: Ed Bullins, Charles Gordone, and, America's most successful African American playwright, **August Wilson**. In 1970 Gordone's *No Place to Be Somebody* became the first African American play to win the Pulitzer Prize. *Somebody*, part black mafia aspiration and part poetic fantasy, played Broadway only briefly. Philip Hayes Dean's *Paul Robeson* (1978), a one-man show with **James Earl Jones**, did slightly better. Ntozake Shange's ***for colored girls who have considered suicide/when the rainbow is enuf*** (1976), a work shaped by both racial and feminist politics, was the most popular African American play of the decade. Shange's 20-part choreopoem began Off-Broadway at the Public Theater in 1975, transferring to Broadway the following year where it ran nearly two years.

Beginning with *Ma Rainey's Black Bottom Blues* in 1984 August Wilson, a struggling writer from Pittsburgh, eventually established a reputation that invited comparisons with Eugene O'Neill, Tennessee Williams, and Arthur Miller. Wilson set out to write a play for each of the ten decades of the twentieth century; each would provide insight into the place of blacks in America in each decade. Nine had Broadway runs. The best-known works in Wilson's cycle include *Ma Rainey*, which is set in a 1925 Chicago recording session with the title character; *Fences* (1987), which uses baseball as a metaphor for achievements of and limitations imposed upon blacks in the 1950s; and *The Piano Lesson* (1990), a 1930s story about the descendants of slaves caught between honoring the past and building toward their future. Both *Fences* and *The Piano Lesson* won Pulitzer Prizes. Several universities and regional theaters have held festivals featuring the entire Wilson play cycle. Shortly after Wilson's death in 2005, Broadway's Virginia Theater was renamed the August Wilson Theater, the first Broadway theater named for an African American.

In the 1980s and 1990s **George C. Wolfe** made his mark on Broadway principally as a director and producer, particularly for the New York Public Theater from 1993 to 2004. However, he wrote the book for the hit musical *Jelly's Last Jam* (1992) and conceived (as well as directed and wrote lyrics for) *Bring in 'Da Noise, Bring in 'Da Funk* (1996). For most of the 1990s Suzan-Lori Parks, who won a succession of Obies for her Off-Broadway plays, seemed doomed to banishment from Broadway by disinterested producers. In 2001, however, Parks resurrected from an earlier play a black character who made his living at carnivals portraying Abraham Lincoln at the moment of his assassination. The result, *Topdog/Underdog* (2002) under Wolfe's guidance, transferred from the Public Theater to Broadway and won the Pulitzer Prize. It was the first play by an African American woman ever so honored and the first play (other than one-woman shows) by an African American woman to appear on Broadway in 33 years. Since then, Parks has maintained a high profile outside of Broadway. Her *365 Plays* (a play a day written between November 2002 and November 2003) received national attention for its creativity and theatrical audaciousness. Lynn Nottage has emerged as another African American playwright with a national audience, but not a Broadway one. The author of *Intimate Apparel*, *Crumbs from the Table of Joy*, and the recent *Ruined*, Nottage's work is very popular with repertory theaters across America. The highly regarded Atlanta native Pearl Cleage (*Flyin' West*, *Blues for an Alabama Sky*, and *Bourbon at the Border*) also has yet to reach Broadway but enjoys a "back-up" career as an Oprah-recognized novelist.

After Miller, Williams, and Hansberry

In the second half of the twentieth century—and particularly after the peak years of Miller, Williams, and Hansberry—it became increasingly difficult to define a Broadway playwright, or even to determine the era to which a writer belonged. The rising cost of Broadway theatrical production, the surge of **European-imported megamusicals** and **Disney** family shows in the 1970s, and the enlarged role of regional and Off-Broadway theaters in nurturing new playwrights during the same period of time blurred the definition of who or what constituted a Broadway dramatist.

The clearest indication of who was a Broadway playwright during this period came from the world of comedy. **Neil Simon**, the most popular playwright in the history of American theater, began his career in live television, for which he never wrote a play. Neil Simon joined Mel Brooks and Woody Allen among others as comedy writers for Sid Caesar's *Your Show of Shows* (1950–1954) on NBC—an experience Simon immortalized in *Laughter on the 23rd Floor* (1993). In 1961 Simon graduated to Broadway with *Come Blow Your Horn*, the first of the 33 plays and books for musicals he was to see staged in the next 42 years (some resurfacing in 28 movies produced from his screenplays). In one six-month period in 1966–1967 Simon had a record four works running simultaneously on Broadway: ***Barefoot in the Park*** (1963), *The Odd Couple* (1965), *Sweet Charity* (1966), and *The*

Star Spangled Girl (1966). Simon's work is often seen as divided between one liner–driven earlier works and more autobiographical later plays referencing his personal experiences and Jewish American heritage, such as his struggle to regain an emotional life after his first wife's death in *Chapter Two* (1977) or family recollections in "the Trilogy" (*Brighton Beach Memoirs* [1983], *Biloxi Blues* [1985], and *Broadway Bound* [1986]). Yet, Simon had always mined his own life for comic inspiration. He and his brother Danny are the models for the two brothers in *Come Blow Your Horn*, and the relationship between Danny and another recently divorced man inspired *The Odd Couple*. Indisputably the premiere playwright of his day, Simon both inspired and overshadowed other contemporary Jewish comedic playwrights, including Herb Gardner (*A Thousand Clowns*, 1962; *I'm Not Rappaport*, 1992) and **Wendy Wasserstein** (*The Heidi Chronicles*, 1989; *The Sisters Rosensweig*, 1993). Following the success of *The Brighton Beach Memoirs* in 1983, the Alwin Theater was renamed the Neil Simon Theater. Simon's last new Broadway play was *Rose's Dilemma* (2003). His last New York play was the aptly named *45 Seconds from Broadway* (2001), and *Lost in Yonkers* was his last play to run on Broadway for a year longer.

Although not Simon's equal in output or popularity, **Edward Albee** has outdistanced his contemporaries as a subject for critical study. Initially an *avant-garde* rather than a mainstream playwright—and often considered as a bridge between Broadway and Off-Broadway theater—Albee was included in Martin Esslin's groundbreaking critical book *The Theater of the Absurd* (1961) before he had written anything longer than a one act. Albee's first play, *The Zoo Story* (1958), premiered on a double bill with Samuel Beckett's *Krapp's Last Tape* in Germany, then Off-Broadway at the Provincetown Playhouse. Absurdism is now rarely mentioned in Albee criticism, but his innovative use of language is. Albee has united critics around the belief that his first full-length play, **Who's Afraid of Virginia Woolf?** (1962), is *the* iconic serious American play of the post–Williams/Miller era. A middle-aged, university couple's after-party drinking gathers momentum in their living room until it explodes into a *Walpurgisnacht*, stripping away of illusions, the chief of which is the fictitious existence of a son who fulfills the needs of his parents. *Virginia Woolf*'s Martha and George have become the paradigm of dysfunctional union held together by destructive passion. It would be another 40 years before an Albee play ran longer than four months on Broadway. In this period Albee's stage adaptations of several books—including Carson McCullers's *The Ballad of the Sad Café* (1963), James Purdy's *Malcolm* (1966), and a musical version of Truman Capote's *Breakfast at Tiffany's* (1966)—opened to little audience or critical interest. He also presented several of his early one acts, the rhythmically hypnotic *Box/Quotations from Chairman Mao Tse-Tung* (1968), and three original full-length plays, *Tiny Alice* (1964), *A Delicate Balance* (1966), and *All Over* (1971). *A Delicate Balance* earned Albee the Pulitzer Prize that many believed he should have won for *Virginia Woolf*. Truly undervalued was Albee's *All Over* (1971), a vigil at the deathbed of a great man conducted by his family, mistress, lawyer, and doctor. Albee's second Pulitzer Prize was awarded to *Seascape* (1975), another play of existential hope that failed to impress Broadway audiences but has succeeded in the world repertoire. *Seascape* was followed by *The Lady from Dubuque* (1980), in which Death appears at the parlor games of a woman dying of cancer. *The Man with Three Arms* (1983) is a seemingly self-referential look into what happens to a celebrity when the freakish singularity that gave him his identity withers away. *The Goat or Who Is Sylvia?* (2002) returned Albee to Broadway after a 19-year absence. The controversial play tests liberal sexual tolerance in that its hero falls in love with a goat. *The Goat* won the Tony Award for Best Play—Albee's first since *Virginia Woolf* four decades earlier.

Playwrights like Albee who began their New York careers after the mid-1950s did so without the safety net of live television drama programs to serve as outlets for their work. Howard Sackler, whose sole Broadway entry, *The Great White Hope* (1968), won a Tony and the Pulitzer Prize, financed the production by selling the screenplay in advance. Albee periodically taught playwriting at the University of Houston in the 1980s and 1990s and became a popular speaker on the reading/lecture circuit. Albert Ramsdell (A. R.) Gurney Jr., whose dramatic milieu is the rarity of well-to-do WASPs from business or academia, taught literature at MIT for over 20 years.

Gay playwrights have been well represented on New York stages—Tennessee Williams, Edward Albee, and Thornton Wilder among them. However, until the 1960s homosexuality as a subject could only be approached metaphorically or in code, and the closer one came to Broadway the more accurate was the designation of "The Love That Could Not Speak Its Name." Even writers like Lanford Wilson and **Terrence McNally**, who sometimes made their sexual preferences clear in their plays, achieved recognition on Broadway only after years in Off-Off and Off-Broadway. McNally shares a penchant for short plays with many writers who began Off-Off Broadway in the 1960s. However, McNally differs from his peers in that he *began* on Broadway—with an adaptation of Alexandre Dumas *fils'* *The Lady of the Camellias* (1963) commissioned by director Franco Zeffirelli when McNally was 23. This recognition paved the way for production of the already-written *And Things That Go Bump in the Night* (1964), about a philosophically murderous family. *The Ritz* (1975), Broadway's first visit to a gay bathhouse (where the protagonist hides out from the mob) ran for a year and was revived on Broadway in 2007. In the 1980s McNally entered into a mutually productive relationship with the Manhattan Theater Club, resulting in *Frankie and Johnny in the Clair de Lune* (which reached Broadway in 2002, five years after its Off-Broadway premiere), and numerous plays, especially on gay themes, that were well received Off-Broadway. Possessed of a keen interest in music, McNally's books for the musicals *Kiss of the Spider Woman* (1993) and *Ragtime* (1998) were Tony winners. *The Full Monty* (2001) was a Tony nominee as was *A Man of No Importance* (2003). McNally also contributed the book for the biographical revue *Chita Rivera: The Dancer's Life* (2005). Still active in his late 60s, McNally's much-publicized *Deuce* (2007), marking **Angela Lansbury**'s heralded return to Broadway after 24 years, met with moderate success.

Even if only half the stories about Sam Shepard's personal life were true, he would be right at home in one of his own plays. He has been a cowboy, a rock and roll drummer, a Pulitzer Prize–winning playwright, and an Academy Award–nominated film actor. Shepard himself grew up on a ranch in Duarte, California. He became enamored of Samuel Beckett's *Waiting For Godot* and quit college to act with a Christian touring troop. By 1964 he was writing plays for such iconic Off-Off and Off-Broadway venues as St. Mark's Church-in-the-Bowery, Café Cino, and La Mama, gaining national attention by the early 1970s. Shepard's 1992 induction into the Theatre Hall of Fame underscores the increasing divide between Broadway and contemporary American playwriting. Broadway has produced only two of his full-length works. Yet Shepard, more than any other playwright, is credited with reinvigorating American drama with a joyously shocking inventiveness and energy not in evidence since Albee erupted onto American stages in the early 1960s.

Women Playwrights

Lillian Hellman found Broadway success both before and after the war, and Lorraine Hansberry forever repositioned African Americans in American theater with *A Raisin in the Sun*. However, no American woman playwright has carved out a sustained Broadway career in the past 50 years even though women have written some of Broadway's most imaginative and compelling plays of that time. Ketti Frings, a screenwriter by profession, won the 1958 Pulitzer Prize for her dramatization of Thomas Wolfe's novel, *Look Homeward, Angel*. While her work appeared on Broadway five times, each play was an adaptation of original material by someone else and only *Look Homeward, Angel* was an unmitigated success. Margaret Edson, the author of the 1999 Pulitzer Prize winner, has even less claim to the title of professional playwright than does Frings. Edson's *Wit*, in which a literary scholar narrates the progress of the ovarian cancer from which she is dying and the parallel growth of her understanding of what it means to be human, was Edson's first and, thus far, only commercial play. By profession she is a kindergarten teacher. Ntozake Shange's *for colored girls who have considered suicide/when the rainbow is enuf* (1976) remains the longest-running Broadway play by a woman since World War II, but Shange has not had a Broadway production since.

Since *A Raisin in the Sun*, the 1980s have been most clearly associated with the success of women playwrights, with Pulitzer Prizes for Drama being awarded to Beth Henley's *Crimes of the Heart* (1981), **Marsha Norman**'s *'night, Mother* (1983), and Wendy Wasserstein's *The Heidi Chronicles* (1988), and Broadway audiences being introduced to works by Tina Howe and Emily Mann. Norman also found success as librettist for two hit musicals, *The Secret Garden* (1993) for which she won the Tony Award for Best Book of a Musical, and *The Color Purple* (2005).

Of the women who emerged in the 1980s, Wasserstein seems to have the most secure place in the annals of playwriting history. Wasserstein wrote over a dozen plays, three of which appeared on Broadway. Her breakthrough work, *Uncommon Women and Others* (1977), deriving from her undergraduate days at Mount

Holyoke College, created a new theater icon—the educated, successful young woman, capable and professional, but riddled with emotional self-doubt that she keeps at bay with stiletto wit. A Wasserstein plot is a stroll through contemporary pop culture exhibits of gender wars, family, politics, and ethnicity with a guide who is part anthropologist and part wiseacre. *Isn't It Romantic* (1979) reduces the dormitory of *Uncommon Women* to a pair of stereotyped roommates: Janie, a slightly frazzled, wisecracking Jewish would-be writer; and Harriet, an elegant, blonde, gentile would-be corporate maven. Both invest less effort in their professional futures than in trying to convince themselves that their current love interests are worth their efforts. *The Heidi Chronicles*, which in addition to the Pulitzer won the Tony Award for Best Play, records one woman's observations of and participation in the first quarter-century of the modern feminist movement (c. 1965–1990). The details of the social evolution through which we follow Heidi Holland may be the best popular history of the period yet produced. Wasserstein's next self-examination involved her Jewish ethnicity in *The Sisters Rosensweig* (1993) and had the largest nonmusical advance booking of any play in Broadway history. The play begins with three sisters gathering to celebrate a birthday (an evocation of the opening scene of Chekhov's *The Three Sisters*). Sara, who is turning 54, is a London-based executive of a Hong Kong bank. Her visiting sisters are Gorgeous (48), who hosts a radio advice show about to make the leap to cable television, and Pfenni (40), a globe-trotting political commentator turned travel writer. Whatever the Rosensweig sisters lack, it is *not* options. Wasserstein's final appearance on Broadway was with *An American Daughter* (1997), who appears to be one of those dynamic women the college students of *Uncommon Women and Others* promised themselves they were going to be. Lyssa Dent Hughes, an eminently successful doctor married to a prominent sociology professor, is on the brink of being named surgeon general of the United States—until it all unravels for reasons no follower of Wasserstein's work will find surprising: a right-wing media looking for a reason to block the appointment of a liberal, pro-choice, woman; a husband's feelings of emasculation in the shadow of a more accomplished wife; and a younger women who uses the ladder built by her feminist forbearers to rise high enough to stab them in the back. The most successful American woman playwright of her era, Wasserstein has also been the most attacked: for relying too much upon her comic abilities and, interestingly, by feminists for not being feminist enough. (The inability of her heroines to be unfulfilled without a man is invariably cited.) However, no one can fault her courage in facing her own prejudices.

Tina Howe began writing plays under the influence of the European Absurdists while a student in Paris in 1960. She has no degree in playwriting, having taught herself by making the production of her plays a condition of her employment as a high school drama teacher in Wisconsin and Maine. Nevertheless, she teaches playwriting at Hunter College and has written numerous, highly regarded plays for Off-Broadway. The successful *Coastal Disturbances* (1986), a Tony Award nominee and her only Broadway credit, is set on a New England beach in August next to a sea that is the source of life. Three generations of lovers are watched over by a "well-endowed" lifeguard (and we are reminded the genesis of a fourth is already present in the eggs of a seven-year-old girl). The artist wife of a couple with nine children and the range of experiences such a long relationship entails attempts to capture on canvas various scenes and goings-on around her, pondering for herself and the audience, "Why does everything have to keep moving?"

Beyond the 1980s

Emily Mann is probably more important as artistic director of Princeton's McCarter Theater Company than she is as a playwright. Five of her six Broadway credits have come since she took charge of the McCarter in 1990, and only one was for a play she had written herself. Nevertheless, Mann deserves recognition for her practice of the "Theater of Testimony," a form of documentary drama reminiscent of the Federal Theatre's Living Newspaper productions. Mann's method is to study a historical event, interview its participants, and portray that event onstage utilizing only the words of those participants. Her first Broadway play, *Execution of Justice* (1986), recreates the 1978 murder of San Francisco Mayor George Moscone and Harvey Milk—the same event upon which the 2008 Sean Penn film *Milk* was based. *Having Our Say: The Delany Sisters' First 100 Years* (1995) is Mann's least typical work and her most successful. Directed by Mann and adapted by her from the autobiography of Sarah and Elizabeth Delany, the play ran on Broadway for over 300 performances to glowing reviews. Mann structured the play around a domestic ritual—the preparation of a dinner (to which the audience is invited)—in celebration of the birthday of the sisters' father. But Sadie and Bessie Delaney are 103 and 101 years old, New York City's first woman high school teacher of color and its second black dentist, respectively. Their story is an American epic, stretching from Reconstruction in the South, through the two World Wars, the Harlem Renaissance, and the Civil and Women's Rights movements. Like most other active American women playwrights of the past 20 years, the aforementioned Suzan-Lori Parks made her reputation Off-Broadway and in experimental theater until *Topdog/Underdog* (2002) transferred to Broadway and won the Pulitzer Prize. Yet, for all the outstanding plays women have written since World War II, even into the twenty-first century authorship of a Broadway play by a woman remains a rare event and a sustained Broadway playwriting career remains virtually unheard of.

Richard G. Scharine

Further Reading

Abbotson, Susan C. W. *Arthur Miller: A Literary Reference to His Life and Work.* New York: Facts On File, Inc., 2007.

Castronovo, David. *Thornton Wilder.* New York: The Ungar Publishing Company, 1986.

Gelb, Arthur and Barbara. *O'Neill: Life with Monte Cristo.* New York: Applause Books, 2000.

Greenfield, Thomas Allen. *Work and the Work Ethic in American Drama, 1920–1970.* Columbia, MO: University of Missouri Press, 1982.

Harris, Andrew B. *Broadway Theatre.* London: Routledge, 1994.

Helburn, Theresa. *A Wayward Quest.* Boston: Little, Brown and Company, 1960.

Krassner, David. *A Companion to Twentieth-Century American Drama.* Malden, MA: Blackwell Publishing, 2005.

Mayorga, Magaret G. *A Short History of the American Drama.* New York: Dodd, Mead, and Company, 1932.

Meserve, Walter J. *An Outline History of American Drama.* New York: Feedback Theaterbooks & Prospero Press, 1994.

Murphy, Brenda. *The Cambridge Companion to American Women Playwrights.* Cambridge, U.K.: Cambridge University Press, 1999.

Nadel, Norman. *A Pictorial History of the Theatre Guild.* New York: Crown Publishers, Inc., 1969.

Poggi, Emil John. *Theatre in America: The Impact of Economic Forces 1870–1967.* Ithaca, NY: Cornell University Press, 1968.

Quinn, Arthur Hobson. *A History of the American Drama: From the Civil War to the Present Day.* New York: Appleton-Century Crofts, Inc., 1936.

Scharine, Richard G. *From Class to Caste in American Drama: Political and Social Themes Since the 1930s.* Westport, CT: Greenwood Press, 1991.

Sponberg, Arvid F. *Broadway Talks: What Professionals Think about Commercial Theater in America.* Westport, CT: Greenwood Press, 1991.

Wharton, John F. *Life among the Playwrights.* New York: Quadrangle/The New York Times Book Company, 1974.

PORGY AND BESS

Broadway Run: Alvin Theatre
Opening: October 10, 1935
Closing: January 25, 1936
Total Performances: 124
Composer: George Gershwin
Lyricists: Ira Gershwin and DuBose Heyward
Book: DuBose Heyward
Musical Director: Alexander Smallens
Director: Rouben Mamoulian
Producer: The Theatre Guild
Lead Performers: Anne Wiggins Brown (Bess), Todd Duncan (Porgy), John W. Bubbles (Sportin' Life), Ruby Elzy (Serena), Warren Coleman (Crown), and Georgette Harvey (Maria)

Porgy and Bess's position as a landmark Broadway show is a peculiar one. Although the production opened in 1935 to great anticipation, it failed to find its footing during its inaugural Broadway run, and each of its main creators—**George Gershwin**, **Ira Gershwin**, and DuBose Heyward—lost his full $5,000 investment. It seemed, initially, to fall through a crack: with its recitatives and operatic voices and orchestra, it was unlike any other contemporary Broadway **musical**, but with its jazzy, vernacular tunes, it did not resemble anything being presented in opera houses of the day. Audiences did not quite know what to make of this mixture of genres. In many ways, *Porgy and Bess* was simply ahead of its time. Today, more than 70 years after its premiere, it is evident that the show opened the door to new approaches on both the musical theater *and* operatic stages.

The début of *Porgy and Bess* was the result of multiple intertwined threads. Its libretto grew out of Heyward's **novel** *Porgy* (1925), which had been inspired by an eccentric southern character in Charleston, Heyward's hometown. The story focused on the handicapped Porgy, who shares his tenement home with the sultry Bess when she is down on her luck, and the two fall in love. They are separated when Porgy is questioned in connection with the murder of Bess's former lover. Bess is convinced that the police will not let Porgy return, so she leaves the tenement, Catfish Row. Heyward's wife, Dorothy, adapted the novel as a play, but gave the plot a more optimistic twist at the end: instead of letting Porgy simply despair over the loss of Bess (who, in the novel, had run off to Savannah with stevedores), Dorothy sent Bess to New York with a drug dealer, Sportin' Life, and let the play conclude with Porgy resolving to go after her. Dorothy's stage play was presented by the **Theatre Guild** in 1927 to much acclaim, and later her more hopeful ending was retained for Gershwin's musical version.

The music itself was a composite of multiple approaches. George Gershwin had been captivated by musical theater ever since hearing **Jerome Kern**'s music as a teenager, but he was also drawn to the exciting sounds of early jazz. Gershwin helped to popularize the blending of jazz with classical music (most famously in his symphonic work *Rhapsody in Blue* [1924]), but he also was one of the composers who helped bring jazz to the Broadway stage as well. Several of Gershwin's shows employed in the orchestra pit some of early jazz's most prominent names: Red Nichols, Benny Goodman, Glenn Miller, Gene Krupa, Jimmy Dorsey, Jack Teagarden, and others. Besides jazz, Gershwin also appreciated other traditional styles of **African American music**, such as spirituals and blues. Gershwin's eclectic taste embraced opera as well, and he had already created a blended form of blues, jazz, and classical music in *Blue Monday*, a one-act "Opera à la Afro-American" that opened on Broadway as part of *George White's Scandals of 1922*. Audiences expecting upbeat entertainment were baffled by this tragic tale sung by white actors in blackface. Producer White pulled *Blue Monday* after one performance, deciding it was too long and too depressing for the rest of the revue. Nevertheless, its mixture of jazz and operatic conventions served as a trial run for Gershwin before he tackled the far more ambitious *Porgy and Bess*.

Heyward had agreed to the musical adaptation of his novel as long as he was permitted to write the libretto; he also wanted to help Ira Gershwin with the lyrics. Compared to most musicals of the era, *Porgy and Bess* underwent a slow development. During the process, George Gershwin approached the Metropolitan Opera to discuss a production of the show. The Met was interested, but felt that they would have difficulty in filling the chorus with African Americans. They wanted to use blackface singers. Gershwin had felt that *Blue Monday*'s use of blackface performers had contributed significantly to its failure, so he refused to consider it. Moreover, his negotiations with the Theatre Guild for a Broadway production were more promising: tickets would be cheaper, and the Guild promised him a longer than usual rehearsal period.

Both drama and music critics attended the premiere of what the creators billed as a "folk opera." In general, the drama journalists were more favorably disposed to the production than the music critics, who condemned many of the operatic aspirations of *Porgy and Bess*. The recitatives came in for particular criticism, and the show closed in the red after 124 performances—an astounding run for an opera, but only a modest achievement for a musical (***Show Boat***, for instance, had closed six years earlier after 572 performances). In 1942, producer Cheryl Crawford revived *Porgy and Bess*, but only after making numerous changes; she reduced the orchestra and chorus and eliminated the recitatives altogether. Crawford's streamlined production set a Broadway record for a revival run. Her modifications clearly shifted the character of *Porgy and Bess* to that of a musical theater work.

The tide began changing soon afterward, however, pulling *Porgy and Bess* back toward the genre of opera. The State Department sent the show (with recitatives restored) on a four-year tour. This production was now billed as an opera, and it played in opera houses worldwide. It was at this point that *Porgy and Bess* was presented at La Scala in Milan, arguably the foremost opera house in the world. This was the first work by an American ever produced on this venerable stage. *Porgy and Bess* subsequently has been revived on Broadway multiple times, and it has enjoyed frequent operatic stagings. A 1985 Metropolitan Opera production celebrated the fiftieth anniversary of the show, and it reinserted every bit of music from the first version that it could find—including a large chunk of material that had been cut before the show premiered. The widely heralded Met production certainly helped cement the show as an American classic.

Porgy and Bess will most likely continue to spark debate between those who admire the rich lyricism of the operatic approach and those who prefer the crisper, faster-paced theatrical setting. However, its lasting influence is multifaceted: it proved that theatrical and operatic scoring could be blended successfully, thus preparing American ears for the sung-through approach of many musicals of the 1970s and 1980s (*Jesus Christ Superstar*, ***The Phantom of the Opera***, *Les Misérables*, *Miss Saigon*, and so forth). Even with jazz in its score, *Porgy and Bess* introduced the label "opera" to Broadway, paving the way for **Andrew Lloyd Webber** and Tim Rice to designate *their* rock-tinged *Jesus Christ Superstar* as a "rock opera." The first production of *Porgy and Bess* had social ramifications as well. As it toured after its Broadway run, the show visited lead actor Todd Duncan's (Porgy) hometown of Washington, D.C. Duncan knew that the city's National Theatre was segregated, and he declared that he would not perform in a venue that he himself could not freely attend. Anne Wiggins Brown (Bess) joined him in his boycott, and despite threats of enormous fines, Duncan was unwavering; he rejected several halfhearted compromises. At last, the theater manager relented and opened the entire house to patrons of any color. To his surprise, not a single white viewer requested a refund. The Civil Rights Act of 1964 lay far ahead, but the courage of the performers in *Porgy and Bess* was one victory in the long struggle toward racial equality, in and out of the world of theater.

Alyson McLamore

Further Reading

Alpert, Hollis. *The Life and Times of Porgy and Bess: The Story of an American Classic.* New York: Knopf, 1990.

Hutchisson, James M. *DuBose Heyward: A Charleston Gentleman and the World of Porgy and Bess.* Jackson, MS: University Press of Mississippi, 2000.

PORTER, COLE (1891–1964)
COMPOSER

Throughout his life, Cole (Albert) Porter offered friends and fans alike a personality as delightful, charming, and lasting as the songs he composed. Whether writing a Broadway **musical** with Moss Hart on a round-the-world junket, composing for Fred Astaire while living in the most exclusive Los Angeles neighborhoods, or hosting royalty with his wife in their Parisian home, Porter consistently served up two items: memorable songs and urbane wit.

Born in Peru, Indiana, Porter was the only child of a wealthy family. His upbringing included piano and violin lessons. When he was an adolescent, his mother sent him to attend Worcester Academy in Massachusetts, an exclusive, prestigious "prep school," where he graduated as class valedictorian. He went on to earn a degree from Yale University. Porter's inclination for composing began early and stood him in good stead; while he was at Yale, as a member of the glee club among other fraternities, he wrote various anthems, including football fight songs.

After a year at Harvard Law School, Porter transferred to their School of Music but never completed a graduate degree. Instead, he headed to New York to mount his first Broadway musical *See America First* (1916). Produced in some haste with undistinguished songs and an inexperienced cast, the show was a critical and commercial flop. After the collapse of the production, Porter claims to have been so desperate as to have joined the French foreign legion. This story seems to have been fabricated by Porter himself, although he did travel to France and does seem to have done some volunteer work delivering food and supplies in areas ravaged during World War I. Postwar Paris enabled Porter to hobnob with other American exiles, many of whom were intellectuals and artists. Here Porter met his future wife, the wealthy widow Linda Lee Thomas. Despite being a 27-year-old gay man, Porter seems to have been captivated by his wife's elegance, taste, and charm. Their marriage, which lasted 34 years until Linda's death in 1954, was filled with both difficulties and love. Early on the two lived as royalty, traveling first class throughout Europe and northern Africa; their luxuries were funded, at least initially, by Linda's fortune. During the 1920s Porter wrote show tunes, which he shared with guests at the many soirees that the couple hosted. While several of his songs were performed in revues, Porter was hardly living the life of a professional composer.

Songwriter Cole Porter is shown circa 1910. (AP Photo)

Upon the couple's return to the United States in 1927, the composer also returned to the Great White Way. At the time, most musical comedies took the form of revues rather than stories with carefully crafted plots with music and dance integrated into the storytelling. The revue format characterized his early shows *Paris* (1928) and *Fifty Million Frenchmen* (1929). Neither show proved lasting but each offered several songs that became part of the Great American Songbook, including: "Let's Do It (Let's Fall In Love)" and "You Do Something to Me." The 1930s proved to be the decade of Porter. His first major show, *The Gay Divorce* (1932), starred Fred Astaire. The production featured one of Porter's biggest hits "Night and Day" and would eventually be adapted to film (1934). Porter next wrote one of his smash success musicals, *Anything Goes* (1934), starring **Ethel Merman** and featuring the songs "Blow Gabriel Blow," "You're the Top," and "I Get a Kick Out of You."

Working on his next show, *Jubilee* (1935), composed on a world cruise, Porter incorporated sounds of the places he visited into his songs, most notably "Begin the Beguine," which was one of Porter's personal favorites. The show reunited Porter with Merman who shared the marquis with Jimmy Durante. Porter followed this with *Red Hot and Blue* (1936), which featured numerous hits including "It's De-Lovely." It was at this time that Porter received a contract from MGM Studios in Hollywood to write scores for movies. His first film score *Born to Dance* (1936) starred Astaire and Eleanor Powell.

While the early and middle 1930s represented professional triumphs for Porter, personal agonies came later in the decade. While visiting friends on Long Island, Porter had both legs crushed by a horse during a riding accident. The rest of his life would be deeply affected by reconstructive surgeries, painkillers, caretakers, and ultimately amputation of one leg. Nevertheless, he ultimately returned to a productive professional life, including composing music for MGM's *Broadway Melody of 1940* as well as the Broadway hit *Du Barry Was a Lady* (1939). *Du Barry* produced the popular song "Friendship," featuring Porter's trademark jarringly clever use of rhymes within a single lyrical line ("friendship . . . perfect blendship," "cook your goose . . . turn me loose").

Porter returned to Hollywood to complete *The Pirate* (1947), starring Gene Kelly and Judy Garland. He followed this film with another Broadway offering, perhaps his greatest success, the Tony Award–winning *Kiss Me Kate*, with such hits as "I Hate Men," "Brush Up Your Shakespeare," and "Too Darn Hot." Despite professional success, in the late 1940s and 1950s Porter lived with unremitting physical pain. More painful still was the steady decline in the health of his wife combined with the sudden death of his mother. Although he continued to write popular shows like *Can Can* (1953), which contained the hit song "I Love Paris" and also made a Broadway star of heretofore unknown chorus dancer **Gwen Verdon**, Porter sunk into a deep depression. *Silk Stockings* (1955) was Porter's last original Broadway show. *Silk Stockings* did not contain one of Porter's most memorable scores but it produced the future Frank Sinatra hit "All of You." Moreover, on the basis of star power (Porter's own and that of 46-year-old film star Don Ameche making his Broadway musical theater debut in the lead role), *Silk Stockings* ran for a very respectable 400-plus performances over the course of 14 months.

The chronic pain and physical problems associated with the riding accident ultimately culminated with Porter's leg being amputated, leaving him in great distress and in need of constant, humiliating physical care.

The last years of Porter's life were less than glamorous, requiring lengthy hospital stays. But that is not the Porter who remains in the popular imagination. Rather, his lasting image is that of the sophisticated wordsmith who, while reveling in his success and celebrity, wrote an amazing variety of memorable tunes and lyrics as well as successful Broadway shows and Hollywood film scores.

Porter's life has been the subject of two Hollywood films. In 1946 Jack Warner produced *Night and Day* with Cary Grant as Porter. The film had little relationship to Porter's actual life beyond the songs. His life has again provided material for a recent Hollywood feature film *De-Lovely* (2004) starring Kevin Kline, which delved into considerable detail about Porter's personal life—including his living fairly openly within the gay/lesbian subcultures on both coasts for most of his adult life.

Porter died in 1964 in Santa Monica, California.

Felicia J. Ruff

Further Reading

Furia, Philip. *The Poets of Tin Pan Alley: A History of America's Great Lyricists*. New York: Oxford University Press, 1990.

McBrien, William. *Cole Porter: A Biography*. New York: Alfred A. Knopf, 1998.

PRINCE, HAROLD (1928–)
DIRECTOR, PRODUCER

Harold "Hal" Smith Prince has been a dominating force on Broadway since 1954 when, at age 26, he produced his first Broadway show, *The Pajama Game*—a hit that earned him the first of his record 21 Tony Awards. From 1954 to 2007 at least one Hal Prince–produced or directed show was playing on Broadway in every calendar year (except 1986). Succeeding with traditional **musicals**, innovative musicals, and straight plays, Prince was the most versatile, innovative, and astonishing Broadway **producer**/director of the last half of the twentieth century.

Born and raised in New York City and drawn to theater from his youth, Prince began his career rather inauspiciously in 1948 as an office assistant for Broadway producer **George Abbott**—working for no salary. Impressing Abbot and his staff early on, and shortly thereafter drawing a salary, Prince remained with Abbott for several years, making connections among the leading lights of Broadway and learning creative and technical intricacies of commercial theater production. He was to become a master of both.

One of the most important contacts Prince made while working for Abbott was with Abbott's stage manager Bobby Griffith, with whom Prince formed a producing partnership. After reading Richard Bissell's **novel** *7 ½ Cents* about a strike in a pajama factory, Prince and Griffith obtained the rights to the book. They set about adapting the novel to a full-scale Broadway musical and persuaded Abbott to direct it, becoming their boss's boss. *The Pajama Game* ran for over 1,000 performances, received rave reviews, and won three Tony Awards including Best Musical. *The Pajama Game* also marked the Broadway choreographing debut of a then obscure young dancer named **Bob Fosse**, who won the Tony for his choreography and became an overnight sensation in his own right.

Prince and Griffith flourished in their collaborations after *The Pajama Game* with a string of musicals that included three major hits: *Damn Yankees* (1955), **West Side Story** (1957), and *Fiorello* (1960). After Griffith's death in 1961 Prince continued to produce shows on his own, finding success the following year with *A Funny Thing Happened on the Way to the Forum*. Prince also tried to hire himself out to other producers as a director. However, after an inauspicious directorial debut (1962's short-lived *A Family Affair*, with music by a not-yet-established **John Kander**), he went back to producing shows—occasionally hiring himself as director. The producing/directing "team" of Hal Prince and Hal Prince started with the moderately successful *She Loves Me* (1963), which is best remembered as one of the stronger scores by the young composer/lyricist team of Jerry Bock and Sheldon Harnick as well the most successful role in journeyman actor/singer Jack Cassidy's career. In 1964 Prince as producer reteamed with Bock and Harnick on the enormous hit, *Fiddler on the Roof*, which ran for eight years and generated several popular songs, including the enduring anthem "Sunrise Sunset." As producer/director, Prince flopped in 1966 with *It's a Bird . . . It's a Plane . . . It's Superman* but later that year made theatrical history as producer and director of *Cabaret*.

Cabaret was a breakthrough musical, expanding the genre's limits in both style and subject. As a backdrop for romance, the rise of the Nazis in Germany from obnoxious street punks to empowered hate mongers, *Cabaret* presented a severe test for musical audiences weaned on the likes of **My Fair Lady** (1956) and *The Sound of Music* (1959) to say nothing of *Fiddler on the Roof*. John Kander and **Fred Ebb**'s musical numbers, instead of just serving character development and dialogue, were used as transitions between realistic scenes, distancing the audience from the characters and underscoring the show's dark themes and foreboding tone. Prince also introduced onstage observers—cast or crew members who would linger conspicuously during scenes and scene changes, disrupting the audience's suspension of disbelief. The entire sensibility of the production was reminiscent of German iconoclast Bertolt Brecht's plays and was decidedly different from the sentimental heart-tugging, lighthearted wit, or uplifting energy to which musical theater audiences had long been accustomed. The original production of *Cabaret* ran for three years. In countless revivals and restagings around the country *Cabaret* "holds up" better than just about any other musical of that decade.

Prince did not produce or direct another major hit until 1970. Working again with **Stephen Sondheim**, the lyricist for *West Side Story*, he produced and directed the musical **Company**. Based on a collection of one-act plays by playwright George Furth, the musical that Prince and Sondheim developed generated something of a revolution in the modern musical. Episodic in form, the show had no clear story line, which, since the heyday of the **Rodgers and Hammerstein** "book musical," had been a *sine qua non* for American musicals. This staged anthology of several characters' relationships in Manhattan helped establish what is often referred to as the "concept musical," in which a controlling idea rather than a linear plot involving one or two main characters centers the play. Sondheim and Prince worked together throughout the 1970s, creating a number of other memorable musicals, including *Follies* (1971), codirected by Prince and choreographer-turned-director **Michael Bennett**; *A Little Night Music* (1973), which featured "Send in the Clowns," one of the biggest hit **show tunes** of the decade; *Pacific Overtures* (1976); and *Sweeney Todd: The Demon Barber of Fleet Street* (1979), which won eight Tony Awards including Best Musical and Best Director. During this same period he also directed **Andrew Lloyd Webber** and Tim Rice's *Evita* (1979), which dominated the 1980 Tonys and ran for almost four years.

Most of the 1980s represented a relatively unsuccessful period for Prince. After *Evita*, he had an eight-year stretch of directing and/or producing unsuccessful original shows, fueling industry and press speculation that the nearly 60-year-old Prince was past his prime. However, in a reversal of fortune worthy of its own staging, Prince directed both the London and Broadway productions of Lloyd Webber's ***The Phantom of the Opera***. *Phantom* opened in Broadway's Majestic Theatre in 1988, having enjoyed a rousing reception in London for the previous two years. The response to *Phantom*, the most successful single show in Broadway history (as well as that of the other two leading English-language theater districts, London and Toronto), was unprecedented to the point of shocking. It is credited with single-handedly accelerating **tourism** in New York City throughout the 1990s and turning the "Broadway" musical (despite its London origins) into an international marketing phenomenon. *Phantom*'s success has become the subject for countless international news stories, academic curriculum, comedy routines, and two generations of Halloween costumes. *Phantom* celebrated its twentieth anniversary at the Majestic Theatre in January 2008, having passed the mind-boggling 8,000 performance mark the year before. It also erased permanently any lingering doubts that Prince was the premiere musical theater director of his era.

In the 1990s and 2000s, Prince pulled back somewhat on his production pace although Broadway revivals of his shows have been plentiful. He still occasionally produces and/or directs new work. His most successful shows post-*Phantom* were *Kiss of the Spider Woman* (1993) and a 1994 revival he directed of the **Jerome Kern**–Oscar Hammerstein II classic ***Show Boat*** (1927). The *Show Boat* revival received strong critical praise, earned Prince a Tony for Best Director of a Musical, and ran for three years. A musical drama, *Lovemusik* (2007), Prince's most recent original Broadway show, which he directed at age 79, received a Tony nomination for its brief run. He suffered a mild stroke in early 2008 but appears to have made a full recovery. Even at 80, Prince was dismissing thoughts of retiring, while conceding that the breakneck a-show-a-year pace he maintained for decades is no longer feasible.

Prince once famously claimed that the purpose of theater is to "astonish" an audience, and no one in modern Broadway history did it in grander style or with greater frequency.

Thomas A. Greenfield and Sarah Provencal

Further Reading

Hirsch, Foster. *Harold Prince and the American Musical Theatre*. Cambridge, England: Cambridge University Press, 1989.

Ilson, Carol. *Hal Prince: A Director's Journey*. New York: Limelight Editions, 2004.

PRODUCERS

Until the latter half of the twentieth century, New York City was the unquestioned center of the American theater, and theatrical production was never anything other than *for-profit*. The theater producer's name was synonymous with the production itself. Producer's names on marquees of theaters—like **Florenz Ziegfeld** or the **Shubert Brothers**—were as important to the success of a show, if not more so, than **critics**' reviews. In the 1940s, 1950s, and 1960s, impresarios like **David Merrick** and Alexander H. Cohen would capably fill the impressive showmaster shoes of those who had gone before them. These producers were entrepreneurs more than storytellers, and their names shared the marquees (and often ownership of the theaters) alongside their productions. Long before general managers and lawyers would shoulder the responsibilities of managing shows and running theatrical production companies these show people did it all. New plays, revivals, and **musicals** originated in New York, on or off Broadway, and then went on the road to the rest of the country—and the world. Eventually, labor unions would stifle the renegade *modus operandi* often exhibited by big producers—which often included paying exploitatively low wages and setting unreasonable work demands of cast and crew. Furthermore, the exponentially rising cost of theatrical production over the ensuing decades would spread both the financial responsibility and control of theatrical production beyond the ability of virtually any individual producer to dominate it in the manner that had characterized Ziegfeld's or the Shuberts' peak years.

As theater-producing organizations grew throughout the first 25 years of the twentieth century, so did organizations representing producers, especially as Actors' Equity Association (AEA, founded in 1913) gained negotiating and bargaining power over performers' working conditions and wages. The League of American Theaters and Producers (now The Broadway League), founded in 1930, came into being when Broadway theater operators came together to promote their common interests and negotiate collective bargaining agreements with theatrical unions and guilds. In subsequent years, the organization's mission expanded to include serving the various needs of theatrical producers in New York as well as producers of national touring shows and presenters of touring productions in cities throughout North America.

Broadway and Off-Broadway Production

The **Off-Broadway** theater movement grew simultaneously alongside Broadway. (Off-Broadway was originally designated as such because of the proximity of said productions to Broadway, but eventually, and logically, designated so because of the size of the theaters themselves.) In a parallel to early Broadway production, Off-Broadway was dominated and driven in the first half of the twentieth century by distinctive personalities (although not necessarily producers) such as the **Provincetown Players' Eugene O'Neill** and Edna St. Vincent Millay—many of whom would also become important figures in commercial Broadway drama. Throughout the 1940s, 1950s, and 1960s Off-Broadway theater became emblematic of antiauthoritarian political movements, rebellion, as well as peace movements and inspired unconventional, often poetic drama. Among the figures who came to prominence in this movement, the most notable were the Living Theatre founders Julian Beck and Judith Malina, who brought fame to their company and the Off-Broadway venues that housed them, such as the Actor's Playhouse and the Cherry Lane Theater.

The Commercial Theater Producer–Nonprofit Producer Relationship

In the first half of the twentieth century, **regional theater** (professional, semiprofessional, or earnest amateur theater productions located, at first, anywhere around the country but not in New York City) consisted largely of academic, community, dinner, and experimental theaters. Beyond road productions, large-scale professional theater was virtually nonexistent outside of New York City. In the 1960s that situation began to change markedly, and the relationship between commercial theater producers and nonprofit theaters that has since emerged profoundly and, by all indications, irreversibly changed American professional theater production. In New York and throughout the United States—with support from such venerated institutions as the Ford Foundation and the National Endowment for the Arts—regional theaters (now commonly called "resident theaters") established themselves in cities across America. The resident theater movement has flourished and grown steadily ever since. Much of the credit for its success is attributed to a theater publicist, Danny Newman, who in the 1960s revolutionized the concept of season-subscription marketing. Subscription marketing (the process by which a theater annually sells ticket packages for an entire season or multiple productions within a season) has since become the backbone of resident theater economics. The resident theater company movement has grown to over 500 theaters that annually produce hundreds of plays, employ thousands of professionals, and serve an audience in the millions (Schulfer 2007, 117).

In addition to adapting shrewd marketing strategies, residential theaters also prospered artistically as previously many New York–based theater professionals moved to more economically friendly communities around the country. As theater artists moved around the country so did the solicitation of investment capital by savvy New York theater entrepreneurs. The production that launched the new trend toward commercial theater producer and nonprofit theater collaboration was Howard Sackler's play *The Great White Hope* (1968), which had been developed and premiered by the Arena Stage in Washington, D.C., as part of its 1967–1968 regular season. Under the leadership of its artistic director, Zelda Fichandler, Arena Stage clearly demonstrated that the artistic quality of a first-rate nonprofit theater could compete with that of a Broadway production. Upon its transfer to New York, *The Great White Hope* garnered Tony Awards for Best Play, Best Actor in a Play (**James Earl Jones**), and Best Actress in a Supporting Role (Jane Alexander), in addition to the 1969 Pulitzer Prize for Drama for **playwright** Sackler.

The 15-month run of the play constituted a commercial as well as an artistic success. However, as the play's run occurred at the very beginning of the collaborative relationship between for-profit and nonprofit theaters, the Arena Stage did not have a contract with the playwright, which specified recognition for Arena's role in the play's development (i.e., "originally produced at Arena Stage"), nor any financial participation in the future of the production created at their venue. Such contract components are now common in agreements among writers of new works, nonprofit theaters, and Broadway producers. In 1975 the musical *A Chorus Line* transferred from Off-Broadway at New York's Public Theater to Broadway's Shubert Theatre under terms decidedly more favorable to the originating company, famously glutting the Public's coffers with more than $25 million. Since then many nonprofits continue to provide, or at least attempt to provide, similar contractual agreements with authors. (While *A Chorus Line* did, in fact, transfer to Broadway with more billing, acknowledgments and other considerations for the show's original creators than had *A Great White Hope*, the legal battle over royalties to the performers who had originated *A Chorus Line's* characters and, by extension, much of the story line, was not completely resolved until decades after the Broadway opening.) Commercial-nonprofit resident theater collaborations rapidly expanded throughout the 1970s and 1980s as producers shopped new productions to resident theaters and looked for possible transfers to Broadway. For commercial producers, these collaborations meant reduced risk and the potential for increased profits. For resident theaters, working with commercial producers provided high-profile productions and revenue from royalties or "enhancement money"—the initial financing provided by a commercial producer to augment the budget of the resident theater (Schulfur 2007, 117).

Over time, such partnerships and arrangements between commercial producers and resident theaters created a seismic shift in American theater. By the mid-1990s, the majority of Broadway productions had their origins in nonprofit theaters. Whereas Broadway productions used to originate out of town merely as a pretext to moving to Broadway (such as in New Haven, Philadelphia, or Boston), the traditional pattern was now reversed—productions came from resident theaters to Broadway and then went out on the road after their New York run. Broadway was largely transformed into a showcase for work that had originated elsewhere, save for productions mounted by monoliths like **Disney Theatrical Productions** that could afford the risk of opening directly on Broadway. Furthermore, nonprofit theaters fostered the emergence of many new playwrights who were able to establish themselves professionally in advance of landing Broadway productions of their plays.

Today, many plays developed by nonprofits have commercial producers attached to them at the very outset. These commercial producers find it far less risky to develop a property in the relative safety of the nonprofit world. They have, in most cases, already acquired commercial stage rights from the author as part of the original production contract. The commercial producers then temporarily waive their exclusive stage rights for the purposes of allowing the nonprofit to premiere the play. For reasons relating to the nonprofit status of the theater company, the commercial theater producer cannot be the producer of, or exert control over, the nonprofit production. However, the commercial producer can and does enhance the nonprofit production financially (Baruch 2007, 280).

9/11 and Beyond

On Thursday, September 13, 2001—two days after the attack on New York's World Trade Center "Twin Towers"—nearly 100 producers, theater owners, general managers, and union leaders gathered at the offices of the League of American Theaters and Producers to talk about the future of the theater in New York, with implications, by extension, for the rest of the country. Their concerns were well founded. The season that concurred with 9/11 saw Broadway's gross decrease by $22 million, marking the first decrease in over ten years. Of particular concern was the sizable reduction in theater attendance from overseas tourists—a critical and growing market for Broadway since the 1990s. However, the basic financial structures and enduring appeal of Broadway held firm. Through the city's and New York state's aggressive promotion of New York's splendors and a gradual easing of anxieties nationwide, New York's tourist industry, and Broadway in particular, recovered and even prospered. Interestingly, the post-9/11 era ushered in a new trend in ticket sales. Specifically, after 9/11 theatergoers began buying theater tickets on the spur of the moment (rather than months in advance) in greater numbers than ever before. Broadway producers and theater managers quickly adjusted their marketing and publicity strategies to meet this trend, and by June 2005 Broadway was exceeding almost every 2001 economic benchmark by a clear margin (Bernstein 2007, 3).

Although much in the post-9/11 Broadway production environment is different than it was beforehand, many basic elements of earlier years remain the same. The **Shubert Organization**, **The Nederlander Organization**, and Jujamcyn Theaters are today, as they have been for several decades (and, in the case of the Shubert Organization, over a century), the largest theater owners on Broadway. The economics and production logistics still trend against "old style" one-person productions. (Companies such as Shubert, Nederlander, and Jujamcyn now routinely put together an entire team to produce a single show, including a general manager, an advertising and/or marketing firm, and a theatrical attorney.) The theatrical producer mainly occupies his or her time raising money—now more than ever a full-time job. Some producing organizations limit individual investments to $10,000 in order to limit liability, but others have no such limitations and will accumulate as many or as few investors as is necessary to meet their production budgets.

Since 2001 the nonprofit-commercial theater relationship has continued to grow exponentially and the production process is decidedly more complex than ever. Although complicated by monoliths such as Disney and Clear Channel, ultimately, theater's newest producers/innovators are the product of a more collaborative, *laissez-faire* network, all in it together to be sure prior to 9/11, and now even more so. The post-9/11 New York theater landscape has seen insurance and theater rental costs skyrocket beyond the ability of most producers, including many sizable organizations, to capitalize them. Generally today's Broadway shows require funding at over $2 million for a relatively small show and up to $20 million for a large spectacular production. Moreover, theatrical production is widely regarded as being among the most undercapitalized industries in America. When a new Broadway show opens, it is the equivalent in another industry of a new product being introduced into the New York market and eventually regional markets throughout the country. The monies allocated to Broadway advertising agencies by producers are a fraction of those that are allocated for advertising in other industries to perform the same function. Nevertheless, operating with a fraction of the budget necessary to get the job done, Broadway agencies are expected to get the title of their latest shows on the lips of everybody in Manhattan in a very short period of time. Miraculously, they often succeed.

The commercial pressures of modern theater production give rise to the kinds of tensions between artistic quality and popular appeal that have dogged the popular arts throughout the twentieth century, and so it is with Broadway in the twenty-first century. The demands of the corporate bottom line often result in what is widely lamented as the homogenization of Broadway theater. The Broadway musical in particular is often faulted for having traded off artistic innovation for mass commercial appeal. Inasmuch as Broadway still sets the agenda and the standard for commercial theater in the United States, the trend in homogenization has extended beyond Broadway to touring companies and sit-down productions all over the country. Even out-of-town shows are produced increasingly by large corporations, offering entertainment sometimes via material recycled from other media, fare that has popular appeals to mass audience tastes and pocketbooks, effectively putting the squeeze on independently owned and operated theaters in New York and throughout the United States. Yet defenders of the current state of affairs are quick to note that, like all mass-marketed goods and services, corporate-produced theater benefits the "consumers" by providing them with a lower-cost product and giving the average American more opportunities to experience theater (artistic considerations aside) than ever before.

As Broadway approaches the second decade of the twenty-first century, the traditional romantic concept of the marquee name Broadway producer has long since given way to modern economic forces and cultural dynamics. Today Broadway productions are financed in a variety of ways: some by many individual investors, others through nonprofit-commercial collaborations, and some by a few angelic benefactors or corporate conglomerates—with no producers knowing exactly the magic formula to use for success. The increasingly growing international market —especially with countries like China becoming more open to world trade and modernization—has led to increased foreign investment in theatrical production, further tightening the competition for investment dollars in American commercial theater. Virtually all producers face increasing frustrations with the slow grind of rule changes at union labor houses and with harsh financial exigencies that can lead to highly controversial cost-cutting measures, such as replacing orchestras with digitally recorded music or hiring nonequity actors for large cast productions. Such cost-cutting and attendant financial pressures have led to a state of constant tension between the labor unions and commercial theater producers, which

FACT (THE FIRST AMERICAN CONGRESS OF THEATRE)

The First American Congress of Theatre ("FACT") of 1974 represented an unusual effort on the part of commercial and nonprofit theater producers, educators, and civic service organizations to resuscitate an ailing American theater industry. Broadway producer Alexander H. Cohen, convener of the four-day conference, warned that all professional theater worked under a "sword of Damocles," which attendees recognized in the combined form of declining revenues even for hit shows, a paucity of new high-quality plays and musicals, staggering production costs, and the deteriorating condition of the Times Square theater district, among other travails.

By the end of the Conference, some clear understandings and informal agreements emerged that would lead, directly or indirectly, to significant changes in American theater. Principal among them was the realization that the for-profit and nonprofit theater worlds could, by working together, achieve certain objectives that neither could achieve on its own.

In the years following FACT the heretofore largely disconnected worlds of commercial and nonprofit theater have forged many cooperative relationships in joint show production, revenue sharing, talent sharing, and cross-promotion, yielding results that have accrued to the benefit of both (see **Regional Theaters**). During this time, the American theater also developed an increased awareness of its need to promote itself as a distinct industry and cultural entity even as it promotes individual shows and companies. In addition, the New York theater community became deeply involved in the city's subsequent efforts to clean up and revitalize Times Square as a tourist and family-friendly attraction.

A Second American Congress of Theater ("ACT II") was convened in 2000 to explore the very relationship between for-profit and nonprofit theater that had evolved since FACT. What came out of ACT II was the sense among some theater professionals that the alliance required further refinement in order to better serve the interests of both commercial and nonprofit theater, but that the alliance was basically sound. However, others felt that the alliance had become a victim of its own success, having by its strength compromised the missions of both commercial and nonprofit theater. The critics' objections notwithstanding, the alliances between commercial and nonprofit that emerged during the original FACT meeting remain very much in force in today's theater.

sometimes boils over into full-blown labor disputes (as when a 19-day stagehands strike in 2007 closed most Broadway houses during the lucrative Thanksgiving vacation season). Inevitably, extra costs are passed along to the ticket buyers, who constitute the only block of participants in Broadway theater currently without union or organizational representation.

Still, Broadway, as all theater, is as unique a live entertainment experience as is to be garnered anywhere, and for all its faults and shortcomings, Broadway still holds its place as the most important theater district in the Western world. As long as there is economic growth in the United States and abroad capable of sustaining the steady flow of tourists and cash into New York City, there is sure to be a Broadway.

Ben Hodges

Further Reading

Baruch, Jason, Esq. "The Arranged Marriage Between Not-for-Profit Theater Companies and Commercial Producers." *The Commercial Theater Institute Guide to Producing Plays and Musicals*, ed. Frederic B. Vogel and Ben Hodges. New York: Applause Theater and Cinema Books, 2007.

Bernstein, Jed. "Forward." *The Commercial Theatre Institute Guide to Producing Plays and Musicals*, ed. Frederic B. Vogel and Ben Hodges. New York: Applause Theater and Cinema Books, 2007.

Conte, David M., and Stephen Langley. *Theater Management*. Hollywood, CA: Quite Specific Media Group Ltd., 2007.

Farber, Donald C. *From Option to Opening: A Guide to Producing Plays Off Broadway*. 5th ed. New York: Limelight Editions, 2005.

Farber, Donald C. *Producing Theater: A Comprehensive and Legal Business Guide*. 3rd ed. New York: Limelight Editions, 2006.

Langley, Stephen. *Producers on Producing*. New York: Drama Book Specialist, 1976.

Little, Stuart W. *After the FACT: Conflict and Consensus*. New York: Arno Press, 1975.

Newman, Danny. *Subscribe Now!: Building Arts Audiences Through Dynamic Subscription Promotion*. New York: Theater Communications Group, 1981.

Schulfer, Roche. "Commercial Producer–Resident Theater Collaborations." *The Commercial Theater Institute Guide to Producing Plays and Musicals*, ed. Frederic B. Vogel and Ben Hodges. New York: Applause Theater and Cinema Books, 2007.

Vogel, Frederic B., and Ben Hodges, eds. *The Commercial Theater Institute Guide to Producing Plays and Musicals*. New York: Applause Theater and Cinema Books, 2007.

THE PRODUCERS (THE MUSICAL)

Broadway Run: St. James Theatre
Opening: April 19, 2001
Closing: April 21, 2007
Total Performances: 2502
Composer: Mel Brooks
Lyricist: Mel Brooks
Book: Mel Brooks and Thomas Meehan
Director: Susan Stroman
Choreographer: Susan Stroman
Produced by Rocco Landesman, SFX Theatrical Group, The Frankel-Baruch-Viertel-Routh Group, Bob Weinstein, Harvey Weinstein, Rick Steiner, Robert F. X. Sillerman and Mel Brooks

Lead Performers: Matthew Broderick (Leo Bloom), Nathan Lane (Max Bialystock), Roger Bart (Carmen Ghia), Gary Beach (Roger De Bris), and Cady Huffman (Ulla)

The Producers came at the tail end of a 20-year period that was marked by fears on the part of Broadway traditionalists that the art of the musical comedy was either dying or dead. During the 1970s and 1980s two kinds of shows had come to dominate Broadway: the **European megamusical**, as represented by **Andrew Lloyd Webber**'s *The Phantom of the Opera* (1988), and the darkly serious concept musical, such as **Steven Sondheim**'s *Company* (1970). *The Producers*, with its emphasis on a straightforward if zany plot, large-scale dance production numbers, jokes, and a conventional romance, invoked the hit musical comedies of the earlier postwar years. Moreover, through its infamous "Springtime for Hitler" production number, *The Producers* resonated deeply with New Yorkers after the events of September 11, 2001, coming to represent the power of the American way of life against those who would destroy it. Its tremendous popularity with both the public and **critics**—the show earned a record 12 Tony Awards, including Best Musical—instigated a resurgence of nostalgic, comedic shows on Broadway stages.

The Producers started life in 1968 as writer and comic Mel Brooks's first feature **film**. Brooks had previously written for such **television** programs as *Your Show of Shows* and *Get Smart*. He enjoyed success in the 1960s performing stand-up comedy as the curiously Yiddish American "Two Thousand Year Old Man" with partner/straight man Carl Reiner. Brooks worked occasionally on Broadway during this time, contributing a sketch to the revue *New Faces of 1952*, cowriting the book for *Shinbone Alley* (1957) starring Eartha Kitt, and authoring the book for the Ray Bolger vehicle *All-American* (1962). But none of these early shows was popular with critics or audiences. After 1968 Brooks focused on making films; he would not return to Broadway for 40 years.

The 1968 film *The Producers* starred Gene Wilder as nebbish accountant Leo Bloom and Zero Mostel as the financially and morally bankrupt Broadway producer Max Bialystock. On stage, Matthew Broderick took the role of Bloom; **Nathan Lane** portrayed Bialystock. Broderick and Lane became so closely identified with their roles that replacement actors had a difficult time maintaining audience interest in the show over the course of its run. The two reprised their roles in 2005 for the film musical adaptation of *The Producers*, directed by **Susan Stroman**. The new film had a mixed reception, suffering from audience memories of the 1968 original film, odious comparisons with the stage musical on which it was based, and formidable box office competition from other holiday-season film releases including ***Rent*** (another adaptation of a hit Broadway **musical**), *Harry Potter and the Goblet of Fire*, and *Brokeback Mountain*.

Overall, the plot of the stage musical closely follows the 1968 film. Bialystock and Bloom come up with a scheme to produce the worst stage musical ever and work to persuade dozens of little old ladies to invest in the show, promising each of them 100 percent of the profits. According to their plan, when the show inevitably fails insurance will cover their losses, making Bialystock and Bloom rich

Nathan Lane (as Max Bialystock), left, and Matthew Broderick (as Leo Bloom) take a curtain call at opening night of The Producers *at the St. James Theatre in April 2001. (AP Photo/Mark Lennihan)*

men. For their surefire flop musical, the pair selects the play *Springtime for Hitler*, written by a former Nazi to honor the fallen Fuehrer. To guarantee its failure, the pair hires the campy Roger De Bris (Gary Beach) to direct the show; on opening night De Bris steps in to play Adolf Hitler when the leading man suffers an accident. To everyone's surprise, *Springtime for Hitler* is taken to be a brilliant satire and is a smash hit, leaving the despondent Bialystock and Bloom unable to pay off their investors. The two are accordingly convicted of fraud and sent to jail, where they proceed to hone their skills in producing musicals with their fellow inmates. In *The Producers'* final moments, Bialystock and Bloom are released from prison and are last seen producing a string of new hit shows.

Brooks made a few changes in adapting the show from screen to stage. Most notably, he added a romance between Bloom and his secretary, the Norwegian blonde bombshell Ulla Swanson (Cady Huffman). Much of the humor from the 33-year-old film was dated so Brooks refreshed his musical with show business in-jokes and references to other musicals. Overall, the tone of *The Producers* the musical was more upbeat than the darkly comic film, emphasizing the "let's put on a show" nature of the story and ensuring a happy ending. Brooks constructed an idyllic view of Broadway musical history through a stream of references to Broadway's past and to Jewish influences on Broadway in particular. The show explicitly places Jews at the center of what makes Broadway work and, thus, is sometimes viewed as an implicit protest against the European megamusical that had flooded Broadway stages in recent decades. Simultaneously a spoof and a highly successful example of traditional "book" musicals, *The Producers* spawned a Broadway resurgence of such shows including *Thoroughly Modern Millie* (2002), *Hairspray* (2002), and *The Drowsy Chaperone* (2006).

As a musical comedy that focuses on the making of a Broadway musical, *The Producers* contains multiple large-scale production numbers. While these numbers often relate to the narrative action, multiple *Ziegfeld Follies*–like moments punctuate and interrupt the plot. These song-and-dance numbers eventually climax with the actual show-within-a-show, Bialystock and Bloom's *Springtime for Hitler*, at the end of Act I. The truncated version of this show that the audience sees comprises a series of set pieces, as when Teutonic women descend a staircase in scanty costumes that represent various aspects of Germany (pretzels decorate the breasts of one chorus girl). These pieces culminate in the Bugsy Berkeley–inspired title number, "Springtime for Hitler," featuring a kickline of chorines in swastika formation. This moment is pure spectacle. It is horrible and horribly funny, and entirely in keeping with what the audience has already witnessed throughout the course of the show. But because Brooks and director/choreographer Stroman frame Hitler and his chorus girls in terms of **vaudeville** and innocuous 1920s musical comedies, the Third Reich is ultimately rendered harmless and pathetic.

At the end of *The Producers*, Bialystock and Bloom walk off into a painted sunset together, singing of their final triumph. Although jailed for fraud, the pair— lovable scoundrels to the end—flourish in jail and become top producers, writing Jews back onto the Broadway stage through such (faux) musicals as *Katz* and *South Passaic*. British megamusicals are deflated, serious concept musicals are ridiculed, and integrated musicals are turned into musical comedies, emphatically reestablishing the traditional American musical comedy as a force on the Broadway stage.

Kathryn Edney

Further Reading

Denman, Jeffrey. *A Year with the Producers: One Actor's Exhausting (but Worth It) Journey from CATS to Mel Brooks' Mega-hit.* New York: Routledge, 2002.

Parish, James Robert. *It's Good to Be the King: The Seriously Funny Life of Mel Brooks.* Hoboken, NJ: John Wiley and Sons, 2008.

PROVINCETOWN PLAYERS
THEATRICAL COLLECTIVE, PRODUCERS

The Provincetown Players was founded in 1915 by wife-and-husband playwrights **Susan Glaspell** and George Cram "Jig" Cook in an effort to develop artistically adventurous and socially conscious dramas for the American stage. Like other "little theater" groups in the New York area, such as the **Neighborhood Playhouse** and the Washington Square Players, the Provincetown Players experimented with naturalism, expressionism, and other late nineteenth-century European theatrical innovations in the hope of counterbalancing the predominance of melodrama and sentimental comedy in New York's commercial theater of the day. During their peak years in the early to mid-1920s, the Players nurtured two of America's first and most important modern **playwrights**, **Eugene O'Neill** and Glaspell, and established a permanent if fragile place on Broadway for innovative theater and literary American playwriting.

Before the advent of the Provincetown Players and the Little Theater Movement, Broadway plays were dominated by imported European productions and (American derivations thereof) as well as heavy use of touring ex-patriot European actors. This was especially true of nonmusical or straight drama productions. American theater **producers** used star power, a common promotion technique even then, in the form of employing European name actors to headline plays in New York. At the same time, talented American actors and playwrights sometimes had difficulty breaking into early legitimate theater and were often forced into less prestigious theatrical fields, such as burlesque or **vaudeville**, if not forced out of theater altogether.

In the 1910s, small (hence "little") theater groups began to crop up in response to the intractability of the commercial theater industry, especially in the New York area but in other cities as well. The movement reflected a growing awareness among American theater artists of the recent intellectual and artistic developments in Europe such as surrealism, naturalism, and the incorporation of new theories of psychology into artistic expression. The little theaters sought to rid themselves of old dramatic modes and find uniquely American ways to save what they took to be an unenlightened, derivative theater controlled by commercial titans, especially the **Shubert Brothers**. The Provincetown Players in particular attempted to create audiences for new American playwrights, designers, actors, and directors.

In the summer of 1915 Glaspell and Cook gathered for this purpose a group of like-minded writers, intellectuals, and artists in Provincetown, Massachusetts. Artistic considerations were paramount to the group, as they wrote, produced, and acted in their own plays using new experimental techniques and theatrical forms. Financially viable at the outset, the Players sustained themselves by staging stripped down, inexpensive productions (disdain for the ornate costumes and sets of commercial Broadway plays was one of their articles of faith). Their first productions, which included Eugene O'Neill's *Bound East for Cardiff*, were mounted in Provincetown and the surrounding area. In 1916, however, the group moved to Greenwich Village in New York City, struggling occasionally but becoming by the end of the 1910s a well-respected, established, if small, theater company.

Central to Glaspell and the Players' vision, however, was taking their innovative plays and productions to mainstream Broadway audiences, and by 1920 they began to do so. Owing in part to Cook's efforts, they were able to mount plays in some of Broadway's smaller theaters as well as their own venue, the Provincetown Theatre in Greenwich Village. Their first recognized commercial Broadway production was O'Neill's expressionistic drama *The Emperor Jones* (1920), which received enthusiastic reviews and ran for over 200 performances. In addition to being an early success for O'Neill, *The Emperor Jones* had the distinction of being the first Broadway drama to star an African American actor, **Charles S. Gilpin**.

O'Neill wrote other important works for the Provincetown Players, including *The Hairy Ape* (1922) and *Desire Under the Elms* (1924). Glaspell, who devoted much of her time in the 1920s to management of the group, also wrote *The Verge* (1921) and *Chains of Dew* (1922) for the Players. By the early 1920s, the Players had gained the respect of New York's leading intellectuals and produced plays by such notable authors as essayist Edmund Wilson and novelist Theodore Dreiser.

Success and public acceptance eventually led to irresolvable conflicts within the group as did the formidable financial demands of running a theater company with a modest if loyal following. Various organizational reconfigurations of the group failed throughout the decade, leading to its collapse in 1929. However, by that time the Players had accomplished their basic mission of launching the careers of new important American writers and staking a claim for bold artistic innovation in the hostile territory of New York's commercial theater.

Thomas A. Greenfield

Further Reading

Kenton, Edna, Travis Bogard, and Jackson R. Bryer. *The Provincetown Players and the Playwrights' Theatre, 1915–1922*. Jefferson, NC: McFarland & Co., Inc., 2004.

Murphy, Brenda. *The Provincetown Players and the Culture of Modernity*. Cambridge, England: Cambridge University Press, 2005.

PUPPETRY

From **vaudeville** marionettes to the recent explosion of the art form, puppetry has had a significant impact on the evolution of theater in America including commercial Broadway. There have been over 80 Broadway productions involving puppets and many significant puppet productions staged **Off-Broadway**, in Lincoln Center, and elsewhere in midtown New York. Often overlooked in reviews, credits, and playbills—even in shows where it makes a conspicuous contribution to the production—puppetry remains one of the least explored and least understood aspects of American theater history and culture.

Historical Overview

Puppetry in America evolved from the theatrical traditions of other countries. During the eighteenth century street puppet theaters performed classical plays and Punch and Judy shows, which have their roots in European puppetry dating back centuries. In the nineteenth century American puppet and marionette artists appeared frequently in theaters and private parlors. In the latter half of the century puppetry gained widespread popularity with the growth of vaudeville and music hall theater. Marionette sketches and ventriloquist acts proved to be audience-pleasing, inexpensive additions to producers' music hall revues and touring variety shows, especially for shows aimed at family audiences. For their part, puppeteers fortunate enough to land a vaudeville or music hall engagement gained measures of security, income, and fame that were heretofore unavailable to them as street or parlor performers.

Until recently ventriloquism has generally played a lesser role than other forms of puppetry on the Broadway stage, despite its popularity in vaudeville. The style of ventriloquism still common today began with the most famous ventriloquist of the early vaudeville era, Harry "The Great" Lester. Lester transformed the medium, which had previously relied upon the puppeteer physically distracting the audience with props, sets, and stage busyness to keep them from watching his ever-moving lips. Lester, however, performed simply, sitting on a chair on an empty stage with one figure on his knee. Significantly, he minimized detectable lip movement to the point of virtually eliminating it from his performance. Ventriloquism in Lester's style remained popular for decades even on the radio in the 1930s and 1940s with the talents of Edgar Bergen, Lester's most famous and successful student. Bergen's success came from his delivery, his wordplay, and his well-developed characters. In the 1950s and early 1960s Paul Winchell, a childhood fan of Bergen's radio shows, continued the tradition as a popular children's **television** star. Jay Johnson became the next major television celebrity ventriloquist on the 1970s sitcom *Soap*. (In 2006 Johnson made a breakthrough on Broadway with his one-actor autobiographical show, *The Two and Only*, garnering rave reviews and a Tony Award for Best Special Theatrical Event.)

Stage Pioneers

Although best known to most Americans as old time radio, television, and comedy club novelty entertainment, puppetry and ventriloquism's legitimate theater roots date back to the early 1900s. Tony Sarg, a highly inventive, sophisticated marionette artist, was among the first to lead Americans to appreciate marionette performances as serious theater art. In 1919 he staged an all-marionette adaptation of English novelist William Makepeace Thackeray's *The Rose and The Ring* in Broadway's Punch and Judy Theatre on 49th Street. The show's three marionette pieces allowed Sarg, the sole puppeteer, to explore what were for most theatergoers of the time new elaborate theatrical approaches to puppetry. (In 1927 Sarg made an altogether different contribution to New York theatrics and culture, if not specifically Broadway, by introducing larger than life gas-filled puppets to the Macy's Thanksgiving Day Parade.)

Puppetry pioneer Remo Bufano's first Broadway marionette production, *Puppets*, opened in 1925. Bufano went on to create puppets for *Last Night of Don Juan* (1925), *El Retablo de Maese Pedro* (1928), and **Eve Le Gallienne**'s *Alice in Wonderland* (1932, and revival 1946). Among his more memorable creations was a 35-foot elephant puppet for **Richard Rodgers** and **Lorenz Hart**'s *Jumbo* (1935) and the famous dinosaur (whom he also played on stage) in **Thornton**

Wilder's Pulitzer Prize–winning play *The Skin of Our Teeth* (1942). Off-Broadway he received accolades for his nine-foot puppets for Edmond Jones's *Oedipus Rex* (1931). He also directed the New York Marionette Division of the WPA's **Federal Theatre Project**, which resulted in not only new jobs for puppeteers but also increased awareness and popularity of puppet theater.

Bil Baird, a protégé of Sarg's, added his talents to many Broadway productions in the 1930s and 1940s. His work was first seen on Broadway in the Federal Theatre's production *Dr. Faustus* (1937), starring and directed by Orson Welles. Baird created some of the spirits who visited Dr. Faustus and received credit as the show's puppet designer. Baird and his puppets appeared in *Ziegfeld's Follies* of 1943. The most successful of the four *Follies* shows produced posthumously under **Florenz Ziegfeld**'s name, the show starred vaudeville colossus Milton Berle and ran for 550 performances. Baird also did work for the short-lived musical *Nellie Bly* (1946) and starred in the puppet-based musical *Davy Jones Locker* (1959). Baird's marionette Clyde was central to the satirical musical *Flahooley* (1951). For the puppet-based production *Man in the Moon* (1963) Baird not only created the puppets but also developed the show's central story. Except for a small contribution to the 1981 flop *Frankenstein* (it closed in one night), Baird's last Broadway show was the well-received Sherlock Holmes musical *Baker Street* (1965), in which his marionettes were the focus of one of the show's highlights, a grand parade scene. The most prominent woman puppeteer to garner Broadway credits in the first half of the twentieth century was marionettist Sue Hastings. Like many of the professional marionette artists who worked with major Broadway theaters and productions, Hastings tried to expand the art form so that it would be seen not just as a source of children's entertainment but also as a part of legitimate theater. Through her "company," Sue Hastings' Marionettes, she created puppets for the 1932 revival of a popular musical revue, *Americana*, and the successful Howard Deitz musical, *At Home Abroad* (1935). Her last Broadway production was her most successful, the Harold Arlen musical *Hooray for What!* (1937), which ran for a respectable 200 performances.

Puppets and Postwar Broadway

The birth of commercial television in the late 1940s and 1950s provided a boon for puppeteers, who found work in the new flourishing genre of children's television programming. Burr Tillstrom, creator of the puppet characters Kukla and Ollie for NBC's long-running hit *Kukla, Fran and Ollie*, is widely viewed as having been the best of the early television puppeteers. His program attracted a surprisingly large adult audience, drawn by Tillstrom's artistry and the overall inventiveness of the show. By the time the show's eight-year network run ended in 1957, Kukla and Ollie were major "celebrities" and Tillstrom was a highly respected member of New York's broadcasting and performing arts communities. In 1960 Tillstrom brought Kukla and Ollie "to Broadway," using a dining room in the Astor Hotel on 44th and Broadway that had been converted to a 200-seat theater for Tillstrom's show. *An Evening with Kukla, Burr and Ollie* offered a children's show for afternoon matinees and more sophisticated entertainment for adults in the evening. The show received rave reviews and developed a cult following for several weeks before interest died down. Tillstrom also performed briefly in *Side by Side by Sondheim* (1977), but his Astor Hotel show with Kukla and Ollie represents the apex of his Broadway career. Tom Tichenor developed something akin to Method Acting for puppets, believing that through puppets he could be anything, anybody, and act his heart out—all without being seen by the audience. Aspiring to make the audience believe as much as possible that his puppets were actually alive, he triumphed in the **Gower Champion**–directed hit *Carnival!* (1961); both the main character and the audience fell in love with Tichenor's hand puppets Carrot Top and Reynardo the Fox. The show, which ran for a hefty 719 performances over the course of two years and earned a Tony Nomination for Best Musical, represents a high point for Broadway puppetry during the 1960s.

The 1970s and 1980s were slow years for puppetry on the Broadway stage, although business was brisk on club and school stages, television, and movies. New programs on public television, including *Mr. Roger's Neighborhood* and *Sesame Street*, brought puppetry and the Muppets into the living rooms of 1980s "Generation Xers." Nevertheless, puppetry did maintain a presence on Broadway even during this relatively lean period A Bunraku (large-headed puppet from Japanese puppet theater) appeared in **Stephen Sondheim**'s *Pacific Overtures* (1976), and a large elephant puppet enhanced the circus setting of the hit musical *Barnum* (1980). New puppet artists were emerging and found some Broadway work as their careers developed. French puppeteer Philippe Genty brought abstract puppet forms manipulated by black velvet–clad performers in *Ahhh Oui Genty*, an imported puppet show produced by Paris troop Compagnie Philippe Genty. American ventriloquist Ronn Lucas lent his talents to *Sugar Babies: The Burlesque Musical* (1982).

A Rebirth of Puppetry on Broadway

Momentum shifted in the 1990s for puppetry in American theater. Barbara Pollitt created puppets and masks for two of the most successful and highly regarded productions of the early part of the decade: *Jelly's Last Jam* (1992) and *Angels in America: Perestroika* (1993). She also did mask and puppet design for British Shakespearean actor (and *Star Trek: The Next Generation* television star) Patrick Stewart's triumphant *The Tempest* in 1996. In 1994 the Famous People Players, a company of Canadian actors with special needs who use various mediums of puppetry in their productions, gave a well-received, limited-run performance of one of their shows, *A Little More Magic*. Shari Lewis, who had come to prominence in the 1960s with a successful children's television program featuring animal puppets Lamb Chop, Hush Puppy, and Charlie Horse, brought her television "cast" to Broadway in 1994. For *Lamb Chop on Broadway*, Lewis's puppets performed alongside full-size versions of themselves.

The 1990s exploded for Broadway puppetry and animation of all sorts when **Disney Theatrical Productions**'s *The Lion King* challenged the theater world and ultimately opened new doors for puppets on Broadway and the American stage. Director **Julie Taymor**'s use of dance, African culture, and puppetry to mix live actors, puppets, shadows, and masks resulted in six Tony Awards for the show and the launching of a Broadway phenomenon. Initially, Taymor wondered if puppetry would interfere with telling the story. However, working with designer Michael Curry and shadow puppeteer Stephen Kaplin, Taymor developed highly innovative ways of enhancing a character's range of expression through puppetry. The show has enjoyed an astonishing level of success. In January 2009, *The Lion King* was the third longest-running show on Broadway behind only *The Phantom of the Opera* and *Chicago*. It has since paved the way for creation of a new modern genre of musical that adeptly portrays children's animated movies through the use of complex scenery, costumes, and puppets. With a catalog of animated movies dating back more than half a century, Disney's new animated live musical theater genre is tailor-made for its corporate history—and puppets. Disney opened *Tarzan* on Broadway in 2006 and then joined forces with producer **Cameron Mackintosh** for *Mary Poppins* and *The Little Mermaid* (both 2008)—all shows that made extensive use of puppetry. Following in kind, DreamWorks Theatricals, a branch of the highly successful DreamWorks Hollywood **film** production company, launched its first Broadway production, *Shrek The Musical* (2009). The show is based on the highly popular animated movie series and features puppets designed by veteran stage costume and scene designer Tim Hatley.

2000 to the Present

While *The Lion King* seemed to augur a new age of animated film-to-stage musicals, Broadway's next surprise puppet hit came out of an entirely different framework. *Avenue Q* (2003) drew directly on 1980s nostalgia for *Sesame Street* and Jim Henson's various Muppets productions, while adding social commentary and adult humor aimed at the now young adult audience that grew up watching those shows. Songwriters/composers Jeff Marx and Bobby Lopez wrote the music and lyrics while veteran film and television puppeteer Rick Lyon designed the puppets. *Avenue Q* breaks conventions by having the puppeteer play the same role as the half-body rod-style Muppet puppet he or she is manipulating on stage in full view of the audience. While puppets have always been able to break conventions and accomplish what a human actor cannot, *Avenue Q* takes this principle farther than it had been seen in any mainstream commercial stage show. In *Avenue Q* only puppets simulate fully naked intercourse on stage, sing the praise of pornography, and push limits of political incorrectness. Audiences have been willing to accept the risqué nature of the lyrics and stage action as performed by cute fuzzy puppet characters. Surprisingly, this avant-garde production took the Tony Award for Best Musical and, in January 2009, was well into the sixth year of its Broadway run. The pioneering spirit of *Avenue Q* lent support for more inventive uses of puppets

Table 4
Broadway Productions with Central or Significant Use of Puppets, 1919–Present (Selected): The following chart lists documented Broadway productions in which puppetry figured centrally or prominently. The year of the show's opening is followed by the title, the chief puppeteer (when known), and the name of the producing theater. Productions where no title appears indicate an evening of puppetry presented by a puppetry company.

1919	*The Rose and the Ring*. Tony Sarg, Punch and Judy Theatre.
1920	*A Midsummer's Night's Dream*. Ellen VanVolkenburg, Little Theatre.
1933	*Teatro dei Piccoli*. Teatro dei Piccoli, Lyric Theatre.
1934	*The Chinese Nightingale*. Remo Bufano, Theatre of Young America.
1959	*Davy Jones Locker*. Bil Baird, Morosco Theatre.
1960	*Kukla, Burr and Ollie*. Burr Tillstrom, Astor Hotel.
1961	*Carnival!* Tom Tichnor, Imperial Theatre.
1963	*Man in the Moon*. Bil Baird, Biltmore Theatre.
	Obraztsov Russian Puppet Theatre (Special). Broadway Theatre.
1966	*Three Penny Opera*. Stockholm Marionettes, Billy Rose Theatre.
1978	*Side by Side by Sondheim*. Burr Tillstrom, Morocco Theatre.
1981	*Frankenstein*. Bil Baird, January 14 (one night), Palace Theatre.
	Aaah Oui Genty. Philippe Genty, Bijou Theatre.
1986	*A Little Like Magic*. Famous People Players, Lyceum Theatre.
1987	Poderecca Puppet Theatre Company, Mark Hellinger Theatre.
1994	*A Little More Magic*. Famous People Players, Belasco Theatre.
	Lamb Chop on Broadway. Shari Lewis, Richard Rogers Theatre.
1996	*Juan Darien*. Julie Taymor, Vivian Veld Theatre.
1997	*The Lion King*. Julie Taymor and Michael Curry, New Amsterdam Theatre.
	Jackie. Big Nazo Puppets, Belasco Theatre.
2000	*The Green Bird*. Julie Taymor, Cort Theatre.
2003	*Avenue Q*. Rick Lyon Puppets, John Golden Theatre.
	Little Shop of Horrors. Martin Robinson Puppets, Virginia Theatre.
2006	*The Two and Only*. Jay Johnson (ventriloquist), Helen Hayes Theatre.
2008	*Shrek The Musical*. The Character Shop, Broadway Theatre.

—*Steve Abrams (Edited from Steve Abrams,* The Puppetry Journal *[2003], updated and reprinted by permission.)*

in subsequent Broadway productions. *The Little Shop of Horrors* (2003) opened three months after *Avenue Q* premiered, following its own very successful Off-Broadway run. The Broadway version used four different puppets to depict the growth of the bloodthirsty, all-too-human plant Audrey II. Martin P. Robinson of

Sesame Street and The Henson Company not only designed the puppets for both the Broadway and Off-Broadway productions but also performed as lead puppeteer. (In the *Playbill* credits for the Broadway show, the puppeteers are listed as "Audrey II-manipulation.")

In the early years of the twenty-first century the presence of puppetry on Broadway appears to be growing healthily. Since the premiere of *The Lion King*, at least 18 Broadway shows have included puppets in some form. The variety of puppet types appearing on stage is expanding as well. While Taymor continued to explore puppetry in the short-lived musical *Green Bird* (2000), her *Lion King* collaborator Michael Curry created the dragon for the hit show *Spamalot* (2005) and various puppets for the popular Christmas season show *Dr. Seuss' How the Grinch Stole Christmas* (2006). In 2004 Marty Robinson explored multiple dimensions of puppetry and costume design in *The Frogs* with the support of puppet enthusiast and the show's composer/lyricist Stephen Sondheim.

Many recent Off-Broadway productions have also employed creative uses of puppetry, maintaining puppetry's newly won high profile in the contemporary New York theater scene. Influential puppeteers frequently perform in major Off-Broadway venues such as La Mama, the Metropolitan Opera, New York City Center, Town Hall, and the Vineyard Theatre. These venues have also hosted international puppet companies, including the Salzburg Marionettes and the Bunraku Theatre of Japan, as well as performances by well-loved American puppeteers such as Charles Ludlam (The Ridiculous Theater), Lee Breuer (Mabo Mimes), Peter Schumann (Bread and Puppet Theatre), and Robert Wilson. In 2003 director Paul Vogel billed his Off-Broadway production, *The Long Christmas Ride Home*, as "a puppet play with actors." Vogel combined theatrical puppetry with Japanese and contemporary theater techniques. Ventriloquist Roman Paska's *The Regard Evening* (also 2003) used an alter-ego puppet to explore the playwright's own aging process.

An ancient and often overlooked art form, puppetry is enjoying something of a renaissance in New York theater, having been a critical factor in the success of some of the most innovative and influential theater productions of the past two decades. As Broadway continues to embrace new popular media, technology, and art forms, the age-old yet newly rejuvenated art of puppetry is better positioned than ever to play its part.

Sharon Peck

Further Reading

Abrams, Steve. "On Broadway." *The Puppetry Journal* 55, no. 2 (Winter 2003): 2–3.

Baird, Bil. *The Art of the Puppet.* New York: The Macmillan Company, 1965.

Bell, John. *Strings Hands Shadows: A Modern Puppet History.* Detroit: Detroit Institute of Arts, 2000.

Eide, Paul, Alan Cook, and Steve Abrams. "A Timeline of Puppetry in America." *The Puppetry Journal* (Special Edition, 2003).

Kaplin, Stephen. "A Puppet Tree: A Model for the Field of Puppet Theatre." *Puppets, Masks and Performing Objects*, ed. John Bell. Cambridge, MA: MIT Press, 2001.

McPharlin, Paul. *The Puppet Theatre in America: A History 1542–1948*. Boston: Plays, Inc., 1969.

Pincus-Roth, Zachary. *Avenue Q The Book.* New York: Hyperion, 2006.

Taymor, Julie. *The Lion King: Pride Rock on Broadway.* New York: Disney Enterprises Inc., 1997.

José Quintero (1924–1999)
Director, Producer

An immigrant from Panama, director Jose Quintero came to prominence in the 1950s and 1960s principally through directing plays by **Eugene O'Neill**. He directed a career total of 19 O'Neill productions on and off Broadway, effectively spearheading America's rediscovery of O'Neill's works, which had been largely ignored after World War II. Quintero is also notable as one of the founders of the Circle in the Square theater in Greenwich Village, which invigorated the **Off-Broadway** theater scene during the 1950s and 1960s.

Quintero was born in Panama City, Panama, in 1924. The son of a politician, Quintero's relationship with his father was strained due to his lack of success as a medical student and his open homosexuality. His father sent him to Los Angeles with an envelope containing $500 and a letter ordering him to never return. Quintero studied theater at the University of Southern California and Los Angeles City College and also spent a year at the Goodman Theatre in Chicago. In the late 1940s he joined with other young theater artists, including future Circle in the Square co-founder Ted Mann, to create the Loft Players, an amateur troop that performed in Manhattan and in the upstate artist colonies near Woodstock, New York.

In 1949, Quintero tried to establish a professional Off-Broadway theater in New York. He found an abandoned lower Manhattan nightclub that had a circular ballroom and three cement pillars in the middle of the floor. He envisioned it as a "Circle-in-the-Square" theater space: a casual theater-in-the-round with a proscenium backdrop and an arena performing area. Some theater friends and a few investors supported his vision and Circle in the Square was born.

Quintero's first hit at the Circle was a 1952 production of **Tennessee Williams**'s *Summer and Smoke*. Although a 1948 Broadway production had failed, Quintero's production was a critical success. The show's popularity led *New York Times* critic **Brooks Atkinson**—at the time the only major New York **critic** who regularly reviewed experimental and Off-Broadway theater—lauded Quintero's creativity in creating an intimate atmosphere with the theater space's unique setup. The next year Quintero directed Victor Wolfson's *American Gothic* (1953), launching his 35-year collaboration with the show's leading actor, **Jason Robards**.

Summer and Smoke's success allowed Quintero to work on Broadway plays in addition to his Off-Broadway projects. His first Broadway productions, which enjoyed only limited success, were Jane Bowles's *In the Summer House* (1953), Alfred Hayes's *The Girl on the Via Flaminia* (1954), William Archibald's *Portrait of a Lady* (1954), and Theodore Apstein's *The Innkeepers* (1954).

A turning point in Quintero's career came in 1956 when a friend suggested he produce O'Neill's *The Iceman Cometh*, a lengthy, "talky," slice-of-life drama about drunken wastrels stuck in the metaphoric hell of a bar that never actually closes. At the time O'Neill's wife, Carlotta, who held the rights to her late husband's works, rarely granted permissions for performances. However, Quintero met with her and earned her trust, securing the rights to *Iceman* and, eventually, other O'Neill plays. Jason Robards starred as Hickey, the barflies' ostensibly reformed ex-drinking pal who hopes to cure his friends of false hope by savaging them with honesty. The play opened at the Circle to critical acclaim. Atkinson and others praised the staging and sophisticated uses of silence to convey a foreboding subtext. Budget-conscious theater manager Quintero and company had fashioned the authentic set by purchasing or scavenging old chairs and cheap barroom furnishings from around the city. While the original Broadway production of *Iceman* (1947) took over two years to prepare, Quintero's adaptation was staged and rehearsed in two months.

Quintero followed *Iceman* with a Broadway staging of O'Neill's posthumously published autobiographical ***Long Day's Journey into Night***. The play involves the Tyrone family, modeled on O'Neill's own family. The play's themes of emotional repression and familial resentment unmistakably point to O'Neill's own feelings about his upbringing. The 1956 production starred Robards, Fredric March, Florence Eldridge, and Bradford Dillman. The play ran for 390 performances, winning the 1957 Pulitzer Prize and Tony Awards for Best Play and Best Actor (March). The production sparked new literary and theatrical interest in O'Neill. To this day it is widely considered to be among the best modern dramatic productions ever staged on Broadway and one of the finest American plays ever written.

In the 1960s Quintero shifted his focus to Broadway. His final production for the Circle in the Square would be a 1963 staging of O'Neill's *Desire Under the Elms*, which ran for an impressive 384 performances but received mixed reviews. His first two Broadway outings in the 1960s, Hugh Wheeler's *Look, We've Come Through* (1961) and Alice Canon's *Great Day in the Morning* (1962), were not successful. He returned to O'Neill in 1963, presenting *Strange Interlude*, the first production for the newly formed **Actors Studio** Theatre. The play involves the controversial theme of abortion and offers an odd representation of characters' thoughts via soliloquies. Critics were mostly positive, either loving or hating Quintero's choice to move ambiguously between soliloquies and action. The show ran for only 93 performances, due in part to a newspaper strike that curtailed advertising. Not always fortunate with O'Neill's work, in 1964 Quintero struggled on Broadway with two O'Neill plays, *Marco Millions* and *Hughie*. *Hughie*, essentially an Off-Broadway style play, particularly displeased theatergoers who paid full price for a 45-minute production. In 1967, perhaps misguidedly, Quintero spent a year adapting O'Neill's unfinished *More Stately Mansions*, an ungainly play at best. Critical and audience response to *Mansions* was disappointing as well.

Quintero would not have another Broadway success until his 1973 production of O'Neill's *A Moon for the Misbegotten*. A pseudo-sequel to *A Long Day's Journey into Night*, *Moon* involves an older version of James Tyrone battling his familiar demons of alcoholism, lust, and self-loathing. The show received overwhelmingly positive reviews with stellar performances by Colleen Dewhurst and Robards. *Moon* ran for 313 performance, winning five Tony Awards. Although he would continue to direct actively on Broadway until 1988, Quintero would not have another Broadway hit. However, he maintained his close associations with O'Neill's plays and Robards into the last phases of his career, directing his favorite actor in three O'Neill revivals: *A Touch of the Poet* (1977), *The Iceman Cometh* (1985), and his last directorial work, *Long Day's Journey into Night* (1988).

Many scholars have explored Quintero's seemingly improbable attraction to O'Neill's plays, considering the two men's distinctly different ethnic backgrounds and the fact they never met. However, historians note that both families were Catholic and both mothers were raised in nunneries. O'Neill's mother tormented Eugene by reminding him that he was the result of an unwanted pregnancy; Quintero's father repudiated José, serially reminding him that the family wanted a daughter.

In his final years Quintero became a professor of theater, teaching at Columbia University, Florida State University, and the University of Houston. Arguably more than any other director working after World War II, Quintero narrowed the gap between the experimental sensibilities of Off-Broadway and the market demands of commercial theater, to the ultimate benefit of both.

He died on February 27, 1999, of throat cancer at his home in Sarasota, Florida.

Thomas A. Greenfield and Robert A. Adamo

Further Reading

McDonough, Edwin J., and José Quintero. *Quintero Directs O'Neill*. Chicago, IL: A Cappella Books, 1991.

Quintero, Jose. *If You Don't Dance They Beat You.* Boston: Little, Brown, 1991 (original, 1974).

RADIO

For generations that have grown up casually regarding the TV set and, more recently, the home computer, as familiar household appliances, the social and cultural impact of radio in its early years is difficult to imagine. For citizens of early twentieth-century America it was nigh on miraculous that this wooden box could summon instantaneous reports of current events and weather forecasts. Still more amazing, professional quality entertainment from the New York stage (or wherever else) could be piped simultaneously into every household from Albuquerque to Zanesville. It was no longer necessary to dress up, step out, and make an occasion of visiting the theater, the recital hall, or the band shell in the park. Not only **vaudeville** but also opera, **Shakespeare**, and the best of Broadway were readily available to be enjoyed privately in dishabille, with family and friends or entirely alone.

Early Radio Broadcasting in America

Although the development of the principal technology for radio dates to the first decade of the twentieth century, radio grew exponentially as a popular medium after World War I. In 1921 there were only 18 broadcast stations in the United States, but by 1923 there were over 500. Their broadcasts were picked up by some one million home sets; a mere two years later that number had increased to 5.5 million. In these early years the airtime utilized by most stations was limited to a few hours a day, but even so the new medium had a voracious appetite for material. It was inevitable that fledgling broadcasters would draw upon established creative personnel of the stage—performers, playwrights, composers, and so on—to fill the seemingly insatiable need for programming.

The early 1920s brought a number of radio "firsts." In February 1922 a musical comedy titled *The Perfect Fool*, which starred veteran stage comic Ed Wynn, became the first Broadway show to broadcast a performance in its entirety. Wynn and his cast traveled to the WJZ studio in Newark, New Jersey, for this special event. With no live audience dead silence greeted Wynn's jokes, an experience that so unnerved the star he avoided radio for a decade afterward. In May of that year WJZ's Bertha Brainard, one of radio's first female announcers, initiated a series of programs devoted to drama criticism, theater news, and interviews with stage notables. Each episode would begin with the hostess's alliterative exclamation: "Bertha Brainard broadcasts Broadway!" (The fact that she was broadcasting from Newark did not fit into this snappy catchphrase, but in any event WJZ itself later moved to midtown Manhattan.) In September a stage troupe known as The Masque from Troy, New York, performed a truncated version of Eugene Walter's play *The Wolf* (1908) at WGY in Schenectady. This broadcast was so popular it led to the first regular series of radio plays. The Masque became the WGY Players, and went on to perform specially adapted audio versions of such Broadway successes as Alexandre Bisson's *Madame X* (1910) and William Archer's *The Green Goddess* (1921). In April 1923 station WEAF of New York broadcast the Otto Harbach and **Oscar Hammerstein II** hit musical *Wildflower* "live" from its accustomed venue, the Casino Theater in Manhattan. Perhaps the show's producers had Ed Wynn's experience in mind, for they made certain an audience was present on this occasion.

Ziegfeld Follies and Radio

The stars of the *Ziegfeld Follies*, the legendary Broadway variety revue shows that ran annually from 1907 through 1931, also began to venture into the new medium. *Follies* favorites **Eddie Cantor** and **Fanny Brice** first tested the waters in 1921, followed by Will Rogers soon afterward. Rogers would simply deliver his comic monologues in the relaxed manner he had perfected on stage, and he soon became a radio favorite. Cantor and Brice, however, each found it necessary to modify their exuberantly theatrical characterizations in order to succeed in radio. The new medium took performers from the remote domain of the stage and put them in a listener's parlor, and thus called for a more intimate delivery. Cantor slowed his frenetic pace and eventually became a calm, avuncular presence—and one of radio's most beloved and top-paid stars. The earthy Brice, whose occasionally risqué material was perfectly acceptable on stage, would run afoul of network censors until she hit upon the character of Baby Snooks, a bratty child who could get away with blunt remarks the grown-up Brice could not. Like Cantor, Brice became enormously successful once she had figured out the demands of the new medium. But for some Broadway headliners stage stardom did not translate into radio success. Celebrities such as Al Jolson, Groucho Marx, and **Ethel Merman** found that their abrasive, larger-than-life personae were too much for this intimate medium, though they made regular appearances as guests on other performers' shows.

Some theater executives viewed the rise of radio with alarm. Vaudeville magnate E. F. Albee, the adoptive grandfather of playwright **Edward Albee**, was among those who forbade performers to accept broadcast offers, fearing an adverse impact on box-office receipts. But ultimately the migration of vaudevillians to radio could not be halted. Radio lent itself readily to a new form of audio vaudeville: songs, jokes, monologues, and sketches, packaged in a regular series format. *The Eveready Hour*, which went on the air in 1923 and lasted for seven years, was radio's first major variety revue, and a precursor to TV's *Ed Sullivan Show* in its heavy reliance on Broadway talent. Listeners could hear **George Gershwin** at the keyboard playing his tunes, stage greats such as **Laurette Taylor** and John Drew in scenes from their best-known plays, grand opera, jazz, excerpts from Shakespeare, and the venerable low comedy duo Weber & Fields, whose career in professional entertainment dated back to the 1880s. This program became the template for the many variety shows that followed, such as Rudy Vallee's *Fleischmann Hour*, which debuted in 1929 and, like the *Eveready* show, featured sequences from current Broadway plays. Vallee's program served as an incubator of sorts for an unusual stage-to-radio success story. One week Vallee showcased excerpts from Clifford Goldsmith's Broadway hit comedy *What a Life* (1938), a comedy concerning a family named the Aldriches. This broadcast proved to be so popular with listeners that Goldsmith wrote several new sketches focusing on the Aldrich family's teenage son Henry. The new sketches led to the long-lasting *Aldrich Family* series, a radio staple that remained on the air until 1953.

Follies impresario **Florenz Ziegfeld**, mentor to Brice, Cantor, and many others, made his own venture into the radio variety field with *The Ziegfeld Follies of the Air*, a half-hour musical comedy show that premiered on CBS in April 1932. In the weeks that followed numerous stars of Ziegfeld's Broadway successes appeared on his program, including **Paul Robeson**, Lupe Velez, Leon Errol, and Ruth Etting. Although this venture brought Ziegfeld into the new world of instant communication, the tone of his program was nostalgic and elegiac, as when he restaged his 1919 *Follies* for radio listeners. The show developed a steady following, but Ziegfeld was in poor health, and the series ended shortly before his death in July of that year. The franchise was briefly revived four years later with a new series featuring a few *Follies* alumnae.

The Depression Era

The Great Depression of the 1930s had a pernicious impact on box-office receipts for live stage productions in New York and throughout the country—and proved to be the final nail in vaudeville's coffin—but radio only became more popular for those families who could no longer afford to go to the theater. By 1932 upwards of one-third of American households owned a radio, a figure that is all the more impressive considering that in-home electricity was not yet universally accessible. This period saw the debuts of two programs that each attempted, in different ways, to bring a taste of Broadway excitement to homebound listeners. Walter Winchell, a former vaudevillian who had switched to journalism during the 1920s, wrote theater reviews and then a highly idiosyncratic syndicated newspaper column that made him extraordinarily powerful. In 1930 he began airing versions of his columns for CBS, switching to NBC's Blue Network (later ABC) in 1932. His early broadcasts, like his early columns, focused largely on theater news and gossip, though as time went on he gradually switched his focus to Hollywood and politics. Even so, during his three-plus decades in broadcasting plugs or pans from Winchell could mean the difference between success and failure for a Broadway production.

A few months after Winchell began his radio career, NBC debuted *The First Nighter*. Capitalizing on listeners' fascination with Broadway glamour, the show's two-minute weekly opening ranks alongside *The Lone Ranger* and *The Shadow* for radio's most famous and fondly remembered intros. It begins with the murmurs of pedestrians and the hectic sounds of midtown Manhattan traffic. The host, Mr. First Nighter, approaches "the little theater off Times Square" just moments before the curtain is to rise. He takes his seat, opens his program, and reads off the title of the evening's play, adding a choice detail or two about what to expect. As an usher calls "Curtain! Curtain!" the show begins. Ironically, the plays presented on *The First Nighter* were original to radio, not Broadway adaptations, and the show was broadcast from Chicago and later Los Angeles, not New York. But the strong quality of the productions and the Broadway mystique the show conjured successfully kept listeners tuned in well into the 1950s.

The popularity of *The First Nighter* inspired several imitations, most notably the *Lux Radio Theater*. Launched in 1934, *Lux Radio Theater* regularly presented truncated versions of actual Broadway hits such as James Barrie's *What Every Woman Knows* (1926) with **Helen Hayes** reprising her starring role, and **George S. Kaufman** and Marc Connelly's *Dulcy* (1921) with film comedienne ZaSu Pitts taking the role **Lynn Fontanne** had played on Broadway. The program also offered broadcast productions of Shakespeare plays and other classic theatrical productions and regularly featured Broadway stars such as **John** and **Ethel Barrymore** as well as the aforementioned Hayes and Pitts. After the second season, however, the program's writers found that current movies lent themselves more readily to radio adaptation, so the show abandoned Broadway and moved to Hollywood.

In the late 1930s radio drama with a very different agenda was born out of a federally funded arts program of President Franklin D. Roosevelt's New Deal. Introduced in August 1935 the **Federal Theatre Project** (FTP) was a product of the Works Progress Administration. It drew controversy and criticism almost from the moment of its inception as conservative critics accused it of mounting left-wing propaganda. Under the directorship of Hallie Flanagan the FTP produced new plays, canonical classics, and a series of stage documentaries on current events known as "Living Newspapers," performed across the country and devoted to political and social topics of the day. A radio division of the FTP was formed and a weekly *Federal Theatre of the Air* was launched in the spring of 1937. This program presented adaptations of some contemporary works from Broadway theater, including **Clifford Odets**'s *Awake and Sing!* (1935) and the FTP's own Living Newspaper project *One Third of a Nation* (1938), along with classic works by Molière, Oliver Goldsmith, Henrik Ibsen, and Anton Chekhov. These programs abruptly left the airwaves in 1939 when Congress gave way to FTP's critics and voted to defund the organization.

In the course of its brief but tumultuous existence, the Federal Theatre Project was instrumental in bringing young Orson Welles to the attention of New York theatergoers and, indirectly, to the listening public across the country. It was under the auspices of the FTP that the 20-year-old wunderkind directed *Macbeth* (1936) in a Harlem theater featuring an all–African American cast. The production caused a sensation among New York theater audiences and the press. Soon afterward, Welles and his business partner, John Houseman, formed their own Mercury Theater troupe and staged several Broadway productions, including Shakespeare's *Julius Caesar* in 1937 and **George Bernard Shaw**'s *Heartbreak House* in 1938 —both of which offered pointed commentary on the rise of fascism in Europe. Early in 1938 Welles agreed to bring his Mercury Theater to CBS, and to produce 9 one-hour adaptations of famous literary works. For a radio version of *Julius Caesar* that fall Welles hired prominent radio commentator H. V. Kaltenborn to narrate, linking the scenes of the play with excerpts from Plutarch's *Parallel Lives*. This served not only to bridge historical gaps, but to give the material the feel of a modern newscast—a device that would, of course, create a genuine sensation when it was used to more shocking effect in the Mercury's *War of the Worlds* broadcast a few weeks later. In December *The Mercury Theater on the Air* became *The Campbell Playhouse*, now sponsored by the soup company, featuring stage and film stars in the lead roles. For example, in 1939 Gertrude Lawrence reprised her Broadway role as Amanda Prynne in a *Campbell Playhouse* adaptation of Noel Coward's *Private Lives* (1931), playing opposite Welles on radio instead of Coward himself, who had starred with Lawrence on Broadway in his own show. In 1940 Welles left New York and radio for new adventures in Hollywood.

During the war years there were new attempts to bring the excitement of the Broadway stage to listeners at home. *The Knickerbocker Playhouse*, which premiered in 1939, began as an ambitious attempt to adapt Broadway successes such as Austin Strong's *Seventh Heaven* (1922) and Robert Sherwood's *Abe Lincoln in Illinois* (1938) to the demands of radio, but after the first season the producers chose to follow the lead of *The First Nighter* and present lightweight original fare instead of legitimate stage plays. A daytime series of 1943–1944 called *Broadway Matinee* initially featured an odd mix of **show tunes** combined with home economics tips, but eventually showcased music only. Broadway musical and **operetta** journeyman **Alfred Drake** could be heard on this New York–based program four days out of five, but could not participate in every broadcast because, ironically, he had to report to the St. James Theater once a week to perform in an actual Broadway matinee, as Curly in *Oklahoma!* During this period another well-known musical comedy star, William Gaxton, appeared in a similar program called *Broadway Showtime*, a half-hour series that featured highlights from noted musicals. The first episode offered a streamlined version of **Richard Rodgers** and **Lorenz Hart**'s *A Connecticut Yankee*, for which Gaxton had played the lead in the 1927 Broadway run.

As the war came to an end in September 1945 a new series was launched, which brought to radio sophisticated theater aimed at adults. Under the seemingly unlikely sponsorship of U.S. Steel, the *Theater Guild of the Air* program was an immediate hit with critics, and gradually caught on with a large audience of discerning listeners across the country. The **Theatre Guild** had been founded in 1919 by Lawrence Langner and Theresa Hellburn with the intention of producing intelligent, innovative, and sometimes provocative dramas, which might not be regarded as commercial prospects by more cautious producers. During its 1920s heyday the Guild brought unconventional works such as Karel Capek's *R.U.R.* (1922), Elmer Rice's *The Adding Machine* (1923), and **Eugene O'Neill**'s *Strange Interlude* (1928) to the attention of Broadway's intelligentsia, but by the 1940s the Guild's artistic directors had become less inclined to select offbeat, challenging material.

The radio venture, under the direction of Langner's wife, Armina Marshall, enabled the organization to revitalize its mission with new energy and bring younger talents to the fore. The series showcased American plays from the period since World War I, that is, the life span of the Theatre Guild itself, although not all of the plays selected for adaptation had originally been presented under the Guild's auspices. The show was only an hour long, which meant that the selected plays had to be expertly condensed and, at times, rewritten to fit the time slot and the demands of the audio medium. The Guild's writers for this project included playwrights Arthur Arent, Kenyon Nicholson, and, during the first season, **Arthur Miller**. Whenever possible, the program featured actors who had appeared in the plays originally, as when **Alfred Lunt** and Lynn Fontanne re-created their 1924 roles in Ferenc Molnár's *The Guardsman*. When this was not possible, the program drew upon the top acting talent available, including such performers as Helen Hayes, Burgess Meredith, June Havoc, and so on. John Gielgud appeared as Hamlet in a special 90-minute episode. The Guild was not above hiring Hollywood names to appear on the program, as long as the stars were suited to their roles and "know how to act" as Marshall quipped. Thus, the Guild's 1946 production of Odets's *Golden Boy* (1937) starred Dana Andrews, a 1950 production of **Thornton Wilder**'s *Our Town* (1938) featured Walter Huston and Elizabeth Taylor, and a 1951 broadcast of **William Inge**'s *Come Back, Little Sheba* (1950) paired Shirley Booth with Gary Cooper. When the Guild ran into occasional problems with network censors over frank material, they always received full support from their sponsor, U.S. Steel. The company regarded the program as an important symbol of cultural prestige and maintained its sponsorship throughout the series' eight-year run on radio. For the 1952–1953 season the show changed its name to *The United States Steel Hour*, and kept that name when it moved to **television** in the fall of 1953. Under that title the show lasted as a TV favorite for another ten years.

The arrival of television in the late 1940s sounded the death knell for audio drama. Instead of accepting radio offers, Broadway stars and vaudeville veterans began to appear on TV's *Colgate Comedy Hour* or Ed Sullivan's *Toast of the Town*. Radio fought back with a final large-scale variety series, *The Big Show*, which premiered on NBC in November 1950 hosted by legendary actress and larger-than-life personality Tallulah Bankhead. *The Big Show* was a weekly 90-minute extravaganza, an expensive program that boasted guest stars from the worlds of Broadway and Hollywood—everyone from show business veterans such as Jimmy Durante and Ethel Merman to fresh young personalities such as Jane Powell and Judy Holliday. The show featured scenes from current Broadway hits in by-now-familiar fashion. The banter between the hostess and her guests was witty and sophisticated, with a sharper edge than listeners were accustomed to hearing in normally innocuous variety shows, but in the end, this strenuous effort to amuse could not persuade the folks at home to ignore their new TV sets and come back to radio. Irrevocably, "listeners" had become "viewers." *The Big Show* lasted for two seasons and then called it quits, passing into radio drama history along with the *The First Nighter*, *The Lux Radio Theater*, *The Theater Guild of the Air*, and the other late, lamented radio showcases for Broadway theater.

William Charles Morrow

Further Reading

Barnouw, Erik. *History of Broadcasting in the U.S.* New York: Oxford University Press, 1968.

Buxton, Frank, and Bill Owen. *The Big Broadcast, 1920–1950.* Lanham, MD: Scarecrow Press, 1997.

Dunning, John. *Tune in Yesterday: The Ultimate Encyclopedia of Old-Time Radio, 1925–1976.* Englewood Cliffs, NJ: Prentice-Hall, Inc., 1976.

Dunning, John. *On the Air: The Encyclopedia of Old-Time Radio.* New York: Oxford University Press, 1998.

Henderson, Amy. *On the Air: Pioneers of American Broadcasting.* Washington, DC: Smithsonian Institution Press, 1988.

MacDonald, J. Fred. *Don't Touch That Dial!: Radio Programming in American Life from 1920 to 1960.* Chicago: Nelson-Hall, 1979.

Maltin, Leonard. *The Great American Broadcast.* New York: Dutton, 1997.

Museum of Broadcast Communication. *Encyclopedia of Radio.* New York: Fitzroy Dearborn, 2004.

Nachman, Gerald. *Raised on Radio.* New York: Pantheon Books, 1998.

Weaver, Pat. *The Best Seat in the House: The Golden Years of Radio and Television.* New York: Knopf, 1994.

Wertheim, Arthur Frank. *Radio Comedy.* New York: Oxford University Press, 1979.

A RAISIN IN THE SUN

Broadway Run: Ethel Barrymore Theatre (March 11, 1959 to October 17, 1959); and the Belasco Theatre (October 19, 1959 to June 25, 1960)
Opening: March 11 1959
Closing: June 25 1960

Total Performances: 530
Playwright: Lorraine Hansberry
Director: Lloyd Richards
Producers: Kenneth Schwartz and Mel Howard
Cast: Sidney Poitier (Walter Lee Younger), Ruby Dee (Ruth Younger), Claudia McNeal (Lena Younger), Diana Sands (Beneatha Younger), Lonne Elder III (Bobo), Louis Gossett Jr. (George Murchison), John Fiedler (Karl Lindner), Ivan Dixon (Joseph Asagai), Glynn Turman (Travis Younger), Douglas Turner (Moving Man), Ed Hall (Moving Man)

A Raisin in the Sun was the first play written by an African American woman to be produced on Broadway, the first to be directed by an African American, and the longest-running Broadway show written by an African American up to that time. With this production **playwright** Lorraine Hansberry and director **Lloyd Richards** ushered in a Renaissance of African American theater activity throughout the country. In the context of a Chicago African American family's confrontation with racial prejudice in the ostensibly liberal North, *A Raisin in the Sun* explores Pan-African philosophy, the politics of ethnic assimilation within the African American community, and the intersection of racial and gender conflicts in society at large. These were themes that were new to Broadway and, in the depth and scope of Hansberry's explorations, rare in published or professionally produced African American drama up to that point. The initial Broadway run of *A Raisin in the*

A curtain call for the Broadway revival of A Raisin in the Sun, *2004, in New York City. Sean "Puffy" Combs, center, is flanked by actresses Audra McDonald, left, and Phylicia Rashad, right. (AP Photo/Diane Bondareff)*

Sun was a singularly important catalyst for the dynamic growth of African American theater that accompanied the Civil Rights Movement of the late 1950s and 1960s.

Although Lorraine Hansberry's professional writing career lasted only a few years and within her lifetime boasted only this one major commercial success, Hansberry and *A Raisin in the Sun* hold a special place in the history of Broadway and American culture. At age 29, Hansberry was one of the youngest people to ever solo author a major Broadway play or garner a Best Play Tony nomination. She is still the youngest person ever to have won the prestigious New York Drama Critics Circle award for Best Play of the Year, which she won for *A Raisin in the Sun.* Born in Chicago into an intellectual and politically active family, Hansberry was living in New York in the mid-1950s when she began writing full time. Among her early literary efforts was a play entitled *The Crystal Stair* (after a line from a poem by Harlem Renaissance author Langston Hughes), to which she would eventually give the title *A Raisin in the Sun* (an allusion to another Hughes poem).

The plot of *A Raisin in the Sun* concerns the Younger family's internal conflicts over how to spend a $10,000 life insurance bequest left to matriarch Lena by her deceased husband. Her son, Walter Lee, a 35-year-old chauffeur for a white businessman, wants the money to fund his own liquor store, which he envisions as an assertion of his manhood and his entrée into that world of entrepreneurship he sees up close every day from his driver's seat. His younger sister, Beneatha, an undergraduate gadfly who seems to skitter from one interest to another, is in fact a committed premedical student; Lena has pledged some of the money for Beneatha's medical school expenses. And Lena herself wants out of their infested, cramped, rundown Chicago apartment and into a suburban house where she can breathe free and tend a garden. Neither the $10,000 nor the family's deep though sorely tested love for each other will cover all their wishes.

The story is based in part on Hansberry's childhood memories of her parents' conflict-ridden attempt to purchase a home in a white Chicago area neighborhood. Written in a naturalistic style that shows the influence of **Arthur Miller**'s kitchen-table poetic dialogue and invokes the subtle character textures of the nineteenth-century Russian playwright Anton Chekhov, *A Raisin in the Sun* introduced Broadway audiences to a complex, profoundly unsentimental examination of contemporary African American life.

The play opened to standing ovations, **critics** raved, and almost everyone connected with the production rose to prominence. Hansberry was pursued for press interviews and hailed as a new young literary voice. Lead actors Sidney Poitier and Ruby Dee, already well-respected actors, earned significant career boosts and became *bona fide* stars. Director Lloyd Richards went on to a highly acclaimed directing, producing, and academic theater career, including award-winning direction of several plays by **August Wilson** in the 1980s and 1990s. Louis Gossett Jr., who had a minor role in the show, has enjoyed a long, successful **film** and **television** career. Actor Lonne Elder III would eventually turn his attention to writing, garnering an Academy Award nomination for writing the screenplay for the movie

Sounder and a Drama Desk Award in 1969 as Most Promising Playwright for his play *Ceremonies in Old Dark Men*. Douglas Turner Ward, who had a minor role in the play, became an award-winning playwright, director, and a co-founder of the historic Negro Ensemble Company. Glynn Turman, who played Walter Lee's young son, has been a fixture in Hollywood for 40 years, especially on network television shows such as *ER*, *Scrubs*, and *In Treatment* (for which he won an Emmy Award).

Rather than waning in influence after its initial run, *A Raisin in the Sun* has risen to iconic stature in American theater and African American culture. The outpouring of critical acclaim for the play's initial Broadway run followed by Hansberry's screenplay for the 1961 film adaptation made her the first African American celebrity playwright and the first major African American Broadway celebrity since the heyday of actor/singer **Paul Robeson** a generation earlier.

Hansberry died of cancer in New York City in 1965 at age 34. A second Broadway production, *The Sign in Sidney Brustein's Window*, ran briefly and closed in 1965. However, Hansberry has had an active posthumous literary and dramatic career, largely through the efforts of former husband and executor of her manuscripts, Robert Nemiroff. In 1970 Nemiroff completed one of her manuscripts in progress, *Le Blancs*, which had a brief Broadway run. *Raisin* (1973), a hit musical version of the original play (with book by Nemiroff), ran for over two years, winning the Tony Award for Best Musical. A highly publicized Broadway revival of the original play was mounted in 2004 starring popular television star Phylicia Rashad and hip-hop artist Sean "P. Diddy" Combs.

The growing recognition and importance of African American writing in the decades since the premier of *A Raisin in the Sun* only enlarged the stature of the play and its author. The production's singular contribution in bringing national attention to African American writing and theater has been acknowledged by virtually every major scholar and critic writing on the subject. University courses on modern American drama and critics' lists of major American plays invariably include *A Raisin in the Sun*, placing it in the rarified company of such American theatrical masterpieces as Arthur Miller's ***Death of a Salesman***, **Tennessee Williams**'s ***A Streetcar Named Desire***, and **Eugene O'Neill**'s ***Long Day's Journey into Night***. The play remains to this day a centerpiece for discussion of twentieth-century literature, African American or otherwise, dramatic or otherwise.

Thomas A. Greenfield and Sue Ann Brainard

Further Reading

Bloom, Harold. *Lorraine Hansberry's A Raisin in the Sun*. New York: Bloom's Literary Criticism, 2009.

Leeson, Richard M. *Lorraine Hansberry: A Research and Production Sourcebook*. Westport, CT: Greenwood Press, 1997.

RAITT, JOHN (1917–2005)
ACTOR

Best known for his leading roles in two major musical hits of the post–World War II era, *Carousel* (1945) and *Pajama Game* (1954), John Emmett Raitt helped set the standard for the virile, broad-shouldered leading man that dominated modern **musicals** from 1943 to 1966. Often compared to other Broadway romantic leading actors of the time, such as **Alfred Drake** (*Oklahoma!*, *Kiss Me, Kate*) and Robert Preston (*The Music Man*, *I Do! I Do!*), Raitt brought a physical, hard-to-

Scene from the prologue of Carousel, *in which John Raitt made his Broadway debut as Billy Bigelow, who gets better acquainted with Julie Jordan (Jan Clayton) as she takes a ride on the carousel. Richard Rodgers and Oscar Hammerstein collaborated on the music and lyrics of* Carousel, *which opened on April 19, 1945, at the Majestic Theater in New York. (AP Photo)*

tame quality to his roles, giving an edge to his performances that complemented his matinee idol looks and operatic voice.

Born in Santa Ana, California, Raitt attended the University of Southern California and the University of Redlands. At both institutions he majored in physical education and competed in school athletics. Possessing a rich, room-filling baritone singing voice from early adulthood, he performed musical theater and light opera in and around Los Angeles during the early 1940s, eventually landing the role of Curly (originated on Broadway by Drake) in an early touring company of *Oklahoma!* The *Oklahoma!* tour led to his Broadway debut as Billy Bigelow in **Richard Rodgers and Oscar Hammerstein II**'s *Carousel*—a rare Broadway instance of an unknown actor debuting as the lead in a major musical and doing so triumphantly. It was to be the most successful and distinctive performance of his career. Raitt gave Billy's character a gruff working-class, antihero quality while still sporting the conventional "look" and sonorous singing voice of a romantic leading man. One of the features of the score for *Carousel* was "Soliloquy" (commonly known as "My Boy Bill"), a six-plus minute solo written by Rodgers and Hammerstein specifically for Raitt's brawny singing style and vocal range. The song, in which Billy agonizes over the challenges of pending fatherhood, jumps from congested half-spoken self-reflection, to cascading braggadocio, to tenderhearted vulnerability. It stopped the show every night and remained a regular feature of Raitt's singing concerts long after he had ceased to be a force on Broadway.

Appearing in three flops after *Carousel*—*Magdalena* (1948), *Three Wishes for Jamie* (1952), and *Carnival in Flanders* (1953)—Raitt scored his second, and only other, hit in *The Pajama Game* as the "cute with spunk" factory superintendent Sid Sorokin. This role was more traditional than that of Billy Bigelow, inasmuch as Raitt played the management half of a management-labor romance. However, a pajama fashion show at the finale, featuring the muscular Raitt topless alongside his barelegged leading lady (modeling two-can-sleep-as-cheaply-as-one pajamas) was for its time a daring if brief foray into beefcake entertainment. Raitt reprised his role of Sid Sorokin—complete with the topless appearance—in the 1957 film adaptation of *The Pajama Game*.

As Broadway musicals began to change in the middle and late 1960s, responding to new social currents in America's attitudes toward ethnicity, diversity, and gender roles, Raitt and other romantic leading men of the time found it increasingly difficult to land major roles. His final Broadway appearances, *A Joyful Noise* (1967) and *A Musical Jubilee* (1975), were unsuccessful, and Raitt never appeared on Broadway again. Nevertheless, he made such an impact in his two hit shows that he maintained an active singing, television, and musical touring career into the 2000s. Signature solos from his two Broadway hits, such as *Carousel*'s "Soliloquy" and "If I Loved You" and *The Pajama Game*'s "Hey There" remained audience favorites for decades. Raitt was the father of popular American blues singer and guitarist Bonnie Raitt, and in his later years the two would occasionally perform together.

Raitt died on February 20, 2005, at his home in Pacific Palisades, California, from complications due to pneumonia.

Thomas A. Greenfield and Sean Roche

Further Reading

Green, Stanley, and Kay Green. *Broadway Musicals: Show by Show.* Milwaukee, WI: Leonard, 1994.

Hischak, Thomas S. *The Rodgers and Hammerstein Encyclopedia.* Westport, CT: Greenwood Publishing Group, 2007.

REGIONAL THEATERS

Modern American regional theater—known also as resident theater—was founded in the 1940s in part to counterbalance Broadway's status as the sole expression of American professional theatrical production. The two theatrical fronts of Broadway and regional theater have remained closely interrelated ever since. For at least the past 25 years it has become increasingly common to find new American plays on Broadway that originated in the regional theater scene. Even many Broadway musicals now originate in American regional theaters although, notably, **Andrew Lloyd Webber musicals** and **Disney Theatrical Productions** generally do not.

Where previously Broadway **producers** would "try out" their shows out of town, with producers, directors, and writers making changes along the way, increasingly resident theaters today function as tryout venues. Generally, resident theater productions become Broadway tryouts in one of two ways. In some instances the resident theater presents a work already destined for Broadway through up-front investment agreements (called "enhancement money") with Broadway producers. In other cases the resident company will mount a new work independently and then solicit commercial interest for transfer to Broadway on the basis of success in the regional run of the show. The regional or resident theater movement today serves not just as an alternative to Broadway but also as its partner and a vital source of discovering new works, new artists, and new audiences.

Regional theaters vary in size and mission, so their exact numbers are difficult to determine. The Theatre Communications Group (TCG), the largest professional association of American professional theaters, has over 480 members ranging from some of the country's largest professional theater companies to small community-based theaters—some with annual operating budgets of less than $100,000. Adding university, semiprofessional community theaters, and other not-for-profit theaters, the number easily exceeds 1,000.

The League of Resident Theaters (LORT) represents those theater companies that operate under an Actors' Equity Association (AEA) agreement and, therefore, generally have longer seasons, longer rehearsal schedules, and larger operating budgets than smaller non-Equity theaters. LORT's 77-member theater companies, many of which also belong to TCG, include several that have established strong reputations for staging world premieres of plays that later transferred successfully to Broadway, including the Guthrie Theater in Minneapolis, Actors Theatre of Louisville, Arena Stage in Washington, D.C., and the Goodman Theatre in Chicago.

1900–1940: The Little Theater Movement and Federal Theatre

While the major period of expansion for the regional theater movement took place after World War II, modern regional theater is also an outgrowth of the Little Theater Movement of the 1910s. These were amateur theaters—some with professional and even commercial aspirations—that emphasized artistic merit and new work over the commercialism of early Broadway. In the 1910s, the **Shubert Brothers** dominated Broadway theatrical production, including commercial tours of Broadway shows throughout the United States. The American Little Theater Movement, inspired by Ibsenism and turn-of-the-century European modernism, provided an alternative to the New York–based tours that emphasized star performers and spectacle. The movement also dovetailed with a surge in community performances, particularly civic spectacles, pageantry, and outdoor theater. Indigenous theaters in Boston, Chicago, Milwaukee, San Francisco, and other cities began to prosper in the 1920s. Some of the theaters established during the Little Theater Movement, like Cleveland Play House (founded in 1916), eventually became fully professional theaters. University theater also grew in significance during this time. Many of the **playwrights** who became prominent during the 1920s and 1930s, including **Eugene O'Neill**, had studied with George Pierce Baker at his famous 47 Workshop playwriting seminar, which he conducted at Harvard from 1906 to 1924. He later moved to Yale and became instrumental in establishing the Yale School of Drama.

The 1920s and 1930s saw a continuation of the Little Theater Movement spirit in the birth of several significant art theaters, most notably the **Theatre Guild**, the **Provincetown Players**, and the **Group Theatre**, which offered alternatives to the light, mainstream entertainment on Broadway. These theaters produced new, foreign, and challenging work in Broadway houses with varying degrees of commercial and critical success. The Theatre Guild, for example, brought Karel Capek's *R.U.R.* to Broadway in 1922, where it ran for four months. The play then became one of the most highly anthologized and widely produced in "little theaters" of the 1920s. While only the Provincetown Players originated outside of New York (and quickly left its Provincetown, Massachusetts, roots behind), these theater groups offered organizational models for the resident theaters of the 1940s and later.

During the 1930s, several theaters were created out of barns and mills, such as Pennsylvania's Bucks County Playhouse (a former gristmill), Connecticut's Westport Country Playhouse (a former tannery), and New Jersey's Paper Mill

Playhouse (indeed, a former paper mill). Often these theaters, located within a hundred miles of Broadway, provided work for Broadway performers off-season as well as testing grounds for future Broadway fare. Broadway playwright Moss Hart was one of the purchasers of the Pennsylvania mill that he transformed into Bucks County Playhouse. Westport Country Playhouse's stage was designed by Broadway designer Cleon Throckmorton to match the specifications of Broadway's Times Square Theater on 42nd Street.

Another significant boost in the growth of regional theaters was provided by the **Federal Theatre Project** (FTP), sponsored by the New Deal Works Project Administration (WPA) to provide employment to out-of-work theater artists. The Great Depression saw the closing of many Broadway houses as well as several out-of-town Shubert houses that hosted "direct from Broadway" **touring productions**. Hallie Flanagan, who ran the Experimental Theater at Vassar and had earlier served as a production assistant to George Pierce Baker at Harvard, oversaw the Federal Theatre Project, which ran from 1935 to 1939. Playwright Elmer Rice, who oversaw the New York City arm of the FTP, first developed a plan for a national theater with regional centers. Flanagan and others modified his plan but put Rice's basic concept in practice. The Federal Theatre Project was national in scope, with five basic areas: New York City (under Rice), the East, the South, the Midwest, and the West. For all intents and purposes, contemporary regional theater still divides itself along those lines.

Much of the output of the Federal Theatre Project took place in New York City, with a Negro unit, a vaudeville unit, a classical performance unit, and more. Through sponsoring the "living newspaper," a style of documentary plays, and emphasizing experimental work, the FTP enhanced the creation of new and original productions across America. A production of *Swing Mikado* (1939) that originated in Chicago eventually transferred to New York. National FTP programs of plays by O'Neill and **George Bernard Shaw** as well as children's plays also met with success. The FTP's funding was canceled in 1939, largely as a result of the House Un-American Committee (HUAC) and its intimations that the FTP was decidedly politicized and left-leaning.

1940s–2000: The Rise of Modern Regional/Resident Theater

During the 1940s Broadway actors and producers continued to work in summer stock companies out of town. Prior to World War II, Broadway's interaction with regional theaters was minimal, although many Broadway shows continued to have out-of-town tryouts and post-Broadway road companies. The regional theater movement took off significantly after World War II with the establishment of three theater companies, all founded by women. In 1947 Margo Jones, who is often credited as the visionary behind the growth of modern regional theater, established the repertory company Theater '47 in Dallas (the theater was later renamed for her). Nina Vance, a former colleague of Jones's, founded the Alley Theater in Houston that same year. In 1950, Zelda Fichandler started the Arena Stage in

Washington, D.C. A few years later in 1952 avant-garde producers Herbert Blau and Jules Irving began the Actor's Workshop of San Francisco. All of these theaters were amateur, non-Equity theaters at first, but each turned professional after they became established. They all used rented facilities, not built as theaters, for their locations. What is particularly striking about these groups is that they were not founded by Broadway producers or performers, but by individuals who, at the time, were rooted in community and university theater.

Unlike Jones, Vance, and Fichandler, Sir Tyrone Guthrie, founding artistic director of the Guthrie Theatre in Minneapolis, was a star personality when he began his pioneering work in American regional theater. He brought a star-studded group of actors, including Broadway giants **Hume Cronyn** and **Jessica Tandy**, to the Guthrie in its first season in 1963. Like Margo Jones, who was a missionary for theater-in-the-round, Guthrie also championed stages that offered alternatives to Broadway's proscenium arch, and emphasized the "thrust" stage that jutted into the audience on three sides. They organized the institutions as not-for-profit corporations and sought to establish permanent companies that would serve their communities through a subscription season made up of a combination of classics and new work. This concept stands to this day as the basic operating model for most regional theaters.

The success of these regional theater companies (and particularly that of the Guthrie) led to an explosion of regional theaters founded across the country. Foundation and government support, which had become increasingly available in the late 1950s, enhanced the stability of regional theater as a viable professional alternative to Broadway theater. Beginning in 1959 the Ford Foundation began awarding three-year matching grants to the Alley, the Workshop, and the Arena, enabling them to hire Equity actors for full-season contracts. The Ford Foundation also allotted funds for the establishment of the aforementioned Theatre Communications Group. Housed in New York City, the member-based organization publishes the magazine *American Theater*, grants financial awards to regional theaters, and serves as the national advocacy association for American not-for-profit professional theaters large and small. In 1966, the League of Resident Theaters established its own contract with Actors' Equity Association, fortifying Broadway and commercial theater's relationship with the larger, better financed not-for-profit regional companies.

At the same time, not-for-profit "regional" theaters in New York City itself set down roots, hiring actors under a new concession called an **Off-Broadway** contract. Instead of alternative theater groups like the Theatre Guild producing work in smaller Broadway houses, Circle in the Square (1951), Roundabout Theatre Company (1965), Manhattan Theatre Club (1970), and Playwrights Horizons (1971) began working, essentially, as regional theaters within the boundaries of New York City. The Repertory Theatre of Lincoln Center operated at the Vivian Beaumont in Lincoln Center as an in-town "regional theater" from 1965 to 1973. Lincoln Center Theater was reestablished in 1985. **Joseph Papp** developed the Public Theater out of his Shakespeare Workshop in 1967. (Because of the New York location of these prominent theaters, the term "resident theater" became increasingly used interchangeably with "regional theater"; it has since become the preferred term for describing the contemporary not-for-profit professional theater scene.)

These theaters naturally made use of Broadway's talent pool on all fronts and altered the context in which Broadway theater was received. The establishment of the National Endowment for the Arts (NEA) in 1965 encouraged the growth of these Off-Broadway theaters, as well as out-of-town not-for-profit theaters and Off-Off-Broadway companies. Many of the playwrights who came to prominence in the latter part of the twentieth century, including **Marsha Norman** and **August Wilson**, were produced in resident companies that found new funds through the NEA. In addition, the Tax Act of 1969 provided an incentive for foundations to find suitable grantees, as they now were required by law to disperse 5 percent of their endowment earnings each year to maintain their advantageous tax status.

Resident theaters founded during this period made a virtue of their differences from Broadway. Most of the resident theaters sought to establish a year-round, resident company of actors, who would inform their repertoire of works that included a selection of Shakespeare, classical, contemporary, and new work. Despite the frequent use of the "repertory" in theater company titles, very few resident theaters operated on a repertory model, in which several shows would open simultaneously and then alternate performances. Instead, most operated on the stock model in which one play opened and closed, and then another was put up in its place. (Shakespeare festivals often were, and are, exceptions to this practice. Oregon Shakespeare Festival and the Utah Shakespearean Festival hire a resident company for the season who perform in all of the shows that run in repertory.)

Another distinguishing characteristic of modern resident theaters has been an emphasis on education. Following in the zealous path of Joseph Papp, who brought free **Shakespeare** not just to Central Park but to communities throughout New York City's five boroughs, many resident theater companies offer discounted tickets to students and offer programs designed to increase community involvement in theater in their own home communities. In addition, offering professional training programs for actors and other aspiring theater artists has been a staple of resident theater programs and services for decades, especially among the larger, better-funded theater companies

With the success of resident theaters on many fronts, they increasingly became Broadway training grounds for artists and technicians. In the past 30 years many of the actors who came to Broadway, such as Tony Award–winners Frank Langella and Jane Alexander, had early career training in resident theaters as did many stage managers and directors. Resident theaters generally offered not only professional training classes, drawing on a national pool of talent, but also provided educational outreach programs to area schools and children. As early as 1966, *Variety* reported that there were more professional actors working in the resident theaters throughout the country than on Broadway.

Despite the emphasis many resident theater managers place on their differences from Broadway, a turning point in the relationship between resident theaters and Broadway came with Howard Sackler's *The Great White Hope*, which originated at Washington, D.C.'s Arena Stage in 1967. It subsequently transferred with great success to Broadway, winning the Pulitzer Prize as well as the Tony Award for Best Play. That commercial producers could profit by the work done in the provinces in the not-for-profit world was a subject that engendered a great deal of ethical debate. Many felt that only by keeping the two worlds separate could the integrity of the resident theaters be maintained, and they sought safeguards to prevent the original ideals of the regional theater movement from being overrun by profit-seeking motives. Others believed that the prestige a Broadway production could bring to a resident theater company would enhance its stability and draw greater resources to that theater, while improving the variety of what Broadway could provide to its audiences. Other resident transfers soon followed. The first rock musical, *Hair* (1968), which opened Off-Broadway at the Public Theater in 1967, transferred to Broadway the following year and became one of the most important and successful musicals of the decade.

Resident theater soon become so important to the health of Broadway and American theater as a whole that in 1976 the **American Theatre Wing**, custodians of the Tony Awards, began granting an annual Special Tony Award for Regional Theater. There had been sporadic, individual industry recognition given for contributions to regional or resident theater beforehand, but the institution of a yearly award regularized the practice. The annual award had the added benefit of ensuring that Broadway audiences and Tony voters would gain some familiarity with the resident theater scene both from the process of voting for the annual winner and from the publicity generated from the award presentation itself. The first Special Tony Award for Regional Theater went to Arena Stage, which, like several other larger regional theaters, was becoming increasingly interested in producing new original plays that would find Broadway production and other forms of national attention.

With the increasing quality of resident theater productions and the benefit to Broadway producers of having someone else stage "out-of-town" tryouts, Broadway transfers of new plays from these theaters became increasingly common in the 1980s and 1990s. Marsha Norman's Pulitzer Prize–winning *'Night Mother* (1983) originated in Actor's Theatre of Louisville and most of August Wilson's Broadway plays premiered at the Yale Repertory Theatre in New Haven, Connecticut. **Tony Kushner**'s *Angels in America*, arguably the most significant American theatrical event of the 1990s, debuted on Broadway in 1993 only after years of development at San Francisco's Eureka Theatre and Los Angeles's Mark Taper Forum. As resident theaters were able to support new play development through enhancement income from Broadway producers, they began to bear the brunt of the start-up process. Where new plays in the 1950s and 1960s opened "out of town" at commercial houses and were revised on the road, increasingly new plays began to be commissioned and developed in resident theaters. Often two or more resident theaters worked together on a new production. The 2008 musical *Passing Strange*, for example, was billed as a joint premiere by Berkeley Repertory Theatre and the Public Theater, before its Broadway transfer. Boston's American Repertory Theatre has had six shows transfer to Broadway; Atlanta's Alliance Theatre has had four. Des McAnuff, while Artistic Director of La Jolla Playhouse near San Diego, transferred such acclaimed original productions as *The Who's Tommy* (1993) and *Jersey Boys* (2006).

Broadway producers increasingly look to resident theater for talent as well as productions. Resident theater alumni starring on Broadway in recent hits include the aforementioned Langella (*Frost/Nixon*, 2007), as well as **Patti LuPone** (*Gypsy*, 2008 revival), and David Hyde Pierce (*Curtains*, 2007). At the same time, few theater companies have been able to maintain a stable, resident company of actors. By the 1990s, most resident theaters were routinely holding auditions for their productions in New York and, in turn, hiring very few actors from their own communities for major roles.

Because of the relatively complex production logistics and costs of mounting musicals as compared to plays, the process of Broadway transfer for new plays and musicals generally differs when commercial money becomes involved. Resident theaters tend to develop new straight plays and then invite producers to invest once a play is up and running. With musicals, more often the resident theaters seek commercial enhancement funds in advance of mounting a full production in their own theaters. Increasingly, this happens not only with new musicals but also with musical revivals that originate in a resident theater. With the exceptions of the aforementioned Disney and Andrew Lloyd Webber productions, it has become increasingly rare for a new musical to debut on Broadway without the involvement of a resident theater on some level. Through this process, the distinction between a resident production and the traditional out-of-town tryout, particularly for musicals, has essentially become blurred.

Twenty-First Century: Resident Theater on Broadway

Since the turn of the twenty-first century, resident theaters and Broadway have worked increasingly in collaboration. Several resident theaters in New York now have Broadway houses, including Manhattan Theatre Club, which programs the Biltmore Theatre, and the Roundabout Theatre, which uses the American Airlines Theatre (formerly the Selwyn) and Studio 54. Lincoln Center's Vivian Beaumont Theatre, located almost two miles from the theater district, became classified as a Broadway theater, making shows there eligible for Tony awards. Many critics believe that the Beaumont's staging of Tom Stoppard's massive Tony Award–winning trilogy, *The Coast of Utopia* (2006), could not have been produced as a commercial venture without the institutional support of a large organization like Lincoln Center. Because of their not-for-profit status, these theaters with Broadway homes still do not pay taxes and are able to pay actors a lower rate than the Broadway minimum, a bone of contention among Broadway producers.

In 2008, of 112 Tony Award nominations, nearly one-third went to productions that originated in these not-for-profit companies. While Broadway producers complain about the not-for-profit encroachment into the for-profit domain, enhancement money from corporations, including for such things as naming rights for a theater, has become an important stimulus for new play and musical development in the not-for-profit world. As new resident theaters are founded, like New Jersey's ReVision Theatre founded in 2008, they are more likely to unabashedly claim Broadway aspirations than define themselves in terms of what Broadway is not.

Gwen Orel

Further Reading

Berkowitz, Gerald M. *New Broadways: Theater Across America: Approaching a New Millennium*. New York: Applause, 1997.

Novick, Julius. *Beyond Broadway: The Quest for Permanent Theaters*. New York: Hill and Wang, 1968.

Schanke, Robert A., ed. *Angels in the American Theater: Patrons, Patronage, and Philanthropy*. Carbondale, IL: Southern University Press, 2007.

Volz, Jim. *The Back Stage Guide to Working in Regional Theater*. New York: Back Stage Books, 2007.

Ziegler, John Wesley. *Regional Theater: The Revolutionary Stage*. Minneapolis: University of Minnesota Press, 1973.

RELIGION

American commercial theater, a decidedly secular endeavor, has had a long and occasionally unsettled relationship with religion. Between 1900 and the early 2000s, Broadway theaters featured more than 150 original plays and musicals in which religious themes and characters contributed significantly—even controversially—to their plots and underlying messages. Audiences have found themselves variously entertained and challenged by works on champions and enemies of religion, crises of faith, Judaism and anti-Semitism, Catholicism, martyrdom, and atheism among other religious themes. Some of America's most important **playwrights** have brought religious subjects to the stage, including **Eugene O'Neill**, **Arthur Miller**, and **Tony Kushner**. Joining them on Broadway have been European masters, including **George Bernard Shaw** and Samuel Beckett. Hit musicals as diverse as Jerry Bock and Sheldon Harnick's *Fiddler on the Roof* (1964), **Andrew Lloyd Webber**'s *Jesus Christ Superstar* (1971), and even *Monty Python's Spamalot* (2005) have drawn inspiration from the sphere of religion.

Late Nineteenth and Early Twentieth Centuries

In the first decade of the twentieth century, Broadway welcomed some 15 religious dramas. The most successful of the turn-of-the-century "toga plays" was William Young's *Ben-Hur* (1899), adapted from Lew Wallace's novel *Ben-Hur: A Tale of the Christ*. The story told of a Roman Jew who converted to Christianity. In the play Jesus "The Nazarene" was represented on stage by a 25,000-candle-power shaft of blue light. The 1900 season also saw a rare instance of two entirely different stage adaptations of the same novel appearing on Broadway in the same year. Henry Sienkiewicz's novel *Quo Vadis?*, a tale of love, persecution, and conversion during the reign of Nero, was staged in April by producer C. F. Whitney. A less successful adaptation by another producer opened in December. Other religious dramas making it to Broadway in the early 1900s included the fifteenth-century morality play *Everyman* (1902) and Paul Heyse's *Mary of Magdala* (1902), whose plot posed Judas as lover of the Magdalene.

The years between 1905 and 1910 saw production of several plays featuring Messianic figures who induced moral and spiritual changes in those around them. James MacArthur's *The Christian Pilgrim* (1907), Charles Rann Kennedy's *The Servant in the House* (1908), and Jerome K. Jerome's *The Passing of the Third Floor* (1909) all explored messianic themes. The 1910s also saw Broadway take a turn toward modern American morality plays and dramatic adaptations of biblical stories. The allegories *Everywoman* by Walter Browne (1911) and *Experience* (1914) by George V. Hobart taught familiar lessons about temptation, false happiness, and true love. Bible stories finding their way into full theatrical production included *Joseph and His Brethren* (1913), written and directed by Louis N. Parker. *Joseph* starred Irish-born heartthrob and press favorite Brandon Tynan, and enjoyed a run of several months. Maurice V. Samuels's *The Wanderer* (1917) retold the biblical tale of the prodigal son. (Featured as Pharaoh was James O'Neill, father of playwright Eugene O'Neill, whom many believe was the inspiration for the character James Tyrone in **Long Day's Journey into Night**.) The Irish playwright Lord Dunsany, who specialized in escapist tales with Asian and Middle East settings, rendered a dramatization of *The Book of Job* (1919) in a repertory series whose religious significance was overshadowed by the exotic faraway sets and costumes.

Towering above these playwrights was Anglo-Irish moralist, agnostic, and provocateur George Bernard Shaw, who in the 1910s saw over 20 productions of his plays mounted on Broadway. Two plays examined religious questions. *Androcles and the Lion* (1915) explored a favorite Shavian topic—the attitude of the established order to anything new—through his humorous depiction of a halfhearted Roman persecution of cheerful, song-filled followers of Jesus. *Major Barbara* (1915), with its spirited discussion-debates on types of religion and forms of salvation, is one of Shaw's two best-known religious plays. It has been revived four times on Broadway, as recently as 2001. (The other is *St. Joan*. See sidebar "Joan of Arc on Broadway.")

The Roaring Religious 1920s

Not withstanding the post–World War I secularization of American culture in general, and Manhattan's night life in particular, religious works thrived on Broadway in the 1920s. However, along with plays about devotional belief, playwrights, producers, and audiences demonstrated an interest in religious issues concerning

JOAN OF ARC ON BROADWAY

No religious figure has graced the stages of Broadway with greater fanfare than Joan of Arc, the fifteenth-century French peasant girl who, guided by saints' voices, led an army to save France only to be burned at the stake for heresy. Lawrence Marston, who would later direct the original productions of the play *Kismet* (1911) and *Abie's Irish Rose*, wrote an unsuccessful adaptation of Joan's tale under the title *Jeanne d'Arc*. In 1907, the Shuberts produced a different adaptation with the same title. The Shubert play, written by Percy Mackaye and starring the popular husband-and-wife acting team of E. H. Sothern and Julia Marlowe, enjoyed more acclaim than Marston's effort. In 1910, 1916, and 1917 Sarah Bernhardt, the legendary French actress, staged limited-run Broadway productions of Emile Moreau's *Le Proces de Jeanne d'Arc*, examining the last days of Joan's life. A 1921 English translation of the play (*The Trial of Joan of Arc*), with which Bernhardt was not associated, ran on Broadway for one month.

George Bernard Shaw's *St. Joan* (1923) is the most famous theatrical rendering of Joan of Arc's legend. One of the most frequently revived modern plays in Broadway history (six times between 1936 and 1993), it is the play most closely associated with Shaw's 1925 Nobel Prize for literature. Inspired by her canonization in 1920, the play whimsically identifies the Roman Catholic saint as the first Protestant, since she had communed with heaven without priestly intermediaries. Moreover, Joan's contentious arguments with church elders about faith and feminism provided Shaw an opportunity to engage his "theater of ideas" technique, in which dramatic action is suspended so characters can debate the politics and philosophy behind their motivations. While Shaw is the playwright most closely associated with the success of Joan of Arc "on Broadway," he held no monopoly. **Maxwell Anderson**'s *Joan of Lorraine* (1946) was also a hit; Ingrid Bergman starred as Joan and co-won (with **Helen Hayes** in *Happy Birthday*) the first-ever Tony Award for Best Actress in a Play. **Lillian Hellman**'s highly regarded English adaptation and translation of Jean Anouilh's biographical drama *The Lark* (1955) earned leading actress Julie Harris a Best Actress Tony Award, rave notices, and a rare (for a Broadway performer) cover story/profile in *Time Magazine*.

tolerance and bigotry. Not uncoincidentally the 1920s saw the emergence of organized protests by religious groups against productions with perceived defamatory content. E. Temple Thurston's *The Wandering Jew* (1921) dramatized the Christian legend of the man who, for taunting Jesus on his way to Calvary, was condemned to roam the earth until the Second Coming. The thirteenth-century *Freiburg Passion Play* (1929) staged the traditional drama of Jesus' last days, prompting members of New York's Jewish community to criticize the play for seemingly reviling their people. Aaron Hoffman's *Welcome Stranger* (1920), although a comedy, was one of the earliest American plays to confront the nation's anti-Semitism, while John Galsworthy's *Loyalties* (1922) examined anti-Semitism in England.

The importance of religious tolerance—including interfaith romance—as a theme in twentieth-century Broadway was made unmistakably clear with the success of *Abie's Irish Rose* (1922), a comedy based on a Jewish-Irish marriage. The author attributed the play's astonishing run (2,327 performances spanning five years) to the spirit of tolerance it celebrated at a time when such an interfaith union seemed improbable in America. By fitting contrast, Elmer Rice's *Street Scene* (1929), a socially conscious melodrama about ethnic and religious intolerance in New York, won the Pulitzer Prize.

The 1920s also saw the rise of **radio** preachers, who began broadcasting on local stations and regional station hookups as early as 1920. Several acquired national audiences and celebrity status with the growth of networks in the late 1920s. Not surprisingly, as preachers became iconic figures, they soon found themselves represented in popular culture. Eternal judgment was the theme of Sutton Vane's *Outward Bound* (1924), in which a minister known as the Examiner conducts individual, soul-searching interviews to determine if passengers aboard a mysterious ship would go to Heaven or Hell. Eugene O'Neill's *Dynamo* (1929) traced a minister's son's search for a religion as he converted from fundamentalism to atheism and, finally, to science. Patrick Kearny's *Elmer Gantry* (1928), adapted from Sinclair Lewis's controversial 1927 novel about an irredeemably hypocritical minister, opened without public controversy but closed quickly due to lack of audience support. In the same year, Sidney Howard and Charles MacArthur's *Salvation* (1928) brought to mind Aimee Semple McPherson and other famous radio preachers of the era.

1930s and 1940s

In the 1930s Broadway productions explored religious themes that were familiar from past decades, although some new issues—particularly race relations—entered the mix. Marc Connelly's Pulitzer Prize–winning *The Green Pastures* (1930) stands in the tradition of staged Bible stories. An African American cast retells Old Testament tales as Green, a white writer, speculates how they might have been rendered by black Christians in the rural South. The rare presence of an all-black Broadway cast performing a work by a contemporary white playwright complicated the religious issues attendant to the play. Critical reaction split along lines that hinted at the emerging, uneasy political alliance between northern white liberals and African Americans. Liberal drama critics generally celebrated the play as a meaningful dramatization of African American religious belief. However, the African American writer Langston Hughes characterized the piece as a demeaning simplification of African American faith.

The martyrdom of the twelfth-century churchman Thomas Becket (canonized 1173) was the subject of T. S. Eliot's first religious drama. *Murder in the Cathedral*

(1936), a Federal Theatre Project production, used liturgical forms, a classical chorus, and morality-play Tempters to examine the sincerity of Becket's actions in embracing self-sacrifice. Jesus' words about being a prophet "without honor . . . among his own kin" (Mark 6:4) expressed the theme of Lenore Coffee and William Joyce Cowen's *Family Portrait* (1939), in which Jesus' brothers and other relatives reject his ministry; only his mother, Mary, the central figure, steadfastly supports him. The theme of humanity's penchant for creating false beliefs is grounded in the biblical warnings of false idols and has certainly found its way into modern literature—famously so in Eugene O'Neill's play *The Iceman Cometh* (1946) with its explorations of the "pipedreams" of self-delusional alcoholic men, self-condemned to the metaphoric hell of a New York flophouse bar.

Two faith-based Broadway musicals bracketed other religious offerings in the 1940s. In Lynn Root, Vernon Duke, and John La Touche's *Cabin in the Sky* (1940)—a medieval morality play in a modern idiom—the forces of good (the Lawd's General and a loving, prayerful wife) vied with the forces of evil (Lucifer Jr., and a sultry temptress) for the soul of a rascally husband given a second chance at life and redemption. Maxwell Anderson and Kurt Weill's *Lost in the Stars* (1949) based on Alan Paton's novel *Cry, the Beloved Country*, told of a black South African minister whose faith was shaken by his son's murder of a white benefactor and of the victim's British father, who acquired faith through his loss.

1950–The Holocaust, the Bomb, and McCarthyism

In the 1950s the Holocaust, the atom bomb, and McCarthyism provided the stimulus for religious dramas, musicals, thought-provoking comedy, and tragicomedy. Jewish Broadway producers and writers, long reluctant to present overtly Jewish content to a mainstream audience, felt freer to do so after the defeat of Adolf Hitler and the liberation of the Nazi concentration camps by Allied forces. The Pulitzer Prize–winning *The Diary of Anne Frank* (1955), dramatized by Frances Goodrich and Albert Hackett, portrayed the communal existence of eight Jews, including young Anne, who survived for two years in an Amsterdam garret during the Nazi occupation. Christopher Fry's *The Firstborn* (1958) told the story of Moses and the Jews in Egypt, culminating in the start of the Exodus. The work was produced in tribute to Israel's tenth anniversary. Paddy Chayefsky's *The Tenth Man* (1959) placed the Jewish fable of the *dybbuk*—possession of a living person by the malevolent soul of a dead person—in a suburban Long Island setting. **Clifford Odets**'s *The Flowering Peach* (1954) presented the spirited Jewish family life of Noah before, during, and after the Flood—here, an allegory of nuclear destruction. The play inspired the 1970 musical *Two by Two*, one of **Richard Rodgers**'s last original full-scale Broadway musicals.

Jewish themes were by no means the only religious content to emerge on Broadway after World War II. In *The Crucible* (1953), Arthur Miller used the seventeenth-century witchcraft trials in Salem, Massachusetts, to explore the roots of intolerance, to attack persecution, and to indict the anti-Communist witch-hunts of HUAC and Joseph McCarthy. The link Miller drew between religious and political bigotry is one of the play's lasting contributions to modern discourse on issues of tolerance in American society. *J.B.* (1958), Archibald MacLeish's Pulitzer Prize–winning modern version of the *Book of Job*, probed the individual's relationship to God amid the misery, injustice, and catastrophes of the atomic age. Inspired by the celebrated 1925 "monkey trial" in Tennessee, Jerome Lawrence and Robert E. Lee's *Inherit the Wind* (1955) pitted Darwin's theory of evolution against the literal interpretation of creation in *Genesis*. Recent controversies over the teaching of Darwin and creationism in schools prompted Broadway revivals in 1996 and 2007.

The Devil enjoyed prominent roles in George Bernard Shaw's amusing *Don Juan in Hell* (1951) and in the **George Abbott**, Richard Adler, and Jerry Ross musical *Damn Yankees* (1955). Shaw's sophisticated Devil engaged the title character in a philosophical debate on the benefits of Hell (love, pleasure, art, beauty) over Heaven (rational discourse) to convert the Puritan Don to a hedonistic existence. In a comically Faustian bargain Mr. Applegate, the Devil in *Damn Yankees*, transforms a middle-aged fan of the hapless Washington Senators ball club into a young, powerful slugger who enables the team to take the American League pennant from the indomitable New York Yankees. A gambler's love for a sister at the Save-a-Soul Mission lies at the heart of **Frank Loesser**'s *Guys and Dolls* (1950). Its songs included the gospel-style number "Sit Down, You're Rockin' the Boat" and the Missionaries' hymn "Follow the Fold."

Along with references to Christ's crucifixion, to salvation, and to damnation, *Waiting for Godot* (1956) by Irish playwright Samuel Beckett implied, in its absurdist world of cruelty and hopelessness, a flickering faith, perhaps in God, to whom the title might allude, and a hope for His coming. Although the original Broadway production received no major awards, the play is widely considered to be among the most influential dramas of the twentieth century.

1960s and 1970s

Broadway in the 1960s and 1970s reflected the social turbulence of those decades in powerful dramas and stirring musicals on potent religious subjects. Among the noteworthy dramas of the time was Robert Bolt's *A Man for All Seasons* (1961) about the imprisonment of English Renaissance writer and religious dissenter, Sir Thomas More. The play won the Tony for Best Play and numerous other awards. The play was revived in 2008 with Broadway veteran Frank Langella starring in the title role. Opposition to either sacred or secular authority drove plays about the Bible's Gideon (Paddy Chayefksy's *Gideon*, 1961) and about St. Thomas Becket (Jean Anouilh's *Becket*, 1960). John Osborne's *Luther* (1963), a biographical play about Martin Luther, also paid homage to religious dissent.

The opening of the Second Ecumenical Council in 1962 by Pope John XXIII brought widespread public attention to the Vatican. Broadway responded with two plays on the papacy. Rolf Hochhuth's *The Deputy* (1964) controversially contended that Pope Pius XII, as God's vicar on earth, was criminally responsible for the deaths of countless Jews for failing to denounce Nazi extermination camps. Police and protesters greeted the Broadway opening, but the play ran for an impressive 316 performances. Peter Luke's hit *Hadrian VII* (1969) offered a decidedly more favorable portrayal of the papacy. Luke's play concerns a fictional early twentieth-century English Pontiff who gives away Vatican treasures to help the poor and reforms the Church. He dies a martyr, after forgiving his assassins.

A number of theatrical works of the 1960s and 1970s reflected the contemporary Black Arts Movement's ethos of African American ownership of their own narratives and theatrical representations. The African American team of Vinnette Carroll, Alex Bradford, and Mikki Grant developed the high-energy *Your Arms Too Short to Box with God* (1976), a contemporary gospel-driven musical loosely based on the *Book of Matthew*. The original production ran for over 400 performances and the show has been revived on Broadway twice. Langston Hughes's *Tambourines to Glory* (1963), adapted from his novel of the same name, filled Broadway's famed Little Theatre with fervent gospel singing in telling the story of the establishment of a street-corner church. In James Baldwin's *The Amen Corner* (1965), impoverished blacks turn to religion for a respite from their sorrows. The play was the source for a short-lived musical adaptation, *Amen Corner* (1983).

The first family in Genesis furnished plots for two noteworthy productions. The frothy "Diary of Adam and Eve" (from Mark Twain's story)—Act I of Jerry Bock and Sheldon Harnick's musical *The Apple Tree* (1966)—followed the couple from their creations, through their fall, their new life in a place Eve called Tonawanda, and offstage events concerning Cain and Abel, to Eve's death. In Arthur Miller's comedy *The Creation of the World and Other Business* (1972), God and Lucifer vied for power, holding Adam, Eve, Cain, and Abel in their sway, as the playwright grappled with questions on the nature of free will and the origins of good, justice, and their opposites.

Two musicals in the 1970s memorably retold the biblical accounts of the life and death of Christ in the contemporary rhythms of the youth culture. Andrew Lloyd Webber and Tim Rice's *Jesus Christ Superstar* (1971) introduced Broadway to **European "megamusicals"** that would become a dominating force on Broadway in the coming decades. John-Michael Tebelak and Stephen Schwartz's *Godspell* (1976) was a devotional adaptation of the life of Jesus. One of the show's songs, "Day By Day," became a mainstream radio hit single, providing a boost to the newly emerging Christian rock music industry. Other musicals of the period that dealt with religious themes included the hit *Fiddler on the Roof*, a musical comedy that, nonetheless, presented a purposeful treatment of one man's struggle to hold on to Jewish religious traditions in a diverse and progressive world. Its major figure, Tevye the dairyman, regularly addresses God in monologues, at once respectful and familiar.

The theme of false religious beliefs found unconventional expressions in two plays from England. *Equus* (1974) by Peter Schaffer criticized dogmatic, repressive Christianity and championed primitive, passionate religious belief through its story about a boy who blinded horses and worshiped an equine god. In a pivotal scene in Bernard Pomerance's *The Elephant Man* (1979), John Merrick, the grotesquely misshaped historical title character, spends the latter half of the play building a model of a church. This rising structure symbolized humankind's aspiration to transcend the earthly.

1980s to the Present

The early 1980s generated a number of Catholic-themed plays and musicals that, while viewed by some as probing or amusing, were seen by many critics and organizations as openly anti-Christian or anti-Catholic. Individually and collectively these works and the controversies surrounding them became part of a larger "culture war" played out in the mass media between the entertainment industry's impulse to market whatever content it chooses and religious traditionalists' commitment to combating public defamation of their beliefs.

John Pielmeier's *Agnes of God* (1982), a discourse on the theme of faith versus reason, questioned the existence of saints and miracles today as well as society's ability to recognize and accept them if they did appear. The Catholic League of America, which surveys entertainment and media for what it considers to be objectionable content, branded the play (and the 1985 film adaptation) as "notoriously anti-Catholic." The previous season's *Mass Appeal* by Bill C. Davis, dramatizing the clash between a worldly senior priest and an idealistic seminarian, drew little controversy. Adding fuel to the controversy over Broadway's representation of Catholicism was the astonishingly successful **Off-Broadway** play *Sister Mary Ignatius Explains It All for You* by Christopher Durang. The longest-running dramatic production in Off-Broadway history (1979 through 1984), the play is a savage farce involving a Catholic school assembly presided over by a cartoonishly sadistic nun. Detractors have labeled the play "a hate letter" to the Church. Later Broadway plays also explored controversial subjects within the Catholic church, but none received anything approaching the level of criticism associated with the controversies of the early 1980s. Diane Shaffer's *Sacrilege* (1995) made the case for the ordination of women to the Roman Catholic priesthood. John Patrick Shanley's Pulitzer Prize–winning and Tony Award Best Play *Doubt* (2005) probed people's suspicions and moral certainties concerning a Roman Catholic priest and his camaraderie with a young male student.

The Catholic Church has hardly been the sole focus of theatrical explorations of religion over the past few decades. Infused with Christian theology, Peter Shaffer's *Amadeus* (1980) dealt extensively with divine injustice, which seemingly bestowed inadequate earthly bounty on the devout, hardworking composer Antonio Salieri, while extravagantly advancing the scatological libertine Mozart, whose name "Amadeus" suggests "the love of God" and "the one whom God loves." Lloyd Webber and Rice's *Joseph and the Amazing Technicolor Dreamcoat* (1982) set to music the previously dramatized Old Testament accounts of Jacob's favorite son and his coat of many colors.

In the 1990s Judaism, the modern church, and gay themes inspired memorable plays. Alfred Uhry's *The Last Night of Ballyhoo* (1997), set in Atlanta, raised the issue of intra-ethnic Jewish prejudices (German Jews versus Eastern European

Jews). The musical *Parade* by Uhry and James Robert Brown (1998) told the true story of Leo Frank, a Brooklyn Jew transplanted to Atlanta, who was lynched in Marietta, Georgia, in 1915 for the murder of a 13-year-old girl, of which he had been falsely accused. His trial, sensationalized by the press, had stirred up anti-Semitic tensions around the state.

Just as several plays and musicals of the past had linked race to questions of morality and religion, more recent works have drawn comparable linkages between attitudes about homosexuality and religion. Tony Kushner's revolutionary two-part **Angels in America** (*Millennium Approaches* and *Perestroika*, both 1993) featured a conservative Mormon lawyer who struggled to reconcile his faith with his homosexuality. Spectacularly interweaving issues of religious prejudice, racial prejudice, and gay/lesbian prejudice, Kushner expanded the concept of the American social drama from a tightly focused, issue-driven narrative to an intellectual and visual spectacle. The play included biblical references, the saying of Kaddish (the Hebrew prayer of mourning the dead), scenes in Heaven, and international angels. The play also linked religious righteousness to respect and social acceptance for AIDS victims. **Terrence McNally**'s Off-Broadway play *Corpus Christi* (1998), like *Sister Mary Ignatius*, generated controversy that reverberated throughout New York's professional theater community. The play imagines the life and death of Jesus from the twentieth-century perspective of a young man named Joshua and his followers, all homosexuals, who spread a gospel of love. The play began and ended in the Texas town of the title which, translated from Latin, means "Body of Christ." Protests and bomb threats in reaction to the Bible story's gay interpretation initially prompted the Manhattan Theater Club (MTC) to cancel the production, citing public safety concerns. Following an outcry from free speech advocates, MTC reversed itself and presented the play, though audiences had to pass through police barricades and metal detectors.

In the new century, religion and Broadway still found a place for one another, and early indications suggest that former tensions may have eased. Preceding Shanley's *Doubt*, the one-actor play *An Almost Holy Picture* by Heather McDonald (2002) explored the expressions that faith could take as a former Episcopal priest sought meaning in his Job-like existence. By jarring contrast, the campy hit musical comedy *Monty Python's Spamalot*(2005), like the movie from which it was adapted (*Monty Python and the Holy Grail*), mocks the centuries-old genre of Christian quest literature with its irreverent plot (the "holy quest" is ultimately a mission to bring a show to Broadway) and purposefully cheesy-looking costumes and sets (including a representation of God as two gigantic, cartoon-drawn bare feet descending from the clouds). Lest Christians feel singled out in the satire, *Spamalot's* pilgrims are warned along the way, in a soft shoe number, that they will not "succeed on Broadway if (they) don't have any Jews."

As they have for more than a century, speculative dramatists, composers, producers, and audiences receptive to theatrical inquiries, celebrations, and even satires in the areas of spirituality and theology will ensure the vitality of plays and musicals about religion for decades to come.

John Spalding Gatton

Further Reading

Adler, Thomas P. " 'The Mystery of Things': The Varieties of Religious Experience in Modern American Drama." In *Themes in Drama* 5: *Drama and Religion*, ed. James Redmond. Cambridge, England: Cambridge University Press, 1983, pp. 139–57.

Atkinson, J. Brooks. "New Negro Drama of Sublime Beauty." *New York Times*, February 27, 1930, p. 20.

Blum, Daniel C. *A Pictorial History of the American Theater: 1860–1985*. New York: Crown, 1986.

Clum, John. "Religion and Five Contemporary Plays: The Quest for God in a Godless World." *South Atlantic Quarterly* 77, no. 4 (1978): 418–32.

Hopper, Stanley Romaine, ed. *Spiritual Problems in Contemporary Literature*. New York: Harper & Row, 1957.

Mayer, David. *Playing Out the Empire:* Ben-Hur *and Other Toga Plays and Films, 1883–1908: A Critical Anthology*. Oxford, England: Clarendon Press, 1994.

Rich, Frank. *Hot Seat: Theater Criticism for* The New York Times, *1980–1993*. New York: Random House, 1998.

Sova, Dawn B. *Banned Plays: Censorship Histories of 125 Stage Dramas*. New York: Facts on File, 2004.

Weales, Gerald. *Religion in Modern English Drama*. Philadelphia: University of Pennsylvania Press, 1961.

RENT

Broadway Run: Nederlander Theatre
Opening: April 29, 1996
Closing: September 7, 2008
Total Performances: 5,123
Book, Music, and Lyrics: Jonathan Larson
Choreographer: Marlies Yearby
Director: Michael Greif
Producer: Produced by Jeffrey Seller, Kevin McCollum, Allan S. Gordon, and New York Theatre Workshop
Cast: Taye Diggs (Benjamin Coffin III), Wilson Jermaine Heredia (Angel Schunard), Jesse L. Martin (Tom Collins), Idina Menzel (Maureen Johnson), Adam Pascal (Roger Davis), Anthony Rapp (Mark Cohen), Daphne Rubin-Vega (Mimi Marquez), and Fredi Walker (Joanne Jefferson)

Rent ran from 1996 to 2008 and introduced mainstream commercial musical theater to Generation X or the MTV Generation: sophisticated young urbanites born after 1960 and presumptively acclimated to racial tolerance, multiculturalism, homosexuality, bisexuality, and casual drug use as cultural norms. Based loosely on Puccini's opera *La Boheme*, *Rent* tells the story of a group of struggling young

The cast of Rent *takes a curtain call after the Pulitzer Prize–winning rock musical opened on Broadway in 1996.* Rent *arrived triumphantly at the Nederlander Theater after a successful run Off-Broadway. It opened a few weeks after the death of its 35-year-old creator, Jonathan Larson. (AP Photo/Wally Santana)*

New York hipsters working menial jobs to support their loftier ambitions as artists and performers. Along the way the ensemble confronts challenges from drug use, poverty, social conformity, sexual identity, and AIDS. Jonathan Larson, who wrote the books, lyrics, and music for *Rent* had the most important and most successful one-show career in the history of Broadway. Having shepherded the show through years of redrafts, workshops, and a successful **Off-Broadway** run, Larson died a few months before the show's Broadway opening. He posthumously won a career's worth of awards for *Rent*, including three Tony Awards (Best Musical, Best Lyrics, Best Score) and a Pulitzer Prize for outstanding drama.

Larson was born in White Plains, New York, in Westchester County to a Jewish family. In high school he performed in school bands and theater productions. He began composing while attending Adelphi University in suburban New York, starting with small student cabaret productions. He later wrote the full score to *Libro de Buen Amor* (*Book of Good Love*), a **musical** written by Jacques Burdick, an Adelphi faculty member and a highly respected director in academic and **regional theater** circles. After graduation and with an Actors' Equity card in hand, Larson moved to New York City and rented a small fifth floor loft without heat in Greenwich Village. Over the years Larson had various impoverished young roommates who shared his loft's harsh conditions. His observations of their comings and goings would later serve as the basis of the characters and multiple plotlines for *Rent*. He supported himself by working as a waiter for ten years at the Moondance Diner, one of the last of midtown Manhattan's "old style" diners (it closed in 2007). Larson met several other aspiring theater artists at the diner including fellow waiter Jesse L. Martin, who would later originate the role of Tom Collins in *Rent* and go on to a prodigious stage, **film**, and **television** career.

Prior to completing *Rent*, which Larson worked on for seven years, he landed a number of solid professional jobs and won several prestigious young artist prizes. A futuristic rock musical, *Superbia*, won a Richard Rodgers Development Grant and earned Larson a coveted workshop staging at New York's Playwrights Horizons. Larson also performed Off-Broadway with an original rock monologue *tick, tick . . . BOOM!* (which, in a 2001 Off-Broadway revival, would earn Larson three posthumous Drama Desk Awards). He also contributed songs to *Sesame Street* and worked on a project for Warner Brothers Animation. Along the way, his work caught the attention of **Stephen Sondheim**, who encouraged Larson throughout the early stages of his career.

Before opening on Broadway in April 1996, *Rent* had an enormously successful Off-Broadway run earlier in the year. However, Larson did not live to see either the Off-Broadway or Broadway staging of his masterwork. On the night of the final dress rehearsal for *Rent*'s Off-Broadway premiere, Larson died suddenly of an aortic aneurysm from Marfan Syndrome, a disorder of the connective tissue.

Rent opened on Broadway to sensational reviews and almost unprecedented nationwide press coverage, expressing nearly universal admiration for the show's energy and originality as well as compassion over the untimely death of its young creator. When it closed on Broadway in June 2008, it had run for over 5,000 performances—the seventh longest-running show in Broadway history and the only one in the top ten written or conceived by an artist with only one Broadway credit. Although a 2005 film adaptation was a critical and commercial failure, the show's signature song "Seasons of Love," with its engagingly quirky lyrical hook (525,600 minutes), is one of the most recognizable Broadway **show tunes** from the 1990s, and *Rent* has been a huge success on national tours and in overseas productions. The show is often compared to the musical **Hair** (1968) in that it attracted large numbers of late teenagers and "twenty-somethings" who heretofore had stayed away from commercial musicals in droves. (Some university theater directors refer to the crop of undergraduates who came of age during the Bill Clinton presidency as "The *Rent* Generation," owing to their powerful identification with the show, its themes, and the short but remarkable life of its young creator.)

Rent also provided important career breakthrough roles for several young original cast members, most notably Idina Menzel, who went on to win the Tony Award for Best Actress in a musical as Elphaba the Green Witch in *Wicked* (2003) and Daphne Rubin-Vega, who later co-starred on Broadway in the critically acclaimed drama *Anna in the Tropics* (2003).

Molly Smith Metzler

Further Reading

Rapp, Anthony. *Without You: A Memoir of Love, Loss, and the Musical* Rent. New York: Simon & Schuster, 2006.

Schulman, Sarah. *Stagestruck: Theater, AIDS, and the Marketing of Gay America.* Durham, NC: Duke University Press, 1998.

RICHARDS, LLOYD (1919–2006)
DIRECTOR, EDUCATOR, THEATER ADMINISTRATOR

Lloyd George Richards was one of the most influential figures in American theater during the latter half of the twentieth century. Although probably best known as a groundbreaking director on Broadway and longtime head of the Yale Repertory Theatre, he was probably most influential in—and most proud of—his role as a discoverer and nurturer of new **playwrights**. As a member of the Playwrights' selection committee of the Rockefeller Foundation and of the New American Plays program of the Ford Foundation, and as Artistic Director of the National Playwrights Conference at the Eugene O'Neill Memorial Theatre, his eye was ever toward discovering and developing both new dramas and new dramatists. The list of those who owe much of their success to his mentorship and far-reaching influence includes many of Broadway's most distinguished playwrights of the past

August Wilson, left, and longtime collaborator, director Lloyd Richards, shown in a 1990 photo taken at New York's Walter Kerr Theatre, where Wilson's play The Piano Lesson, *directed by Richards, was performed. The play won the 1990 Pulitzer Prize for drama. (AP Photo/David Cantor)*

50 years, such as **Lorraine Hansberry**, **Wendy Wasserstein**, **August Wilson**, Athol Fugard, and John Guare.

The unequivocal respect that Lloyd Richards earned in both New York's highly competitive theater industry and academia came after a series of lateral moves that took him from a childhood of poverty to a life of relative ease. Richards was born in Toronto, Canada, in 1919 to Albert and Rose Richards, Jamaican immigrants, who moved the family to Detroit, Michigan, when he was four. His father found work in a Detroit automobile factory but died a few years later, leaving the family in dire financial straits. At 13, Richards went to work during the height of the Depression to help support his struggling family. He shined shoes and swept floors in a barbershop while his widowed mother found work as a domestic. His mother eventually lost her eyesight, making him the sole breadwinner for a household of five siblings and himself. Nonetheless, Richards succeeded in supporting his family and, after high school, enrolled in Wayne State University. Upon graduation, Richards enlisted in the army toward the end of World War II, becoming one of the military's first black pilots. After discharge, he returned to Detroit and became active in **radio** drama and **regional theater**.

Richards later moved to New York City in the 1950s where, between acting and directing, he worked a host of menial jobs to sustain his cash flow. He studied with Paul Mann, a proponent of the Stanislavsky method of acting, eventually becoming a teacher at Mann's Actors Workshop. Except for a one-week Broadway stint in an evening of one-acts in 1950, Richards worked Off-Broadway throughout the 1950s. His debut in a full-length Broadway play came in 1957 with a minor role in Molly Kazan's *The Egg Head*. The production folded quickly but Richards found himself in the company of some of Broadway's leading artists, including the play's star, Karl Malden, and director, **Hume Cronyn**.

Following Mann's advice, Richards moved toward directing as well as theater education. In 1959, he directed Lorraine Hansberry's *A Raisin in the Sun* (1959). The play was a sensation, vaulting Hansberry and Richards into the center of New York theater circles. The production has since earned a place of distinction in American theater history for, among other reasons, marking the first time an African American directed a major Broadway play. The play won the New York Critics Circle Award for the 1958–1959 season and generated numerous professional and educational opportunities for Richards. He became head of actor training at the New York University School of the Arts from 1966 to 1972 and later professor in the department of theater and cinema at Hunter College in New York. Throughout the 1960s and 1970s his reputation as a talent scout and mentor of young theater professionals spread throughout New York's theater network and beyond. Largely on the basis of his rapport with students, in 1969 he was called upon to head the Eugene O'Neill Theater Center in Waterford, Connecticut.

In 1979 Yale University invited Richards to head both the Yale School of Drama and the Yale Repertory Theatre. That he was African American later surprised the theater community; that he was qualified did not. Richards distinguished himself with his inclusive approach to working with students and his serious-minded approach to both the academic and artistic demands of theater education. He also established the Yale Repertory Theatre as a leading regional proving ground for future Broadway plays, including Athol Fugard's *Master Harold and the Boys* (1982), Lee Blessing's *A Walk in the Woods* (1988), and most famously the plays of August Wilson.

Richards' long search for a major new American playwright led him to Wilson in 1982 and came to fruition in 1984 with the production of *Ma Rainey's Black Bottom*, first at the Yale Repertory Theatre and later that year on Broadway. The historic collaboration between playwright and director began in 1982, when Wilson submitted the script of *Ma Rainey's Black Bottom* to the O'Neill Theater Center summer workshop. Richards and Wilson blended their talents to create a string of critically acclaimed plays that also included *Fences* (1987), *Joe Turner's Come and Gone* (1988), *The Piano Lesson* (1990), and *Two Trains Running* (1992). Wilson wrote the plays and Richards directed and polished them in workshops such as those at the Yale Repertory Theatre and regional theaters throughout the country. Richards directed six of Wilson's Broadway productions, earning a Tony Award for Best Direction of a Play for *Fences* and numerous other awards and plaudits for that distinguished body of work.

In 1991 Richards retired with distinction from his 12-year post as Dean of the Yale School of Drama with an unprecedented flurry of media attention. In the minds of many of his peers, he had made the school into the leading theater education program in the country, giving it a reputation for exceptional commitment to cultivating new talent and diversifying the talent pool in all areas of theater. As a gesture to commemorate his indelible impact upon the direction of its drama program, Yale established an endowed chair in Richards's name—the first of its kind for an African American. He continued to serve as Artistic Director of the Playwrights Conference at the O'Neill Center until 1999.

Richards died of heart failure on his 87th birthday, June 29, 2006, in New York City.

Sandra G. Shannon

Further Reading

Bartow, Arthur. "Lloyd Richards." *The Director's Voice: Twenty-one Interviews*. New York: Theatre Communications Group, 1988.

Shannon, Sandra G. "Richards, Lloyd George." *Encyclopedia of African-American Culture and History*, Vol. 4, ed. Jack Salzman et al. New York: Macmillan, 2002.

ROBARDS, JASON, JR. (1922–2000)
ACTOR

Also known simply as Jason Robards, Jason Robards Jr. achieved success as an actor in **radio**, **television**, and **film**, but established himself as a major American

Jason Robards, right, chats with cartoonist-playwright-screenwriter Herb Gardner, on the film set of A Thousand Clowns, *in a studio outside New York, July 6, 1964, which was turned into a movie after its successful run on Broadway in 1962. (AP Photo)*

actor in Broadway and **Off-Broadway** theater. His well-crafted, commanding acting style and strong stage presence kept him in demand in New York and in Hollywood for over 40 years. Although he acted in works by many major American **playwrights**, Robards is best known for his critically acclaimed performances in the later plays of **Eugene O'Neill**. These performances helped inspire a revival of popular interest in O'Neill's work after the playwright's death in 1953. Between 1957 and 1978 Robards was nominated for eight Tony Awards, the most ever for a male actor. Four of those eight nominations were for roles in O'Neill plays.

Robards was born in Chicago, the son of stage and screen actor Jason Robards Sr. Robards's interest in O'Neill and his desire to become an actor were sparked while serving in the navy during World War II. He came upon a copy of O'Neill's *Strange Interlude* in the ship's library and felt an immediate affinity for the playwright's work. When Robards left the navy he moved to New York and enrolled in the American Academy of Dramatic Arts, where he was taught acting by some of the same instructors who had taught his father years earlier. He began his professional career in the 1950s, working in Off-Broadway theater, radio, and prestige network television productions such as *Studio One*, *Omnibus*, and *Philco Television Playhouse*. His ascent to theatrical stardom came in 1956 when he appeared Off-Broadway as Hickey, the enigmatic shatterer of pipe dreams in a revival of Eugene O'Neill's *The Iceman Cometh*. Directed by **José Quintero** at the Circle in the Square Theatre, this enormously successful revival eclipsed the lackluster 1946 Broadway original, conferring new prestige and credibility upon Off-Broadway theater in general and establishing both Robards and Quintero as major figures in New York theatrical circles.

The critical and popular acclaim accorded this production restored O'Neill's public reputation, which had reached its height in 1931 with the premier of *Mourning Becomes Electra* but began to decline two years later after the successful production of *Ah, Wilderness!* Although O'Neill was awarded the Nobel Prize for Literature in 1936, no new plays of his were produced on Broadway between 1934 and 1956 other than the 1946 production of *Iceman*.

Robards attributed his success in interpreting O'Neill's complex and tortured characters to his ability to discern subtleties of theme and character embedded in O'Neill's dialogue and stage directions. Robards was also aware of similarities in personality and experience between himself and O'Neill—an actor father, a distant mother, a career at sea, multiple marriages, and serious bouts of alcoholism. Some commentators believe these similarities resonated in his interpretations, particularly in the role of Jamie in ***Long Day's Journey into Night***.

Robards also credited his success to his directors, most notably Quintero. Following the success of *The Iceman Cometh*, Robards and Quintero became hot properties on Broadway and one of the most formidable actor/director pairings in American theater history. In addition to their collaboration on *Iceman*, they worked together on a string of successful productions, including Broadway stagings of O'Neill's *Long Day's Journey into Night* (1956), *Hughie* (1964), *A Moon for the Misbegotten* (1974), and *A Touch of the Poet* (1977).

Because of his craftmanship, presence, and resonant voice, many critics and theatergoers view Robards as America's greatest actor in the classical style since **John Barrymore**. Robards was the first American to work at the **Shakespeare** Festival in Stratford, Ontario, Canada. During the 1958 Stratford season, he appeared as Hotspur in *Henry IV, Part I* and as Polixenes in *A Winter's Tale*. In addition to his work in O'Neill's plays, Robards demonstrated remarkable range in other notable Broadway appearances. He won the Tony Award for Best Actor in a Play starring in Budd Schulberg's *The Disenchanted* (1958). Other Broadway successes included **Lillian Hellman**'s *Toys in the Attic* (1960), Herb Gardner's comedy *A Thousand Clowns* (1962), which was later turned into a movie also starring Robards, A. R. Gurney's *Love Letters* (1993), and Harold Pinter's *No Man's Land* (1994), which was his final Broadway appearance. As an original member of the Lincoln Center Repertory Theatre, he helped launch the company's first season starring in **Arthur Miller**'s *After the Fall* (1964).

Robards enjoyed a long and successful career in the movies despite his professed disdain for Hollywood, which he called "The Land of the Living Dead." He reprised his role as Jamie in Sidney Lumet's film version of *Long Day's*

Journey into Night (1962), winning the best actor award at the Cannes Film Festival. He received Academy Awards for his supporting roles in *All the President's Men* (1976) and *Julia* (1977).

In 1999, the year before his death, Robards received the Kennedy Center Honors in recognition of his lifetime of contributions to American culture. His last and perhaps most fitting honor, the first annual O'Neill Foundation Monte Cristo Award for his Contribution to American Theater, was bestowed upon him in October 2000.

At the end of the twentieth century scholars and critics of American theater predictably launched their debates to determine the best American plays of the twentieth century. High on virtually every serious list were O'Neill's *The Iceman Cometh* and *Long Day's Journey into Night*—both of which owe much of their lasting critical acclaim to Robard's riveting star performances.

Robards died of lung cancer in Bridgeport, Connecticut, on December 26, 2000.

Ellen Herzman

Further Reading

Black, Stephen A., et al., eds. *Jason Robards Remembered: Essays and Recollections.* Jefferson, NC: McFarland & Co., 2002.

Shafer, Yvonne. *Performing O'Neill: Conversations with Actors and Directors.* Rev. ed. New York: Palgrave Macmillan, 2000.

ROBBINS, JEROME (1918–1998)
CHOREOGRAPHER, DANCER, DIRECTOR

Jerome Robbins left a powerful imprint in the theater world, choreographing and directing some of Broadway's most successful **musicals** and introducing important innovations in Broadway staging and choreography. Throughout the 1950s and 1960s Robbins developed his pioneering humor, eclectic mixing of dance traditions, and conceptual approach to choreography simultaneously in both concert dance and musical theater. A pioneer in merging the roles of Broadway choreographer and director, he enlarged the importance of dance and expanded the varieties of dance forms in the modern popular musical. As choreographer and/or director for such shows as *The King and I* (1951), *The Pajama Game* (1954), *Peter Pan* (1954), *Bells Are Ringing* (1956), **West Side Story** (1957), **Gypsy** (1959), and *Fiddler on the Roof* (1964), he elevated the theatrical and conceptual quality of Broadway show dancing, making of it something akin to a modern art form in and of itself.

Born Jerome Rabinowitz to an immigrant Jewish family in New York City, Robbins developed a love for the performing arts from childhood, learning to play the violin and piano and studying interpretative dance. He attended New York

University but dropped out in 1936 due to family financial pressures. Following the lead of his sister Sonia, a professional dancer, Robbins danced professionally in and around New York and Pennsylvania for the next few years. During this time he took small roles in Broadway shows including *Great Lady* (1938), *Stars in Your Eyes* (1939), *Keep Off the Grass* (1940), and *The Straw Hat Revue* (1940). Although none of these productions enjoyed more than moderate success, they afforded Robbins opportunities to work with some of the most influential Broadway talents of the day, including actress **Ethel Merman**, director **Joshua Logan**, and choreographer **George Balanchine**. Each would figure prominently in his success.

At the same time Robbins pursued his career and passion as a concert ballet dancer and choreographer. In the summer of 1940 he joined the new American Ballet Theatre (ABT), where he flourished for several years as a company member, solo performer, and choreographer. His comical, high energy 1944 dance piece "Fancy Free," choreographed with the then unknown composer **Leonard Bernstein**, was a sensation with ABT audiences and became the basis for his first major Broadway show, *On the Town* (1944). The show, choreographed by Robbins with music by Bernstein, was a success and effectively unleashed the two young classical but decidedly iconoclastic artists upon the Broadway world.

Over the next five years Robbins choreographed four solid hit musicals: *Billion Dollar Baby* (1945), *High Button Shoes* (1948) for which he won the first of his three Tony Awards for Best Choreography, *Look Ma, I'm Dancin'* (1948), and *Call Me Madam*(1950), in which he was reunited with Ethel Merman. All this time, he remained active as a leading ballet performer and choreographer, leaving the American Ballet Theatre in 1949 to join George Balanchine's New York City Ballet. He eventually became a star choreographer and dancer for the company as well as associate artistic director.

The 1950s marked an astonishing period for Robbins as he achieved greater renown as a ballet choreographer while directing and/or choreographing some of the most important musicals of the modern era. In 1951 he choreographed *The King and I*, a lavish spectacle set in Siam (now Thailand) that ran for three years and became his biggest Broadway hit to date. In 1954 he codirected *The Pajama Game* with **George Abbott**, one of Broadway's most successful producer/directors. This labor-management romance won the Tony Award for Best Musical and ran almost as long as *The King and I*. Notably, the show also launched new choreographer (and Robbins protégé) **Bob Fosse** toward Broadway stardom. Later that year Robbins directed and choreographed *Peter Pan*, in which he dazzled audiences and peers with choreography for a "flying" cast suspended in midair by thin wires controlled by stagehands. Although the original show ran for only 152 performances, television broadcasts of the original cast with **Mary Martin** and decades of successful tours (especially those starring gymnast-turned-actress Cathy Rigby in the 1980s and 1990s) seared images of Robbins's aerial ballet into America's consciousness. (Robbins's work on *Peter Pan* anticipated the current popularity of aerial choreography in such shows as Cirque du Soleil performances and the

Brenda Angiel Aerial Dance Company.) Almost lost in the shadow of *Peter Pan* and his other successes in the 1950s was *Bells Are Ringing* (1956), directed by Robbins and cochoreographed with Fosse, which ran for over 900 performances.

The only blemish on Robbins's soaring reputation during this period proved to be a serious one. In 1953 the House Un-American Activities Committee (HUAC) subpoenaed Robbins in its ongoing investigation of alleged communist activity in the entertainment industry. He testified to his own prior affiliation with the Communist Party and named eight others as members or "fellow travelers," including some colleagues from his past shows. His testimony remains an indelible part of his biography and later in life he expressed regret for having named people. Several people never forgave him (including actor Zero Mostel, who later worked with him regardless), but the impact of his theatrical successes combined with the fact that HUAC held decidedly less influence over the theater industry than it did over film and broadcasting minimized industry and public resentment of Robbins's actions.

Amazingly, with five major Broadway hits between 1950 and 1956, Robbins's most distinctive achievements of the decade were yet to come. *West Side Story* (1957), directed and choreographed by Robbins with music by Bernstein and lyrics by newcomer **Stephen Sondheim**, is widely viewed as the most innovative musical of the 1950s—largely as a result of Robbins's direction and choreography. Conceived by Robbins as an updated retelling of **Shakespeare**'s *Romeo and Juliet* (but with New York white and Puerto Rican street gangs taking the place of the warring Capulet and Montague families), *West Side Story* was the most uncompromising exploration of American racial and social tensions in a mainstream musical since ***Show Boat*** (1927). Robbins's innovations in dance and staging were no less adventurous. Ever since **Agnes de Mille**'s breakthrough choreography of ***Oklahoma!*** (1943), Broadway choreographers had been developing dance numbers centered on characterization and other literary elements of a show. Robbins had certainly been mindful of this approach in his own work. In *West Side Story*, however, Robbins determined that his choreography would make a quantum leap forward to conceptually represent the story's literary dynamics as an integrated whole.

Robbins used the scenographic elements of urban neighborhoods—alleyways, fire escapes, and tiny window landings—to create crowded, explosive choreography that accumulated energy as the story headed for the climactic street rumble. The legendary "Tonight" quintet, in which Robbins stages five simultaneously interconnected mini-scenes around Bernstein's five-part orchestration of a single song, still stands as a landmark scene in American musical theater history. Moreover, to this day directors, choreographers, scholars, and students study videos of the *West Side Story* as well as the 1961 movie adaptation (codirected by Robbins) and even archived Robbins's rehearsal tapes to glean lessons from this ageless production.

Following *West Side Story*, Robbins directed and choreographed *Gypsy* (1959), starring Merman as larger-than-life stage mother of Mama Rose. Compared to other Robbins hits, *Gypsy*'s 702-show run was not exceptional, and the show won no Tonys in any category. However, over the decades *Gypsy* has gradually captured the adoration of the American public. Robbins's masterful choreographic mapping of daughter Louise's evolution from clumsy child singer to world-class stripper and the rarity of its enduring lead role for a middle-aged actress have given *Gypsy* a greater durability in revivals than even *West Side Story* or *The King and I*. *Fiddler on the Roof*, the story of a turn-of-the-century Russian Jewish family, was his next big hit as director/choreographer. *Fiddler* saw Robbins further applying the conceptual story-line choreography that had become his trademark. With over 3,200 performances, *Fiddler* was the longest-running Broadway show of the entire decade and provided a rare instance of Jewish artists (Robbins along with composer Jerry Bock and lyricist Sheldon Harnick) using specifically Jewish content as the central focus of a mainstream Broadway musical.

Robbins essentially stopped choreographing new Broadway shows in the mid-1960s, turning his attention to ballet. Nevertheless, his Broadway legend grew on its own momentum through 15 Broadway revivals of his shows mounted from the mid-1960s until his death in 1998. Robbins did make one final return to Broadway in 1989 with a retrospective of his own musical theater career, *Jerome Robbins' Broadway*. The show won rave reviews and Tony Awards for Best Musical and Best Director for Robbins. An audience favorite for two seasons, *Jerome Robbins' Broadway* aptly demonstrated that Robbins, an ostensibly behind-the-scenes talent as director and choreographer, had become as famous for his artistry as the most recognizable Broadway star actors, composers, and lyricists. The high level of appreciation and recognition accorded to later choreographers/directors—including Fosse, **Michael Bennett**, and **Susan Stroman**—stands as a critical part of Robbins's legacy to Broadway.

More than a decade after his death, Robbins remains a looming presence in musical theater. Broadway and regional revivals of his hits are among the safest investments any producer can make. (*Peter Pan* and *Fiddler* alone have been revived on Broadway nine times between them, and a 2008 *Gypsy* starring Broadway veteran **Patti LuPone** drew some of the best reviews of any revival in years.) His preeminent positions in the traditionally disparate worlds of show dancing and concert dancing combined with his ability to fuse the two in ways that advanced the state of both make of Robbins a singular talent in the history of musical theater.

Thomas A. Greenfield and Nicole Katz

Further Reading

Jowitt, Deborah. *Jerome Robbins: His Life, His Theater, His Dance*. New York: Simon & Schuster, 2004.
Vaill, Amanda. *Somewhere: The Life of Jerome Robbins*. New York: Broadway Books, 2006.

ROBESON, PAUL (1898–1976)
ACTOR

Paul Robeson was the first African American to achieve career-long stardom in legitimate theater, **film**, and music. One of the most extraordinary figures in twentieth-century American cultural history, Robeson garnered acclaim for a handful of historically significant Broadway roles even as he earned international fame as a concert singer. For much of his career, achievements and public acceptance as an artist clashed with his political activism on behalf of racial equality and other presumptively radical causes. He is widely considered to have had more impact on theater than any other twentieth-century African American artist.

Robeson was born in Princeton, New Jersey. His father was a minister, having fled slavery in North Carolina as a boy. Robeson graduated high school in Somerville, New Jersey, and enrolled in Rutgers University, one of the first African Americans to attend that institution. A standout as a student and athlete, he finished first in his graduating class and played several varsity sports including football, for which he won All-American honors. After graduation in 1919, he studied law at Columbia University, supporting himself as a singer, actor, and semiprofessional athlete.

During this period, Robeson made his Broadway debut in *Taboo* (1922), a drama about Africa and the South. He starred opposite Margaret Wycherley, a leading actress of the London and Broadway stages. The play closed quickly in New York, but that summer Robeson joined the company for a successful London production. Although he eventually completed his law degree and worked briefly in a law firm, starring in *Taboo* led him to choose a performing career over law.

In the 1920s Robeson established himself as an acting and singing star. His music career soared as he applied his rich baritone/bass voice to concert performances of spirituals, becoming a pioneering solo interpreter of African American folk music to general audiences. In theater he achieved considerable success in starring roles that paired him with the emerging giant of American playwriting, **Eugene O'Neill**. Robeson starred in O'Neill's *All God's Chillun Got Wings* (1924), which, despite a controversial scene wherein Robeson kissed a white actress's hand, earned Robeson sterling reviews and a 100+ performance run. Robeson also starred in the first revival of O'Neill's *Emperor Jones* in 1925 (**Charles S. Gilpin** starred in the original). In 1926 Robeson played the husband in a melodramatic tale of an interracial couple's travails in *Black Boy* (which has no connection to the Richard Wright novel of the same name). In 1928 Robeson appeared briefly in the Broadway play *Porgy*, which would later be the source for the **Gershwin musical *Porgy and Bess***. In 1930, Robeson starred in **Shakespeare**'s *Othello* in London, where he was already a singing sensation, earning high praise for his performance.

For the next six years Robeson worked primarily on his singing career, developing a worldwide reputation as a masterful concert singer of classical pieces, popular songs, and African American folk songs. He also began making commercial films during this period. Robeson returned to Broadway in 1932 as Joe, a stevedore in the first Broadway revival of **Jerome Kern** and **Oscar Hammerstein**'s *Show Boat* (1927). Robeson's showstopping solo, "Ol' Man River," has become so famous that many people mistakenly believe that Robeson originated the role. (Jules Bledsoe, a largely forgotten actor/singer, played in the original.) The song became Robeson's signature piece for the remainder of his singing career.

Aside from a one-week run starring in *John Henry* (1940), a forgettable musical that overly sentimentalized the legendary railroad man, Robeson spent the decade after his *Show Boat* triumph making films and expanding his renown as a concert singer. His films in this period included starring roles in the adaptation of *The Emperor Jones* (1933), the adaptation of *Show Boat* (1936), and *King Solomon's Mines* (1937). He also undertook concert tours of Europe, Asia, and Africa, often singing translated lyrics for his audiences.

During the 1930s Robeson also began using his fame as a forum for speaking out on political, and often controversial, causes. Although principally concerned with racial injustice in America, Robeson spoke on behalf of impoverished Welsh miners and antifascist Spanish Brigades fighting Francisco Franco's regime. As Robeson became increasingly associated with left-wing causes, public protests, FBI investigations, and negative press began to impact his professional opportunities—and would continue to do so for the remainder of his performing career. Robeson did manage to avoid fatally damaging backlashes against his activism long enough to achieve another milestone achievement, his 1943 portrayal of Othello. Margaret Webster, one of the most successful directors of serious drama on Broadway, chose Robeson for the lead, notwithstanding either his notoriety for political activism during wartime or the racial barriers that had heretofore limited starring Shakespearean roles in commercial theater to whites (except for the occasional "all-black cast" production). Robeson performed brilliantly. Reviews heralded both the production's historic importance and artistic triumph. *Othello* ran for 296 performances—a record for a Broadway revival of a Shakespearean play. Robeson's Othello also helped open the door, if only slightly, for considerations of color-blind casting on Broadway. Moreover, Robeson's performance affirmed that African American actors could carry a major classical theatrical production. Later stage successes in the 1950s and early 1960s by Sidney Poitier, **Ossie Davis**, and **James Earl Jones** among others owe a significant debt to Robeson's Othello. Robeson and Webster revived the show in 1945; it was Robeson's final Broadway appearance.

During the Cold War, Robeson openly praised socialist governments of Russia and Eastern Europe, including Stalin's regime. The House Un-American Activities Committee (HUAC) questioned him on his politics, the FBI extensively investigated his activities, and demonstrations occurred at some of his appearances. His passport was revoked for nearly ten years. He was for all intent and purposes blacklisted through the 1950s, losing work and professional visibility. By 1960, his passport had been reinstated and the ban against him and other blacklisted performers had eased. Robeson returned to singing but ill health and changing musical tastes led to a waning of his performing career, which was effectively over by 1970.

Robeson died of a stroke in Philadelphia on January 23, 1976. A one-actor biographical play, *Paul Robeson* (1978), written by Philip Hayes Dean and starring James Earl Jones in the original production has had three Broadway stagings.

Thomas A. Greenfield

Further Reading

Boyle, Sheila Tully, and Andrew Bunie. *Paul Robeson: The Years of Promise and Achievement.* Amherst: University of Massachusetts Press, 2001.
Duberman, Martin B. *Paul Robeson: A Biography.* New York: Knopf, 1989.

RODGERS, RICHARD (1902–1979), AND HAMMERSTEIN, OSCAR, II (1895–1960)
COMPOSER; LYRICIST

Richard Rodgers and Oscar Hammerstein II comprised the most successful and influential composer-lyricist team in the history of Broadway. Their string of hit groundbreaking shows form a canonical listing of what is often called "the Golden Age" of Broadway **musicals**: *Oklahoma!* (1943), *Carousel* (1945), *South Pacific* (1949), *The King and I* (1951), *Flower Drum Song* (1958), and *The Sound of Music* (1959). More than any other composer-lyricist team, Rodgers and Hammerstein brought a new literacy and artistic maturity to the Broadway musical, moving away from the traditional almost haphazard linking of songs and dances with a contrived plot and toward a coherence of music, song, dance, strong story line, and well-developed characters.

Richard Charles Rodgers was born in New York City on June 28, 1902. In 1920 he began writing professionally for Broadway productions, including musicals with lyricist **Lorenz Hart**. The team of Rodgers and Hart enjoyed Broadway success through the 1920s and especially the 1930s with such shows as *On Your Toes* (1936), *Babes in Arms* (1937), which featured the hit songs "The Lady Is a Tramp" and "My Funny Valentine," *The Boys from Syracuse* (1938), and their best-known show, *Pal Joey* (1940), which featured the now classic torch song "Bewitched, Bothered and Bewildered." Rodgers and Hart were among the most successful writers of witty rhyme-driven **show tunes** that characterized the Tin Pan Alley–influenced musicals of the day. Yet Rodgers's success with Hart ultimately paled in comparison to what he would achieve in his partnership with Oscar Hammerstein, which commenced in 1943 after Hart's health and professional reliability fell into decline.

Richard Rodgers, seated, and Oscar Hammerstein II are shown at work in New York City in June 1949. (AP Photo)

Oscar Hammerstein II was born in New York City on July 12, 1895, into a show business family. His grandfather, Oscar Hammerstein I, was an important theater owner and opera producer in New York City. His uncle Arthur Hammerstein produced Broadway **operettas** and musicals, including *Wildflower* (1923), one of his nephew Oscar's first hits. Prior to teaming with Rodgers, Oscar Hammerstein II had collaborated on songs for Broadway and **film** with various composers, including Otto Harbach, **George Gershwin**, and **Jerome Kern**. Notwithstanding the fact that he and Kern made Broadway history with their revolutionary musical *Show Boat* (1927), it was through his partnership with Rodgers that Hammerstein achieved legendary status. That partnership lasted until Hammerstein's death in 1960.

Prior to 1943 Rodgers and Hammerstein had never collaborated with each other, but within the small community of Broadway songwriters they knew each other and each other's work. In the years since *Show Boat* Rodgers had been decidedly more successful than Hammerstein, whose lyrical style leaned more toward the emotional imagery of European operetta than the devilishly clever rhyming and cocktail party wit of Hart, **Cole Porter**, and other leading Broadway lyricists of the day. Each had independently developed an interest in a well-respected 1931 **Theatre Guild** play, *Green Grow the Lilacs* by Oklahoma-native Lynn Riggs. *Green Grow the Lilacs*, a "play with songs" rather than a full musical, had run for only 64 performances but enjoyed some measure of prestige as a Theatre Guild production. After Hart declined Rodgers's invitation to develop a musical from the play, Rodgers persuaded Hammerstein to work with him on it, thus effectively ending his 25-year collaboration with Hart.

The result was *Oklahoma!* (1943), which ran for a record-setting 2,212 performances and ushered in radical changes in American musical theater. What followed was a period that is widely considered to be the apex of the Broadway musical in the twentieth century. "The Rodgers and Hammerstein Era," as it is sometimes called, took Broadway by storm in the 1940s and 1950s, implanting itself in the minds and musical tastes of many Americans for generations to follow. Rodgers and Hammerstein wrote musicals consistently over the next 16 years, ending with *The Sound of Music* in 1959. The sophistication of their shows set a new standard for Broadway musicals and all but ended the heretofore common practice of bundling together songs for a show with little regard for continuity between the songs and the characters who sang them or the relationship of the songs to a coherent story. Hammerstein's ability to write lyrics for specific characters and particular moments within a story caused Rodgers to adapt his composing to a more openly operatic and sonorous style than that which he had developed with Hart. With Hammerstein's lyrics Rodgers could compose lush yet controlled melodies and arrangements whose development revealed the motives, thoughts, and desires of the characters singing them. Within the framework of a three-minute song, Hammerstein's lyrics could give full voice to an aging gentleman's sudden realization of what a final, unexpected chance at love can mean (*South Pacific*'s "Some Enchanted Evening"), a teenager's awkward yet irrepressible coming of age (*The Sound of Music*'s "Sixteen Going on Seventeen"), or the flirtatiously bemused but thoroughly self-aware confessions of a man-crazy single girl (*Oklahoma!*'s "I Can't Say No").

For his part, Rodgers's melodies are so engaging that arrangements of many of his show songs, from "My Funny Valentine" to "My Favorite Things," have become easy listening, pop, and jazz instrumental standards, still performed by countless singers and dance bands. Musical historians credit him with rescuing the waltz from the doldrums of antiquity with eminently modern updates such as "Out of My Dreams" (*Oklahoma!*) and "I'm in Love with a Wonderful Guy" (*South Pacific*). The opening strains of "Some Enchanted Evening" (*South Pacific*), "People Will Say We're in Love" (*Oklahoma!*), and "You'll Never Walk Alone" (*Carousel*) are among the many Rodgers melodies that are instantly recognizable to generations of **radio** and recording listeners, with or without the words. More than anyone else, Rodgers and Hammerstein proved that the American musical was a serious dramatic genre and not simply a showcase for popular songs dropped intermittently between "gags and girls."

The awards and kudos accorded Rodgers and Hammerstein, both within their lifetimes and posthumously, reflect their generation-leaping popularity and iconic status in American culture. Between them they earned 34 Tony Awards, 15 Academy Awards, 2 Pulitzer Prizes, and 2 Grammy Awards. Even 50 years after their last show premiered on Broadway, their musicals remain staples of regional, community, and school theater programs as well as summer stock companies, not just in the United States but worldwide.

In 1995 revivals of three of their musicals played on Broadway simultaneously: *Show Boat*, *The King and I*, and *State Fair*. Their most successful shows, including *Oklahoma!*, *Carousel*, *The King and I*, and *The Sound of Music*, were adapted by Hollywood into internationally successful films, and the hit original cast soundtrack albums of these shows remain among the most popular of the genre. In 1998 *Time Magazine* listed the pair among the 20 most influential artists of the twentieth century. Estimates of the numbers of licenses and permissions sold and granted for the professional use of their songs, shows, and scores runs in the hundreds of thousands in the past 25 years alone.

Rodgers and Hammerstein's impact on American culture and American music is incalculable. Not long after their retirement from creating new musicals the landscape of American musical theater turned toward dance, nonlinear plotlines, and spectacle. According to many musical theater critics, that change brought along with it a corresponding decline in the literary sophistication that characterized the Rodgers and Hammerstein musical and defined a generation of Broadway musical theater.

Hammerstein died on August 23, 1960, in Doylestown, Pennsylvania. Rodgers died on December 30, 1979, in New York City.

Alison Jones Peña

Further Reading

Hischak, Thomas A. *The Rodgers and Hammerstein Encyclopedia.* Westport, CT: Greenwood Press, 2007.

Nolan, Frederick. *The Sound of Their Music: The Story of Rodgers and Hammerstein.* New York: Applause Theatre & Cinema Books, 2002.

S

SHAKESPEARE

While rarely the biggest hit of the season, Shakespearean drama has always held a singular appeal to Broadway **producers**, writers, composers, performers, and audiences. Since 1900 there has scarcely been a Broadway season that did not feature at least one production and/or adaptation of a Shakespeare play. In the first five years of the twenty-first century alone, Shakespeare scored five different Broadway writing credits—more than perennial White Way favorites **Eugene O'Neill**, **Arthur Miller**, **Neil Simon**, **Edward Albee**, or **George Bernard Shaw** garnered during the same period of time. Nearly four centuries after his death, the Bard is truly a "working" Broadway **playwright**.

The history of modern professional Shakespearean performance on Broadway emerged in three overlapping phases. From the turn of the century up until the Depression, Shakespeare's presence on the commercial stage in New York was dominated by a few privately owned or patron-supported Shakespearean theater companies from out of town and even overseas. During a transitional period from the 1930s to World War II, commercial companies shared the Bard with emerging not-for-profit American theatrical enterprises. Since the 1950s Shakespeare play production on Broadway has been all but monopolized by not-for-profit theater.

As the "not-for-profits" assumed a preeminent position in the latter half of the century, other significant trends in Broadway Shakespeare production evolved. "Star power"—casting a celebrity actor or actress from commercial theater, **film**, or **television** fame in the lead role—has become almost a *sine qua non* for new Broadway Shakespeare productions. At the same time, mainstream commercial Broadway has been experimenting for over half a century—at times quite successfully—with musical and other adaptations of Shakespeare's plays.

1900 to 1930: The Era of the Shakespearean Theater Company

During the first two decades of the century, New York often hosted three very active British-based Shakespearean companies that dominated Broadway production of Shakespeare plays. While not quite repertory groups in the modern sense of the term, they nonetheless restaged Shakespearean plays with little or no deviation from established texts, featuring the same lead performers over an extended run. The first touring Shakespearean performer and impresario to have had a major impact on early-twentieth-century New York was Ben Greet, a British actor and manager who toured widely with his Ben Greet Repertory, also known as the Elizabethan Stage Society of England. Among the places visited by his group in addition to New York were Chautauqua, Newport, Harvard, and the White House. From 1904 to 1910, Greet produced at least eight Shakespearean plays in repertory. He maintained a presence in New York commercial theater through 1913 with other Elizabethan, Restoration era, and even some new plays. Greet's presence in U.S. theater ended when in 1914 he returned to London to assume the directorship of the Old Vic Theatre. Members of his Broadway casts had included some of the most distinguished British actors of the day, including Edith Wynne Matthison, Dame Sybil Thorndike, and Sydney Greenstreet (who in later years would enhance his stage career with a series of successful roles as a character actor in Hollywood, most notably in the Humphrey Bogart classics *The Maltese Falcon* and *Casablanca*).

A husband-and-wife team, British actress Julia Marlowe and American-born actor/producer E. H. Sothern, closely rivaled Greet with their eponymous repertory company, which produced Shakespeare on Broadway from 1910 to 1913. Marlowe herself first appeared in *Henry IV Part 1* as early as 1895 and first performed Shakespeare with Sothern in a 1904 *Hamlet*. Between the work of their own company and that produced by others, Marlowe and Sothern appeared in several dozen Shakespeare productions. Although their production company repertoire was similar to that of their contemporaries (emphasizing *Hamlet*, *Macbeth*, *Twelfth Night*, *Merchant of Venice*, *As You Like It*, and *Much Ado about Nothing*), they also revived *Cymbeline* (1923) and *The Taming of the Shrew* (several times, beginning in 1905), two plays not performed on Broadway by the other contemporary Shakespearean repertory companies.

Marlowe and Greet productions were more favored by **critics** than those of their older competitor, Scotsman Robert Mantell, who began performing in the New York commercial theater as early as the 1880s. Not very successful in his native land, he produced his first Shakespeare play in New York in 1904, a production of ***Othello*** in which he also starred. Mantell performed in and around Broadway until 1923, producing at least 11 different Shakespeare plays and a musical spectacular at Lewisohn Stadium in uptown Manhattan called *Caliban of the Yellow Sands* (1916). That show featured an amalgamation of Shakespeare's characters, teaming Cressida (from *Troilus and Cressida*) with Perdita (from *A Winter's Tale*), Romeo, Mistress Ford (from *The Merry Wives of Windsor*), King Henry V, and Cleopatra, among many others. In his more traditional productions, Mantell favored *Julius Caesar, Othello, Hamlet, King Lear, Macbeth, Twelfth Night,* and *Merchant,* thus surpassing Greet's comparatively meager tragedy repertoire that consisted only of *Macbeth* and *Julius Caesar.* Significantly, Mantell also introduced to commercial New York theater three history plays: *Henry V, Richard III,* and *King John.* The fact that neither Greet's company nor Marlowe and Sothern's company had produced any Shakespearean history plays in those first decades of the twentieth century suggests that "the histories" (as Shakespeare's plays about the political and military travails of English monarchs are collectively known) are decidedly less commercially viable than Shakespeare's major tragedies and better-known comedies—a phenomenon still largely true to this day.

Several of Mantell's casts featured Fritz Leiber, who performed with Ben Greet as early as 1905 and also acted in Marlowe's company. He built a thriving career in New York, during which time he made an unusually early transition to Hollywood in 1916. He landed his first film role as Mercutio in a silent *Romeo and Juliet.* He performed at least 19 Shakespeare roles on stage before founding his own Chicago Civic Shakespeare Society in the 1920s under the patronage of Harley Clarke, president of the large holding company Chicago Utilities Power and Light. Leiber brought his Chicago-based troupe to Broadway in 1930 and 1931 to perform nine different plays at the Shubert, Ambassador, and Royale Theaters. Like Greet's and Mantell's companies, Leiber's was essentially an out-of-town troupe that used Broadway to expand its renown and build its audience. Thus an abiding pattern was established early in the century: a closely networked set of actors headed up performing companies that dominated professional performances of Shakespeare in New York. Touring and patronage provided additional financial support although Marlowe and Sothern's troupe, on the strength of their renown, sustained themselves on Broadway from 1912 to 1923.

The presence of these companies did not wholly exclude other producers from mounting successful Shakespeare productions on Broadway. As actors Marlowe and Sothern, when not performing in their own company's Shakespeare productions, were particular favorites of the **Shubert Brothers**, the powerful American producers and theater owners. The Shuberts began including Shakespearean plays in their extensive list of Broadway productions in 1907. In 1904 producer Charles Frohman, a producer and founding member of the powerful **Theatrical Syndicate**, began adding the occasional Shakespeare play to his extensive Broadway offerings of comedy, **operetta**, and original dramas.

The selection of Shakespeare plays for commercial performance was somewhat different in the early twentieth century than it is today, with almost no histories represented in the early years and with the currently very popular *Romeo and Juliet* then only occasionally performed. It is noteworthy that *Merchant of Venice,* now rarely performed professionally in New York, was a regular attraction in the first third of the century. This receding of interest in *Merchant*—one of only a few Shakespeare plays that invites consideration of themes of ethnic prejudice—may well reflect contemporary sensitivities toward issues of immigration or anti-Semitism that were decidedly less controversial in mainstream American society prior to 1930.

Star power casting, although a dominating force in contemporary Broadway stagings of Shakespeare, has been alive and profitable for a century or more. Producer Arthur Hopkins presented **John Barrymore** in both *Richard III* and *Hamlet* between 1920 and 1923. These performances are widely considered to have advanced Barrymore's reputation as a serious actor. Hopkins also placed Barrymore's brother Lionel in *Macbeth* for 28 performances during the 1921 season.

1930s and the World War II Era: Transition into Not-for-Profit Shakespeare

The domination of New York Shakespeare by a small set of professional companies dissolved after the 1920s as new forms of Shakespearean performances took hold. Between 1930 and 1954 (the year that **Joseph Papp** established New York Shakespeare Festival), no one force for Shakespeare emerged in New York. In 1936 the **Federal Theatre Project**, created as part of the Roosevelt administration's New Deal to counter the devastating effects of the Depression on the theater industry, produced a highly successful and inventive production of *Macbeth* from the Project's New York–based Negro Theatre Unit. Set in Haiti, directed by Orson Welles, and performed with an all–African American cast, the production was enormously successful and is widely viewed as a landmark event in the history of African American professional theater.

During this period there was a number of performances staged at the New Century Theater located in the Times Square theater district, including a 1946 Old Vic import of parts 1 and 2 of *Henry IV* starring British theatrical legends Laurence Olivier as Hotspur, Ralph Richardson as Falstaff, and Margaret Leighton as Lady Percy. At the same theater, producer Hall Shelton presented *Merchant*, *As You Like It*, and *King Lear* in repertory during early 1947. Star power casting, which was to become the dominant *modus operandi* for staging Shakespeare on Broadway after World War II, was showing its potential in the 1930s. Katharine Cornell, a Broadway star since the early 1920s, produced *Romeo and Juliet* in 1936 for herself and actor Maurice Evans, who himself then produced *Richard II*, *Hamlet*, *Henry IV*, and *Macbeth* (with Judith Anderson coproducing and starring as Lady Macbeth) in the 1930s and 1940s. Anderson also performed opposite John Gielgud in a 1936 *Hamlet*. These star turns were harbingers of things to come. Because the Depression and World War II encouraged lighter fare and made touring less feasible for theater companies, regular repertory visits to Broadway, especially Shakespearean or "Classical" European companies, gave way to star power casting in straightforward Shakespeare productions and increasingly popular adaptations or appropriations of Shakespeare's work to **musicals** and other idioms.

World War II and Beyond

After the decline of the pre–World War II Shakespeare repertory companies, star power casting sustained the production of Shakespeare on Broadway. **Paul**

Robeson's *Othello* (1943) at the Shubert Theater in New York, a production that ran a record-setting impressive 296 Broadway performances for a Shakespearean production, used Robeson's name recognition and 20-year career as a nationally known theater, film, and music star to full advantage. The production also featured **José Ferrer** as Iago and **Uta Hagen** as Desdemona. The 1940s saw just three productions of *As You Like It*, each running for just a few performances, until Katharine Hepburn carried a production in 1950 to 145 performances. In 1940 Laurence Olivier independently produced *Romeo and Juliet* for himself and Vivian Leigh. At the time Leigh had no Broadway experience and only two film roles to her credit but had become a major star by virtue of the fact that one of those film roles was Scarlett O'Hara in 1939's *Gone With the Wind*. The famous pair returned in 1951 for *Anthony and Cleopatra*, which played in repertory with George Bernard Shaw's *Caesar and Cleopatra*.

If star power had emerged as a dominant force for getting Shakespeare produced commercially in New York, so had the practice of appropriating (or bearding) Shakespearean plays into altogether different shows. Although Broadway adaptations of Shakespeare became more common after World War II, some early experiments anticipated the later trend. In 1938, **Richard Rodgers** and **Lorenz Hart** brought to the stage what were then daring jokes and situations by creating the musical *The Boys from Syracuse* out of *The Comedy of Errors*. The following year, the revue *Swingin' the Dream* (a loose variation of *A Midsummer Night's Dream* set in turn-of-the-century New Orleans) appeared in 1939 at Center Space in Rockefeller Center. It was commercially unsuccessful even though it featured some of the most popular African American stars of the day: Louis Armstrong, Butterfly McQueen, the Dandridge sisters, and music by Count Basie as well as by Benny Goodman. **Cole Porter** revived his Broadway career in 1948 with *Kiss Me Kate*, based on *The Taming of the Shrew*. *Kiss Me Kate* ran for 1,077 performances over a period of two and a half years and featured two of Porter's most famous songs from the latter part of his career, "Too Darn Hot" and, appropriately enough, the enduring novelty song "Brush Up Your Shakespeare."

Most famous among the modern Broadway Shakespeare appropriations is **Leonard Bernstein** and **Stephen Sondheim**'s *Romeo and Juliet* adaptation, ***West Side Story*** (1957), one of the dozen or so most important musicals in the history of Broadway and the last musical to appropriate a Shakespearean tragedy. With its mix of "high" and "low" cultures and its updated setting and content (featuring gang violence peppered with verbal street slang invented especially for the production), it epitomizes Broadway's Shakespearean appropriations.

The last unqualified success for a musical appropriation of Shakespeare was *Two Gentlemen of Verona* (1971), which producer Joseph Papp brought from downtown to the St. James Theater in Times Square. **Off-Broadway**, *Your Own Thing* (1968) brought *Twelfth Night* to rock music for over 900 performances. Less financially successful but innovative for their own times have been the Off-Broadway musicals, *Bomb-ity of Errors* (1999), a rap musical, and *Lone Star Love* (2005), based on the *Merry Wives of Windsor*.

Today, the two biggest forces for producing professional Shakespeare in venues in New York City are Papp's Public Theater/New York Shakespeare Festival and Lincoln Center, both nonprofit groups. They have outlasted the American Shakespeare Theatre (AST), which occasionally sent plays from its home in Stratford, Connecticut, to Broadway. Before it went bankrupt in 1985, AST produced *Othello* on Broadway in 1982, with **James Earl Jones** in the title role, Christopher Plummer as Iago, Dianne Wiest as Desdemona, and Kelsey Grammer as Cassio. Len Cariou had preceded them starring in an AST Broadway production of *Henry V* in 1969.

Founded in 1954 by Joseph Papp, the New York Shakespeare Festival (NYSF) has produced every one of Shakespeare's plays, often with popular success, equally often to negative academic criticism. The NYSF sometimes brings its plays uptown to Broadway, as was the case for its *Much Ado*, with Sam Waterston and Kathleen Widdoes, in 1972 and for *The Tempest* in 1995, with Patrick Stewart. Like the NYSF, Lincoln Center (at the Vivian Beaumont) has recently relied on actors whose star power transcends Broadway. A 2003–2004 *Henry IV* brought film star Ethan Hawke to the role of Hotspur, while film and stage star Kevin Kline played Falstaff and Michael Hayden, the Prince. Television sitcom star Helen Hunt played Viola in a 1998 *Twelfth Night*. Lincoln Center has, though, been producing Shakespeare since its 1968 *King Lear* with **Lee J. Cobb**, who had achieved enormous fame 20 years earlier for his signature role as the original Willy Loman in ***Death of a Salesman*** (1947). Broadway denizens saw Blythe Danner in a 1972 *Twelfth Night*, and Rosemary Harris and Christopher Walken as Portia and Bassanio in a 1973 *Merchant of Venice*.

During the 1996 season, in a rare throwback to the early twentieth-century practice of staging touring Shakespeare repertory company productions on Broadway, the Kennedy Center for the Performing Arts helped bring in a "starless" production of *Midsummer Night's Dream* from England's Royal Shakespeare Company (RSC) for a limited run in Times Square. The cast was composed of RSC repertory players who had virtually no experience on Broadway or Hollywood and, thus, no real name recognition in the United States. Neither the RSC nor any Broadway producer has sought to repeat this effort since. Lincoln Center occasionally coproduces Shakespeare imported from Canada's Stratford Festival as it did with a 2004 *Lear* starring Christopher Plummer and a 1987 *Comedy of Errors* from Chicago's Goodman Theatre, which featured several performers who had recently garnered a following on Broadway as part of the *Flying Karamazov Brothers* postmodern "New Vaudevillian" comedy revues in the early 1980s.

Shakespeare on Broadway continues to flourish because it gives established stars a means for shaping their public image and sharpening "their chops" or skills as actors. In addition, it provides young actors visibility in the New York media center. Not-for-profit theater companies remain committed to classical theater and can usually find responsive audiences and sympathetic press coverage for a quality production, especially if a celebrity actor is cast in the starring role and performs well. Since midcentury, however, the production cost factor has narrowed the range of plays that get produced and increased Broadway's reliance on celebrity actors from beyond the realm of theater. Recent examples of such star power Broadway productions include film heartthrob Jude Law as *Hamlet* (2009), British theater actor (and *Star Trek* leading man) Patrick Stewart in *Mac-Beth* (2008), and Oscar-winning actor Denzel Washington in *Julius Caesar* (2005). As long as "name" stars, many of whom had performed Shakespeare early in their careers, are willing to take the inevitable pay cut to headline a big-time New York Shakespeare production, the Bard is likely to remain a Broadway force to be reckoned with.

Richard Finkelstein

Further Reading

Brown, Stephen J. "The Uses of Shakespeare in America: A Study in Class Domination." In *Shakespeare: Pattern of Excelling Nature*, ed. David Bevington and Jay Halio. Newark: University of Delaware Press, 1978, pp. 230–38.

Dunn, Esther Cloudman. *Shakespeare in America*. New York: Macmillan, 1939.

Hill, Erroll. *Shakespeare in Sable: A History of Black Shakespearean Actors*. Amherst: University of Massachusetts Press, 1984.

Internet Broadway Database. http://www.ibdb.com/person.asp?ID=8638.

Levine, Lawrence. "William Shakespeare and the American People: A Study in Cultural Transformation." In *The Unpredictable Past: Explorations in American Cultural History*. New York: Oxford University Press, 1993, pp. 139–71.

Shattuck, Charles. *Shakespeare on the American Stage*, 2 vols. Washington: Folger Press, 1976, 1987.

Sturgess, Kim. *Shakespeare and the American Nation*. New York: Cambridge University Press, 2004.

Teague, Frances. *Shakespeare and the American Popular Stage*. New York: Cambridge University Press, 2002.

SHANGE, NTOZAKE

See *for colored girls who have considered suicide/when the rainbow is enuf*.

SHAW, GEORGE BERNARD (1856–1950)
PLAYWRIGHT

Irish-born Bernard Shaw (he did not like to use "George") was the most important and most prolific of the major modern European **playwrights** in terms of Broadway production history and overall impact on Broadway's theatrical traditions. From the 1890s through the 1920s, his witty comedies and occasional serious dramas energized the emerging American commercial theater with a sophisticated body of dramatic literature years before American professional playwriting came into its own. Shaw's plays are so beloved by American theater professionals and playgoers that his works are still regularly produced on Broadway and around the world to this day. With over 120 (and counting) Broadway productions in a span of 115 years, Shaw is Broadway's most-produced twentieth-century playwright.

Raised in Dublin, Ireland, Shaw was one of a number of Irish authors and artists who fled Ireland to England and other parts of Europe at the turn of the century in the hopes of making an impact on the larger world. Having established himself in the 1880s as a highly regarded London arts critic and political essayist (whose profound interests in socialism, women's rights, and pacifism found their way readily into his dramatic work), Shaw did not turn to playwriting until he was in his late thirties. From the outset, Shaw took advantage of the nascent Broadway theater's demand for imported European plays to fill its stages. Only three years after his London debut as a professional playwright, Shaw's plays began running on Broadway, starting with the 1894 American premier of *Arms and the Man.* Shaw's early Broadway successes, which also included *The Devil's Disciple* (1897) and *You Never Can Tell* (1905), whetted American audiences' appetite for witty modern parlor comedies—updated versions of the English eighteenth-century *Comedy of Manners*—and laid the groundwork for Broadway successes by fellow Englishman Noel Coward, James M. Barrie, and Somerset Maugham as well as later Americans such as Booth Tarkington and even **George S. Kaufman**.

By reputation the most important of Shaw's plays in American popular culture —and Broadway history in particular—is *Pygmalion* (1914). *Pygmalion* tells the satiric tale of English linguist Professor Henry Higgins's efforts to pass off London street urchin Liza Doolittle as a blue-blooded noblewoman after subjecting her to a few months of his intense instruction in diction and comportment. Notwithstanding its successful original run in New York and the generally positive reception of its five subsequent revivals (including a production in 2007), *Pygmalion* is best known as the source and inspiration for the **Lerner and Loewe** classic 1956 **musical *My Fair Lady***. (The album cover to the original *My Fair Lady* soundtrack famously bore a cartoon likeness of the deceased Shaw perched on clouds pulling marionette strings tied to actor **Rex Harrison** [the original Higgins] while Harrison, in turn, is drawn similarly as puppeteer to a marionette **Julie Andrews** [the original Liza Doolittle].) The musical, in turn, spawned an Oscar-winning **film** adaptation in 1964.

Notwithstanding the legendary status of the *Pygmalion–My Fair Lady* connection, *Pygmalion* was not Shaw's most successful Broadway play. Shaw's first Broadway play, *Arms and the Man*, not only enjoyed six Broadway revival productions in the twentieth century but also inspired a well-regarded musical/**operetta** adaptation, *The Chocolate Soldier* (1909). *The Chocolate Soldier* was revived on Broadway five times between 1910 and 1947. The Shaw play that has enjoyed by far and away the largest number of Broadway stagings is the decidedly less well-known comedy *Candida*, which has seen a mind-boggling 13 revivals since its

1903 premier. *Candida*'s popularity with producers can be explained in part by its relatively undemanding production requirements: a small cast and one interior set. But its greatest appeal certainly lies in the engaging feminist (or even female supremacist) twists Shaw applies to the boilerplate comedy of manners conflict: old husband and dashing youthful would-be cuckholder vie for the affections of a young wife. At the end, neither husband nor suitor prevails as Shaw turns the test of wills between the two men into a dissertation on their mutual unworthiness of the wittier, wiser, and more principled young Candida. Over the years the title role has been played on Broadway by such distinguished actresses as Olivia de Havilland, Katharine Cornell, Joanne Woodward, and Celeste Holm.

Broadway's interest in Shaw has waned since the mid-1990s, but only relatively speaking. Between 2000 and 2007 three different Shaw revivals appeared on Broadway. Most notable among these was the 2006 staging of the subtle, if somewhat rambling, antiwar satire and cautionary tale, *Heartbreak House*, which Shaw wrote in response to events surrounding World War I. This most recent New York production directed by Robin Lefèvre appeared to invoke Shaw's lifelong pacifist sentiments in the context of America's ongoing military conflicts in Iraq and Afghanistan.

Shaw wrote over 50 plays during his lifetime. Throughout his playwriting career he continued publishing essays, newspaper columns, public letters, and famously argumentative prefaces to the published editions of his plays.

Shaw died in 1950 at age 94 in his home in Ayot St. Lawrence, England, from complications arising from a fall off a ladder while working in his garden.

Thomas A. Greenfield

Further Reading

Bloom, Harold. *Bernard Shaw*. New York: Chelsea House Publishers, 1987.
Davis, Tracy C. *George Bernard Shaw and the Socialist Theatre*. Westport, CT: Greenwood Press, 1994.

SHOW BOAT

Broadway Run: Ziegfeld Theatre
Opening: December 27, 1927
Closing: May 4, 1929
Total Performances: 572
Music: Jerome Kern
Lyrics: Oscar Hammerstein II
Book: Oscar Hammerstein II; based on the novel *Show Boat* by Edna Ferber
Producer: Florenz Ziegfeld Jr.
Lead Performers: Norma Terris (Magnolia), Howard Marsh (Gaylord Ravenal), Helen Morgan (Julie), and Jules Bledsoe (Joe)

Broadway and the American theater turned a significant corner in **Florenz Zieg-feld**'s 1927 production of *Show Boat*. Challenging the Broadway **musical** tradition of spectacle for its own sake, *Show Boat*, a stage adaptation of an epic **novel** by Edna Ferber, dared take on social issues embedded in the very fabric of American society. Its plot deals with decidedly unfamiliar Broadway musical fare for its time: issues of class, racial prejudices, miscegenation, alcoholism, and spousal abandonment. The show's biggest hit, "Ol' Man River," took on a cultural legacy of its own as the career-defining song for **Paul Robeson**, who played in the 1928 London production and the 1932 Broadway revival. The show launched Robeson's career, which, to this day, remains the most historically significant theater of any African American actor.

No less groundbreaking in its production history, *Show Boat* became one of the first Broadway shows with an integrated black and white cast. Moreover, as the first major Broadway musical hit in which songs were crafted to serve as integral parts of story and character development, *Show Boat* laid important groundwork for the 1940s to 1960s era of the book musical—a form lyricist **Oscar Hammerstein II** would come to dominate with eventual partner **Richard Rodgers**. Many historians view *Show Boat* as the first authentically American musical, representing one of the genre's most significant breaks from its nineteenth-century **vaudeville** and European **operetta** traditions.

Although a significant departure from the familiar Broadway musical, *Show Boat* was a logical extension of the careers of its principal creators. By 1927 **Jerome Kern** was a well-established Broadway composer, having contributed songs to revues and musicals since 1904. He cowrote music for his first full musical in 1908 and had been a contributor of songs for *Show Boat* producer Ziegfeld's *Follies* throughout the 1910s. From 1915 to 1918 Kern was the composer for "the Princess musicals," a series of small well-received shows including *Nobody Home* (1915) and *Oh Lady! Lady!* (1918), staged at New York's Princess Theatre. The Princess was a small, almost club-sized Broadway venue that allowed Kern and his lyricist collaborators to experiment with the then radical notion of creating credible story lines supported by a score that advanced the stage action. For his part producer Ziegfeld, a notorious Broadway rule breaker and trendsetter, was coming off some weak seasons and attendant financial difficulties. Kern and Hammerstein had recently collaborated on the 1925 hit *Sunny* for a rival producer, which at 517 performances surpassed anything Ziegfeld had mounted in several years. Although wary of the Kern-Hammerstein show, given its potentially controversial content, Ziegfeld was accustomed to taking chances on something new. Hammerstein, a disciple of European operetta, had the least iconoclastic production record of the three. However, by 1927 with ten years and over a dozen Broadway shows to his credit, Hammerstein felt that both he and the genre in which he labored could use some new direction.

The story line of *Show Boat* follows Ferber's novel very closely ("slavishly" the *New York Times* declared in the opening night review). Spanning the 1880s to the 1920s, the musical follows the loves and losses of a riverboat's (*Cotton*

Blossom) cast and crew of touring entertainers, gamblers, passengers, workers, and hangers-on. The main plot focuses upon Magnolia (Nola) Hawks, daughter of ship "Cap'n" Andy Hawks, who wins the heart of rakish gambler Gaylord Ravenal. They fall in love and, for a time, perform as the stars of the *Cotton Blossom*'s traveling shows. Eventually, they have a daughter and move to Chicago. Later, Gaylord loses all his money and abandons his wife and daughter. A protracted tale of reconciliation and reunion of the estranged family resolves the main story line.

Interwoven into the main plot is a miscegenation theme reminiscent of the "tragic mulatto" tales Broadway had seen occasionally in melodramas but never before in a mainstream musical. Early in the show Julie, a mulatto passing for white and the traveling show's leading lady at the outset of the story, has her racial identity exposed by an unsuccessful suitor. A sheriff seeks to enforce local segregation laws and customs forbidding performances of racially integrated shows. Julie (with her white husband/co-star, Steve) leave the *Cotton Blossom*, turning the show's starring roles over to Gaylord and Magnolia. Also featured prominently in the musical is an African American couple, Joe (a stevedore) and Queenie, who provide Greek chorus–like commentary and folk wisdom to and about the principal characters. Joe's "Ol' Man River" offers a knowing philosophical perspective on the trials and tribulations of the principal characters (to say nothing of a show-stopping masterpiece).

Show Boat was a hit from the outset. In addition to the healthy (for its time) 572-performance run, Ziegfeld quickly arranged for a post-Broadway tour. He also mounted productions in London and a Broadway revival in 1932 (both with Robeson, whose presence added significantly to the show's legendary status as well as his own). *Show Boat* has seen a total of six Broadway revivals, including a solid yearlong run from 1946 to 1947 produced by Kern and Hammerstein themselves. **Hal Prince**'s 1993 revival, which ran for 947 performances over a span of two-and-half years and won five Tony Awards, is the longest run of the show in history. *Show Boat* remains among the most frequently produced musicals in regional, university, and community theaters, notwithstanding the tendency of such organizations to shun musicals that predate World War II.

Notwithstanding its critical and popular success, *Show Boat* did not immediately depose Broadway's decades-long fondness for revues and song showcases. Through World War II, Broadway would still see an abundance of musical scores that provided launching pads for radio and Tin Pan Alley hits or stage "moments" for big name stars at the expense of story and character development. But composers, librettists, lyricists, **producers**, and audiences took notice of *Show Boat*'s innovations. Thanks in large measure to that breakthrough production, the modern integrated book musical gradually evolved into the predominating form of the genre. Hammerstein would play a major role in that evolution through his legendary partnership with Richard Rodgers. Together they launched the much heralded "Golden Age of Musicals" beginning with ***Oklahoma!*** in 1943.

Thomas A. Greenfield and Tracy L. Paradis

Further Reading

Block, Geoffrey. *Enchanted Evenings: The Broadway Musical from Show Boat to Sondheim.* New York: Oxford University, 2004.

McLamore, Alyson. *Musical Theater: An Appreciation.* Upsaddle River, NJ: Prentice-Hall, 2004.

SHOW TUNES: FROM TIN PAN ALLEY TO POP RADIO

It has been decades since songs from Broadway **musicals** routinely became independently popular through **radio** play and record sales. **Stephen Sondheim**'s last "hit" song was "Send in the Clowns" from his 1973 musical *A Little Night Music.* Since then Sondheim has turned out a string of successful shows, but none has produced a hit song. Sondheim's record is typical of Broadway songwriters during the past 50 years—occasional hit "singles" emerge from a Broadway show but, for the most part, a show's song list takes on no life of its own beyond the show itself and its soundtrack album. Yet during the so-called "Golden Era of American popular music," roughly from the mid-1920s through the mid-1950s, songs from Broadway musicals dominated the popular music charts. For much of that era, a successful stage musical was measured by the number of hit songs it produced, songs that sold significant copies of sheet music and recordings, and that were aired on radio programs such as *Your Hit Parade.*

Many of these Broadway show "hit" songs, moreover, have managed to do what few other popular songs have done—*stay* popular long after public interest in the original show has waned. The whole idea of a "popular" song, after all, is that its popularity is ephemeral; after it has caught the public's ear for a brief period, it is displaced by newer songs. Paul Dresser, probably the most successful songwriter of the 1890s (and brother of American novelist Theodore Dreiser), is a case in point. Notwithstanding his enormously successful output for the American sheet-music industry (known as Tin Pan Alley) only one Dresser song is familiar today—"On the Banks of the Wabash"—primarily because it was adopted by Indiana as its state song.

But the next generation of songwriters—**Irving Berlin**, **Jerome Kern**, and **George and Ira Gershwin**—would write songs that have endured beyond their initial era of popularity to become "standards" (in Britain they are called "evergreens"). Such songs comprise what has been called "The Great American Song Book," the classic songs that are the bedrock of the jazz repertory but also have been reinterpreted by such diverse popular singers as Frank Sinatra and Willie Nelson, Linda Ronstadt and Rod Stewart, Carly Simon and Ella Fitzgerald. The key to such musical transcendence was that these and other songwriters—the duo of **Richard Rodgers** and **Lorenz Hart**, **Cole Porter**, E. Y. "Yip" Harburg (1896–1981), and Harold Arlen (1905–1986)—wrote for the Broadway stage. In 1914, George Gershwin is said to have quit his job as a piano "plugger" on Tin Pan

Alley, demonstrating his sheet-music company's latest songs to **vaudeville** performers in search of new material, when he heard Jerome Kern's "They Didn't Believe Me." Kern's song was an interpolation—a song added to the existing score of a Broadway musical that Kern had not written (*The Girl from Utah* [1914]). "They Didn't Believe Me" made Gershwin realize that songs written for the Broadway stage had more depth and sophistication than those written for the popular sheet-music sales of Tin Pan Alley. Many Tin Pan Alley songsmiths, notably Irving Berlin, could not read music, while Broadway composers such as Gershwin, Kern, and Porter were classically trained musicians. Similarly, lyricists such as Ira Gershwin, Lorenz Hart, and Howard Dietz were schooled in the rigors of light verse. In writing for the characters and dramatic situations of Broadway musicals, such lyricists found that their songs had what they called "particularity," as opposed to the simple "I love you" formulas of Tin Pan Alley wordsmiths. They could write lyrics that rivaled those of their idol, English lyricist W. S. Gilbert (1836–1911) of the immortal **operetta** composing team **Gilbert and Sullivan**, even though they had to do it the hard way. Gilbert and Sullivan always started a song with the words, and Sullivan's job was essentially to set one of Gilbert's light-verse poems to music. In American songwriting, it was the music that usually came first, and a lyricist had to find the syllables, words, and verbal phrases that matched his collaborator's melody as if he were working a musical crossword puzzle.

The Broadway musical had long been off limits to Tin Pan Alley. Except for the thumpingly American musicals of **George M. Cohan**, with their vernacular songs such as "Give My Regards to Broadway" (1904) and "You're a Grand Old Flag" (1906), the Broadway stage was dominated by European operetta, either imports such as Franz Lehar's *The Merry Widow* (1907) or homegrown imitations such as **Victor Herbert**'s *Naughty Marietta* (1910). Occasionally a song from an operetta, such as "Ah! Sweet Mystery of Life" (1910), became popular through sheet-music sales, but for the most part songs that churned out of the assembly lines of Tin Pan Alley's publishing houses were marketed in vaudeville, the working-class and middle-class variety theater that had displaced the minstrel show of the mid-nineteenth century.

Songs from Tin Pan Alley were based on simple, streamlined formulas that were more urban and urbane than the formulas of earlier songs. Nineteenth-century songs usually consisted of verses, which told a story ("In a cavern, in a canyon, excavating for a mine, lived a miner forty-niner . . . ," and a brief lyrical refrain of 8 or 16 bars ("Oh, my darlin', oh, my darlin', oh, my darlin' Clementine . . ."). By 1910, Tin Pan Alley had replaced that strophic formula with songs built on a chorus of 32 bars. The chorus was frequently preceded by a brief verse, but that verse served only to introduce the chorus, the "money" part of the song in Alley parlance. The 32-bar chorus was divided into four 8-bar musical units where two or more melodies alternated in an ABAB, ABAC, or, more rarely, ABCD, pattern. The most common pattern was AABA where an 8-bar musical phrase was introduced, then repeated, then varied with an 8-bar B melody called the "bridge" or "release," which then returned the listener back to the A melody for the final eight bars. Such insistent and insinuating melodies gave lyricists only 50 to 75 words, so instead of narrating stories, lyricists rang variations on romantic formulas. As one lyricist put it, "Ya gotta say 'I Love You' in thirty-two bars."

The extraordinary success of Tin Pan Alley's wares—1 million copies of sheet music sold for "After the Ball" (1893) then 2 million for "Alexander's Ragtime Band" (1911)—would have eventually found a home in the American musical, but that welcome was precipitated by World War I. American audiences were disenchanted with European operettas (often disparagingly called "Viennese schmaltz") and the musical stage embraced contemporary stories laced with the kind of popular song that had become identifiably American. A series of musical shows at New York's Princess Theatre as well as other houses by composer Jerome Kern, lyricist P. G. Wodehouse, and librettist Guy Bolton inspired young lyricists and composers to write songs for the Broadway stage that, even though they were built on Tin Pan Alley formulas, sparkled with the wit and sophistication of Gilbert and Sullivan. By the mid-1920s, it was clear that a "renaissance" in popular music was underway as songs by Rodgers and Hart, the Gershwins, Cole Porter, Jerome Kern, **Oscar Hammerstein II**, and others, including the remarkably adept Irving Berlin, emanated from the Broadway stage then went on to dominate Tin Pan Alley's sheet-music sales.

The apogee of this union of Tin Pan Alley and "Shubert Alley" (a slang reference for Broadway theater as a whole from the famous alley and meeting point in the heart of the Times Square theater district) came in 1927 when Roaring Twenties prosperity and optimism welcomed 20 Broadway musical premieres during one week—11 on the evening of December 26 alone. Among the shows opening that night were DeSylva, Brown, and Henderson's *Good News* and Kalmar and Ruby's *The 5 O'Clock Girl*. A good show in those heady days was simply a show with a lot of good songs, many of which would go on to become independently popular on radio, records, and sheet-music sales. Songs were not tied too closely to character and dramatic situation in a musical, lest such "integration" inhibit their chances of becoming "hits" on Tin Pan Alley. Most songs, in fact, were given "androgynous" lyrics so that they could be popularized by both male and female singers. Within the stage musical, there would be a "boy's" verse and a "girl's" verse but the all-important chorus would be "unisex"—"*you* do something to *me*."

The elegant and literate songs of this era, "Fascinating Rhythm," "Manhattan," "Let's Do It," and others—received an additional boost by the advent of radio and the development of the microphone. Songs were no longer something that had to be boomed out to the last row of the balcony by performers such as Al Jolson. Instead they could be what Irving Berlin called intimate "sob ballads" aimed at the solitary listener of radio or phonograph. Berlin saw this shift in song coming when his 1921 hit "All By Myself" sold as many copies of records as it did of sheet music. Radio, which had started out in 1921 by broadcasting sporting events, church services, and elections, finally reached its public by playing popular songs —"free music"—in the evenings. From $60 million in sales in 1922, radio sales reached $506 million in 1926. Berlin described the shift as one where America moved from a country that "produced" its own songs—by playing sheet music on the family parlor piano—to one that "consumed" music by listening to songs on the phonograph or the radio. The bulk of the music heard on recordings and radio emanated from the Broadway musical, so that had there been a "Your Hit Parade" of 1927, virtually every one of the "Top Ten" songs would have been part of a Broadway score.

Yet one of the musicals that opened during that banner final week of 1927 challenged the premise that a good Broadway show was a showcase for the wares of Tin Pan Alley. Jerome Kern and Oscar Hammerstein's **Show Boat** returned to the tradition of operetta and provided songs that grew integrally out of character and dramatic situation. Songs such as "Ol' Man River" and "Can't Help Lovin' Dat Man" might be built on a brief verse and an AABA chorus of 32 bars but they are intimately tied to the story of the musical. "Ol' Man River" not only must be sung by a male performer but a black male performer; "Can't Help Lovin' Dat Man" is the song that provides the first hint that the character Julie LaVerne is a mulatto. Producer **Florenz Ziegfeld** was sure that *Show Boat* would be a flop, but it turned out to be the most successful of his productions.

Such integration between song and show might have become more commonplace on Broadway were it not for the market crash of 1929 and the ensuing Depression. For much of the 1930s the lavish "book musical" was replaced by the sophisticated, intimate, and more economical "little revue," such as Dietz and Schwartz's *The Little Show* (1929) and *The Band Wagon* (1931). These revues, with their simple sets, contemporary costumes, and small casts maintained the tradition of the "unintegrated" song, such as "Dancing in the Dark" or Irving Berlin's "Easter Parade," that could be the basis of a production number but then go on to independent popularity.

That "hit song" tradition was also maintained by another development of 1927 —the advent of sound **films** with Warner Bros.' *The Jazz Singer*. Although it is frequently acclaimed as the first "talkie," *The Jazz Singer* is essentially a silent film with a few song sequences in sound and a synchronized musical soundtrack. As Jack Warner purportedly said when he and his brothers considered adding sound to movies, "Nobody wants to pay money to hear actors *talk*." All the Warner brothers wanted to do was to add a Vitaphone musical soundtrack to their films so that theaters could show silent movies with a full orchestral soundtrack and dispense with having to pay local piano players and pit bands to provide accompaniment. But since their first venture into a feature film with such a soundtrack was a movie version of a successful Broadway play about a cantor's son who rejects his heritage to sing popular songs, Warner Bros. decided to have Al Jolson sing several songs in synchronized sound. It was while singing Irving Berlin's "Blue Skies" to his on-screen mother that Jolson began talking as well as singing and that impromptu moment gave birth to talking—as well as singing—pictures.

But presenting a song in a film posed problems that would ultimately be solved by Broadway. As the movie *Singin' in the Rain* hilariously depicted early sound films, the noise of the camera had to be muffled by enclosing both camera and cameramen in a soundproof box. Microphones had to be concealed in props or costumes, and actors huddled around them to be heard. While those technical problems would be remedied in a few years, the aesthetic problem posed by song persisted. Sound had brought a new realism to film. Silent movies had transported audiences to another world where, for one thing, people did not talk out loud. This new realism made it hard for audiences to accept actors moving from dialogue into singing—then back to dialogue—without the applause that cushions such transitions in the musical theater. For years, Hollywood solved this aesthetic problem by decreeing that actors had to have a realistic excuse to sing, and the most common excuse was that they were putting on a Broadway musical as part of the movie plot.

When movie actors in such movies sang, therefore, it was because they were rehearsing or performing a Broadway show—*Broadway Melody*, *42nd Street*, or the endless series of *Gold Diggers* musicals. These "backstagers," as such films were dubbed, gave Broadway musicals—and their songs—new life on the screen. Hollywood studios bought up the Tin Pan Alley song publishing firms, moved their songwriters to the West Coast, and worked their catalog of songs into both musical and dramatic films. Even in contemporary films such as *When Harry Met Sally* and *Sleepless in Seattle* Broadway standards are incorporated into the soundtrack, giving those songs even greater longevity.

Even though the depression took its toll on Broadway, several musicals of the 1930s brimmed over with hit songs. The Gershwins' *Girl Crazy* (1930) featured "I Got Rhythm," "Embraceable You," "Bidin' My Time," and "But Not for Me." Porter's *Anything Goes* (1934) had the title song, "You're the Top," "All Through the Night," "Blow, Gabriel, Blow," and "I Get a Kick Out of You." Rodgers and Hart's *Babes in Arms* (1937) was even richer in hit songs: "My Funny Valentine," "Where or When," "Johnny One-Note," "The Lady Is a Tramp," and "I Wish I Were in Love Again." Even shows that had only one hit song could survive on its strength; Porter's *Gay Divorcé* was nicknamed "The 'Night and Day' Show" because audiences came to hear Fred Astaire sing Porter's most famous song.

By the 1940s, however, shows such as Rodgers and Hart's ***Pal Joey*** (1940) and Ira Gershwin and Kurt Weill's *Lady in the Dark* (1941) were striving for full integration between song and story yet still managed to produce hit songs such as "Bewitched, Bothered, and Bewildered" and "My Ship." The show that established the principle of integration, however, was Rodgers and Hammerstein's ***Oklahoma!*** (1943). As librettist as well as lyricist, Hammerstein could tailor character and dramatic situation to coalesce into song. The collaborators also struck upon a new way of working; instead of working from the music first, as Rodgers had done with Hart and Hammerstein with Kern, a song started with Hammerstein's lyric, which Rodgers would then set to music. Such lyrical primacy made for even greater integration between song and story.

The songs from *Oklahoma!* do what songs from few previous Broadway musicals do: heard apart from the show, they conjure up their dramatic moment of stage performance. "I Can't Say No," "Kansas City," "People Will Say We're in Love," "Oh, What a Beautiful Mornin'" are so closely tied to the story and characters that they are indelibly identified with their moment in the show. In earlier decades, such thoroughly integrated songs would not have become independently popular. But a new development, the original cast recording, made the full score of Broadway shows available to listeners who had never seen the original production. Originally consisting of elegantly boxed sets of 78-rpm records, such cast recordings had liner notes that told the story of the show, and radio stations made hits of such "integrated" songs as "There Is Nothin' Like a Dame" and "Bloody Mary" from *South Pacific* (1949).

In the early 1950s, the recording industry created two new types of recordings—and record players—that paralleled a division in the world of popular music. The LP (long-playing record) could hold an entire symphony as well as a Broadway score on a single disk, and these records were marketed to adult audiences to be played on expensive "hi-fi" (high fidelity) record players. The newly prosperous teenage market played 45-rpm "singles" on inexpensive players that had a large spindle so records could be stacked high for continuous play. Original cast recordings of Broadway shows of the 1950s were enormously popular, and such unlikely numbers as "The Rain in Spain" from *My Fair Lady* (1956) and "Ya Got Trouble" from *The Music Man* (1957) become independently popular hits through radio play.

The LP also became a vehicle for former Big Band singers such as Frank Sinatra, Doris Day, and Ella Fitzgerald who, in turn, made productive use of Broadway tunes in the post-band-singer phases of their careers. While these singers had occasional hit "singles," the advent of rock 'n' roll prevented them from dominating the pop charts as at least Sinatra once had. Instead, they turned to the LP and recorded a collection of 12 to 15 songs in what would now be called "concept" albums such as Sinatra's *Only the Lonely.* Instead of recording current hits, such singers, guided by arrangers such as Nelson Riddle at Capitol Records, turned to the songs of Broadway from the 1920s, 1930s, and 1940s. By singing "I Get a Kick Out of You," "My Funny Valentine," "Someone to Watch Over Me," and other show tunes, Sinatra and other singers helped transform them into timeless standards. In return, such songs gave singers more "character" than they had had as Big Band singers warbling the hits of their day. Many of Sinatra's standards, for example, were originally sung in Broadway musicals by female performers. For example, when Sinatra recorded "April in Paris" (originally sung by an actress in the 1932 Broadway Revue *Walk a Little Faster*), the lyrics gave his singing persona a new tenderness and vulnerability he lacked as an idol of the bobby-soxers. While Sinatra could render such feminine-tinged songs by Porter, Rodgers and Hart, and the Gershwins, he seldom ventured to record the more integrated songs of the post-*Oklahoma!* era. "Particularity" rather than "integration" was the quality he sought in the songs of the earlier Broadway musical.

It was Hollywood that, along with the original-cast recording, made that later era of Broadway musicals—and their songs—familiar to a nationwide audience. Faced by the threat of **television** in the early 1950s, Hollywood studios became very conservative in making musicals—the most expensive kind of cinematic enterprise with its retinue of singers, dancers, and musicians. Studios seldom ventured on new movie musicals with untried songs; it was safer to build a musical around a proven body of Broadway work such as that of Arthur Schwartz and Howard Dietz in *The Band Wagon* (1931) and the Gershwins in *American in Paris* (1950). Safer still was to make a film adaptation of a proven Broadway success such as **West Side Story** (1957) or **Gypsy** (1961). In making such film adaptations, Hollywood often adhered slavishly to the stage production, particularly in the performance of songs. While such film adaptations often won Academy Awards and enthralled audiences, they were the worst of both worlds—filmed versions of stage productions. It is a tribute to the power of a Broadway song—even in a comparatively lifeless filmed rendition—that generations of filmgoers around the world have come to love the scores of Broadway musicals even if many of them have never actually seen a Broadway show.

The rift that opened between Broadway and the popular song market in the 1950s has grown increasingly wider down to the present. It is rare that even the most successful Broadway musical produces an independent hit song in the traditional sense. The days when Irving Berlin considered *Annie Get Your Gun* (1946) a hit show because almost every one of its songs became independently popular have been gone for a long time. Yet during the heyday of the 1920s, 1930s, and 1940s, Broadway shows produced most of the hit songs of the day. Preserved by revivals of those shows, by Hollywood films that incorporate them onto their soundtracks, by jazz musicians who find their harmonic chord progressions an inspiration for improvisation, even by television commercials, these Broadway "show tunes" comprise the closest thing America has to a body of classical song that has been reinterpreted by each subsequent generation of singers and musicians.

Philip Furia

Further Reading

Furia, Philip. *The Poets of Tin Pan Alley A History of America's Great Lyricists.* New York: Oxford University Press, 1990.

Furia, Philip, and Michael L. Lasser. *America's Songs: The Stories Behind the Songs of Broadway, Hollywood, and Tin Pan Alley.* New York: Routledge, 2006.

Hischak, Thomas S. *The Tin Pan Alley Song Encyclopedia.* Westport, CT: Greenwood Press, 2002.

Jasen, David. *Tin Pan Alley: An Encyclopedia of the Golden Age of American Song.* New York: Routledge, 2003.

Kanter, Kenneth. *The Jews on Tin Pan Alley: The Jewish Contribution to American Popular Music, 1830–1940.* New York: Ktav Publishing House, 1982.

SHOW TUNES: THE ROCK ERA, DISNEY, AND DOWNLOADS

In the years since **Stephen Sondheim**'s *A Little Night Music* (1973) introduced the world to "Send in the Clowns," Broadway **musicals** have produced numerous songs that have become hits by climbing the music charts, earning great sums of money, finding an audience through new technology, and otherwise making an impact on popular culture. With few exceptions, however, today's "hit" show tunes generally lack the prominence in the music industry they held during the heyday of Tin Pan Alley (1920s–1940s) or the so-called Golden Age of musicals (1940s–mid-1960s).

The Broadway show tune's loss of cultural status and market share over the past several decades is largely a factor of the explosion of diverse popular music genres, formats, and delivery technology that have overtaken the popular music industry since Sondheim sent in the clowns. While it may no longer be culturally or technologically possible for Broadway's top composers to assume the command over American popular music they enjoyed between the 1920s and the dawn of rock and roll, Broadway hit songs continue to find sizable audiences—often by morphing into new musical styles and accommodating new marketing technologies that may actually have little to do with the Broadway shows or soundtrack albums in which they originated.

Rock Musicals and Dance Tunes: The 1970s

The Broadway musical scene in the 1970s offered an eclectic mix including rock musicals, traditional book musicals, and Stephen Sondheim (1930–). Arguably the biggest hit song from this decade was Sondheim's "Send in the Clowns," but it was the rock musicals that produced most of the decade's other hit Broadway songs. *Hair* (1968), with its rousing title song, is generally considered to be the first rock musical. British newcomers Tim Rice (1944–) and **Andrew Lloyd Webber** (1948–) started a trend when they released the soundtrack of their groundbreaking rock opera *Jesus Christ Superstar* (1971) in 1970, before the stage show was even fully conceived. Containing rock and classical elements, the soundtrack appeared on major musical charts for two years, spending eight weeks as the No. 1 best-selling album in the United States. Two songs from the show became hits. The original cast recording of the title song "Jesus Christ Superstar" received a lot of **radio** airplay as did two versions of "I Don't Know How to Love Him." Original cast member Yvonne Elliman's version received considerable radio and **television** exposure. More notably, pop singer Helen Reddy's "cover" (a recording of a song previously recorded and released commercially by another artist) also became a big hit, spending 20 weeks on the *Billboard* charts and launching the Australian singer to stardom in the United States. There have been numerous other recordings made of the song over the years.

"Day by Day," from Stephen Schwartz's religious rock musical *Godspell* (1971), was resurrected over 20 years after first becoming a hit. Originally released as a single in 1972, the song spent 14 weeks on the *Billboard*'s Hot 100 chart. With its soft rock arrangement and only mildly religious lyrics, "Day by Day" helped expose the new specialty market genre of Christian rock to a mass audience. Some 20 years later, the song found a whole new generation of fans when the Christian rock group dc Talk included it on their influential 1995 album *Jesus Freak*.

The Wiz (1975), an all-black cast adaptation of *The Wizard of Oz*, generated excitement with its soul- and jazz-influenced score by jazz pianist Charlie Smalls. The cast recording of the dance-friendly signature song "Ease on Down the Road" spent 14 weeks (several at No. 1) on the *Billboard* Hot Dance Club Play chart—a new music chart created in the 1970s to track business generated by disco and dance club music. The song helped forge a heretofore unknown and unimaginable linkage between Broadway show tunes and the disco and techno dance club scenes of the 1970s, 1980s, and 1990s.

The practice of turning show tunes into dance remixes for clubs and dance-track recordings became a common practice in the 1970s, making surprise hits of many songs. Remixes, recordings of songs with certain elements altered electronically, may feature changes in tempo or chord progression, or certain instruments may be strengthened or diminished, and so forth, but the essence of the song remains the same. The practice continues to this day. "Don't Cry for Me Argentina" from Lloyd Webber and Rice's smash hit *Evita* (1979) is a case in point. The original cast record of the song did well with radio audiences as did a cover version by pop singer Olivia Newton-John in 1977. But the song became a phenomenal success as a dance tune 20 years later, when Madonna recorded a disco version after starring in the 1996 **film** adaptation of the musical. Even "Hard Knock Life," an up-tempo ensemble piece from the traditional book musical hit *Annie* (1977), made the charts in 1999 when hip-hop artist Jay-Z reinterpreted it as a dance tune and gave it the subtitle "Ghetto Anthem." It spent an impressive 56 weeks on the *Billboard* Hot Rap Singles charts (another new post–Rock Era measure of song popularity), reaching No. 2.

Sondheim was back on Broadway by the end of the 1970s with *Sweeney Todd* (1979). While the rich score attracted devoted fans from the start and won a Grammy Award for Best Cast Recording in 1979, it was not until the 2007 film adaptation was released that a large national audience embraced the show's songs. In the two months following the release of the film, millions of fans logged on to YouTube to watch streaming videos of cast members singing the ballad "Not While I'm Around" (in all likelihood, the song Sondheim intended as the pop hit) and other songs. The film also stirred up new interest in the original Broadway production, as nearly 500,000 viewers logged onto a You Tube clip of the *Sweeney Todd* original cast singing "A Little Priest" within a few months after the movie opened.

Broadway shows of the 1970s produced some songs that have earned a distinctive notoriety in popular culture but are arguably not high revenue–generating "hits." **A Chorus Line** (1975) produced two very well-known songs: "What I Did For Love" and "One," with its unforgettable melody and first line, "One . . . singular sensation, every little step she takes." That much-loved song is referred to repeatedly in popular media from television shows *The Simpsons* and *Scrubs* to the *Shrek* films. Similarly, the single recording of "Tomorrow" from *Annie* did not get extensive radio airplay nor did it sell very well. However, the song enjoys wide recognition in popular culture and is regularly performed or parodied in popular media, including television shows *South Park*, *Friends*, and *Survivor* as well as the 1998 Tom Hanks/Meg Ryan hit movie *You've Got Mail*.

Heavy on Hydraulics, Light on Hits—The 1980s

The 1980s brought flashy **megamusicals** from Europe, but there were some home-grown musicals that produced hit songs as well. The cast recording of "And I'm Telling You I'm Not Going," a powerful R&B song with gospel overtones from *Dreamgirls* (1981), propelled 21-year-old singer Jennifer Holliday to stardom, winning her accolades from critics, a Grammy Award, and a spot on *Billboard*'s Hot 100 chart for 14 weeks. A hit film adaptation starring newcomer and television reality show *American Idol* finalist Jennifer Hudson, was released over 20 years later in 2005. Hudson's rendition from the film received extensive radio airplay and landed on numerous *Billboard* charts, including the newly created "Hot Ringtones" chart (to measure purchased songs downloaded for use on personal mobile phones).

La Cage aux Folles (1983), a traditional musical comedy with a nontraditional plot, became part of a new trend that persisted throughout the decade—targeting a show tune as a hit for a specific segment of the audience. *La Cage*, composed by *Hello, Dolly!* creator **Jerry Herman** (1931) included "I Am What I Am," a showstopper intended to inspire gay/lesbian audience members. It did. Disco singer Gloria Gaynor, who had a large following in gay dance clubs, recorded the song while the show was still running. Her version spent ten weeks on the Hot R&B/Hip Hop charts. Twenty years later, digital downloads would propel a 2003 remake of the song by Linda Eder back up the charts, prompting some to call it a "gay anthem."

The biggest Broadway story of the 1980s was the "British invasion." Andrew Lloyd Webber brought five musicals to Broadway in this decade, of which three produced hit songs. Though many critics argue that the emphasis in these shows is on visual stage hydraulics rather than music, cast recordings of Webber shows generally sold briskly. "Memory" from *Cats* (1982) has become a standard, recorded by dozens of performers over the years. The London and Broadway cast recordings of the ballad generated strong sales and radio airplay. The song became an even bigger hit when it was recorded by Barbra Streisand in 1982 and then by Barry Manilow in 1983. Manilow's recording stayed on *Billboard*'s Hot 100 chart for 14 weeks.

Another song from a Lloyd Webber musical, "Any Dream Will Do" from *Joseph and the Amazing Technicolor Dreamcoat* (1982), has been recorded successfully by many performers, including Donny Osmond (who toured nationally as Joseph for years) and 1980s soft rock singer Andy Gibb. Singer Lee Mead, winner of a *London* reality show that decided who would play the lead in a London revival of *Joseph*, resurrected the song in 2007. Another European import, *Les Misérables* (1987), was very popular with theatergoers. Told almost entirely in pop-operatic songs with elaborate, quickly moving sets, *Les Mis* mesmerized audiences. "I Dreamed a Dream" was recorded by rock crooner Neil Diamond in 1987 almost as soon as the cast recording was released. Diamond's version spent 15 weeks on *Billboard*'s Hot Contemporary charts. The haunting "Castle in the Sky," sung in the show by the child Cosette, is arguably the show's most memorable melody, principally because of the aggressive marketing campaign that put commercials for the show featuring that song on every American television for years. The choral piece "One Day More" is highly recognizable as well and is parodied often, most notably in the Broadway spoof musical *Urinetown* (2001).

Lloyd Webber's ***The Phantom of the Opera*** (1988), the longest-running show in Broadway history, is told almost entirely in opera-inspired pop songs, several of which became hits with wide audiences. Streisand had two hits from *Phantom*. Her cover of "All I Ask of You," a traditional love song that does not depend on the show's plot, did extremely well on radio. She also joined Michael Crawford, who played the Phantom on Broadway and London, in a very popular recording of "The Music of the Night." Several artists recorded the title song "Phantom of the Opera," which was marketed successfully as a dance club remix in 1993 and again in 2005.

The popularity of the quirky song "One Night in Bangkok" from the Benny Andersson, Bjorn Ulvaeus (both formerly of ABBA), and Tim Rice musical *Chess* (1988) outlasted the Broadway production, which ran for a disappointing 68 performances. Targeted for a more youthful audience than would likely have attended the Broadway show, the song hit No. 3 on the *Billboard* Hot 100 charts, lasting a total of 20 weeks. By the end of the 1980s, as "mass appeal" music continued to give way to audience segmentation, Broadway composers and producers had become adept at targeting specific audiences for potential hit songs in the increasingly stratified markets of popular music.

Disney and the Corporate Musicals: The 1990s

In the 1990s conditions were ripe for the Disney Corporation to move into Broadway and set up house, which they did when they adapted their 1991 animated film *Beauty and the Beast* (1994) to Broadway. The title song "Beauty and the Beast" was recorded for the film by pop vocalists Celine Dion and Peabo Bryson and is frequently sung in concert by other pop singers. It was a big hit on the radio and generated healthy sales before and after the Broadway show opened. The song "Be Our Guest" is also highly recognizable and can be heard frequently in television commercials.

Disney's next Broadway production, *The Lion King* (1997), was also based on a Disney animated children's film. "Circle of Life" and "Can You Feel the Love Tonight," pop ballads with African rhythms, were written for the film and show by pop rocker Elton John and Tim Rice. Both songs were wildly popular, enjoying considerable radio airplay and huge record sales before the Broadway show opened. Even the unlikely song "Hakuna Matata," a song whose title at least is inextricably tied to the characters and plot of the show, earned sufficient radio airplay to spend 11 weeks on *Billboard*'s Hot Adult Contemporary chart in 1995. For both *Beauty and the Beast* and *The Lion King*—two of the top-ten longest-running shows in Broadway history—the Disney-owned hit songs from the Disney-owned films served as advertising for the Disney-owned Broadway musicals, inducing listeners to travel to New York to experience the familiar as new again. After the musicals opened, the songs became associated with the shows instead of the films.

Other corporate-produced musicals in the 1990s included the relatively small-scale but long-running ***Rent*** (1996) by **Jonathan Larson**. The show was extremely popular with hip young urban adults and is credited with attracting a new generation (sometimes called "Generation X" or "Reagan-era babies") to Broadway musicals. The *Rent* cast recording spent 22 weeks on the *Billboard* charts. The original cast recording of the song "Seasons of Love" (widely known by its improbable opening lyric, "525,600 minutes") appeared on numerous charts for 30 weeks, and was recorded several times, most notably by Stevie Wonder. A film adaptation debuted in 2005 and, although panned by the **critics**, revived public interest in the music. At one point in December 2005 five songs from *Rent* charted on *Billboard*'s Pop 100 chart simultaneously. The music video showing the cast singing "Seasons of Love" was viewed on YouTube over 2 million times in the year following the release of the film.

The Twenty-First Century: Disney Rolls, Jukeboxes Rock, and Hair Sprays

The first big hit of the new century was another **Disney production**, the first one not based on an animated film. Elton John and Tim Rice's *Aida* (2000) retells the Verdi opera with pop rock tunes that stylistically pull from reggae, Motown, gospel, and African music. Elton John recorded and prereleased the songs from *Aida* a year before it opened on Broadway. Two of the songs did well in the charts. "A Step Too Far," sung by Elton John and Heather Headley (the original Broadway Aida), spent 10 weeks on the *Billboard* charts while John's solo of "Written in the Stars" reached No. 4 during its 10 weeks on the charts. Deborah Cox (a replacement Aida) released a version of "Easy as Life" that spent 13 weeks on the dance charts.

Hairspray (2002), a critical and financial success, produced a strong-selling cast album that spent many weeks on the *Billboard* charts. Additionally, the soundtrack for the 2007 film adaptation of the musical *Hairspray* (which was itself based on a 1988 John Waters nonmusical film) stayed on the *Billboard* 200 Top Album chart for 35 weeks, peaking at No. 2. The film made hits of "You Can't Stop the Beat" and "Without You" from the original score, principally through downloads and YouTube clips from the film and stage performances.

Composer Stephen Schwartz's *Wicked* (2003) contains "Defying Gravity," released as a single by the show's co-star Idina Menzel. The song was extremely popular with young music fans, spending over 10 weeks on the *Billboard* Hot

Singles Sales chart as well as 15 weeks on the Hot Dance Club Play charts, peaking there at No. 5. As with other Broadway shows from this decade, fans flocked to YouTube to hear their favorite numbers. By 2008, over a million and a half people had viewed Menzel singing the song on YouTube. Other songs from the show, such as "Popular" and "What Is This Feeling," established strong YouTube followings as well.

Jukebox musicals, which had appeared sporadically on Broadway since the 1980s, became something of a trend in 2000–2010, owing to the phenomenal success of *Mamma Mia!* (2001), thus far the longest-running musical to open in the new century. Jukebox musicals create full Broadway shows (with generally less than full story lines) from earlier hit songs of established rock or pop artists. *Mamma Mia!* revives the songs of 1970s soft rock group ABBA. Original ABBA radio and club hits, including "Dancing Queen," "Waterloo," and "Mamma Mia," have become international hits all over again as show tunes, owing to the musical's marathon runs in New York and London and relentless touring throughout North America and Europe. Other recent jukebox musicals include Broadway hits *Movin' Out* (2002), based on the songs of pop music giant Billy Joel, and *Jersey Boys* (2005), based on the songs of the 1960s group the Four Seasons. In 2009 *Rock of Ages*, a musical based on "hair band" and "metal" songs of the 1980s, opened to strong reviews. By contrast *All Shook Up* (2005), based on Elvis Presley's songs, struggled through a six-month run, and a dismally received *The Times They Are a Changing* (2006), inspired by the songs of folk/rock icon Bob Dylan, closed in three weeks. While jukebox musicals represent a reasonable, although not guaranteed, hedge against financial failure (producers already know the songs are popular), many find the trend disturbing since the shows add no new music to Broadway.

While it has been generally true throughout Broadway musical history that for a show to succeed it needs at least one signature "hit song," a number of musicals opening since 2000 have disproved that point. Hit shows like *The Full Monty* (2000), **The Producers** (2001), *Urinetown* (2001), *Monty Python's Spamalot* (2005), and critically acclaimed shows such as *Assassins* (2004), *A Light in the Piazza* (2005), *The 25th Annual Putnam County Spelling Bee* (2005), and Disney's *The Little Mermaid* (2008) do not have a truly solid hit song among them. While some of these soundtrack albums sold reasonably well, none of these shows made a major impact on the music scene or added a signature song (whether in original form, dance remix, ringtone, or other mutated iteration) to the ever-expanding honor roll of Broadway hit show tunes. Nevertheless, Broadway composers, producers, and audiences, still look actively for *the* song that will have crowds singing their way out of the theater and heading straight to their record store, computer, or iPod Nano to recapture the magic of the live performance.

Broadway songs have come a long way since rock and roll virtually evicted Broadway show songs from radio and shoved soundtrack albums into the back bins of record stores. To turn show tunes into popular hit songs in the twenty-first century, composers and producers have combined venerable established practices with new marketing and production strategies. They continue to release classy

NEW WAYS TO DETERMINE A "HIT" SONG IN THE TWENTY-FIRST CENTURY

The music industry looks very different in the twenty-first century than it did in the latter part of the twentieth century, a fact that complicates how to determine if a show tune, or any tune, is a hit. By the closing decades of the twentieth century, pop music had fragmented into a multitude of subgenres (e.g., alternative rock, hard rock, urban, rhythm and blues, etc.) each with devoted listeners who often tend to ignore other genres. Technology for delivering music from its creators to its audience have diversified as well. Digital downloads, onto iPods and other MP3 players, peer-to-peer file transfers, Internet radio, and YouTube have all rendered staples of traditional "hit" calculations—radio airplay statistics and sales of recordings or sheet music (in the Tin Pan Alley days)—far less influential than they had been in years past.

Billboard Magazine's Music Charts. Expanding its chart categories and measurement methods to accommodate evolving tastes and technology, _Billboard_ maintains its 70-plus-year status as the preeminent industry adjudicator of American song popularity. _Billboard_ updates and publishes weekly charts that rank songs, albums, videos, and ringtones based on sales (including digital sales since 2007), radio airplay, and dance club play using music industry statistics. The "Hot 100" songs is the most general, combining rock, hip-hop, country, pop, and other music genres. (_Billboard_ has been tracking hit singles since the 1940s.) _Billboard_ also produces genre-specific charts such as Top 40 Mainstream, Pop 100, Hot Country Songs, Hot Rhythm and Blues, Hot Dance Club Play, Hot Digital Sales (started in 2005), Hot Ringtones (started in 2004). _Billboard_ also continues to chart top-selling albums, as it has since the 1940s, currently under the chart name of the Top 200.

Ringtones. Other recent ways of playing Broadway music include ringtones, digital sound clips that signal incoming calls on cell phones. Ringtones have become big business, with most popular songs, including Broadway show tunes, available for downloading. _Billboard_ began tracking sales of the most popular ringtones in 2004.

YouTube. The free video streaming service that allows users to view and listen to short video/audio clips on the Internet has led to thousands of music fans posting clips of casts of Broadway musicals singing songs from the shows, allowing other fans to view them freely. Some of the clips are illegally obtained by fans smuggling video cameras into theaters, while others are captured from television programs.

original-cast soundtrack albums (with at least one or two songs designated as the "hits"), encourage cover recordings by popular artists, and maintain robust connections with Hollywood musical film producers. At the same time, Broadway has had to adapt to the new diversity of popular music markets and rapidly evolving, youth-centered forms of music distribution technology. Although no longer a dominant force in popular music, the Broadway show tune still holds its own as a competitive player in contemporary music—and for fans of Broadway, that is something to sing about.

Sue Ann Brainard

Further Reading

Billboard. www.billboard.com.

Broadway Theatre League. www.broadwayleague.com.

Bruno, Antony. "How to Define a Hit." *Billboard* 119 (2007): 18.

Internet Broadway Database. www.ibdb.com.

Murrells, Joseph. *Million Selling Records from the 1900s to the 1980s: An Illustrated Directory*. New York: Arco, 1984.

Recording Academy. www.grammys.com.

Siskin, Steven. *Show Tunes: The Songs, Shows, and Careers of Broadway's Major Composers*. New York: Oxford University Press, 2000.

Stewart, John. *Broadway Musicals, 1943–2004*. Jefferson, NC: McFarland, 2006.

Studwell, William E. *Popular Song Reader: A Sampler of Well-Known Twentieth Century Songs*. New York: Haworth, 1994.

YouTube. www.youtube.com.

SHUBERT BROTHERS
PRODUCERS, THEATRE OWNERS

At the turn of the twentieth century, the three Shubert Brothers—Sam S. (c.1876–1905); Lee (Levi, c.1873–1953); and Jacob J. (J. J., aka Jake, c.1878–1963)—founded a theatrical dynasty whose impact on Broadway and the American theater continues today. As children, the brothers immigrated to Syracuse, New York, from Eastern Europe with their parents, David (1845–1913), an itinerant pack peddler, and Catherine (1849–1914).

Sam S. Shubert was reportedly the most charming and extroverted of the three male siblings and was the driving force behind the Shuberts' foray into the theater business. Beginning as a program boy in a local Syracuse playhouse, he quickly worked his way into the box office, eventually becoming the Treasurer of the Wieting Theatre, the largest professional theater venue in Syracuse. His passion for the stage led him to producing. In the mid-1890s he negotiated with **playwright** Charles Hoyt for the touring rights to his play *A Texas Steer*, which became the first big hit for Shubert management. Eventually Sam lured his brother Lee away from his haberdashery business and into the box office, and within a few years set his sights on Broadway. In May 1900, the brothers acquired the lease to the Herald Square Theatre and then, with the financial assistance of some Syracuse businessmen, set about adding other theaters to their management. Youngest brother J. J.

remained upstate and managed the family's venues in Rochester, Utica, Syracuse, and Albany.

Once in New York City, the Shuberts had to deal with the **Theatrical Syndicate** (generally known as "the Syndicate"), headed by Marc Klaw and Abraham Erlanger, which dominated the American theater at the time through its booking business. Initially the Shuberts tried to cooperate with Klaw & Erlanger but soon realized that their interests and those of the Syndicate conflicted. The brothers began challenging the Syndicate by leasing or buying theaters on the road. They also enticed many performers, playwrights, and **producers** who were disgruntled with K&E's strong-arm practices to join them in what they called an "Open Door" policy. The Shuberts' audacity in taking on the Syndicate reaped rewards, and Sam was able to persuade several key theatrical figures to join him in his fight. The Shuberts, then, were making great strides in building up their company when Sam died suddenly in a train accident at age 29.

His death was a major blow to the Shubert brothers and their burgeoning theater enterprise. Although distraught, Lee and J. J. (who relocated to Manhattan after Sam's death) rose to the occasion and dedicated themselves to fulfilling Sam's dream of realizing a company that would eventually destroy the Syndicate and become the dominating force in the American theater. By 1911 they controlled 17 theaters in New York City, and at the height of their empire in the late 1920s they owned, leased, or booked productions into over 1,000 theaters in North America. The Syndicate officially dissolved in 1919. In the ensuing years many in the industry accused the Shuberts of being as abusive of their power as the Syndicate had been.

In addition to owning and managing theaters, Lee and J. J. Shubert produced numerous plays, revues, and **musicals** to fill their stages. While J. J.'s main interests were with the musical productions, especially **operettas**, which he loved, it was Lee who often strove for more serious and artistic material. By and large, however, what the Shuberts offered was mainstream fare. Some of their more popular successes include *The City* (1909), *The Blue Bird* (1910), *Maytime* (1917), *Blossom Time* (1921), *The Student Prince* (1924), *Death Takes a Holiday* (1929), *As You Desire Me* (1931), *At Home Abroad* (1934), *Life Begins at 8:40* (1935), *Hellzapoppin'* (1939), *Ten Little Indians* (1944), and the various editions of the *Passing Show* and *Artists and Models* revues. Among the stars they discovered or nurtured were Fred and Adele Astaire, Ray Bolger, **Fanny Brice**, Cary Grant, Willie and Eugene Howard, Al Jolson, Bert Lahr, Beatrice Lillie, Jeanette MacDonald, Marilyn Miller, Carmen Miranda, Alla Nazimova, Olson and Johnson, and Mae West.

Lee also realized early the money-making potential of motion pictures. His foresight led to the Shuberts' involvement in major **film** enterprises such as the Shubert Feature Film Booking Company, the World Film Corporation, Loew's Incorporated, the Goldwyn Picture Company, and Metro-Goldwyn-Mayer. Among many other business ventures that Lee and J. J. undertook were real-estate investment in New York and other major cities, and the operation of several subsidiary entertainment-related companies including the Shubert Music Publishing Company and the Century Library, a play-renting enterprise.

The Shuberts were severely hurt by the Depression. In 1931 the Shubert Theatrical Corporation went into receivership and had to sell some theaters, give up the leases on others, and scale back its producing activities. But Lee, astute and determined, formed a new company called Select Theatres, and bought the assets of the old Shubert Theatrical Corporation at a bankruptcy auction. From this point on, the Shuberts produced fewer shows, and aside from several successful productions in the 1930s and 1940s, were content to remain behind the scenes as investors in other people's shows, as landlords, and as participants in sundry business enterprises. The post-Depression Shuberts operated an extremely profitable company.

Although many regarded Lee and J. J. as ruthless businessmen, they cared deeply about theater and were extremely charitable. In 1945, they established the Shubert Foundation, which today, through its grant program, is one of the largest financial supporters of the performing arts in America. In 1950 the U.S. government filed an antitrust suit against the Shuberts. Lee, who died in 1953, never saw the end result of that litigation, which required the divestiture of several theatrical properties in New York and other cities. Lee had no offspring. J. J.'s only son, John Shubert, co-ran the company with his father in the 1950s and early 1960s until his untimely death in 1962. J. J. continued his involvement in the business until his death in 1963, when his grandnephew, Lawrence Shubert Lawrence Jr., assumed control.

In 1972, the Shubert Foundation appointed Gerald Schoenfeld and Bernard B. Jacobs, former lawyers for Lee and J. J., to head the company, which was reorganized into an entity called The Shubert Organization. Schoenfeld died in 2008 and was succeeded by Philip J. Smith and Robert E. Wankel who were named Co-Chief Executive Officers of the Organization.

Lee, J. J., and Sam S. Shubert played a key role in defining and establishing the modern Broadway theater industry. Were it not for their contributions, the business structure of Broadway, and even its physical appearance, would be radically different than it is today.

Maryann Chach

Further Reading

MacNamara, Brooks. *The Shuberts of Broadway: A History Drawn from the Collections of the Shubert Archive.* New York: Oxford University Press, 1990.

Wilmeth, Donald B., and C. W. E. Bigsby. *The Cambridge History of American Theatre: 1870–1945.* Cambridge, England: Cambridge University Press, 1999.

SHUBERT ORGANIZATION

See **Shubert Brothers**.

SHUFFLE ALONG

Broadway Run: 63rd Street Music Hall
Opening: May 23, 1921
Closing: July 15, 1922
Total Performances: Approximately 484
Librettists: Flournoy Miller and Aubrey Lyles
Composer: Eubie Blake
Musical Director: Eubie Blake
Lyricist: Noble Sissle
Dance arrangements: Charles Davis and Lawrence Deas
Director: Walter Brooks
Producer: Nikko Producing Company
Cast: A. E. Baldwin (Soakum Flat, Syncopating Sunflower); Edna Battles (Majestic Magnolia); Mildred Brown (Jazz Jasmine); Hazel Burke (Majestic Magnolia); Charles Davis (Uncle Tom, Syncopating Sunflower), Noble Sissle (Tom Sharper), and Billy Williams (Strutt)

Although it contained many elements of nineteenth-century black minstrelsy and **vaudeville** in its writing and staging, *Shuffle Along* is generally considered to be the first modern-era **musical** written and developed by an **African American** creative team—and certainly the first to become a blockbuster New York hit. Staged in the small, almost unknown 63rd Street Music Hall—a movie, music, and lecture house 20 blocks north of Times Square—*Shuffle Along*'s unexpected popularity with white audiences helped stimulate a new level of respect and acceptance for black creativity in theater, music, and other arts. The show is credited with creating a permanent niche for black musicals on Broadway and catalyzing a surge of white interest in "uptown" African American entertainment that eventually produced much of the Harlem Renaissance's lasting influence on American culture.

Prior to its extraordinary 480-plus performance New York run (the exact number of performances is the subject of some scholarly dispute), the presence of black music and comedy performance in New York commercial theater had been largely confined to black minstrel shows, revues, and other entertainments from the black music circuit tours. Although the rare African American mainstream vaudeville act (most notably **Bert Williams**, who starred in *Ziegfeld's Follies* throughout the 1910s) would make an occasional appearance in a major commercial midtown theater, black music and comedy entertainment on Broadway was in short supply throughout the 1910s.

Shuffle Along established the fact that Broadway's white audiences would not only support but enthusiastically embrace a black-composed, black-written, all-black cast musical—even with a heretofore unthinkable straightforward love story between a black man and a black woman. Broadway theater managers, other black composers and writers, and the New York press could not help but marvel at the surprise hit of the season, and the modern Broadway black musical was born.

In 1921 composer Eubie Blake (born 1883) and lyricist Noble Sissle (born 1889) were veteran vaudeville and minstrel musicians, having worked both individually and as a team for years in numerous **touring** companies and music halls. In addition to his work in vaudeville and minstrel shows, Blake was a highly regarded music hall jazz pianist and a pioneering ragtime player and composer. Librettists Flournoy E. Miller and Aubrey Lyles, both about the same age as Blake and Sissle, were among the day's most successful African American vaudeville writers and performers, having toured extensively in the United States and Europe with various shows and companies. Miller and Lyles developed the plot for *Shuffle Along*—a conventional musical romance story set against the backdrop of a farcical small-town mayoral election—from one of their vaudeville routines. Dance managers Charles Davis and Lawrence Deas, who also played small parts in the show, were experienced minstrel and vaudeville performers as well.

Much about the production reflected the vaudeville and minstrelsy performing backgrounds of its creators, including black actors performing in blackface, dance numbers based on popular steps of the day, the casual sacrifice of plot depth and coherence for showcase musical numbers, and traditional plantation humor aimed at white audiences familiar with the conventions of minstrel shows. However, Blake and Sissle did not imbue *Shuffle Along* with race-specific "coon songs" (songs capitalizing on white stereotypes of blacks and black life), which had been a staple of minstrelsy and black vaudeville since the mid-1800s. Instead, they wrote race-neutral, mainstream Tin Pan Alley–type songs, including the evening's showstopper "Love Will Find a Way" and the up-tempo classic "I'm Just Wild about Harry" (which reinvigorated the show's legacy when Harry Truman selected it as his presidential campaign theme song in 1948).

Like most African American shows that played anywhere in Manhattan at that time, *Shuffle Along* had been touring prior to its arrival in New York. While popular among African American audiences in Philadelphia and Washington, D.C., there was no indication from these road stops that the show was going to draw a huge following among white theatergoers in New York or anywhere else. Yet once in New York, reviews were favorable, noting not only the show's exceptional songs and performances but also its relatively "clean" wife-and-family friendly humor, for which many road revues—black or white—were not generally known. The show became a spectacular hit, at first on its own merits and then as a prestigious Manhattan word-of-mouth "must see" event for theatergoers and those "in the know." The 14-month rush of white patrons uptown to support a black event or performance of any kind was a new phenomenon and, as the Harlem Renaissance would bear out in the decade ahead, a milestone in white audience acceptance of and respect for African American artists.

The success of *Shuffle Along* as part of the flourishing of African American creativity in Harlem in the 1920s opened up numerous theatrical opportunities for African American composers, lyricists, musicians, and stage performers. Blake, Sissle, Lyles, and Miller all had several more Broadway credits in the 1920s and 1930s. Jazz pianist Thomas "Fats" Waller began placing songs in both black and predominantly white musicals in the late 1920s. Ragtime pianist James P. Johnson, composer of the dance-craze song "The Charleston," wrote music for several Broadway revues in the 1920s, including a moderately successful Miller and Lyles "sequel" to *Shuffle Along, Keep Shufflin'* (1928). African American Broadway stars whose onstage personas showed little or no ties to minstrelsy or coon show traditions emerged on the scene. **Paul Robeson**, who appeared briefly in a small replacement singing part in the original *Shuffle Along*, saw his Broadway career begin in earnest in 1922. A teenaged Josephine Baker, who toured in *Shuffle Along* directly after its Broadway run, soon thereafter became the toast of Europe as an enigmatic and alluring singer, dancer, and actress.

The show is also distinctive, if not unique, in the annals of Broadway in that it single-handedly transformed an out-of-the-way, all-but-unknown music and movie hall into one of Broadway's legitimate theaters. After *Shuffle Along*'s 14-month, traffic-stopping run at the 63rd Street Music Hall, some of Broadway's most successful producers, **playwrights**, and composers began bringing shows into the now popular and well-known venue. Among the more notable productions to take up residence at the 63rd in the wake of the *Shuffle Along* juggernaut were the **Provincetown Players'** original production of **Eugene O'Neill**'s *Desire Under the Elms* (1925), Mae West's historically controversial play *Sex* (1926), Miller and Lyles follow-up effort *Keep Shufflin'*, and the **Federal Theatre Project**'s revival of **Clifford Odets**'s hit *Awake and Sing* (1935). The venue remained an active legitimate theater until it closed in 1941.

Thomas A. Greenfield

Further Reading

Sotiropoulos, Karen. *Staging Race: Black Performers in Turn of the Century America.* Cambridge, MA: Harvard University Press, 2006.

Wintz, Cary D., and Paul Finkelman. *Encyclopedia of the Harlem Renaissance.* London: Taylor & Francis, 2004.

Simon, Neil (1927–)
Playwright, Producer

Neil Simon is the most prolific and by far the most commercially successful contemporary **playwright** in the world. He has earned the most money, has written the largest number of Broadway plays (at least 40, including originals, musicals, and adaptations), and is the only playwright ever to have had four plays running on Broadway simultaneously. Principally a writer of comedies, Simon at his best is without peer in his ability to enrich everyday American middle-class dialog with breathtakingly funny repartee that is as wise and wistful as it is hilarious.

Neil Simon poses for a picture at the reception for the Eugene O'Neill Theater Center's Monte Cristo Award in New York, April 21, 2008. The award, given in recognition of distinguished careers, was given to playwright Simon. (AP Photo/Seth Wenig)

Marvin Neil Simon was born and raised in the Bronx, New York, which he immortalized in a number of his plays that often hinted at—and at times practically documented—events of his youth. Before writing for Broadway Simon started as a young night club and **television** comedy writer in the 1950s, most famously as a member of the historic comedy writing team on Sid Caesar's *Your Show of Shows* along with comedy superstars-to-be Woody Allen, Mel Brooks, Larry Gelbart, and Carl Reiner. The experience of writing for weekly television grounded Simon in the sensibilities of America's middle-class mass audience, whose affection he captured throughout his playwriting career notwithstanding the pronounced New York City flavor of many of his most successful works. In addition to dealing with the tamer elements of daily life, Simon's plays confront sex, betrayal, infidelity, failure, and death without sacrificing wit nor necessitating that children be excluded from the audience.

Simon's initial Broadway successes in the 1960s and early 1970s included a string of now internationally famous hits: *Come Blow Your Horn* (1961), *Little Me* (1962), **Barefoot in the Park** (1963), *The Odd Couple* (1965), *Last of the Red Hot Lovers* (1969), *The Prisoner of Second Avenue* (1971), and *The Sunshine Boys* (1972). In addition to energizing Broadway with the shear magnitude of its success, this body of plays has for the past five decades provided the nation's summer stock companies, community theaters, and high school drama clubs with a library of budget-friendly "family plays" that, nonetheless, has brought to America's hometowns the most influential stage comedy writing of the twentieth century. The wide-scale acceptance of these plays also invigorated "wisecrack" comedy writing on Broadway (and film comedy as well) as readily seen in the work of other successful Broadway comedy writers such as Herb Gardner (*A Thousand Clowns, I'm Not Rappaport*) and **Wendy Wasserstein** (*The Heidi Chronicles*).

During the 1970s and mid-1980s Simon continued to write for the stage although he actually enjoyed more public attention and commercial success as a screenwriter for adaptations of his plays as well as some original scripts. He had a resurgence of commercial and critical Broadway success in the mid-1980s when he produced a very well received autobiographical trilogy: *Brighton Beach Memoirs* (1983), *Biloxi Blues* (1985), and *Broadway Bound* (1986). These later plays are often characterized as Simon's "serious comedies" in that, while still very funny, family themes and characterizations are drawn more deeply and subtly than they had been in earlier works. Moreover, the later plays show a mature easing up on the staccato **vaudeville**-esque comic pacing that characterized much of his work in the 1960s. Simon's 1991 play *Lost in Yonkers* followed in this more serious vein and became Simon's most critically acclaimed play, having won the Tony Award, the Pulitzer Prize, and the Drama Desk Award for Best Play.

The unprecedented level of Simon's audience popularity, particularly at the outset of his career, defied the scolding of some **critics** and theater scholars, many of whom took a decade or more to recognize the extraordinary craftsmanship and artistry of Simon's writing. Widely dismissed early on as a hack or formula writer, Simon's quotable laugh lines and mass appeal made him an easy target for "intellectuals" intent on championing theater—including comedy—as high art. However, Simon's body of work outlasted its critics and, by the end of the 1980s, Simon began receiving the critical praise and attention commensurate with his accomplishments. In addition to the aforementioned Tony Award and Pulitzer Prizes, Simon received prestigious Kennedy Center Honors recognition in 1995 and was the subject of one of the Public Broadcasting System *American Masters* profiles. Moreover, by the 1990s a generation of drama scholars raised on "Simon-esque" comedy began including him in university courses on American drama, alongside the likes of **Arthur Miller**, **Tennessee Williams**, and **Edward Albee**, and essays on Simon's work began making their way into serious scholarship on American theater and drama.

Since the 1990s Simon has not exerted nearly the level of influence over Broadway and American theater that he did during his peak periods in the 1960s and the 1980s. Recent new works, such as *The Dinner Party* (2000) and *45 Seconds from Broadway* (2001), were unsuccessful and a 2006 revival of one of his early signature hits, *Barefoot in the Park*, had an undistinguished Broadway run. In 2009, a revival of *Brighton Beach Memoirs* closed in one week. Yet Simon remains a uniquely important force in American theater. Revivals of his plays abound throughout the country every year. His legacy is enhanced with each new work irrespective of its success on Broadway or lack thereof. More than any other stage comedy writer Simon refined the quick wisecracking comeback humor of American vaudeville, 1930s radio comedy, and the television sitcom so that it could support full dramatic plots, memorable stage characters, and rich human relationships. In so doing, he has set the standard for American comedy playwriting in the modern era.

Simon lives in Los Angeles with his fourth wife, actress and television personality Elaine Joyce-Simon (formerly Elaine Joyce).

Thomas A. Greenfield

Further Reading

Bloom, Harold. *Neil Simon*. Broomall, PA: Chelsea House Publishers, 2002.

Koprince, Susan Fehrenbacher. *Understanding Neil Simon*. Columbia: University of South Carolina Press, 2002.

SOLO PERFORMANCES

Solo performances (also known as monodramas or "one-actor-shows"), in which a single performer commands the stage for an entire show, are the exception among Broadway productions. The demands of a one-character performance and requisite marquee appeal limit the number of viable candidates who can star in a solo Broadway show and carry it to success. Broadway audiences are generally attracted to the spectacle of large cast-and-chorus **musicals** or comedies and dramas rendered by a dynamically interactive cast. Broadway **producers** are often reluctant to invest the funds and energy required to mount a production in a novelty or nontraditional format such as the solo performance show. Nevertheless, throughout the past 40 years, a number of solo performance shows have run successfully on Broadway, expanding the idea of what a Broadway hit can be and adding some special dimensions to modern American professional theatrical performance.

Central to the commercial and artistic success of a one-character show is the actor's relationship to the script. While many solo performance shows have been initiated by the starring actor, others are written independently of the actor who will perform the show. Thus, the performer's relationship to the script ultimately determines the type of production. Solo performers who wrote their own shows include Whoopi Goldberg, whose eponymous Broadway debut in 1984 was a surprise Broadway hit, and the late Spalding Gray, whose *Monster in a Box* (1991) and *Gray's Anatomy* (1994) brought national attention to the edgy, New York club comic and performance artist. Veteran stand-up comic Jackie Mason periodically brings a solo show to Broadway, most famously in *Jackie Mason's The World*

Julie Harris won a Tony Award for Best Actress in a Play, 1977, for her portrayal of Emily Dickinson in her solo performance in The Belle of Amherst. *(AP Photo)*

According to Me! (1986), which won a special Tony Award. In other instances a **playwright** develops a one-actor script independently of the actor or actress who will perform it. This was the case in **Julie Harris**'s Tony Award–winning performance as Emily Dickinson (and numerous other characters) in William Luce's *The Belle of Amherst* (1976). The final script of a solo performance can also result from a collaborative effort involving the performer and the writer, as indeed was the successful collaboration of actress Vanessa Redgrave, director David Storey, and author/playwright Joan Didion in adapting Didion's autobiographical best seller *The Year of Magical Thinking* (2007) for the stage. Recently many solo performances on Broadway have tended toward the Spalding Gray model, wherein the actor draws upon his or her own life for the show's primary source material. These kinds of one-actor shows, some of which have been both commercially and critically successful, have played an important role in bringing Off- and Off-Off-Broadway ingenuity to the attention of Broadway audiences and broadening the boundaries of legitimate commercial theater.

Precursors to modern Broadway's solo performance can be traced to a number of U.S. popular performance traditions: circuit Chautauqua, circus sideshows, medicine shows, as well as **vaudeville**. Early twentieth-century audiences were generally familiar with vaudeville's solo comedian routines as well as with traveling sideshow "talkers," who lured patrons into the performance tent through persuasive and entertaining speech. During a medicine show—a paratheatrical event presented before, between, or after a music or theatrical entertainment—a lecturer would sell "medicine" to rural audiences where such wares were in scarce supply. These captivating speakers, who learned from one another's oratory and performing skills, were in a sense popular entertainers for those in towns across the country that had little by way of live or professional amusement. Targeting a more highbrow audience in the early twentieth century, touring circuit Chautauqua(s) often included a mixture of lectures, music, and drama. Celebrity lecturers, such as Mark Twain, whose public stature could draw crowds with their orations, were essentially solo performers, repeating their show at each stop on the circuit. Several Chautauqua speakers, and Twain in particular, would later serve as source material for one-actor dramatic productions. In turn, audiences for early solo performance on Broadway already had come to view professional readings and lectures as a form of entertainment and elocution excellence as a performing art.

One of the earliest and most acclaimed actors of the one-actor show was Ruth Draper. From the 1920s to midcentury, Draper performed monologues for Broadway that she alone carefully crafted to tell a story. She created imaginary circumstances on stage by portraying a few characters and having those characters react to other characters left unseen to the audience. She never addressed the audience directly. Instead, Draper would transform quickly from one character to another with only simple onstage costumes changes and set pieces to assist her. Her productions included minimal stage makeup and lighting design, as she relied upon her impersonation to suggest the imaginary fourth wall. Her shows set an early precedent for solo performance that Broadway shows and performance art in general would copy in varying degrees. She is not well-known today outside of theater circles because she did not publish her writing nor did she ever make a film. But her influence on contemporary solo performance and performance art was considerable.

For most of the twentieth century Draper's "cast of characters" was the exception in Broadway solo performance. In the mid-twentieth century biographical sketches became the mode *du jour* for one-character shows, a result at least in part of the rise of Method Acting in America and its focus on the replication of real emotions in performance. Among the actors who made a career as monologuists, Hal Holbrook stands out. Holbrook, a major **television** and **film** star since the 1960s, has also endeared himself to theater audiences through his portrayals of figures from U.S. history. By far the most famous of his characterizations is Mark Twain, immortalized in his *Mark Twain Tonight!* (1966, revival 1976), a show Holbrook toured with for years before and after its first Broadway run. Holbrook began his career by imitating historical figures like Abraham Lincoln, but he struck gold with *Mark Twain Tonight!*

With each historical re-creation, Holbrook conducts extensive research to find his character's mannerisms and point of view. The result is empathetic portrayals of men whose integrity Holbrook admires. Holbrook attributes his audiences' enduring interest in his Twain show to Twain himself, the man's agile mind and wit. Holbrook tailors each new *Mark Twain Tonight!* tour or revival to suit the sociopolitical atmosphere of the day. In the 1960s, for example, Holbrook toured the South with a version that emphasized Twain's writings on slavery. Holbrook's sensitivity to the cultural landscape in which he performs represents but one example of the possibility for the biographical sketch. Others include actor/playwright Emlyn Williams (1905–1987) in *Emlyn Williams as Charles Dickens.* Williams privileged his own interpretation of the figure's work and reflected in performance his close, scholarly like reading of primary and secondary source material about Dickens.

Perhaps the most celebrated Broadway representation of an historical figure is Julie Harris's performance in William Luce's *The Belle of Amherst: A Play Based on the Life of Emily Dickinson* (1976). Given the poet's legendary life of solitude, Dickinson was well suited as a source for the monodrama. Harris as Dickinson speaks directly to the audiences, making of them her guests and confidants in her house. Luce compiled much of the script from Dickinson's poems and journals and invented the rest for dramatic action. Harris won a Tony Award for her performance as Dickinson. The success of the play, with its Broadway run and tours, not only helped establish the one-actor show as a viable Broadway entity but also familiarized a general audience with the internal life of a complex female protagonist. With the women's movement very much in the public's consciousness during the 1970s, *The Belle of Amherst* helped call attention to the relative dearth of well-drawn female roles in stage and film. More recently, actress Tovah Feldshuh portrayed Israeli Prime Minister Golda Meir for two years in the longest-running one-woman show in Broadway history, *Golda's Balcony* (2003). Written by William Gibson, *Golda's Balcony* examines Meir's personality in the context of events surrounding the Yom Kippur War of 1973.

In the last quarter of the twentieth century, the one-actor show on Broadway broadened to include exceptional "performance artists," solo performers whose show is drawn from their personal observations, experiences, feelings, and thoughts; performance artists tend to rely far less on a text or script than improvisation and multimedia presentation. Spalding Gray became synonymous with "performance art" in the 1980s. He first appeared solo on Broadway in one of the most venerable Broadway houses, Lincoln Center's Vivian Beaumont Theater, with *Monster in a Box* followed by *Gray's Anatomy*. He also appeared solo at the Vivian Beaumont in *It's a Slippery Slope* (1996) and *Morning, Noon, and Night* (1999). Thoughts of suicide and his own phobias were common subjects in Gray's performances. *Monster in a Box* delves into Gray's humorous double negativity, in which he describes his inability to accomplish any of his numerous projects, from conducting interviews for an HBO special to writing a novel thinly masked as fiction about a man who cannot take a vacation. In 2004 Gray committed suicide by leaping off of the Staten Island Ferry. A posthumous **Off-Broadway** show based on his writings, *Spalding Gray: Stories Left to Tell*, was performed successfully as recently as 2007, and books of his writings still sell briskly.

Lily Tomlin's *Appearing Nightly* (1977) and the better-known *The Search for Signs of Intelligent Life in the Universe* (1985) exemplify the solo show crafted through actor-writer collaboration. *The Search for Signs* was written for Tomlin by playwright Jane Wagner, Tomlin's life partner. Tomlin attributes all the writing of her Broadway shows to Wagner, although the two have been collaborating on Tomlin's characters throughout Tomlin's career. The shows display the skillful characterizations and impeccable comic timing that earned Tomlin enormous fame on the television comedy show *Laugh-In* from 1969 to 1973. Although *The Search for Signs*, a multiple-character show, resembles Ruth Draper's approach to monodrama, Tomlin is more of a comedian than was Draper and decidedly more interested in exploring feminist themes. Tomlin won a "special" Tony Award for *Appearing Nightly*, a Best Actress Tony for the original production of *The Search for Signs*, and shared a third Tony with Wagner for the 2000 revival for *The Search for Signs*.

Solo performance on Broadway has also helped jump-start careers. Oscar-winning film star, comedian, television celebrity, and producer Whoopi Goldberg is a case in point. In 1984, a then all-but-unknown Goldberg brought her self-titled monodrama *Whoopi Goldberg*, in which she portrays a melting pot of complex "everyman" and "everywoman" characters, from obscure comedy clubs and Off-Off Broadway venues to Broadway's venerated Lyceum Theatre. The show received rave reviews and garnered national publicity for her unusual and heretofore undiscovered talent. Goldberg has been a star and a formidable show business presence ever since, translating her initial Broadway triumph into success in the burgeoning comedy club–and-cable industry of the 1980s, live and series television, and hit films such as *Ghost, Sister Act*, and *The Color Purple*. Goldberg remains one of only a handful of African American women ever to achieve sustained high-level success in the entertainment industry and is the only African American to have won an Oscar, an Emmy, a Grammy, and a Tony Award (as co-producer of the Broadway show *Thoroughly Modern Millie*). She returned to the scene of her first triumph in 2004, when she revived *Whoopi Goldberg* for a twentieth-anniversary salute to the show that made her career.

The one-actor show format has enabled other performers of color besides Goldberg to create their own vehicles for attracting producers. Actress Meryl Streep produced shows by African American performance artist Sarah Jones and helped her move to Broadway in 2006 with *Bridge and Tunnel*. Popular performance artist John Leguizamo began his solo shows in downtown performance venues in the early 1990s. However, when he garnered financial backing to bring *Freak* (1988), a performance art–based solo show, to Broadway, he achieved great success with mainstream theater audiences and critics. His second Broadway performance art show, *Sexaholic* (2001), was also successful. Broadway audiences were very receptive to Leguizamo's humorous depictions of urban Latino characters. Shaped by the people he knew growing up in Queens and the Bronx in the 1970s, Leguizamo's solo shows caricature men and women of different races as they confront racism, poverty, sexism, homophobia, and each other. Prior to his Broadway debut with *Freak*, Leguizamo had created characters that were largely fictional, although informed by his boyhood upbringing in neighborhoods that were less than friendly to Colombian immigrants like himself. Both of Leguizamo's Broadway shows are explicitly autobiographical and told in the first person. Leguizamo took an unusual step for Broadway in an effort to diversify his audience, setting aside a set number of discounted tickets for each of night of his runs to attract a culturally and economically diverse audience. This measure widened his fan base and, indeed, audiences for Leguizamo's Broadway performances tended to be more ethnically and culturally diversified than most Broadway audiences.

Like Leguizamo, Anna Deavere Smith, an African American, had a large following as a performance artist prior to her Broadway show *Twilight: Los Angeles* (1994). Smith's work echoes Draper's performance style of capturing the speech pattern of individual characters. Smith, however, introduced to Broadway "solo docu-theater" with *Twilight: Los Angeles 1992* (1994), in which Smith portrayed several real people whom she interviewed regarding the infamous 1991 beating of Rodney King, an African American cab driver, by Los Angeles police officers. (Film of the beating was broadcast on television, leading to criminal charges and a trial for the police officers involved. When the officers were acquitted of all charges, several days of rioting broke out in southern Los Angeles.)

Recent one-actor shows have not been as overtly political as Smith's piece nor as artistically innovative as Leguizamo's works, but they still show an interest in current culture. *The Year of Magical Thinking* with Vanessa Redgrave represented a successful effort to bring writer Joan Didion's 2005 best-selling memoir to the stage while the book was still in vogue. Chazz Palminteri's *A Bronx Tale* (2007) gave the veteran New York actor an opportunity to portray everyone in his colorful family, neighborhood, and even the local mob in the fast-paced solo memoir. *Thurgood* (2008) allowed playwright George Stevens Jr. an opportunity to comment on race relations in America in his star vehicle for actor Laurence Fishburne as the first African American Supreme Court Justice.

Leah Garland

Further Reading

Canning, Charlotte M. *The Most American Thing in America: Circuit Chautauqua as Performance*. Iowa City: University of Iowa Press, 2005.

Dolan, Jill. "Finding Our Feet in the Shoes of (One An) Other: Multiple Character Solo Performers and Utopian Performatives." *Modern Drama* 45, no. 4 (2002): 495–518.

Fusco, Coco. "Macho Mouth." *The Village Voice* 36, no. 15 (April 9, 1991): 24.

Gentile, John S. "Early Examples of the Biographical One-Person Show Genre: *Emlyn Williams as Charles Dickens* and Hal Holbrook's *Mark Twain Tonight!*" *Literature in Performance* 6, no. 1 (1985): 42–53.

Harris, Julie. Quoted in "Twenty Questions for Julie Harris." *American Theater* (May/June, 2001): 88.

Hornsby, Richard. "Chronicles—Theater—Ruth Draper Recordings." *The Hudson Review* 55, no. 1 (2002): 173–183ff.

McNamara, Brooks. "Talking." *The Drama Review* 31, no. 2 (1987), 39–56.

Meyer, Howard N. "A Second Look at *The Belle of Amherst*." *The Midwest Quarterly* 21 (1980): 365–70.

Rogers, Neville. "The Art of Ruth Draper." *The Ohio Review* 19, no. 1 (1978): 6–23.

Ward, Andrew. "With Mark Twain You Can Get away with Murder." *American Heritage* (September 2003): 48.

SONDHEIM, STEPHEN (1930–)
COMPOSER, LYRICIST

From the 1970s to the early 2000s Stephen Sondheim was the most successful and influential American composer of Broadway **musicals**. Although befriended and mentored in his youth by both **Richard Rodgers** and **Oscar Hammerstein II**, Sondheim's innovations in conceptualizing and composing musical scores introduced new forms to Broadway that rendered the literary or book-driven musical (i.e., "the Rodgers and Hammerstein type musical") all but passe after the 1960s.

Sondheim was born to a family of Jewish garment workers with roots in New York's Lower East Side. His parents achieved some prosperity prior to his birth, and Sondheim was raised in relative affluence on Manhattan's Upper West Side. However, his youth was filled with emotional difficulty in the family that ultimately led to his parents' divorce. Stephen and his mother later moved to Bucks County, Pennsylvania. A small blessing came in his friendship with Jamie Hammerstein, son of Oscar Hammerstein II, with whom Stephen and his mother were now neighbors. The Hammerstein home and family provided Stephen with a frequent refuge from his difficult mother.

Beyond the emotional relief found at the world-renowned lyricist/composer's home, the young Stephen found a musical mentor. He was in their home in 1943 as Richard Rodgers and Hammerstein began work on their first collaboration—*Oklahoma!* Shortly, Sondheim watched the pair in rehearsal on *Allegro* (1947),

Actress-singer Bernadette Peters, star of Sunday in the Park with George, *leans forward to discuss the recording of the Broadway show's album with composer-lyricist Stephen Sondheim, left, and producer of the album Thomas Z. Shepard in New York City, in 1984. (AP Photo/Marty Reichenthal)*

an experiment in form that inspired Sondheim. At the age of 16, Sondheim left his mother's home and moved in with his father in Connecticut, enrolling in Williams College where he studied music. After graduation, he spent a brief time in Hollywood as a television scriptwriter before returning to the East Coast to launch his composing and songwriting career.

Sondheim's early professional collaborators included many of the great composers, lyricists, and book writers of the time and led to prodigious early successes. While still in his twenties, he had written the lyrics for two of the most important musicals in modern Broadway history: *West Side Story* (1957) with composer **Leonard Bernstein** and book writer **Arthur Laurents** and *Gypsy* (1959) with composer **Jule Styne**. His work on *A Funny Thing Happened on the Way to the Forum* (1962) matched him with another creative team that included Burt Shevelove and Larry Gelbart as writers. In 1965, he composed the music to Richard Rodgers's lyrics on *Do I Hear a Waltz*.

His artistic associates on the production side of Broadway also included the giants of the profession. **Jerome Robbins** had already established himself as a great choreographer and director when Sondheim first worked with him on *West Side Story*. It was on the same production that he began a professional association with **Harold Prince**, who was just breaking into producing; through Prince, Sondheim's musicals were interpreted visually by designer Boris Aronson. *A Funny Thing Happened on the Way to the Forum* (1962) gave him the opportunity to work with **George Abbott**, who is among the two or three most prolific musical producers and directors in Broadway history.

Firmly established as a major Broadway composer and lyricist by his early thirties, Sondheim helped to turn the Broadway musical in a new direction, now known as the "Concept Musical"—a musical based on vignettes and controlling ideas rather than plot complications. His next shows such as ***Company*** (1970) and *Follies* (1971) develop around themes rather than plotlines and drew widespread attention for this innovative approach. As Sondheim broke out on his own, he consistently applied experimental compositional techniques to sophisticated subject matter. His signature style became the intricate linking of form with content as seen in his next work *A Little Night Music* (1973), based on the Ingmar Bergman film *Smiles of a Summer Night* where he composed the score largely in 3/4 waltz time. This show offered Sondheim's most popular hit "Send in the Clowns."

His later concept musicals created in collaboration with Prince include the successes *Pacific Overtures* (1976), about cultural imperialism through Commodore Matthew Perry's opening of Japan to the West, and *Sweeney Todd* (1979), based on a British pulp novel (called "Penny Dreadfuls") that ranges from serial killing and cannibalism. The unsuccessful *Merrily We Roll Along* (1981) brought an end to the Prince-Sondheim musicals.

With *Sunday in the Park with George* (1985), about nineteenth-century French artist George Seurat and his pointillism painting technique, Sondheim began an artistic association with director and librettist James Lapine. Later collaborations with Lapine included *Passion* (1994), a musical partly in the epistolary form and based on an Italian film *Assassins* (1990) about presidential assassinators in the United States, and the often-performed *Into the Woods* (1987).

A self-described maverick of the form, Sondheim writes musicals, even one like *Into the Woods*, which retells famous faerie tales, with a focus on mature and intellectually challenging ideas; he deliberately avoids the fluff typically associated with the commercial goals of the Broadway musical. While each of his musicals features complex harmonies and sophisticated craftsmanship, Sondheim's rhythms and rhyme schemes singularly and intricately reflect each character as well as their inner life. His love of word games, mathematics, and murder mysteries are legendary in Broadway circles; in part because of his fascination with murder mysteries, Sondheim cowrote a film script with Anthony Perkins titled *The Last of Sheila* (1973). He also wrote numerous songs for films such as the movies *Reds*, *Dick Tracy*, and *The Birdcage*.

Awarded all the notable statues and prizes, Sondheim has received Oscars, Grammys, and a Pulitzer as well as the Kennedy Center Award and a Special Tony for Lifetime Achievement. But perhaps his greatest recognition comes in his successors and imitators for whom he opened up new possibilities in the genre. Like Hammerstein who encouraged young Sondheim, he has motivated a new generation of musical creators like *Parade* (1998) composer **Jason Robert Brown** and *Rent* (1996) composer **Jonathan Larson** whose posthumous Off-Broadway work *tick . . . tick . . . boom!* uses Sondheim's blessing as the barometer for success in the musical theater world.

Felicia J. Ruff

Further Reading

Horowitz, Mark Eden, and Stephen Sondheim. *Sondheim on Music: Minor Details and Major Decisions*. Lanham, MD: Scarecrow Press in association with Library of Congress, 2003.

Secrest, Meryle. *Stephen Sondheim: A Life*. New York: Knopf, 1998.

SPORTS

Though the number of Broadway plays and **musicals** that have used sport as a major or minor backdrop is relatively small, there is a surprisingly high percentage that have captured Tony awards for best drama, for musical, or for leading roles. This does not mean, of course, that using sports as a vehicle ensures success in a play. It does show, however, that sports is a topic that can easily lend itself to Broadway. Sport-themed plays have been able to capture and present difficult social issues, and these topics, plus excellent writing and acting, have been recognized and lauded for having done so. There are many powerful stories in American sport history and some will surely become topics of Broadway plays in the next decade and beyond.

Following World War I, many Americans experienced a significant increase in their leisure time as a result of the industrial growth of the United States and the concomitant growth in labor unions. The United States had been largely unaffected by the devastation of the war that destroyed large sections of Europe and had suffered fewer casualties. The incremental growth in the U.S. economy and the expanding middle class led to a great increase in leisure time for many. Two beneficiaries of this expansion were sports and theater, which both saw rapidly increasing popularity and commercialization in the late 1910s through the 1920s

Background

Sports were a part of American life from colonial times, but up until the latter half of the nineteenth century most contests were regional and only played by children or by adults in their few free hours of leisure. One of the best cultural synthesizers of sports and games proved to be the Civil War. Men from around the country shared their local or regional games and negotiated the varying rules of similar games, enabling them to play during the long hours of boredom between battles. The resulting impact of the Civil War on the nationalization and commercialization of sports was almost immediate.

In 1869 the Cincinnati Red Stockings, a local amateur baseball team, reformed itself into the nation's first professional baseball team and played both locally and on tour. By the 1870s the National League of Professional Baseball Players, forerunner to the modern National League, was overseeing competition among professional teams from New York, Boston, Philadelphia, Chicago, and elsewhere. Professional basketball teams and leagues sprang up at the turn of the century as did small professional football associations. Boxing or prize fighting, a staple of American frontier culture and county fairs since the eighteenth century, also morphed into an ostensibly organized professional sport at the end of the nineteenth century, awarding "undisputed" world championship titles and crowning official champions. By 1920, the economic and cultural foundations of modern American "big time" sports were firmly established and well positioned to seize upon the national explosions in personal wealth, mass media, and commercial stage entertainment that were soon to come.

Sports Stars on Stage

The 1920s saw the rise of the first great American sports heroes, and through **radio**, newsreel footage, and newspapers their various exploits became nationally known. Seeking to capitalize on the national interest in sports that had risen dramatically during the decade, some Broadway producers thought that bringing top sports stars onto the stage might bring more fans into the theaters. During this time burlesques and **vaudeville**-type revues such as *Ziegfeld's Follies* still commanded a healthy share of the Broadway audience although competition from other forms of entertainment posed a constant threat. Made up of anywhere from 8 to 15 acts of various types, these shows lent themselves to brief marquee appearances by celebrity athletes who could sing a song, or tell a few jokes or stories, and then exit before the audience's or their own patience wore thin. Moreover, vaudeville and burlesque had employed athletes as "dumb acts" for years: strongmen, strongwomen, and acrobats who performed wordlessly ("dumb") to music while customers wandered in and out between shows. But the move to book celebrity athletes for vaudeville represented an early application of sports star power, drawing on the athlete's celebrity status rather than athletic ability *per se* to please audiences.

By far the most popular and well-known sports star of the era (or possibly ever) was Yankees star George Herman "Babe" Ruth. Ruth appeared occasionally in vaudeville revues in New York and elsewhere from 1921 to about 1927. In the winter of 1922 Ruth even joined a vaudeville tour but quit the show when spring training started. Harold "Red" Grange, the football immortal and one of the first professional athletes to secure the services of a business agent to broker his off-the-field enterprises, headlined a vaudeville tour that operated mostly in the Midwest. Boxing champion Jack Dempsey, a midtown New York celebrity fixture during his championship reign in the early 1920s, periodically performed in New York vaudeville houses with well-received comedy sketches. Dempsey was so enamored of his star status in the Manhattan limelight that upon his retirement from boxing he opened Jack Dempsey's Broadway Restaurant, where he held court for 40 years as host to the famous from all walks of life, signing autographs and telling stories of his glory days. (Some boxing historians speculate that Dempsey's show business celebrity activities detracted from his training for his historic 1926 fight with Gene Tunney. Dempsey lost his crown to Tunney in one of heavyweight boxing's legendary upsets.) Mildred "Babe" Didrikson, then as now widely heralded as the best woman athlete of all time, followed suit in the 1930s with a "folksy" act that included onstage banter, a brief harmonica performance, and a tune sung while she jogged on a treadmill.

The demise of vaudeville in the 1930s significantly curtailed the practice of putting athletes on the Broadway stage for their star appeal alone, but it did not eliminate it entirely. In a well-publicized throwback to vaudeville-type sports star promotion, the prestigious Theater in the Square cast retired New York Jets quarterback "Broadway" Joe Namath in a featured role in their revival of *The Caine Mutiny* (1983). By most accounts Namath, dubbed "Broadway Joe" by sportswriters during his playing days for his high-living "lady's man" off-the-field exploits, delivered an acceptable if undistinguished debut performance. Thereafter Namath generally restricted his show business appearances to television commercials and sports broadcasting.

Without question the most remarkable transition from sports stardom to commercial theater success belongs to Olympic gymnast Cathy Rigby. Rigby was an athletic superstar in the late 1960s and early 1970s. She anchored the U.S. women's gymnastics Olympic team in 1968 and medaled in national and world competitions in the early 1970s. She became very famous through press coverage of the Olympics and numerous televised appearances on ABC's *Wide World of Sports* and other mainstream sports programs. However, unlike sports stars of the past who had dabbled in theater for a lark or pin money, Rigby, still in her early twenties, made a purposeful career move in the early 1970s to retire from sports and move into acting.

In 1974 she played the title role in a professional touring production of the Carolyn Leigh/Mark Charlap classic musical *Peter Pan* (1954). A daunting, athletic part that requires the actor playing Peter to fly suspended by wires while singing, acting, and literally dancing in midair, Rigby proved to be a natural for it. The 1974 tour never appeared on Broadway, but it introduced Rigby to the Broadway musical touring business, which for decades has played a critical role in providing Broadway with a national market for major shows. Rigby continued playing the eternal child Peter for 30 years, eventually becoming a co-producer as well as the show's star. Although she principally mounted the show as a **touring production**, she brought *Peter Pan* to Broadway four times in the 1990s. As co-producer and lead actress she earned a highly respectable three Tony nominations for these productions. She also appeared in a featured role in the Broadway musical *Seussical* (2000). Rigby's *Peter Pan* shows were beloved across the nation by local host producers of touring Broadway shows, and Rigby became a highly respected figure in the national touring theater side of the industry. Rigby's tours with *Peter*

Pan evolved into "can't miss" big sellers for local venues, drawing families and school groups while boosting all-important subscription and package ticket sales. In 2004 Rigby was awarded a Lifetime Service Award from Broadway's League of American Theaters and Producers (now known as The Broadway League) in recognition of commercial contributions to Broadway and professional theater. In 2005, after more than 30 years with *Peter Pan*, she completed her self-described farewell tour.

Plays and Musicals about Sports

The growth of professional sports in the 1920s and 1930s generated a corresponding expansion in sports writing. Beyond reporting scores sportswriters wrote of the heroic and mythic qualities of sports competition. They drew allegorical connections between sports victories and personal triumphs, and offered rags-to-riches narratives and tales of moral redemption in their profiles of star athletes. American **playwrights** followed suit and sports-based stories eventually found their way into Broadway plays and musicals.

Among the first of the noteworthy literary representations of sports on Broadway was *Golden Boy* by **Clifford Odets** (1937). A young second-generation Italian American, Joe Bonaparte, must choose between pursuing the violin and boxing as a career. The latter holds the prospect of immediate financial benefit for his family as well as instant acceptance into "mainstream" America, while the former represents Joe's dream. The play was later made into a **film** in 1939. In 1964, the play was adapted into a successful musical with a predominantly African American cast. Boxer Joe Bonaparte became Joe Wellington, the setting was moved from the Italian neighborhoods of lower Manhattan uptown to Harlem, and singer Sammy Davis Jr., the most famous African American stage and club entertainer of the decade, starred in the lead role. The musical version also stressed the importance of facing life's difficult choices as when Joe's family and friends sing a slightly ironic plea for him to remember his roots when entering the netherworld of sports stardom ("Don't forget 127th Street . . . whatever you may do").

In 1949 **Arthur Miller** made effective use of sports in what many people believe to be the most important American drama of the twentieth century, ***Death of a Salesman***. The play has as its theme the examination of aging salesman Willy Loman's pursuit and failure to achieve the American dream for himself and his sons. Sports figure prominently in Willy's worldview. He is an overly committed believer in the kind of dream-come-true tales of athletic stardom that American sportswriters had been promulgating for years. His older son Biff was a high school football star weaned on his father's belief that physical attractiveness and sports stardom trumped honesty and hard work as America's winning virtues. Young Biff seemed on his way to achieving the American dream through school sports glory. However, the family's misguided values doom both father and son to a tragic confrontation with the false promises of shallow appearance and empty fame. The drama relies heavily on Miller's dichotomous presentation of the role that sports can play in the achievement of success or the perpetuation of adolescent fantasy and false hope. Even with all the governing bodies and media scrutiny surrounding modern sports, the shady world of gambling and other illegal activity has never been far from the American sports scene. Gambling, in fact, has been a part of sports from the beginning of sport contests, dating back to the ancient Greeks. The presence of gambling was often a specter that cast a shadow on contests that might have been "fixed" by gamblers seeking a big pay off. The 1919 World Series is a prime example, but gambling, horse racing, and "fixing" were long a part of the sport scene. This truism formed the basis of one of the most dynamic musicals of the postwar Broadway era, the **Frank Loesser** classic *Guys and Dolls* (1950). Based on a story and characters of the great sportswriter turned fiction writer Damon Runyon, the musical was an instant hit. The story involves hustlers, horse race handicappers, and low-level gamblers in New York, and the love that develops between a Salvation Army sister and a gambler. The show was produced as a film in 1955 and revived in 1965 and again in 1976 with an all-black cast. All three productions won Tonys for Best Musical or Musical Revival. A surprisingly successful 1992 revival ran almost as long as the original (1,143 performances and 1,200 performances, respectively) and conferred musical comedy stardom upon actor **Nathan Lane** in the "second banana" role of gambler Nathan Detroit.

In 1954 a new musical opened on Broadway, which had no deeper meaning, it seemed, than sport, itself. This was *Damn Yankees*, based on Douglass Wallop's novel *The Year the Yankees Lost the Pennant*. From 1949 to 1953, the New York Yankees won the American League Championship and, subsequently, defeated the National League champions to claim the World Series title. To Yankee fans, it was glorious, but to most other Americans, it bordered on unfair practices. The musical played to this anti-Yankee animus by having the lowly Washington Senators, at the time perpetual bottom finishers of the American League, capture the pennant as their star player, young Joe Hardy, makes a pact with the devil to make the dream of a Senators' pennant come true. (How else could the Yankees lose?) *Damn Yankees* won the 1955 Tony Award for Best Musical and then the 1994 Tony for Best Musical Revival.

The next year (1956) saw **Alan Jay Lerner and Frederick Loewe**'s *My Fair Lady* debut on Broadway. The musical was based on British playwright **George Bernard Shaw**'s turn-of-the century satire *Pygmalion*, wherein a "speech coach" bets that he can turn a young Cockney girl into being mistaken for royalty. Though sport only comes into play in a single scene, it is an important one. The newly tutored Eliza Doolittle makes her public debut in British society at the Ascot Race Course, a symbol of the wealth and leisure time of the royal and upper classes. Eliza's earnest yet unsuccessful effort to exercise proper decorum at the august racing event represents one of the musical's more faithful representations of Shaw's socialist antipathies toward the British class system, as well as an effective reminder of how tightly sport and leisure were woven into that system during the Victorian era.

The Best Musical of 1957, *The Music Man*, is one of the most famous musicals ever produced. Its central figure, Harold Hill, proposes to improve the quality of life in a small Iowa town by giving music lessons and organizing a first-rate marching band. One of the town's big problems is young men playing pool in the pool hall and associating with "unsavory" characters. Hill's observation of pool is the subject of the famous song, "Trouble Right Here in River City" and plays cleverly, if tamely by comparison, on the *Guys and Dolls* thematic associations of sports and leisure with unsavory and degenerative behavior. The show was revived in 1980 and 2002, the first of which won the Tony Award for Best Musical Revival.

The 1960s and 1970s: Social Issues and Sports

The social upheavals in the 1960s and 1970s that brought a number of sensitive issues, particularly race relations, to the fore of American culture was reflected in some noteworthy Broadway productions with sports themes and settings. One of the most powerful of these was Howard Sackler's *The Great White Hope* (1969). The play starred **James Earl Jones** as "Jack Jefferson" in a thinly veiled biographical drama about Jack Johnson, the first black heavyweight champion of the world (1908–1915). Johnson was controversial for his outspokenness, his flaunting of his "blackness," his dating and marrying of white women, his intelligence (he wrote an autobiography and read voraciously), and his powerful boxing skills. Even Congress was fearful of the implications of his boxing reign. In 1920 he was arrested and imprisoned for violation of the Mann Act, which involved "the transportation of women across state lines for immoral purposes." The act was passed in 1910 to deter aspects of prostitution, but Johnson was prosecuted for providing a rail ticket for his white girlfriend at the time to travel from Pittsburgh to Chicago to be with him. He was released from jail a year later. The play addresses the issues of race and the many implications and nuances of race that Johnson confronted in his life. The name of the play comes from the boxing press's and promoters' futile search for a "great white hope," a white boxer, to defeat Johnson in the ring. The play won both the Tony Award and the Pulitzer Prize for Best Play. Both Jones and Jane Alexander (as his white love interest) won Tony Awards as Best Actor and Best Supporting Actress, respectively, and went on to earn Oscar nominations for their reprisal of these roles in a 1970 film adaptation of the play.

Three years later, Jason Miller's *That Championship Season* (1972) also explored the connection between sports and race, albeit more understatedly than did *The Great White Hope*. The play features five middle-aged white men from central Pennsylvania—four members of a 1950s championship high school basketball team and their coach. The setting is the coach's house, where they return each year for a reunion. Missing is the team's star player who has left the area, never to return. These five men seem to have had their lives peak with this championship and their various adult failures are assuaged by the coach noting that "they can never take that (championship) away from us." Echoing *Death of a Salesman*, the play uses youthful sports heroics as a substitute for success in adult life. These men have never grown up emotionally. They use their memories of school days sports glory to numb the pain of adult failures and justify moral lapses into dishonesty and racism.

A different game and a different social issue were the focus of D. L. Coburn's Pulitzer Prize–winning *The Gin Game* (1977). The husband and wife acting team of **Hume Cronyn** and **Jessica Tandy** have often been closely identified with this two-person play, which takes place in a retirement home. As newly acquainted retirement home residents, Weller Martin and Fonsia Dorsey seek to build a friendship over successive games of gin rummy. As they do, their conversations become increasingly personal and then hostile. Martin has taught Dorsey the game, yet, to his seething resentment, she wins every hand. We eventually learn that both have been essentially "dumped" at the home by uncaring children. The game emerges as the highlight of their waning lives even as the dynamics of their competition reveal the complexities of coping with end-of-life changes. The repeated, ritualistic competition of the card games offers riveting and poignant insights into the lives that keep bringing Martin and Dorsey back to the gaming table.

The 1980s through the beginning of the Twenty-first Century

The musical *Chess* began as a concept album in 1984 by Benny Andersson and Bjorn Ulvaeus of ABBA with lyrics by Tim Rice. It then became a hit musical in London in 1986 and then came to Broadway in 1988. The play was modified significantly before coming to Broadway and was not well received, closing after 68 regular performances. The musical was inspired by the world famous 1972 chess match between American star Bobby Fischer and Russian champion Boris Spassky. The match, which was covered internationally as a metaphoric Cold War confrontation between the world's contending superpowers, influenced the Broadway version, which placed considerable emphasis on the cloak and dagger workings of the CIA and their Russian KGB counterparts. Chess itself is less important than loyalty and relationships, which are subsequently destroyed by the callousness and political expediency of both secret agencies.

The interplay of race and sports would appear on Broadway again in **August Wilson**'s *Fences* (1987), his second play to appear on Broadway and the fourth in Wilson's ten-play Pittsburgh cycle. The play takes place in the front yard of Troy Maxson, an African American in his fifties who was once a great ball player in the Negro Leagues but was born too soon to play in the majors. Maxson represents many African Americans who were outstanding in sports or other areas but were victimized by "legal" segregationist policies and unchecked discrimination prior to the 1960s Civil Rights Movement. Maxson also uses baseball metaphors for his philosophy of life. In addition, Maxson's son, Cory, is a high school football star whom Maxson stops from playing. He wants his son to rely on education, not sports, to advance himself. *Fences* was yet another play that drew upon issues raised in *Death of a Salesman* and serves as further testimony to the impact of the Miller play. *Fences* received both the Tony Award and the Pulitzer Prize for drama in 1987. The original role of Troy Maxson was played by James Earl Jones, who won a Tony Award for his role.

Gay-lesbian themes began to appear in Broadway shows in the late 1970s and 1980s, but Richard Greenberg's *Take Me Out* (2003) was the first major commercial play to merge sports and societal discrimination against **gay** people. The play focused upon the vexing issue of the fear among gay athletes that their sexual orientation might be discovered. In *Take Me Out* Darren Lemming is of mixed race and plays for the New York Empires. The entire play takes place in the Empires' locker room over the course of a season and depicts what might occur were a top professional star to "come out" while still playing major league baseball. The issue is not fully resolved in the play nor in sport to this day.

Murry R. Nelson

Further Reading

Broadway . . . A History of the American Musical with host Ron Husmann. DVD. Irvine, CA: Chesney Communications, 1990.

Frommer, Harvey, and Myrna Katz Frommer. *It Happened on Broadway; An Oral History of the Great White Way.* New York: Harcourt, 1998.

Johnson, Jack. *Jack Johnson Is a Dandy; The Autobiography of Jack Johnson.* New York: Chelsea House, 1969.

Peterson, Robert. *Only the Ball Was White.* New York: Gramercy, 1999.

Rader, Benjamin. *American Sports from the Age of Folk Games to the Age of Televised Sports.* 5d. Upper Saddle River, NJ: Prentice-Hall, 2003.

Sackler, Howard. *The Great White Hope.* New York: Dial press, 1968.

Wallop, Douglass. *The Year the Yankees Lost the Pennant.* New York: W. W. Norton, 2004 (originally 1954).

STRASBERG, LEE (1901–1982)
DIRECTOR, PRODUCER, ACTING TEACHER

Despite having little professional acting experience, Lee Strasberg had a profound impact on the training of American actors and the modernization of American acting theory. Strasberg was the most influential and most controversial of a handful of New York–based acting teachers who sought to replace formal, classical stage acting techniques with naturalistic psychology-rooted, nuanced approaches originated by Russian director Konstantin Stanislavsky's System. As the head acting instructor of the **Group Theatre** in the 1930s and artistic director of the **Actors Studio** from the 1950s through the early 1980s, Strasberg became the principal driving force in bringing what came to be called Method Acting to the fore in American stage and film.

Strasberg was born on November 17, 1901, in Budanov, Austria-Hungary. In 1908 his family moved to the United States and lived on the Lower East Side in New York City. In his late teens and early twenties Strasberg participated in Yiddish theater and little theater groups in lower Manhattan. In 1923 he saw a performance by a touring company from Stanislavsky's Moscow Art Theatre (which included Stanislavsky himself). Responding with an intensity that would later famously characterize his teaching and directing styles (as well as relationships with many colleagues), Strasberg quickly started conceptualizing a psychology-based theory of acting and an ensemble-centered approach to production, notwithstanding the fact that he was at the time an obscure semiprofessional neighborhood actor. He soon enrolled to study at the American Laboratory Theater in New York, which had been established by Russian immigrants and former Moscow Art Theatre members, director Richard Boleslavsky and actress Maria Ouspenskaya. Strasberg's studies with the America Laboratory further reinforced his commitment to developing new principles for actor preparation and training.

From 1925 to 1931 Strasberg performed in a few productions as a member of the **Theatre Guild**, at the time a prestigious, relatively progressive yet nonetheless commercial New York production cooperative. By 1931 Strasberg and some like-minded Guild members, especially **Harold Clurman** (a classmate of Strasberg's at the American Laboratory Theater) and Cheryl Crawford, had grown impatient with what they took to be the Guild's resistance to experimental plays and disinterest in adventurous production methods. The trio of Clurman, Crawford, and Strasberg left the Guild to form the Group Theatre, which quickly evolved into, among other things, a laboratory in which Strasberg as head acting instructor would test his radical theories of actor training and ensemble theater. Strasberg's approach relied heavily on an actor's comprehensive understanding of character motivation, both on and off stage, and reliance on "emotional memory" or "affective memory" (exploration of the actor's own emotional responses to past life situations as the raw material for developing a psychologically true characterization).

Although fraught with internal conflict and financial difficulty, the Group Theatre held its ensemble largely intact for a full decade, officially terminating its operations in 1941. Its saving graces were Clurman's sober and reassuring leadership, Crawford's remarkable management skills, Group **playwright Clifford Odets**'s powerful dramas, and Strasberg's iron-willed commitment (detractors would call it rigidity) to the teaching of his theories. The Group nurtured some of twentieth-century theater's most noteworthy figures, including Strasberg, playwright Odets, director **Elia Kazan**, actor **Lee J. Cobb**, and future acting teachers (and critics of Strasberg's approach) Stella Adler and **Sanford Meisner**. Despite the unevenness of the Group's production record, most of its members found their theatrical reputations and skills significantly enhanced for having survived its tumultuous run. Strasberg was certainly numbered among them.

With the demise of the Group Theatre and the end of World War II, three alumni of the Group, Robert Lewis, Elia Kazan, and Cheryl Crawford, founded the Actors Studio in 1947. Strasberg became the Artistic Director of the Actors Studio in 1950 and supervised the Studio's principal activities, training young actors and developing the skills of established actors eager to hone their craft. Strasberg's tenure with the Group Theatre had already given Method Acting a foot-in-the-door of American theater. In the 1940s, Group veterans Harold Clurman and Elia Kazan had directed, respectively, on Broadway *Truckline Café* (1946) and *A Streetcar Named Desire* (1947). The two productions each highlighted a compelling performance by a young gifted "method" actor named **Marlon Brando**. (Brando would later renounce Strasberg as a teacher, citing Stella Adler as his true mentor.) However, it was during Strasberg's 30-year tenure with the Actors Studio that the Method became the predominant teaching philosophy for succeeding generations of Broadway and Hollywood's leading performers. While Strasberg claimed he never specifically intended to "create stars" at the Actors Studio or establish the Studio as "a temple of the method," he also acknowledged the obvious; he had (Strasberg 1975). Actors such as **Julie Harris**, Al Pacino, Marilyn Monroe, Kim Stanley, James Dean, Dustin Hoffman, Jane Fonda, Burgess Meredith, Alec Baldwin, Robert DeNiro, and Uma Thurman, trained either with Strasberg at Actors Studio or in one or more studios or institutes founded on his teachings.

Strasberg's success in the 1950s and 1960s brought with it dissent from inside the profession. Common critiques of his teaching held that he had misinterpreted, distorted, or overemphasized Stanislavsky; his methods overfed actors' egos at the expense of the play's text; he failed to sufficiently modify his own theories with changing times; and he had effectively driven out of the modern acting curriculum valuable alternative forms of instruction, such as classical, Shakespearean, or period acting. Stella Adler and Sanford Meisner were among the more prominent figures to adapt teaching approaches that pointedly differed from Strasberg's.

The criticisms aimed at Strasberg did little to diminish the spread of Method Acting or Strasberg's association with it. While teaching at the Actors Studio, he became a much sought-after speaker and guest artist, giving lectures and conducting seminars in Europe, South America, Israel, and all over the United States. He founded a West Coast branch of the Actors Studio in 1966. Three years later he founded the Lee Strasberg Theatre and Film Institute in New York and Los Angeles. To this date, the central focus of the Institute's curriculum is Strasberg's "method."

During the 1960s, in what proved to be a controversial and less than successful move, Strasberg and the Actors Studio ventured beyond the realm of workshops and instruction and mounted a few full professional productions. In 1963, the Actors Studio collaborated with director **José Quintero** in a well-received Broadway revival of **Eugene O'Neill**'s *Strange Interlude*, starring Actors Studio members Jane Fonda and Ben Gazzara. In 1964 Strasberg directed an Actors Studio production of Anton Chekhov's *The Three Sisters*, which was very well reviewed in New York. However, in an historically disastrous attempt to mount the production in London the following year, a combination of actor illness, problems with the London theater, and some ungracious remarks Strasberg made about London theater in the London press led to an audience rebellion of outright booing and catcalling on opening night. Strasberg and the Actors Studio quickly got out of the big time theater production business and stayed out.

Strasberg never formally retired. He was still the director of the Actors Studio up until his death. At Al Pacino's urging he had reinvigorated his acting career in his seventies, appearing most famously opposite Pacino as Hyman Roth in *Godfather II* (1974). In 1979, at age 77, he starred opposite Ruth Gordon (four years his senior) in a small dramatic film *Boardwalk*. In the year before his death, he had a role in a made for **television** movie, *Skokie* (1981).

Strasberg died of a heart attack in New York City in 1982. Today, some acting teachers and directors view his theories as part an archival piece of theater history, while many see them as vibrant and quite relevant to this day. What rests beyond dispute is Strasberg's towering influence over the reshaping of twentieth-century American acting in both theory and practice.

Thomas A. Greenfield and Nicole Katz

Further Reading

Bartow, Arthur. *Training the American Actor*. New York: Theatre Communications Group, 2006.

Hirsch, Foster. *A Method to Their Madness: The History of the Actors Studio*. New York: Norton, 1984.

Strasberg, Lee. "Lee Strasberg on the Actors Studio." *Actors Studio Website*. 1975. Retrieved June 20, 2009, from http://www.actors-studio.com/strasberg/.

A STREETCAR NAMED DESIRE

Broadway Run: Ethel Barrymore Theatre
Opening: December 3, 1947
Closing: December 17, 1949
Total Performances: 855
Playwright: Tennessee Williams
Scene Designer: Jo Mielziner
Composer: Alex North
Director: Elia Kazan
Producer: Irene M. Selznick
Lead Performers: Jessica Tandy (Blanche Du Bois), Marlon Brando (Stanley Kowalski), Kim Hunter (Stella Kowalski), Karl Malden (Harold Mitchell, "Mitch")

Widely recognized as a classic of the modern stage, *A Streetcar Named Desire* transformed the American theater and left a lasting imprint on American culture. **Tennessee Williams**'s poetic drama about the clash between a faded Southern belle and her brutish, working-class brother-in-law startled audiences in the 1940s with its overt presentation of sexual themes, including male and female sexual desire, homosexuality, and rape. The play also broke taboos in its celebration of the male body. **Marlon Brando**, who rocketed to stardom with his performance as the hypermasculine Stanley Kowalski, captivated theatergoers with his attractive, muscular physique—highlighted onstage by tight-fitting jeans and T-shirt. Not only was Williams's subject matter daring, but his style was innovative. Departing from traditional realism (as he had done two years earlier in *The Glass Menagerie*), Williams offered audiences a striking blend of realism and expressionism—juxtaposing the gritty world of the Kowalski apartment with Blanche Du Bois's inner world of illusion and presenting the heroine's tragic story in rich, lyrical language. Staged by an extraordinary creative team, the 1947 Broadway production of *Streetcar* was so perfectly realized that it stood on its own as a unique experience in the American theater. As **playwright Arthur Miller** later noted, the production "*became* the play."

The origins of *A Streetcar Named Desire* can be found in earlier works by Williams such as "Blanche's Chair in the Moon" and "Portrait of a Madonna"—the latter of which focuses on a repressed Southern belle whose sexual dreams cause her to be taken to an asylum. More broadly, the play is rooted in the anguished life of Williams himself, whose experience was marked by sexual promiscuity, loneliness, alcohol dependence, and mental instability. Blanche and Stanley are often viewed as reflecting two sides of Williams's identity—the fragile, feminine side

The final scene of the original 1947 Broadway production of Tennessee Williams's play A Streetcar Named Desire, *with Marlon Brando as Stanley Kowalski, Kim Hunter as Stella, and Jessica Tandy as Blanche. (AP Photo)*

that venerated art and poetry, and the rough-hewn, masculine side that was governed by sexual appetite. Although Blanche and Stanley appear as polar opposites in the play—suggesting a contest between the spirit and the flesh, or between the vanishing culture of the Old South and a harsh new industrial society—these characters are actually more alike than one might suspect. Blanche, the audience learns, has a promiscuous past and shares Stanley's strong sexual urges. Stanley, it is revealed, can be tenderhearted and vulnerable, especially when he fears that his wife, Stella, might abandon him. Together, Blanche and Stanley express the desperate need for human connection that is at the heart of all of Williams's plays and that Blanche herself calls "the kindness of strangers."

Williams began writing *Streetcar* in 1945 during the Broadway run of his first major success, *The Glass Menagerie* (1945). Over the course of the next two years he revised the play (which he originally titled *The Poker Night*)—shifting his focus from a group of crude, working-class poker players to the cultivated, yet emotionally unstable Blanche. After meeting with producer Irene Selznick, Williams argued that the best choice for a director would be **Elia Kazan**, a prominent figure in theater and film who had recently impressed Williams with his direction of Arthur Miller's drama *All My Sons*. After agreeing to take on the project, Kazan involved himself personally with every aspect of the production, assembling a superb cast led by **Jessica Tandy** and Marlon Brando and working closely with scene designer Jo Mielziner, costumer Lucinda Ballard, and composer Alex North. With the production of *Streetcar*, Williams and Kazan began a collaboration that would last for more than a decade.

Under Kazan's direction, the Broadway production of *A Streetcar Named Desire* artfully integrated script, scene, music, and acting in order to create the stylized realism that Williams had envisioned. Jo Mielziner's set, which featured two shabby rooms and a spiral staircase leading up to another flat, reflected the grim reality of the Kowalski home as well as the dream-like atmosphere that surrounded it. Transparent walls provided the audience with a view of the French Quarter outside the apartment, symbolically calling attention to the exterior and interior worlds of Williams's heroine; and intricate lighting effects punctuated Blanche's movement in and out of a world of illusion. Music also contributed to the play's blend of realism and expressionism. A live, four-piece jazz band played the music of "real-life" New Orleans outside the Kowalski apartment. But the eerie Varsouviana polka tune (played backstage on a Novachord, or early synthesizer) was audible only to Blanche and the audience and signified her descent into insanity.

Contrasting acting styles were prominently featured in the Broadway production. Jessica Tandy, in the role of Blanche, was a classically trained British actress whose performance was theatrical, precise, and meticulously planned. Marlon Brando, a Method-trained American actor, was much more improvisational and lifelike in his portrayal of Stanley—striving for the psychological realism that was at the heart of the Method technique. A co-founder of the **Actors Studio**, Kazan clearly favored the naturalistic style of Brando and others in the cast. But he was convinced that the competing styles of the two lead actors ultimately enhanced the production, underscoring the fundamental contrast between Blanche (the decadent Southern aristocrat) and Stanley (her crude, proletarian antagonist). Moreover, Tandy's classical style served to highlight Blanche's outsider status—her old-fashioned aura amid the coarse, modern world of New Orleans.

When the curtain fell on the opening night performance of *Streetcar*, the audience at the Ethel Barrymore Theatre applauded for 30 minutes. The play quickly became a box-office hit—running on Broadway for more than two years and touring the nation with two different road companies. Initial reviews of the Broadway production were overwhelmingly positive. Although a few critics were troubled by the play's sensational content, most hailed *Streetcar* as a significant new American drama. Some pointed to the play's larger-than-life quality and its affinity with classical tragedy. Howard Barnes, writing for the *New York Herald Tribune*, even argued that Williams was the **Eugene O'Neill** of the current generation. Earning Williams a Pulitzer Prize as well as the prestigious New York Drama Critics' Circle Award, *Streetcar* cemented Williams's reputation as a major figure in the American theater.

The far-reaching impact of *A Streetcar Named Desire* can be seen by its translation into other media—including a 1952 ballet, two teleplays (in 1984 and 1995), and a 1998 opera by André Previn. The most significant adaptation is the classic 1951 film version, directed by Kazan and starring Vivien Leigh (of *Gone with the Wind* fame) and three members of the original Broadway cast: Marlon Brando, Kim Hunter, and Karl Malden. During the filming, Williams and Kazan were forced to battle with movie industry censors who demanded that they tone down the play's erotic content, remove any reference to homosexuality, and punish Stanley for his rape of Blanche. Despite these restrictions (which Kazan circumvented, to some extent, through clever cinematic symbolism), the film version of *Streetcar* captures the power of the original Broadway production and stands as the first "adult" Hollywood movie. It was also the first film to showcase the techniques of Method Acting. Brando's magnetic performance popularized and validated the Method style—revolutionizing the craft of acting for a post–World War II generation. Appropriately, the American Film Institute has identified *A Streetcar Named Desire* as one of the top 50 films in American history.

Since its Broadway premiere in 1947, *Streetcar* has been performed on countless stages around the globe, with major New York revivals in 1956, 1973, 1992, and 2005. The play has also inspired a host of unconventional adaptations, including African American, multiracial, and cross-gendered versions—the latter presenting Blanche Du Bois as a drag queen. Williams's masterpiece has likewise left its mark on popular culture in America—evidenced by the T-shirt craze that followed Brando's legendary performance, by allusions to *Streetcar* on **television** shows such as *Seinfeld* and *The Golden Girls*, and by a musical spoofing of the play in a 1992 episode of *The Simpsons*. These wide-ranging responses to *Streetcar* are a testament to the play's universal appeal and its central place in the national consciousness. Indeed, in 1999, the American Theatre Critics Association voted *A Streetcar Named Desire* the most influential drama of the twentieth century.

Susan Koprince

Further Reading

Kolin, Philip C., ed. *The Influence of Tennessee Williams: Essays on Fifteen American Playwrights.* Jefferson, NC: McFarland, 2008.

———. *Tennessee Williams: A Guide to Research and Performance.* Westport, CT: Greenwood Press, 1998.

STROMAN, SUSAN (1954–)
CHOREOGRAPHER, DIRECTOR

Since the early 1990s, Susan Stroman ("Stro" to friends) has been Broadway's most consistently successful choreographer in both commercial and artistic terms. The four shows for which she has won the Tony Award for Best Choreography stand as a testimony to her creative versatility. She has updated classical Broadway works (1992's Gershwin tribute *Crazy for You* and 1994's triumphant revival of ***Show Boat***), pioneered new uses for dance in theatrical storytelling (2000's *Contact*), and crafted physical camp and chaos for the most outlandish musical comedy in recent history (2001's ***The Producers***), Since 2000, Stroman has been directing as well as choreographing most of her shows. While earning industry-wide respect as a director, Stroman is best known for her artistic and commercial achievements in musical choreography, which for contemporary choreographers stand in a class by themselves.

"Stro" was born in Wilmington, Delaware, into an artistically inclined family. Her father, a pianist, was a fan of Fred Astaire movies

Susan Stroman, the director and choreographer of the musical The Producers, *and Mel Brooks, creator of the show, pose with their Tony Awards after the musical won a record 12 Tony Awards at the 55th annual Tony Awards ceremonies Sunday, June 3, 2001, in New York. (AP Photo/Richard Drew)*

and passed his interest in movie **musicals** on to his daughter. As a child Stroman studied ballet, jazz, and tap, which led to her choreographing productions in high school and in college. Set on a dancing career, she moved to New York in 1977 shortly after graduating college and joined Broadway's legions of gypsy show dancers trying to break into the business.

During the late 1970s and early 1980s, Stroman carved out a promising if unspectacular early career. She performed in regional theater on the East Coast, and premiered on Broadway in 1979 as an ensemble dancer in *Whoopie*, a revival of a 1920s **Flo Ziegfeld** musical. She also performed in a **touring production** of **Bob Fosse**'s *Chicago*—one of the premiere showcase musicals for dancers of the past 30 years. In 1980, at age 25, she landed the multiple roles of assistant director, assistant choreographer, and dance captain for a Broadway show, *Musical Chairs*, a backstage Broadway musical that flopped badly. Stroman did not appear again on Broadway for another 12 years. During that period she worked principally in New York, dancing and choreographing for **Off-Broadway** shows and the New York City Opera. In 1987, she choreographed a well-received Off-Broadway revival of **John Kander and Fred Ebb**'s *Flora the Red Menace* (1965). She followed *Flora* by choreographing the New York City Opera's 1990 revival of **Stephen Sondheim**'s *A Little Night Music* (1973) and another Kander and Ebb Off-Broadway show, *And the World Goes 'Round*.

Stroman made the leap from respected working New York dancer/choreographer to Broadway dynamo in 1992 when she cocreated *Crazy For You* with director (and future husband) Michael Ockrent. A loosely constructed original story set to some of **George** and **Ira Gershwin**'s most familiar Broadway songs—including "I Got Rhythm" and "They Can't Take That Away from Me"—the show's appeal and ingenuity rested largely on Stroman's choreography. **Critics** and audiences loved it. Stroman won the first of her four Best Choreography Tony Awards, and the show ran for four years. In 1994, she choreographed **Hal Prince**'s elaborately updated staging of *Show Boat*, the **Jerome Kern** and **Oscar Hammerstein** musical whose 1927 historic premiere represented one of Broadway's first major breaks from European **operetta** conventions. Prince and Stroman's revival—the most recent of six Broadway revivals of that show—was the most successful. It ran for 947 performances, by far the longest of any major production of the show, including the original. The production also introduced new audiences to the classic score, and rejuvenated touring and regional theater interest in the show. In addition to earning a Tony Award, Stroman received a generous share of the credit for the show's impact. At age 40 Storman was now a formidable presence on Broadway.

Recent triumphs notwithstanding, Stroman had two successive disappointments in the mid-1990s. Despite reuniting professionally with director Ockrent and joining with lyricist Richard Maltby Jr. (*Miss Saigon*, 1991), Stroman's choreography for *Big* (1996) could not save the expensive stage adaptation of the 1988 hit movie. The show folded in six months. She next collaborated again with Kander and Ebb, but this time for a full-scale Broadway production and not an Off-Broadway piece. *Steel Pier* (1997), the story of a young female dance marathon competitor in the 1930s, appeared to be tailor-made for Stroman's talents. But the show was criticized harshly for lacking the energy and edge normally associated with Kander and Ebb's or Stroman's best work. The show folded in two months.

In a "third act" of its own Stroman's career turned again with the new century, and she soon eclipsed her earlier Broadway successes. *Contact* (2000), an uncompromising dance-as-storytelling concept musical was not so much inspired by the long-running *A Chorus Line* as it was emboldened by it. Three different love stories woven together by dance and passion gave Stroman, as show conceiver, director, and choreographer, more creative latitude for dance staging than she had ever had in a major show. Audiences and critics were enthralled with the energy and innovativeness of the show, which won Tony Awards for Best Musical and Best Choreography. Her Tony nomination as Best Director and the startling 1,000-plus performance run of the show allowed her to recover any lost momentum from her two previous failures and establish herself as a well-regarded, if neophyte, Broadway director as well. In the same year, Stroman extended her directorial reach by mounting a revival of one of Broadway's classic book musicals, Meredith Wilson's *The Music Man* (1957). This production, too, was an audience favorite and enjoyed a healthy 699 performance run.

Even with the strong career momentum built up with *Contact* and *Music Man*, neither Stroman nor Broadway could have anticipated what happened next. Stroman and now husband Mike Ockrent agreed to choreograph and direct, respectively, Mel Brooks's musical adaptation of his 1968 film *The Producers*. Many people had doubts about whether this project could amount to more than a novelty show. Although Brooks was a topflight **television** and **film** comedy writer, he had not written for Broadway in 40 years and never successfully when he did. Moreover, the film—with its intentionally inexorable staging of a musical about Adolf Hitler and the Nazis—was one of the most disappointing of Brooks's career in terms of box office and critical reception. But Brooks speculated that the combination of New York's rough-edged sensibilities, Broadway's love for musicals about itself, and the passage of an additional 30 years might give new life to this story of two theater producers' miscalculated exercise in excruciatingly bad taste. Complicating matters for Stroman as production began, however, was the fact that Ockrent was diagnosed with leukemia. Ockrent died shortly thereafter, and Stroman finished the show in dual roles as director and choreographer. The show's reception was absolutely mind-boggling. *The Producers* won a record 12 Tony Awards, including Best Musical, Best Director, and Best Choreographer. It ran for six years and over 2,500 performances, making it the second longest-running Broadway show to open in the twenty-first century (behind *Mamma Mia!*, 2001). The show solidified Stroman's position as both the most successful choreographer on Broadway and a top-level director. The unexpected spectacular success of the show became a leading story in all of entertainment news, and Stroman found herself interviewed and profiled on television and in mass market magazines, making of her that rare Broadway choreographer or director whose name and face are well-known outside the world of live theater.

Her recent projects have yielded uneven results. A short-lived 2004 production of *Frogs* (an expanded revival of a 1974 novelty musical—itself a loose adaptation of Aristophanes's ancient play) was followed by her reunion with Brooks for his next film-to-Broadway effort, *Young Frankenstein* (2007). Although its 14-month run would represent a satisfactory showing for most productions, inflated industry expectations for Brooks and Stroman and a widely reported bloated production budget ultimately made it unsuccessful. Nevertheless, Stroman's place in Broadway history is quite secure and, still highly energetic at 50-plus, she has time to build on her already astonishing career.

Thomas A. Greenfield and Nicole Katz

Further Reading

Bryer, Jackson R., and Richard Allan Davison. *The Art of the American Musical: Conversations with the Creators.* New Brunswick, NJ: Rutgers University Press, 2005.

Fliotsos, Anne L., and Wendy Verow. *American Women Stage Directors of the Twentieth Century.* Urbana: University of Illinois Press, 2008.

STYNE, JULE (1905–1994)
COMPOSER, PRODUCER, DIRECTOR

Jule Styne's multifaceted composing career exemplified the interrelationships of film, Broadway, and pop songs that helped make Broadway an essential part of American popular culture throughout the twentieth century. One of American musical theater's most prolific and successful songwriters, Styne wrote scores and songs for many of the most memorable Broadway **musicals** of the 1950s and early 1960s, including *Peter Pan* (1954), *Gypsy* (1959), and *Funny Girl* (1964). However, unlike many other Broadway composers of his day—including **Leonard Bernstein**, **Frederick Loewe**, and Richard Adler—Styne earned his songwriting pedigree by first writing scores and hit songs for film musicals. Numerous Styne compositions, especially songs from his early Hollywood musicals, had become top-selling hits before he ever ventured into writing Broadway musicals.

Styne (Julius Stein) was born on New Years' Eve, 1905, in London. His family moved to the United States and he was raised in Chicago, where he received the majority of his musical training. Styne proved to be a prodigy, even performing as soloist with the Chicago Symphony Orchestra as a child, but turned his back on classical music to join touring dance bands. He formed his own band in 1931 and found his way to the West Coast, eventually working as a songwriter, vocal coach, and music staffer for Hollywood studios. During the late 1930s and early 1940s Styne provided tunes for many forgettable films at 20th Century Fox, Paramount, Universal, and Columbia. While the films themselves were generally unsuccessful, several of the tunes he wrote for them became signature songs of the World War II era, particularly "I Don't Want to Walk Without You" from the noir potboiler *The Glass Key* (1942) and "I'll Walk Alone" from *Follow the Boys*

(1945), which earned him one of his nine Best Song Academy Award nominations. Upon this success, Styne and his most frequent Hollywood collaborator, Sammy Cahn, wrote songs for the multinominated *Anchors Aweigh* (1945), an MGM musical starring Gene Kelly, Kathryn Grayson, and Frank Sinatra and earned another Academy Award nomination for "I Fall in Love Too Easily."

Styne was 41 years old and well-established in Hollywood when, collaborating again with Cahn, he made a sensational Broadway debut with *High Button Shoes* (1947). The show ran for 727 performances and teamed Styne for the first time with wunderkind choreographer-producer-director **Jerome Robbins**. Styne ended the 1940s working with lyricist Leo Robin on the songs for *Gentleman Prefer Blondes* (1949), a musical adaptation of Anita Loos's 1926 popular stage comedy. *Gentleman* ran for almost two years on Broadway. It included the materialist's anthem "Diamonds Are a Girls Best Friend" and was adapted to a career-making film for Marilyn Monroe in 1953. By the early 1950s, Styne was a middle-aged Broadway newcomer and a force to be reckoned with.

The 1950s and 1960s were the most successful decades for Styne, from a professional standpoint. He deepened his working relationship with Robbins by contributing songs to Robbins's hit production of *Peter Pan* (1954), including the show's most memorable song "Never Neverland." The show also connected him to the lyricist team of **Betty Comden and Adolph Green**. The quartet of Robbins, Comden, Green, and Styne would work together on *Bells Are Ringing* (1956), a vehicle for the unique comic gifts of actress Judy Holliday. Between these triumphs, Styne would set Cahn's lyrics to music for the theme song to 20th Century Fox's *Three Coins in the Fountain* (1954), for which the two won the Academy Award for Best Song. Styne would finish out the decade by writing music for his most famous musical, *Gypsy* (1959), based on the memoirs of famed stripper Gypsy Rose Lee. *Gypsy* has become one of the most popular shows in musical theater history and features a career's worth of hit songs: "Let Me Entertain You," "Everything's Coming Up Roses," "Small World," and "Together Wherever We Go," among them. Styne would continue his success into the next decade by writing an equally strong score for *Funny Girl* (1964), which gave the show's 21-year-old star Barbra Streisand the signature song of her career, "People." His efforts on *Hallelujah, Baby!* (1967) would finally bring him a Tony Award as a Broadway composer. *Hallelujah, Baby!* was named Best Musical of 1967, earning Styne a second Tony Award as its producer. Styne had a success in 1972 with *Sugar*, which ran for over 500 performances but was overshadowed that year by **Stephen Sondheim**'s *A Little Night Music*. Styne's *Lorelei* (1974), a sequel to *Gentleman Prefer Blondes* (with Carol Channing reprising her original starring role), failed to generate sustained interest and ran a respectable but undistinguished ten months.

In the 1970s, as Broadway turned away from the integrative, story- and character-driven musicals of the previous 30 years, Styne and his generation of composers could no longer match their early successes. Nevertheless, Styne remained active as a composer on Broadway up until a year before his death, opening his last show *The Red Shoes* in 1993. His early hits enjoy revivals; *Bells re Ringing*, *Funny Girl*, and *Gypsy* have all been restaged on Broadway since 2000.

Styne's numerous awards reflect the distinctive breadth of his achievement in popular culture. In addition to receiving Kennedy Center Honors in 1990, Styne was elected to the Songwriters Hall of Fame in 1972 and the Theatre Hall of Fame in 1981. He was presented a special lifetime achievement Drama Desk Award in 1990 by theater **critics** and writers.

Styne died on September 20, 1994, of heart failure in Manhattan, New York.

Darryl Kent Clark

Further Reading

Styne, Jule. *Jule Styne*. Alexandria, VA: Time-Life Books, 1981.

Zinsser, William. *Easy to Remember: The Great American Songwriters and Their Songs*. Jaffrey, NH: David R. Gordine Publisher, 2006.

Sullivan, Ed (1901–1974)
Television Host, Columnist

Best known for producing and hosting *The Ed Sullivan Show* from 1948 to 1971, Edward Sullivan was a master at recognizing and promoting talented performers in all entertainment fields—even though he was notoriously devoid of any such talent of his own. An influential New York newspaper theater gossip columnist prior to becoming internationally famous as a **television** host, Sullivan often featured Broadway stars and scenes from their shows as part his program's weekly talent lineups. In so doing, Sullivan provided Broadway with one of its few national showcases during the 1950s and 1960s—a period when many believe the Broadway **musical** reached its peak as an indigenous American art form.

Sullivan was born on September 28, 1901, in Harlem. He grew up in Port Chester, New York, but returned to New York City after graduating high school. Working for several New York area newspapers throughout his career, Sullivan started out as a sports reporter in the 1920s as one of a rapidly expanding cadre of writers covering the

Ed Sullivan, whose television show and newspaper column promoted Broadway entertainment, gained a 2009 postage stamp honoring him for his contributions to American popular culture. (AP Photo/USPS)

burgeoning New York City professional sports scene. In 1931, while working at the now defunct *New York Graphic*, he succeeded the well-known Broadway columnist Walter Winchell. From the outset Sullivan declared that his column, "Ed Sullivan Sees Broadway," would save Broadway reporting from its woeful, salacious prurient state. Cultivating both admirers and enemies, Sullivan immediately became a major figure in Broadway circles and remained so for the rest of his career.

The *Graphic* closed in 1932, and Sullivan was hired to write a Broadway column for *The New York Daily News*. In the same year, he hosted a **radio** program, *Broadway's Greatest Thrills*, which was canceled after six months due to low ratings. In the 1940s Sullivan even produced two shows on Broadway. *Crazy with the Heat* (1941) and *Harlem Cavalcade* (1942), which featured all-black casts, experienced only short runs. Sullivan also periodically guest hosted New York **vaudeville** shows from 1932 to 1948.

Sullivan's CBS television variety show, originally called *Toast of the Town*, debuted on June 20, 1948. In deference to Sullivan's success and celebrity, it was renamed *The Ed Sullivan Show* in 1955. Despite the show's high ratings and Sullivan's popularity, he was criticized by reviewers for his apparent ineptitude as a master of ceremonies and his decidedly nonphotogenic facial expressions (which earned him the nickname "The Great Stone Face"). Unfazed, Sullivan never made any apparent effort to polish his onstage persona. He indulged numerous comic impressionists who mimicked him on his own show and endeared himself to many entertainers who knew that, unlike fellow (and rival) television hosts Jack Parr or Johnny Carson, Sullivan would never try to upstage or "top" his guests during their appearances. As a television personality, he was at least tolerable if not appealing to all segments of the national audience and presided over the most successful family-oriented variety program in television history.

As the success of *The Ed Sullivan Show* grew over the years, so did its importance to popular culture. He gave Dean Martin and Jerry Lewis, the most famous comedy team of the television era, one of their earliest exposures to a national audience. Elvis Presley's "censored-from-the-waist-down" appearance in 1956 and the Beatles' American debut in 1964 are milestone events in the history of rock music. He featured African American and other minority talents at a time when national television appearances for nonwhite entertainers were rare.

Sullivan also made a particular point of educating the American public about Broadway, encouraging his national audiences to see these "great shows" when they come to New York. Owing to the fact that *The Ed Sullivan Show* broadcast live from the New York theater district on Sunday nights when the theaters were dark, Broadway producers could readily arrange live, original cast television appearances for Sullivan whenever the opportunity presented itself. During the 1950s and 1960s Sullivan presented original cast scenes from ***My Fair Lady***, *Carousel*, *Gentleman Prefer Blondes*, ***West Side Story***, *Camelot*, *Man of La Mancha*, and *Annie Get Your Gun*, among others with such stars as **Julie Andrews**, **John Raitt**, **Ethel Merman**, **Carol Channing**, and Carol Lawrence. (Many of these Sullivan original cast appearances enjoy a revived currency through

YouTube.) Broadway luminaries, such as composers **Richard Rodgers** and **Leonard Bernstein** or lyricist **Oscar Hammerstein**, would occasionally be seated in Sullivan's live studio audience to receive an on-camera acknowledgment, a round of applause, and a quick plug from the host for their latest projects. The continuous exposure on Sullivan's show helped Broadway maintain a strong national presence in popular culture during the early years of the television era.

As broad "family" television programming gave way to narrower target-marketed programming, Sullivan's ratings started to decline by the late 1960s. CBS canceled the show in 1971. (Broadway star Bernadette Peters and choreographer Peter Gennaro were among Sullivan's guests in his final shows.) Sullivan later hosted some television specials, including his final televised appearance in 1973, *Ed Sullivan's Broadway.* The show aired on the same day as his wife Sylvia's unexpected death. Soon thereafter, Sullivan began suffering from depression and deteriorating physical health. Sullivan died in New York City on October 14, 1974, of cancer of the esophagus.

The theater in which he hosted his legendary television show, located on Broadway and 53rd Street in the New York theater district, was renamed for Ed Sullivan in 1967 and has been the home to CBS's *Late Show with David Letterman* since 1993. In 2003, 32 years after *The Ed Sullivan Show* had been off the air, Buena Vista Home Video company released on DVD *The Best of Broadway Musicals: Original Cast Performances from The Ed Sullivan Show*—a collection of over a dozen appearances by Broadway original casts. A brisk seller in the specialty home video market, the video provided further confirmation of Sullivan's important role in keeping Broadway musical theater at the forefront of modern American popular culture.

Thomas A. Greenfield and Christy E. Allen

Further Reading

Bowles, Jerry G. *A Thousand Sundays: The Story of the Ed Sullivan Show.* New York: Putnam, 1980.

Maguire, James. *Impresario: The Life and Times of Ed Sullivan.* New York: Billboard Books, 2006.

TANDY, JESSICA (1909–1994)
ACTRESS

Jessica Tandy's Broadway career spanned 55 years, 40 of them in starring roles. The English-born actress is best known on Broadway for her masterful performance as the original Blanche DuBois in **Tennessee Williams**'s *A Streetcar Named Desire* (1947), widely considered to be one of the best female dramatic roles in the canon of American drama. From the 1950s through the 1980s Tandy performed frequently with fellow actor and husband **Hume Cronyn**, usually to the delight of audiences and **critics**. Their heralded onstage partnership resulted in the pair succeeding **Alfred Lunt and Lynn Fontanne** as Broadway's premiere acting couple. A frequent performer on both English and Canadian stages as well as an Oscar-winning **film** actress, for half a century Tandy imbued Broadway with her wide-ranging talent, a refined aristocratic elegance, and the prestige of her international renown.

Born in London, England, in 1909, Jessie Alice Tandy was a teenager when her parents enrolled her in the Ben Greet Academy of Acting in London. She spent the next several years training and acting in small London and English **regional theaters**. In 1929, she debuted in London's West End in *The Rumor* by C. K. Munro, a minor contemporary English playwright. The following year she came to New York and made an inauspicious Broadway debut in two failed **Shubert Brothers** productions, *The Matriarch* (1930) by G. B. Stern and *The Last Enemy* (1930) by Frank Harvey. She returned to England, polishing her acting skills in numerous dramatic and comic roles ranging from Shakespeare to modern comedy. She did not appear on Broadway again for eight years.

From the late 1930s until 1947, Tandy appeared in several Broadway and **Off-Broadway** productions, periodically flying to Hollywood and London for additional work. During a brief Broadway run in A. J. Cronin's *Jupiter Laughs* (1940), she met and fell in love with Canadian-born actor Hume Cronyn, who had been working steadily on Broadway for several years. They were married in 1942, although they did not begin appearing on stage together until years later.

Tandy's first starring role on Broadway as Williams's damaged, enigmatic Southern belle Blanche DuBois in *Streetcar* brought her rave reviews, sudden fame, and the first of her three Tony Awards for Best Actress in a play. Notwithstanding the accolades she earned for the role, Tandy was passed over for the 1951 film version in favor of the better-known Hollywood actress Vivien Leigh. Despite the snub, Tandy's haunting performance is still widely remembered as the definitive interpretation of the role.

Tandy and Cronyn began performing together in the early 1950s and were immediately embraced as an outstanding couple acting by both critics and audiences. They first co-starred on Broadway in Jan de Hartog's sophisticated two-character marriage comedy *The Fourposter* (1951). The play was a sensation, running 632 performances over 18 months. Except for *Streetcar*, *The Fourposter* was the longest-running Broadway show of Tandy's career. Tandy and Cronin followed *Fourposter* on Broadway as co-stars in several productions: an evening of short plays (*Triple Play* [1959]), Hugh Wheeler's *Big Fish, Little Fish* (1962), and *Hamlet* (1963). Their 1977 performance in D. L. Coburn's *The Gin Game*, another two-character play, yielded Tandy her second Best Actress Tony in one of the most highly regarded stage dramas of the decade.

In between appearances with Cronin, Tandy also had numerous stage and film successes on her own. Between 1944 and 1994 she acted in 25 movies. She won the Oscar for Best Actress for the 1989 film *Driving Miss Daisy*—at age 80 the oldest actress ever to receive that award.

Between 1981 and 1986 Tandy followed *The Gin Game* with her final four Broadway appearances. None matched the impact of her earlier stage hits, but she earned strong reviews and Tony nominations for Andrew Davies's *Rose* (1981) and Brian Clark's *Petition* (1986), her final Broadway appearance. (Appropriately, with *Petition* she closed out her Broadway career in a two-character marriage play performing opposite her husband.) She won her third Best Actress Tony for *Foxfire*, written by Susan Cooper and Hume Cronyn (1981).

Diagnosed with ovarian cancer in 1990, Tandy still worked occasionally in film and **television** in the last few years of her life. She earned an Oscar nomination for Best Supporting Actress in *Fried Green Tomatoes* in 1991. A few months before her death, the **American Theatre Wing** honored her with a special Tony Award for Lifetime Achievement.

Tandy died of cancer in Easton, Connecticut, on September 11, 1994.

Thomas A. Greenfield and Laura Lonski

Further Reading

Barranger, Milly S. *Jessica Tandy: A Bio-bibliography.* Westport, CT: Greenwood Press, 1991.

Staggs, Sam. *When Blanche Met Brando: The Scandalous Story of "A Streetcar Named Desire."* New York: Macmillan, 2005.

TAYLOR, LAURETTE (1884–1946)
ACTRESS

Despite being almost unknown today, Laurette Taylor was among the most highly respected dramatic actresses in the first half of the twentieth century. Her career was highlighted by two roles performed 33 years apart: the title role in the comedy *Peg O' My Heart* (1912) and Amanda Wingfield in **Tennessee Williams**'s *The Glass Menagerie* (1945). Through her performance in *Menagerie* Taylor earned a legendary, iconic place among Broadway actors and directors who came a generation after her. Such luminaries as Maria Seldes, **Hal Prince**, **Uta Hagen**, and Maureen Stapleton have publicly proclaimed her the most gifted, natural American stage actress of her time and a major influence on the post–World War II generation of Broadway actors.

Taylor was born Loretta Cooney in New York City. She was a child vaudeville performer in the 1890s. In 1901, at age 17, she married Charles Taylor, a successful melodrama writer and **producer** 20 years her senior. For the next decade she performed throughout the country, principally in shows written and produced by her husband. They had two children, but Taylor took little time away from performing. The Taylors were very successful during this period but within a few years the rigors of raising children on the road and her impatience with the popular but unchallenging roles her husband was writing for her caused a fissure in the marriage. By the time of her first Broadway appearance in 1909, the Taylor marriage and business partnership were on the verge of collapse. They divorced in 1910.

Taylor debuted on Broadway in *The Great John Ganton* (1909) by English playwright J. Hartley Manners, whom she married shortly after her divorce from Taylor. Laurette appeared in several Broadway plays over the next few years, notably *Alias Jimmy Valentine* (1910) and *The Bird of Paradise* (1912), both of which had respectable 100-plus performance runs and earned Taylor critical and audience acclaim. She became a star in Manners's comedy *Peg O' My Heart*. Manners wrote the tale of an Irish teenager visiting England specifically for the 28-year-old Taylor. The show was one of the biggest hits of the decade, running a then record 603 performances. For the next 15 years, Taylor appeared regularly on Broadway, often in plays by Manners: *The Harp of Life* (1916), *Out There*

(1917), *Happiness* (1917), *One Night in Rome* (1919), a 1921 revival of *Peg*, and *National Anthem* (1922). These plays enjoyed varying degrees of success (*Happiness*, which ran for 136 performances, being the strongest among them). Although none matched the success of the original *Peg*, Taylor remained one of the most popular and highly regarded Broadway actresses in the 1910s and 1920s. As a result of her Broadway fame, Taylor went to Hollywood in 1922 to make silent film versions of her most famous shows: *Peg O' My Heart*, *Happiness*, and *One Night in Rome*. Taylor received particularly strong reviews for the film adaptation of *Peg*.

Manners died in 1928 and Taylor, now wealthy from the success of *Peg* and other projects, took a four-year hiatus from performing. She reemerged with moderate success in two James M. Barrie plays, *Alice Sit-By-The-Fire* and *The Old Lady Shows Her Medals* (both 1932). But by the mid-1930s, Taylor was battling alcoholism and serious emotional problems. She virtually disappeared from Broadway from 1932 until 1945. Her lone Broadway appearance in this period was a small part in *Outward Bound* (1938), for which she received glowing press reviews and raves from fellow actors. However, Taylor squandered much of the momentum she gained from *Outward Bound* and did not accept another of the hundreds of scripts submitted to her until she read *Menagerie* by the then unknown Williams. Taylor understood the potential in the play and the role of Amanda immediately and immersed herself in the play to astonishing results. Reviews of the Chicago tryout alone heralded her performance as among the best veteran **critics** had ever seen. The Broadway reception was even stronger. Critics raved about the understated complexity and power of Taylor's Amanda. Audiences adored the play and Taylor's performance. For a year fellow actors saw the show repeatedly to watch what became one of the most heralded dramatic performances in modern Broadway history. *Menagerie* ran for 18 months, giving Taylor a new stature and marketability in the theater. But she had become ill during the run and died of complications following a heart attack in New York City on December 7, 1946, four months after *Menagerie* closed.

No film recording was ever made of her performance in *Menagerie*, and she was never asked to make movies after the silent film era. Thus, Taylor remains a looming, legendary figure in the oral recollections of Broadway veterans who saw her perform.

Thomas A. Greenfield and Christy E. Allen

Further Reading

Courtney, Marguerite. *Laurette*. New York: Limelight Editions, 1984. (Original, New York: Rinehart, 1955.)

Menefee, David W. *The First Female Stars: Women of the Silent Era*. Westport, CT: Praeger, 2004.

TAYMOR, JULIE (1952–)
DIRECTOR, COSTUMER, PUPPETEER, SCENIC DESIGNER

Best known for her imaginative concept and staging of the **Walt Disney Theatrical Productions** smash hit *The Lion King* (1997), Taymor is the first woman ever awarded a Tony for Best Direction in a Musical. Apart from this singular achievement, Taymor is one of the most innovative and highly respected American theater artists of the past two decades. Often blurring the lines between puppets and human stage characters and artfully melding Western and non-Western performance traditions, Taymor's work on stage and in **film** has brought new, influential ideas to contemporary stagings of **Shakespeare**, opera, **musicals**, and plays.

Raised in the Boston area, Taymor had a highly eclectic education. Before she entered college she had participated in Boston Children's Theatre, studied Asian theater in Sri Lanka and India on an international student program, and took instruction in mime from Jacques Lecoq in Paris. She returned to the United States to study folklore and mythology at Oberlin College. While still a student she auditioned for Herbert Blau's company, one of the country's most venerated experimental theater troupes, and became its youngest member at that time. After graduation, she studied **puppetry** in Japan before traveling to Indonesia. While

Lion King director Julie Taymor interacts with a South African actor during a rehearsal of The Lion King *at Pretoria's National Theater in Pretoria, South Africa, in 2007. The first production with an all–South African cast, some new costumes, choreography, and songs was as successful as the theatrical adaptation of Disney's animated film when it opened on Broadway in 1997. (AP Photo/Jerome Delay)*

there she founded an international dance-mask troupe, the Teatr Loh, and remained in Indonesia as director of the troupe for four years.

She returned to the United States in 1979 and quickly became involved in experimental theater productions with a number of like-minded artists. Among her more notable works during the 1980s was the elaborate *The King Stag*, a staged adaptation of an eighteenth-century Venetian children's tale, which was directed by Andrei Serban and for which Taymor worked on costumes, makeup, large puppets and stage movement. The show, which opened in Cambridge, Massachusetts, has since toured widely. With composer Elliot Goldenthal she staged *Transposed Heads* in 1980 and *Juan Darien: A Carnival Mass* in 1988. The latter show, a puppet-laden fantasy staging of a story by Uruguayan writer Horacio Quiroga, won an Obie award when it opened **Off-Broadway**. It was mounted on Broadway in 1996, marking Taymor's Broadway debut. The production received an impressive five Tony nominations, including Best Musical, Best Score (for Goldenthal), and Best Director and Best Scenic Design for Taymor, but no wins.

In 1992 Taymor staged Stravinsky's opera *Oedipus Rex* in Japan. The production was broadcast nationally in the United States, earning Taymor an Emmy Award. She staged several other operas during the 1990s and, in 1994, she directed a highly regarded, innovative Off-Broadway stage production of Shakespeare's *Titus Andronicus*.

Intrigued by her string of critical successes, her mastery of Asian and African theatrical idioms, and her command of visual representation through mask and puppetry, Michael Eisner, Chair of the Walt Disney Company, approached Taymor about staging their planned musical adaptation of the animated film hit *The Lion King*. She agreed and proceeded to fashion one of the most visually and aurally distinctive Broadway musicals in recent memory. Her design once again blurred the lines between actor, puppet, and costume. The final "look" and visual style of the production—which has now achieved near iconic stature in popular culture and is familiar even to people who have never seen the show—is in its totality the product of Taymor's vision.

The success of *The Lion King* amazed everyone involved. The production won six Tony Awards, including Best Musical and the historic Best Direction of a Musical for Taymor. The show celebrates its twelfth anniversary on Broadway in 2009 and will almost certainly reach its 5,000th Broadway performance in 2010. It has been one of the great boons to the Broadway touring industry, and one of the few musicals that can hold its own on the road against the likes of *Cats*, *Les Misérables*, and ***The Phantom of the Opera***. The show also has garnered for Taymor financial rewards and mainstream fame commensurate with the "inside" reputation she had within the theatrical community as an independent, cutting-edge, avant-garde artist for 15 years.

Taymor has since directed some films, including a film version of *Titus Andronicus* (1999). She has also returned to staging opera with *The Magic Flute* (2004) for the New York Metropolitan Opera and *Grendel* (2006), an original opera she directed and cowrote with poet J. D. McClatchy, based on the epic poem *Beowulf*. (*Grendel* premiered in Los Angeles.) Taymor's next scheduled Broadway directorial project is *Spider-Man: Turn Off the Dark* (2010), a musical extravaganza (with an estimated one-show record budget of $50 million) based on the cartoon and film superhero.

To this day, one can easily trace Taymor's most heralded and best-known artistic achievements back to her multicultural education and earliest days as a publicly unknown but professionally respected global theater artist. The journey from the commercial nether regions of non-Western theater to mainstream box-office glory is a highly improbable one—a fact that makes Taymor's remarkable talent, past achievements, and future prospects all the more extraordinary.

Thomas A. Greenfield, Sarah Provencal, Brian Balduzzi

Further Reading

Blumenthal, Eileen, and Julie Taymor. *Julie Taymor, Playing with Fire: Theater, Opera, Film.* New York: H. N. Abrams, 1995.

Gold, Sylvianne. "Julie Taymor: A Woman in Charge." *Women in American Theatre*, ed. Helen Krich Chinoy and Linda Walsh Jenkins. New York: Theatre Communications Group, 2006.

TELEVISION

From its very beginnings, American television has looked to the Broadway stage as a potent source of programming. Hit dramas, **musicals**, and comedies were a natural source of prime-time material, particularly since they had proven their worth in the theatrical marketplace. The issue quickly emerged, however, of the best way to televise works originally created for the Great White Way. Should the home audience watch the proceedings from an ideal seat in the fourth row of the orchestra? Should TV cameras penetrate the proscenium stage and break the fourth wall? How would a large cast fit on a small screen? What is the best way to adapt a three-act play to a substantially reduced, commercially interrupted, running time? How faithful should an electronic medium be to the live, dramatic vision of the theater? The answers to these questions would vary from decade to decade, and from network to network, but they reflected the shifting, but significant, roles Broadway would play for at least the first 40 years of American television.

During the late 1930s, the stage was a leading player in the still experimental medium of television. Early New York City broadcasters showcased their Broadway connections, offering excerpts from leading productions, such as a 1938 NBC telecast of a 22-minute selection from **Rachel Crothers**'s *Susan and God* (1937), complete with members of the original cast including Gertrude Lawrence. After World War II, and the gradual development of commercial broadcasting, the New York–based networks continued to utilize the glamour of live theater conveniently located only a few blocks from their studios. All three networks launched

Broadway-themed programming. NBC coproduced a series of dramas with the **Theatre Guild**; ABC's *Actors Studio* (1948–1950) featured live stage adaptations with leading members of the recently formed **Actors Studio**; while CBS's *Tonight on Broadway* (1948–1949) offered excerpts from current productions as well as interviews with the cast conducted by theater critic John Mason Brown. None of these efforts was very successful (finding sponsors was a continuing problem), but they led the way to the chief source of theatrical television programming for the next decade: the live anthology drama series.

Prestige Dramas and Anthology Programs

Programs like *Philco Television Playhouse* (1948–1955), *Ford Theatre Hour* (1948–1951), *Kraft Television Theatre* (1947–1958), *Pulitzer Prize Playhouse* (1950–1952), and *Celanese Theatre* (1951–1952), much like their earlier **radio** counterparts *Mercury Theatre on the Air/The Campbell Playhouse* (1938–1940) and *Lux Radio Theater* (1934–1955), looked frequently to the Broadway stage to fill their prodigious need for material. The *Philco Television Playhouse*, for example, broadcast a star-studded version of Elmer Rice's *Counselor at Law* and Sidney Howard's *The Late Christopher Bean* (both with Paul Muni). *Kraft Television Theatre* did numerous Broadway play adaptations throughout its 11 years, including J. M. Barrie's *Dear Brutus* (1918) and Emlyn Williams's *Night Must Fall* (1936). The approaches varied, from *Philco Television Playhouse*'s distinguished revivals, often with original cast members, to *Ford Theatre Hour*'s use of leading stage actors like **Eva Le Gallienne** and Burgess Meredith in one-hour theater adaptations. Fidelity to the text was a pressing concern, with frequent complaints from **playwrights** and performers not only about the wholesale dropping of plotlines and characters to conform to the pressures of a 30- or 60-minute time slot, but also about prudish sponsors eager to remove even the slightest hint of controversy or suggestiveness from their eponymously titled showcases. *Celanese Theatre* on ABC attempted a different approach by actively consulting the original playwrights, some of whom even worked on the television script adaptations—a task facilitated by the fact that the program's script editor was Mabel Anderson, the wife of dramatist **Maxwell Anderson** (who adapted two of his plays for the series).

In addition to the weekly anthology series, Broadway was frequently utilized for special event programming throughout the 1950s, particularly when the networks were eager to exhibit their glossiest, crowd-pleasing wares. NBC's *Producer's Showcase* (1954–1957) was network president Sylvester "Pat" Weaver's effort to lure audience with unique TV spectaculars, including a revival of Noel Coward's *Tonight at 8:30* starring Ginger Rogers, a staging of *Cyrano de Bergerac* (1898) with **José Ferrer** recreating his triumphant 1946 performance in the title role, and most memorably of all, a 1955 telecast of James M. Barrie's *Peter Pan* (1954), imported right after its Broadway closing, with original star **Mary Martin** and the rest of the Broadway cast intact. In the same year, the series took the bold step of refashioning **Thornton Wilder**'s *Our Town* (1938), which had already been televised three times in the previous seven years, into an original musical, with a score by Jimmy Van Heusen and Sammy Cahn, starring a clearly uncomfortable Frank Sinatra as the Stage Manager. Not to be outdone, CBS launched its first program in color, *The Best of Broadway* (1954–1955), with a series of big-star revivals, such as the **George S. Kaufman** and Edna Ferber comedy *The Royal Family* (1927) with **Helen Hayes** and Fredric March, and Kaufman and Moss Hart's *The Man Who Came to Dinner* with Merle Oberon and Joan Bennett.

The Best of Broadway made a point of stressing its theatrical roots, leaving the proscenium arch intact and placing the cameras in the midst of a studio audience. But other programs, like CBS's *Studio One* (1948–1958) and NBC's *Hallmark Hall of Fame* (1951–), were also experimenting with a more innovative and intimate approach to televised drama, penetrating the stage walls and allowing the cameras to fluidly explore the playing areas in provocative and exciting ways. Directors like Delbert Mann, George Schaeffer, and Alex Segal specialized in this form of intense dramatic exploration, and the results led to a new type of "tele-theater" that roughly translated the emotional power of the stage to the small screen.

Nevertheless, by the late 1950s, the era of prominent Broadway showcases and exploratory directorial techniques was coming to an end. The networks still televised occasional musical specials. In 1957 CBS commissioned Richard Rodgers and Oscar Hammerstein to create *Cinderella*, an original musical for television broadcast (the celebrated production drew an astonishing viewership of 107 million). In the same year NBC broadcast a 90-minute version of *Annie Get Your Gun* (1946) starring **Mary Martin** (which drew 60 million viewers). In the following year CBS telecast *Wonderful Town* (1953) with Rosalind Russell and NBC mounted a *Hallmark Hall of Fame* presentation of *Kiss Me Kate* (1948) with original stars **Alfred Drake** and Patricia Morrison. But within a year, most of the live New York anthology programs, with their occasional forays into Broadway revivals, were off the air, replaced by less expensive, studio- and company-produced TV series from Hollywood.

Network Specials and Ed Sullivan

Special event dramas and the more difficult to produce musicals would also grow increasingly rare, as the commercial networks would now view the stage as a pricey indulgence, best carted out in times when the Nielsen ratings were shut off (as they were a couple times a year back then) or when public outcry over low-quality fare became especially pronounced. The only reliable TV venue for Broadway during the next decade would be the *Ed Sullivan Show* (1948–1971). Prior to his broadcast career, **Ed Sullivan** was a celebrated Broadway theater and nightlife newspaper columnist. His attachment to the Great White Way was one of the signatures of his long-running variety program, whether he was introducing to viewers leading Broadway figures seated in his audience or featuring excerpts from the latest hit contemporary musicals, complete with performances by the original casts.

CBS's reduced New York theater offerings during the 1960s were typical of network programming trends at the time. Still wearing, however uneasily, the mantle of the "Tiffany network," CBS linked up with prominent producer David Susskind for a series of prestigious, but infrequently scheduled, Broadway revivals. These included a 1966 production of **Tennessee Williams**'s *The Glass Menagerie* (1945), with cuts approved by the author so that the play fit into a two-hour time slot. Broadcasts of **Arthur Miller**'s *Death of the Salesman* (1949) and *The Crucible* (1953) were adapted directly by the author himself. CBS also televised two critically acclaimed, one-man shows—John Gielgud's *The Ages of Man* (1958) and Hal Holbrook's *Mark Twain Tonight!* (1966)—which had recently completed sold-out Broadway engagements. The other broadcast networks offered even less in the way of stage drama, other than occasional *Hallmark Hall of Fame*'s theatrical adaptations on NBC or a 1968 ABC telecast of a revival of Michael V. Gazzo's *Hatful of Rain* (1955) starring Sandy Dennis and Peter Falk.

Perhaps the most interesting TV theater event of the 1960s was not a retread or a reworking but an unusually ambitious, short-lived series called *ABC Stage 67* (1966–1967). Launched with great fanfare by ABC president Leonard Goldenson, the avowedly upscale cultural program featured intriguing original dramas by Broadway playwrights Murray Schisgal and **Arthur Laurents**, as well as a variety of musical and comedy revues. Its unquestionable highlight, however, was **Stephen Sondheim**'s 1966 made-for-TV musical, *Evening Primrose*, which told, in an exquisite score, the story of a department store mannequin's brief journey into life.

Public Television and Notable Experiments

As the commercial networks turned away from theater, except for publicity-driven special events, educational television became the primary venue for stage-based programming by the mid-1960s. Even with minimal funding and a scattered collection of affiliates, NET (the ramshackle predecessor to PBS) leapt into the fray with *NET Playhouse* (1966–1972), offering viewers for the first time the chance to see uncut, commercial-free, contemporary theatrical productions. The series stressed collaborations with leading playwrights like **Edward Albee** and skilled TV directors, and featured a variety of distinguished theater companies from throughout the country. Highlights included works by Ronald Ribman and Tennessee Williams. With the creation of the Public Broadcasting Service in 1969, and the merger of NET with New York's public station, serious theatrical programming on the new network would increase dramatically. As part of *Great Performances* (1972–), *Theater in America* (1973–1979) continued the approach of *NET Playhouse*, showcasing innovative productions from the country's lively regional theater scene, including adventurous New York troupes like the Negro Ensemble

Company, the Repertory Theater of Lincoln Center, and the Circle Repertory Company.

Interestingly, at the very time PBS was embarking on its theatrical ventures, one of Manhattan's leading **Off-Broadway** companies, the New York Shakespeare Festival, decided to take a chance with the more alluring realm of commercial television. In 1972, its founder and head, **Joseph Papp**, signed an impressive $7 million deal with CBS to produce 13 full-length plays over the next four years. However, both Papp and CBS would soon regret this sudden attempt to reestablish the network's dramatic credentials. To inaugurate the series, Papp decided to televise his current Broadway mounting of *Much Ado about Nothing*, chipping in $60,000 of his own money to cover the elaborate production costs. While not a ratings powerhouse (it attracted a modest 15 million viewers), its effect on the theater box office was decisive (attendance dropped by nearly two-thirds) and the Broadway show was forced to close. Papp's next telecast would prove to be his last. David Rabe's *Sticks and Bones* may have won the Tony Award for Best Play in 1972, but its controversial story of a blind Vietnam War veteran was hardly typical commercial television fare, and CBS, spurred by the unfavorable reaction of its affiliates, canceled the program three days before its scheduled broadcast in March 1973. It was eventually shown the following August, with no sponsors and only half of the network's stations willing to air it. Papp and CBS parted ways soon afterwards.

Several noteworthy developments in televised theater appeared during the 1980s. The first was a curious throwback to the era of live TV drama 30 years before. *NBC Live Theater* (1980–1984) was a series of annual two-hour specials, broadcast live from various regional stages and shot primarily from the audience's proscenium perspective. Productions included Preston Jones's *The Oldest Living Graduate* (1976) featuring Henry Fonda and Timothy Hutton; Tad Mosel's *All the Way Home* (1960) with Sally Field and William Hurt from USC; and Carson McCullers's *A Member of the Wedding* (1950) with Pearl Bailey and Dana Hill.

More promising was the growth of the pay cable networks. Similar to the early days of commercial television, newly launched pay cable networks like HBO and Showtime turned to the Broadway stage as a way to attract attention and lure potential subscribers. Showtime was by far the most ambitious with its series *Broadway on Showtime* (1979–1987), which presented nearly 50 recent or revived dramas. Productions varied from light Broadway comedies, television-star based revivals, interesting Off-Broadway attractions, and shot-in-the-theater presentations of selected Broadway productions including Stephen Sondheim's *Sweeney Todd* (1979) and *Sunday in the Park with George* (1984). Many of these programs would later appear on PBS series like *Great Performances* and *American Playhouse* (1980–1996). HBO's initial theater efforts were far more modest. Its *Standing Room Only* (1981–1982) was designed to offer one stage production a month, from **Neil Simon** dinner-theater perennials, to unusual Off-Broadway fare, to a lavish, $3 million production of the recent Broadway revival of *Camelot* (1960). The high cost of the latter, however, convinced the network to quickly abandon televised theater in favor of more popular made-for-TV movies. It would return only once more with an extraordinary 2003 film version of **Tony Kushner**'s *Angels in America* (1993), directed by **Mike Nichols**.

Theater was also a featured attraction on several short-lived cable networks of the early 1980s. ARTS (a co-venture of ABC and Hearst) often showcased edgy, Off-Broadway productions, including two plays by Frank South, *Rattlesnake in a Cooler* and *Precious Blood*, videotaped for television by their stage director Robert Altman. The Entertainment Channel (before its 1984 merger with ARTS to form A&E in 1984) presented several costly Broadway productions. And CBS Cable, premiering in 1981 and lasting less than a year, presented a variety of sophisticated productions from London and New York stages.

The costly collapse of these high-toned cable ventures and the shift in direction at HBO left PBS (and its occasional production partner Showtime) as the primary venue for televised theater. During the next decades, its showcase series *Great Performances* and *American Playhouse* provided a diverse menu of dramatic attractions, ranging from reworked stage productions to taped-in-the-theater musicals to imported, "in concert" performances of Broadway hits. There were also documentary specials, such as 1986's fascinating backstage portrait *Follies in Concert*, as well as an epic six-part series *Broadway: The American Musical* in 2004 that traced the entire history of the Great White Way. The network's other primary performing arts series, *Live from Lincoln Center* (1976–), also presented many events direct from the Center's premiere stage venue, the Vivian Beaumont Theater, including **Susan Stroman**'s *Contact* and Adam Guettel's *Light in the Piazza* (2005).

The broadcast networks showed little interest in the stage from the mid-1980s onwards, except for a few well-received musicals from the production team of Craig Zadan and Neil Meron. Their first was a 1993 film version of *Gypsy* (1959) for CBS, starring Bette Midler. Four years later they switched networks to ABC and produced the second remake of Rodgers and Hammerstein's made-for-TV musical *Cinderella*, with pop singer Brandy Norwood and Broadway musical comedy veteran Bernadette Peters. Its success led to two more televised musicals for the network, including *Annie* (1959) in 1999 and *The Music Man* (1957) in 2003.

Though Broadway has been a scarce commodity for decades on the broadcast networks during prime time (except for CBS's annual telecasts of the perennially low-rated *Tony Awards Show* [1967–]), it has, surprisingly enough, made an impact on New York–based network daytime and late night TV. Programs like *Late Night with David Letterman* (1993–), *Live with Regis and Kathie Lee/Kelly* (1989–), *The View* (1997–), and the traditional early morning network stalwarts *The Today Show* (1952–) and *Good Morning America* (1975–) have often featured excerpts from current midtown musicals. Perhaps no program in recent memory has done more to celebrate Broadway than *The Rosie O'Donnell Show* (1996–2002), thanks to the boundless enthusiasm of its theater-infatuated host. During its six seasons on the air, O'Donnell presented more than 50 original-cast appearances, each showcased with vivid camerawork and lighting.

While it is difficult to predict the future of televised theater, given its dramatic ups and downs on American TV since the 1940s, there is little doubt that Broadway will hold some kind of special attraction on home screens for years to come.

Brian G. Rose

Further Reading

Beck, Kirsten. *Cultivating the Wasteland*. New York: American Council for the Arts, 1983.
Rose, Brian. *Televising the Performing Arts*. Westport, CT: Greenwood Press, 1992.

THEATRE GUILD

Before the Theatre Guild hit its stride as a production company in the early 1920s, most plays staged on Broadway were conventional in both style and content. To be certain, experimental "little theaters" such as the **Provincetown Players** and Washington Square Players were just starting up in small venues (rarely in actual permanent theater buildings) in lower Manhattan. However, most of New York's theatrical endeavors were presented by **producers** who had little interest in stretching the boundaries of what was considered possible in the theater and no desire to challenge audience assumptions or prejudices. But the adventurers who formed the Guild just after World War I seized the opportunity to stretch those boundaries and challenge their audiences as a matter of course, and for many years they were surprisingly successful at doing so, both aesthetically and commercially.

Several of the Theatre Guild's founders were, in fact, veterans of the Washington Square Players, a company of Greenwich Village bohemians who in the mid-1910s mounted productions that addressed charged topics of the day, such as gender relations and the ethics of birth control. This company disbanded in 1918, but in December of that year one of its members, lawyer and sometime **playwright** Lawrence Langner, gathered the nucleus of the group that would become the Theatre Guild: literary manager Theresa Helburn, scenic designer Lee Simonson, actress Helen Westley, banker Maurice Wertheim, and director Philip Moeller. In a break with earlier companies, which were usually run by a single, forceful personality, the Guild was run by a committee of forceful personalities, six opinionated individuals who sometimes clashed sharply over the choice of material and its manner of presentation. The Guild's first production, *The Bonds of Interest* (1919), featured two players who would become Guild regulars, board member Helen Westley and Dudley Digges, along with poet Edna St. Vincent Millay. The show was not a success, but Langner, whose practice as a patent attorney was lucrative, put up the funds to keep the Guild afloat.

At about this time the formation of Actors' Equity caused a rift on Broadway when most producers refused to recognize the union. The Theatre Guild not only

A dance scene from Oklahoma!, *a Theatre Guild production, during its original run in 1943–1944. (Library of Congress LC-USW331-054949-ZC)*

recognized Equity but practiced a union-approved profit-sharing arrangement with its actors and crew. Consequently, when a major Equity strike erupted in August 1919, shutting down most of New York's theaters, the only play permitted to continue its run was the Guild's second production, St. John Ervine's drama *John Ferguson*. With virtually no competition for audiences, the play drew packed houses nightly. This situation lasted for a month, and the fluke success established the Theatre Guild's reputation and ensured its survival for the foreseeable future.

The Guild reinforced its maverick image by eschewing the star system that prevailed elsewhere; posters advertising Guild productions listed only the title and playwright, not the actors. It was also widely noted in this early period that the company was inclined to choose material by non-American authors that was decidedly highbrow and eccentric by Broadway standards: plays by Georg Kaiser, Henrik Ibsen, August Strindberg, Leo Tolstoy, and so on. During one period so many Hungarian plays were presented that wags dubbed the Theatre Guild "the Budapest House." The Guild's decision to stage the world premiere of **George Bernard Shaw**'s massive *Back to Methuselah* in 1922 sealed its reputation for boldness. This opus consisted of a cycle of five full-length plays spanning thousands of years of human history, from Adam and Eve into the distant future. The Guild split *Methuselah* into three sections, each performed for a week in alternation. Shaw himself quipped that the Guild were "lunatics," but this production resulted in a lasting professional bond between the company and the playwright. Shaw allowed the Guild to present the world premiere of his *Saint Joan* the following year and a number of his works thereafter.

In time the influence of the European avant-garde was reflected in new American drama, leading to such memorable and influential Theatre Guild productions of the mid-1920s as Elmer Rice's drama *The Adding Machine* (1923) and John Howard Lawson's *Processional* (1925). In the latter Dudley Digges played Mr. Zero, a hapless accountant who turns homicidal when he learns he is to be replaced by a machine. The Guild's production of *The Adding Machine* featured the kind of stylized performances and Expressionistic sets found in some of the German and Soviet silent **films** of the period.

Not all of the Guild's successes were so artistically ambitious, however. In 1924, **Alfred Lunt** and his wife, **Lynn Fontanne**, scored a triumph in an adaptation of Ferenc Molnár's frothy comedy *The Guardsman* under the Guild aegis. After this the "no star" policy went by the wayside as the Lunts became the company's in-house headliners. Around this time the Guild built its own theater in the Broadway theater district and attempted to establish an ongoing repertory company, but without success. (The Guild Theatre building, which still stands on 52nd Street near 7th Avenue, is the current August Wilson Theatre.) The Guild produced more works by American playwrights as the 1920s rolled on, including Sidney Howard's *They Knew What They Wanted* (1924), *Porgy* (1927) by DuBose and Dorothy Heyward, and **Eugene O'Neill's** *Strange Interlude* (1928).

As the 1930s began, a number of factors began to pull the Theatre Guild away from its founding principles and undercut its commitment to producing challenging work. The rise of **radio** drama and the advent of talking pictures drained writing talent from the theater and from New York, just as the Depression's impact began to be felt at the box office. By this time, too, some of the Guild's strong-willed founding members had developed interpersonal conflicts, and several departed. A group of top playwrights affiliated with the Guild left to form their own organization, the Playwrights' Company, while some of the Guild's younger and more politically progressive talents left to form the **Group Theatre**. The change was not immediately noticeable while the successes continued: Lunt and Fontanne in *Reunion in Vienna* (1931), O'Neill's *Mourning Becomes Electra* (1931) and *Ah, Wilderness!* (1933), S. N. Behrman's *Biography* (1932), and so on, but it was obvious to observers that the Guild's former boldness was no longer evident in stagecraft or selection of material.

Despite its newfound caution, by 1939 the Theatre Guild was nonetheless facing bankruptcy. Ironically, the company was rescued that year by a conventional comedy featuring a Hollywood star. *The Philadelphia Story*, featuring Katharine Hepburn, ran on Broadway for a full year—the first Theatre Guild production ever to do so. In the war years the Guild presented the premieres of two highly innovative **Richard Rodgers and Oscar Hammerstein** musicals, *Oklahoma!* and *Carousel*, and it continued to offer Broadway regular doses of Shaw and O'Neill. But by 1950, the company's days as a daring, innovative, and influential force on Broadway were effectively over. By the 1960s the Theatre Guild was simply a production company much like any other, and the task of challenging audiences with startling new works had long since passed to other hands.

At the peak of its powers, especially in the 1920s, the Guild emboldened other producers by proving repeatedly that there was a healthy market for provocative, offbeat, and sometimes controversial drama in this country. **Critic Brooks Atkinson** even credited the Guild with annihilating "provinciality in the American theater." While that point may be debatable, it is a matter of record that the Guild's greatest successes demonstrated that artistically ambitious works can indeed reap rewards at the box office.

William Charles Morrow

Further Reading

Atkinson, Brooks. *Broadway.* New York: Macmillan, 1970.
Banham, Martin, ed. *The Cambridge Guide to Theatre.* Cambridge, England: Cambridge University Press, 1995.

THE THEATRICAL SYNDICATE (THE SYNDICATE)
PRODUCERS, THEATER OWNERS

The so-called Theatrical Syndicate (never called that by its members) was formed in 1896 by six leading theater magnates: Marc Klaw (1858–1936), Abraham Lincoln Erlanger (1860–1930), Al Hayman (1847–1917), Charles Frohman (1860–1915), Samuel F. Nixon (born Nirdlinger) (1848–1918), and J. F. Zimmerman (1843–1925). The firm of Klaw & Erlanger had existed since the late 1880s, booking theater and producing attractions. Nixon and Zimmerman were longtime partners in Pennsylvania theater ownership. Frohman and Hayman had been affiliated in all aspects of the business for more than a decade. Collectively they saw an opportunity to bring order out of what was at the time a chaotic, decentralized, unstructured, unprofessional commercial theater industry. They largely succeeded, at the same time making a great deal of money for themselves and alienating much of the theatrical community.

At the time of the Syndicate's founding, chaos in the commercial theater business had been growing for almost a quarter century. As commercial theater business developed from local stock companies into regional or nationwide touring companies (called "combinations"), producers and managers urgently needed some degree of centralization. By the late 1870s, New York City's Union Square in lower Manhattan—about 30 blocks or two miles downtown from today's Times Square theater district—had developed into the Mecca for all things theatrical. Booking agents took desk space in nearby buildings during the summer months. Sometimes they would simply loiter out on the Square to receive owners trying to fill their theaters or for a season and attraction managers trying to put together a touring route. It was a haphazard and inefficient though colorful system, often resulting in nonsensical routing for attractions and many unfilled weeks for theaters. Through the 1880s many theaters became affiliated with circuit bookers and managers with offices on Union Square. These new operations promised sensible logistics and full schedules for theater houses and performers alike.

Klaw, Erlanger, Frohman, and Hayman learned their trade in the Union Square milieu. They variously sold tickets, hawked opera glasses, and worked as advance men for minstrel shows and melodramas that crisscrossed the country. As the men worked their way up the industry ladder, they formed large circuits of their own, booking attractions nationwide. By 1896, they could collectively bring many hundreds of theaters of their own to the Syndicate table, to combine with the rivals-but-soon-to-be-partners Nixon & Zimmerman's many first-rank theaters. Besides bricks and mortar, Klaw, Erlanger, Frohman, and Hayman brought a great many productions as well; Frohman was by then one of Broadway's preeminent American producers, and the team of Klaw & Erlanger was not far behind.

The Syndicate's formation from this highly cohesive group of theatrical entrepreneurs was fairly straightforward. The Syndicate's members could help theaters coast to coast—both small-town theater owners presenting one-nighters and big-city managers with full weeks to fill—by offering giant, well-planned touring routes that catered to the needs of all concerned. And a touring show or act could expect to be on the road for a full 40-week season, without many off nights or inefficient double-back routes. Veteran theater men like Abe Erlanger or "C. F." Frohman knew the minutiae of the touring logistics road—transport, lodging, local support services—so intimately that they could juggle the planning for several routes at a time in their heads, seldom needing to refer to notes or schedules or a timetable or a directory. In the Syndicate members' minds there was no one better suited to take on the daunting challenge of reforming the theater business, bringing rationality to such an inefficient muddle, for the benefit of all, including the theatergoing public.

That was the theory, and for many theater owners and performers it worked according to plan. As advertised, many "provincial" theatergoers were able to see productions that otherwise might not have reached their cities and towns. But rivals and some disgruntled clients and employees of the Syndicate's sharp-eyed insiders quickly labeled the new high-end approach as greed cloaked in altruism. The Syndicate partners, they claimed, were looking out for themselves first and foremost. The Syndicate organization operated similarly to the trusts and vertical monopolies formed by the industrialist robber barons of the day. The Syndicate owned outright, or had interests in, many of the theaters and attractions it was booking, besides controlling the overall distribution of theatrical product nationwide. Favoritism was built into the structure at its very foundation. Certainly other attraction managers and theater owners could be part of the Syndicate game, as long as they played by the Syndicate's rules, which were heavily slanted toward the Syndicate partners' interests. For example, Syndicate partners were systematically double dipping, charging booking fees to theaters as well as fees to attractions for the privilege of being booked. Such fees invariably favored Syndicate allies who received better rates, thus financially hobbling rivals who needed access to the Syndicate's touring routes, theaters, and services. Less-favored theaters and attractions often had to make substantial payments to Syndicate partners in order to get services at all, a practice the partners vehemently denied even in the face of the evidence. At times the Syndicate blatantly tried to ruin those they viewed as competition. (Their professional persecution of such theatrical luminaries as playwright/producer **David Belasco**, actress/producer **Minnie Maddern Fiske**, and actress Sarah Bernhardt became the stuff of theatrical legend.) Other players had to endure blatantly unfair business practices if they were to survive in the business at all.

This radical disconnect between altruistic theory and self-serving practice caused widespread discontent with the Syndicate's high-handed practices. Resentment simmered for years in the theater industry, sporadically coming to a boil but invariably fought back by the cagey moguls.

As time went on, the Syndicate partners' increasing arrogance led to a contemptuous attitude toward business and public alike. More and more theater people were disillusioned or bankrupted by corrupt Syndicate practices, and theatergoers nationwide began to question the fairness, for example, of paying top dollar to attend third-rate road companies billed as "direct from New York's Broadway." The Syndicate's stubborn rigidity, and its preferred methods of steamrollering all competition, sowed the seeds of its own destruction. It took rival producers and theater owners the **Shubert Brothers** to stand up to the Syndicate and break its stranglehold.

As early as 1903, Abe Erlanger boasted that the Shubert Brothers, who had moved to New York City from Syracuse in 1900 to set up shop against the Syndicate, would soon be out of business. He and his partners completely underestimated the young "upstarts," ignoring the growing dissatisfaction in the theatrical world and the Shuberts' ingenuity. The "wars" between the Shuberts and the Syndicate, gleefully reported blow by blow in the daily press, went on for a decade and a half, concluding only with the demise of the Syndicate after the end of World War I. By that time, Frohman and Hayman were dead, Zimmerman was pursuing his own interests, and Klaw & Erlanger were on the verge of breaking up their partnership.

The Theatrical Syndicate had succeeded in bringing a large measure of order to the chaotic business practices of the 1870s and 1880s. While many of the Syndicate's innovations still govern commercial theater, the giant company ultimately toppled because of the public's and the industry's revulsion at the partners' hubris and unadorned greed. Their successors sometimes manifested the same faults. Still, for all their considerable shortcomings, modern Broadway could hardly have developed without them.

John Tenney

Further Reading

Poggi, Jack. *Theater in America: The Impact of Economic Forces, 1870–1967*. Ithaca, NY: Cornell University Press, 1968.

Witham, Barry. *Theatre in the United States: 1750–1915: Theatre in the Colonies and United States*. Cambridge, England: Cambridge University Press, 1996.

TONY AWARDS

See **American Theatre Wing—Tony Awards**.

TOURING PRODUCTIONS

In the United States a touring hit play or **musical** generally follows a successful New York commercial run. If during its Broadway, or in some cases its **Off-Broadway**, tenure the show generates some combination of good ticket sales, positive press attention, audience appeal, and/or the interest of a name lead actor or actress willing to tour, the show becomes a likely touring property. At this point a tour producer (the organizer and packager of the touring production) and local presenters (the theater managers, owners, or other entities that host the show during its run in each venue) work together to bring "Broadway" theater entertainment to communities across the country. According to the Broadway League, each year upwards of 240 large, medium, and even some small-sized cities in every region of the continental United States and Canada host at least one Equity Broadway touring show (a production of a show that either is currently playing or has played on Broadway). Non-Equity tours of varying quality also make the rounds each year, usually to smaller communities, university campuses, or small theaters in larger cities and towns.

The most visible of the touring concerns are the annual "Broadway seasons" presented as a series marketed largely through subscription sales by local presenters and theater managers. Each such season is likely to highlight one or two newly licensed first national tours of recent Broadway hits (*Legally Blonde*, which opened on Broadway in 2007, was touring nationally in the fall of 2008). The season is then fleshed out with older shows in their second, third, or perhaps tenth season of touring and the occasional Broadway-themed special event or concert. In larger touring cities, the Broadway series is often presented in a high-profile, multifunctional venue, which may intersperse the touring Broadway shows with performances by local or regional orchestras, dance companies, opera companies, and/or touring artists and concert acts.

A successful national or even regional tour can extend the commercial life and theatrical legacy of a show or its touring star well beyond its record of New York openings and revivals. Touring shows also provide desperately needed training grounds and employment opportunities for theater artists whose touring numbers on any given evening can outnumber those of the performers actually appearing in Broadway theaters. Furthermore, although a smash hit on Broadway is still a performer's surest road to theatrical stardom in America, a number of veteran touring artists—including Cathy Rigby (*Peter Pan*), Donny Osmond (*Joseph and the Amazing Technicolor Dreamcoat*), and the late Robert Goulet (*South Pacific* and *Man of La Mancha*)—garnered enough nationwide acclaim after years on the road to become *bona fide* "Broadway musical" stars without actually having spent very much time performing on Broadway.

While the thrill of seeing a new original hit, a breakthrough performance, or even a major revival on Broadway will likely never lose its singular allure, the re-creation of the "Broadway experience" through national tours remains one of Broadway's most important revenue generating enterprises and a key factor in Broadway's impact on American popular culture.

Historical Overview of American Touring Professional Theater

Professional theater in the United States was a road business years before any American city could support even a semiprofessional residential theatrical community on a permanent basis. Professional theater introduced itself to the colonies in the mid-1700s through English companies that toured or immigrated permanently to America, playing road adaptations of Shakespeare plays, melodramas, and comedy hits from the London stage. The English company of Walter Murray and Thomas Kean, generally viewed as the first professional company to perform in America, debuted in Philadelphia in 1749 (McDermott 1988, 186). Lewis Hallam's famous London Company of Comedians followed shortly thereafter, establishing itself as the first major entrepreneurial professional theater company in the colonies. Others followed thereafter. The paucity of theater venues in the eighteenth century meant that traveling companies often performed in pubs, open town squares, and courthouses (a touring tradition memorialized by the numerous active performance venues bearing the name "Courthouse Theater" in communities as diverse as St. Louis, Missouri; Appomattox, Virginia; Kingston, Rhode Island; Concord, North Carolina; Hudson Falls, New York; and Niagara-on-the-Lake, Ontario).

The eighteenth-century touring strategy was not appreciatively different from modern touring strategies: extended stays in the growing colonial population centers of New York, Boston, Philadelphia, or Williamsburg until business dried up or local licenses expired and, when available, the occasional short-term booking or one-night appearance in smaller communities along the way. These short stopovers added to company revenues, eased the rigors of extended travel, and instilled a nascent appetite for live theater in small, relatively isolated rural American communities. In the 1750s David Douglass, an enterprising British actor and **producer** in Hallam's company, took it upon himself to oversee construction of theater venues in some of the locales where his troop performed. Douglass was also a skilled negotiator of local political sensibilities and was a major force in bringing live theater to communities where Puritan resistance to entertainment—and theater in particular—was especially pronounced. (Douglass's bold self-insertions into local affairs in order to advance his theatrical interests anticipated by more than a hundred years absentee control of local theater production—a phenomenon that would play a large role in the centralization of American professional theater in New York at the end of the nineteenth century.)

The Revolutionary War curtailed most theatrical activity in the colonies. However, the period immediately following the ratification of the Constitution was marked by a population explosion throughout the new states, theater construction in numerous cities and towns, and an enlarged demand for live entertainment across the new country (McConachie 1998, 130–131). Circuses, acrobats, human "curiosities," variety shows, and star music hall singers all found their way into the turn-of-the-century touring business along with theater troupes. American-owned theater companies with both English and American actors sprang up after the Revolutionary War and new works by American-born **playwrights** entered into touring repertoires. By 1800, what could reasonably be called "theater districts" were forming in New York, Philadelphia, and Boston. Nevertheless, touring companies and actors remained the primary means by which professional theater established its place in early American culture, especially as the new country expanded westward.

1800s: Critics and Celebrity Culture

The first half of the nineteenth century brought forth newspaper theater criticism whose earliest practitioners included William Coleman writing for the *New York Evening Post* and Washington Irving writing under the pseudonym Jonathan Oldstyle in New York's *Morning Chronicle*. The practice of writing reviews and general news stories about touring shows and performers soon spread to more cities and even some smaller towns that played host to touring performers. Published reports of performances both in New York and on the road helped stars, plays, playwrights, and theater companies expand their reputations and their markets. By the mid-nineteenth century, a famous star or popular touring company could generally expect to be greeted in Baltimore, Denver, or St. Louis with some pre-arrival publicity and/or a review in the local papers. Increasing theatrical coverage throughout the century inevitably increased the fame of performers who—through heralded performances in the theater capitals of America and Europe, tours across the country, and occasional rumored tales of scandalous behavior—became the country's first generation of celebrity actors.

Celebrity status made it easier for topflight actors to tour as individuals rather than as members of a full touring production company. Touring companies competed, often unsuccessfully, with stars who traveled alone or with one or two assistant actors, filling in other parts with local performers. **Edwin Forrest** (1806–1872) toured successfully as a leading man in the South and Midwest while still in his teens, eventually playing major roles to great acclaim in New York,

Philadelphia, and London by the time he was 30 years old. Forrest was a highly visible member of East Coast and European social sets. Rumors and documented incidents of his scandalous personal life were fodder for newspaper articles and back-fence gossip for years. Charlotte Cushman (1806–1876), a self-taught actress, began her career as a resident actress in New York City and spent several years in London theater before returning to the United States to become a very successful independent touring star in the years following the Civil War. **Edwin Booth** (1833–1893), a highly regarded tragedian was adored as an actor until his brother, also an actor, assassinated Abraham Lincoln in 1865. Booth toured aggressively in the 1870s and 1880s to reestablish his reputation and recoup financial losses he incurred in various family enterprises. Between 1882 and 1913 James O'Neill (1847–1920), father of playwright **Eugene O'Neill**, became wildly famous touring across the country in *The Count of Monte Cristo*, performing the role over 6,000 times. (James's career became associated with the alcoholic patriarch in son Eugene's ***Long Day's Journey into Night*** [1956]. However, theater historians debate the extent to which the fictional father, whose talent and health had been thoroughly decimated on the road, reflected James O'Neill's actual experience as a touring actor.)

By the end of the Civil War, American theater was still a largely decentralized enterprise. In the late nineteenth century upwards of 200 touring stars and companies toured regionally or nationally throughout the country in any given year, and professional resident stock companies flourished in cities and some small communities from coast to coast (Poggi 1968, xv). Touring stage theater shared the road, and later the rails, with vaudeville shows, lecturers and educational programs such as lyceums (and later Chautauquas), minstrel shows, and variety shows. In the meantime, tour management and route or "circuit" planning was becoming a subindustry in and of itself as more theatrical venues great and small sprang up around the country.

In the latter half of the nineteenth century, the success of the touring star actor had put intense competitive pressure on resident theater companies in all but the largest cities as well as companies that toured as ensembles without major celebrity stars. The increased power of the touring star actor accrued to the benefit of New York's theater industry, which was increasingly drawing theatrical talent, investors, and entrepreneurs to Manhattan. By 1870 New York already had the largest population of any American city as well as the greatest number of theaters and resident theater companies. Nevertheless, several other communities were still supporting strong resident companies that could produce their own successful original and touring productions. But that would not last long.

The management of tour routing, logistics, and economics had become increasingly complex by the 1870s and 1880s—one of many factors leading to the all but total disappearance of original large-scale professional theatrical production outside of New York City by the end of the century. Touring performers who had seen to their own booking and tour management responsibilities began turning those operations over to professional booking agents and tour managers. The major agencies operated out of New York, adding to the City's bounty of theatrical talent and resources. The expansion of the American railroad in the mid to late nineteenth century made touring an increasingly rail-dependent enterprise, providing further incentive for touring actors to live near the country's East Coast railroad hubs, one of which was, of course, New York. New York–based producers and investors were purchasing theaters throughout the country along the primary touring roots, further squeezing out locally based operations and centralizing more power in New York. In addition, the rush of immigrants arriving from Europe and settling in New York after the 1840s included many who found New York's burgeoning entertainment business more accepting of foreigners than many other lines of work.

The consecration of New York's permanent status as America's undisputed and unrivaled capital of all theater production—residential and touring—would come in the late nineteenth and early twentieth centuries in the form of an epic battle between two giant forces: the **Theatrical Syndicate** (known to admirers and detractors as "the Syndicate") and the **Shubert Brothers**.

The Syndicate and the Shubert Brothers

In 1896, six highly successful New York theater businessmen—each with varied interests and concerns in the industry—joined forces to establish the Theatrical Syndicate. Led by Abraham Erlanger, Charles Frohman, and Marc Klaw, the Syndicate sought to bring efficiency and order to what had become the chaotic multi-faceted business of professional theater. Among their numbers were show producers, financiers, theater owners, tour booking agents, and talent managers. Previously, at various times they had worked together and in competition with one another but now sought to unify their myriad theatrical operations while eliminating competition (or forcing competitors to operate on their terms). The Syndicate succeeded in solidifying their power very quickly. By 1900 they had consolidated financial control of the most profitable touring routes in the East and Midwest. By 1907 they could claim a near monopoly on theater production in America, controlling the operations of some 1,500 theaters and contractual management of many of the theater's most popular and famous performers. Increasingly, American touring theater became composed of Syndicate-managed tours of Syndicate-produced and licensed New York hits, touring with artists performing on Syndicate terms traveling on Syndicate-booked routes to theaters controlled all or in part by Syndicate members. (During the same period of time, vaudeville impresarios B. F. Keith and E. F. Albee exercised a comparable level of monopolistic control of vaudeville circuits and theaters. See **Vaudeville** entry.)

The Syndicate's monopolistic, iron-hand business practices earned them many enemies within the industry and critics in the general public. Nevertheless, the Syndicate had no significant rivals until the Shubert Brothers from Syracuse, among the few prosperous independent theater owners operating during the Syndicate era, decided to move to New York City and expand their operations into theater production, management, venue ownership, and tour booking.

The Shuberts moved most of their operations to New York City in 1900 while still maintaining control of the handful of theaters they owned in upstate New York. Through their considerable industriousness and ability to woo legions of disgruntled performers, producers, investors, and independent theater owners fed up with the Syndicate monopoly, the Shuberts mounted a purposeful challenge to the Syndicate in virtually all major facets of theater production and management. Tough competitors and businessmen, the Shuberts were nonetheless generally more accommodating in their dealings with associates and less hostile in dealings with competitors than had been the Syndicate. By 1911 the Shuberts reached near parity with the Syndicate, controlling 17 theaters in New York City and garnering increasing control and influence over all aspects of commercial theater. Beset by antimonopoly litigation from the government, intense competition with the Shuberts, and the death of Frohman on the ill-fated ship *Lusitania* in 1915, the Syndicate ultimately lost power to the Shuberts. By 1920 the Shuberts boasted ownership, management, or booking control of over 1,000 theaters in North America.

Like the Syndicate, the Shuberts maintained the marketing concept of touring theater as direct-from–New York entertainment to local hometowns, even if that meant a Broadway Shubert production that originated in a Broadway Shubert theater touring via Shubert booking arrangements to Shubert-owned or operated theaters in Minneapolis, Boston, Cleveland, etc. The Shuberts held their monopoly until the mid-1950s when, faced with federal antitrust suits, they were forced to relinquish control of many of their theater holdings and booking operations. Today the **Shubert Organization**, the name given to the reorganized operation when the Shubert family withdrew from the business, owns 17 Broadway theaters and a handful of theaters nationwide.

Although some large touring production companies operating today, like Broadway Across America and the **Nederlander Organization**, have interests in many cities and/or theaters nationwide, no single company or conglomerate holds the kind of control over Broadway touring today that the Syndicate or the Shuberts exerted in the late nineteenth and early to mid-twentieth century. But the concept of American professional touring theater as an aftereffect of New York success remains a lasting if not indelible legacy of the Syndicate-Shubert rivalry and the solidification of New York's permanent place as *America's* theater district.

Depression Era to Post–World War II

The Depression Era and the War years had cut into theatrical touring as many theaters throughout the country folded or converted to higher-profit, lower-maintenance movie houses. The Shuberts, the dominant force in both Broadway and touring theater even in the lean years of the 1930s, faced some competition in touring from producers eager to dislodge them from their perch. In 1939 New York Opera impresario Fortune Gallo and Denver theater owner Arthur Oberfelder launched the Legitimate Theatre Company of New York, declaring their company would "bring back the road" to the pre-Depression glory days. The Company put together an ambitious touring program featuring **Eva Le Gallienne** re-creating her Broadway performance in Henrik Ibsen's *The Master Builder*. They also sent out a touring company of **Clifford Odets**'s 1937 hit *Golden Boy* (but with none of the stars of the original production going out on this tour). The Legitimate Theatre Company's touring operation was well funded, well promoted, and well organized, but it, too, fell victim to the Depression and competition with movies playing in their tour destinations. The company folded its touring operations in less than two years.

In the Midwest, circle stock theater companies filled a void left by closed or reconverted theaters by skillfully negotiating the financial risks of touring in the geographically expansive and thinly populated heartland states. These companies offered vaudeville type revues, improvisational skits, new plays by local playwrights, but also stripped down versions of plays that had run on Broadway years earlier. Circle stock theater companies were locally owned enterprises that repeatedly toured a limited-mileage regional circuit of small theaters and summer tent venues throughout a season (i.e., a two-week Kansas circuit or a three-week Eastern Minnesota circuit). The Kansas-based Chick Boyes Players, which toured circuits in Kansas and Nebraska, was among the more durable of these companies during the 1930s and 1940s. In any given season Boyes would tour a mix of new works from Midwest authors and regional publishing companies as well as older Broadway fare, such as the popular 1920s family comedies *Why Men Leave Home* and *Getting Gertie's Garter* by Avery Hopwood and *Six-Cylinder Love* by William Anthony McGuire (Magnuson 1995, 73). They reached the peak of their popularity in the mid to late 1930s but were still prevalent in rural regions during the 1940s and the 1950s. Their "Broadway" plays were popular but never pretended to offer a New York style theatrical experience. The stripped down traveling sets and sparse costuming reflected the economics of the times, and national name actors were neither available nor affordable. The circle stock companies anticipated the role that **regional theaters** would play after World War II as testing grounds for new works, as they encouraged local or regional playwrights to provide original (and cheap or even free) plays for the circuit stock companies to perform. The circle stock companies began to die out after World War II. The burgeoning popularity of the new "Golden Age" of musicals of the 1950s combined with postwar economic recovery stimulated a growing national market for "New York quality" tours with name shows and name stars.

Postwar and Post-Shubert

The loosening of the Shubert Brothers' monopoly on American city touring operations in the mid-1950s gradually opened up the business of touring to new entrepreneurs and new ways of presenting shows across the country. The League of America Theatres and Producers (now called the Broadway League) established the nonprofit Independent Booking Office (IBO) in New York in 1957, which filled the void of booking operations that had previously been controlled by the Shuberts.

The IBO, which served as a clearinghouse for Broadway shows touring out of New York, would work with New York producers eager to get shows out on the road. The League and its affiliate presenters throughout the country used a touring season formula generally consisting of two musicals (such as *My Fair Lady* and *Li'l Abner*), a comedy (*No Time for Sergeants*), and a mystery or drama (*The Diary of Anne Frank*). Collecting fees from both the presenting theaters and the New York producers, the IBO ensured local theaters could accommodate the demands of touring shows (and vice versa), oversaw financial negotiations and payments, and generally spared the New York producer and local presenter the inconvenience of having to deal directly with one another over long distances. Most medium- and large-sized cities had one or more prewar vintage auditorium that could accommodate the relatively modest (by today's standards) logistical demands of new, major touring shows, and the IBO succeeded in opening up new markets and venues for touring. Business generally rose and fell with the availability of hit name shows and popular stars.

Although some years proved stronger than others in the 1960s, popular first national tours of such shows as *The Sound of Music*, *Camelot*, *Mame* (with **Angela Lansbury**), and *Hello, Dolly!* (with **Carol Channing**) gave the touring industry a reasonably strong foundation in the years immediately following the breakup of the Shubert monopoly. The IBO began to wane in influence in the 1970s and was out of business by 1985. Touring was becoming a more diversified enterprise. Some New York producers wanted to become more directly involved in what appeared to be the new, promising growth of the touring business and increasingly began working directly with the host presenters across the country. For their part, many local presenters grew more ambitious about their own operations, especially as cities began renovating, upgrading, or replacing old, vaudeville-era theaters.

The reconfiguration of touring business in the absence of a single controlling national monopoly, such as the Shuberts or the Syndicate, created opportunities for new entrepreneurs who did not operate on a monopolistic business model. American Theater Productions (ATP) and NAC Entertainment, two independent tour producers and promoters founded in the 1970s, succeeded in the post-Shubert era without aspiring to gain control of every theater, agent, tour route, or artist with whom they worked. American Theater Productions was established in Chicago by Tom Mallow in 1965 but soon thereafter relocated to New York. ATP specialized in "bus and truck" tours (second-run or second -class tours, generally less expensively produced than first national tours, that usually go up after a first national tour has been on the road for a while. ATP earned a reputation for upgrading the production values of second-class tours, which historically had a hit and miss reputation with local presenters and audiences. ATP specialized in bringing high-quality Broadway touring productions to middle-sized towns like Cincinnati, Louisville, and Columbus. ATP mounted tours of recent Broadway hits, usually featuring noted theater or Hollywood performers but not the original Broadway lead actors. The company had early success with a tour of Ira Wallach's sophisticated comedy *Absence of a Cello* (Broadway 1964, tour 1965). The show starred Hans Conried, a veteran stage and film comic who had in recent years become famous for memorable roles in top-rated television sitcoms such as *I Love Lucy* and Danny Thomas's *Make Room for Daddy.* Arguably, Conried's tour did more to enhance the play's legacy than had the Broadway production, which starred a highly capable but less well-known comic actor, Fred Clark. Hitting full stride in the mid to late 1960s, ATP put together a very successful tour of *Hello, Dolly!* (Broadway 1964, tour 1968) starring film legend Dorothy Lamour. ATP also mounted the first-ever bus and truck tour of *Hair* (Broadway 1968, tour c.1970). The Company maintained its niche as a premiere "Broadway show" tour producer for medium-sized cities through the 1970s and 1980s and is credited with greatly expanding the national market for high-quality touring Broadway productions in smaller communities.

Founded in 1976 in Binghamton, New York, NAC Entertainment has sustained a remarkable longevity as a producer and presenter of premiere quality, Equity touring shows for a specific region. Maintaining a touring strategy reminiscent of the circle stock companies of the 1930s, NAC confines its primary touring interests to a seasonal circuit in upstate New York (Buffalo, Rochester, Syracuse, and Binghamton) and western Pennsylvania (Erie and Scranton), for whom NAC provides the communities' premiere Broadway season. NAC supplements its small Broadway touring circuit with regional presentations of major touring specials or "family shows" (Ice Capades, Harlem Globetrotters, etc.). Founder and CEO Albert Nocciolino also occasionally coproduces Broadway productions, most notably the 2007 Broadway hit *Legally Blonde*. But producing and booking Broadway tours for its home region is NAC's signature business. The company's longevity has allowed it to establish strong partnerships with local presenters. The managers of Buffalo's Shea Performing Arts Center and the Rochester (NY) Broadway Theatre League both credit the NAC-Broadway series as critical factors in the marshalling of funds and community support for major renovations in their venues.

Although many producers remember the early 1970s as a slow and struggling period for Broadway in general and touring in particular, the late 1970s presented the first rumblings that the Broadway touring industry was going to experience rapid growth in expense, logistical complexity, and audience expectation. The successful first tours of *Grease* in 1973 and 1974, *A Chorus Line* in 1976, and *Annie* in 1978 were among the harbingers of a new era of prosperity, tumult, and change.

1980–2000: Megamusicals and Megachanges

The sea change in modern touring would occur in the 1980s when the **European megamusicals** produced by Londoner **Cameron Mackintosh** began touring in the United States. The staggeringly successful New York openings of Mackinstosh's **Cats** (1982), *Les Misérables* (1987), and **The Phantom of the Opera** (1988) had an immediate transformational impact on Broadway. The shows featured dazzling, distractingly elaborate sets and special effects that overshadowed considerations of star performances or script/song continuity. The shows made Broadway a favorite destination for family vacations and school trips, a perpetually elusive market for Broadway (especially in the years before the redevelopment and "clean up" of Times Square in the 1980s and 1990s). Mackintosh branded and marketed his shows to the general public, rather than just the theatergoing public, as if each show were a separate multinational corporation. All of this was new to Broadway. That these productions would have a seismic effect on touring once they went on the road was inevitable. And, indeed, they did.

The national tours of *Cats*, the first of which went out in 1983, changed the Broadway touring business forever. Within a few weeks of the start of the first tour, demand for the show from all over the country was unprecedented. Markets accustomed to presenting first national tours were joined in their eagerness to book the show by new would-be presenters. Communities with little or no experience in high-end Broadway touring, were suddenly hungry to get in on the new phenomenon. Many markets that could secure a booking of the show realized their local audiences could probably support the show for weeks—in some cases even months—rather than the typical run of several days to a few weeks that a new touring hit might normally run. Mackintosh mounted another company several weeks after the first national company went out, and the two companies stayed out for more than two years.

When a third company of *Cats* went on the road the following year, Mackintosh and many local presenters were prepared to accommodate expanded stays of several weeks. Many local presenters and venues had to tailor their entire seasonal offerings to accommodate the new scheduling configurations brought about by extended bookings for *Cats*. In addition, Mackintosh was now requiring that road presentations of his shows replicate to near exactitude the Broadway production. He oversaw the modification of the design of his touring sets to accommodate many older host venues that otherwise would have had trouble even fitting his sets through their loading doors much less mounting the production. Mackintosh was also able to modify the setup and strike time of his productions so that even smaller venues could host *Cats* for a week without having to close the theater for days just to get the show in and out of the building. *Cats'* voluminous junkyard set and signature heaven-bound hydropowered gigantic tire were rendered manageable for cities with older theaters.

Cats generated previously unheard of levels of business "for the road." Mackintosh and his presenters made a lot of money and more was on the way. In 1987, Mackintosh sent out *Les Misérables*, his next megamusical, complete with an enormous cast and a rotating barricade wall the size of a small apartment building. *Cats* had already prepared local presenters and audiences for another precedent-shattering road success, and "*Les Miz*" did not disappoint. One North American touring company stayed out on the road for over 15 years while international productions and tours proliferated throughout the globe. Mackintosh's continued insistence that local productions mirror the original production gave local audiences and presenters ever-greater confidence that they were seeing a *bona fide* Broadway show—confidence that translated readily into higher ticket prices at touring venues and more people willing to pay them.

By 1989 *Cats* and *Les Miz* were still doing excellent road business with multiple profit-making touring companies and sit-down productions (open-ended, long runs playing in what would normally be touring venues) of both shows going strong. *The Phantom of the Opera* had opened on Broadway in 1988 and a tour was scheduled for 1990. By this time the theater industry had realized that what had started as a one-show phenomenon with *Cats* had redefined, for good and ill, the manner in which all high-end Broadway show touring would be conducted from here on out. As extraordinary as had been the touring success of *Cats* and *Les Miz*, the first *Phantom* tours set, again, whole new levels of income and expectation. By 1992, two national tours were filling houses across the country. A sit-down company had been established in Los Angeles and another in Toronto (it would stay in Toronto for ten years). By this time, many local communities were floating bond issues to radically upgrade their venues and/or build lavish performing arts centers to ensure a suitable nesting place for *Phantom* and whatever touring miracles might follow in the years ahead. By 1994, the Broadway League was reporting that gross annual touring revenues had tripled since 1987 and the number of ticket sales of touring productions had more than doubled in the same period of time. Perhaps more significantly, as one Midwest producer observed, in cities and even smaller communities across the country a quality annual Broadway season had come to be seen as a key factor in downtown redevelopment planning and a *sine qua non* for any state-of-the-art performing arts renovation or construction project.

Although still a prolific producer to this day, Mackintosh has not developed any new shows of the production or marketing magnitude of his "big three" megamusicals: *Cats*, *Les Misérables*, and *Phantom*—all of which have aged well on the road. In 2009, at least one company of each musical was touring successfully in North America. The Disney Company, inspired by Mackintosh's success with visually splendid, mass-appeal musicals, entered into the theatrical business in the 1990s, forming **Disney Theatrical Productions** as its theater producing unit. Disney's first hit, *Beauty and the Beast*, which opened on Broadway in 1994 and went on national tour in 1995, was highly successful and helped sustain within the industry some of the psychological and financial momentum of Mackintosh's earlier touring juggernauts.

However, by this time, the string of superhits for touring was running short. New Broadway successes like *Sunset Boulevard*, *Rent*, and *Kiss of the Spider Woman* did not tour as well as Mackintosh's monsters, lacking the broad appeal and visual thrall of the giants that had preceded them. Of course, some new productions and new revivals were successful on tour during the 1990s. Cathy Rigby, star and producer of her own *Peter Pan* revival, became one of the most bankable, "subscription leader" touring shows of the decade. But it would be after the turn of the new century before Broadway would send out *The Lion King*—another touring blockbuster reminiscent of the kind that had reshaped the touring industry in the 1980s.

In the meantime, the overall expense of touring, with ever more costly payments required to producers of touring shows and higher overhead at newly renovated or constructed performing arts venues, meant that in some cities theater tickets for touring productions started to rise precipitously. Presenters had a harder time

THE BROADWAY BRAND

In 1995, the Broadway League (then known as the League of American Theatres and Producers) under the leadership of its president, Jed Bernstein, attempted to elevate the term "Broadway" from the amorphous colloquialism it had been for over a century to a quasi-corporate brand, complete with a logo and national campaign to promote Broadway theater as an entity in and of itself. Broadway would now be called "Live Broadway," a brand that for promotional purposes would encompass all shows and subsidiary theater activities conducted by the League and its member producers. Modeling its campaign after Major League Baseball, which had been successfully promoting itself as an entity (rather than just promoting its franchise teams), the Live Broadway campaign sought to make of "Broadway" an institution and an icon.

Most of the campaign's initiatives were New York City–based (i.e., soliciting corporate sponsorship of the League itself, an annual outdoor Kids' Night on Broadway concert, etc.), but the campaign had spillover benefits for the touring end of the industry. Most local presenters offering annual seasons of touring Broadway shows had been using the term "Broadway" in their promotions for years, either on their own or through the aegis of their touring producers ("Broadway Season," "Broadway Series," "Direct from Broadway," etc.). The national branding campaign only strengthened the promotional impact of the term in local markets. News within the industry of League successes in garnering corporate sponsorships and partnerships for its own enterprises as well as those of member producers provided new incentives, strategies, and encouragement for local presenters to accelerate their solicitations of local sponsorships. Moreover, Bernstein had felt that touring was a generally underappreciated and underserved aspect of Broadway theater relative to the revenue it generated for producers and its value as a promoter of tourism for New York and Broadway. Bernstein increased the research and data collection the League does on behalf of touring shows and instituted a series of annual awards for touring production (Best New Touring Musical, Best Play, Best Direction, etc.).

selling full subscriptions in the new economy of the 1990s as local theatergoers increasingly began to pick and choose a headline show (such as *Peter Pan* or *A Chorus Line*) and perhaps one or two other scheduled shows rather than buy an entire subscription at the beginning of the season. Both producers and presenters lamented that by the mid-1990s, there was no longer any such thing as a low-cost touring Broadway show, and the days of having a full season's expenses met in advance by brisk subscription sales had all but faded.

2000 to the Present

By the turn of the century, the cost of Broadway touring had risen as rapidly as had the expectations of the Broadway touring audience. The extraordinary production values of the first megamusicals, now touring for 15 years, had led audiences to demand a higher level of product even in shows where spectacular effects were not a key selling point. Moreover, through computer video, DVD sales, and You-Tube, local audiences—even those who had not seen a particular production on Broadway—have a strong sense of what an original Broadway production looks like and sounds like (or believe they do), and both producers and local presenters are faced with meeting that demand. Touring revenues declined between 1997 and 2001, largely because the new hits going on tour during that period (such as the aforementioned *Rent*, *Kiss of the Spiderwoman*, *Sunset Boulevard*) often did not generate the business on the road that producers and presenters had hoped for. Industry concerns surfaced to the effect that the paucity of top demand shows and the vicissitudes of any given season might make touring all but impossible especially for small- or medium-sized producing and booking companies.

In an effort to reduce costs for both New York producers and presenters (and, thus, reduce producers' incentives to send out lower-cost, non-Equity tours), Actors' Equity, long resistant to compromising the provisions of its production contracts, negotiated a compromise with producers. In 2004, League producers and Equity agreed to an experimental "tiered" contract that permits tour produc-ers, in certain shows and under specific conditions, to hire Equity actors at less than the terms dictated by the standard Equity production contract. Despite initial skepticism on the part of some Equity members, by 2008 the association acknowl-edged that the new agreement had kept a higher number of Equity actors on tour and helped Equity maintain its health benefits and other services to its actors. The compromise is now widely considered to be a necessary trade-off against the benefits of keeping Equity actors employed on the road (Gans and Hetrick 2008). As much as the touring business has reinvented itself over the years, a few truisms seem to hold up under any circumstances. A strong touring season that offers appealing, road-friendly new shows generally means a healthy year. Since 2000, *Mamma Mia!* (first national tour 2002), Disney's *The Lion King* (first national tour 2002), and *Wicked* (first national tour 2005) have been among the biggest box-office road hits, spawning follow-up tours and filling 3–6 week stays (or longer) in large and even medium-sized communities. *Jersey Boys* (first national tour 2006) and *Legally Blonde* (first national tour 2008) have also started strong and show signs of having several good years on the road. On the other hand, the first national tours of **The Producers** (2002), *Hairspray* (2003), and *The 25th Annual Putnam County Spelling Bee* (2006) were disappointments, despite enormous pop-ularity with general audiences during their New York runs.

Notwithstanding periodic warnings about the unfeasibility of touring in the twenty-first century economic environment, American communities have just entered their fourth century of welcoming touring theater troupes into their midst. The historical precedent and cultural imperative for professional actors to tour should militate against a complete collapse of the enterprise. Certainly changes in production, presenting, and marketing are likely to maintain their frenetic pace as the industry adapts to highly uncertain economic conditions. But as long as Broadway lives by the motto "the show must go on," it might as well add as an approved contract rider "the show must also go on the road."

Thomas A. Greenfield

Further Reading

Broadwayworld.com.

Broadway League Touring Broadway Statistics. Retrieved October 25, 2009, from http://www.broadwayleague.com/index.php?url_identifier=touring-broadway-statistics.

Conte, David M., and Stephen Langley. *Theatre Management: Producing and Managing the Performing Arts*. Hollywood, CA: EntertainmentPro, 2007.

Gans, Andrew, and Adam Hetrick. "Actors' Equity and Broadway League Reach Tentative Agreement; Highlights Announced." *Playbill Online*, July 2, 2008. Retrieved March 1, 2009, from http://www.playbill.com/news/article/119141.html.

Isaacson, Mike. "The Road Not Taken." *Guide to Producing Plays and Musicals*, ed. Frederic B. Vogel and Ben Hodges. New York: Applause Theatre & Cinema Books, 2006. League of American Theaters and Producers/Touring.

Leonhardt, David. "Broadway's Touring Shows Find Seats Harder to Sell." *NYTimes.com*, August 20, 2006. Retrieved March 8, 2009, from http://www.nytimes.com/2006/08/20/theater/20leon.html?_r=1&scp=1&sq=%22touring%20shows%20f ind%20seat s%20harder%20to%20sell%22&st=cse.

Magnuson, Linus. *Circle Stock Theater: Touring America Small Towns, 1900–1960*. Jefferson, NC: McFarland, 1995.

McConachie, Bruce. "American Theatre in Context, from the Beginnings to 1870." *The Cambridge History of American Theatre: Vol 1. Beginnings to 1870*, ed. Don B. Wilmeth and C. W. E. Bigsby. Cambridge, England: Cambridge University Press, 1998.

McDermott, Douglas. "Structure and Management in the American Theatre from the Beginnings to 1870." *The Cambridge History of American Theatre: Volume I Beginnings to 1870*, ed. Don B. Wilmeth and C. W. E. Bigsby. Cambridge, England: Cambridge University Press, 1998.

Micocci, Tony. *Booking Performance Tours: Marketing and Acquiring Live Arts and Entertainment*. New York: Allworth Press, 2008.

Poggi, Jack. *Theater in America: The Impact of Economic Forces, 1870–1967*. Ithaca, NY: Cornell University Press, 1968.

Robertson, Campbell. "We All Got Together and Put on a Brand." *NYTimes.com*, July 2, 2006. Retrieved March 8, 2009, from http://www.nytimes.com/2006/07/02/theater/02robe.html.

Shagan, Rena. *Booking & Tour Management for the Performing Arts*. New York: Allworth Press, 2001.

Travis, Steve. "The Rise and Fall of the Theatrical Syndicate." *Educational Theater Journal*, 10, no. 1 (March 1958): 35–40.

Wilson, Garff B. *Three Hundred Years of American Drama and Theater from Ye Bare and Ye Cubb to Chorus Line*. 2nd ed. Englewood Cliffs, NJ: Prentice-Hall, 1982.

The editor gratefully acknowledges and thanks Michael D. Kobluk, formerly of American Theater Productions and the Spokane Opera House; Gary McAvay of Columbia Artists Theatricals; Albert Nocciolino of NAC Entertainment; Leslie Broecker of Broadway Across America; and Robert Sagan and Linda Glosser D'Angelo of the Rochester Broadway Theatre League in Rochester, New York, who contributed important information for this entry in nonpublished form.

TOURISM

Over the course of the last century tourists have been drawn to New York City to visit famous landmarks and museums, to shop and dine, and to see Broadway productions. Since establishing itself as the beating heart of the nation's theater district, Times Square has undergone enormous transformations to lure tourist dollars. As of January 2007, Times Square was named the most popular tourist attraction in the world according to the *Forbes Traveler*'s 50 Most Visited Attractions List, with more than 35 million visitors a year. Broadway's commercial success has been a key factor in the ever-climbing number of tourists descending upon New York City despite its beginnings as a local center of entertainment. The story of the ebb and flow of Broadway tourism is inextricably tied to the changing landscape of Times Square and the promotion of tourism within the wider framework of America's history and culture.

Early Broadway and Its Audience

At the turn of the twentieth century, commercial Broadway was off to a promising start. Theaters were located mainly downtown from Long Acre Square, which was renamed Times Square with the opening of the *New York Times* building in 1904. Some 40 "legitimate" Broadway theaters stretched from 13th Street uptown to 45th Street, and approximately 100 productions opened in the 1900–1901 season. While this number may sound high, production turnover was common, and the majority of plays and **musicals** offered little in the way of literary substance or artistic merit. For the most part local audiences attended the sentimental dramas and comedies, and most came to see headline star performers rather than the productions themselves. Broadway theater audiences paid $1.50 to $2 for the best seats, with many other affordable entertainments competing for their money within the span of a few years. Nickelodeon theaters (showing short silent films) and **vaudeville** theaters were charging pocket change for admission and enjoyed a sizable audience. At the other end of the spectrum, the opera catered to the upper class at $5 a seat. Music and spectacle dazzled audiences in such entertainments as **operettas**, revues, extravaganzas, and follies. One of the most famous, the *Ziegfeld Follies*, reincarnated itself annually for decades, drawing audiences to see scantily clad beauties in the chorus as well as top-name singers, dancers, and comedians.

In this early period, the Great White Way earned a reputation for opulence and decadence. (The "Great White Way" was a nickname given to the Broadway theater area in the early 1900s either because of the dazzling new electric lights around Times Square or because of a 1902 newspaper report of the area after a massive snowstorm.) Rich men frequented the follies, propositioning chorus girls with lavish gifts, living expenses, and occasional offers of marriage. Conservative factions of the community spoke out about the lack of decency on stage. Salacious plays were occasionally shut down by the police, though such controversy usually created a demand for tickets. Broadway became a center of excitement and titillation. With a wealth of variety in theatrical offerings, early Broadway had something for everyone.

The draw of tourism to New York City was still in its infancy in the earliest part of the twentieth century. Though the first Broadway audiences were predominantly residents of New York City or business travelers, rapid developments soon brought out-of-town tourists as well. One significant development was the opening of the subway system to the theater district in 1904, making access to the Great White Way easy and affordable. With Times Square as both a commercial crossroads and a blossoming entertainment empire, the marketing and promotion of New York City as a tourist destination began growing in the first decade of the twentieth century. New York City already boasted such landmarks as the Statue of Liberty, the Metropolitan Museum of Art, and Central Park, and Broadway fed into the mix of diversions that made it a "world-class" destination for travel. Early promotions were rather primitive by modern standards. Picture postcards promoted the city as a center of culture and entertainment, and promotions that tied in rail tickets with hotel stays helped lure travelers to the city for more than a day trip. Based on rail and hotel records, by 1910 an estimated 100,000 to 200,000 tourists a day visited the city.

Broadway theater continued to gain momentum, and by the 1920s Broadway was booming, as were national **touring productions** based out of New York City. The festive attitude of the roaring 1920s provided the perfect platform for commercial entertainment, and new theater buildings were built at a record rate. Follies shows, especially **Florenz Ziegfeld**'s, were wildly popular as were roof garden theaters with late-night entertainments—a fad of the extravagant times. By 1923 an estimated 700,000 people a day were attending New York City theaters, at least one-quarter of them nonresidents. Broadway openings reached an all-time high, with more than 260 productions in the 1927–1928 season. The wide variety of entertainment was key with offerings ranging from spectacle-based extravaganzas to the rich literature of **Shakespeare**. Stars, particularly beautiful actresses, remained a major attraction, supported by the glorification, gossip, and scandals about actors published in newspapers and magazines.

Off Broadway, the Little Theater Movement—a movement toward artistic rather than purely commercial theater—was blossoming both in New York City and around the country. As these small art theaters experimented with European modernism, a new rank of American **playwrights**, directors, and actors came to the fore, some eventually finding their way to the Broadway stage. One prime example was playwright **Eugene O'Neill**, who got his start at the Provincetown Playhouse before seeing his first of many plays performed in Broadway's more commercial venues.

The 1920s continued to roar on Broadway until the one-two punch hit theaters in 1929: the stock market crash and the advent of "talkies," or talking pictures.

The Depression and the War Years

During the Depression, construction of new Broadway theaters, which had been flourishing for two decades, stopped dead in its tracks. Many of the palatial theaters that had recently been built either closed or became movie or burlesque houses. Burlesque, an adult variety genre, degenerated into striptease and raunchy sketch comedy. Although catering to tastes of working-class men, burlesque also enticed businessmen, college students, servicemen, and a few women to attend, thus threatening to take a portion of the "legitimate" Broadway audience including the few tourists who remained. Times Square eventually turned into a series of low-grade entertainment venues and diners, more akin to a street carnival than a glamorous entertainment capital. To aggravate matters, a flood of theater artists migrated to Hollywood to seek work in films. Despite the quality of many stage productions, the number of Broadway openings declined during the 1930s, making commercial profit on Broadway an uphill battle. By the 1940–1941 season, the *New York Times* reported only 49 new productions opened, down from a record of 264 in the 1920s.

Amid the dire effects of the Great Depression, a few bright spots remained for Broadway audiences. Major American playwrights such as Eugene O' Neill, **Lillian Hellman**, **Maxwell Anderson**, **George S. Kaufman**, and Moss Hart premiered some of their best works. Jack Kirkland's *Tobacco Road*, about a poor family of sharecroppers in rural Georgia, struck a chord with Depression-era audiences and played for a record-breaking run of 3,182 performances in 1933. Several musicals also stand out from this period, reflecting the times. One of the first was the political satire *Of Thee I Sing* (1931), which won the 1932 Pulitzer Prize for Drama for writers George S. Kaufman and Morrie Ryskind and lyricist **Ira Gershwin**. Set in the White House, it presented a president who put a new spin on public relations. Perhaps the most unusual Broadway musical of the period was *Pins and Needles* (1937), produced and performed by the International Ladies' Garment Workers' Union and Labor Stage Inc. At a time when unionization was controversial, this musical revue took a pro-union stance toward current events. A melodic score by Harold Rome and enthusiastic word of mouth brought audiences in for 1,108 performances. Other unique plays and musicals included works of the **Federal Theatre Project** (FTP), a part of President Franklin D. Roosevelt's Works Progress Administration (WPA) to get Americans back to work. Unfortunately, Congress accused the FTP of a leftist slant and pulled their funding, closing the FTP in 1939.

When the United States entered World War II, Broadway responded with escapist comedies and thrillers, along with patriotic revues. One production that celebrated Americana was composer **Richard Rodgers** and lyricist **Oscar Hammerstein**'s first collaboration: *Oklahoma!* (1947). Audiences came in droves to see the groundbreaking musical, which played for five years and broke all existing Broadway records. Rodgers and Hammerstein proved that song and dance could be integrated to support the plot and that the story was the most important component of a musical. *Oklahoma!* set new standards for producers, creators, and fans of musical theater, and in the Golden Era of musicals that followed in the years thereafter tourists to Broadway enjoyed musicals such as *Annie Get Your Gun* (1946), *Kiss Me Kate* (1948), *South Pacific* (1949), *Guys and Dolls* (1950), *My Fair Lady* (1956), and *West Side Story* (1957). Musicals became the golden draw for audiences, offering story, song, dance, spectacle, and stars. Foreign visitors could also enjoy musicals without knowing English, a concept that was capitalized upon in the 1980s with spectacle-heavy productions such as *Cats* (1982), *Starlight Express* (1987), and *The Phantom of the Opera* (1988).

Post–World War II: New Marketing Strategies

The booming post–World War II American economy brought a new tide of tourists to New York City. In addition to the draw of musicals, Broadway gained critical and artistic renown with a group of new American playwrights, including **Tennessee Williams**, **Arthur Miller**, and **William Inge**. Although **television** competed against theater as a form of entertainment, it occasionally helped promote Broadway productions. In particular, *The Ed Sullivan Show*, which ran live on Sunday nights and, thus, did not compete with Broadway theater performances, welcomed Broadway actors, composers, and playwrights. **Ed Sullivan** often broadcast scenes from popular productions with the current Broadway casts and, thereby, introduced Broadway to living rooms across America. (Sullivan had a long-standing connection with Broadway, having been a highly influential newspaper theater reporter and New York gossip columnist before launching his television show.) Rapid transit, a postwar economy, and increased leisure time made New York City a destination for a new type of tourist: the American family. Unfortunately, many of the down-at-the-heels establishments of Times Square from the previous era could not be considered family fare.

By mid-twentieth century New York City was marketing and promoting Broadway to tourists as a consumer product. Posters had long been used to promote Broadway shows and continued to do so. By the early 1970s, when crime and general degeneration of the Times Square area had scared away tourists, television commercials began promoting Broadway musicals, boosting ticket sales. On the heels of the first TV commercials, the Theater Development Fund opened its first TKTS booth for discounted same-day tickets in 1973, again luring tourists to downtrodden Broadway with the hopes of scoring a bargain for increasingly pricey theater tickets, especially for hit shows. The "half-price" booth, as it is generally known, does a thriving business to this day.

To battle New York City's deteriorating image, the "I ♥ NY" advertising campaign took off in 1977, its icon remaining popular on T-shirts, hats, and buttons for decades after. The merchandising of Broadway T-shirts and memorabilia also grew, with some 4.95 million people attending Broadway shows in the 1976–1977 season. Tourism brought $4.5 billion into the city in 1977, with more than 16.5 million visitors. Mayor Edward I. Koch and city planners saw that the commercial draw of New York must continue, and soon the plans for Times Square redevelopment were underway.

Times Square Renovation

The history of Times Square's reinvention is so complex that it has become the subject of several books and essays. Before city plans developed, Playwrights Horizons, a theater group formed in 1971, moved to 42nd Street, pioneering a group of small theaters there known as Theater Row. This row of Off- and Off-Off-Broadway theaters was developed in conjunction with the nonprofit group called the 42nd Street Development Corporation (founded 1976). Together they formed the first link in a chain that led to further revitalization and economic growth.

When city and state officials became involved, as did private corporations, a tension of interests developed and complicated the planning process. In 1980 Mayor Koch rejected a plan by The City at 42nd Street, Inc., an offshoot of the 42nd Street Development Corporation. The plan called for the creation of, essentially, a high-tech urban amusement park. Koch withheld his approval based on the planned demolition of historical theaters and loss of local culture. The mayor held that tourists coming to Times Square should not experience Florida's Disney, but something unique to New York City—that visitors should "have seltzer instead of orange juice." With Koch's input, plans went forward with a new goal: to restore historic theaters and thereby revive the turn-of-the-century flavor of the Great White Way.

In 1984 new plans were approved, and none too soon for Broadway, which was in a slump. Sex shops, greasy spoons, and downtrodden businesses were evicted for the construction of gigantic versions of American chains, including Toys "R" Us and Applebee's. In 1995 the Disney Corporation officially announced the refurbishing of the New Amsterdam Theater, a palatial venue located dead center in the theater district at 42nd Street and Broadway. It had been built in 1903 but had since fallen into disrepair. A grand reopening ceremony took place in 1997, complete with a Disney parade on 42nd Street, and soon the New Amsterdam became home to the long-running Disney musical, *The Lion King* (1997). In 1998 the Ford Center for the Performing Arts (renamed the Hilton Theatre in 2005) opened, sponsored in part by the Ford Motor Company. It was constructed on the sites of the former Lyric and Apollo Theaters in Times Square and incorporated some architectural aspects of both turn-of-the-century theaters.

Despite the renewed prosperity of a "cleaned up" Broadway, critics have lamented that the flavor of New York City—its many cultures and classes—has been distilled to a family-friendly, homogeneous pseudoculture. Although Broadway has always been a commercial venue, they argue that the glamour of Broadway during its heyday in the 1920s, including some degree of its adults-only, untamed edginess, has been lost to corporate sponsorship and mass marketing strategies for attracting national and international tourist dollars.

Post-9/11

Despite criticism from Broadway traditionalists, the revitalized Times Square steadily drew audiences back to Broadway throughout the 1990s until September 11, 2001. The city came to a standstill as everyone grappled with the implications of the terrorist attack on the World Trade Center. Broadway went dark. Performers questioned how they could act, sing, and dance as if nothing had happened. The highly anticipated opening of a Broadway revival of **Stephen Sondheim**'s Off-Broadway hit *Assassins*, a musical based on the assassinations of U.S. presidents, was deemed inappropriate for a post-9/11 audience and was postponed. (It opened on Broadway in 2004.) Mayor Rudolph W. Giuliani stepped forward to urge that life go on as usual, asking that theaters reopen on September 13. Many producers and companies complied but the once-thriving tourist economy had been decimated. People were afraid to fly on planes at all, and New York City was perceived as a potential target for another attack that could occur at any moment. Fearing financial collapse, Broadway executives marched to their city and state governments for money and were successful, in part because hotels, restaurants, and other businesses relied on Broadway tourism. At a time when budget deficits loomed on the horizon, the city bought 50,000 Broadway tickets ($2.5 million) and the state gave $1 million toward a promotional campaign. Without the same commercial clout, Off-Broadway theaters did not fare well, and many were forced to close productions without extra funding.

Broadway's road from decimation back to commercial viability was a bumpy one. On September 28, actors from every Broadway show gathered in Times Square to sing "New York, New York," from the **Betty Comden and Adolph Green** musical *On the Town* (1949), for a television commercial campaign that aired in 20 countries. The subsidies and the campaign eventually paid off, and audiences gradually returned. Predictably, American audiences came back to Broadway first as domestic traveling fears began to ease in the months following 9/11. However, it took four years to get foreign tourists back to the pre-9/11 level. By 2005–2006 the League of American Theaters and Producers (now called the Broadway League) reported that 57 percent of the 12 million tickets were bought by tourists. International visitors accounted for 1.32 million tickets, compared to 525,834 international visitor ticket sales in the 2001–2002 season.

Despite this turnaround, ticket sales took another hit in November 2007 when the stagehands union went on strike and shut down most of Broadway for three weeks during the peak Thanksgiving/pre-Christmas holiday season. City officials estimated that the city lost $2 million in revenue each day. Angry tourists left with invalid, expensive show tickets along with decimated vacation plans. Many canceled or shortened their trips, spent their time and money away from the theater district, or even strode down to the closed theaters to take souvenir photographs along the picket lines.

Luring Tourists with Movie Titles

As a commercial venue, Broadway's chief objective has always been to fill seats. In the twenty-first century, Internet advertising and sales of tickets have literally put Broadway planning at tourists' fingertips, boosting sales and changing marketing strategies. In addition, producers targeted tourist dollars by developing a successful formula: the conversion of movies to the Broadway musical stage, often featuring well-known TV and movie stars. Broadway's movie-based musicals in the early part of the twenty-first century include *The Full Monty* (2000), ***The Producers*** (2001), *Hairspray* (2002), *Legally Blonde* (2007), *Young Frankenstein* (2007), and *Billy Elliot* (2008)—all created and marketed with the tourist dollar in mind. In a capitalistic twist, a few Broadway musicals of this ilk have been converted back into movie musicals, including *The Producers* (2005) and *Hairspray* (2007). Of course, the Disney Company, producing actively on Broadway through **Disney Theatrical Productions** since the 1990s, has its entire library of well-known movies that it has been tapping for theatrical adaptation with considerable success (including the aforementioned *The Lion King, Mary Poppins* [2006], and *The Little Mermaid* [2008]). For traditionalists of the Rodgers and Hammerstein era, the moneymaking formula continues in the other direction as well: from original stage production to screen. In recent years this has been the case with *The Phantom of the Opera* (2004), ***Rent*** (2005), *Dreamgirls* (2006), and *Sweeney Todd* (2007). Ironically, "talking pictures," which threatened to steal Broadway's audience and artists in the 1930s, seem to work in a symbiotic relationship with Broadway in the twenty-first century. Producers from both Hollywood and Broadway are counting on it.

Anne Fliotsos

Further Reading

Bell, John. "Disney's Times Square: The New American Community Theater." *TDR* 42, no. 1 (1998): 26–33.

Bianco, Anthony. *Ghosts of 42nd Street: A History of America's Most Infamous Block.* New York: Harper, 2005.

Harris, Neil. "Urban Tourism and the Commercial City." In *Inventing Times Square: Commerce and Culture at the Crossroads of the World*, ed. William Robert Taylor. New York: Russell Sage Foundation, 1991, pp. 66–82. [Note: Harris provides information on the history of early New York tourism found in this essay.]

League of American Theaters and Producers Web site. www.livebroadway.com.

Progrebin, Robin. "How Broadway Bounced Back after 9/11; but Downtown Theater Lacked the Right Ties." *New York Times*, May 22, 2002, E1.

Reichl, Alexander J. *Reconstructing Times Square: Politics and Culture in Urban Development.* Lawrence: University Press of Kansas, 1999.

Sagalyn, Lynne B. *Times Square Roulette: Remaking the City Icon.* Cambridge, MA: MIT Press, 2001.

Times Square Alliance. *Times Square: Then and Now.* www.timessquarenyc.org/then_-now/then_now_theater_notable.html.

TUNE, TOMMY (1939–)
DANCER, CHOREOGRAPHER, DIRECTOR, ACTOR, WRITER

Thomas James (Tommy) Tune has been a major force in musical theater dance since his debut in the Sherlock Holmes musical *Baker Street* in 1965. Since then, the 6 foot 6 inch actor has established himself as a marquee performer and an innovative director and choreographer for musicals and straight plays. Tune has an infectious smile and a joy when he dances that connects immediately with audiences and transcends the conventional limitations of "dancer"—a fact borne out by his status as the first person in history to win Tony Awards in four categories—choreography, direction, best actor, and featured actor in a musical.

Tap dancer-choreographer Tommy Tune and actress-singer Twiggy pose together during rehearsal of the broadway musical My One and Only *at the St. James Theater in New York City in 1985. (AP Photo/Richard Drew)*

Born in Wichita Falls, Texas, Tommy Tune (his real name) began dancing at the age of 5. Growing up, he studied in private dance studios, performed in school functions, and attended touring performances in Houston of such notable companies as the Ballet Russe de Monte Carlo and American Ballet Theatre. By the time he was in college, he was performing at the Dallas Summer Musical, a prestigious regional venue for musicals, where he met **Carol Channing**, whom he later described as his theatrical godmother. After completing a B.F.A. in Drama at the University of Texas in Austin, he left Texas for New York in 1965.

That same year he made his Broadway debut in *Baker Street*, which was directed by **Hal Prince** and choreographed by cutting-edge modern dancer Lee Becker Theodore—a truly auspicious beginning. By the following year, he was performing in *A Joyful Noise* (1966), where he established a long-term mentor relationship with the more advanced, although younger, choreographer **Michael Bennett**. In 1967 Tune danced for director **George Abbott** and choreographer Gillian Lynne, later of *Cats* fame, in the musical *How Now, Dow Jones*. In 1973 Bennett gave Tune a featured role and an opportunity to extend his talent as an associate choreographer in the musical *Seesaw*. Tune won the Tony for Best Featured Actor in a Musical and stole the show with "androgynous charm" and "ageless flow" (Long 2001, 256).

In addition to stage work, Tune appeared in the **film** adaptation of *Hello, Dolly!* directed by Gene Kelly and later in Ken Russell's film *The Boy Friend*. He also danced on **television**, directed and choreographed summer stock musicals, and appeared in his own one-man show, *Tommy Tune Tonite!* (1992). After meeting with poet Eva Merriam, he decided to direct an unusual theater piece **Off-Broadway** in which women played men and then later appeared as men playing women. *The Club* shared the 1977 Obie Off-Broadway award for distinguished theatrical production. These experiences prepared him to come into his own as a choreographer and director of Broadway musicals.

That first directing opportunity came in 1978 in the form of a musical with the unlikely title of *The Best Little Whorehouse in Texas*. Choreographed by Tune and co-directed with one of its writers, Peter Masterson, he achieved his first *bona fide* long-running Broadway hit. The show is based on an incident in Texas in which a popular whorehouse was closed in the 1970s due to the efforts of a morals crusader. Tune created out of this material some of the most comically effective dances seen on Broadway in years, including a kick line with female dancers in cheerleading outfits accompanied on each arm with life-size cheerleading dummies. The musical ran for over three years; Tune had arrived.

Over the next several years, he would choreograph, direct, and occasionally perform in some of Broadway's most successful musicals of that period. Two of the most unusual were *A Day in Hollywood/A Night in the Ukraine* (1980) and *Nine* (1982). The first of these was composed of two strangely paired one acts—the first takes place in the lobby of Hollywood landmark Grauman's Chinese Theatre and is a pastiche of Hollywood musical films, while the second act takes place in the Ukraine and, among other oddities, places the Marx Brothers in an Anton Chekhov short story. Both Tune and co-choreographer Thommie Walsh received the Tony Award for Choreography.

With *Nine* Tune won the 1982 Tony Award for Best Direction of a Musical, beating out his mentor, Michael Bennett, who had directed and choreographed *Dreamgirls* that year. Based on the character Guido Contini, film director Federico Fellini's alter ego in his signature work *8 ½*, *Nine* had one male character, played by Raul Julia, and 21 women. Set in a spa in Venice, the show follows a film director experiencing a midlife crisis and features the collage-like appearances of numerous women who had made an impact on his life. Although the musical received mixed reviews, Tune's ingenious staging earned him enormous respect among his peers and the admiration of musical theater enthusiasts eager to see Broadway push its edges.

In addition to experimenting with the unusual, Tune's work also exhibited a deep affection for musical theater's past, as demonstrated in such musicals as *My One and Only* (1983), *Grand Hotel* (1989), and *The Will Rogers Follies* (1991). With *My One and Only*, Tune teamed up with 1960s British "cover girl" Twiggy (Leslie Hornby) to play the leads. He codirected and choreographed the musical with longtime collaborator Thommie Walsh. Gently spoofing 1920s style Broadway revues with the music of **George Gershwin**, Tune and Walsh contrived one cleverly constructed dance metaphor after another. The musical was further enhanced by the appearance of legendary tap dancer Charles "Honi" Coles teaching Tune's character how to tap dance to the title song.

With *Grand Hotel*, Tune stayed in the 1920s but with a very different tone. This was Berlin in 1928, and the musical centered on the interweaving lives of five principal characters. The musical comments on their ups and downs, loves and losses, and, ultimately, on life and death. Tune wove dance and movement with narrative vignettes that overlapped in one continuous motion. The show received both critical praise and popular appeal, earning Tune Tony Awards for Direction and Choreography.

The *Will Rodgers Follies* completed Tune's trio of musicals set in the past. In this production, Tune centers the story on Will Rodgers and **Flo Ziegfeld** against a backdrop of early twentieth-century America. Tune again won Tonys for Direction and Choreography. The show enjoyed a 981 performance run, although critics faulted the production's lack of care that they had come to expect from Tune.

Tune last performed on Broadway in a well-received, New Year's week retrospective, *Tommy Tune Tonight!* (1992). His last turn as a Broadway director/choreographer came in the ill-fated sequel to *Best Little Whorehouse—The Best Little Whorehouse Goes Public* (1994). Reviews were dismal and Tune, usually a critics' favorite, was singled out for lackluster work. The show closed in two weeks. Since then Tune continued writing and performing occasionally, although not on Broadway. But his legacy as a great innovator of the choreographer/director era of the 1980s and the 1990s is secure. Tune on Broadway was a 6 foot 6 inch graceful, humor-filled, inventive theater artist who towered over the stage in more ways than one.

Ray Miller

Further Reading

Long, Robert Emmett. *Broadway the Golden Years: Jerome Robbins and the Great Choreographer-Directors 1940 to the Present*. New York: Continuum, 2001.
Tune, Tommy. *Footnotes: A Memoir.* New York: Simon and Schuster, 1997.

V

Vaudeville

Vaudeville was the first truly mass entertainment in the United States. It had varieties that appealed to all classes and both genders. It created ethnic stereotypes even as it gave new immigrants a place to bond with their countrymen and gain exposure to American ideals. It started during the nineteenth century in the historic, ethnically diverse Bowery district in downtown New York City. As commerce, culture, and immigrant populations moved uptown, so did vaudeville, attracting more of the upper class to its performances and eventually moving right into the center of what would become the **Broadway theater district**. Although the exact dates of the vaudeville era are subject to dispute as is the definition of "vaudeville" itself, American vaudeville can be roughly dated from the mid-nineteenth century through the mid-twentieth century. During its heyday in the early twentieth century it was the most popular entertainment in the country, with local artists and touring stars reaching almost every small town in the United States.

Vaudeville had a significant impact on the development of the Broadway theater. Many Broadway stars, writers, and **producers** got their start in vaudeville. Vaudeville performance styles and comic "schtick" (a Yiddish word meaning "small piece" adapted by Jewish comics as a catchall term for comedic stage expressions, gestures, and gimmicks) later found homes in the "legitimate" houses of Broadway. Vaudeville performers traveled the country, playing the same material from New York to Richmond to San Francisco, providing the first American-grown live entertainment shared by the nation as a whole. Stereotypes, jokes, and sentimental songs traveled the country through vaudeville, providing the basis for a common American culture.

The History of Vaudeville

Vaudeville grew in the mid-nineteenth century out of the myriad of popular entertainments, both American and imported, that held the attention of the lower classes. Much of this entertainment was targeted at men who were attracted by the coarse humor and attractive (and hopefully available) women. American minstrelsy contributed to vaudeville performance styles (such as ethnic satire) and performers (such as the "blackface" duo McIntyre and Heath and minstrel performer/producer Lew Dockstader). Vaudeville also adapted a number of aspects of the minstrel show format including the musical afterpiece and the comic stump speech, both used in various forms throughout the life of vaudeville. German beer gardens provided a model for family-friendly variety entertainment, which they had been providing for German Americans and tourists to New York City throughout the nineteenth century. The English music hall showed that variety entertainment could appeal to all classes. And the French vaudevilles—short musical playlets performed "in the French style"—were regularly seen on downtown New York stages by the 1850s. Concert saloons provided their predominantly male clientele with racy variety entertainment along with alcohol and occasionally gambling. The variety theater of the mid-nineteenth century influenced and was influenced by all of these traditions.

The differences between nineteenth-century variety entertainment and the vaudeville theater are largely a matter of definitions and do not readily lend themselves to hard and fast classification. However, it is generally considered that variety entertainment became vaudeville when it cleaned up all the coarser elements of its shows, including double entendres and bad words, and started appealing to women and middle-class audiences. Producer **Tony Pastor** is generally credited with beginning this trend when he opened Tony Pastor's Opera House on the Bowery in 1865. He refused to call his performances "vaudeville" until his second theater opened further uptown ten years later, considering the term "sissified" and French. Other managers who contributed to the development of what would eventually be called "big-time vaudeville" include B. F. Keith and E F. Albee (grandfather by adoption of the famous contemporary playwright). This expansion began in the 1880s and 1890s with "circuits" of theaters controlled by managers such as Keith and Albee. They made good use of the new, far-reaching American railway system to stage their shows throughout the country and develop vaudeville as a truly national popular form of entertainment.

Vaudeville began the twentieth century at the height of its popularity. Big-time vaudeville of the 1910s and 1920s was sophisticated, appealed to all levels of society, and enjoyed a very close, sometimes indistinguishable, relationship with the legitimate theater. The first challenge to the then time-honored structure of vaudeville shows came from silent films, which at the beginning of the twentieth century were seen regularly in vaudeville theaters, especially those owned by B. F. Keith. Vaudeville offered the perfect playing space for films because early films were short—about the length of a typical vaudeville sketch—and made good use of the house orchestra. And while silent films became very popular in vaudeville, even occupying the star slot at times, they did not challenge the basic existence of the theater. That did not occur until sound became standard in film in the late 1920s. At that point film outgrew what the standard vaudeville theater could easily provide. As theaters became equipped for sound and managers realized the wider profit potential in film over theater, vaudeville theaters quickly gave way to movie palaces.

Many vaudeville performers were thrown out of work unceremoniously, but others found work in the new media of **radio** and **film** or made the move (or the move back) to legitimate theater. Soon after the emergence of "talking pictures" the phenomenon of network radio also hastened the demise of vaudeville. By the early 1930s, radio networks were broadcasting regularly scheduled music, comedy, and variety shows throughout the week, and Americans acclimated quickly to the idea of enjoying such entertainment at home for free rather than in theaters. Eager to hire established entertainers to fill their rapidly expanding programming schedules, the New York City–based radio networks welcomed seasoned vaudeville performers, many of whom had to do little more than cross the street to revitalize their careers in the emerging lucrative medium of broadcasting. Comics Bob Hope, Jack Benny, and George Burns & Gracie Allen as well as ventriloquist Edgar Bergen were among the vaudeville veterans who earned even greater fame and fortune in broadcasting than they had ever achieved in the vaudeville circuits. However, not everyone made the transition successfully. Some vaudeville performers were not able to maintain their success in radio because national audiences and weekly appearances meant that material that had lasted them for years on the road was used up after one broadcast performance.

The networks' early reliance on vaudeville talent accounts in large part for the fact that the structure and performance style of vaudeville lived on in radio and **television**, particularly in the television variety shows of the 1950s and 1960s. Moreover, most modern slapstick comedy—whether on television, film, or Broadway—can be traced back to vaudeville and its ancestors.

The Structure of a Vaudeville Show

Although the structure of a vaudeville bill changed over the years and from theater to theater, a standard bill throughout the period of vaudeville's dominance generally contained about a dozen acts. Often the show would start with a dumb act—an act composed of nonverbal elements, such as acrobats, animal acts, or instrumental musical numbers—that could still be enjoyed as a noisy crowd was coming in. The dumb act would be followed by a series of unrelated, successively more popular acts of a wide variety of styles. Song and dance acts were very common as were monologuists (similar to contemporary stand-up comedians). Comic duos, often sporting "ethnic" personas, made up a large portion of vaudeville performers. Minstrel acts were particularly popular in the nineteenth century, and sophisticated musical performances gained prominence in the twentieth century. "Freak" acts brought over from circuses and freak shows showcased performers who were armless (such as Prussian musician Carl Unthan who played the violin with his feet), or legless, or hirsute ("Jo-Jo the Dog-faced Boy"). Unlike freak shows, however, acts in vaudeville had to have performance value to hold audience attention.

Novelty acts also had to come up with a performance. Well-known personalities like Babe Ruth and Carrie Nation, who supplemented their incomes by appearing in vaudeville shows, had to have some kind of act or patter to entertain audiences, who were not content to just stare at the famous. Magicians such as Harry Kellar, Herrmann the Great, and Harry Houdini had places on vaudeville bills throughout its lifetime. Other performers became famous for unusual talents they perfected, such as the regurgitator Hadji Ali, the "mentalist" John T. Fay, and female impersonator Julian Eltinge. Physical acts—acrobats, contortionists, jugglers, funambulists, gymnasts, strongmen, and so on—were omnipresent throughout the life of vaudeville, but rarely achieved widespread fame. (The strongman Sandow was one exception to this trend.) Once vaudeville "went continuous" by running shows all day long, poorly performed dumb acts were often used by managers to drive audiences out of the theater in order to make room for new paying customers.

Every vaudeville house had live musical accompaniment, which ranged from a single piano player to a full orchestra. Typically the vaudeville house band consisted of perhaps five to seven musicians playing a combination of the current hits of the day (many of which were burlesqued by having their lyrics changed), music written specifically for individual acts and sketches, and background music for dumb acts.

Audiences watched vaudeville bills from a variety of vantage points. Wealthier patrons could afford boxes or the parterre (today called the orchestra) while the lower classes sat in the galleries. Upper galleries were reserved for the cheapest seats or for African Americans in those theaters where they were even permitted to attend.

The Business of Vaudeville

In the early days of vaudeville, company managers were independent, usually managing only one company and, if they were lucky, owning one theater. The more ambitious managers, especially those in New York, took their companies on tour during the off-season. (Vaudeville's "season" ran during the same months as that of the legitimate theater, but theater owners also rented out their venues to other companies in the summer and occasionally hosted "special performances" in their own houses.)

Each vaudeville manager generally had his own company made up of regular performers comprising a variety of specialties. The "regulars" were supplemented by independent performers hired on a weekly basis. The regular company members drew local audiences who liked performers they were familiar with. The regulars also populated the majority of roles in afterpieces, later known more commonly as playlets: parodies of current legitimate plays, or sentimental melodramas, or knock-about farces. Afterpieces were a staple of early vaudeville bills.

Managers used the afterpieces to entice famous actors from the legitimate stage to appear in their shows. Although vaudeville was considered a step down in prestige for most legitimate actors, the high pay (for stars) and easy work schedule (for those appearing only in playlets) were too good to resist. B. F. Keith was one manager who used the playlet to great advantage, drawing to his shows both legitimate theater stars and, consequently, higher-class audiences.

What is known as "big vaudeville" began with the formation of the Association of Vaudeville Managers in 1901, after at least a year of negotiations among the most powerful and fiercely independent managers to gain control of bookings and contract terms of the vaudeville performers they hired. The Association essentially combined the forces of the already strong Keith and Orpheum circuits, along with several other managers, to form a virtual monopoly that many performers felt stifled by. Resident companies had already been abandoned by most managers because of their high operating expense, and continuous vaudeville had lower-level performers doing their acts sometimes five or six times a day. Additional professional hazards like being abandoned by a bankrupt manager while on tour or having their act continually censored meant that vaudeville performers no longer functioned as independent artists as they once had. A group of vaudeville performers, led by singer George Fuller Golden, began meeting as soon as they heard of the managers' plans and managed to form their own organization, the White Rats (modeled on Britain's music-hall performers' union, the Grand Order of the Water Rats) nearly a year before the managers formalized their agreement.

Big vaudeville culminated in construction of the Palace Theatre, which opened on Broadway in 1913 as part of a deal between two major vaudeville companies, the Orpheum and Keith circuits. After a rocky start the theater grew to become the pinnacle of vaudeville performance venues and remained so until the late 1920s. After that it limped along as a vaudeville/movie house until the mid-1960s, when theater owner James Nederlander made it a house for mainstream Broadway shows and limited-run special performances. Under Nederlander's ownership, the Palace has housed such hit musicals as *Sweet Charity* (1966), *La Cage aux Folles* (1983), *Beauty and the Beast* (1994), *Aida* (2000), and *Legally Blonde* (2007).

The Stars of Vaudeville

Vaudeville performers of virtually every specialty appeared on or influenced the Broadway stage. Some performers, like Cliff "Ukulele Ike" Edwards, Al Jolson, Sophie Tucker, and Fred and Adele Astaire, began in vaudeville and then moved to Broadway. Many other performers, like **Fanny Brice**, made the short hop from vaudeville to the *Ziegfeld Follies*. Conversely, performers from the legitimate stage often moonlighted on vaudeville to make extra money. A top star from Broadway could earn the same amount of money or more in vaudeville for much less work, and high-profile performers like **Ethel Barrymore** and Sarah Bernhardt often took advantage of that fact.

Arguably, vaudeville's most famous gift to Broadway was **George M. Cohan**. Cohan began as a child in vaudeville in the 1880s, performing musical numbers and comedy sketches with his parents and sister as The Four Cohans. Cohan became the primary writer for the group. He also sold his songs and sketches professionally, first hearing his songs performed by famous entertainers while he was still in his teens. Cohan's sketches grew longer and more elaborate, and in 1901 he brought the family to Broadway in a full-length version of their popular sketch "The Governor's Son." He was a highly successful writer, songwriter, and producer on Broadway through the 1930s. His song, "Give My Regards to Broadway" from *Little Johnny Jones* (1904)—for which Cohan wrote the book, music, and lyrics as well as directed and starred—remains one of the best-known show tunes in American theater history. A statue honoring Cohan's contributions and legacy to Broadway has stood in Times Square since 1959, the only such public memorial to a single performer in the New York theater district.

Other vaudeville performers created material used on Broadway and in the movies for decades to come. Joe Weber and **Lew Fields** were two of the earliest Jewish performers to succeed in popular theater. At the turn of the twentieth century Weber and Fields were playing to high-class audiences. Their burlesques were the predecessors of Broadway musical revues and comedies. Lew Fields continued to innovate in his productions throughout his life, combining the elements of revue, **operettas**, vaudeville, and burlesque, to create a foundation for musical theater that profoundly influenced future Broadway artists such as Oscar Hammerstein II, **George and Ira Gershwin**, and **Cole Porter**.

Vaudeville had all but vanished from New York City by the end of the 1930s. But its performers and material continued on into commercial theater as well as radio, film, and television. Television's variety shows of the mid-twentieth century were direct descendants of vaudeville as were screwball comedies in film. Intermittently over the past two decades "conceptual performers" such as Bill Irwin, David Shiner, the Flying Karamazov Brothers, and Avner the Eccentric (sometimes categorized as "new vaudevillians") have returned some of the styles, techniques, and material of vaudeville to Broadway with special one-night-only or limited run Broadway shows, including Irwin and Shiner's *Fool Moon* (1993) and the Karamazovs' *The Flying Karamazov Brothers Do the Impossible* (1994).

Susan Kattwinkel

Further Reading

Snyder, Robert W. *The Voice of the City: Vaudeville and Popular Culture in New York.* New York: Oxford University Press, 1989.

Wertheim, Arthur Frank. *Vaudeville Wars: How the Keith-Albee and Orpheum Circuits Controlled the Big-Time and Its Performers.* New York: Palgrave Macmillan, 2006.

Zellers, Parker. *Tony Pastor: Dean of the Vaudeville Stage.* Ypsilanti, MI: Eastern University Press, 1971.

VERDON, GWEN (1925–2000)
DANCER, SINGER, ACTRESS

Eulogized by many as the best female dancer in American **musical** history, Gwen Verdon was the premier Broadway dancer/actress of the 1950s and 1960s. With collaborator director/choreographer **Bob Fosse**, to whom she was married from 1960 to 1987, Verdon created memorable musical roles that blended the seemingly incongruous qualities of sly sexuality, robust athleticism, and impish humor—all rendered with a mastery of deceptively complicated dance techniques and movements. Although not an elite, gifted stage singer, she imbued her vocal performances with penetrating energy and wit that fully complemented her remarkable dancing. Two of her showstopping numbers, "Whatever Lola Wants" from *Damn Yankees* (1955) and "If My Friends Could See Me Now" from *Sweet Charity* (1966), are among the finest song and dance numbers from Broadway's Golden Age of musicals. With starring or featured roles in only seven Broadway shows, Verdon won a remarkable four career Tony Awards as Best Actress or Featured Actress in a Musical.

Gwyneth Evelyn Verdon, was born in Culver City, California, and studied dancing all through childhood. In the late 1940s and early 1950s she was a student and assistant for Hollywood and Broadway choreographer Jack Cole, working with him on some of his studio film musicals and serving as his assistant choreographer for a Broadway musical *Magdalena* (1948)—her first Broadway credit. Cole, whose sensual and exotic choreography well suited the charismatic redheaded Verdon, cast her as a dancer in his Broadway revue *Alive and Kicking* (1950). Although the show ran only two weeks, the production brought Verdon into contact with many established figures on Broadway, including director Robert Gordon and musical director Lehman Engel. In 1953 **Abe Burrows** and **Cole Porter** cast Verdon from auditions as the second lead female role in *Can-Can*, behind the show's star, the French dancer Lilo. Verdon stole the show from the French diva with a fierce Apache number in the second act, earning critical raves, her first Tony Award (Best Actress in a Featured Role), and star status she would enjoy for the remainder of her career.

Her next role as Lola, the devil's temptress aide-de-camp in *Damn Yankees* (1955), represented her first legendary performance and, not coincidentally, her first Broadway collaboration with Fosse. Fosse, fresh off his first triumph as choreographer for *Pajama Game* (1954), had seen Verdon in *Can-Can* and fell in love with her dancing—and with Verdon herself not long afterwards. Verdon's Lola became one of the defining female Broadway performances of the decade. She won the Tony for Best Actress in a musical and re-created the role in the 1958 film adaptation. The show cemented Fosse and Verdon as Broadway's most dynamic creative performing team of the time. They followed *Damn Yankees* with the somewhat less successful *New Girl in Town*, producer **George Abbott**'s adaptation of **Eugene O'Neill**'s Pulitzer Prize–winning play *Anna Christie* (1922). The show ran a respectable 431 performances and won Best Actress Tony Awards for both

Gwen Verdon, right, and Chita Rivera rehearsing the musical Chicago *in Philadelphia in 1975. (AP Photo)*

female co-stars, Verdon and Thelma Ritter. But historically the show has been overshadowed by Fosse and Verdon's more famous works.

After making the film adaptation of *Damn Yankees* together, Fosse and Verdon returned to Broadway for *Redhead* (1959). As with *New Girl in Town*, the new show had a solid run for a year, sweeping the Tony Awards for musicals (including Best Actress for Verdon, Best Choreography for Fosse, Best Actor for male lead Richard Kiley, and Best Musical). However, no signature number emerged to immortalize either the show or the performances.

After *Redhead*, Verdon took a hiatus from Broadway to care for her and Fosse's daughter Nicole, born in 1963. She returned to Broadway in 1966 under Fosse's direction and choreography for the second of her two most famous performances, the title role in *Sweet Charity.* The show was a huge critical and commercial success, enhancing the 40-year-old Verdon's legend for staying power as well as artistry and fortifying the already imposing reputation of the Fosse-Verdon team (she received a Best Actress Tony nomination while Fosse won for Best Choreography). With the exception of a one-night flop in a drama, *Children! Children!* (1972), Verdon did not return to Broadway until 1975 when, at age 50, she made her final Broadway appearance as Roxie in Fosse's *Chicago.* The show's two-year run consecrated the now 20-year choreographer-dance partnership as the premiere Broadway team of its kind since World War II.

The Fosse-Verdon legend was revived in popular culture in later years with Fosse's direction of the 1979 semiautobiographical film *All That Jazz,* a 1991 tribute Broadway musical *Fosse* (for which Verdon is credited as an artistic advisor), and the phenomenal success of *Chicago*'s 1996 Broadway revival, which exceeded 5,000 performances in 2008.

Verdon died of natural causes in October 2000 at her daughter's home in Woodstock, Vermont.

Thomas A. Greenfield

Further Reading

Everett, William A., and Paul R. Laird. *The Cambridge Companion to the Musical.* Cambridge, England: Cambridge University Press, 2008.

Gottfried, Martin. *All His Jazz: The Life and Death of Bob Fosse.* New York: Da Capo, 2003.

W

WASSERSTEIN, WENDY (1950–2006)
PLAYWRIGHT, NOVELIST, TELEVISION WRITER, ESSAYIST

Wendy Wasserstein's plays articulate a complex, comical vision of well-educated women and their efforts to negotiate the world of careers, relationships, family, and society. Her most successful play, *The Heidi Chronicles* (1989), earned her the Pulitzer Prize for drama as well as the Tony Award for Best Play. Her facility with crisp, fast-paced dialog powered by showstopping wisecracks reflected the influence and tradition of earlier Jewish comic **playwrights** from **George S. Kaufman** to **Neil Simon**. Through her plays and other writings, Wasserstein became a distinctive literary voice for the American feminist movement of the latter part of the twentieth century, which saw a nationwide surge of new women writers, feminist presses, women's poetry collectives, and feminist theater groups. Of the emerging women playwrights of that period, Wasserstein established the strongest presence on Broadway and the New York theater scene.

Wasserstein was born in Brooklyn on October 18, 1950. Her father, a textile manufacturer, invented a unique fabric and became financially successful. The Wassersteins then moved to Manhattan's fashionable Upper East Side where Wasserstein was educated in an exclusive private school. She later earned a Bachelor of Arts in history from Mount Holyoke College in Massachusetts and then studied creative writing at City College of New York. Her first play, *Any Woman Can't*, was discovered and produced in 1973 by Playwrights Horizons, an **Off-Broadway** company famous for presenting works by new young playwrights. Shortly thereafter, Wasserstein attended the Yale School of Drama, earning a Master of Fine Arts degree in 1976.

Wendy Wasserstein in New York in 2000. (AP Photo/Gino Domenico)

After Yale, Wasserstein returned to Manhattan. Her first major New York success came in 1977 with her play *Uncommon Women and Others*, produced Off-Broadway by the Phoenix Theatre. PBS's *Great Performances* taped and telecast the production of the play, providing impetus to Wasserstein's career as well as those of its then relatively unknown stars, Glenn Close, Jill Eikenberry, and Swoosie Kurtz. Depicting a reunion of several graduates of Mount Holyoke that flashes back to events from their college days, the play drew the admiration of both **critics** and audiences who were moved by the 26-year-old Wasserstein's ability to convey complexities of sadness, disappointment, and frustration through witty dialog and a sharp-edged political point of view. This comical yet political tone would become the cornerstone of Wasserstein's work, and her ability to make an audience laugh—while shedding light on topics ranging from feminism to pop culture—would become her trademark.

In 1989, Wasserstein became an internationally renowned dramatist when *The Heidi Chronicles* opened on Broadway. The plot follows one Heidi Holland over a period of 20 years from mid-1960s high school wisecracker to her career as a noted art historian. The play's main themes deal with the changing role of women during this time period, tracing Heidi's encounters with feminism, career, friends, and lovers through the 1970s and 1980s. The play opened Off-Broadway in 1988 starring Joan Allen as Heidi. In March of the following year the play moved to the Plymouth Theatre (now the Gerald Schoenfeld Theatre), marking Wasserstein's Broadway debut. The original Broadway cast featured Cynthia Nixon, who years later would star in the cast of the groundbreaking (and Wasserstein-influenced) HBO television series *Sex in the City*. The multiple award-winning play ran for 622 performances and has since become a staple of college theater and English classes studying literature of the American women's movement.

In her next play, *The Sisters Rosensweig* (1993), Wasserstein continued her exploration of contemporary women, this time focusing on Jewish American identity. Invoking some surface features and the symphonic-like movements of *The Three Sisters* by Anton Chekhov—one of Wasserstein's literary idols—the play concerns three Jewish American sisters each struggling in her own way to come to terms with her religious and ethnic roots. *Rosensweig* starred Broadway and Hollywood mainstays Jane Alexander and Madeleine Kahn. Kahn's performance won her the Tony for Best Actress in a play, beating out fellow cast member Alexander who was also nominated for the same show. *Rosensweig* ran for 556 performances over the course of 15 months and earned Wasserstein a Tony nomination for Best Play.

Wasserstein's third and last full-length Broadway play, *An American Daughter* (1997), was her most overtly political and by far the least successful of the three. Set in the nation's capital and concerned with sexist power mongering among D.C.'s political and media elite, *An American Daughter* was so steeped in the "other worldliness" of Washington that neither Wasserstein's generous supply of high-end wisecracks nor Kate Nelligan's commendable performance in the title role could make the play connect with audiences. Reviews were harsh and the play closed in ten weeks.

Wasserstein's other plays include *Isn't It Romantic*, *Old Money*, and her final staged work, *Third*, none of which was produced on Broadway. However, *Third*, starring Dianne Wiest as a professor confronted with challenges to some of her long-held ethical beliefs, had a prestigious, well-received run at Lincoln Center in 2005. Both Wiest and Wasserstein won praise for their textured exploration of the now "middle aged" late twentieth-century feminist movement with which Wasserstein had come to be closely identified.

Wasserstein also wrote for **television** and **film**, most notably penning the screenplay for the 1998 film adaptation of Stephen McCauley's novel *The Object of My Affection*. Jennifer Aniston starred in the film. Wasserstein also wrote two collections of essays, *Bachelor Girls* (1990) and *Shiksa Goddess: Or, How I Spent My Forties* (2001).

Wasserstein was hospitalized with lymphoma in December 2005. She died on January 30, 2006, at the age of 55. The following night, Broadway lights were dimmed in her honor. In 2007, Wasserstein was posthumously inducted into the American Theatre Hall of Fame.

Molly Smith Metzler

Further Reading

Barnett, Claudia. *Wendy Wasserstein: A Casebook*. New York: Garland, 1999.

Wasserstein, Wendy. *Shiksa Goddess: Or, How I Spent My Forties—Essays*. New York: Random House USA Inc., 2002.

WEST SIDE STORY

Broadway Run: Winter Garden Theatre (September 26, 1957 to February 28, 1959); Broadway Theatre (March 2, 1959 to May 10, 1959); Winter Garden Theatre (May 11, 1959 to June 27, 1959)

Opening: September 26, 1957
Closing: June 27, 1959
Total Performances: 732
Composer: Leonard Bernstein
Lyricist: Stephen Sondheim
Book: Arthur Laurents
Choreography: Jerome Robbins
Director: Jerome Robbins
Producer: Robert E. Griffith and Harold S. Prince; in arrangement with Roger L. Stevens
Lead Performers: Larry Kert (Tony), Carol Lawrence (Maria), Chita Rivera (Anita), Mickey Calin (Riff), Ken Le Roy (Bernardo)

West Side Story is widely regarded as one of America's 20th-century musical theater masterpieces. It is an outstanding example of how collaboration between artists produced a result that transcended their individual contributions. **Arthur Laurents** and **Stephen Sondheim**'s book and lyrics challenged audiences to recognize the multifaceted nature of contemporary gang rivalry. **Jerome Robbins** refocused attention on choreography, proving that dance could speak for characters in ways that words could not always express. Several of *West Side Story*'s songs became immediate standards, and composer **Leonard Bernstein** blended classical, theatrical, Latin American, and jazz approaches in a score that seemed both fresh and powerful. Nevertheless, *West Side Story* initially sparked mixed reactions after its 1957 opening. This updated version of *Romeo and Juliet* recast **Shakespeare**'s feuding Italian families as modern New York gangs, so audiences could not lose themselves in a theatrical fantasy world. Instead, they were confronted with many of the upsetting social issues that awaited them outside the theater, and some found this an appalling experience. Only gradually, as the initial shock wore off, did most viewers begin to recognize what many audience members and numerous **critics** had noted from the first: that *West Side Story* was a landmark achievement in its integration of words, music, and dance.

Prior to its Broadway opening, the show had undergone a long, slow gestation. The initial idea for a modernized approach to Shakespeare's powerful tragedy originated with Jerome Robbins early in 1949. Robbins proposed a conflict between New York Catholics and Jews, calling the project *East Side Story*. Bernstein immediately declared it "a noble idea," but as Laurents started writing the early scenes, both he and Bernstein recognized that the concept was not working. The hotbeds of ethnic tension that the Manhattan-born Robbins knew from his youth were shifting to new neighborhoods, and the **musical**'s religious conflict seemed dated. Progress on the show ground to a halt, and the prospective partners moved on to other projects. The idea for the show kept percolating, however. While Bernstein was on the West Coast in 1955, he ran into Laurents and began to discuss the project yet again. Sitting beside a hotel pool, they spotted a newspaper article covering gang violence in Los Angeles, and suddenly a new strategy seemed clear: they could focus the story around New York Puerto Rican gangs and

Carol Lawrence, right, as Maria, and Chita Rivera, as Anita, are shown in the original Broadway production of West Side Story *at the Winter Garden Theatre in New York City in 1957. (AP Photo)*

the rising tide of juvenile delinquency. As Bernstein noted in his diary, "Suddenly it all springs to life."

Robbins was thrilled to hear about the new approach to the adaptation. Since 1949, Manhattan's worst trouble spots had moved west to the area known as "Hell's Kitchen," so the project was at first rechristened *Gangway!* and, eventually, *West Side Story.* Bernstein initially intended to write the lyrics as well as the score, but Robbins, choreographing the show, required a great deal of dance music as well as songs. Bernstein realized that the task was too massive for him to accomplish alone. At about the same time Laurents mentioned the *Romeo and Juliet* project to Sondheim at a cocktail party. Laurents had heard and admired some of Sondheim's lyrics and thought the young songwriter might be able to handle the lyrics for this show. But there was a problem. Although today Sondheim is one of musical theater's most respected artists, in 1956 he was a Broadway unknown (his first and only show had derailed before opening night when the producer died of leukemia). Moreover, like Bernstein himself, Sondheim wanted to write both words *and* music; he had no desire to serve as someone else's lyricist. However, Sondheim's mentor was the venerable **Oscar Hammerstein II**, who told his protégé that he would be working with some of Broadway's brightest luminaries. All parties agreed, if somewhat cautiously, and Sondheim became the lyricist.

Other hurdles had to be crossed before *West Side Story*'s début. One of the producers, Cheryl Crawford, withdrew her support not long before rehearsals were to start, but Sondheim was able to enlist the help of producers **Harold Prince** and Robert Griffith. Prince then had to persuade Robbins to continue as choreographer. Robbins felt the dual tasks of director and choreographer were too big to manage by himself, but Prince knew that "Choreography by Jerome Robbins" was an important box-office draw. Prince agreed to let Robbins have some help with the choreography and eight weeks of rehearsal time rather than the customary four.

When the fruit of the collaborators' labors premiered on Broadway in late September, the reaction was mixed. *West Side Story* had capitalized on shock value with its gritty, brooding stage sets (designed by Oliver Smith), dramatic lighting by Jean Rosenthal, and the eerie, unexpected opening "Prologue" that contains no overture. Moreover, Bernstein's jazz- and Latin-American-tinged orchestral score is often harsh and at times almost discordant. The sounds of snapping fingers added to the "Prologue" and the agitated opening choreography underscore the hostility and violence that have characterized the lives of the gangs over the preceding months. By the time the white teenagers take the stage and sing the "Jet Song," the rationale for their hostility toward the Puerto Rican Sharks is abundantly clear. Similarly, when the girlfriends of the Sharks argue over the benefits and drawbacks of life in "America," they capture the fracture between the fabled "American Dream" and the harsh prejudice that many immigrants encounter. Although Sondheim later disparaged his lyrics for some of the songs as being too clever or complex for the uneducated characters who sang them, his poetry for "America" describes painful realities that, sadly, are still often the case today, more than 50 years after the show premiered.

The characters in *West Side Story* expressed themselves not only through words but also through Robbins's brilliant and daring choreography. He had used method-acting techniques as he directed the show, giving each gang member a distinct identity (many paralleling characters in Shakespeare's play) and segregating the gangs from each other through much of the rehearsals. When the gangs finally came together on stage, they already instinctively distrusted each other. Costume designer Irene Sharaff further emphasized their division with the clothing colors worn by each gang. The character Anybodys, played by Lee Becker, was a wanna-be Jet, but was rejected by them because she was female; Becker found herself ostracized and eating lunch alone during many rehearsals.

As early as opening night, a number of critics recognized the powerful way that the dance movements conveyed the emotions of the inarticulate teenagers. The important role of the choreography meant that it often supplanted more traditional dialogue. For example, in the first meeting of the doomed hero and heroine, Tony and Maria silently dance a delicate cha-cha, oblivious to the raucous school dance surrounding them.

The songs were equally important in creating the show's impact. It was often in their lyrics that glimpses of Shakespeare's earlier images could be spotted. The Jets cryptically declare their lifelong loyalty to one another in slogans such as "Womb to tomb," resembling Friar Lawrence's lines, "The earth that's nature's mother is her tomb; / What is her burying grave, that is her womb." The songs also helped to control the dramatic pacing; just as Shakespeare used clowns to leaven his tragedy, the Jets use the rambunctiously satiric song "Gee, Officer Krupke" to escape momentarily the horror and tragedy of the growing death toll that surrounds them. The song had its detractors, who felt it was too frivolous for the dark story, but others defended it, arguing that people often resort to sardonic humor to cope with desperate situations.

Although much of the music is well-known today, Bernstein's use of unusual intervals, clusters of notes, and shifting rhythms made it hard to walk out of the theater whistling the tunes—another factor that delayed the widespread appreciation that *West Side Story* now enjoys.

Although various critics have found fault with certain aspects of *West Side Story*, the fact remains that the show simply "clicks" at a level that few other musicals have achieved. It fuses the expert contributions of its many skilled collaborators in a mesmerizing, heart-wrenching story. Many of its songs continued to live as independent standards. In 1975, cast member Lee Becker (using her married name "Lee Becker Theodore") founded the American Dance Machine to preserve the choreography of *West Side Story* and that of many other musicals. The show's explosive energy, balanced by a compelling love story, generated a realism that is seldom matched on the Broadway stage.

Alyson McLamore

Further Reading

Bernstein, Burton, and Barbara Haws. *Leonard Bernstein: American Original*. New York: Collins, 2008.

Laurents, Arthur. *Original Story by: A Memoir of Broadway and Hollywood*. Milwaukee: Hal Leonard Corporation, 2001.

WHO'S AFRAID OF VIRGINIA WOOLF?

Broadway Run: Billy Rose Theatre
Opening: October 13, 1962
Closing: May 16, 1964
Total Performances: 664
Author: Edward Albee

Director: Alan Schneider
Producers: Richard Barr and Clinton Wilder (Theater 1963); A. B. W. Productions, Inc. and Pisces Productions, Inc.
Lead Players: Uta Hagen (Martha), Arthur Hill (George), George Grizzard (Nick), Melinda Dillon (Honey)

Edward Albee's *Who's Afraid of Virginia Woolf?* defied Broadway conventions of the time and marked a critical turning point in both the **playwright**'s career and American playwriting in general. Arriving on Broadway during the reign of traditional book **musicals**, flashy scenery, large casts, and short running-time stage comedies, *Woolf* placed four characters in one room for over three hours as its discomfortingly adult content and language delivered a dark portrait of the American family. The play brought to the American living room drama an intensity of psychological desperation that could stand toe to toe with the most wrenching plays of **Arthur Miller**, **Tennessee Williams**, and **Eugene O'Neill**. The play served as the 34-year-old Albee's abrupt introduction to the general theatergoing public and started him on a storied evolution from *enfant terrible* of the American theater to the country's most important playwright of the past 50 years.

The three-act play is set in the New England college town of New Carthage, widely believed to be modeled after Trinity College in Hartford, Connecticut. George and Martha, respectively, a late-middle-aged history professor and his wife (who is also the daughter of the unseen but ever-present college president) invite Nick, a young biology professor, and Honey, his pregnant wife, over for drinks after a party. During the course of the evening Martha and George drink heavily and engage in relentless acts of verbal and occasional physical abuse while Nick and Honey watch in fascination, embarrassment, and horror. The First Act "Fun and Games" primarily deals with Martha's taunting of George, exposing in a teasingly but unmistakably cruel manner his various career failings. The Second Act is called "Walpurgisnacht," a reference to a pagan holiday when the boundaries between the living and dead are weakened. In this act we learn several pieces of information about the two couples, including that George may have accidentally killed his father and that Nick married Honey believing her to be pregnant—only to discover hers was an "hysterical" pregnancy. In the Third Act, "The Exorcism," George "kills off" the couple's shared imaginary son because Martha mentioned him to the guests, a breach of one of their numerous protective arrangements by which the knowing couple survives the daily horror of living with one another.

Who's Afraid of Virginia Woolf? was Albee's first Broadway play. He had had some short plays staged **Off-Broadway** (most notably his first play *The Zoo Story*) for which he was hailed by the American avant-garde as this country's leading proponent of European postwar Theater of the Absurd. Before devoting himself to playwriting, Albee had been living in New York writing fiction and poetry. A fortuitous opportunity to receive some guidance from playwright and novelist **Thornton Wilder**, whose work Albee admired, helped move him toward playwriting. Five years later, shortly before his thirtieth birthday and after several failed attempts, Albee finally succeeded in completing *The Zoo Story*, his first short play. Unable to debut it in America, he passed the play to friends who in 1959 arranged a premiere in Berlin, Germany. The Berlin performance was very successful and within a few months *The Zoo Story* was staged in New York Off-Broadway. Other short plays and Off-Broadway stagings followed shortly thereafter.

Two producers Albee had worked with Off-Broadway, Richard Barr and Clinton Wilder, wanted to produce his first full-length play, *Who's Afraid of Virginia Woolf?* on Broadway. They managed to pull the venerated stage actress **Uta Hagen** away from her teaching duties at HB Studio in New York to play Martha. Veteran stage and film actor Arthur Hill agreed to the part of George. Notwithstanding the strains of frequent script changes, rehearsal scheduling conflicts with a movie Hill was finishing in Europe, and the firing of the original actress cast as Honey (Lane Bradbury, replaced by Melinda Dillon), the cast clicked. The producers decided not to mount the traditional pre-Broadway out-of-town tryout but, instead, scheduled ten preview performances. They set low ticket prices to attract fans of Albee's Off-Broadway plays, and the cast and crew strongly encouraged theater people to come to the first preview. The audience for the first preview performance found no printed program of any kind; they were greeted with a pre-curtain speech announcing the actors. Notwithstanding the low-key promotion, the audience was thrilled by the play. Word spread through the New York theater community and soon all previews were sold out.

On opening night, Albee and Barr nervously paced backstage while the actors took over. The show was three and a half hours long, and Broadway **critics**, who would over time come to accept and sometimes admire the harrowing toughness of Albee's dialogue, did not know what they were in for. Reviews were mixed. Notices ranged from howls of excoriation ("sick" and "dirty-minded") to predictions—which would prove accurate—that the play had launched a major American playwright. The Broadway community clearly sided with the play's supporters, conferring five Tony Awards on the production (Best Play, Best Director, Best Actor, Best Actress, and Best Producer). Nonetheless, controversies spawned by the negative reviews persisted throughout the run and may have even helped foster interest in the production. *Woolf* ran for over a year and a half; it remains Albee's longest-running Broadway production to date.

Although Albee has been variously in and out of favor with mainstream critics and audiences in the decades following his Broadway debut, the original *Who's Afraid of Virginia Woolf?* is indisputably one of the most important dramatic productions of the latter half of the twentieth century. Prior to the play's opening on Broadway, six years had elapsed since the posthumous staging of O'Neill's ***Long Day's Journey into Night*** generated excitement and revived serious interest in the power of American playwriting. Although Arthur Miller and Tennessee Williams were still writing actively, by 1962 their most influential work was behind them. American playwriting was in need of a new voice and a new direction. *Woolf* brought a postmodern sensibility to American theater. The play presented a masterful interweaving of naturalistic settings and middle-class characters with language that operated on several levels at once. Moreover, the play eschewed the

American social drama tradition of staging newsworthy issues and, instead, explored fearlessly the perilous labyrinth of human communication as a sociopolitical issue in and of itself. Albee's career, and *Who's Afraid of Virginia Woolf?* in particular, inspired and influenced an entire generation of American playwrights, including Pulitzer Prize winners Sam Shepard, David Mamet, and **Tony Kushner**, while bringing back to Broadway—even if only occasionally—revolutionary, exciting, and challenging drama.

Carissa Cordes

Further Reading

Bottoms, Stephen J. *Albee: Who's Afraid of Virginia Woolf?* Cambridge, England: Cambridge University Press, 2000.

Gussow, Mel. *Edward Albee: A Singular Journey.* New York: Simon & Schuster, 1999.

WILDER, THORNTON (1897–1975)
PLAYWRIGHT, NOVELIST

Thornton Wilder was a distinguished novelist and **playwright** who defied prevailing theatrical trends of psychological and social realism in the mid-twentieth century by writing plays characterized by overt theatricalism, metaphysical themes, and unconventional dramatic uses of time. His best-known work is the Broadway and American literary classic ***Our Town*** (1938), which remains among the most frequently produced and read plays in American schools and community theaters. His play *The Matchmaker* (1955) was the source for the smash hit **musical** *Hello, Dolly!* (1964). An admirer of novelist James Joyce, Wilder is one of the first successful American playwrights to anticipate modernistic and postmodern departures from naturalistic and realistic drama.

Wilder was born in Madison, Wisconsin, on April 17, 1897. He attended Oberlin College and Yale University, where he earned his B.A. in 1920. Upon graduation Wilder continued his studies at the American Academy in Rome in 1920 and later earned an M.A. in French literature at Princeton University in 1925. His erudition and appreciation of world travel would inform his writing throughout his life.

Wilder wrote his first full-length play, *The Trumpet Shall Sound*, while at Yale, and managed to get it produced for a brief run in New York. However, he first found literary acclaim through his novels. *The Cabala* (1926) was praised for its uniquely measured and complex tonal qualities, anticipating the reception he would later receive for his plays. His second novel, the best seller and Pulitzer Prize–winning *The Bridge of San Luis Rey* (1927), made him a major literary celebrity.

Thornton Wilder in 1931. (AP Photo)

Success as a dramatist came in the 1930s. His first Broadway credit after *The Trumpet Shall Sound* was *Lucrece* (1933), a translation of a modern French play. His adaptation of Henrik Ibsen's *A Doll's House* (1937) was the second-longest running production of the play's ten Broadway revivals in the twentieth century. Wilder's first original Broadway successes came in 1938, when he had two Broadway openings. *The Merchant of Yonkers* played for only 28 performances but would return as a hit in 1955 under a new title, *The Matchmaker*. His Pulitzer Prize–winning masterpiece, *Our Town*, appeared the same year and represented a major departure from typical dramatic fare. The set was relatively barren and a character called "The Stage Manager" spoke throughout the play as an intermediary between the onstage action and the audience. (Wilder, who occasionally played the Stage Manager as a replacement in the original production, would later play the role in some regional productions as well.) Notwithstanding the play's unusual staging and foreboding existentialist exploration of death and loss, critics and audiences responded favorably. *Our Town* has since had three Broadway revivals, two film adaptations, numerous television adaptations, and countless amateur and professional restagings around the world.

The Skin of Our Teeth (1942) won Wilder his third Pulitzer Prize, his second for drama. The play concerns the survival of the human race as represented by the seemingly ordinary, modern Antrobus family, who contend against various forces of disaster and metaphorically live out eternal human struggles on behalf of the audience. In 1948 the *Happy Journey to Trenton and Camden*, a poignant, minimalist one-act play written some 15 years earlier, played on Broadway as part of a two-play evening with French existentialist Jean-Paul Sartre's *The Respectful Prostitute*. The small production ran for an astonishing 318 performances, about as long as the original run of *Our Town*. Wilder revised the failed *Merchant of Yonkers* into *The Matchmaker* in 1955. The revised play was a major hit, running for 486 performances. The play focuses on Dolly Levi, a professional matchmaker, attempting to secretly set herself up with a well-known businessman in Yonkers. **Jerry Herman**'s smash hit musical adaptation, *Hello, Dolly!*, immortalized the character of Dolly Levi in American popular culture (helped along by the hit title song and actress **Carol Channing**'s immersion into the role she would play thousands of times on Broadway and on tour). Wilder's final New York production, *Someone from Assisi*, *Infancy*, and *Childhood*—assembled under the title *Plays for Bleeker Street* (1962), played Off-Broadway to favorable reviews but never transferred to Broadway.

Wilder continued to write novels throughout his career, publishing five after *The Bridge of San Luis Rey*. He also published two books of short plays, *The Angel That Troubled the Waters* (1928) and *The Long Christmas Dinner and Other Plays* (1931).

Wilder died of natural causes on December 7, 1975, in Hamden, Connecticut.

Thomas A. Greenfield and Christy E. Allen

Further Reading

Bloom, Harold. *Thornton Wilder*. Philadelphia: Chelsea House, 2003.
Konkle, Lincoln. *Thornton Wilder and the Puritan Narrative Tradition*. Columbia, MO: University of Missouri Press, 2006.

WILLIAMS, BERT (1874C.–1922)
PERFORMER, COMPOSER, LYRICIST

Bert Williams was one of the most successful and inventive performers in vaudeville and early Broadway **musicals** and revues. An African-American, Williams is the first performer to gain fame and widespread audience acceptance in both black musicals and "mainstream" (predominantly white-cast or integrated) shows. He is also the first African American Broadway performer to earn star billing and compensation comparable to that of white headline performers over a sustained period of time. A skilled singer, composer, comic, mime, and dancer, Williams's performing legacy was sometimes reviled during the Harlem Renaissance and even as late as the Civil Rights Era by **critics** who felt his comedic routines, most performed in blackface, perpetuated antiblack stereotypes. However, recently scholars have praised Williams's subtle revolt against the most egregious theatrical stereotypes as well as his trailblazing success as Broadway's first African American star.

Born in the British West Indies, Williams's family moved to the United States when he was a child, raising their family in California. Largely self-taught as a performer, Williams entered the world of entertainment at age 18 as a banjo player and offstage hand for Martin and Selig's Mastodon Minstrels, a relatively small

Black vaudeville comedian Bert Williams in a publicity photo for the Ziegfeld Follies *of 1910. (AP Photo)*

blackface troop based in San Francisco. Shortly thereafter, a Kansas-born entertainer of approximately the same age, George Walker, joined the Minstrels. The two became fast friends and worked up several two-man routines, relying heavily on African-influenced dance and stage movements. The pair left the Mastodon Minstrels and, billed as Williams and Walker, performed from 1893 to 1895 in what small-time medicine shows and all-black cast revues they could land in the West and Midwest. The pair eventually honed a popular two man minstrelsy-influenced act, calling themselves ''The Two Real Coons'' and featuring the light-skinned Walker in blackface. Although hardly prosperous, the pair developed an increasingly popular regional following with Walker generally serving as straight man and overly dressed buffoon as Williams offered punch lines, wisely comic observations, and, at times, even dramatic pathos.

In 1896 Williams and Walker made their New York stage debut, improbably, in a musical by **Victor Herbert**, who was still a few years shy of becoming Broadway's foremost American composer of European-style **operettas**. During rehearsals of Herbert's *The Gold Bug*, producers felt the show was lackluster and—on word of mouth recommendations—hired Williams and Walker to do a variation of one of their stage routines in the show to spice it up. The show flopped but Williams and Walker were a hit. They earned enough credibility with their brief appearance to headline high-end **vaudeville** tours and launch a Broadway performing career.

No longer using "The Two Real Coons" for New York theater billing purposes —although they continued to mine the improvisational skills and performance timing they had developed during those years—Williams and Walker wrote the book, music, and lyrics for the musical comedy *The Policy Players* (1899), which played in two of lower Manhattan's major music halls. They followed up with *The Sons of Ham* (1900, revived in 1901), which they wrote, composed, and starred in, taking it for two separate New York runs. In 1902, the pair wrote songs for the longest-running Broadway show (100 performances) they would enjoy as a team, *Sally in Our Alley*. They also starred in African-themed musicals written by African American classical composer Will Marion Cook. Cook's *In Dahomey* (1903) created something of a stir inasmuch as it was the first musical with an all-black cast and creative team staged in an uptown, mainstream Broadway theater venue (the New York Theatre on 44th Street and Broadway) rather than a music hall or vaudeville house in lower Manhattan. The play was well received in New York and also proved popular on tour. Williams and Walker headlined the show in London, a trip that earned Williams, a British subject by his own declaration, a private meeting with King Edward VII. Williams and Walker also starred in two more all-black cast Broadway shows composed by Cook, *Abysinnia* (1906) and *Bandanna Land* (1908).

In the years between *The Gold Bug* and *Bandanna Land* Williams and Walker refined their performances, building upon their minstrelsy and small-time vaudeville stage routines to develop more fully realized stage characterizations. Williams in particular developed a stage persona of a comically ironic, philosopher-everyman observer of life. In songs such as "Nobody" or "I'm a Jonah Man" he would implicitly and, for the time, boldly comment on racial conditions but in an abstract, nonaccusative manner that would not offend his enraptured white audiences. Williams would receive occasional criticism, especially from African American writers, for what they saw as the blackface pandering that marked his career, but the inventiveness and subtlety of his performances, especially during the period between 1905 and 1910, is now widely recognized and admired.

Shortly after *Bandanna Land*, Walker became ill and withdrew from performing; he died in 1911. Although professionally and emotionally tied to his partner for nearly 20 years, Williams's career accelerated unexpectedly when **Flo Ziegfeld** invited Williams to join the cast of the 1910 *Follies*. Racially integrated casts were unheard of at the time and, although many white performers complained, Ziegfeld was quick to remind them of their dispensability. Williams became a featured member of the *Follies* cast, garnering stage time, billing, and salary comparable to those of fellow *Follies* giants **Eddie Cantor** and **Fanny Brice**. Williams remained with Ziegfeld throughout the 1910s, appearing in ten of the annual shows and gaining ever greater fame as the *Follies* shows grew in stature and popularity.

By the time he left the *Follies* in 1920, Williams was an elite-level Broadway star who happened to be black, not a star of black musicals and minstrelsy.

Williams died unexpectedly in 1922 in New York City at age 47, having pioneered the ascension of black performers from minstrelsy to black musicals to full Broadway stardom.

Thomas A. Greenfield

Further Reading

Onuorah Chude-Sokei, Louis. *The Last "Darky": Bert Williams, Black-on-Black Minstrelsy and the African Diaspora*. Durham, NC: Duke University Press, 2006.

Forbes, Camille F. *Introducing Bert Williams: Burnt Cork, Broadway, and the Story of America's First Black Star*. New York: Basic Civitas, 2008.

WILLIAMS, TENNESSEE (1911–1983)
PLAYWRIGHT

Often hailed as America's greatest **playwright**, Tennessee Williams (Thomas Lanier Williams III) had a total of 11 plays produced on Broadway between 1945 and 1961. Virtually all were successful with **critics** and audiences. Several earned Williams major awards: Pulitzer Prizes for *A Streetcar Named Desire* (1947) and *Cat on a Hot Tin Roof* (1955), a Best Play Tony Award for *The Rose Tattoo* (1951), and dozens of other accolades. Commercially successful Hollywood **films** were made of almost all of Williams's plays from that period, starring A-list actors such as Elizabeth Taylor, **Marlon Brando**, and Paul Newman. The 1951 film of *A Streetcar Named Desire*, directed by **Elia Kazan** and starring Vivian Leigh and Marlon Brando (re-creating his historic role from the Broadway production), left an indelible stamp on American culture, winning three Oscars and earning the American Film Institute's recognition as one of the 50 greatest films ever made. Best remembered on Broadway for his earlier dramas, Williams is considered a pioneer in American letters for his courageous explorations of sexuality and violence as well as his willingness to forego mainstream commercial success for artistic experimentation in the latter stages of his career.

Thomas Lanier Williams was born on March 26, 1911, in Columbus, Mississippi, the second child of Cornelius Coffin Williams and Edwina Dakin Williams. In 1918, the family moved to St. Louis after Williams's father took a job as manager of the International Shoe Company. Williams later used his experiences in St. Louis as the background for his first major play, *The Glass Menagerie* (1945). He attended the University of Missouri in Columbia from 1929 to 1932, where he majored in journalism and entered playwriting contests. After he failed ROTC, however, his father took him out of the university and forced him to work at the International Shoe Company, a job that lasted for three years and made Williams

Tennessee Williams in 1955. (AP Photo)

miserable. In 1935, while staying with his grandparents in Memphis, Williams had his first play—*Cairo! Shanghai! Bombay!*—produced in a backyard by a neighborhood theater group. He returned to school, attending Washington University in St. Louis and the University of Iowa, from which he graduated with his B.A. in 1938. In 1939, Tom Williams adopted the pen name "Tennessee" when he submitted a set of three plays to the **Group Theatre** playwriting competition under the title *American Blues*. He won a $100 prize for his submissions, which led him to sign on with literary agent Audrey Wood—a partnership that would propel him to success and last for many years.

After World War II, Williams burst onto the Broadway theater scene with a string of successful plays, some achieving masterpiece status during their first run. *The Glass Menagerie* ran for 563 performances, a hit by any standard and a landmark achievement for the debut work of an unknown author. **Laurette Taylor**'s moving portrayal of the tormented and flawed Amanda Wingfield remains to this day a legendary performance in the memories of theatergoers and Taylor's fellow actors. Williams's next play, *You Touched Me* (1945), was not a major success, but 1947 saw the premiere of *Streetcar*. **Jessica Tandy** as Blanche DuBois, in her first Broadway starring role, mesmerized audiences. Moreover, the explosive troika of Tandy, Marlon Brando as Stanley Kowalski, and Kim Hunter as Stella Kowalski opened Broadway drama to new levels of sophistication and honesty in adult relationships. *Summer and Smoke* (1948), which Williams later revised and re-entitled *Eccentricities of a Nightingale*, had an undistinguished four-month run. His next new play, however, the Tony Award–winning *The Rose Tattoo* (1951), was a hit and made a Broadway star of lead actress Maureen Stapleton. *Cat on a Hot Tin Roof* (1955), another bold theatrical exploration of adult relationships, ran for 20 months and won the Pulitzer Prize. *Sweet Bird of Youth* (1959) and *Night of the Iguana* were also popular with critics and audiences.

Despite Williams's success during the 1940s and 1950s, none of his plays after *The Night of the Iguana* ever achieved the critical or popular acclaim that the early works had, and the main products of these later years closed after only a few performances. Some of Williams's post *Night of the Iguana* plays had Broadway openings, but as the years progressed, more and more were produced in small playhouses **Off-Broadway**, Off-Off-Broadway, and in cities other than New York. Even though some productions did receive good reviews, all were essentially commercial and critical failures in comparison to the plays of his early period.

The later works that played on Broadway included *The Milk Train Doesn't Stop Here Anymore* (1963); *Slapstick Tragedy* (1966), which earned Broadway newcomer Zoe Caldwell the first of her four acting Tony Awards; *The Seven Descents of Myrtle* (1968); and *Out Cry* (1973). *Eccentricities of a Nightingale* (1976) drew some extra preproduction press attention as a reworking of 1948's *Summer and Smoke*, but the new play closed in three weeks. *Clothes for a Summer Hotel* (1980), the last original Williams play to open on Broadway during the author's lifetime, also failed despite the formidable talents of director **José Quintero** and lead actress Geraldine Page.

Williams was acutely aware of the divide between the critical reception of his earlier and later works and was devastated by the critical reception he received during the 1960s, 1970s, and 1980s. In the 1960s he claimed to be moving deliberately away from what the critical establishment saw as the essentially realistic dramatic forms that dominated his early career to a more antirealistic, fragmented, and playful type of drama characteristic of new theater movements of the time. His later plays responded to the changing social climate of the 1960s and 1970s, as well as to his own personal growth and artistic development. Critics, however, failed to evaluate these works on their own terms and often dismissed them altogether, commenting instead on Williams's lifestyle and reductively claiming that his use of alcohol and drugs was destroying his creative powers. While Williams's homosexual identity was a more or less open secret throughout his life, attacks on his "lifestyle" intensified in the press after he officially came out as a gay man in 1970 on a national television talk show. Williams himself insisted that the deliberate changes in style and presentation since his early plays disturbed the majority of critics, and that their nostalgia for plays such as *The Glass Menagerie* prevented them from accepting his later experiments with language and dramatic form.

In 1999 Williams received a measure of posthumous mainstream acceptance when Trevor Nunn directed a Broadway production of *Not About Nightingales*, a previously unproduced play that Williams had written in 1938—prior to any of his Broadway successes. The intensely violent play based on an actual hunger strike in a Philadelphia prison received favorable reviews and ran for 125 performances—the longest Broadway run of a new Williams play since *Iguana* 38 years earlier.

Williams kept writing diligently and continued to oversee productions of new plays until his death in 1983. In recent years Williams's publisher, New Directions, has been publishing much of the work that had previously been available only in manuscript form: *Fugitive Kind* (1937), *Candles to the Sun* (1937), *Spring Storm* (1938), *Not About Nightingales* (1939), *Stairs to the Roof* (1941), and *The Notebook of Trigorin* (1981). A collection of Williams's previously unpublished one-act plays, *Mister Paradise and Other One-Act Plays*, was released in 2005, and a collection of previously unpublished later plays, *The Traveling Companion and Other Plays*, came out in 2008. Continuing interest in these volumes attests to the legacy that Williams left to modern American literature beyond the considerable impact of his early Broadway hits.

Williams died on February 25, 1983, at the Hotel Elysée in New York City, apparently from asphyxiation after accidentally swallowing the cap of a medicine bottle.

Annette J. Saddik

Further Reading

Kolin, Philip. *The Tennessee Williams Encyclopedia*. Westport, CT: Greenwood Press, 2004.

Saddik, Annette J. *The Politics of Reputation: The Critical Reception of Tennessee Williams' Later Plays*. Madison, NJ: Fairleigh Dickinson University Press, 1999.

WILSON, AUGUST (1945–2005)
PLAYWRIGHT

August Wilson is the best-known and most widely read African American **playwright** in history and the first African American whose critical and commercial success places him among the elite of America's most venerated dramatists. His ten-play cycle, a decade-by-decade depiction of twentieth-century African American life (often referred to as the Century Cycle or The Pittsburgh Cycle) consumed almost the entirety of his professional playwriting career. Nine of his ten cycle plays have been produced on Broadway. Moreover, in as much as all of Wilson's plays had premiers and/or other pre-Broadway runs in repertory and **regional theater** companies, Wilson was a key figure in the rejuvenation of American regional theater in the 1980s and 1990s.

Frederick August Kittel was born and raised in Pittsburgh, Pennsylvania, whose predominantly African American Hill District became the inspiration and setting for most of his plays. After his father died in 1965 he took his mother's maiden name, Wilson, as his surname. He began his writing career as a poet and amateur community theater group member during the Black Power movement in the late 1960s. He did not take up playwriting seriously until the relatively late age of 31. However, Wilson made up for lost time with the instantaneous success of his second professional play, *Ma Rainey's Black Bottom Blues*, which premiered in 1984 at the Yale Repertory Theatre under the direction of "Yale Rep's" artistic director **Lloyd Richards**. Wilson and Richards took the play to Broadway in the fall of the same year. Subsequently, Richards oversaw the development and transfer of Wilson's next four plays from Yale to Broadway: *Fences* (1985) for which Wilson won a Tony Award for Best Play and his first Pulitzer Prize for drama, *Joe Turner's Come and Gone* (1988), *The Piano Lesson* (1990) for which Wilson won another Pulitzer Prize for drama, and *Two Trains* (1992).

By the mid-1990s, word of Wilson's ambition to complete an entire cycle of ten plays representing each decade of African American life had reached the

Playwright August Wilson discusses his new work at the Yale Repertory Theatre in New Haven, Connecticut, 1985. Wilson's play, Ma Rainey's Black Bottom, *had been unveiled a year previously at the Yale Rep and went on to successful performances on Broadway. (AP Photo/Bob Child)*

American theater community and beyond, and the pursuit of that ambition became a focal point of virtually every interview, review article, and academic discussion that featured him. Unlike most successful playwrights who, for commercial and/ or artistic reasons, expand their creative reach into **film**, **television**, and other media, Wilson was almost single-minded in his devotion to completing his play cycle. For the remainder of his career he wrote few creative works of any kind other than the plays dedicated to the cycle. (A notable exception is the 1995 tele-vised adaptation of *The Piano Lesson*, for which he served as **producer** and writer of the teleplay. It is the only film or television adaptation of his plays Wilson ever permitted.) Wilson lived to see *Radio Golf*, the tenth and final play of the cycle, have its premier at the Yale Repertory Theatre in 2005 but died two years before its Broadway opening in 2007.

Wilson claimed that his plays were not straightforward political dramas, but he openly acknowledged his debt to American social drama traditions. His plays' recurring themes of African Americans struggling to reconcile their present-day social and economic conditions with their cultural and ethnic heritage ground his work in the social and political theater of the **Group Theatre**, **Clifford Odets**, **Arthur Miller**, **Lorraine Hansberry**, and the Black Arts Movement of the 1960s. Yet his plays also show a romantic quality reminiscent of nineteenth-century Russian playwright Anton Chekhov and Americans **Eugene O'Neill** and **Tennessee Williams**. Wilson is famous for his haunting, lyrical speeches

Table 5
August Wilson's Ten-Play Century Cycle

Title	Decade of Setting	World Premiere	Original Broadway Run
Jitney	1970s	Allegheny Repertory Theatre (Pittsburgh), 1982	None
Ma Rainey's Black Bottom Blues	1920s	Yale Repertory Theatre, 1984	October 11, 1984 – June 9, 1985
Fences	1950s	Yale Repertory Theatre, 1985	March 26, 1987 – June 26, 1988
Joe Turner's Done Come and Gone	1910s	Yale Repertory Theatre, 1986	March 27, 1988 – June 26, 1988
The Piano Lesson	1930s	Yale Repertory Theatre, 1987	April 16, 1990 – January 27, 1991
Two Trains Running	1960s	Yale Repertory Theatre, 1990	April 13, 1992 – August 30, 1992
Seven Guitars	1940s	Goodman Theater, Chicago, 1995	Mar 28, 1996 – September 8, 1996
King Hedley II	1980s	Pittsburgh Public Theatre, 1999	May 1, 2001 – July 1, 2001
Gem of the Ocean	1900s	Goodman Theatre Chicago, 2003	December 6, 2004 – February 6, 2005
Radio Golf	1990s	Yale Repertory Theatre, 2005	May 8, 2007 – July 1, 2007

Sources: Internet Broadway Database. http://www.ibdb.com/, May 2007. Theatre Database. Theatredatabase.com, May 2007.

emanating from characters who often enter and exit as if cued by the plays' spirituality as much as the demands of plot conflict.

Wilson died of cancer on October 2, 2005, in Seattle, Washington, where he had lived for the last 15 years of his life. He was survived by his third wife of 11 years, Costanza Romero, a costume designer whom he met on the set of the television taping of *The Piano Lesson*. Shortly after his death, the Jujamcyn Amusement Corporation, owners of the Virginia Theatre on Broadway, renamed the venue the August Wilson Theatre, making Wilson the first African American to have a Broadway theater named in his honor.

In 2009 a controversy arose over a revival of Wilson's play *Joe Turner Done Come and Gone*. Romero, the executive of her late husband's estate, for the first time granted permission for a white director, Bartlett Sher, to direct a Broadway production of an August Wilson play. During his lifetime, Wilson had strictly prohibited white directors from mounting Broadway productions of his works fearing, according to friends, that if it happened once, Broadway producers would never hire another African American director for his plays. Black cast members were publicly supportive of Sher's approach to the production, but many black directors decried the seemingly gratuitous underscoring of their underutilization in commercial theater.

Thomas A. Greenfield

Further Reading

Bryer Jackson R., and Mary C. Hartig, eds. *Conversations with August Wilson*. Jackson: University Press of Mississippi, 2006.

Healy, Patrick. "Director's Race Adds to Drama for an August Wilson Revival." *New York Times*, April 23, 2009. Retrieved April 23, 2009, from http://theater.nytimes.com/pages/theater/index.html.

Shannon, Sandra G. *The Dramatic Vision of August Wilson*. Washington, DC: Howard University Press, 1996.

WOLFE, GEORGE C. (1954–)
DIRECTOR, PRODUCER, WRITER

George C. Wolfe is one of the most highly decorated stage directors on and off Broadway; he has also directed **films**, written plays and librettos, and acted. He is best known for his tenure as Artistic Director and Producer (and heir to the legacy of **Joseph Papp**) of the Public Theater/Shakespeare in the Park from 1993 to 2004. He is African American and openly gay. He has worked on important productions in which race or sexual orientation are foregrounded, but he does limit his subject matter in any respect. He has been nominated for the Best Director Tony Award five times, winning twice for the 1993 *Angels in America, Part 1: Millennium Approaches* and the 1996 *Bring in 'Da Noise, Bring in 'Da Funk*. He earned Tony Nominations for *Jelly's Last Jam* (1992), *Angels in America, Part 2* (1993), and *Caroline, or Change* (2004).

Wolfe was born in Frankfort, Kentucky, the son of a teacher and government clerk. While attending Frankfort High School he began writing, acting, and directing. After a single year at Kentucky State University, he transferred to Pomona College in California where he earned his B.A. in Theatre. He worked for several years in Los Angeles at the Inner-City Cultural Center before moving to New York City, where he enrolled in the M.F.A. in Dramatic Writing and Musical Theatre programs at NYU's Tisch School of the Arts.

Wolfe wrote a **musical** and a play right out of graduate school, both of which were produced **Off-Broadway**: *Paradise* (1985) and *The Colored Museum* (1986), the latter of which remains a widely studied and frequently performed satire on African American identity in the 1980s. He then earned an Obie Award for directing his adaptation of Zora Neale Hurston stories, *Spunk* (1989). He has

George C. Wolfe in 2007. (AP Photo/Stuart Ramson)

written the book for the Broadway musicals *Jelly's Last Jam* (1991) and *The Wild Party* (2000) with co-author Michael John LaChiusa. He directed both productions. He was also the principal creative force behind the commercially successful "dance musical" *Bring in 'Da Noise, Bring in 'Da Funk.*

Wolfe's directing career has been his main focus, and it is here he has won most acclaim. Along with the plays and musicals that won him his Tony Awards and Tony Nominations for directing, he has directed Suzan-Lori Parks's *Topdog/Underdog* (2002) and the Off-Broadway **Tony Kushner** translation of Bertolt Brecht's *Mother Courage and Her Children* (2006). He also has a long-standing association with performer/author Anna Deavere Smith, producing and directing her Broadway play *Twilight: Los Angeles 1992* (1994) and adapting her Off-Broadway play *Fire in the Mirror* for **television** in 1993.

Wolfe's tenure as Artistic Director and Producer of the Public Theater is widely viewed as an important, even historic, catalyst for diversifying content, personnel, and audiences in New York theater, both off and on Broadway. (Of his vision for the Public Theater, for years the premiere Off-Broadway theater in New York, Wolfe wryly said his goal was to make the lobby look like a New York subway stop.) He was a fervent advocate and practitioner of color-blind casting, an adventurous backer of experimental and potentially controversial plays, and a legendary nurturer of new playwrights from diverse backgrounds. Parks, **David Henry Hwang**, Nilo Cruz, and Diana Son are among the better known playwrights who benefited from early collaborations with Wolfe.

His most successful shows in terms of Broadway runs and mainstream awards were his own *Bring in 'Da Noise, Bring in 'Da Funk*, created with and for dancer/choreographer Savion Glover, and Parks's Pulitzer Prize–winning *Topdog/Underdog*, both of which he moved to Broadway after developing the first productions at the Public Theater. In all, Wolfe moved 11 shows from the Public Theater to Broadway during his tenure, directing most of them.

His extraordinary artistic achievements and community-minded outreach efforts belie his exceptional talents as a manager. Wolfe, who inherited a weak financial situation at the Public Theater when he took over in 1993, managed to eliminate the theater's debt and build its endowment before handing over the reigns to Oskar Eustis in 2004—an astonishing achievement in modern not-for-profit theater management.

Wolfe left the Public Theater in 2004 to work in film and do more writing. In 2005 he directed the film *Lackawanna Blues*, based on a play he had produced at the Public, for HBO. *Nights in Rodanthe*, his feature film directorial debut, was released in 2008. Yet, thus far, Wolfe's major contributions to American theater and American culture lie in the rare achievement of bringing the diversity of the City to its professional stages and guiding important new playwrights into the ever-growing library of American literature.

Melanie N. Blood

Further Reading

Green, Jesse. "Where Have You Gone, Impresarios?" *New York Times Magazine*, October 3, 2004. Retrieved June 15, 2009, from http://www.nytimes.com/2004/10/03/magazine/03PUBLIC.html.

Hill, Erroll, and James Vernon Hatch. *A History of African American Theatre*. Cambridge, England: Cambridge University Press, 2003.

WOMEN AND BROADWAY: THE EARLY YEARS, 1845–1939

Prior to women securing the right to vote in 1920, theater was one of the few forums in which women enjoyed a public presence. By the mid to late nineteenth century New York City was affirming its status as both the capital of American commercial theater and a major center for women's political activism. The emergence of women on Broadway during this time intersected with two important feminist political movements: the suffragist movement (approximately 1848–1920), in which women fought for the legal right to vote, and the New Woman movement (approximately 1875–1930) in which women reimagined themselves as equals with men beyond the right to vote: in career, in family life, and in sexual freedom. As women became more aware of the need to establish their own public voice, New York's commercial theater became an increasingly politically charged forum wherein women could achieve social and economic autonomy. Many notable women did—principally as actresses but also as directors, theater managers, and **playwrights**.

The careers of several women of this period both embody and symbolize the paradoxical situation in which women in theater found themselves, representing both traditional nineteenth-century Victorian values and twentieth-century progressive values at the same time. Actresses in particular occupied a paradoxical place in the American imagination. Offstage, the image of actresses loomed in stark contrast to prevailing Victorian feminine social norms; they were often seen more or less in league with prostitutes selling their time and physical presence for public consumption. Onstage, however, within the social vacuum of a play's performance, actresses enjoyed the privilege of being seen and heard in front of an audience without violating the rules of acceptable feminine behavior.

Women Pioneers in Theater in the 1800s

A breakthrough event in the history of women on Broadway and American culture occurred in 1845 when Anna Cora Mowatt's (1819–1870) play *Fashion* was produced at New York's Park Theatre. It is generally considered to be the first commercially successful American play written by a woman. (The first known professional play written by an American woman was Mercy Otis Warren's *The Ladies of Castile* in 1784.) A newspaper announcement of Mowatt's play speaks to the reception a woman playwright could expect in the nineteenth century: "A Native American Comedy, by a Mrs. Mowatt, is rumored to be in rehearsal . . . We have little confidence in female dramatic productions . . . but we wish the lady a happy debut" (Barlow 1985, ix). Mowatt proved the doubters wrong and the play was a success. Mowatt later moved from playwright to actress, an unusual transition for the time. However, her decision to do so garnered her a reputation as one of the first "gentlewomen" to take the stage professionally, an action that to some extent called into question the moral taint often associated with actresses.

The next significant woman in Broadway history, **Laura Keene** (1826–1873), pioneered the emergence of women in Broadway theater management. In 1855 Keene, a successful New York and touring actress, leased her first Broadway theater (the Metropolitan in lower Manhattan), assigning herself the position of actress-manager. As such, Keene selected her own roles and controlled the overall artistic vision of all in-productions at the venue. She was the first woman to do so for any major Broadway theater. Her managerial career lasted eight years during which time she mounted numerous crowd-pleasing productions. Her most famous show, ***Our American Cousin*** (1858), was one of the first long-running plays at a major Broadway theater. (The play is, of course, notorious as the show Abraham Lincoln attended in Washington, D.C., on the night of his assassination in 1865.)

By laying the groundwork for women's entry into theatrical management, Keene bore the public shock and resentment of male managers against whom she competed, often successfully. Keene fought back against her critics, adapting a traditional feminine public role of decrying her critics' lack of chivalry and pleading for public sympathy. Behind the scenes, however, she rejected Victorian feminine vulnerability, overseeing every detail of her tightly run, efficient operation and molding an ensemble-based acting company behind her starring roles. When Keene retired from management, she passed the leadership baton to actress Mrs. John Wood (Matilda Vining, 1836c.–1915, who went professionally by her married name). Mrs. Wood successfully ran Keene's former operation for three years.

Keene's choice to hire a woman successor represents a strategy women in commercial theater came to rely upon: an "Old Girls' Network" of mentoring, hiring, and promoting other women. Mrs. Wood had learned managerial skills from Keene as a member of Keene's theater company before being hired by Keene as theater manager. As time went on, Broadway women drew more heavily on the power of female networking as the number of women in positions of leadership increased.

The feminist implications of actress-managers' work rippled outward in multiple directions. Actress Charlotte Cushman (1816–1876), for example, not satisfied with the parts available to her, managed productions so that she might take Shakespearean male roles, displaying a woman onstage who assumed male power and privilege. Mrs. Woods was able to take her three years of managerial success as Laura Keene's successor and to open her own theater in England. In the nineteenth century virtually anything that relocated women from the private to the public sphere sent a message about gender that likely contradicted social norms.

Those actresses who did not become actress-managers also found venues—or venues found them—in which they challenged gender norms. Fanny Kemble (1809–1893), from the time she first stepped out onto Broadway stages in 1832, challenged the notion that women on the stage were morally questionable. Her artistry in parts such as **Shakespeare**'s Juliet and Portia and the dutiful daughter Julia in Sheridan Knowles's *The Hunchback* (1832) earned her respect from audiences and **critics** alike. Actress and author Olive Logan (1841–1909) fought the notion that acting was synonymous with immorality. Logan penned books about her life as a stage actress and wrote opinion pieces in newspapers arguing that it was possible to both uphold moral standards and earn a living from acting on the stage.

On the other end of the spectrum, Adah Isaacs Menken (1835–1868), instead of fighting the perception that actresses were morally loose because they showed their bodies for public consumption, embraced the idea of the female body as spectacle. In so doing she drew audiences, publicity, and the wrath of some feminist critics (including Olive Logan). Menken began a movement that embraced women using their bodies as spectacle in New York commercial theater, making herself into a star. The novelty and shock value of her performances underscored most of her reviews, both positive and negative. Menken's most famous role, that of the male lead in *Mazeppa* (1866), had her strapped to the back of a horse seemingly nude (she wore skin-colored tights and a skin-colored body suit). The show toured the United States and Europe before coming to Broadway. New York critics excoriated her vulgarity, which had the presumably unintended result of enhancing her fame, visibility, and *bona fides* as a spokeswoman on political issues. Menken used her fame to publicly air her views on women, disparaging female domesticity as antithetical to female independence.

While Menken was a superstar of bodily display, the general phenomenon of the "leg show" began in earnest the same year as Menken's Broadway debut as Mazeppa. The first Broadway leg show was also Broadway's first **musical, *The Black Crook***, which debuted in 1866. Whereas audiences had previously judged actresses on their elocution skills, when *The Black Crook* hit the stage with female dancers in short costumes, audiences were not attending to the actresses' voices. Plotline and play quality took a backseat to costumes that revealed the bodily shape of the women performers. Although those legs were heavily hosed, in the nineteenth century any formfitting view of the shape of a woman's body was considered, depending on the audience, gloriously titillating or morally reprehensible.

Lydia Thompson (1838–1908) and her British Blondes followed Menken and *The Black Crook*, inaugurating what was to become the modern burlesque show.

Soon, leg shows and burlesque shows competed for audiences by pushing the boundaries of what constituted "legitimate" displays of the female body. Within this context, female performers were recruited based on their bodily dimensions and movement skills without much regard to their skills as actresses—to the dismay of Olive Logan and many other legitimate stage actresses. By the 1870s, the leg show and large-scale spectacles had begun to deplete opportunities for serious stage actresses. With the new emphasis on youth and beauty generated by the leg show, actresses found it increasingly difficult to establish long-lasting stage careers. (Such spectacles also laid the foundation and public interest for twentieth-century showgirl productions—most notably those by **Florenz Ziegfeld** [1867–1932], whose wildly popular *Follies* shows capitalized on the female form as commercial entertainment.)

Toward the end of the nineteenth century, while Menken and those who followed in her footsteps were making their living from female sexuality, a genre of thoughtful drama examining women's lives and experiences began to emerge. The collision of the titillating and the cerebral forms of women's performance was a microcosm of a larger battle of genres on Broadway: Spectacle versus drama. Each form offered vastly different opportunities for women and each represented a different vision of women in the American cultural imagination: spectacle presented women as commodities to be looked at and desired, while drama demanded that audiences consider women as intellectual beings with complex lives worthy of the same serious attention as men's. Serious drama, or what came to be known as "the theater of ideas," attracted actresses who found themselves advocating not only for particular roles in plays but for new ways in which theater could represent women on stage. This was no easy task.

The 1894 Broadway production of Henrik Ibsen's *A Doll's House*, although written in Norway, marked a turning point in American drama. When **Minnie Maddern Fiske** (1865–1932) as Ibsen's heroine Nora famously slammed the door on husband and home in favor of autonomy and self-awareness, she created a social uproar among audiences. That one gesture signaled a new day and age for actresses in search of roles that examined the complexity of female life. Among the most highly regarded American-born female theatrical personalities at the turn of the century, Mrs. Fiske (as she was known) created a public image for herself as an intelligent, strong-willed, autonomous woman. Her superb performances in serious roles and her success as a theatrical producer, director, and writer gave her sufficient fame and credibility to participate openly in political debates and major business disputes, acquitting herself as a witty debater and formidable business competitor. Widely seen as an underdog who was strong and intelligent, Mrs. Fiske often gave speeches on stage about the evils of the **Theatrical Syndicate**, the notoriously monopolistic organization that dominated American commercial theater production from the 1890s to the 1910s.

Actress and suffragist Mary Shaw (1854–1929) also found that curtain calls of her theatrical performances were a powerful platform from which to deliver women's rights speeches. Shaw, more so than any other actress of her day, explored the multiple feminist possibilities the stage offered. As each role Shaw played on stage increased her fame as a Broadway actress, she used her notoriety and influence to champion two causes: strong roles for actresses and women's rights in general. Recognizing the unique political opportunity afforded her as a successful actress, Shaw had earned great fame and admiration for performing in and championing the plays of Henrik Ibsen and **George Bernard Shaw** (no relation). Inasmuch as Ibsen and Shaw were playwrights whose major works dealt with issues particular to women, Mary Shaw championed their works as intellectually stimulating, uplifting havens for actresses within the male-dominated arena of Broadway. Such a stance reflected her belief in theater's largely untapped power to communicate women's experiences and concerns.

Actresses and Activism in the Early 1900s

In 1913, Mary Shaw announced the opening of the Gamut Club, a hybrid organization that brought together the culture of the women's club movement, the activist spirit of the suffragist and feminist movements, and theater productions specifically addressed to women's issues and audiences. As New York's earliest explicitly feminist theater group, the Gamut Club strived for progressive political change. At its peak, the Gamut Club boasted over 250 members and included the brightest female names in Broadway theater: actress Lillian Russell; playwright, actress, and director Edith Ellis; actress and director **Ethyl Barrymore**; and playwright and actress Olive Logan. These women rivaled the popularity and visibility of male political and theatrical figures of the day.

Fiske, Logan, and Shaw laid the groundwork for other actresses to use their fame in pursuit of specific political goals. In 1912 the Women's Political Union, a high-profile New York–based suffragist organization, held a tea in honor of many of Broadway's leading pro-suffrage actresses. Europe and Broadway stage legend Sarah Bernhardt spoke out for women's suffrage and marched in the 1913 New York suffrage parade. (Virtually all of the numerous New York City suffragist parades in the 1910s had an actress section and each one was largely populated by Broadway actresses.)

Prior to 1920 the successful actress had at her disposal two assets that she could parlay into other activities in public venues: her position as an actress, which allowed her the possibility of economic autonomy without breaking established gender norms, and her fame, which categorized her as a public figure and provided her with a far stronger public voice than that of other women, working or not. Female playwrights on Broadway also had the opportunity to directly voice their thoughts to a large audience but could do so without the moral reprimands actresses often faced. However, far fewer women playwrights found acceptance on Broadway than did actresses.

Of all the female playwrights of the time, **Rachel Crothers** (1878–1958) stands out as the most prolific and the most commercially successful. Beginning in 1906 with *The Three of Us*, her first Broadway play, and ending with her final Broadway hit, *Susan and God* in 1938, Crothers was the first American woman to carve out an enduring successful commercial career as a playwright. Like so many of the actresses of the early twentieth century, Crothers used her success as a Broadway playwright to gain control over other aspects of her productions, including directing and acting as well as authorship. Crothers's career was founded on feminist principles born out of necessity—tools needed in order to overcome the obstacles in front of her as a female nonactress trying to succeed in the theater industry. She continually drew upon resources available to her through female networking, a kind of "practical" or "survivalist" feminism.

As a young playwright in 1907 Crothers joined the Society of Dramatic Authors, a female-dominated group that modeled itself after the all-male American Dramatists' Club, the most prestigious club for male playwrights at the time. Crothers's membership in the society shaped her awareness of her position as a woman director, with all its political and social implications. As a result of Crothers's successful networking within the society, Broadway actress-manager Maxine Elliot hired Crothers to direct Crothers's own play, *Myself Bettina* (1908), in which Elliot starred. This initial opportunity provided Crothers with sufficient credibility within New York theater circles to hire herself as director for most of the other plays she wrote (18 between 1908 and 1938, of which she directed 13). Crothers's plays explored female characters' struggles to negotiate conflicting societal messages of how to live, love, and exist. Her mainstream yet feminist mentality is best exemplified in her 1910 play *A Man's World*, which she wrote and directed, which ran on Broadway for a respectable 71 performances. *Young Wisdom* (1914) pushed the boundaries of Broadway's moral tone and yet stayed within mainstream expectations, a particular Crothers specialty. Gail, a young woman with highly progressive attitudes about women, insists on a "trial marriage" (i.e., premarital sex) with her fiancé. Crothers's plot exposed truths about women who contradicted American Victorian-era mores and espoused the values of the emerging New Woman of the suffragist and women's rights movements: that women were not satisfied with either pure domesticity or pure autonomy. However, the play also reinforced broadly acceptable Victorian beliefs about women as the moral keepers of society. Many of Crothers's plays found success because the topics and character dilemmas mirrored well-known social problems. Unlike most commercial theater productions, Crothers's productions seldom ended with satisfying resolutions. Instead, what happiness her female characters were able to find generally came with great sacrifice, usually resulting in a compromise of whatever goals the female character set out with in the beginning of the play.

By the late 1910s and 1920s, thanks in part to the pioneering efforts of Crothers, women playwrights were beginning to see productions of their works mounted in New York's commercial theaters. In most cases these plays explored women's lives and kept women as a focal point in the commercial and profit-driven Broadway arena. Zona Gale won the Pulitzer Prize in drama for her play *Miss Lulu Bett* (1921), the first woman to earn that honor. Anne Nichols's *Abie's Irish Rose* (1922) ran for 2,327 performances, becoming the longest-running Broadway play up to that time and earning Nichols the title of the "million-dollar playwright." (The play still ranks as the third longest-running nonmusical production in Broadway history.) Comedy playwright Anita Loos scored early career hits with *The Whole Town's Talking* (1923) and *Gentlemen Prefer Blondes* (1926). Lillian Trimble Bradley wrote melodramas that had moderately successful runs on Broadway, including *The Wonderful Thing* (1921) and *Izzy* (1924). Yet even into the 1930s women playwrights still found commercial theater to be a hostile environment, with one critic claiming that women playwrights "rarely philosophize, their social consciousness is rarely apparent; . . . they don't raise you to the heights of aesthetic emotions" (Barlow 1985, xxx).

Prior to World War II women playwrights found a more hospitable environment in the Little Theater Movement, a specifically noncommercial genre of theater that began in the 1910s. Women served in these companies as set designers, directors, playwrights, and, of course, actresses without having to go through Broadway's various hoops and obstacles. In New York City, the **Neighborhood Playhouse** was run by five women and the **Provincetown Players**, a group formed to encourage American playwrights, had a membership consisting of close to 50 percent women, including playwrights **Susan Glaspell**, Neith Boyce, Rita Wellman, and Djuna Barnes, as well as a female set designer. No matter how successful on the little theater stage, most plays did not transfer well to Broadway, with a few exceptions (mostly from Provincetown playwright **Eugene O'Neill**). However, Susan Glaspell's *Trifles* (1913) a one-act produced in repertory with other short plays in one of the **Shubert Brothers'** Broadway theaters, has survived as a defining work of American social drama and feminist theater.

While a select group of women were writing, acting, and directing serious, woman-centered dramas, the successor of the leg show—the chorus girl—was becoming a fixture on Broadway. Whereas Crothers, Fiske, Mary Shaw, and others wrote and performed complex social plays reflecting individual women's lives, chorus girls represented the opposite end of the spectrum: long lines of identically clad female bodies performing identical movements. In the 1910s and 1920s, Ziegfeld ruled the chorus girl world, even introducing nudity onto the Broadway stage. Broadway, however, found itself in a precarious position when presenting explicitly sexualized images of women on stage. While the female chorus girl's existence was based on her ability to arouse desire, Broadway standards dictated some restraint in presenting sexual content. Male audience members needed to be able to enjoy female images without the taint of immorality. More than any other sexualized stage show, *Ziegfeld's Follies* made staged female sexuality acceptable by giving chorus girls "a detached aristocratic allure keeping them nearly motionless on stage" (Hamilton 1992, 89). In addition, the young women on stage seemed sexually nonthreatening because of their anonymity. Owing to their shear numbers and uniform presentation, they charmed the viewer with dazzling spectacle rather than seductive allure. More explicitly sexual entertainers such as Mae West (1893–1980) and Adah Menken, as well as the strong feminist Minnie Maddern Fiske, forced a specific female identity into the public realm. Both before and after women gained the right to vote, a woman who projected a strong individual identity, whether sexually or intellectually generated, on stage or elsewhere, created an explicitly political and potentially disruptive intrusion into broadly accepted middle-class expectations and norms of female behavior.

With few exceptions, women who performed on Broadway after 1920 found themselves either boxed into a sexualized role (in musicals and revues) or serious-actress role (in literate dramas)—dubbed the Ibsen versus Gibson girl dilemma after the esteemed Norwegian playwright and a popular pinup girl magazine illustrator, respectively. Chorus girls generally had less career mobility than serious actresses, although some managed the unlikely move from anonymous stage female body to theatrical star. The most famous of these was **Fanny Brice** (1891–1951) who, after several years as a chorus girl, became a solo star of the *Ziegfeld Follies* and the most successful comedienne of her day. Brice represented and largely originated a new role for women on stage, in which the actress interacted with the audience by making them laugh, sustaining her persona as the central element of the performance. Brice used her Jewish ethnicity—a potential disadvantage to her career otherwise—as a source of humor in her self-representation. Like Brice, many other comediennes created comedy with their bodies, personalities, and/or culture in ways that were contrary to the idealized image of the chorus girl. Marie Dressler and Trixie Friganza were overweight. Eva Tanguay created the antitheses of femininity by proving that she could be as verbally and physically aggressive on stage as any man. Also like Brice, Beatrice Lillie (1894–1989), who first traveled to New York from London in 1924 as a member of a touring English burlesque revue, played Broadway as a comedienne from the 1930s through the 1950s, commanding enormous audience and industry respect. **Ethel Merman** (1908–1984), another musical star whose career drew on the tools of the comedienne, debuted on Broadway in 1930 **George and Ira Gershwin**'s *Girl Crazy*. She went on to star in numerous Broadway shows, becoming a Broadway legend for her stage-consuming diva persona and her show-stopping "belt it out" singing style.

In the years between the two World Wars women were less inclined to protest for equal rights than they had been only a few years earlier. Having won the vote in 1920, there was no vote to fight for. Thus, theatrical women in this period, as a whole, were less politically vocal than those in the generation that preceded them. Yet during this period women in theater built on these previous advances. For example, in 1928 Ethyl Barrymore opened the Ethyl Barrymore Theatre, which still bears her name. While theatrical management opportunities for all actors diminished as the Theatrical Syndicate and other businessmen took over the management end of the business, female directors were appearing on Broadway in increasing numbers. Mary Shaw directed a successful revival of *Mrs. Warren's Profession* (1922). Lillian Trimble Bradley directed three Broadway productions between the years 1921 and 1925. Agnes Morgan, **Eva Le Gallienne**, Margaret Wycherly, Winifred Lenihan, Auriol Lee, Cheryl Crawford, and Antionette Perry (for whom the Tony Awards are named) also made their mark as directors prior to World War II. Margaret Webster (1905–1972) entered the directing scene in the 1930s and proved herself to be one of the most capable directors of the twentieth century. Webster, who primarily directed classical plays, made history when, in

1943, she cast **Paul Robeson** as the first black Othello in her Broadway production of the Shakespeare classic.

Although the women-friendly Little Theater Movement of the first two decades of the century was struggling by 1920, in its wake a new theater group emerged, melding the goals of the Little Theater Movement with the commercial opportunities offered by Broadway. The **Theatre Guild**, including board members Helen Westley and Theresa Helburn, leased the Garrick Theater in 1919 and began bringing serious drama to the commercial venue of Broadway. The original Theater Guild members included several women with ties to the Little Theater Movement, including Edna St. Vincent Millay and Ida Rauh (both formerly of the Provincetown Players), actress Helen Freeman, and actress/director Eva Le Gallienne. The Guild trained and employed Cheryl Crawford, who later became one of the founders of the now legendary Group Theater. The Guild also staged Lillian Sabine's *The Rise of Silas Lapham* (1919) and produced Dorothy and DuBose Heyward's *Porgy* (1927), one of the few Broadway dramatic productions before World War II to employ African American actors. The play starred **Rose McClendon** (1885c.–1936) the leading African American stage actress of her time. Theresa Helburn proved to be an important figure in the Guild, directing productions and coming up with the idea to transform Lynn Rigg's *Green Grows the Lilacs* (1931) into a musical—eventually titled *Oklahoma!* (1943). The production changed the face of the American musical. Notwithstanding its historic contributions and numerous successes, the Guild was financially floundering by the end of World War II and many of the founding members had left for more financially stable prospects.

For playwrights, Broadway in the 1920s and 1930s proved fickle, but several women made their mark and a few made history. Zoe Akins won the Pulitzer Prize for *The Old Maid* (1935), edging out playwright **Lillian Hellman**'s controversial Broadway success *The Children's Hour* (1934). Hellman, however, bounced back from the loss, becoming one of the most influential playwrights of the twentieth century. Hellman's other Broadway productions included *The Little Foxes* (1939) about the implications of greed for a Southern family; *Watch on the Rhine* (1941), a powerful anti-Nazi play; *Another Part of Forest* (1946), a continuation of the *Foxes* drama that Hellman also staged; and *The Autumn Garden* (1951), a humorous drama set in a resort in New Orleans. Her plays spoke about difficult subjects and challenged audiences to reconsider their comfortable American values. Each of her plays, save one, earned a place in critic Burns Mantle's influential annual collection *Best American Dramas*. In her plays, her numerous other writings, and her public persona, Hellman was confrontational and uncompromising on matters of politics, war, and sexuality, and like many of her suffragist predecessors, a highly controversial public figure.

The 1930s: The Depression, Musicals, and the Call of Hollywood

Much of the revolutionary spirit that animated women's early contributions to and participation on Broadway dipped beneath the surface by the end of the 1920s.

Commercialism and the return to domestic values after the vote was won paved the way for a quieter, less politicized feminist presence on Broadway. By the 1930s actresses who in previous decades might have traded fame for leadership positions in theater, abandoned Broadway for Hollywood. Gertrude Lawrence, Katharine Hepburn, and Katharine Cornell are among the more notable performers whose cinema fame eclipsed their Broadway beginnings. Yet **Helen Hayes** (1900–1993), who had been successful as a child **vaudeville** star and a light comedy ingenue in the 1920s, came into her own as "First Lady of the American Theater" with riveting title role performances in the historic dramas *Mary of Scotland* (1933) and *Victoria Regina* (1935).

In the early years of Broadway, women explored the possibilities that American commercial theater offered them to be represented and to represent themselves. Gender, in particular women's role in society, was constructed and deconstructed through productions that ranged from *A Man's World* to *Mazeppa* to *Ziegfeld's Follies*. All of these performances forced a woman's presence into the public arena, raising and often answering the question of what is women's place—and what are women's places—in the theater and the world.

Pamela Cobrin

Further Reading

Auster, Alibert. *Actresses and Suffragists: Women in the American Theater 1890–1920*. New York: Praeger Publishers, 1984.

Barlow, Judith E. "Introduction." *Plays by American Women 1900–1930*, ed. Judith E. Barlow. New York: Applause, 1985, p. ix.

Curry, Jane Kathleen. *19th Century American Women Theater Managers*. Westport, CT: Greenwood Press, 1994.

Dudden, Faye. *Women in the American Theater; Actresses and Audiences 1790–1870*. New Haven, CT: Yale University Press, 1994.

Glenn, Susan A. *Female Spectacle: The Roots of Modern Feminism*. Cambridge, MA: Harvard University Press, 2000.

Hamilton, Marybeth. "Mae West Live: Sex, The Drag, and 1920s Broadway." *The Drama Review*, 36, no. 4 (Winter 1992): 89.

Hapgood, Norman. *The Stage in America*. New York: The Macmillan Company, 1901.

WOMEN AND BROADWAY: THE LATER YEARS, 1940–PRESENT

The Baby Boom Years: 1940–Mid-1960s

Although women made inroads working in Broadway theater through the 1940s, the 1950s saw a vast disparity between the employment levels of men and women, especially in terms of playwriting and directing. Many women who did manage to earn recognition on Broadway in the postwar era had established solid careers prior to the war. The decline in the women's workforce was not specific to Broadway, of course, but emblematic of a larger social phenomenon. As thousands of men returned from the war, they reestablished their positions in the American workforce or entered college on the G.I. Bill, giving them a substantial advantage upon graduation. Women who were employed during the war were now largely relegated back to traditional duties of housewife and mother. Marriages increased, along with the legendary baby boom from 1946 to 1964, producing some 79 million babies in the United States. The shifting images and economic realities of women making the transition from workers in the war effort to contented homemakers had an impact on women in commercial theater much as it did in most aspects of American life.

Salary discrimination against women, a staple of commercial theater economics since the days of **vaudeville** and follies persisted well into the postwar era. Women performers also faced issues of inequality beyond issues related to compensation. Women appearing on stage were generally limited to the roles of supportive mothers and wives or objects of sexual desire that male writers and producers created for them. In addition, the shear number of substantial roles for women paled in comparison to the number of roles for their male counterparts.

Despite these inequities, many women gained fame for their talents on Broadway in the years following World War II. When the **American Theatre Wing** established the Antoinette Perry Awards (Tony Awards) in 1947, male and female performers were presented with a rare equal opportunity to win recognition for Broadway work. By 1951, the now standard four categories of Tony Awards for actresses (Best Actress and Best Actress in a Featured Role for a play and a musical, respectively—identical categories with males) were firmly in place. Women winning the Tony for leading dramatic roles in the early years of the Tony included **Helen Hayes**, **Jessica Tandy**, **Uta Hagen**, **Julie Harris**, and Joan Plowright. The musical theater also boasted an array of Tony Award–winning female leads, among them **Mary Martin**, **Ethel Merman**, Rosalind Russell, **Gwen Verdon**, and **Carol Channing**.

Although they were paid less and were generally less visible than their male counterparts on Broadway, women have periodically earned comparable recognition with men, and even occasional preeminence, in technical fields. Somewhat surprisingly, three women were considered leaders in the world of lighting design during the postwar era. Jean Rosenthal, who had received her technical training with the **Federal Theatre Project** in the 1930s, became a highly respected designer of both dance and theater lighting. After her Broadway debut in 1942 with the **operetta** *Rosalinda*, she designed lighting for such hit productions as *West Side Story* (1957), *The Sound of Music* (1959), *Barefoot in the Park* (1963), *Fiddler on the Roof* (1964), and *Hello, Dolly!* (1964). A leader in the field, Rosenthal designed more than 75 Broadway productions by 1980. Another pioneering designer, Peggy Clark, worked in both costume and scenic design before settling on lighting. Her Broadway debut came as a lighting designer for *Beggar's Holiday* in 1946. Her major Broadway credits in the postwar years include some of the most successful and significant shows of the era, including *Brigadoon* (1947),

Gentlemen Prefer Blondes (1949), *Paint Your Wagon* (1951), *Wonderful Town* (1953), *Peter Pan* (1954), *Auntie Mame* (1956), *Bells Are Ringing* (1956), *Flower Drum Song* (1958), *Bye Bye Birdie* (1960), and *The Unsinkable Molly Brown* (1960). Also in the postwar era, Tharon Musser began a long Broadway career that would span more than five decades. Musser made her Broadway debut as a lighting designer for **Eugene O'Neill**'s *A Long Day's Journey into Night* in 1956. She designed regularly on Broadway, accumulating an impressive 118 lighting design credits by 2007. Despite the success of women lighting designers, only one woman, Jean Eckart, gained acclaim as a scenic designer in this period, and her credits were shared with her husband, William Eckart. In addition to scenic design, they occasionally shared lighting and costume design credits as well. The Eckharts designed lights, costumes, and scenery for the 1959 production of *Fiorello!*

The burgeoning "golden age of **musicals**" from the mid-1940s to the mid-1960s increased opportunities for costume designers and choreographers, fields that had traditionally included women. Irene Sharaff earned a Tony Award for Costume Design in 1952 for *The King and I*, in addition to four other Tony nominations in the 1950s and 1960s. In an extraordinary, and probably not repeatable, Tony Award sweep, costume designer Lucinda Ballard won the first-ever Tony Award for Costume Design for her collective work on five different shows in the same season. She also won in 1962 for the play *The Gay Life*. Choreographer **Agnes de Mille**, a giant in the world of concert modern dance, became famous for her pioneering choreography in *Oklahoma!* (1943) as well as other hit shows such as *Carousel* (1945), *Brigadoon* (1947), and *Gentlemen Prefer Blondes* (1949). Other women achieved success as choreographers during this period. Most notable among them was Onna White who earned eight Tony nominations during her career, for musicals such as *The Music Man* (1958), *Irma La Douce* (1961), and *Mame* (1966).

Women **playwrights** and directors were a distinct rarity on Broadway during the postwar era, but a few pioneering women found critical acclaim. Playwright Bella Cohen Spewack began writing Broadway plays before the war, including the smash hit *Boy Meets Girl* (1935). She continued getting both plays and musicals produced in the postwar years. Her biggest hit was the Tony-winning musical *Kiss Me Kate* (1949), coauthored by husband Samuel Spewack. Writer Anita Loos also made her Broadway debut in prewar years, but found a hit with the 1949 musical *Gentlemen Prefer Blondes*, based on her novel of the same name. In 1951 she opened a stage version of *Gigi*, adapted from the novel by the French author Colette, followed in 1959 by another adaptation of Colette's *Chéri*. British-born playwright Enid Bagnold earned a Tony nomination in 1956 for *The Chalk Garden*, and Frances Goodrich, along with co-author and husband Albert Hackett, won the Tony Award that same year for *The Diary of Anne Frank*.

Although Goodrich had an illustrious writing career, mainly in **film**, her Broadway success was eclipsed the following year by the next woman to win a Tony nomination for Best Play, Lorraine Hansberry. Her drama *A Raisin in the Sun* (1959), told the story of a black family's struggles for social and economic advancement in postwar Chicago. Hansberry made history as the first African

American woman to have a play produced on Broadway, and she won a New York Drama Critics Circle Award for the play. Today the play is considered to be a landmark work of modern American drama and a definitive play in the canon of African American drama and literature. She followed up her Broadway debut with the decidedly less successful *The Sign in Sidney Brustein's Window*. Her death of cancer in 1965, at age 34, deprived Broadway of one of its most revered and promising young talents.

In the world of musical theater, only a few women writers gained attention, including **Richard Rodgers**'s daughter Mary, who made her Broadway debut in 1959 as the composer of *Once Upon a Mattress*. By the end of World War II, lyricist and book writer Dorothy Fields already had a string of Broadway credits (cowriting with her brother, Herbert Fields). She had a big hit in 1946 with *Annie Get Your Gun*, followed by such well-known shows as *A Tree Grows in Brooklyn* (1951), *Redhead* (1959; Tony Award for Best Musical), and *Sweet Charity* (1966). Lyricist and writer **Betty Comden**, along with her partner **Adolph Green**, made her Broadway debut (as the writer of the book and the lyrics as well as a performer) in 1944 with *On the Town*, launching an illustrious career that included *Wonderful Town* (1953; Tony for Best Musical), *Peter Pan* (1954), and *Bells Are Ringing* (1956).

The story of women directors on Broadway is quite sobering. Historian Helen Housely tabulated that from 1945 to 1950 women directed an average of 11.6 percent of Broadway productions, but from 1951 to 1961 the average plummeted to 2 percent (Housely 1993, 112). Women had more difficulty getting hired to direct musicals on Broadway owing to producers' reluctance to entrust women with the ever-increasing production budgets and the attendant increased pressure for generating a substantial box-office return. In one example, director Mary Hunter was hired to direct the new musical *High Button Shoes* (then under a different title), but she was abruptly fired when producers decided they could make more money by replacing her with renowned director **George Abbott**.

New Voices, New Movements: The 1960s to the 1970s

In the 1960s several benchmark events set the stage for the American women's liberation movement to come. The introduction in 1960 of the birth control pill followed by new groundbreaking publications, such as Helen Gurley Brown's *Sex and the Single Girl* in 1962 and Betty Friedan's *The Feminine Mystique* in 1963, fueled many women's desire to revolt against traditional social and sexual norms. Yet as women slowly gained ground on issues involving their sexuality, they found they still had little voice in the public sphere, even within larger civil protest movements, and certainly had not achieved equity in the workplace. Friedan helped change that in 1966 as a co-founder of the National Organization for Women (NOW), which recognized and fought sexism in the legal system, in employment practices, and in portrayals of women in media and popular culture. By the 1970s many women were eager to explore new identities, inspiring a number of women playwrights and other women artists to call for social change by creating new works.

Given Broadway's history of white male privilege, it is not surprising that during the 1960s, the new feminist movement notwithstanding, women continued to be underrepresented on the Great White Way. With the exception of the rock musical *Hair* (1968), few plays or musicals involving countercultural themes or serious challenges to societal norms came to the Broadway stage. Most experimental works, including those by newly formed women's theaters, were found Off-Off-Broadway and in small theaters around the country, where salaries and production budgets were small and commercial success was rarely a driving force or a practical possibility. However, as women gained voice and experience through these smaller venues, a few found their way to Broadway, particularly when a production became a hit in a remote venue and moved up the ranks to larger commercial performance theaters.

The Tony Awards continued to draw recognition to exceptional female leads in straight plays, including **Julie Harris**, Colleen Dewhurst, Irene Worth, and Maureen Stapleton. Their counterparts in musical theater who enjoyed the Tony spotlight included Liza Minnelli, **Angela Lansbury**, Leslie Uggams, and Lauren Bacall. However, all of these women performed in roles written for them by men. Few women playwrights found representation on Broadway during this period, though there were exceptions. In 1974 Marjorie Barkentin earned a Tony nomination for Best Play for *Ulysses in Nighttown*, a dramatization of James Joyce's *Ulysses*. A more notable success was Ntozake Shange's *for colored girls who have considered suicide/when the rainbow is enuf*, which earned a Tony nomination as Best Play in 1977. Thematically her piece, a self-described "choreopoem" combining choreography and dramatization through poetry, revolved around the lives of black women, their joys, and their disappointments. Shange's choreopoems were first performed in San Francisco bars before the production took shape at New York's New Federal Theater. *For colored girls* next gained momentum at **Joseph Papp**'s Public Theater, at the time New York's most prestigious **Off-Broadway** venue. The show transferred to Broadway in 1976 and has since become a canonical work of African American drama.

Another African American woman to make Broadway history during the 1970s was actor/director/writer Vinnette Carroll, who became the first black woman to earn a Tony nomination as a director for *Don't Bother Me, I Can't Cope* (1973). She created the gospel-inspired musical with Micki Grant at the Urban Arts Corps, which Carroll helped found in Harlem in 1968. Carroll went on to create many popular gospel-style musicals with Grant, and she again won Tony nominations for both directing and writing *Your Arms Too Short to Box with God* in 1977. Only three other women earned Tony nominations for directing plays and musicals during the 1960s and 1970s: British director Joan Littlewood, performer June Havoc, and composer/creator Elizabeth Swados. In addition to Grant, Swados was one of the few women to earn recognition from the Tony Awards for music or lyrics during this period. Swados wrote, directed, choreographed, composed, wrote lyrics, and played guitar in her musical *Runaways*, earning three Tony nominations for her work in 1978. That same year the veteran team of Betty Comden and Adolph

Green won the Tony Award for *On the Twentieth Century*, for which they wrote both book and lyrics.

Lighting designers Rosenthal, Clark, and Musser continued to work regularly during the 1960s and 1970s, and Jennifer Tipton, who came to lighting design primarily through dance performance lighting, made her Broadway debut in 1969 with a revival of **Our Town**. Tipton rapidly gained recognition, winning a Tony Award for Lincoln Center's *The Cherry Orchard* in 1977 and critical praise for her work in *for colored girls* (1977) during this period.

Women scenic designers remained scarce, though three women made successful Broadway debuts. Marjorie Bradley Kellogg made her debut as an assistant scenic designer in 1968, and followed with her debut as scenic designer in 1974, for the revival of the musical *Where's Charley?* For the next two decades she designed 25 Broadway productions. Tanya Moiseiwitsch, a British costume and scenic designer who had made her Broadway debut in 1946, earned a Tony nomination for Best Scenic Design of *The Misanthrope* in 1975. Another Tony Award–winning designer was Franne Lee, who made her Broadway debut in 1972 and only two years later won both Drama Desk Awards and Tony Awards for Best Costume Design and Best Scenic Design for a revival of the musical *Candide*. In 1979 Lee also won a Tony for her costume designs in the musical *Sweeney Todd*.

To the Millennium and Beyond

The 1980s saw Broadway in a slump with audience numbers dwindling even as ticket prices skyrocketed. Although a few notable women had broken Broadway's glass ceiling and attitudes about women's roles were starting to change, the numbers of women working on Broadway increased only marginally. A large discrepancy remained between the number of men and women employed, particularly in positions of authority. Women continued to fare much better in not-for-profit theaters, where budgets and salaries were lower. Some women chose not to pursue Broadway theater because their goals did not lie in the realm of commercial theater.

As more women took the helm as either producers or artistic directors in the nation's **regional theaters**, many consciously opted to stage works by women and hire more women than had most of their male predecessors. Though not all women leaders shared this agenda, little by little the numbers of women working behind the scenes grew, especially in nonprofit theaters. By the 1980s, with rising costs and a widely perceived lack of quality productions on Broadway, more producers looked to transfer successful plays and musicals from Off-Broadway theaters and regional theaters, giving women on those creative teams new opportunities to break into the Broadway circle of playwrights, composers, lyricists, choreographers, designers, and directors. In a sense, a back door to Broadway opened a bit wider. **Marsha Norman**'s Pulitzer Prize–winning *'night Mother* (1983) originated in Actors Theater of Louisville, and **Wendy Wasserstein**'s Tony Award–winning satire *The Heidi Chronicles* (1989) moved to Broadway after a successful run Off-Broadway exemplified this trend.

During this period both veteran and aspiring stage actors faced a new challenge: a resurgence of "star power" on Broadway. Broadway producers discovered that by casting celebrities from film, **television**, and music, ticket sales increased and runs could be extended. Soon they were substituting television stars (or past stars) into their casts every few months, and the formula seemed to work. Savvy journeymen stage performers like Bebe Neuwirth crossed over and worked in television and then returned newly famous to Broadway in starring roles. In the early part of her stage career, Neuwirth appeared in ensemble, replacement, understudy, and supporting roles, but once she played the sharp-tongued psychologist Lilith on the hit television show *Cheers*, she returned to Broadway in leads. She starred as Lola in a revival of *Damn Yankees* in 1994. Soon after she reprised her role of Lilith on the *Cheers* television spinoff *Frasier* and then starred as Velma in the 1996 Broadway revival of *Chicago*, for which she won her second Tony Award. While not all actors followed this successful path, the trend became clear when celebrities such as Madonna made their Broadway debuts (*Speed-the-Plow*, 1988).

Still a major factor in keeping actresses highly visible on Broadway, the Tony Awards in recent decades have recognized a mix of past Broadway stars and crossover celebrities. Winners for lead roles in straight plays have included stage veterans Zoe Caldwell and Judi Dench as well as crossover stars Glenn Close, Stockard Channing, Lily Tomlin, and Linda Lavin. On the musical stage, Tonys went to Broadway veterans such as **Patti LuPone**, Chita Rivera, and Bernadette Peters as well as to film and television stars Lauren Bacall, Tyne Daly, and Natasha Richardson.

In the 1980s and 1990s, women playwrights were not only seeing Broadway productions of their work but getting critical recognition as never before (see Table 6).

In 1991 *The Secret Garden* made history for having a nearly all-female creative team—a not uncommon phenomenon in regional theater or Off- and Off-Off-Broadway but all but unheard of in big-time Broadway production. Marsha Norman wrote book and lyrics; Lucy Simon composed the music; Heidi Landesman (now Ettinger) both produced and designed scenery; Theoni V. Aldridge designed costumes; Tharon Musser designed lighting; and Susan H. Schulman directed the production, which won three Tony Awards and played more than 700 performances. Set in colonial India, it tells the story of a girl, Mary, who goes to live at her uncle's manor and discovers dark secrets about the house and its inhabitants. Schulman took over for a male director who failed to mesh with the rest of the creative team. She framed the action through the eyes of Mary, responding to the emotional discoveries Mary makes on her journey.

The year 1998 marked something of a watershed for recognition of women in theater. Yasmina Reza won the Tony Award for Best Play (*Art*) and Paula Vogel won the Pulitzer Prize for *How I Learned to Drive*. Garry Hynes (*The Beauty Queen of Leenane*) and **Julie Taymor** (*The Lion King*) became the first women to win Tony Awards for directing (play and musical, respectively), with Taymor winning an additional Tony for costume design. Lyricist Lynn Ahrens shared a Tony with composer Stephen Flaherty for the musical score of *Ragtime*, and a

Table 6
Women Playwrights Nominated for the Tony Award for Best Play 1980–2008

Tony Award	Best Play (nominees)
1982	*Crimes of the Heart*, by Beth Henley [Pulitzer Prize, 1981]
1983	*'night Mother*, by Marsha Norman [Pulitzer Prize, 1983]
1984	*Play Memory*, by Joanna Glass
1987	*Costal Disturbances*, by Tina Howe
1989	*The Heidi Chronicles*, by Wendy Wasserstein [Tony Award Winner, Pulitzer Prize, 1989]
1991	*Our Country's Good*, by Timberlake Wertenbaker
1993	*The Sisters Rosensweig*, by Wendy Wasserstein
1994	*Twilight: Los Angeles, 1992*, by Anna Deavere Smith
1995	*Having Our Say*, by Emily Mann
1997	*Stanley*, by Pam Gems
1998	*Art*, by Yasmina Reza (Tony Award Winner)
2000	*Dirty Blonde*, by Claudia Shear
2002	*Metamorphoses*, by Mary Zimmerman
2002	*Topdog/Underdog*, by Suzan-Lori Parks [Pulitzer Prize, 2002]
2003-2008	No women nominees for Tony Award for Best Play. No women Pulitzer Prize winners for drama.
2009	*God of Carnage*, by Yasmina Reza,

In addition to those noted above, Paula Vogel won a Pulitzer in 1998 for *How I Learned to Drive* and Margaret Edson won for *Wit* in 1999, neither of which have had a Broadway production.
Sources: International Broadway Data Base (IBDB.com). Pulitzer Prize official Web site. http://www.pulitzer.org/bycat/Drama.

number of women shared in celebration of these victories through their roles as producers and co-producers.

Since the year 2000 several other women have gained recognition for their work in Broadway musicals, include composer Jeanine Tesori, director/choreographer Graciela Daniele, director/choreographer Kathleen Marshall, and director/choreographer Susan Stroman. Stroman raised eyebrows in 2000 when she earned four Tony nominations (one each for directing and choreography) for both *Contact* and her revival of *The Music Man.* She won the Tony Award for choreography of *Contact* (her third Tony) and the following year walked away with two Tonys for directing and choreographing **The Producers**.

Despite the high profile of many women on Broadway at the turn of the twenty-first century, a 2002 study conducted by the New York State Council on the Arts presented a more sobering account of women's overall success in commercial theater. While Taymor, Stroman, and others were highly acclaimed, the percentage of women working on Broadway as designers, playwrights, and directors in particular has remained low. The study concluded that while progress was being made in raising women's representation on Broadway, such progress was slow and inconsistent. The study called for renewed attention to the obstacles women face in the theater—a call likely to generate some progress yet unlikely to obliterate long-standing, institutionalized barriers to women's equality on the Great White Way.

Anne Fliotsos

Further Reading

Chinoy, Helen Krich, and Linda Walsh Jenkins. *Women in American Theater.* 3rd ed. New York: Theater Communications Group, 2006.

Coleman, Bud, and Judith Sebesta, eds. *Women in American Musical Theater: Essays on Lyricists, Librettists, Arrangers, Choreographers, Designers, Directors, Producers and Performance Artists.* Jefferson, NC: McFarland Press, 2008.

Dialogues with Notable Women in American Theater. Women in Theater, Series One. [Videorecording.] New York: Theater Communications Group, 2006.

Fliotsos, Anne, and Wendy Vierow. *American Women Stage Directors of the Twentieth Century.* Urbana: University of Illinois Press, 2008.

Housely, Helen M. "The Female Director's Odyssey: The Broadway Sisterhood." *Women and Society* (Proceedings from the Second Annual Conference on Women). Poughkeepsie, NY: Marist College, 1993.

New York State Council on the Arts Theater Program. "Report on the Status of Women: A Limited Engagement? Executive Summary." December 31, 2002. http://www.womensproject.org.

Robinson, Alice M., Vera Mowry Roberts, and Milly S. Barranger. *Notable Women in the American Theater.* New York: Greenwood Press, 1989.

Wild, Larry. *A Brief Outline of the History of Stage Lighting.* March 16, 2008. www.northern.edu/wild/LiteDes/ldhist.htm.

Z

_

ZIEGFELD, FLORENZ (1867–1932)
THEATRICAL PRODUCER

Nowadays only historians and show business trivia buffs are familiar with such once-famous stage producers as **David Belasco** or Charles Frohman, but Florenz "Flo" Edward Ziegfeld Jr. has defied the passage of time as the sole showman of his era whose name is not only remembered but remains synonymous with a specific style of theatrical extravaganza. Even in the twenty-first century a mention of the _Ziegfeld Follies_ paints an image of lavish sets, spectacular costumes, and, above all, a procession of beautiful showgirls marching across the stage in a thrilling yet dignified promenade. However, Ziegfeld was more than just a producer of ephemeral crowd-pleasing shows. He was a fearless, rule-breaking showman whose productions greatly advanced the state of theatrical spectacle and stagecraft in American theater, especially in the areas of scenic and lighting design.

The _Follies_ were also known for witty sketches filled with topical humor performed by some of the era's greatest comedians. Although Ziegfeld's revues resembled vaudeville in structure, their content was considerably more refined and sophisticated. Unlike most of vaudeville, _Follies_ audiences included New York's social and political elite. Ziegfeld was a prolific producer with many other projects to his credit, but it is the legend of the _Follies_ that has kept alive his reputation as the "Glorifier of the American Girl."

Ziegfeld was born in Chicago, son of middle-class European immigrant parents. His father established a renowned music seminary, but Flo did not inherit his musical talent. Ziegfeld made his debut as a theatrical impresario at the Chicago World's Fair of 1893 while in his twenties. Assigned to provide music for the fair, he unexpectedly made his mark through vigorous promotion of Eugen Sandow, a charismatic muscleman who created a sensation. The next major object of Ziegfeld's professional attention was Polish-born performer Anna Held. Ziegfeld starred the petite, delicate beauty in his first Broadway production, a play called *A Parlor Match*, in 1896. Over the next ten years Ziegfeld produced shows with and without Held, who became his common-law wife.

In 1906 Held suggested that he mount a Folies Bergère style revue designed to showcase beautiful American women and satirize current trends. The name was suggested not by the Parisian music hall but by a New York newspaper column called "Follies of the Day." Ziegfeld mounted a show with songs, comic sketches, and a chorus line of 50 girls. When it opened as *The Follies of 1907* in July of that year, the show was a resounding success. One critic warned readers about the racy tone of the entertainment but allowed that "the action of the *Follies* is so fast that a state of delirious acquiescence is induced." Ziegfeld mounted a second *Follies* in 1908, this time making his name part of the title, and when the third *Ziegfeld Follies of 1909* proved to be another hit he decided to make the show an annual event.

In 1913 the *Follies* took up residence in the ornate New Amsterdam Theatre in the heart of the Times Square theater district, where it would remain until 1927. As successive editions were mounted, the series became known as a cultural trendsetter, popularizing such songs as "Shine On, Harvest Moon" and "A Pretty Girl is Like a Melody" and such dances as the fox-trot, the tango, and the shimmy. World-class scenic designer Joseph Urban began working for Ziegfeld in 1914 and achieved spectacular results with dappled, Seurat-style pointillage and bold lighting effects. Urban's innovations had an impact beyond the theater, influencing domestic interior design and the burgeoning Art Deco movement.

Ziegfeld, always a ladies' man, focused primarily on his female performers. Amid the cavalcade of singers, dancers, and comics that graced the Follies stages, Ziegfeld featured beautiful girls wearing the outfits of "Lucile" (Lady Duff Gordon), the era's supreme couturier. (Lucile was credited with creating the modern fashion show—a stately parade of statuesque poker-faced, gorgeously attired beauties—which Ziegfeld happily appropriated for his *Follies*.) He lavished personal and professional attention upon his leading female stars, such as Lillian Lorraine, Ann Pennington, and especially Billie Burke, whom he courted and married in 1914. It was said that Ziegfeld had no heartfelt appreciation for comedy and seldom laughed, yet he signed and showcased America's top comedians: Will Rogers, W. C. Fields, **Eddie Cantor**, **Fanny Brice**, and many others. Comedy sketches in the *Follies* often featured blackface routines and racial humor typical of the era, but it is notable that in 1910 Ziegfeld hired the great black comedian **Bert Williams**, who became the first African American performer to receive featured status in the *Follies*.

While continuing to mount annual editions of his namesake show in the 1920s, Ziegfeld demonstrated more range in his theatrical projects with *Sally* (1920), a vehicle for singer-dancer Marilyn Miller, and *Kid Boots* (1923), a showcase for the talents of Cantor. Both were highly successful, but a subsequent series of flops and related financial difficulties hampered Ziegfeld's career in the mid-1920s. He rebounded spectacularly during the 1927–1928 season with a string of record-breaking smash hits: *Rio Rita*, *Rosalie*, *Whoopee!*, and, most memorably, the epochal **Jerome Kern–Oscar Hammerstein II** musical *Show Boat*, which premiered at his sumptuous new Ziegfeld Theatre, which Ziegfeld had built with financing from newspaper magnate William Randolph Hearst. *Show Boat* was notable not only for its beautiful score but also for the seriousness of its libretto, a surprise from a producer with Ziegfeld's track record.

Show Boat marked the pinnacle of his career but also served as an untimely finale. When the stock market crashed in October 1929 Ziegfeld was wiped out, ruined beyond his ability to recover. Later productions such as *Simple Simon* (1930) starring Ed Wynn and *Smiles*, featuring the team of Fred and Adele Astaire with perennial favorite Marilyn Miller, could not draw sufficient audiences to restore the showman's fortunes. Ziegfeld made one final attempt to revive the old *Follies* format in 1931, after a four-year hiatus. This last edition featured Ruth Etting, the dance team of Buck and Bubbles, the usual complement of beautiful women, and a herd of elephants. It ran for over four months and was regarded as something of a comeback for the 64-year-old impresario. Nonetheless, when he died the following year Ziegfeld was deeply in debt, and his creditors continued to hound his widow for years thereafter.

The nature of Ziegfeld's gift is difficult to define. He was not a dramatist nor was he a stage director in the modern sense of the term. Instead, like Walt Disney, he was an exacting perfectionist who brought out the best in his handpicked team. His shows were extravagant, romantic, a little vulgar, and fresh. His influence endures in **film** musicals, **television** variety shows, parades, beauty pageants, and elaborate public spectacles of all kinds.

William Charles Morrow

Further Reading

Golden, Eve. *Anna Held and the Birth of Ziegfeld's Broadway*. Lexington, KY: University Press of Kentucky, 2000.

Mordden, Ethan. *Ziegfeld: The Man Who Invented Show Business*. New York: St. Martin's Press, 2008.

Glossary of Selected Historical and Technical Terms

Actors' Equity Association ("AEA" or "Equity") AEA is the primary union for stage actors in the United States. Founded in 1913, AEA seized upon the theme of "equity" in response to the callous treatment of actors by many producers and booking agents of the day, particularly the Theatrical Syndicate. The colloquial term "an Equity show" refers to a production staged in accordance with Actors' Equity Association contracts, codes, and/or agreements.

American Society of Composers, Authors, and Publishers (ASCAP) Founded in 1914, ASCAP originally organized to enforce current copyright laws and lobby for new stronger protections of original work. Among its members in its early years were some of Broadway's leading composers, including Victor Herbert, Otto Harbach, and Irving Berlin. With the growth of radio and the recording industry, ASCAP's mission evolved to the point where its current principal function is the collection of royalties for performances of its members' works.

backstage musical This term refers to any musical whose main plot or subject matter deals principally with the inner workings of show business and theater. *Gypsy* (1959), *A Chorus Line* (1975), and *Dreamgirls* (1981) are famous examples of backstage musicals.

blackface (or black face) Identified with nineteenth- and early twentieth-century minstrelsy, the term "blackface" refers to both (a) any form of entertainment in which an actor artificially darkens his/her face to comically grotesque African Americans and (b) the specific act of darkening the face for such a performance. Originally viewed as wholesome family entertainment, blackface faded after World War I as blacks and many whites increasingly expressed revulsion over the racial denigration of black people embodied by such performances.

blacklist (verb) The term "blacklist" generically means to identify specific individuals to be denied a benefit or opportunity available to others. The term is commonly associated with an effort on the part of the federal government, communications and entertainment corporations, and self-declared patriotic citizens groups in the 1940s and 1950s to rid America's entertainment industries of alleged communists and communist sympathizers. This effort had greater impact upon the film and broadcast industries than it did upon commercial theater. Nevertheless, many notable Broadway figures, including Elia Kazan, Lee J. Cobb, Arthur Miller, Jerome Robbins, and Lillian Hellman were either blacklisted or threatened with blacklisting if they did not "name names" of friends and associates whom they knew to be sympathetic to communist ideas at some time in their lives. *See also* HUAC in this glossary.

book musical A book musical refers to a musical dominated by a coherent story line and clearly drawn characters (as those likely to be found in a traditional novel or short story). The elements of stage production, including songs and dance numbers, are generally developed in service of the plot and characters. Richard Rodgers and Oscar Hammerstein (*Oklahoma!*, *South Pacific*) elevated the book musical to preeminence during the "Golden Age of Musicals" from the 1940s to the mid-1960s.

burlesque In American theater, "burlesque" most commonly refers to revues and variety shows from the mid-nineteenth century to the 1920s that featured raucous adult humor and lines of young attractive women in alluring and/or revealing attire. Starting with "leg shows" in the nineteenth century and moving into striptease performances in the twentieth century, the term "burlesque" is generally identified with the sexual presentation of women for the entertainment of men, even though the term's European roots also encompass traditions of farce and satire.

bus and truck tour (alternately, second or third national touring company) Bus and truck tours generally go on the road after the first national tours have been out for some time. Bus and truck or second tours are usually less expensively produced than first national tours and often play in communities that cannot afford to house a first national tour. The bus and truck tour derives its name from 1950s and 1960s companies that toured with the performers in a bus and the costumes and sets in one or more trucks. *See also* first national tours in this glossary (Conte and Langley 2007, 190; Micocci 2007, 163).

combination company A combination company was an early model of a theatrical touring company that would prepare only one show and perform it exclusively on tours. Common in the United States in the first half of the nineteenth century, many combination companies organized and played their first performances in New York before taking the production out to other locations. In so doing, the combination company anticipated the "direct from Broadway" marketing ethos that would characterize modern commercial theater touring.

concept musical "Concept musical" refers to a musical that focuses on a theme or idea, rather than a linear plot. A concept musical will typically feature several characters, instead of a leading man and/or woman, exploring the controlling idea from a variety of perspectives. The term is often associated with post–Golden Era Broadway of the 1970s and 1980s, and many works by composer/lyricist Stephen Sondheim (*Company*; *Assassins*). Andrew Lloyd Webber's *Cats* is often cited as a concept musical as well.

Drama Critics Circle (Officially New York Drama Critics Circle) and Drama Critics Circle Award Founded in 1935 by New York drama critics furious over recent Pulitzer Prize drama selections, the Drama Critics Circle has been presenting an annual award to the "best new play by an American playwright produced in New York" ever since. Notwithstanding the noteworthy people who have overseen the awards, the Drama Critics Circle Award has nowhere near the national recognition or cultural cache of either the Pulitzer Prize or the Tony Award for Best Play. Nevertheless, within the American professional theater community, Drama Critics Circle Awards (which now include Best Play, Best Musical, and Best Foreign Play) are valued highly.

Equity production A descriptive term that denotes a production as being staged under Actors' Equity Association contracts and agreements. *See* Actors' Equity Association in this glossary.

first national tour The first national tour (alternately, national tour, first North American tour, first-class tour) is the first touring production of a successful Broadway (or occasionally Off-Broadway) show. First national tours generally "go out" during or shortly after the show's original New York run. National tours are generally booked into their touring locations for a fixed run—a predetermined length ranging from several days to several months. In some cases, producers and local presenters will negotiate a sit-down production, open-ended run lasting as long as the show generates sufficient box office to merit staying in the touring location. The producer of the original Broadway show usually produces or otherwise controls the first national tour (Conte and Langley 2007, 189–190).

47 Workshop "47 Workshop" is the name of the first known playwriting course ever taught at an American college or university. George Pierce Baker taught his playwriting workshop and other dramatic arts at Harvard University from 1905 to 1924, when Yale outbid Harvard for Baker's services. Eugene O'Neill, George Abbott, and S. N. Behrman were among the heralded alumni of Baker's classes and seminars.

golden age of musicals (also golden era of musicals) An often-used term referencing the ascent of the American musical from its roots in European operetta and American vaudeville/revue to a sophisticated, wildly popular, and distinctly American art form. In many texts, including this one, the Golden Age begins with Rodgers and Hammerstein's landmark "book musical" *Oklahoma!* (1943) and ends in the middle to late 1960s as the book musical makes room for new innovations such as the rock musical (*Hair*, 1968) and the concept musical (*Company*, 1970). Other scholars place the starting point earlier, often citing Jerome Kern's and Oscar Hammerstein's *Show Boat* (1927) and the 1930s musicals of Cole Porter, Irving Berlin, et al. as the first architects of the modern American musical.

Great White Way A famous nickname for the Times Square theater district, believed to be coined around 1900. The origin of its popular use as slang for Broadway and the theater district is uncertain. Historians cite two possibilities: (1) a two-point vortex of the extravagant blaze of electric lighting that, by the turn of the century, was setting Times Square (then called Long Acre Square) aglow every night as part of the attraction of a night out in New York; and (2) a 1902 newspaper report describing Broadway in the aftermath of an enormous snow storm (Allen 1995, 58–59). Whatever its beginning, the name has stuck. The phrase has also been used ironically to reference the invisibility of racial minorities in Broadway productions and audiences relative to their numbers in New York City's general population.

gypsy Slang term for show dancers who survive by going from show to show and audition to audition in one of the more grueling, competitive aspects of performing on Broadway. The musical *A Chorus Line* (1975), based on taped interviews with gypsies talking about their livelihood, demystified the Broadway dancers' lives even as it immortalized them through the show's enormous success.

Harlem Renaissance A period (1917c.–1930c.) of flourishing African American arts and culture in the Harlem district of New York City and in African American communities across the country. Mainstream Broadway plays and musicals soon showed some increased involvement of African Americans in productions and a growing influence of jazz and other aspects of African American culture. Actors Paul Robeson and Charles S. Gilpin, dramatist Zora Neale Hurston, composer Eubie Blake, actress Rose McClendon, and actress/singer Ethel Waters were among the artists associated with Broadway theater and the Harlem Renaissance during this period.

HUAC (House Un-American Activities Committee) A committee of the U.S. Congress, HUAC was created in 1938 to investigate alleged subversive and treasonous acts among citizens and organizations. With the advent of the Cold War after World War II, the committee began focusing on alleged communist activities and affiliations. From 1947 to 1955, the entertainment and broadcast industries came under particular scrutiny. Many Broadway figures were called before the Committee to defend themselves against charges of communist affiliations and/or identify ("name names") of others so affiliated. *See also* blacklist in this glossary.

interpolation An interpolation is a song added to an existing musical after the musical has been running. The term often implies that the composer/lyricist of the new song was not the primary composer or lyricist for the musical. Interpolation was a relatively common practice in the 1920s when Broadway shows were the principal source of showcasing popular tunes.

jukebox musical A variation of the rock musical, the jukebox musical is created from a catalog of familiar rock and pop hits usually by a single artist or group (although the score for the musical *Rock of Ages* [2009] is an anthology of

1980s rock songs by various artists). By far the most successful jukebox musical is the long running *Mamma Mia!* (2001) based on the songs of the 1970s dance/pop group ABBA. *Jersey Boys* (2005), a biographical musical based on the lives and music of the 1960s soft rock group Frankie Valli and the Four Seasons, also found enormous success on Broadway and on tour.

legitimate theater An elastic term that can be applied simply to distinguish plays (or "straight dramas") from musicals, revues, or dance performances. However, the phrase usually refers to the professional production of full three-to-five act plays and often implies that the plays, companies, and/or theatrical venues so designated carry a certain measure of prestige among theater professionals and audiences. The term derives from the English Restoration when Charles II issued licenses to only two theater companies for the performance of spoken drama and shut down unlicensed companies.

libretto More commonly associated with opera than musical theater, the libretto is the entire written text (often "the book") of a musical, including dialog, song lyrics, and any other textual matter attendant to the work.

Little Theater Movement Dating from the 1910s, the Little Theater Movement was a reformist movement among American theater artists who hoped to bring new approaches to playwriting and dramatic production to commercial theater. Viewing the current American theater of the time as nonintellectual, derivative, and impervious to change from within, they formed small experimental theater groups, principally in cities that had functioning commercial theater districts such as New York and Chicago. Over time, the main New York little theaters—The Provincetown Players, the Washington Square Players, and the Neighborhood Playhouse—helped establish an audience and a niche on Broadway for new, serious-minded American plays.

LORT League of Resident Theatres. LORT is the leading professional association of resident (or regional) American theater companies. *See also* regional theater in this glossary.

Method Acting The term by which most Americans know the late nineteenth-century Russian director Konstantin Stanislavsky's system of teaching and preparing actors for performance. Relying on the actor's ability to create a complete internal psychological life for his or her character and dispensing with classical postures and grand stage poses, Stanislavsky's system revolutionized modern acting in both Europe and the United States. While his principal American disciples—Lee Strasberg, Sanford Meisner, Cheryl Crawford, and Stella Adler among them—often disagreed vehemently on how to interpret and teach Stanislavsky's theories, their collective efforts redefined the art and practice of American acting from the 1930s to the present.

New York Drama Critics Circle. *See* Drama Critics Circle in this glossary.

Off-Broadway The term was first associated in connection with experimental New York theater productions in small theaters or makeshift venues (churches, reconverted restaurants) outside of the Times Square theater district. While the term is believed to have originated as early as the 1930s, the formation of the now defunct Off-Broadway Theatre League in 1949 helped bring the term into formal professional theater parlance. Today, by standards of the League of Off-Broadway Theatres and Producers and Actors' Equity Association contract terms, Off-Broadway refers to professional productions in Manhattan theaters with 100–499 seats. *See also* entry Off-Broadway in the encyclopedia.

Off-Off Broadway Refers to any professional New York production staged in a venue with fewer than 100 seats. From this single criterion it is possible to stage an Off-Off Broadway play in Times Square. However, as a colloquial term, Off-Off Broadway generally implies a location away from the theater district. Under Actors' Equity Association Codes, Actors' Equity often grants permission for its members to participate in approved Off-Off Broadway shows without an Equity contract.

regional (resident) theater Although sometimes broadly applied to almost any United States theatrical enterprise housed outside of the New York City area, the term "regional theater" generally refers to professional, permanent, not-for-profit theater companies that are, indeed, located outside of metropolitan New York. Regional theaters are typically characterized by a serious-minded artistic and/or community mission that through the 1960s seemed pointedly at odds with Broadway's commercialism. However, since the late 1960s, Broadway producers and regional theaters have established partnerships and other symbiotic relationships in order to develop new works and nurture emerging theater artists. The Guthrie Theatre in Minneapolis and Arena Stage in Washington, D.C., are among the best-known regional theater companies. With the rise of high quality not-for-profit professional companies in New York City, such as Joseph Papp's the Public Theater, the phrase "resident theater" has evolved as a synonymous or, to many, a more precise term than "regional theater" for describing American professional not-for-profit theater.

repertory Refers to a specific plan for presentation of productions by a theater company whereby the company prepares two or more works and offers them in alternation or rotation, usually on successive days. Typically some or all cast members will appear in two or more company productions playing "in repertory" at the same time. Theater companies working in this manner are called, and often name themselves, repertory theaters (i.e., San Jose Repertory Theatre, Tennessee Repertory Theatre). The terms "stock company" or "stock productions" are often used synonymously with "repertory."

rock musical A musical theater production whose songs and scores are written and arranged in rock (or rock and roll) music idioms and styles. *Hair*, which premiered on Broadway in 1968, is widely considered to be the first musical to bring the heretofore alien worlds of rock music and youth counterculture to mainstream Broadway. *Jesus Christ Superstar* (1971), *Grease* (1972), and *Rent* (1996) were also hit rock musicals. *See also* jukebox musical in this glossary.

schtick (shtick) From a Yiddish word meaning "small piece," the word "schtick" was adapted by early twentieth-century Jewish stage comics as a catchall term for comedic stage expressions, gestures, and gimmicks. It is now a somewhat dated generic term for comedic stage business, or even any noticeable theatrical trait or special interest, even though its Jewish/Yiddish origin is unmistakable.

score The score is the complete music content of a musical (or opera, operetta, dance performance, etc.) in written notation form with all parts arranged and laid out in sequence for performance.

Shubert Alley A slang reference for Broadway theater as a whole, but originally the phrase referred specifically to the famous alley and meeting point outside of the Shubert Theatre in Times Square.

sit-down productions Open-ended runs of Broadway "touring" shows in touring venues outside of New York City. Technically a touring show, a successful sit-down production may run for years in the same out-of-town theater. (A sit-down production of *The Phantom of the Opera* occupied the Pantages Theatre in Toronto from 1989 to 1999.)

song plugger. A fixture in the era of Tin Pan Alley, the song plugger was a piano player engaged by a publisher to promote new songs to performers and producers. Jerome Kern and George Gershwin worked as song pluggers before they became famous as composers of Broadway musicals and popular songs.

star power Refers to the ability of a famous actor or actress to generate box-office sales and pre-opening excitement for a production by the mere fact of his or her appearance in it. The casting of Daniel Radcliffe, star of the Harry Potter movies, in the 2008 London and Broadway revivals of *Equus* is a recent example of star power in action, although the practice in America dates back to the nineteenth century.

stock company *See* repertory in this glossary.

tour, first national *See* first national tour in this glossary.

workshop A formal theatrical term, both noun and verb. Under Actors' Equity Association agreements, a workshop is a scaled-down experimental staging of a new script that a producer has under development. Presented in one or more "sessions" to a by-invitation-only audience, neither the general public nor critics on assignment may view the show. Workshops are generally used to refine or test the feasibility of a script before the producer decides whether or not to attempt a full production.

yellowface Analagous to blackface, yellowface is the practice of non-Asian performers (usually white) using makeup, costumes, properties, and so-called "acting techniques" to represent onstage stereotypical images of Asian or Asian American characters. Although now viewed as racially denigrating, yellowface nevertheless persisted in popular American theater even after blackface entertainment ceased to be considered acceptable by the general public. *See also* entry Asians and Asian Americans in the encyclopedia.

References

Allen, Irving Lewis. *The City in Slang: New York Life and Popular Speech*. New York: Oxford University Press, 1995.

Conte, David M., and Stephen Langley. *Theatre Management: Producing and Managing the Performing Arts*. Hollywood, CA: Entertainment Pro, 2007.

Micocci, Tony. *Booking Performance Tours*. New York: Allworth Press, 2008.

Other Books or Sites with Theater Glossaries (Selected)

Barranger, Milly S. *Theatre: A Way of Seeing*. Belmont, CA: Wadsworth/Thomson Learning, 2002.

Tupelow Community Theatre Online Glossary. Retrieved June 4, 2009, from http://www.tctwebstage.com/glossary.htm.

Viagas, Robert. *The Back Stage Guide to Broadway*. New York: Back Stage Books, 2004.

Vogel, Frederic B., and Ben Hodges. *The Commercial Theater Institute Guide to Producing Plays and Musicals*. New York: Applause Theatre & Cinema Books, 2006.

Wilson, Edwin, and Alan Goldfarb. "Theatre the Lively Art, 4e: Glossary." McGraw-Hill Online Learning Center. Retrieved, June 4, 2009, from http://highered.mcgraw-hill.com/sites/0072407182/student_view0/glossary.html.

General Bibliography

General Histories, References, and Thematic Studies

Abbotson, Susan C. W. *Masterpieces of 20th-Century American Drama*. Westport, CT: Greenwood Press, 2005.

Bartow, Arthur, ed. *Training of the American Actor*. New York: Theatre Communications Group, 2006.

Bianco, Anthony. *Ghosts of 42nd Street: A History of America's Most Infamous Block*. New York: Harper, 2005.

Bigsby, C. W. E. *A Critical Introduction to Twentieth-Century American Drama: Volume 1 1900–1940*. Cambridge, U.K.: Cambridge University Press, 1982.

———. *A Critical Introduction to Twentieth-Century American Drama: Volume II, Williams, Miller, Albee*. Cambridge, U.K.: Cambridge University Press, 1984.

———. *A Critical Introduction to Twentieth-Century American Drama: Volume III, Beyond Broadway*. Cambridge, U.K.: Cambridge University Press, 1985.

Block, Geoffrey. *Enchanted Evenings: The Broadway Musical from Show Boat to Sondheim*. New York: Oxford University Press, 1997.

Bordman, Gerald. *American Operetta: From H.M.S. Pinafore to Sweeney Todd*. New York: Oxford University Press, 1981.

———. *American Musical Theatre: A Chronicle*. New York: Oxford University Press, 2001.

Brown, John Russell, ed. *The Oxford Illustrated History of the Theatre*. Oxford, England: Oxford University Press, 1993.

Bryer, Jackson R., and Richard Allan Davison. *The Actor's Art: Conversations with Contemporary American Stage Performers*. New Brunswick, NJ: Rutgers University Press, 2001.

———. *The Art of the American Musical: Conversations with the Creators*. New Brunswick, NJ: Rutgers University Press, 2005.

Citron, Stephen. *Sondheim and Lloyd-Webber: The New Musical*. Oxford, England: Oxford University Press, 2001.

Clum, John M. *Something for the Boys: Musical Theater and Gay Culture*. New York: Palgrave, 2001.

Cobrin, Pamela. *From Winning the Vote to Directing on Broadway: The Emergence of Women on the New York Stage, 1880–1927*. Newark, DE: University of Delaware Press, 2009.

Connolly, Thomas F. *George Jean Nathan and the Making of the Modern American Theatre*. Madison, NJ: Fairleigh Dickinson University Press, 2000.

Denkert, Darcie. *A Fine Romance*. New York: Watson-Guptill, 2005.

Dunne, Michael. *American Film Musical Themes and Forms*. Jefferson, NC: McFarland, 2004.

Everett, William A., and Paul R. Laird. *The Cambridge Companion to the Musical*. Cambridge, England: Cambridge University Press, 2008.

Fliotsos, Anne L., and Wendy Verow. *American Women Stage Directors of the Twentieth Century*. Urbana: University of Illinois Press, 2008.

Furia, Philip. *The Poets of Tin Pan Alley: A History of America's Great Lyricists*. New York: Oxford University Press, 1990.

Gavin, Christy. *African American Women Playwrights: A Research Guide*. New York: Garland, 1999.

Gewirtz, Arthur, and James J. Kolb. *Experimenters, Rebels, and Disparate Voices*. Westport, CT: Praeger, 2003.

Grant, Mark N. *The Rise and Fall of the Broadway Musical*. Boston: Northeastern University Press, 2004.

Green, Stanley. *Encyclopedia of the Musical*. London: Cassell & Co., 1976.

Grody, Svetlana Mclee, and Dorothy Daniels Lister. *Conversations with Choreographers*. Portsmouth, NH: Heinemann, 1996.

Hay, Samuel A. *African American Theatre*. New York: Cambridge University Press, 1994.

Henderson, Mary C. *The City and the Theatre: The History of New York Playhouses*. 2nd ed. New York: James T. White & Co., 1973.

Hill, Errol, ed. *The Theatre of Black Americans*. New York: Applause, 1987.

Jensen, Amy Petersen. *Theatre in a Media Culture: Production, Performance and Perception since 1970*. Jefferson, NC: McFarland, 2007.

Jones, John Bush. *Our Musicals, Ourselves: A Social History of the American Musical Theatre*. Lebanon, NH: Brandeis University Press, 2003.

Kenrick, John. *Musical Theatre: A History*. New York: Continuum, 2008.

King, Woodie, Jr. *The Impact of Race: Theatre and Culture*. New York: Applause, 2003.

Kislan, Richard. *Hoofing on Broadway: A History of Show Dancing*. New York: Prentice-Hall Press, 1987.

Knapp, Raymond. *The American Musical and the Formation of National Identity*. Princeton, NJ: Princeton University, 2005.

Krasner, David. *A Beautiful Pageant: African American Theatre, Drama, and Performance in the Harlem Renaissance, 1910–1927*. New York: Palgrave Macmillan, 2002.

Lee, Esther Kim. *A History of Asian American Theater*. Cambridge, U.K.: Cambridge University Press, 2006.

Lerner, Alan Jay. *The Musical Theatre: A Celebration*. New York: McGraw-Hill, 1986.

McLamore, Alyson. *Musical Theatre: An Appreciation*. Upper Saddle River, NJ: Pearson Prentice Hall, 2004.

McMillin, Scott. *The Musical as Drama*. Princeton, NJ: Princeton University Press, 2006.

Miller, Scott. *From Assassins to West Side Story: The Director's Guide to Musical Theatre.* Portsmouth, NH: Heinemann, 1996.

Mordden, Ethan. *The Happiest Corpse I've Ever Seen: The Last Twenty-five Years of the Broadway Musical.* New York: Palgrave MacMillan, 2004.

Most, Andrea. *Making Americans: Jews and the Broadway Musical.* Cambridge, MA: Harvard University Press, 2004.

Murphy, Brenda, ed. *The Cambridge Companion to American Women Playwrights.* Cambridge, U.K.: Cambridge University Press, 1999.

Patinkin, Sheldon. *"No Legs, No Jokes, No Chance": A History of the American Musical Theater.* Evanston, IL: Northwestern University Press, 2008.

Peterson, Bernard L. *A Century of Musicals in Black and White: An Encyclopedia of Musical Stage Works By, About, or Involving African Americans.* Westport, CT: Greenwood Publishing Group, 1993.

Prono, Luca. *Encyclopedia of Gay and Lesbian Popular Culture.* Westport, CT: Greenwood Publishing Group, 2008.

Ramirez, Elizabeth C. *Chicana/Latinas in American Theater.* Bloomington: Indiana University Press, 2000.

Roudane, Matthew Charles. *American Drama Since 1960: A Critical History.* Woodbridge, CT: Twayne, 1996.

Schulman, Sarah. *Stagestruck: Theater, AIDS, and the Marketing of Gay America.* Durham, NC: Duke University Press, 1998.

Snyder, Robert W. *The Voice of the City: Vaudeville and Popular Culture in New York.* New York: Oxford University Press, 1989.

Sternfeld, Jessica. *The Megamusical.* Bloomington: Indiana University Press, 2006.

Suskin, Stephen. *More Opening Nights on Broadway.* New York: Schirmer Books, 1997.

———. *Opening Night on Broadway.* New York: Schirmer Books, 1990.

Swain, Joseph P. *The Broadway Musical: A Critical and Musical Survey.* Rev. and expanded ed. Lanham, MD: Scarecrow Press, 2002.

Traub, James. *The Devil's Playground: A Century of Pleasure and Profit in Times Square.* New York: Random House, 2004.

Vogel, Frederic B., and Ben Hodges, eds. *The Commercial Theatre Institute's Guide to Producing Plays and Musicals.* New York: Applause Theatre & Cinema Books, 2006.

Wilmeth, Don B., and Tice L. Miller, eds. *The Cambridge Guide to American Theatre.* Cambridge, England: Cambridge University Press, 1993.

Woll, Allen. *Black Musical Theatre: From Coontown to Dreamgirls.* Baton Rouge: Louisiana State University Press, 1989.

Selected Biographical, Autobiographical, and Single-Themed Sources

Banfield, Stephen, and Geoffrey Holden Block. *Jerome Kern.* New Haven, CT: Yale University Press, 2006.

Block, Geoffrey Holden, ed. *The Richard Rodgers Reader.* New York: Oxford University Press, 2002.

Bloom, Harold. *Bernard Shaw.* New York: Chelsea House Publishers, 1987.

————. *Neil Simon*. Broomall, PA: Chelsea House Publishers, 2002.

Brater, Enoch. *Arthur Miller's America Theater and Culture in a Time of Change*. Ann Arbor: University of Michigan Press, 2005.

Clurman, Harold. *The Fervent Years: The Story of the Group Theatre and the Thirties*. New York: Harvest ed. New York: Harcourt Brace Jovanovich, 1975. (Reprint of original New York: Harvest, 1945.)

Courtney, Marguerite. *Laurette*. New York: Limelight Editions, 1984. (Original, New York: Rinehart, 1955).

Coven, Brenda, Christine E. King, and Donna M. Albertus. *David Merrick and Hal Prince: An Annotated Bibliography*. New York: Garland Publishing, 1993.

Forbes, Camille F. *Introducing Bert Williams: Burnt Cork, Broadway, and the Story of America's First Black Star*. New York: Basic Civitas, 2008.

Furia, Philip, and Graham Wood. *Irving Berlin: A Life in Song*. New York: Schirmer Books, 1998.

Gilvey, John Anthony. *Before the Parade Passes By: Gower Champion and the Glorious American Musical*. New York: St. Martin's Press, 2005.

Gottfried, Martin, and Martha Swope. *Stephen Sondheim*. New York: Harry N. Abrams, 2000.

Gould, Neil. *Victor Herbert: A Theatrical Life*. New York: Fordham University Press, 2008.

Gussow, Mel. *Edward Albee: A Singular Journey*. New York: Simon & Schuster, 1999.

Hischak, Thomas S. *The Rodgers and Hammerstein Encyclopedia*. Westport, CT: Greenwood Press, 2007.

Horn, Barbara Lee. *Joseph Papp: A Bio-bibliography*. Westport, CT: New York: Greenwood Press, 1992.

Kattwinkel, Susan. *Tony Pastor Presents: Afterpieces from the Vaudeville Stage*. Westport, CT: Greenwood Press, 1998.

Kazan, Elia. *Elia Kazan: A Life*. New York: Knopf, 1988.

Kissel, Howard. *David Merrick: The Abominable Showman*. New York: Applause, 1993.

Koprince, Susan Fehrenbacher. *Understanding Neil Simon*. Columbia: University of South Carolina Press, 2002.

McBrien, William. *Cole Porter: A Biography*. New York: Alfred A. Knopf, 1998.

McCabe, John. *George M. Cohan: The Man Who Owned Broadway*. New York: Da Capo Press, 1980.

Miller, Arthur. *Timebends: A Life*. New York: Grove Press, 1987.

Murphy, Donn B., and Stephen Moore. *Helen Hayes: A Bio-bibliography* Westport, CT: Greenwood Press, 1993.

Oja, Carol J. *Leonard Bernstein*. New Haven, CT: Yale University Press, 2007.

Peters, Margot. *The House of Barrymore*. New York: Knopf, 1990.

Rapp, Anthony. *Without You: A Memoir of Love, Loss, and the Musical Rent*. New York: Simon & Schuster, 2006.

Roudane, Matthew Charles. *The Cambridge Companion to Tennessee Williams*. Cambridge, U.K.: Cambridge University Press, 1997.

Schickel, Richard. *Elia Kazan: A Biography*. New York : HarperCollins Publishers, 2005.

Shannon, Sandra Garrett. *The Dramatic Vision of August Wilson*. Washington, DC: Howard University Press, 1995.

Sheaffer, Louis. *O'Neill, Son and Playwright*. Boston: Little, Brown, 1968.

Snelson, John, and Geoffrey Holden Block. *Andrew Lloyd Webber*. New Haven, CT: Yale University Press, 2004.

Turan, Kenneth, and Joseph Papp. *Free for All: Tales from the New York Shakespeare Festival*. New York: Broadway Books, 2009.

Vaill, Amanda. *Somewhere: The Life of Jerome Robbins*. New York: Broadway Books, 2006.

Ziegfeld, Richard E., and Paulette Ziegfeld. *The Ziegfeld Touch: The Life and Times of Florenz Ziegfeld, Jr*. New York: H. N. Abrams, 1993.

Selected Online Sources

Actors' Equity Association homepage. http://www.actorsequity.org/.

The American Society of Composers, Authors, and Publishers (ASCP). http://www.ascap.com/index.aspx.

American Theatre Wing homepage. http://americantheatrewing.org/.

The site contains a searchable compendium of the Tony Awards since their inception.

Andrew Lloyd Webber.com. http://www.andrewlloydwebber.com/.

The Arthur Miller Society. http://www.ibiblio.org/miller/.

Association for Theatre in Higher Education. http://www.athe.org.

Broadway League. http://www.livebroadway.com/.

The national trade association for Broadway theater producers. The site contains data and research information on the theater business both on Broadway and on tour.

The Drama League. http://www.dramaleague.org/.

The Web site for the 90+-year-old support organization that advances professional theater through awards, theater education, support of young theater talent, and other activities.

The Dramatists Guild of America. http://www.dramatistsguild.com/.

The online home for the 80+-year-old association devoted exclusively to authors, composers, and lyricists writing specifically for the live stage.

eOneill.com: An Electronic Eugene O'Neill Archive. http://www.eoneill.com/.

The Federal Theatre Project. http://novaonline.nvcc.edu/eli/spd130et/federaltheatre.htm.

A general history of the FTP maintained by North Virginia Community College.

Federal Theatre Project Materials. http://sca.gmu.edu/finding_aids/ftpscripts.html.

A research guide to original FTP materials and documents housed at George Mason University's library in Fairfax, Virginia.

Internet Broadway Database. http://ibdb.com/index.php.

Conceived and maintained by the Broadway League, "IBDB" is a comprehensive, searchable Web site for significant information about every Broadway show ever produced: creators, cast, numbers of performances, theatrical venue, etc.

League of Resident Theatres Web site. http://www.lort.org/.

Musicals101.com. http://www.musicals101.com.
A comprehensive online encyclopedia of musicals created and maintained by theater historian John Kenrick.

New York Times online. http://www.nytimes.com/.
Broadway reviews, profiles, and theater feature back to the mid-nineteenth century are easily accessed by site search feature. Some older articles require fee payment for downloading or viewing.

PBS American Masters Series. http://www.pbs.org/wnet/americanmasters/.
The site contains substantial background material on the televised series' subjects, many of which include people and events from Broadway.

Playbill Online. http://www.playbill.com/index.php.
The online version of the familiar feature magazine handed to every playgoer in attendance at a Broadway show.

The Rodgers and Hammerstein Organization. http://www.rnh.com/index.asp.
Sondheim.com. http://www.sondheim.com/.
Theatre Communications Group. http://www.tcg.org/.
A national organization of over 450 theater companies, TCG's Web site includes online versions of numerous publications and reports on the state of professional theater.

Theatre Historical Society of America. http://www.historictheatres.org/.
The Web site is dedicated to the study and appreciation of America's historical theater buildings, on Broadway and beyond.

The Thornton Wilder Society. http://www.tcnj.edu/~wilder/.
Victor Herbert: Music for the Soul. http://vherbert.com/.

About the Editor
and Contributors

The Editor

Thomas A. Greenfield is Professor of English and American Studies and a Lecturer in music at the State University of New York (SUNY)–Geneseo. He is the author of *Work and the Work Ethic in American Drama, 1920–1970* (1982) and *Radio: A Reference Guide* (1989) in Greenwood Press's American Popular Culture reference series as well as numerous articles and essays on drama, theater, media, and popular culture. He is a recipient of the SUNY Chancellor's Award for Excellence in Teaching.

The Contributors

Susan C. W. Abbotson is Assistant Professor of Modern and Contemporary Drama at Rhode Island College. She has written extensively on Arthur Miller, and American drama in particular, and her books include *Student Companion to Arthur Miller* (2000), *Thematic Guide to Modern Drama* (2003), *Masterpieces of Twentieth Century American Drama* (2005), and *A Critical Companion to Arthur Miller* (2007).

Steve Abrams is Associate Editor of *Puppetry Journal* and past president of Puppeteers of America. He is also the North American editor of the *World Encyclopedia of Puppetry Arts*.

Robert A. Adamo is currently a second-year student at Pace Law School.

Christy E. Allen is a senior at SUNY–Geneseo majoring in Psychology and Sociology and minoring in English.

Brian Balduzzi is pursuing graduate study at Pennsylvania State University.

Milly S. Barranger is the author of books on theater history and biography, including *Margaret Webster: A Life in the Theater*, *Theatre: A Way of Seeing*, *Understanding Plays*, and *Unfriendly Witnesses: Gender, Theater, and Film in the McCarthy Era*. She is Distinguished Professor Emerita at the University of North Carolina, Chapel Hill, where she served as chair of the Department of Dramatic Art and producing director of PlayMakers Repertory Company.

Melanie N. Blood is Professor of Theatre and Associate Dean of the School of the Arts at SUNY–Geneseo. She is also Coordinator of the Women's Studies Program at Geneseo. She has published in the *Journal of American Drama and Theatre*, *Modern Drama*, *Angels in the American Theatre*, *The Gay and Lesbian Theatrical Legacy*, and she is a past officer of the Association for Theatre in Higher Education.

Sue Ann Brainard, a member of numerous community theater production teams, is an Associate Reference Librarian at SUNY–Geneseo, specializing in instruction of research technology and skills.

Chase Bringardner received his PhD in Theatre History and Criticism from the University of Texas at Austin in May 2007. In the fall of 2007, he served as an assistant curator on a major exhibit of Arthur Miller's works and papers entitled "Rehearsing the Dream" at the Harry Ransom Center in Austin, Texas. He is currently a Visiting Instructor at Auburn University.

Kenneth James Cerniglia is dramaturg and literary manager for Disney Theatrical Productions as well as a writer and director. His recent independent projects include *Psyche*, a new chamber opera created with Seattle's Fisher Ensemble and *ReEntry*, a docudrama about returning from war, at Two River Theatre Company in Red Bank, New Jersey. For Disney he has developed over 20 shows for professional and school productions, including *Tarzan*, *High School Musical*, *The Little Mermaid*, *Beauty and the Beast JR.*, *The Aristocats KIDS*, and *Peter and the Starcatchers*. He holds a Ph.D. in theater history and criticism from the University of Washington and has published in *Theatre Journal* and *Theatre Annual*.

Maryann Chach is currently the Director of The Shubert Archive in New York City. Chach co-edited with Stephen M. Vallillo, *Pleasure Gardens* (Theatre Library Association 1998) and has contributed articles to several publications. With her colleagues at the Shubert Archive, she collaborated on the book *The Shuberts Present* (Abrams 2002). In 2006 The Theatre Library Association awarded her the Distinguished Achievement in Service and Support of Performing Arts Libraries Award.

Darryl Kent Clark is Assistant Professor of Dance at Missouri State University in Springfield, Missouri.

Pamela Cobrin is a Senior Lecturer at Barnard College, where she teaches in the English and Theatre Departments and is Director of the Writing and Speaking Programs. She is the author of *From Winning the Vote to Directing on Broadway: The Emergence of Women on the New York Stage, 1880–1927* (Delaware 2009). She has also published in *The Drama Review*, *American Theatre Magazine*, *Theatre Insight*, and *Women and Performance: A Journal of Feminist Theory*, where she currently serves on the editorial board.

Thomas F. Connolly is Associate Professor of English at Suffolk University and Visiting Professor of Literature at the Institute of English Philology, University of Ostrava, Czech Republic. He serves as a theater history consultant for *The New Yorker*, NPR, CBS, and the BBC and has contributed to *The Cambridge Guide to American Theatre*, *The Oxford Encyclopedia of Drama and Performance*, *The Encyclopedia of New England*, and numerous other reference works. He is the author of *George Jean Nathan and the Making of Modern American Drama Criticism* and *British Aisles*. He is the recipient of the Parliamentary Medal of the Czech Republic.

Francis Rexford Cooley is the Dean of the College at Paier College of Art in Hamden, Connecticut.

Don Corathers is editor of *Dramatics*, a monthly magazine for students and teachers of theater, which is published by the Educational Theatre Association.

Carissa Cordes is an actor and theater artist currently residing in New York City. She holds a B.F.A. in theater from NYU.

Kevin Cunningham graduated from SUNY–Geneseo.

Zachary A. Dorsey earned an M.A. and a Ph.D. in Theatre History and Criticism from the University of Texas at Austin. His dissertation, "Embodied Resistance: A Historiographic Intervention into the Performance of Queer Violence," won U.T.'s 2008 Outstanding Dissertation Award. He is a Visiting Assistant Professor at St. Lawrence University and is also a dramaturg and fight choreographer.

Kathy Dreifuss is a technical services librarian at Grant County Public Library in Williamstown, Kentucky.

Michelle Dvoskin is a doctoral student in Theatre and Dance at the University of Texas, Austin. Her dissertation focuses on musicals that explicitly take up historical narratives. Her other areas of interest include television musicals, U.S. popular culture, queer and feminist theory in performance, and directing.

Kathryn Edney is completing her Ph.D. at Michigan State University in the American Studies Program. Her dissertation is entitled "Gliding Through Our

Memories: American Musical Theater Does 'History.' " She is managing editor for *The Journal of Popular Culture* and has published on the musicals *Urinetown*, *City of Angels*, and *The Color Purple*.

Richard Finkelstein is Professor and Chair of the Department of English at SUNY–Geneseo. He has written numerous articles and reviews on Shakespeare and Renaissance Drama, including essays on Shakespearean appropriations and the history of Shakespearean publishing.

Anne Fliotsos is Associate Professor of Theatre at Purdue University. Her co-authored musical, *Oedipus! A New Musical Comedy*, was produced in New York City and is published by Baker's Plays. In addition to publishing articles and book chapters, she has co-edited *Teaching Theatre Today* (Palgrave 2004) and co-authored *American Women Stage Directors of the 20th Century* (Illinois 2008).

Gerard Floriano is an accomplished conductor in the orchestral, choral, and operatic arenas. He has led numerous choral and orchestral performances in the United States and Europe He has directed critically acclaimed productions of several operas and operettas, including Jerome Kern's *Show Boat* and Leonard Bernstein's *Candide*. He serves as the Director of Choral Activities at the State University of New York at Geneseo, where he recently was awarded the SUNY Chancellor's Award for Scholarship and Creative Activity.

Marisa Fratto is a graduate of SUNY–Geneseo in Musical Theatre and English. She currently resides in New York City where she is pursuing an acting career.

Philip Furia is a professor in the Department of Creative Writing at the University of North Carolina Wilmington. He is the author of *The Poets of Tin Pan Alley: A History of America's Great Lyricists*, as well as biographies of Ira Gershwin, Irving Berlin, and Johnny Mercer. He has lectured on American popular song at the Library of Congress, the New York Historical Society, and many colleges and universities and has appeared on *Larry King Live*, AMC's *Biography*, NPR's *All Things Considered* and *Fresh Air with Terry Gross*, as well as on other national television and radio programs.

Michael G. Garber holds a Ph.D. in Theatre and a Certificate in Film Studies from the City University of New York, where he wrote his dissertation on "Reflexive Songs in the American Musical, 1898–1947." He is an adjunct instructor on theater, film, and music at colleges in the New York area, including Manhattanville College and the State University of New York, Purchase College. He is also a diplomate of the Institute for Music and Health, through which he teaches the holistic approach to the arts developed by Dr. John Diamond. He is also the founder of the Tin Pan Alley Project Web site, and lectures frequently on American musical theater, film, and popular songs of the first half of the twentieth century.

Leah Garland, Ph.D., is a graduate from NYU's Department of Performance Studies. She is the author of *Contemporary Latina/o Performing Arts of Moraga, Tropicana, Fusco, and Bustamante* (Peter Lang 2009).

John Spalding Gatton is Professor of English at Bellarmine University in Louisville, Kentucky. He has published essays on Lord Byron as poet, prose writer, and dramatist; on Delacroix's interpretations of Byron's works; on Oscar Wilde; and on nineteenth-century theater. He is the translator-annotator of *Aventures de l'esprit* (1929), as *Adventures of the Mind* (1992), a volume of literary memoirs by Natalie Clifford Barney.

Kristen Gentry's short stories and poems have been featured in *The Matrix Anthology* and *The Crab Orchard Review*. She is a visiting Assistant Professor of English at SUNY–Geneseo where she teaches creative writing.

Isa Goldberg's interviews with playwrights have aired on PBS's *In The Life*, and her conversations with entertainers and performers have been broadcast on Reuters International Television. Her theater reviews and feature stories have appeared in the *New York Daily News*, *Newsday*, and *The Advocate* and are syndicated in newspapers in the Philadelphia area and upstate New York. Currently her theater reviews air on radio stations throughout the New York, New Jersey, Connecticut tri-state area, and she can be heard on the Web at womensradio.com.

Mary Hanrahan is a student at SUNY–Geneseo.

Ellen Herzman. She is an adjunct lecturer in English and formerly an adjunct lecturer in theater at SUNY–Geneseo. She also acts in professional and semiprofessional theater productions.

Jessica Hillman has written and published on musical theater and Jewish representation. She currently teaches theater at State University of New York at Fredonia.

Ben Hodges is editor in chief of *Theatre World*, the oldest annual pictorial and statistical record of the American theater. He co-edited *The Commercial Theater Institute Guide to Producing Plays and Musicals*. He is the editor of two anthologies of gay and lesbian plays, *Forbidden Acts* and *Out Plays*. He is the recipient of a 2003 Special Theatre World Award, and was a 2004 finalist for the Lambda Literary Award for Drama.

Helen Isolde has an M.A. in English from the University of Rochester. She is also a freelance writer of popular nonfiction. She is the author of *How to Have a Perfect Christmas* (Dutton 1996) and a number of articles that have appeared in various journals. She is currently at work on a memoir entitled *Dear Santiago*.

Amy Petersen Jensen is an Assistant Professor in the Department of Theatre and Media Arts at Brigham Young University in Provo, Utah. She is the author of *Theatre in a Media Culture: Production, Performance, and Perception since 1970* (2007).

Randy Barbara Kaplan is Associate Professor of Theatre at the State University of New York at Geneseo where she also serves as Founding Artistic Director of GENseng, Geneseo's Asian American Performance Ensembles. She has written and lectured extensively on the history of Asian American theater and theater artists.

James A. Kaser is Professor and Archivist at the College of Staten Island, a senior college of the City University of New York. He is the author of *The Washington, D.C. of Fiction: A Research Guide* (2006) and *At the Bivouac of Memory: History, Politics, and the Battle of Chickamauga.* (1996).

Susan Kattwinkel is Associate Professor of Theatre History and Director of the First-Year Experience at the College of Charleston in Charleston, South Carolina. She is the author of *Tony Pastor Presents: Afterpieces from the Vaudeville Stage* (Greenwood 1998). She has also contributed articles and chapters to the "Library Chronicle" of the University of Texas at Austin, the journal *Theatre Symposium*, and the book *Interrogating America Through Theatre and Performance* (ed. William W. Demastes, Palgrave/Macmillan 2006).

Nicole Katz is currently pursuing a Master's Degree at SUNY–Albany.

Shannon Kealey is an Instructional Services Librarian for Birnbaum Library at Pace University, home of the Actors Studio M.F.A. program. She has a Master of Library Science from SUNY–Buffalo and is also an actress and a professional singer/songwriter.

Caitlin Klein is a student at SUNY Geneseo.

Susan Koprince is Professor of English at the University of North Dakota, where she teaches courses in modern American fiction and drama. She is the author of *Understanding Neil Simon* (South Carolina 2002) and articles on American playwrights such as August Wilson, William Inge, and Susan Glaspell. Her publications on Tennessee Williams include essays on "Domestic Violence in *A Streetcar Named Desire*," "Tennessee Williams's Unseen Characters," and "Neil Simon's Parodies of Tennessee Williams," printed in *The Influence of Tennessee Williams: Essays on Fifteen American Playwrights* (2008).

Michael Lasser is an independent music historian and the co-author, with Philip Furia, of *America's Songs: The Stories Behind the Songs of Broadway, Hollywood,* *and Tin Pan Alley*. His nationally syndicated public radio program, *Fascinatin' Rhythm*, has been on the air since 1980, and is the recipient of a 1994 Peabody Award. He is at work on a new book, *The Pleasant Ache: How Love Song Lyrics Sang About Us, 1900–1950*.

Megan Lee recently graduated from SUNY–Geneseo.

Laura Lonski recently graduated from SUNY–Geneseo.

Stephen Marino is the editor of *The Arthur Miller Journal*. His work on Miller has appeared in *Modern Drama*, *The South Atlantic Review*, and the *Dictionary of Literary Biography*. He is the editor of *The Salesman Has a Birthday: Essays Celebrating the Fiftieth Anniversary of Arthur Miller's Death of a Salesman* and the author of *A Language Study of Arthur Miller's Plays, The Poetic in the Colloquial*.

Alyson McLamore is a music professor and recipient of the Distinguished Teacher Award at California Polytechnic State University, San Luis Obispo, and has published *Musical Theater: An Appreciation* (Prentice-Hall) and essays in the *Royal Musical Association Research Chronicle*, *Notes, New Dictionary of the History of Ideas*, *Music Franca: Essays in Honor of Frank A. D'Accone*, and *Music Observed: Studies in Memory of William C. Holmes*. She has presented papers at meetings of the American Musicological Society and College Music Society. She also writes program notes and gives preconcert talks for several performing organizations.

Molly Smith Metzler received an M.F.A. in Dramatic Writing from NYU and is currently a Lila Acheson Wallace playwright in residence at The Juilliard School and an Associate Editor with *American Theatre Magazine*. Her play *Training Wisteria* was produced as part of the Cherry Lane Mentor Project in 2007. Her play *Close Up Space* was selected for the Manhattan Theatre Club 2009 7@7 Reading Series.

Ray Miller is a professor of theater, a choreographer, and a director at Appalachian State University in North Carolina. He has directed and/or choreographed over 200 plays, musicals, operas, and dance concerts. His work has been published in *Dance Research Journal*, *Theatre Journal*, *Text and Performance Quarterly*, and *Dance Chronicle*.

William Charles Morrow is a longtime staff member with the Performing Arts Library at Lincoln Center, where he catalogs moving image material for the Theatre on Film and Tape Archive. He has written numerous articles on theater and cinema. In the 1980s he wrote and directed radio plays for WBAI in New York City. His musical, *The Ministry of Progress*, was produced Off-Broadway in 2004;

a one-act (nonmusical) version of that play has been staged in Indiana, Kentucky, and Florida, as well as New York.

Monica Moschetta is co-author with Thomas A. Greenfield of "Theater and Performance" in *The Greenwood Encyclopedia of World Popular Culture* (2007).

Phillip Moss is the head of the creative and performing arts department at University Liggett School in Michigan. He has directed numerous state and national award-winning plays and productions, and is a member of the Educational Theatre Association's Hall of Fame.

Murry R. Nelson is Professor of Education and Department Head of Curriculum and Instruction at Pennsylvania State University. His most recent publications include *The Encyclopedia of Sports in America*, which he edited for Greenwood Press (2008) and *The National Basketball League: A History, 1935–1949.*

Aaron Netsky is a graduate of SUNY–Geneseo. His great-uncle, Harold Karr, wrote the music for the Broadway musical *Happy Hunting* (1956).

Gwen Orel holds a Ph.D. in Theatre from the University of Pittsburgh. She has worked as literary manager of Alabama Shakespeare Festival and City Theatre, Pittsburgh, as well as an AEA stage manager. Her writing has appeared in the *New York Times*, *Wall Street Journal*, *Pittsburgh Post-Gazette*, *American Theatre*, *Time Out New York*, *Back Stage*, and numerous other publications.

Tracy L. Paradis is Senior Assistant Reference and Instruction Librarian at SUNY–Geneseo.

Sharon Peck is an Assistant Professor of literacy in the Shear School of Education at SUNY–Geneseo. A professional puppeteer, she is the North East Regional Director for the Puppeteers of America. She performs as a puppeteer in New England and lectures to teachers on integrating puppetry into classroom instruction.

Alison Jones Peña graduated from the University of Wisconsin–Stevens Point in English and Theater. A USDA-Natural Resources Conservation Service Easement Program Specialist by profession, she acts, directs, and has served on the Board of Directors for Riverside Players Community Theater.

Nicholas J. Ponterio is a student at SUNY–Geneseo.

Sarah Provencal is currently a teacher, actress, and director in Charlotte, North Carolina.

Michael Radi is a student at SUNY–Geneseo. He recently wrote his first musical, an adaptation of Tennessee Williams's *A Streetcar Named Desire*.

Sean Roche is a recent graduate from SUNY–Geneseo.

Brian G. Rose is a professor in the Department of Communication and Media Studies at Fordham University. He is the author of *Television and the Performing Arts* and *Directing for Television*, among other books.

Felicia J. Ruff chairs the Department of Theatre and Speech at Wagner College. In 2007 she received a grant to attend the NEH summer seminar "The Wilde Archive" at UCLA's Clark Library. Her writing has appeared in *Theatre Symposium: Comedy Tonight* (Alabama 2008) and *Theatre Journal*. She has extensive production experience, including opening the Center for the Arts at the College of Staten Island.

Alice Rutkowski is Assistant Professor of English at SUNY–Geneseo where she teaches American literature and Women's Studies. She has published on Civil War and Reconstruction literature and popular culture.

Annette J. Saddik is an Associate Professor in the English Department at New York City College of Technology (City University of New York). She is the author of *Contemporary American Drama* (Edinburgh 2007) and *The Politics of Reputation: The Critical Reception of Tennessee Williams' Later Plays* (Associated University Presses 1999). She also edited *The Traveling Companion and Other Plays*, a collection of Tennessee Williams's previously unpublished later plays (New Directions 2008). She serves on the Editorial Board of *Theatre Topics*, and has published several essays in various journals, edited collections, and encyclopedias.

Richard G Scharine is Emeritus Professor of theatre and Adjunct Professor of ethnic studies at the University of Utah. He has served as interim chair of the Theatre Department, Director of Graduate Studies, head of the B.A. program, and co-founder of the London Study Abroad Program. He is the author of a number of books and articles on British contemporary theater, American political theater, and African American theater. He has received numerous professional honors including Outstanding Educator of America, Senior Fulbright Lecturer in Poland, College of Fine Arts Faculty Achievement Award, University of Utah Diversity Award winner, and Distinguished University Professor. Co-director of People Productions, an African American themed theater, he has directed over 80 plays and has acted in ten states and seven foreign countries.

Sandra G. Shannon is Professor of Dramatic Literature and Criticism in the Department of English at Howard University. She is the author of *The Dramatic*

Vision of August Wilson (Howard University Press 1995), *August Wilson's Fences: A Reference Guide* (Greenwood 2003), and *August Wilson and Black Aesthetics* (Palgrave-McMillan 2004). She has also contributed to *The Influences of Tennessee Williams* (McFarland 2008); *Contemporary African American Playwrights* (Routledge 2008); *Critical Reflections on the Fiction of Ernest Gaines* (Georgia University Press 1994); and *August Wilson: A Casebook* (Garland 1994) as well as numerous scholarly journals. She is currently editing *Approaches to Teaching the Plays of August Wilson* to be published by the Modern Language Association. Dr. Shannon is editor of the journal *Theatre Topics* and is Immediate Past President of the Black Theatre Network.

Kaitlin Snyder teaches English in the Waterloo, New York Central School System.

Joseph P. Swain won ASCAP's Deems Taylor Award for *The Broadway Musical: A Critical and Musical Survey* (Oxford 1990) in 1991 and since then has written *Musical Languages* (Norton 1997), *Harmonic Rhythm* (Oxford 2002), *A Historical Dictionary of Sacred Music* (Scarecrow 2006), and *Sacred Treasure: Understanding Catholic Liturgical Music* (Notre Dame 2010).

John Tenney is a professional musician and great grandson of Marc Klaw, one of the founders of the Theatrical Syndicate. He conducts research on Klaw and his producing partner A. L. Erlanger as well as the Syndicate. Tenney has developed a book-length manuscript on Klaw and Erlanger's turn of the century blockbuster stage production of *Ben-Hur.*

Ian Scott Todd is currently a doctoral candidate in English at Tufts University, where his research interests include twentieth-century literature and film. He has recently published pieces on Alfred Hitchcock and the Hollywood western.

Daniel Yurgaitis is an associate professor of theater at Northern State University in Aberdeen, South Dakota. A professional director, he has directed over 300 productions in theaters across the United States.

Megan Zeh recently graduated from SUNY–Geneseo.

Index

∽